Philip Jodidio

100 CONTEMPORARY
GREEN
BUILDINGS

100 Zeitgenössische Grüne Bauten
100 Bâtiments Verts Contemporains

VOL 1

TASCHEN

CONTENT VOLUME I

INTRODUCTION	Einleitung/Introduction	**6**
24H ARCHITECTURE	Panyaden School *Chiang Mai*	**12**
70F	Petting Farm *Almere*	**18**
EFFAN ADHIWIRA	Green School *Badung*	**24**
AFF	"Hutznhaisl" *Tellerhäuser*	**32**
AGENCE BABYLONE	Active Nature *Saclay*	**38**
ALDINGER ARCHITEKTEN	Cafeteria and Day Care Center, Waldorf School *Stuttgart*	**44**
EMILIO AMBASZ	Ospedale dell'Angelo *Venice-Mestre*	**48**
AUER+WEBER+ASSOZIIERTE	Buildings in Chenshan Botanical Garden *Shanghai*	**54**
PIETA-LINDA AUTTILA	Wisa Wooden Design Hotel *Helsinki*	**62**
BALMORI ASSOCIATES	The Garden That Climbs the Stairs *Bilbao*	**68**
SHIGERU BAN	Papertainer Museum *Seoul* / Nomadic Museum *New York; Santa Monica; Tokyo*	**74**
CHARLES BARCLAY	Kielder Observatory *Kielder*	**84**
BARLINDHAUG CONSULT AS	Svalbard Global Seed Vault *Longyearbyen*	**90**
SEBASTIAN BERGNE	LEGO Greenhouse *London*	**98**
BIG	The Mountain *Copenhagen*	**104**
PATRICK BLANC	CaixaForum Vertical Garden *Madrid*	**110**
BOHLIN CYWINSKI JACKSON	Grand Teton Discovery and Visitor Center *Grand Teton National Park* / Combs Point Residence *Finger Lakes Region*	**114**
VINCENT CALLEBAUT ARCHITECTURES	Anti-Smog *Paris* / Perfumed Jungle *Hong Kong*	**126**
CARNEY LOGAN BURKE ARCHITECTS	Laurance S. Rockefeller Preserve *Grand Teton National Park*	**138**
CARTER + BURTON ARCHITECTURE	Shenandoah Retreat *Warren County*	**144**
MARCO CASAGRANDE	Chen House *Sanjhih*	**150**
CASEY BROWN	Permanent Camping *Mudgee*	**158**
EDWARD CULLINAN	Downland Gridshell *Singleton*	**164**
DECOI ARCHITECTS	One Main *Cambridge*	**170**
DILLER SCOFIDIO + RENFRO	Hypar Pavilion Lawn *New York*	**178**
VLADIMIR DJUROVIC	Samir Kassir Square *Beirut*	**182**
DRN ARCHITECTS	La Baronia House *Quintero* / House at Punta Chilen *Chiloé Island*	**188**
DUMAY + FONES + VERGARA	Fuente Nueva Chapel *Lake Rupanco*	**202**
ECOSISTEMA URBANO	Ecoboulevard of Vallecas *Madrid*	**208**
SHUHEI ENDO	Bubbletecture H *Sayo-cho*	**216**
ETH-STUDIO MONTE ROSA / BEARTH & DEPLAZES	New Monte Rosa Hut SAC *Zermatt*	**222**
FELIX-DELUBAC	Ecolodge *Siwa*	**228**
FLOAT	Watershed *Willamette Valley*	**236**
NORMAN FOSTER	Chesa Futura *St. Moritz* / Masdar Institute *Abu Dhabi*	**244**
FRANK O. GEHRY	Serpentine Gallery Pavilion *London*	**254**
GLAVOVIC STUDIO	Young Circle ArtsPark *Hollywood*	**260**
NICHOLAS GRIMSHAW	The Eden Project *St. Austell*	**266**
GUSTAFSON GUTHRIE NICHOL	Lurie Garden *Chicago* / Robert and Arlene Kogod Courtyard *Washington, D.C.*	**272**
HEBERLE MAYER	U6 Berlin Penthouse *Berlin*	**282**
ANNA HERINGER AND EIKE ROSWAG	Handmade School *Rudrapur*	**286**
STEVEN HOLL	Vanke Center / Horizontal Skyscraper *Shenzhen* / HEART: Herning Museum of Contemporary Art *Herning*	**292**
HOTSON BAKKER BONIFACE HADEN	Nk'Mip Desert Cultural Center *Osoyoos*	**304**
HWKN (HOLLWICH KUSHNER)	Wendy *Long Island City*	**320**
IROJE KHM ARCHITECTS	Lim Geo Dang *Go Yang* / Hye Ro Hun *Gwangju*	**320**
JUNYA ISHIGAMI	Greenhouses, Japanese Pavilion *Venice*	**330**
JACKSON CLEMENTS BURROWS	Cape Schanck House *Cape Schanck*	**338**
CHRIS JACOBS	Vertical Farm *Harlem*	**344**
CREDITS		**348**

90 **Barlindhaug Consult AS**, Longyearbyen

54 **Auer+Weber+Assoziierte**, Shanghai
478 **Morphosis**, Shanghai
492 **Neri & Hu**, Shanghai
686 **Zhu Xiaofeng Scenic Architecture**, Qingpu

582 **Saunders & Wilhelmsen**, Hardanger Fjord
366 **Jensen & Skodvin Architects**, Tautra Island
374 **Jensen & Skodvin Architects**, Gudbrandsjuvet
562 **PUSHAK**, Måsøy 562
440 **Lassila Hirvilammi Architects**, Kärsämäki
576 **SARC Architects**, Joensuu
378 **Emma Johansson and Timo Leiviskä**, Mikkeli

74 **Shigeru Ban**, Seoul
320 **IROJE KHM Architects**, Go Yang
326 **IROJE KHM Architects**, Gwangju
464 **Ken Sungjin Min**, Gangwon-do
548 **Dominique Perrault**, Seoul

62 **Pieta-Linda Auttila**, Helsinki
300 **Steven Holl**, Herning
104 **BIG**, Copenhagen
404 **Kempe Thill**, Rostock
282 **Heberle Mayer**, Berlin
32 **AFF**, Tellerhäuser
588 **SeARCH**, Rheden
390 **Françoise-Hélène Jourda**, Herne
44 **Aldinger Architekten**, Stuttgart
612 **Werner Sobek**, Tieringen

568 **Hiroshi Sambuichi**, Inujima
216 **Shuhei Endo**, Sayo-cho

182 **Vladimir Djurovic**, Beirut
Li Xiaodong, Lijiang 454
80 **Shigeru Ban**, Tokyo
506 **Nikken Sekkei**, Tokyo
228 **FELIX-DELUBAC**, Siwa
250 **Norman Foster**, Abu Dhabi
430 **Kengo Kuma**, Yusuhara

150 **Marco Casagrande**, Sanjhih
536 **Sergio Palleroni**, Taipei

132 **Vincent Callebaut Architectures**, Hong Kong
294 **Steven Holl**, Shenzhen

470 **MODUS**, Bressanone
640 **Matteo Thun**, Lana, Merano

12 **24H Architecture**, Chiang Mai

286 **Anna Heringer and Eike Roswag**, Rudrapur

48 **Emilio Ambasz**, Venice-Mestre
330 **Junya Ishigami**, Venice

626 **Studio Mumbai**, Nandgaon

244 **Norman Foster**, St. Moritz
512 **Rolf Karl Nimmrichter,** Dietlikon

Effan Adhiwira, Badung 24

158 **Casey Brown**, Mudgee

222 **ETHStudio Monte Rosa / Bearth & Deplazes**, Zermatt

Jackson Clements Burrows, Cape Schank 338
Taylor Cullity Lethlean, Cranbourne 634

434 **Lacaton & Vassal**, Mulhouse

38 **Agence Babylone**, Saclay
126 **Vincent Callebaut Architectures**, Paris

100 CONTEMPORARY
GREEN
BUILDINGS

IMPRINT

PROJECT MANAGEMENT
Florian Kobler and
Inga Hallsson, Cologne

COLLABORATION
Harrient Graham, Turin

PRODUCTION
Ute Wachendorf, Cologne

DESIGN
Sense/Net Art Direction,
Andy Disl and Birgit
Eichwede, Cologne
www.sense-net.net

GERMAN TRANSLATION
Caroline Behlen, Berlin;
Christianè Court, Frankfurt;
Karin Haag, Vienna;

Kristina Brigitta Köper,
Berlin; Nora von Mühlendahl,
Ludwigsburg; Laila Neubert-
Mader, Ettlingen; Annette
Wiethüchter, Berlin; Holger
Wölfle, Berlin

FRENCH TRANSLATION
Jacques Bosser, Montesquiou
Claire Debard, Freiburg

© 2013 TASCHEN GMBH
Hohenzollernring 53
D–50672 Cologne
www.taschen.com

This book is in large part
a compilation from
TASCHEN's previously
published **ARCHITECTURE
NOW!**-series.

CONTENT VOLUME II

JAMES CORNER FIELD OPERATIONS / DILLER SCOFIDIO + RENFRO   The High Line *New York* **354**

MICHAEL JANTZEN   Homestead House **362**

JENSEN & SKODVIN ARCHITECTS   Tautra Maria Convent *Tautra Island* / Juvet Landscape Hotel *Gudbrandsjuvet* **366**

EMMA JOHANSSON AND TIMO LEIVISKÄ   Anttolanhovi Art and Design Villas *Mikkeli* **378**

JOHNSEN SCHMALING ARCHITECTS   Camouflage House *Green Lake* **384**

FRANÇOISE-HÉLÈNE JOURDA   Mont-Cenis Academy and Municipal District Center *Herne* **390**

RAYMOND JUNGLES   Coconut Grove *Coconut Grove* **396**

KEMPE THILL   Hedge Building *Rostock* **404**

KIERANTIMBERLAKE   Sidwell Friends Middle School *Washington, D.C.* **410**

MATHIAS KLOTZ   La Roca House *Punta del Este* **416**

KENGO KUMA   Glass Wood House *New Canaan* / Yusuhara Marché *Yusuhara* **424**

LACATON & VASSAL   Social Housing, Cité Manifeste *Mulhouse* **434**

LASSILA HIRVILAMMI ARCHITECTS   Kärsämäki Church *Kärsämäki* **440**

NIC LEHOUX AND JACQUELINE DARJES   The Lilypad *Point Roberts* **446**

LI XIAODONG   Yuhu Elementary School *Lijiang* **454**

MIII ARCHITECTEN   Environmental Education Center *Hoorn* **460**

KEN SUNGJIN MIN   Kumgang Ananti Golf & Spa Resort *Gangwon-do* **464**

MODUS   Damiani Holz & Ko Headquarters *Bressanone* **470**

MORPHOSIS   Giant Interactive Group Corporate Headquarters *Shanghai* **478**

ALBERTO MOZÓ   BIP Computer Office and Shop *Santiago de Chile* **486**

NERI & HU   The Waterhouse at South Bund *Shanghai* **492**

VICTOR NEVES   Reorganization of the Riverside of Esposende *Esposende* **500**

NIKKEN SEKKEI   Sony City Osaki *Tokyo* **506**

ROLF KARL NIMMRICHTER   S House *Dietlikon* **512**

OFFICE DA   Helios House *Los Angeles* **518**

CARLOS OTT   Playa Vik *Faro José Ignacio* **528**

SERGIO PALLERONI   Zhong Xiao Boulevard Urban Ecological Corridor *Taipei* **536**

PERKINS+WILL   1315 Peachtree Street *Atlanta* **544**

DOMINIQUE PERRAULT   Ewha Womans University *Seoul* **548**

RENZO PIANO   Renovation and Expansion of the California Academy of Sciences *San Francisco* **556**

PUSHAK   Lillefjord *Måsøy* **562**

HIROSHI SAMBUICHI   Inujima Art Project Seirensho *Inujima* **568**

SARC ARCHITECTS   Metla, Finnish Forest Research Institute *Joensuu* **576**

SAUNDERS & WILHELMSEN   Summer House *Hardanger Fjord* **582**

SEARCH   Posbank Tea Pavilion *Rheden* **588**

SELGASCANO   Studio in the Woods *Madrid* / Mérida Factory Youth Movement *Mérida* **594**

KEN SMITH   Santa Fe Railyard Park and Plaza *Santa Fe* **606**

WERNER SOBEK   H16 *Tieringen* **612**

GERMÁN DEL SOL   Hotel Remota *Puerto Natales* **620**

STUDIO MUMBAI   Palmyra House *Nandgaon* **626**

TAYLOR CULLITY LETHLEAN   Royal Botanic Gardens *Cranbourne* **634**

MATTEO THUN   Vigilius Mountain Resort *Lana* **640**

MICHAEL VAN VALKENBURGH   Connecticut Water Treatment Facility *New Haven* **644**

KOEN VAN VELSEN   Media Authority Building *Hilversum* **648**

WHY ARCHITECTURE   Grand Rapids Art Museum *Grand Rapids* **654**

WMR   Till House *Los Arcos* / Mandakovic House *Los Arcos* **660**

KYU SUNG WOO   Putney Mountain House *Putney* **672**

WORK ARCHITECTURE COMPANY   Public Farm 1 *Long Island City* **678**

ZHU XIAOFENG SCENIC ARCHITECTURE   The Green Pine Garden *Qingpu* **686**

INDEX **692**

CREDITS **696**

INTRODUCTION

WHERE THE GRASS IS GREENER

Green, green, it's green they say
On the far side of the hill
Green, green, I'm going away
To where the grass is greener still.

Barry McGuire, The New Christy Minstrels, 1963

The trouble with "green" is what does it mean? Standards for measuring the environmental "friendliness" of architecture of course exist and take into account such factors as energy consumption in a clear, statistical manner, together with a number of other criteria that tend to vary from country to country. And yet, can "sustainability" be defined in a generally acceptable way? Those who read about architecture regularly encounter lengthy descriptions of the benefits derived from "passive energy strategies," such as orienting a house so that it does engender maximum solar gain. Well, the good news is that people have been doing that since the dawn of time, with just a little common sense on their side. Concrete poured in great quantities notably saves energy through "thermal mass." Thick stone or mud walls did the same thing thousands of years ago with far fewer environmental risks. It would seem that just as architects have come in recent years to understand that references to history are not taboo, the *tabula rasa* of Gropius notwithstanding, so, too, there has been a great liberation in the area of returning to age-old common sense in building. It is ok to have operable windows even if they disturb the slick surfaces of modern buildings, and turning the structure just so it avoids the noonday sun has become a terrific sales argument. Aren't we green and sustainable and squeaky clean and new!

Well, yes, do read the instructions carefully before swallowing that delightful little green pill—you know the warning about how this fine medicine can cause internal bleeding, temporary blindness, and sudden loss of consciousness. The truth is that there are heavy metals in your photovoltaic cell and that corn ethanol may starve the planet before it reverses global warming. Perhaps the grass is greener on the other side of the hill.

GREEN AND LEAN

Now, now, let us not be too sarcastic, there is surely much to be gained from a LEED Platinum rating, even if the downside of certain "green" products has not been fully elucidated, and may never be because somebody out there is making a tidy profit. LEED (Leadership in Energy and Environmental Design) certification, initiated by the US Green Building Council (USGBC), entails a point system that measures performance in the following areas: Sustainable Sites, Water Efficiency, Energy and Atmosphere, Materials and Resources, Indoor Environmental Quality, Locations and Linkages, Awareness and Education, Innovation in Design, and Regional Priority.[1] Rather complex, surely because it touches on categories that approach the subjective, the LEED system has nonetheless made considerable headway. Nor is it the only standard employed in the world; far from it. The USGBC states: "With nearly 9 billion square feet (836 127 000 m²) of building space participating in the suite of rating systems and 1.6 million feet (148 645 m²) certifying per day around the world, LEED is transforming the way built environments are designed, constructed, and operated […] from individual buildings and homes, to entire neighborhoods and communities. Comprehensive and flexible, LEED works throughout a building's life cycle."[2] There, wasn't that simple? Feel better?

WOOD IS GOOD

This book, derived in part from earlier volumes written by the same author, tries to ask the billion-dollar question "What is green?" in a different way. Yes, there are LEED-certified buildings published here of course, and an emphasis is put on how and why they are "sustainable." But there are also gardens and temporary structures that do not exist long enough to survive the LEED certification process. You have to imagine that Shigeru Ban's Nomadic Museum, made of paper tubes and recycled shipping containers, cannot have had all that negative an impact on the environment even if no rating system can prove it. There are buildings made of wood or out of rammed earth in this book as well. Wood is known to pose an environmental problem if it is improperly harvested, but, there too, rating systems like FSC Forest Management Certification and others exist, and are gaining ground. Wood might otherwise be considered the ultimate renewable resource, in particular if it is disposed of in a responsible manner after usage.

TECHNICIANS OF THE KILOWATT-HOUR UNITE!

There are parks like the small Samir Kassir Square in Beirut (Vladimir Djurovic), and even greenhouses, including one made of LEGO bricks in this book, because what grows inside them is green. This is not an exaggeration—green buildings are not just the ones that use high-tech gadgetry to reduce energy consumption. They are also structures and even spaces that participate willfully and happily in the natural equilibrium of things, a balance that rampant development has lost sight of in most places. The French botanist Patrick Blanc has proven again and again with his elegant vertical gardens that even city centers can be a place for nature. No, this is not a book for technicians of the kilowatt-hour, although some might be inspired by taking the time to look at the 100 projects published here. Let us say that it is a book about *looking back*, back to the ways that have always been used in buildings to make them comfortable, even when it is hot or cold outside. It is also a book about *looking forward* at the active search for technological means to control global warming in the area of construction, which accounts for a significant percentage of the emission of greenhouse gases in the world. Perhaps best said, it is a book about *looking up*, at the sky and the sun, *and then down*, at the earth and grass, which may well be quite green beneath our feet, even where we stand.

1 http://www.usgbc.org/DisplayPage.aspx?CMSPageID=1989 accessed on August 12, 2012.
2 http://www.usgbc.org/DisplayPage.aspx?CMSPageID=1988 accessed on August 12, 2012.

EINLEITUNG

WO DAS GRAS GRÜNER IST

Green, green, it's green they say
On the far side of the hill
Green, green, I'm going away
To where the grass is greener still.
Barry McGuire, The New Christy Minstrels, 1963

Was genau meinen wir, wenn wir von „grün" sprechen? Ohne Frage, es gibt klare Standards für „umweltfreundliche" Architektur, die Faktoren wie den Energieverbrauch statistisch aufschlüsseln, ebenso wie ergänzende Kriterien, die von Land zu Land variieren. Doch die Frage bleibt: Wie lässt sich „Nachhaltigkeit" auf eine allgemein verbindliche Formel bringen? Wer sich regelmäßig mit Architektur befasst, kennt die üblichen wortreichen Beschwörungen „passiver Energiestrategien", etwa die Optimierung des Wärmegewinns durch entsprechende Orientierung von Bauten. Glücklicherweise ist dies eine Strategie, die dank gesundem Menschenverstand im Grunde schon immer praktiziert wurde. Auch das Wärme speichernde Potenzial von massivem Beton durch seine „thermische Masse" ist längst bekannt. Massive Stein- oder Lehmmauern leisten seit Jahrtausenden nichts anderes – noch dazu mit geringeren Umweltrisiken. Fast scheint es, als hätten Architekten erst in den letzten Jahren verstanden, dass historische Rückbezüge kein Tabu sein dürfen – trotz des bekannten Gropius-Worts von der Tabula rasa. Dass heute in der Baukunst wieder auf jahrtausendealte Weisheiten zurückgegriffen wird, ist ein entscheidender Befreiungsschlag. Fenster, die sich öffnen lassen, sind wieder eine Option, auch wenn sie die glatten Fassaden moderner Bauten stören mögen. Einen Bau so auszurichten, dass er die gleißende Mittagssonne meidet, hat sich zum cleveren Verkaufsargument gemausert. Sind wir nicht grün und nachhaltig, politisch korrekt und am Puls der Zeit?

Dennoch lohnt es, den Beipackzettel der verlockenden grünen Pille aufmerksam zu lesen, bevor man sie schluckt – denn der Wunderwirkstoff kann Nebenwirkungen haben: innere Blutungen, temporäre Erblindung, plötzlicher Bewusstseinsverlust. Tatsache ist, dass unsere Solarzellen Schwermetalle enthalten und Maisethanol unseren Planeten womöglich in noch größeren Hunger treibt, bevor es gelingen wird, die Erderwärmung in den Griff zu bekommen. Vielleicht ist das Gras auf der anderen Seite doch grüner?

GRÜN UND SCHLANK

Doch allzu viel Sarkasmus ist sicher nicht hilfreich, und zweifellos spricht einiges für LEED-Zertifikate, auch wenn die Nebenwirkungen bestimmter „grüner" Techniken und Produkte nicht abschließend geklärt sind (und vielleicht nie geklärt werden, weil sie erhebliche Profite versprechen). Der US-amerikanische Zertifizierungsprozess nach LEED-Maßstäben (Leadership in Energy and Environmental Design), initiiert vom Green Building Council (USGBC), beruht auf einem Punktesystem, das Effizienz in den folgenden Kategorien misst: nachhaltige Bauplätze, sparsamer Wasserverbrauch, Energieeffizienz, Materialauswahl, Raumklima im Bau, Lage und Anbindung, Information und Vermittlung, innovative Gestaltung sowie die Priorisierung regionaler Aspekte.[1] Trotz hoher Komplexität, auch weil etliche Kategorien eher subjektiv sind, hat sich das LEED-System weithin durchsetzen können. Dennoch ist es international längst nicht der einzige Standard. Das USGBC erklärt: „Mit fast 836 127 000 m² gebauter Fläche, die nach unserem Punktesystems geplant werden, und täglich 148 645 m² zertifizierter Projekte weltweit trägt LEED dazu bei, Planung, Bau und Betrieb [...] von Gebäuden, privaten Wohnbauten, ganzen Stadtteilen und Gemeinden grundlegend zu verändern. LEED ist umfassend und flexibel und berücksichtigt die gesamte Lebensdauer eines Bauwerks."[2] Ist doch ganz leicht, oder? Und schon fühlt man sich besser.

HOLZ IST GUT

Dieser Doppelband fußt zum Teil auf früheren Publikationen des Autors und will sich der milliardenschwer dotierten Preisfrage „Was ist grün?" aus einem neuen Blickwinkel nähern. Natürlich werden hier LEED-zertifizierte Bauten vorgestellt, doch es geht darum, auf welche Weise und warum sie „nachhaltig" sind. Darüber hinaus finden sich hier Gärten und temporäre Bauten, deren Lebensdauer zu kurz ist, als dass sie für den LEED-Zertifizierungsprozess in Frage kämen. Es leuchtet ein, dass Shigeru Bans Nomadic Museum aus Pappröhren und recycelten Schiffscontainern vermutlich keine besonders negativen Auswirkungen auf die Umwelt hatte, auch wenn sich dies nicht mit einem Punktesystem belegen lässt. In diesem Band finden sich außerdem Bauten aus Holz oder Stampflehm. Holz als Baustoff ist bekanntlich dann problematisch, wenn es nicht aus verantwortungsvoll praktizierter Forstwirtschaft stammt. Doch auch hier gibt es inzwischen Punktesysteme wie das Zertifikat des FSC (Forest Stewartship Council) und andere, die sich zunehmend durchsetzen. Grundsätzlich kann Holz als ultimative erneuerbare Ressource gelten, was insbesondere bei verantwortungsvollem Recycling gilt.

ELEKTROTECHNIKER, VEREINIGT EUCH!

In diesem Buch finden sich außerdem Grünanlagen wie der kleine Park am Samir Kassir Square in Beirut (Vladimir Djurovic) und sogar Gewächshäuser, darunter eines aus LEGO-Steinen, denn was in ihnen wächst, ist grün. Dies ist nicht etwa eine Überzeichnung – grüne Bauten sind eben nicht nur solche, die aufwendige technische Spielereien nutzen, um den Energieverbrauch zu senken. Grün sind auch Bauten oder Räume, die sich bewusst und harmonisch in das natürliche Gleichgewicht fügen, ein Gleichgewicht, das wir durch unkontrolliertes Wachstum vielerorts aus dem Blick verloren haben. Der französische Botaniker Patrick Blanc stellt mit seinen eleganten vertikalen Gärten immer wieder unter Beweis, dass selbst in unseren Stadtzentren Platz für Natur ist. Nein, dies ist kein Buch für Elektrotechniker, auch wenn die 100 hier vorgestellten Projekte durchaus Inspiration für deren Branche versprechen. Bei diesem Buch geht es vielmehr darum *zurückzublicken* auf Methoden, die in der Baukunst von jeher zum Einsatz kommen, um Bauten wohnlicher zu machen, auch in kalten oder warmen Klimazonen. Außerdem gilt es *vorauszuschauen*, gilt es, engagiert nach technischen Möglichkeiten zu forschen, der Erderwärmung entgegenzuwirken, und dies gerade in der Architektur, einem Bereich, der weltweit für einen hohen Anteil der Treibhausgasemissionen verantwortlich ist. Doch vielleicht ist dies am ehesten ein Buch, das *nach oben* schauen will, zum Himmel und zur Sonne, und schließlich *nach unten,* auf das Gras unter unseren Füßen, das womöglich dort, wo wir stehen, im Grunde ziemlich grün ist.

1 http://www.usgbc.org/DisplayPage.aspx?CMSPageID=1989, Zugriff am 12. August 2012.
2 http://www.usgbc.org/DisplayPage.aspx?CMSPageID=1988, Zugriff am 12. August 2012.

INTRODUCTION

LÀ OÙ L'HERBE EST PLUS VERTE

Vert, vert, c'est vert disent-ils
De l'autre côté de la colline
Vert, vert, je m'en vais
Là où l'herbe est plus verte encore.

Barry McGuire, The New Christy Minstrels, 1963

Le problème avec le terme « vert », c'est qu'on ne sait pas ce qu'il veut dire. Bien sûr, il existe des normes pour mesurer le degré de respect de l'environnement de l'architecture, elles sont basées sur des facteurs tels que la consommation d'énergie qui sont pris en compte selon des méthodes statistiques claires, ainsi que de nombreux autres critères qui ont tendance à varier selon les pays. Mais la « durabilité » peut-elle pour autant être définie d'une manière acceptable par tous ? Les lecteurs habitués des textes sur l'architecture se heurtent régulièrement à d'interminables descriptions des avantages que procurent les « stratégies énergétiques passives », comme celle consistant à orienter une maison de manière à bénéficier d'un apport solaire maximal. La bonne nouvelle, c'est que les hommes ont recours à ces pratiques depuis la nuit des temps, pour peu qu'ils aient une once de bon sens. On sait par exemple que le béton coulé en grandes quantités permet d'économiser de l'énergie grâce à la « masse thermique ». Il y a des milliers d'années, d'épais murs de pierre ou de terre rendaient le même service avec bien moins de risques pour l'environnement. Il semblerait donc que, au moment même où les architectes commencent à comprendre (depuis quelques années) que les références à l'histoire ne sont pas taboues, la *tabula rasa* de Gropius mise à part, on assiste à une véritable libération du retour au bon sens séculaire dans la construction. Les fenêtres peuvent aujourd'hui parfaitement s'ouvrir, même si cela rompt les surfaces lissées des bâtiments modernes, et orienter une structure afin d'éviter le soleil de midi est devenu un argument de vente extrêmement puissant : ne sommes-nous pas verts et durables, et propres comme des sous neufs !

Bien sûr, il importe de lire attentivement le mode d'emploi avant d'avaler les délicieuses petites pilules vertes – vous savez bien, la mise en garde que cet excellent médicament peut causer des hémorragies internes, une cécité temporaire et de brusques pertes de conscience. La vérité, c'est que les cellules photovoltaïques contiennent des métaux lourds et que l'éthanol de maïs pourrait bien affamer la planète avant d'inverser le processus de réchauffement climatique. Alors, peut-être bien que l'herbe est plus verte de l'autre côté de la colline.

VERT ET MAIGRE

Tout cela est bel et bien beau, mais ne soyons pas trop sarcastiques, il y a certainement beaucoup à gagner à une certification LEED platine, même si les inconvénients de certains produits « verts » n'ont pas encore été complètement élucidés – et pourraient bien ne jamais l'être parce que quelqu'un en tire par ailleurs un joli bénéfice. La certification LEED (Leadership in Energy and Environmental Design), lancée par le Conseil américain pour les bâtiments verts (USGBC), est attribuée selon un système de points qui mesurent les performances des constructions dans les domaines suivants : aménagement écologique des sites ; gestion efficace de l'eau ; énergie et atmosphère ; matériaux et ressources ; qualité des environnements intérieurs ; emplacements et liaisons ; sensibilisation et formation ; innovation des processus de conception et priorité régionale [1]. Malgré sa complexité, car les catégories prises en compte restent assez subjectives, le système LEED a accompli des progrès considérables. Ce n'est pas la seule norme de mesure de la durabilité des bâtiments utilisée dans le monde, loin de là, mais l'USGBC déclare : « Avec 836 127 000 mètres carrés d'espace construit pris en compte dans les différents systèmes de notation et 148 645 mètres carrés d'espace certifié par jour dans le monde, le système LEED transforme la manière dont les environnements construits sont conçus, bâtis et exploités [...], des bâtiments et maisons individuels aux quartiers et communautés entiers. À la fois globale et souple, la norme LEED tient compte de l'ensemble du cycle de vie d'un bâtiment [2]. » Et voilà, n'est-ce pas plus simple ? Vous vous sentez mieux ?

LE BOIS, C'EST BIEN

Ce livre, tiré en partie de précédents ouvrages du même auteur, tente d'apporter une réponse nouvelle à la question à un million de dollars : « C'est quoi, être vert ? » Bien sûr, des constructions certifiées LEED y sont publiées et l'accent est mis sur la question de comment et pourquoi elles sont « durables ». Mais on y trouve aussi des jardins et des structures temporaires qui ne restent pas assez longtemps en place pour survivre au processus de certification LEED. Il faut bien voir par exemple que le Musée nomade de Shigeru Ban, fait de tubes de papier et de conteneurs maritimes recyclés, ne peut pas avoir eu un impact aussi négatif sur l'environnement, même si aucun système de notation ne peut le prouver. Enfin, on trouve aussi dans ce livre des bâtiments en bois ou en pisé. Le bois est connu pour poser un problème environnemental s'il n'est pas récolté correctement, mais là aussi, il existe des systèmes de notation comme la certification FSC de gestion des forêts et ils sont de plus en plus répandus. D'un autre côté, le bois peut être considéré comme la ressource renouvelable suprême, surtout s'il est éliminé de manière responsable après usage.

TECHNICIENS DU KILOWATTHEURE UNISSEZ-VOUS !

On trouve dans les pages qui suivent des parcs, comme la petite place Samir Kassir à Beyrouth (Vladimir Djurovic), ou encore des serres, dont une en briques LEGO, parce que ce qui y pousse est vert. Il ne faut voir là aucune exagération – les seuls bâtiments verts ne sont pas ceux qui ont recours à des gadgets high-tech pour réduire leur consommation d'énergie. Certaines structures, ou même certains espaces, contribuent délibérément et avec bonheur à l'équilibre naturel des choses – que le développement effréné a perdu de vue à bien des endroits. Le botaniste français Patrick Blanc ne cesse ainsi de prouver encore et toujours avec ses élégants jardins verticaux que le centre des villes peut lui aussi être un lieu de nature. Non, décidément non, ce livre n'est pas destiné aux techniciens du kilowattheure, même si certains pourraient être bien inspirés de prendre le temps de regarder les cent projets publiés. Disons que c'est un livre qui *porte un regard en arrière* sur les moyens utilisés depuis toujours pour rendre les bâtiments confortables, même s'il fait trop chaud ou trop froid dehors. C'est aussi un livre qui *porte un regard en avant* sur la recherche active de moyens techniques pour contrôler le réchauffement climatique dans la construction – elle est responsable d'un pourcentage significatif des émissions de gaz à effet de serre dans le monde. Mais peut-être la meilleure façon de le qualifier consiste-t-elle à dire que c'est un livre qui *porte un regard vers le haut*, vers le ciel et le soleil, puis *vers le bas*, vers la terre et l'herbe, parfois bien verte sous nos pieds, même à l'endroit où nous nous tenons.

1 http://www.usgbc.org/DisplayPage.aspx?CMSPageID=1989 consulté le 12 août 2012.
2 http://www.usgbc.org/DisplayPage.aspx?CMSPageID=1988 consulté le 12 août 2012.

24H ARCHITECTURE

24H Architecture
Hoflaan 132
3062 JM Rotterdam
The Netherlands

Tel: +31 10 411 10 00
Fax: +31 10 282 72 87
E-mail: info@24h.eu
Web: www.24h.eu

MAARTJE LAMMERS was born in 1963 and graduated from the Technical University of Delft in 1988. **BORIS ZEISSER**, born in 1968, graduated from the same institution in 1995. The pair worked in several architectural offices before founding 24H Architecture on January 1, 2001, such as (EEA) Erick van Egeraat Associated Architects, Mecanoo, and the Office for Metropolitan Architecture (Rem Koolhaas). Describing their work as inspired by the forms of nature and Art Deco, the firm currently employs 16 people. Their work includes the Ichthus Business Center (Rotterdam, The Netherlands, 2002); Dragspelhuset Holiday House (Arjang, Sweden, 2004); Soneva Kiri, Eco Holiday Resort (Koh Kood, Thailand, 2009); Panyaden School (Chiang Mai, Thailand, 2010–11, published here); Rijkswaterstaat Office (Assen, The Netherlands, 2011); and the Environmental Education Center (Assen, The Netherlands, 2012). Ongoing work includes Salt Cay Resort for Six Senses (Turks and Caicos Islands, 2013); and the Cité des Deux Mers (Morocco, 2013).

MAARTJE LAMMERS wurde 1963 geboren und schloss ihr Studium 1988 an der Technischen Universität Delft ab. **BORIS ZEISSER**, geboren 1968, machte seinen Abschluss 1995 an derselben Hochschule. Bevor sie am 1. Januar 2001 ihr eigenes Büro 24H Architecture gründeten, arbeiteten die beiden für verschiedene Büros, darunter für EEA (Erick van Egeraat Associated Architects), Mecanoo und das Office for Metropolitan Architecture (Rem Koolhaas). Als Einflüsse nennt das Team die Formen der Natur und den Art déco, das Büro beschäftigt derzeit 16 Mitarbeiter. Zu ihren Projekten zählen das Ichthus Business Center (Rotterdam, Niederlande, 2002), das Ferienhaus Dragspelhuset (Arjang, Schweden, 2004), die ökologische Ferienanlage Soneva Kiri (Koh Kood, Thailand, 2009), die Panyaden School (Chiang Mai, Thailand, 2010–11, hier vorgestellt), ein Bürogebäude für die Rijkswaterstaat-Behörde (Assen, Niederlande, 2011) sowie das Zentrum für Umwelterziehung (Assen, Niederlande, 2012). Aktuelle Projekte sind u. a. der Salt Cay Resort for Six Senses (Turks- und Caicosinseln, 2013) und die Cité des Deux Mers (Marokko, 2013).

MAARTJE LAMMERS, née en 1963, est diplômée de l'Université de technologie de Delft (1988), comme **BORIS ZEISSER**, né en 1968 et diplômé en 1995. Le couple a travaillé dans plusieurs agences, dont Erick van Egeraat Associated Architects (EEA), Mecanoo et l'Office for Metropolitan Architecture (Rem Koolhaas), avant de créer 24H Architecture le 1er janvier 2001. Le travail de l'agence, qui emploie 16 collaborateurs, s'inspire des formes de la nature et du style Art déco. Parmi leurs réalisations : l'Ichthus Business Center (Rotterdam, Pays-Bas, 2002) ; la maison de vacances Dragspelhuset (Arjang, Suède, 2004) ; le complexe d'écovacances Soneva Kiri (Koh Kood, Thaïlande, 2009) ; l'école de Panyaden (Chiang Mai, Thaïlande, 2010–11, publiée ici) ; les bureaux du Rijkswaterstaat (Assen, Pays-Bas, 2011) et un Centre d'éducation environnementale (Assen, Pays-Bas, 2012). Ils travaillent actuellement aux projets du Salt Cay Resort for Six Senses (îles Turks et Caicos, 2013) et de la Cité des Deux Mers (Maroc, 2013).

PANYADEN SCHOOL

Chiang Mai, Thailand, 2010–11

Address: 218 Moo 2, T. Namprae, A. Hang Dong, Chiang Mai 50230, Thailand, +66 5342 6618, www.panyaden.org
Area: 5000 m². Client: Yodphet Sudsawad. Cost: not disclosed
Collaboration: Olav Bruin, Andrew Duff

Built in a former orchard, the **PANYADEN SCHOOL** was conceived as a kindergarten and primary school for 375 students in a layout inspired by the shape "of the tropical antler horn fern." Classroom pavilions have load-bearing rammed-earth walls, which are connected by free-shaped adobe walls. All floors are of rammed earth and bamboo roof structures are related in their form to nearby mountains. The assembly hall and canteen are entirely made of bamboo with single bamboo or bundled bamboo columns, giving the feeling of walking through a bamboo forest. All materials are sourced locally and the overall carbon footprint of the project is a 10th of a comparable school. Panyaden School aims to deliver a holistic education that integrates Buddhist principles and environmental awareness with international academic standards.

Die **PANYADEN SCHOOL** wurde auf einer ehemaligen Obstplantage als Kindergarten und Grundschule für rund 375 Schülerinnen und Schüler geplant, ihr Grundriss ist der Form des „tropischen großen Geweihfarns" nachempfunden. Die tragenden Wände der Klassenraumpavillons wurden aus Stampflehm errichtet, zwischen ihnen verlaufen frei geformte Wände aus Lehmziegeln. Sämtliche Böden sind ebenfalls aus Stampflehm, während die Dachkonstruktion aus Bambus formal an die nahe Berglandschaft anknüpft. Aula und Kantine wurden mithilfe von Bambussäulen oder Säulenbündeln vollständig aus Bambus errichtet, sodass der Eindruck entsteht, durch einen Bambuswald zu laufen. Sämtliche Materialien sind lokalen Ursprungs, der gesamte ökologische Fußabdruck des Projekts beträgt rund ein Zehntel eines vergleichbaren Schulbaus. Die Panyaden School will ganzheitliche Bildung bieten und dabei buddhistische Prinzipien und Umweltbewusstsein mit internationalen akademischen Standards verbinden.

Établie dans un ancien verger, l'**ÉCOLE DE PANYADEN** est un jardin d'enfants et école primaire conçu pour recevoir 375 élèves. Son plan s'inspire de la forme d'une fougère tropicale, la *Platycerium superbum*. Les pavillons des classes ont des murs porteurs en pisé et des murs de façade de forme libre en adobe. Tous les sols sont en terre battue et les toitures en bambou rappellent le profil des montagnes avoisinantes. La salle de réunions et la cantine sont entièrement en bambou. La toiture est soutenue par des colonnes simples ou à fûts multiples réalisées dans ce même matériau, ce qui donne l'impression de se trouver dans une forêt de bambous. Tous les matériaux sont d'origine locale et l'empreinte carbone du projet n'est que le dixième de celle d'une école traditionnelle comparable. L'établissement délivre un enseignement holistique qui intègre à la fois des principes bouddhistes et des méthodes académiques internationales pour favoriser la prise de conscience environnementale des élèves.

The school blends into its jungle background in the image above. Right page, the undulating roof is seen in a closer image and in the elevation and section drawings below. A site plan shows the disposition of the elements of the complex.

Die Schule fügt sich harmonisch in die Dschungelkulisse (oben). Rechts das geschwungene Dach aus geringerer Distanz sowie auf Querschnitten unten. Ein Lageplan zeigt die Anordnung der baulichen Elemente des Komplexes.

Image ci-dessus : l'école se fond dans l'arrière-plan de la jungle. Page de droite : le toit ondulé en vue rapprochée et en élévation et en coupe dans les plans techniques. Un plan du site montre la disposition des diverses composantes du complexe.

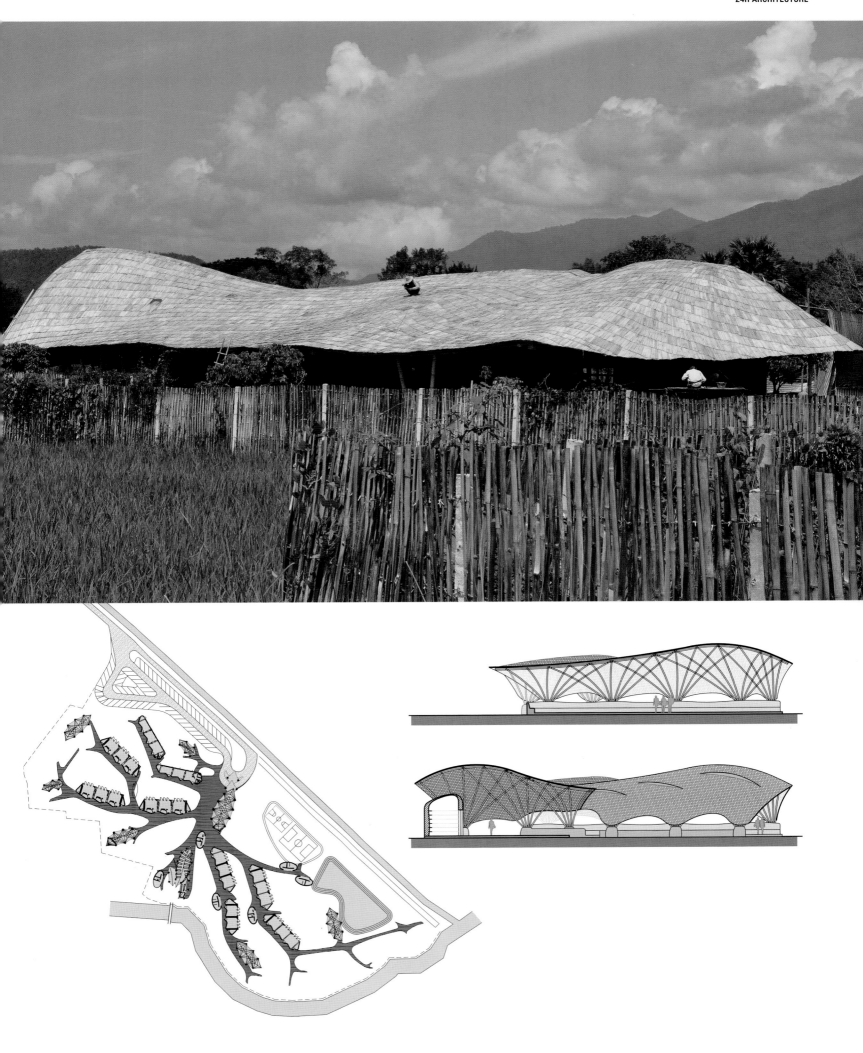

People gathered in the assembly hall with its bundled bamboo columns and low arching roof. Rammed-earth walls mark classroom areas. Local materials and a simple, intelligent form of construction make the carbon footprint of the complex very low.

Eine Versammlung in der „Aula" mit ihren gebündelten Bambusstützen und dem tief heruntergezogenen Dach. Wände aus Stampflehm markieren die Klassenräume. Lokale Materialien und einfache, intelligente Bauformen sorgen für eine ausgesprochen niedrige CO_2-Bilanz.

Assemblée dans la salle de réunions à colonnes à fûts multiples en bambou et à toiture à retombées surbaissées. Des murs en pisé délimitent les salles de classe. Grâce aux matériaux locaux et à un procédé de construction simple et intelligent, l'empreinte carbone du projet reste très basse.

The design of the assembly hall,
seen in plan and image (above),
encourages the natural circulation
of air and is inspired by the forms
of local vegetation.

*Die Konstruktion der Aula auf einem
Grundriss und im Bild (oben). Die von
regionaltypischen Pflanzen inspirierte
Bauform fördert die natürliche Luft-
zirkulation.*

*La forme de la salle de réunions vue
en plan et en image (ci-dessus)
s'inspire des formes végétales
locales et encourage la circulation
naturelle de l'air.*

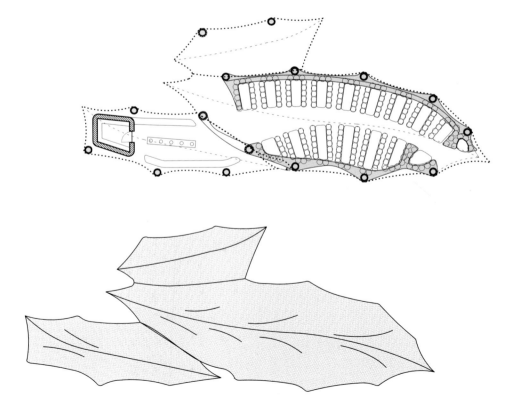

70F

70F
Stamerbos 34
1358 EP Almere
The Netherlands

Tel: +31 36 540 29 00
Fax: +31 36 540 70 20
E-mail: info@70F.com
Web: www.70F.com

BASTEN BRINKE was born in Amsterdam, the Netherlands, in 1972 and received his degree in Architecture at the Technical University in Eindhoven in 1995. **CARINA NILSSON** was born in Lund, Sweden, in 1970 and received her degree in Architecture at Chalmers Technical University, Gothenburg, in 1998. Before that she studied sculpture, drawing, and jewelry making at Lawrence University in the United States. The pair worked in several different offices in the Netherlands before founding 70F in 2000. Their current work includes several villas in the Netherlands; a group of 25 holiday homes in southern Sweden; a Sheep Stable (Almere, 2007); a Petting Farm (Almere, 2008, published here); the EBG Church in Amsterdam (2012); and a luxury spa with five holiday homes, a villa, and a sheep stable in central Italy (Aquilonia, Avellino, 2010–).

BASTEN BRINKE wurde 1972 in Amsterdam geboren und erhielt 1995 sein Diplom in Architektur an der Technischen Universität Eindhoven. **CARINA NILSON** wurde 1970 in Lund, Schweden, geboren und machte 1998 ihr Diplom in Architektur an der Technischen Hochschule Chalmers in Göteborg. Davor hatte sie Bildhauerei, Zeichnen und Schmuckdesign an der Lawrence University in den USA studiert. Bevor das Paar 2000 sein eigenes Büro 70F gründete, arbeitete es bei verschiedenen Architekten in den Niederlanden. Zu den aktuellen Arbeiten von 70F zählen mehrere Villen in den Niederlanden, eine Gruppe von 25 Ferienhäusern in Südschweden, ein Schafstall (Almere, 2007), ein Kinderbauernhof (Almere, 2008, hier vorgestellt), die Kirche der Herrnhuter Brüdergemeine in Amsterdam (2012) und eine luxuriöse Wellnessanlage mit fünf Ferienhäusern, einer Villa und einem Schafstall in Mittelitalien (Aquilonia, Avellino, ab 2010).

BASTEN BRINKE, né à Amsterdam en 1972, est diplômé en architecture de l'Université polytechnique d'Eindhoven (1995). **CARINA NILSSON**, née à Lund (Suède) en 1970, est diplômée en architecture de l'Université polytechnique de Göteborg (1998). Elle avait précédemment étudié la sculpture, le dessin et la joaillerie à l'université Lawrence aux États-Unis. Le couple a travaillé dans différentes agences néerlandaises avant de fonder 70F en 2000. Parmi leurs travaux récents : plusieurs villas aux Pays-Bas ; un ensemble de 25 résidences de vacances en Suède méridionale ; une bergerie (Almere, 2007) ; un minizoo (Almere, 2008, publié ici) ; l'église EBG à Amsterdam (2007–12) et un spa de luxe accompagné de cinq résidences de vacances, une villa et une bergerie dans le centre de l'Italie (Aquilonia, Avellino, 2010–).

PETTING FARM

Almere, The Netherlands, 2008

Address: Den Uylpark, Almere, The Netherlands
Area: 114 m². Client: Municipality of Almere. Cost: €180 000

The architects were approached in 2005 to design a **PETTING FARM** structure on the site of an earlier building that had been destroyed by fire in the early 1980s. Built entirely using money from sponsors, the building makes use of the preexisting foundations. The architects state: "We designed a wooden box with an open façade system for the upper half of the building, allowing the wind to ventilate the whole farm continuously." The stable occupies half the building, with offices, storage space, and toilets making up the rest of the project. With no doors but six shutters, two for the public and four for the animals, the shutters can be opened automatically or manually in the morning and are closed at night. The animals are visible on both sides as the public passes through the middle of the building. With its slat structure, the Petting Farm glows from within at night. The architects conclude: "One could say that the box, a building extensively reduced in aesthetic violence, wakes up and goes to sleep every day."

Die Architekten wurden 2005 beauftragt, ein Gebäude für den **KINDERBAUERNHOF** auf dem Gelände eines Anfang der 1980er-Jahre abgebrannten Altbaus zu planen. Für das ausschließlich mit Spendengeldern errichtete Bauwerk wurden die vorhandenen Fundamente genutzt. Die Architekten erklären: „Wir planten eine hölzerne Kiste mit einem offenen Fassadensystem für die obere Hälfte des Gebäudes, damit der Wind ständig den ganzen Bauernhof durchlüften kann." Der Stall nimmt die Hälfte des Bauwerks ein, in dem anderen Teil befinden sich Büros, Lagerraum und Toiletten. Der Bau hat keine Türen, sondern nur sechs Klappläden, zwei für Besucher und vier für die Tiere. Sie können morgens automatisch oder manuell geöffnet und nachts geschlossen werden. Besucher werden mittig durch das Gebäude geführt, die Tiere sind an beiden Seiten untergebracht. Bei Nacht dringt das Licht durch die Lattenkonstruktion nach außen und lässt das Gebäude leuchten. Abschließend erklären die Architekten: „Man kann sagen, dass diese in ihrer ästhetischen Wirkung extrem reduzierte Kiste jeden Tag aufwacht und schlafen geht."

C'est en 2005 que les architectes avaient été consultés pour la création de ce **MINIZOO** pour animaux domestiques sur le site d'un bâtiment détruit par un incendie au début des années 1980. Entièrement financée par des sponsors, la construction repose sur les fondations préexistantes. « Nous avons conçu cette boîte en bois à système de façade ouvrante en partie supérieure, ce qui permet au vent de le ventiler en permanence », expliquent les architectes. L'étable proprement dite occupe la moitié de l'installation, des bureaux, un espace de stockage et des toilettes se partageant le reste. Pas de portes mais six volets, deux pour le public et quatre pour les animaux, qui s'ouvrent automatiquement ou manuellement le matin et sont refermés le soir. Les animaux sont visibles des deux côtés d'un passage central emprunté par le public. Habillée de lattes de bois, la ferme semble illuminée de l'intérieur pendant la nuit. « On pourrait dire que cette boîte, bâtiment largement dénué de toute agressivité esthétique, se réveille le matin et s'endort le soir, chaque jour », concluent les architectes.

The Petting Farm gives an impression of having almost blank, wooden façades, but in this case, large doors fold up, revealing the interior.

Der Kinderbauernhof zeigt fast geschlossene Holzfassaden. In diesem Fall können jedoch große Türen aufgeklappt werden, um den Blick ins Innere freizugeben.

Le minizoo donne l'impression de se cacher derrière des façades de bois presque aveugles, mais ici de grandes portes se soulèvent pour donner accès à l'intérieur.

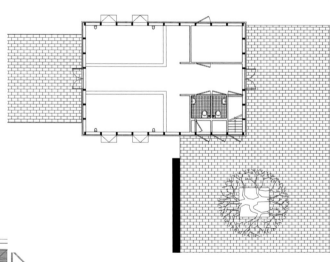

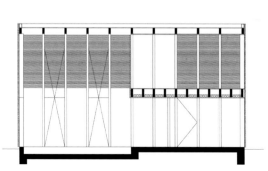

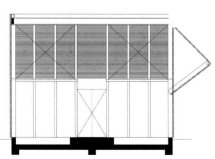

EFFAN ADHIWIRA

Effan Adhiwira
PT Bamboo Pure
Br. Piakan, Sibang Kaja, Abiansemal
Badung
Bali 80352
Indonesia

Tel: +62 36 146 9874
E-mail: info@ibuku.com
Web: www.ibuku.com

EFFAN ADHIWIRA was born in 1982. He received his B.Arch degree from the Faculty of Engineering, Gadjah Mada University (Jogjakarta, Indonesia, 2000–05). He worked as an architect for the firm Toma House from 2005 to 2007. He has been the Senior Architect at PT Bamboo Pure since 2007. Recent work includes the Green School (Badung, Bali, 2007, published here); Kaba-Kaba house (Tabanan, Bali, 2009); VW House (Gianyar, Bali, 2009); and the Tanduk House (Payangan, Bali, 2010). Current work includes the Alphonse Island Resort (Alphonse Island, Seychelles, 2010–); Live Media Theater, a portable 30-meter-diameter bamboo dome theater; the Pemulung House(s) (Denpasar, Bali, 2010–); and the Green Village (Sibang, Bali, 2011–), all in Indonesia unless stated otherwise.

EFFAN ADHIWIRA wurde 1982 geboren und machte seinen B.Arch. an der Fakultät für Ingenieurwesen an der Universität Gadjah Mada (Jogjakarta, Indonesien, 2000–05). Von 2005 bis 2007 war er als Architekt bei Toma House tätig. Seit 2007 ist er leitender Architekt bei PT Bamboo Pure. Jüngere Projekte sind u. a. die Green School (Badung, Bali, 2007, hier vorgestellt), das Kaba-Kaba House (Tabanan, Bali, 2009), VW House (Gianyar, Bali, 2009) sowie das Tanduk House (Payangan, Bali, 2010). Derzeit in Arbeit sind u. a. das Alphonse Island Resort (Alphonse Island, Seychellen, ab 2010), das Live Media Theater, ein mobiler Theater-Bambuskuppelbau mit einem Durchmesser von 30 m, die Pemulung House(s) (Denpasar, Bali, ab 2010) sowie das Green Village (Sibang, Bali, ab 2011), alle in Indonesien, sofern nicht anders angegeben.

EFFAN ADHIWIRA, né en 1982, a obtenu son B.Arch. à la faculté d'ingénierie de l'université Gadjah Mada (Jogjakarta, Indonésie, 2000–05). Il a travaillé pour l'agence Toma House de 2005 à 2007 et, depuis cette date, est architecte senior chez PT Bamboo Pure. Parmi ses réalisations récentes : l'École verte (Badung, Bali, 2007, publiée ici) ; la maison Kaba-Kaba (Tabanan, Bali, 2009) ; la maison VW (Gianyar, Bali, 2009) et la maison Tanduk (Payangan, Bali, 2010). Actuellement, il travaille sur les projets de l'Alphonse Island Resort (Alphonse Island, Seychelles, 2010–) ; du Live Media Theater, un théâtre mobile à coupole en bambou de 30 m de diamètre ; des Pemulung House(s) (Denpasar, Bali, 2010–) et du Village vert (Sibang, Bali, 2011–), tous en Indonésie sauf mention contraire.

GREEN SCHOOL

Badung, Bali, Indonesia, 2007

Address: Sibang Kaja, Abiansemal, Badung, Bali, Indonesia, +62 36 146 9875, www.greenschool.org
Area: 7542 m². Client: Yayasan Kulkul. Cost: $30 212 million

PT Bamboo and the related Meranggi Foundation were founded by John and Cynthia Hardy, designers and environmentalists from Bali. PT Bamboo is a design and construction company that uses bamboo, while the Meranggi Foundation seeks to develop bamboo timber plantations. They decided to build a school to demonstrate their interest in the use of sustainable materials for construction, and to educate children in sustainable life patterns. The bamboo used for the school was transformed by local artisans. Such materials as recycled rubble or car windshields are employed and landscaping includes an organic garden, a wastewater garden, and living tree fences. Bamboo columns are set on top of natural river stones to avoid insect- and humidity-related degradation of the wood. Steel bars drilled through the support rocks connect the columns to the foundation. Outward leaning columns and large roof overhangs reduce solar gain.

PT Bamboo und die mit dem Büro assoziierte Meranggi Foundation wurden von John und Cynthia Hardy gegründet, Designern und Umweltschützern auf Bali. Während PT Bamboo als Gestaltungs- und Baufirma mit Bambus arbeitet, bemüht sich die Meranggi Foundation um die Schaffung von Bambus-Bauholzplantagen. Die Entscheidung zum Bau der Schule entstand aus dem Interesse an der Verwendung von nachhaltigen Baumaterialien und dem Wunsch, Kindern nachhaltige Lebensweisen zu vermitteln. Der für den Schulbau verwendete Bambus wurde von ortsansässigen Kunsthandwerkern verarbeitet. Auch Materialien wie recycelter Bauschutt oder Autowindschutzscheiben kamen zum Einsatz. Die Landschaftsgestaltung umfasst u. a. einen Biogarten, einen Brauchwassergarten und „lebende" Zäune. Um die Schädigung des Holzes durch Insektenbefall oder Feuchtigkeit zu verhindern, wurden die Bambusstützen auf Steine aus einem Flussbett gesetzt. Durch Stahlstäbe, die durch die Steine gebohrt wurden, sind die Stützen im Fundament verankert. Dank der Außenneigung der Stützen und dem großzügigen Dachüberhang wird die Erwärmung des Baus durch Sonneneinstrahlung reduziert.

PT Bamboo et la Meranggi Foundation affiliée ont été fondées par John et Cynthia Hardy, designers et écologistes installés à Bali. PT Bamboo est une agence de design et de construction qui utilise le bambou, tandis que la Meranggi Foundation cherche à en développer les applications. Ensemble, ils ont voulu construire une école pour illustrer l'intérêt de l'utilisation de matériaux durables dans la construction et former les enfants à des modes de vie durables. Le bambou a été transformé par des artisans locaux. D'autres matériaux comme des moellons ou des pare-brise d'automobiles de récupération ont été utilisés. L'aménagement paysager comprend un jardin biologique, un jardin de traitement des eaux usées et des haies vives. Les colonnes de bambou s'appuient sur des pierres trouvées dans la rivière pour éviter les attaques des insectes et les effets de l'humidité. Des tiges d'acier qui traversent ces supports en pierre solidarisent les colonnes aux fondations. Les importants débords de la toiture soutenue par des colonnes inclinées réduisent le gain solaire.

The school blends into the tropical vegetation much in the way that purely indigenous architecture might. Modulated building sizes and the materials employed assure this symbiotic appearance.

Die Schule verschmilzt mit der tropischen Vegetation, wie es eine rein indigene Architektur tun würde. Dieser symbiotische Eindruck wird durch die Modulation unterschiedlicher Proportionen und Materialien erreicht.

L'école se fond dans la végétation tropicale à la manière de l'architecture indigène. La dimension raisonnable des constructions et les matériaux utilisés expliquent cette impression de symbiose.

Spiraling fernlike patterns mark the plan and little distinction can be made between interior and exterior spaces, with bamboo columns offering ample ceiling heights.

Die Form des Grundrisses erinnert an Farnwedel. Außen- und Innenraum sind dank der Bambusstützen und großzügigen Deckenhöhe kaum zu unterscheiden.

Le plan en spirales rappelle le développement des fougères et la distinction entre les espaces intérieurs et extérieurs est floue. Les colonnes de bambou permettent de généreuses hauteurs de plafonds.

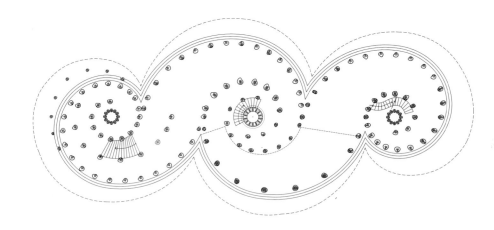

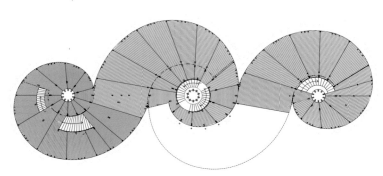

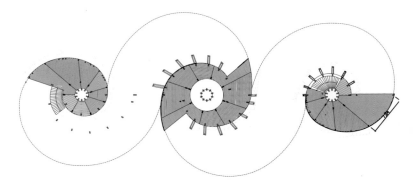

The design of the large arching roof, seen in the images above and the drawing on the right, brings to mind very modern design, albeit here erected using only sustainable materials.

Das Design der hohen, geschwungenen Dachkonstruktion (Abbildungen oben und Zeichnung rechts) wirkt wie ein hochmoderner Entwurf, wurde jedoch ausschließlich mit nachhaltigen Materialien realisiert.

Le design de la vaste toiture en arc (photos ci-dessus et dessins de droite) rappelle des projets d'esprit contemporain, malgré l'utilisation exclusive de matériaux durables.

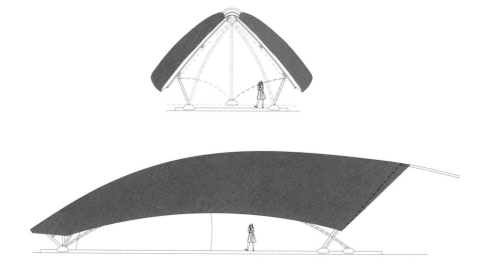

With its generous, open walls and high ceilings, the Green School certainly defies the usual image of sustainable architecture, which might be imagined as being dull and dark. Elevations (right) give an idea of the large scale of the buildings.

Mit ihren offenen Wänden und hohen Decken entspricht die Green School sicherlich nicht den üblichen Vorstellungen von nachhaltiger Architektur, die mitunter fälschlich für fade und dunkel gehalten wird. Aufrisse (rechts) vermitteln einen Eindruck vom Maßstab der Gebäude.

Par ses ouvertures sur la nature et ses plafonds élevés, l'École verte est un défi à l'image habituelle des constructions durables, souvent jugées ennuyeuses et peu lumineuses. Les élévations (à droite) donnent une idée de l'importance de l'échelle de ces bâtiments.

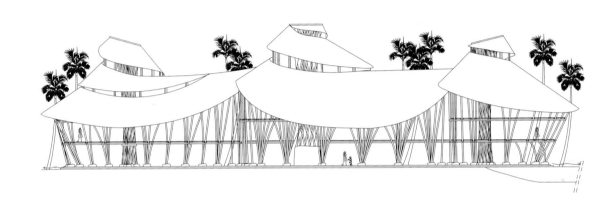

Bundled and assembled in a spiraling pattern, bamboo poles offer an obvious lightness and strength to the building. Daylight and fresh air are also omnipresent in this architecture.

Durch die spiralförmig angeordneten Bambussäulenbündel wirkt der Bau ausgesprochen hell und belastbar. Allgegenwärtig in dieser Architektur sind Tageslicht und frische Luft.

Liés et assemblés en torsades, les piliers de bambou confèrent au bâtiment un sentiment de légèreté et de solidité. La lumière et la ventilation naturelles animent en permanence l'architecture.

Curving desks echo the form of the buildings, while the curvature and slating of the roofs assures that potentially heavy monsoon rains can be carried off without overloading the structure.

Die geschwungenen Tische greifen die Form der Bauten auf. Schwung und Neigung der Dächer wiederum sorgen dafür, dass Wasser bei heftigen Monsunregen abfließen kann, ohne die Konstruktion zu überlasten.

Les bureaux incurvés rappellent la forme des bâtiments tandis que la courbure et l'inclinaison des toits protègent des fortes pluies de la mousson et assurent leur évacuation sans surcharger la structure.

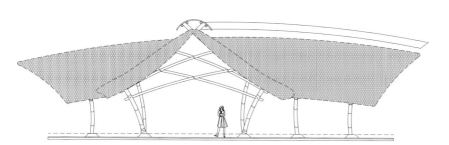
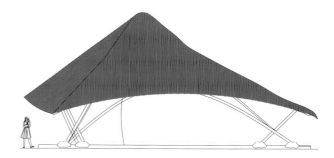
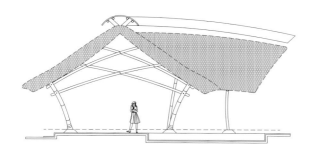
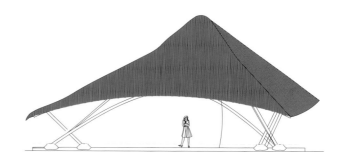

AFF

AFF Architekten
Wedekindstr. 24
10243 Berlin
Germany

Tel: +49 30 27 59 29 20
Fax: +49 30 275 92 92 22
E-mail: berlin@aff-architekten.com
Web: www.aff-architekten.com

AFF ARCHITEKTEN was founded in 1999 by Martin Fröhlich (born in 1968 in Magdeburg, Germany), Sven Fröhlich (born in 1974, also in Magdeburg), and Torsten Lockl (born in 1973 in Gotha, Germany), graduates of the Bauhaus University Weimar. They state that: "In accordance with the workshop tradition, we wanted to establish a firm that would produce architecture with character through the collaboration of committed architects." Their work includes Typological Houses (Weimar, 2006); Anna-Seghers Comprehensive School (Berlin, 2008); Freudenstein Castle (Freiberg, 2008); the exhibition "Terra Mineralia" (Freudenstein Castle, Freiberg, 2008); and the Protective Hut on Fichtelberg Mountain (Tellerhäuser, Oberwiesenthal, 2008–09, published here), all in Germany.

AFF ARCHITEKTEN wurde 1999 von Martin Fröhlich (1968 in Magdeburg geboren), Sven Fröhlich (1974 ebenfalls in Magdeburg geboren) und Torsten Lockl (geboren 1973 in Gotha) gegründet. Die Absolventen der Bauhaus-Universität Weimar erklären: „Im Sinne der Werkstättentradition wollten wir ein Büro gründen, das durch die Kollaboration engagierter Architekten Architektur mit Charakter entwirft." Zu ihren Projekten zählen Typologische Wohnhäuser (Weimar, 2006), die Gemein-schaftsschule Anna Seghers (Berlin, 2008), das Schloss Freudenstein (Freiberg, 2008), die Ausstellung *Terra Mineralia* (Schloss Freudenstein, Freiberg, 2008) sowie die Schutzhütte am Fichtelberg (Tellerhäuser, Oberwiesenthal, 2008–09, hier vorgestellt), alle in Deutschland.

L'agence **AFF ARCHITEKTEN** a été fondée en 1999 par Martin Fröhlich (né en 1968 à Magdeburg, Allemagne), Sven Fröhlich (né en 1974 à Magdeburg) et Torsten Lockl (né en 1973 à Gotha, Allemagne), diplômés de l'université Bauhaus à Weimar. « Dans l'esprit de la tradition de l'atelier, nous souhaitions créer une agence qui produise une architecture de caractère grâce à la collaboration active d'architectes engagés dans le projet », expliquent-ils. Leur œuvre comprend entre autres : les Maisons typologiques (Weimar, 2006) ; l'école secondaire Anna-Seghers (Berlin, 2008) ; le château Freudenstein (Freiberg, 2008) ; l'exposition « Terra Mineralia » (châ-teau Freudenstein, Freiberg, 2008) et le refuge de montagne du Fichtelberg (Tellerhäuser, Oberwiesenthal, 2008–09, publié ici), tous en Allemagne.

"HUTZNHAISL"

Protective Hut on Fichtelberg Mountain, Tellerhäuser, Oberwiesenthal, Germany, 2008–09

Address: Tellerhäuser Str. 5, Tellerhäuser, 09484 Oberwiesenthal, Germany
Area: 70 m². Client: not disclosed. Cost: €60 000

As befits this winter scene, the building exudes an austerity that is itself undeniably cold.

Passend zur winterlichen Szene ist der Bau formal von einer Strenge, die ohne Frage kalt wirkt.

Comme il convient sans doute à cette scène hivernale, le petit bâtiment exsude une austérité glaciale.

A photo and drawing sum up the extremely simple form of the architecture, cast in concrete with no visible frills.

Aufnahme und Zeichnung zeigen die extrem schlichte Architektur, die offenkundig ohne Extras auskommt und in Beton gegossen wurde.

Cette photo et le dessin ci-dessous illustrent l'extrême simplicité de l'architecture en béton coulé, sans le moindre ornement visible.

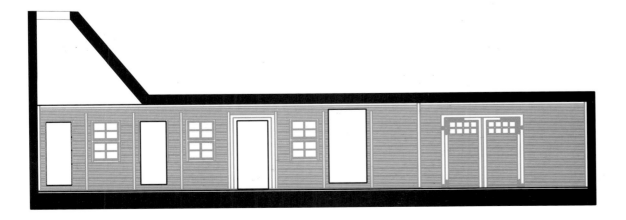

The architects state: "The hut appears to have been wrestled from the surrounding landscape, a concrete sculpture at the side of the road from Rittersgrün and Oberwiesenthal through the Ore Mountains in Saxony." The structure opens toward the forest "like a bus stop opens only to the street, always in the direction of the intended destination." Intended to accommodate six to eight people, the structure is spartan to say the least, with its concrete walls and ceilings and locally cut spruce floorboards. Recycled switches, lights, chairs, and washbasins are used. It has no "daring technical features" in a willful architectural distancing from modern urban life. The concrete of the structure bears the imprint of the former wooden hut that stood on the site, recalling work like that of the English sculptor Rachel Whiteread.

Die Architekten erklären: „Wie der Landschaft abgetrotzt erscheint die Hütte als Betonskulptur am Saum der erzgebirgischen Landstraße zwischen Rittersgrün und Oberwiesenthal." Der Bau öffnet sich zum Wald, „so wie sich eine Bushaltestelle ausschließlich zur Straße öffnet, immer in die Richtung des anvisierten Ziels". Der für sechs bis acht Personen ausgelegte Bau ist gelinde gesagt spartanisch mit seinen Wänden und Decken aus Beton und den Holzdielenböden aus vor Ort geschlagener Fichte. Schalter, Leuchten, Sessel, Stühle und Waschschüsseln sind recycelt. Hier gibt es keinerlei „gewagte technische Besonderheiten"; es ist die bewusste Distanzierung vom modernen, urbanen Leben durch Architektur. Auf dem Baukörper aus Beton zeichnet sich der Abdruck des Vorgängerbaus ab, ebenfalls eine Hütte – eine Reminiszenz an Arbeiten wie etwa die der englischen Künstlerin Rachel Whiteread.

« Sculpture en béton posée au bord de la route qui travers les monts Métallifères de Saxe, entre Rittersgrün et Oberwiesenthal, le refuge semble se mesurer au paysage qui l'environne », commentent les architectes. Il s'ouvre sur la forêt « comme un arrêt de bus s'ouvre sur la rue, toujours dans la direction de la destination supposée ». Prévu pour six à huit personnes, l'aménagement de ce refuge aux murs et plafonds en béton et sols en épicéa d'exploitation locale est pour le moins spartiate. Les éviers, les éclairages, les sièges et même les interrupteurs sont de récupération. Dans sa prise de distance par rapport à la vie urbaine moderne, ce refuge ne présente pas de « caractéristiques techniques audacieuses ». Le béton porte encore l'empreinte de l'ancien refuge en bois qui se trouvait sur le même site et rappelle le travail d'artistes comme la sculptrice britannique Rachel Whiteread.

The architects willfully eschew most comforts of modern life, while using casts of elements from the former wooden hut located on the same site, recalling work of artists such as Rachel Whiteread and her piece Ghost (1990).

Ganz bewusst verzichten die Architekten weitgehend auf modernen Komfort. Dank der Nutzung von Bauteilen des Vorgängerbaus, einer alten Holzhütte, als Schalungselemente erinnert der Bau an Arbeiten der Künstlerin Rachel Whiteread wie etwa Ghost (1990).

Les architectes ont volontairement renoncé à la plupart des conforts de la vie moderne et utilisé des éléments moulés à partir de l'ancien refuge en bois qu'ils remplaçaient. Ces interventions rappellent certaines œuvres d'art comme la pièce Ghost (1990) de Rachel Whitehead.

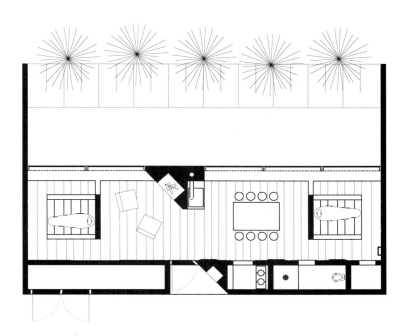

AGENCE BABYLONE

Agence Babylone
56 rue de Paradis
75010 Paris
France

Tel: +33 1 49 23 51 01
Fax: +33 1 43 40 31 31
E-mail: contact@agencebabylone.com
Web: www.agencebabylone.com

Jeoffroy de Castelbajac was born in 1957. He obtained his degree in Landscape Architecture from the École Nationale Supérieure du Paysage de Versailles in 2003. He worked from 1980 to 2000 as a composer. Henri de Dreuzy was born in 1974, and also obtained his Landscape Architecture degree in 2003 from the Versailles school. Adrien Fourès was born in 1978, and completed the same studies as Castelbajac and Dreuzy the same year. This is also the case of Vincent Léger, born in 1978. The four landscape architects are co-managers of **AGENCE BABYLONE**. As they explain their work, Agence Babylone "intervenes essentially in the urban environment, be it on the scale of a town square or an entire region, with a passion for ecology that guides them in the development of new synergies between the city and nature." Along with their winning project Active Nature (Saclay, 2007, published here), their current work includes a park in Cormeilles-en-Parisis (2004–09); an avenue, gardens, and a square in Liévin (2006–09); gardens for the ZAC des Ponts Jumeaux (Toulouse, 2006–10); a redesign of public spaces in Rouen (2005–10), Villeneuve-le-Roi (2006–10), and in Chauray (2007–10); and the Saint-Louis Square in Choisy-le-Roi (2007–10), all in France.

Jeoffroy de Castelbajac wurde 1957 geboren. Er schloss sein Studium der Landschaftsarchitektur 2003 an der École National Supérieure du Paysage de Versailles ab. Von 1980 bis 2000 arbeitete er als Komponist. Henri de Dreuzy wurde 1974 geboren und beendete sein Studium der Landschaftsarchitektur ebenfalls 2003 an der École National Supérieure du Paysage de Versailles. Adrien Fourès wurde 1978 geboren und schloss den gleichen Studiengang wie Castelbajac und Dreuzy im selben Jahr ab. Dasselbe gilt für Vincent Léger, der 1978 geboren wurde. Gemeinsam leiten die vier Landschaftsarchitekten die **AGENCE BABYLONE**. Nach eigener Aussage „greift [die Agence Babylone] im Grunde in die urbane Umwelt ein, sei es nun in der Größenordnung eines Marktplatzes oder einer ganzen Region, und zwar mit einer Leidenschaft für Ökologie, die ihr Leitschnur bei der Entwicklung neuer Synergien zwischen Stadt und Natur ist". Neben ihrem preisgekrönten Projekt Nature Active (Saclay, 2007, hier vorgestellt) gehören zu ihren jüngeren Aufträgen ein Park in Cormeilles-en-Parisis (2004–09), eine Allee, Gärten und ein Platz in Liévin (2006 bis 2009), Gärten für die ZAC des Ponts Jumeaux (Toulouse, 2006–10), Umgestaltungen des öffentlichen Raums in Rouen (2005–10), in Villeneuve-le-Roi (2006–10) und in Chauray (2007–10) sowie die Place Saint-Louis in Choisy-le-Roi (2007–10), alle in Frankreich.

Né en 1957, Jeoffroy de Castelbajac est paysagiste DPLG de l'École nationale supérieure du Paysage de Versailles (2003). Il a été compositeur de musique de 1980 à 2000. Henri de Dreuzy, né en 1974, est également paysagiste DPLG de l'École nationale supérieure du Paysage de Versailles (2003). Adrien Fourès, né en 1978, a accompli les mêmes études que Castelbajac et Dreuzy et a été diplômé la même année. C'est également le cas de Vincent Léger, né en 1978. Les quatre architectes paysagistes dirigent ensemble l'**AGENCE BABYLONE**. Celle-ci, expliquent-ils, « intervient essentiellement en milieu urbain, de l'échelle du square à celle du territoire, avec une passion pour l'écologie qui nous guide dans le développement de nouvelles synergies, pérennes et actives, entre ville et nature ». En dehors du projet Nature Active (Saclay, 2007, publié ici), leurs réalisations, toutes en France, comprennent un parc à Cormeilles-en-Parisis (2004–09) ; une avenue, des jardins et une place à Liévin (2006–09) ; des jardins pour la ZAC des Ponts-Jumeaux (Toulouse, 2006–10) ; la remise en forme d'espaces publics à Rouen (2005–10), Villeneuve-le-Roi (2006–10) et Chauray (2007–10) ainsi que la place Saint-Louis à Choisy-le-Roi (2007–10).

ACTIVE NATURE

Saclay, France, 2007

Site area: 360 km². Client: OIN Massy Palaiseau, Saclay, Versailles, Saint-Quentin-en-Yvelines
Cost: not disclosed. Collaboration: SoA architects, Alter Développement, Biodiversita

The OIN (Opération d'Intérêt National) or Operation of National Interest, a grouping of 49 towns in the suburbs of Paris, launched a competition in 2007 for ideas concerning its development over the next 30 years. With a projected increase in population of 350 000 people during the period, the region has placed a clear emphasis on sustainable development and ecology. Participants were asked to envisage the creation of 5000 homes per year over the 30-year span, while conserving 2000 hectares of existing farmland. Agence Babylone, with an emphasis on landscape design and urban development, worked on this competition with SoA architects, Biodiversita ecological engineers, and Alter Développement engineers. The team won the competition in the category for best use of the resources and natural patrimony of the site. Their idea was to make the maximum possible use of the "productive capacities of nature." Rather than imagining only the overall situation, they used a principle of successively larger zones, each responsible for its own resources. Existing forest areas would be preserved, and agricultural areas for fruit and vegetables added to urban zones. Agricultural zones, crossed by "ecological corridors" intended to protect the natural environment, would be used only for local production. A system of "green batteries" (piles vertes) produces energy in the process of treating waste water and garbage. New housing, coupled with retail and office space, would be concentrated in dense 120 x 160 meter "islands," allowing the overall population density of the region not to exceed 41 inhabitants per hectare.

OIN (Opération d'intérêt national) oder Operation im nationalen Interesse, ein Zusammenschluss von 49 Stadtgemeinden im Umland von Paris, schrieb 2007 einen Wettbewerb aus, um Ideen für die kommenden 30 Jahre zu entwickeln. Prognosen sagen für diese Zeitspanne ein Wachstum der dortigen Bevölkerung um 350 000 Menschen voraus, weshalb die Region besonderen Wert auf eine nachhaltige, ökologische Entwicklung legt. Prämisse für die Wettbewerbsteilnehmer war die Schaffung von 5000 Wohnungen innerhalb der kommenden 30 Jahre und zugleich die Erhaltung von 2000 ha Agrarland. Die Agence Babylone mit ihrem Schwerpunkt auf Landschaftsgestaltung und Stadtentwicklung arbeitete für diesen Wettbewerb mit SoA architectes, dem ökologischen Ingenieurbüro Biodiversita sowie dem Ingenieurbüro Alter Développement zusammen. Die Gruppe gewann den Wettbewerb in der Kategorie beste Nutzung von Ressourcen und des landschaftlichen Erbes des Areals. Ihre Idee war es, die „produktiven Kapazitäten der Natur" maximal zu nutzen. Statt nur die Gesamtsituation zu betrachten, arbeiteten sie nach einem Prinzip immer größer werdender Zonen, von denen jede für ihre eigenen Ressourcen verantwortlich ist. Bestehende Waldgebiete sollen erhalten, urbane Zonen um landwirtschaftliche Nutzflächen für Obst und Gemüse ergänzt werden. Landwirtschaftszonen, die ausschließlich der lokalen Versorgung dienen, werden von „ökologischen Korridoren" zum Schutz der Umwelt durchzogen. Ein System „grüner Batterien" („piles vertes") erzeugt Energie durch die Aufbereitung von Brauchwasser und Abfall. Die neuen Wohnanlagen, kombiniert mit Geschäfts- und Büroflächen, sollen sich auf „Inseln" von 120 x 160 m konzentrieren, sodass die Bevölkerungsdichte der Region 41 Bewohner pro Hektar nicht übersteigt.

L'OIN (Opération d'intérêt national) de Massy-Palaiseau, Saclay, Versailles et Saint-Quentin-en-Yvelines regroupant 49 communes de l'ouest de la banlieue parisienne a lancé un concours d'idées en 2007 pour préfigurer l'aménagement de son territoire sur les 30 prochaines années. Pour répondre à un accroissement prévu de la population de 350 000 personnes, l'accent a été mis sur le développement durable. Les participants devaient envisager la création de 5000 logements par an, tout en conservant 2000 ha de terres agricoles. L'agence, spécialisée dans le paysage et le développement urbains, a travaillé pour cette compétition en collaboration avec SoA architectes, les ingénieurs en écologie Biodiversita et les ingénieurs d'Alter Développement. L'équipe a remporté le concours dans la catégorie de la mise en valeur des ressources et du patrimoine naturel. Leur idée était d'utiliser au maximum « les capacités productives de la nature ». Plutôt que de n'imaginer que la situation globale, ils ont défini un principe de zones de plus en plus grandes, chacune en charge de ses propres ressources. Les zones forestières existantes seraient préservées et des secteurs agricoles de maraîchage créés à proximité des zones urbaines. Les terres agricoles, traversées par des « corridors écologiques », protégeraient l'environnement naturel et seraient cultivées pour la consommation locale. Un système de « piles vertes » produirait de l'énergie par le traitement des eaux et des déchets. Les nouveaux logements couplés à des bureaux et des commerces seraient concentrés en « îles » de 120 x 160 m permettant de ne pas dépasser une densité globale de population de 41 habitants par hectare.

An "aerial" view of the project shows its scale and also the close integration of green areas into and around the built-up areas.

Eine „Luftaufnahme" des Projekts macht dessen Dimensionen sowie die enge Integration der Grünflächen in und um die bebauten Zonen deutlich.

Une vue « aérienne » du projet montre son échelle et l'intégration étroite des espaces verts dans et autour du bâti.

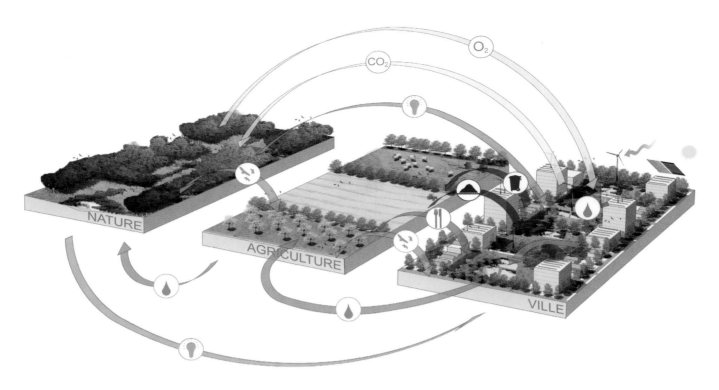

NATURE

AGRICULTURE

VILLE

A diagram and a rendering emphasize the close connection of the complex to nature. In the diagram, the flow of energy and sustenance from field and forest to built-up areas is depicted as a natural cycle.

Diagramm und Rendering veranschaulichen die Anbindung des Projekts an die Natur. Das Diagramm stellt den Energie- und Versorgungsfluss zwischen Feld und Wald sowie bebauten Zonen als natürlichen Zyklus dar.

Ce schéma et l'image de synthèse montrent les interactions entre le projet et la nature. Ci-dessus, les flux d'énergie et de production des cultures et de la forêt vers les zones construites sont représentés comme un cycle naturel.

The biodiverse green areas surrounding the city can assimilate
part of the CO_2 it produces and
generate 34% of the oxygen needs.
Forests and farms can provide food
for 350 000 people, becoming an
"agricultural garden".

Die biologisch vielfältigen Grünflächen um die Stadt absorbieren einen
Teil des dort ausgestoßenen CO_2
und produzieren 34 % des benötigten
Sauerstoffs. Wälder und Bauernhöfe
liefern Lebensmittel für 350 000
Menschen und werden zum
„landwirtschaftlichen Garten".

Les zones vertes de biodiversité
entourant la ville peuvent absorber
une partie du CO_2 qu'elle émet et
produire 34 % de sa consommation
d'oxygène. Des forêts et des fermes
produisent la nourriture pour
350 000 habitants et deviennent
un « jardin agricole ».

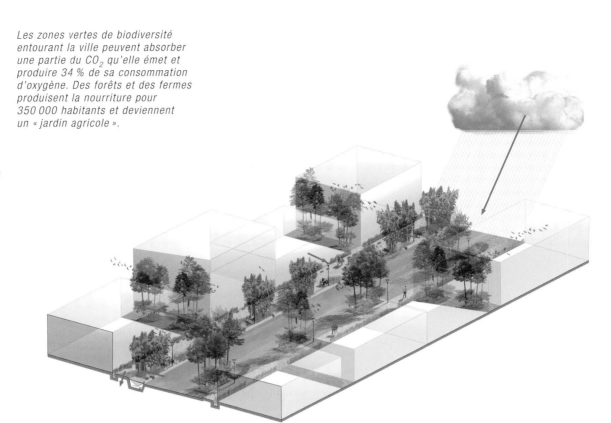

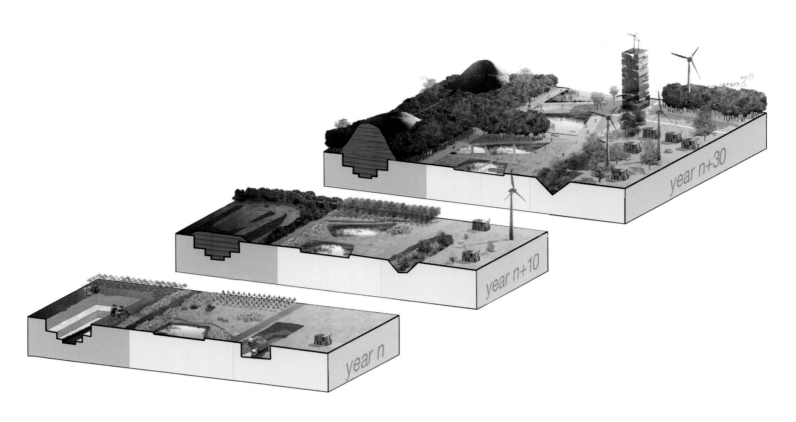

year n+30

year n+10

year n

ALDINGER ARCHITEKTEN

*aldingerarchitekten
Große Falterstr. 23a
70597 Stuttgart
Germany*

*Tel: +49 711 97 67 80
Fax: +49 711 97 67 83 3
E-mail: info@aldingerarchitekten.de
Web: www.aldingerarchitekten.de*

JÖRG ALDINGER was born in Stuttgart, Germany, in 1955. He completed his architectural studies at the University of Stuttgart (1975–80) and worked as a freelance architect, creating Aldinger & Aldinger in 1983, as a professor of Building Physics and Design at the Biberach University of Applied Sciences (1994), and as a visiting professor at California State Polytechnic University (Los Angeles, 1999) before founding Aldinger Architekten in 2009. **DIRK HERKER** was born in 1964 in Bremen, Germany. He studied architecture at the University of Stuttgart (1984–87), and then at Arizona State University (Phoenix, 1987–88). He returned to the University of Stuttgart (1988–91) for further studies and became a partner at Aldinger Architekten in 2009. **THOMAS STRÄHLE** was born in 1966 in Nellingen, Germany, and studied at the Biberach University of Applied Sciences (since 1994). Like Dirk Herker he worked with the earlier firm Aldinger & Aldinger before becoming a partner of Aldinger Architekten in 2009. In addition to the Cafeteria and Day Care Center, Waldorf School (Stuttgart, 2005–07, published here), current work of the firm includes the reconstruction and creation of an annex for an administrative and retail building in Bietigheim-Bissingen (2009–11); the restoration of castles in Meersburg (2010–11) and Schwetzingen (2009–12); and a school in Bad Aibling (2009–13), all in Germany.

JÖRG ALDINGER wurde 1955 in Stuttgart geboren. Nach Beendigung seines Architekturstudiums an der Universität Stuttgart (1975–80) arbeitete er als freischaffender Architekt und gründete 1983 das Büro Aldinger & Aldinger; er war Professor für Bauphysik und Entwerfen an der Hochschule Biberach (1994) und Gastprofessor an der California State Polytechnic University (Los Angeles, 1999). 2009 gründete er die Firma Aldinger Architekten. **DIRK HERKER** wurde 1964 in Bremen geboren. Er studierte Architektur an der Universität Stuttgart (1984–87) und danach an der Arizona State University (Phoenix, 1987–88). Dann kehrte er zu weiteren Studien an die Universität Stuttgart zurück (1988–91) und wurde 2009 Partner bei Aldinger Architekten. **THOMAS STRÄHLE** wurde 1966 in Nellingen geboren und studierte (ab 1994) an der Hochschule Biberach. Ebenso wie Dirk Herker arbeitete er im früheren Büro Aldinger & Aldinger, bevor er 2009 Partner bei Aldinger Architekten wurde. Außer der Cafeteria und der Tagesstätte der Waldorfschule (Stuttgart, 2005–07, hier vorgestellt) umfasst das aktuelle Werk des Büros u. a. den Umbau und die Erweiterung eines Verwaltungs- und Geschäftshauses in Bietigheim-Bissingen (2009–11), die Restaurierung von Schlössern in Meersburg (2010–11) und Schwetzingen (2009–12) sowie eine Schule in Bad Aibling (2009–13), alle in Deutschland.

JÖRG ALDINGER, né à Stuttgart (Allemagne) en 1955, a étudié l'architecture à l'université de Stuttgart (1975–80) et travaillé en free-lance avant de créer l'agence Aldinger & Aldinger en 1983. Il a été professeur de conception et de physique de la construction à l'Université des sciences appliquées de Biberach (1994), professeur invité à la California State Polytechnic University (Los Angeles, 1999) et a fondé Aldinger Architekten en 2009. **DIRK HERKER**, né en 1964 à Brême (Allemagne), a étudié l'architecture à l'université de Stuttgart (1984–87) et à l'Arizona State University (Phoenix, 1987–88). Il est revenu compléter ses études à l'université de Stuttgart (1988–91) avant de devenir partenaire d'Aldinger Architekten en 2009. **THOMAS STRÄHLE**, né en 1966 à Nellingen (Allemagne), a commencé ses études à l'Université des sciences appliquées de Biberach en 1994. Comme Dirk Herker, il a travaillé pour Aldinger & Aldinger avant de devenir partenaire d'Aldinger Architekten en 2009. En dehors de la cafétéria et de la garderie de l'école Waldorf (Stuttgart, 2005–07, publiée ici), l'agence a réalisé le projet de reconstruction-création d'une annexe pour un immeuble de bureaux et de commerces à Bietigheim-Bissingen (2009–11) ; la restauration de châteaux à Meersburg (2010–11) et Schwetzingen (2009–12) ainsi que la construction d'une école à Bad Aibling (2009–13), tous en Allemagne.

CAFETERIA AND DAY CARE CENTER, WALDORF SCHOOL

Stuttgart, Germany, 2005–07

Address: Haussmannstr. 44, 70188 Stuttgart, Germany, +49 711 21 00 20, www.waldorfschule-uhlandshoehe.de
Area: 1200 m². Client: Waldorf School Uhlandshoehe Association. Cost: €3.4 million
Collaboration: Maren Pettenpohl

The architects have used a "villa-typology" to better integrate this **ADDITION TO THE CAMPUS OF THE WALDORF SCHOOL** "Uhlandshöhe" into its neighborhood. An existing playground has been redefined to provide the main access to the structure that provides after-school care and houses a cafeteria, kitchen, high-school library, and a multipurpose room. A central staircase and an elevator also lead up to the top floor which includes a meeting area and access to a roof terrace. Although this is a three-story, reinforced-concrete building, it is clad in larch, has wood window frames, and a green roof. Inside built-in wooden furniture and colored, glazed concrete surfaces create a warm atmosphere.

Die Architekten verwendeten eine „Villentypologie", um diese **ERWEITERUNG DER WALDORFSCHULE** auf der Stuttgarter Uhlandshöhe besser in ihre Umgebung zu integrieren. Ein vorhandener Spielplatz wurde umgeplant zur Haupterschließung des Gebäudes, das zur Betreuung der Schüler nach dem Unterricht dient und eine Cafeteria, eine Küche, die Schulbibliothek und einen Mehrzweckraum enthält. Eine zentral angeordnete Treppe und ein Fahrstuhl führen bis ins oberste Geschoss, in dem sich ein Versammlungssaal befindet und der Zugang zu einer Dachterrasse. Obgleich es sich hier um einen dreigeschossigen Betonbau handelt, wurde er mit Lärchenholz verkleidet und hat Fensterrahmen aus Holz sowie ein begrüntes Dach. Innen sorgen das hölzerne Mobiliar und die farbigen, lasierten Betonwände für eine warme Atmosphäre.

Les architectes ont opté pour une « typologie de villa » afin de mieux intégrer cette **NOUVELLE CONSTRUCTION** à l'environnement du **CAMPUS DE L'ÉCOLE WALDORF**. Un terrain de jeux existant a été redessiné pour dégager l'accès principal au bâtiment qui regroupe une garderie, une cafétéria, une cuisine, la librairie du collège et une salle polyvalente. Un escalier central et un ascenseur conduisent au niveau supérieur qui comprend une salle de réunion et un accès à une terrasse en toiture. Réalisé en béton armé, ce petit immeuble de trois niveaux est habillé de mélèze, équipé d'huisseries en bois et d'une toiture végétalisée. À l'intérieur, un mobilier en bois intégré et des plans de couleur vernis créent une atmosphère chaleureuse.

As seen from most exterior angles, the school does, indeed, resemble a large private house or small apartment building. Here, larch is used as a cladding material, while the structure is in concrete and steel.

Aus fast allen Richtungen gesehen gleicht die Schule eher einem großen Privathaus oder einem kleinen Mehrfamilienhaus. Hier wurde Lärchenholz als Verkleidung gewählt, das Tragwerk ist aus Beton und Stahl.

Vue sous la plupart des angles, cette école fait penser à une grande résidence privée ou à un petit immeuble d'appartements. La structure est en acier et béton, le parement en mélèze.

EMILIO AMBASZ

Emilio Ambasz & Associates, Inc.
295 Central Park West, Suite 14D
New York, NY 10024, USA
E-mail: info@ambasz.com / Web: www.ambasz.com

EMILIO AMBASZ was born in 1943 in Argentina, and studied at Princeton University. He completed the undergraduate program in one year and received an M.Arch from the same institution the next year. He taught at Princeton University's School of Architecture, was a Visiting Professor at the Hochschule für Gestaltung in Ulm, Germany, and has lectured at several American universities. Ambasz served as Curator of Design at the Museum of Modern Art in New York (1970–76) and was a two-term President of the Architectural League (1981–85). Founded in 1976, Emilio Ambasz & Associates, Inc., offers a full range of design services, including building design, consulting, lighting, landscape, exhibition, graphic, and product design. Ambasz states: "It is my deep belief that design is an act of invention. I believe that its real task begins once functional and behavioral needs have been satisfied. It is not hunger, but love and fear, and sometimes wonder, which make us create. Our milieu may change from generation to generation, but the task, I believe, remains the same: to give poetic form to the pragmatic." His projects include Nichii Obihiro Department Store (Hokkaido, Japan, 1987, unbuilt); Lucille Halsell Conservatory at the San Antonio Botanical Center (San Antonio, Texas, USA, 1988); Mycal Sanda Cultural and Athletic Center (Hyogo Prefecture, Japan, 1990–94); and Fukuoka Prefectural International Hall (Fukuoka, Japan, 1995, winner of the 2001 DuPont Benedictus Award). More recently, he has built the Nuova Concordia Residential and Hotel Complex in Apulia (2001–03); the Casa de Retiro Espiritual (Casa de Cordoba, Seville, Spain, 1975/2003–05); an advanced ophthalmological research laboratory (Banca dell'Occhio, Venice-Mestre, 2003–08); and a 680-bed hospital (Ospedale dell'Angelo, Venice-Mestre, 2005–08, published here), all in Italy unless stated otherwise.

Der 1943 in Argentinien geborene **EMILIO AMBASZ** studierte Architektur in Princeton, wo er binnen eines Jahres sein Grundstudium absolvierte und bereits im Jahr darauf mit dem M.Arch. abschloss. Ambasz lehrte an der School of Architecture der Princeton University, war Gastprofessor an der Hochschule fur Gestaltung in Ulm und lehrte an verschiedenen amerikanischen Universitäten. Von 1970 bis 1976 war Ambasz Kurator für Design am Museum of Modern Art in New York, zweimal amtierte er als Präsident der Architectural League of New York (1981–85). Sein 1976 gegründetes Büro Emilio Ambasz & Associates, Inc. offeriert die unterschiedlichsten Dienstleistungen in Sachen Design, vom Entwurf und der Architekturberatung über Landschaftsgestaltung, Lichtkonzeption und Ausstellungsplanung bis hin zu grafischen Konzepten und Produktdesign. Ambasz selbst erklärt: „Ich bin davon überzeugt, dass Design vor allem mit Erfinden zu tun hat. Ist die Anforderung nach Funktionalität und Handhabbarkeit erfüllt, beginnt in meinen Augen erst die eigentliche Aufgabe des Designs. Nicht der Hunger, sondern die Liebe und die Angst – und manchmal das Staunen – machen uns kreativ. Unsere Umwelt mag sich in jeder Generation verändern, aber die Aufgabe bleibt meiner Ansicht nach stets die gleiche: dem Praktischen eine poetische Form zu verleihen." Zu Ambasz' Projekten gehören das Kaufhaus Nichii Obihiro (Hokkaido, Japan, 1987, nicht realisiert), das Lucille-Halsell-Gewächshaus im Botanischen Garten von San Antonio (Texas, USA, 1988), das Kultur- und Sportzentrum Mycal Sanda (Präfektur Hyogo, Japan, 1990–94) und die Fukuoka Prefectural International Hall (Fukuoka, Japan, 1995), für die Ambasz 2001 den DuPont Benedictus Award erhielt. Zuletzt entstanden die Wohn- und Hotelanlage Nuova Concordia in Apulien (Italien, 2001–03), die Casa de Retiro Espiritual bei Sevilla (Spanien, 1975/2003–05) und die beiden Bauten in Venedig-Mestre (Italien), die Banca dell'Occhio, ein Forschungsinstitut für Augenheilkunde (2003–08) und das hier vorgestellte 680-Betten-Krankenhaus Ospedale dell'Angelo (2005–08).

Né en 1943 en Argentine, **EMILIO AMBASZ** a étudié à l'université de Princeton. Il y a accompli ses études de licence en un an et obtenu son mastère en architecture l'année suivante. Il a enseigné à l'École d'architecture de Princeton, a été professeur invité à la Hochschule für Gestaltung d'Ulm (Allemagne), et a donné des cours dans plusieurs universités américaines. Conservateur pour le design au Musée d'art moderne de New York (1970–76), il a présidé l'Architectural League pendant deux mandats (1981–85). Fondée en 1976, l'agence Emilio Ambasz & Associates, Inc. offre une gamme complète de services en conception architecturale, consultance, éclairage, aménagement du paysage, expositions, graphisme et design produit. Ambasz a déclaré : « Je crois profondément que le design est un acte d'invention. Je crois que sa vraie tâche débute une fois les besoins fonctionnels et comportementaux satisfaits. Ce n'est pas la faim, mais l'amour, la peur et parfois l'émerveillement qui nous font créer. Notre milieu peut évoluer de génération en génération, mais la tâche reste pour moi la même : donner une forme poétique au pragmatique. » Parmi ses projets : le grand magasin Nichii Obihiro (Hokkaido, Japon, 1987, non construit) ; la serre Lucille Halsell au San Antonio Botanical Center (San Antonio, Texas, 1988) ; le Mycal Sanda Cultural and Athletic Center (préfecture de Hyogo, Japon, 1990–94) ; le Hall international de la préfecture de Fukuoka (Fukuoka, Japon, 1995) qui a remporté le prix DuPont Benedictus 2001. Plus récemment, il a réalisé l'hôtel et ensemble résidentiel Nuova Concordia dans les Pouilles (Italie, 2001–03) ; la Casa de Retiro Espiritual (Casa de Cordoba, Seville, Espagne, 1975/2003–05) ; un laboratoire de recherches avancées en ophtamologie (Banca dell'Occhio, Venise-Mestre, 2003–08) et un hôpital de 680 lits (Ospedale dell'Angelo, Venise-Mestre, 2005–08, publié ici).

OSPEDALE DELL'ANGELO

Venice-Mestre, Italy, 2005–08

Address: Nuovo Ospedale di Mestre, Via Don Tosatto 147, 30174 Mestre, Venice, Italy, +39 41 965 71 11, www.nuovospedalemestre.it
Area: 92 903 m². Client: Regione Veneto. Cost: €500 million
Collaboration: Studio Altieri (Architect of Record, Alberto Altieri, Principal)

This is a 680-bed facility billed as the "world's first green general hospital." It features an entrance hall 200 meters in length and 30 meters high, conceived as a "veritable winter garden." Fully half the patients have a view of this garden from their rooms, and lounges placed on each floor also overlook it. The other rooms have plant-covered containers outside their windows. The basic plan of the facility is rectangular, but its sloping façades and its emphasis on green elements make the structure both inviting and pleasant to look at, quite the contrary of most hospital architecture. The project took almost 40 years to realize, with three other architectural firms having been involved before Emilio Ambasz took on the task. Service facilities, parking, laboratories, and operating rooms are covered with earth and plants on three sides and their roof space so as not to interfere with the agreeable central areas containing the rooms. The hospital is located across a street from the Banca dell'Occhio, another project by the same architect.

Das Ospedale dell'Angelo wird nicht umsonst „als die erste grüne Klinik der Welt" gepriesen: Ist da doch zunächst einmal seine 200 m lange und 30 m hohe Eingangshalle, die als „veritabler Wintergarten" angelegt ist. Dessen Grün lässt sich nicht nur von den auf jeder Ebene eingerichteten Lounges aus genießen – nicht weniger als die Hälfte der Patienten hat von ihren Zimmern einen direkten Blick auf den Garten. Vor den Fenstern der übrigen Zimmer sind großzügig begrünte Pflanzenkübel angebracht. Mag der Grundriss des Gebäudes auch schlicht rechteckig sein, bietet sich dank der schrägen Fassaden und der Betonung naturgrüner Elemente ein ungewohnt positiver, ja einladender Anblick – ganz im Gegensatz zu den meisten sonstigen Krankenhäusern. Die Umsetzung des Projekts hat sich über beinahe 40 Jahre hingezogen; bevor Emilio Ambasz die Sache endlich in die Hand nahm, hatten sich bereits drei andere Architekturbüros daran versucht. Die Parkplätze, Haustechnik, Labore und Operationssäle sind so in den Erdraum eingelassen, dass nur ihre Vorderseite freiliegt, uneinsehbar für den Zentralbereich mit den Patientenzimmern, dessen angenehme Atmosphäre somit ungestört bleibt. Gleich gegenüber der Klinik befindet sich auf der anderen Straßenseite Ambasz' Banca dell'Occhio.

Cet hôpital de 680 lits, qualifié de « premier hôpital général écologique du monde », s'ouvre par un hall d'entrée de 200 m de long et 30 m de haut conçu comme un « véritable jardin d'hiver ». La moitié des patients bénéficient d'une vue sur ce jardin de leur chambre comme des salons aménagés à chaque étage. Les autres chambres sont dotées de jardinières plantées devant leurs fenêtres. Le plan d'ensemble est rectangulaire, mais l'inclinaison des façades et l'importance accordée à la verdure rendent le bâtiment accueillant et agréable à regarder, contrairement à l'architecture habituelle de la plupart des hôpitaux. Le projet a mis plus de quarante années avant de naître, trois autres agences d'architecture s'y étaient succédé avant l'intervention d'Ambasz. Les services, les parkings, les laboratoires et les salles d'opérations sont recouverts de terre et de plantations sur trois côtés et leur toiture, ce qui les isole de la zone centrale qui regroupe les chambres. L'hôpital est séparé de la Banca dell'Occhio du même architecte par une avenue.

The Ospedale dell'Angelo shares with its neighbor, the Banca dell'Occhio, surprising slanted façades. Right, the glazed surface of the hospital.

Das Ospedale dell'Angelo besitzt ähnlich wie sein Nachbar, die Banca dell'Occhio, ungewohnt schräge Wände. Rechts die Fassadenverglasung des Krankenhauses.

L'Ospedale dell'Angelo partage avec la Banca dell'Occhio voisine d'étonnantes façades inclinées. À droite, la façade de verre de l'hôpital.

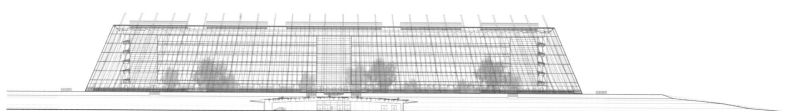

AUER+WEBER+ASSOZIIERTE

Auer+Weber+Assoziierte
Sandstr. 33
80335 Munich
Germany

Tel: +49 89 38 16 17 0 / Fax: +49 89 38 16 17 38
E-mail: muenchen@auer-weber.de
Web: www.auer-weber.de

FRITZ AUER, born in Tübingen, Germany, in 1933, became a partner in the firm of Behnisch & Partner in 1966 and created Auer+Weber in 1980. **CARLO WEBER** was born in Saarbrücken, Germany, in 1934 and attended the Technische Hochschule in Stuttgart, before going to the Beaux-Arts in Paris. Like Auer, he became a partner at Behnisch & Partner in 1966. They have worked extensively on urban renewal in Bonn, Stuttgart, and other cities. The firm, with offices in Munich and Stuttgart, currently employs 100 to 120 people and includes managing partners Moritz Auer, Philipp Auer, Jörn Scholz, Achim Söding, and Stephan Suxdorf. They completed the Gut Siggen Seminar Building (Siggen, 2007); the façade of the ECE Stadtgalerie (Passau, 2008); the Altstadt-Palais, an office building (Munich, 2008); additions and alterations to the Olympic Hall (Munich, 2008); Central Facilities on the Martinsried Campus (Ludwig-Maximilians University, Munich, 2009); the Central Bus Terminal in Munich (2009); buildings in Chenshan Botanical Garden (Chenshan, Shanghai, China, 2010, published here); and the Small Olympic Sports Hall, Olympic Park (Munich, 2011). Current work includes Bielefeld University of Applied Sciences Campus (Bielefeld, 2013); the ESO Headquarters Garching (Munich, 2013); the extension to the Federal Ministry of Defense (Berlin, 2013); the Alliance Campus (Unterföhring, 2014); Centre Universitaire des Quais (Lyon, France, 2014); and Grandes Combes (Courchevel, France, 2014), all in Germany unless stated otherwise.

FRITZ AUER, 1933 in Tübingen geboren, wurde 1966 Partner bei Behnisch & Partner und gründete 1980 sein Büro Auer+Weber. **CARLO WEBER**, geboren 1934 in Saarbrücken, studierte zunächst an der Technischen Hochschule Stuttgart, anschließend an der École Nationale Supérieure des Beaux-Arts in Paris. Auch er wurde 1966 Partner bei Behnisch & Partner. Das Büro war und ist an vielen Stadterneuerungsprojekten in Bonn, Stuttgart und anderen Städten beteiligt. Die Bürogemeinschaft mit Sitz in München und Stuttgart beschäftigt derzeit 100 bis 120 Mitarbeiter, darunter die Geschäftsführer Moritz Auer, Philipp Auer, Jörn Scholz, Achim Söding und Stephan Suxdorf. Zu den realisierten Projekten zählen das Seminargebäude Gut Siggen (Siggen, 2007), die Fassade der ECE-Stadtgalerie (Passau, 2008), das Bürogebäude Altstadt-Palais (München, 2008), Erweiterung und Umbau der Olympiahalle (München, 2008), das Zentralgebäude auf dem Campus Martinsried der Ludwig-Maximilians-Universität (München, 2009), der Zentrale Omnibusbahnhof München (2009), Bauten im Botanischen Garten Chenshan (Schanghai, China, 2010, hier vorgestellt) sowie die Kleine Olympiahalle im Olympiapark (München, 2011). Aktuelle Projekte sind u. a. der Campus der Fachhochschule Bielefeld (2013), die Erweiterung des ESO-Hauptquartiers in Garching (München, 2013), die Erweiterung des Bundesministeriums der Verteidigung (Berlin, 2013), der Allianz-Campus (Unterföhring, 2014), das Centre Universitaire des Quais (Lyon, Frankreich, 2014) und ein Neubau an der Seilbahnstation von Grandes Combes (Courchevel, Frankreich, 2014), alle in Deutschland soweit nicht anders vermerkt.

FRITZ AUER, né en Allemagne à Tübingen en 1933, est devenu partenaire de Behnisch & Partner en 1966 et a créé Auer+Weber en 1980. **CARLO WEBER** est né à Sarrebruck, Allemagne, en 1934 et a suivi les cours de l'Université technique de Stuttgart avant d'aller aux Beaux-Arts de Paris. Comme Auer, il est devenu partenaire de Behnisch & Partner en 1966. Ils ont beaucoup travaillé à la rénovation urbaine de Bonn, Stuttgart et d'autres villes. L'agence a des bureaux à Munich et Stuttgart, elle a 100 à 120 employés dont les associés dirigeants Moritz Auer, Philipp Auer, Jörn Scholz, Achim Söding et Stephan Suxdorf. Ils ont réalisé : le centre de séminaires Gut Siggen (Siggen, Allemagne, 2007) ; la façade du centre commercial ECE Stadtgalerie (Passau, Allemagne, 2008) ; un immeuble de bureaux (Altstadt-Palais, Munich, 2008) ; des ajouts et modifications au Centre olympique (Munich, 2008) ; des équipements centraux du campus de Martinsried (université Ludwig-Maximilian, Munich, 2009) ; la gare routière de Munich (2009) ; des bâtiments du Jardin botanique de Chenshan (Shanghai, 2009, publiés ici) ; la petite salle olympique du Centre olympique (Munich, 2010). Leurs travaux actuels comprennent notamment : la salle omnisports (Antibes, 2012) ; le campus de l'Université des sciences appliquées de Bielefeld (2013) ; le siège de l'ESO à Garching (Munich, 2013) ; l'extension du ministère fédéral de la Défense (Berlin, 2013) ; le campus Alliance (Unterföhring, 2014) ;le centre universitaire des Quais (Lyon, 2014) et le site des Grandes Combes (Courchevel, 2014), tous en Allemagne sauf si précisé.

BUILDINGS IN CHENSHAN BOTANICAL GARDEN

Chenshan, Shanghai, China, 2007–10

Area: 66,000 m² (Visitor Center, Greenhouses, Research Building)
Client: Chenshan Botanical Garden, Shanghai
Cost: €65,000,000

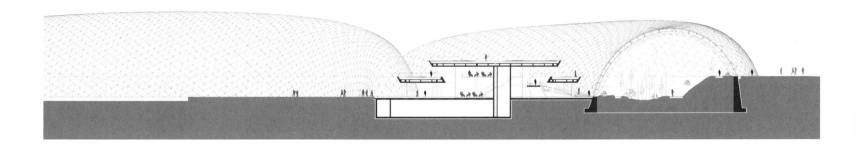

As photos and a section drawing (top left) show, the architectural elements designed by Auer+Weber are inserted into the landscape. A greenhouse with its operable windows in the open position assumes a spiked appearance.

Aufnahmen und Querschnitt (oben links) zeigen die in die Landschaft integrierte Architektur von Auer+ Weber. Die geöffneten Fenster eines Gewächshauses wirken wie Stacheln.

Comme le montrent les photos et un schéma en coupe (en haut à gauche), les éléments architecturaux créés par Auer Weber s'insèrent dans le paysage. Les fenêtres en position ouverte d'une serre prennent l'aspect de pointes.

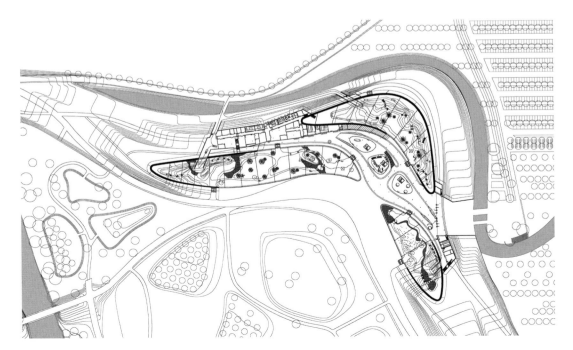

The visitor center, greenhouses, and research building by Auer+Weber are located in the 202-hectare grounds of the Chenshan Botanical Garden designed by the Munich firms Valentien + Valentien and Straub-Thurmayr. The buildings are integrated into a "ring of gardens" within the park, embedded into the undulating landscape. The architects explain, "The dynamic forms and arrangement of the buildings and the change of materiality between concrete, as a supporting element of the landscape and glass that acts as a filling between the openings of the ring, integrates the architecture within the landscape design." On the southern side of the park, the visitor center includes an education area, exhibition space, and administrative offices. The research center is on the north, while to the northeast, the architects have placed a series of greenhouses near the Shen Jing He Canal. An open-air amphitheater is situated in a former quarry. Apartments and villas for researchers and guests are in the meadows to the south of the center of the park. The architects state that the Chenshan Botanical Garden "can become an example in using renewable energies and intelligent climatic concepts to save resources," but in any case, the theme of the botanical garden itself forcibly involves the protection and study of nature.

Empfangsgebäude, Gewächshäuser und Forschungszentrum von Auer+Weber verteilen sich über das 202 ha große Gelände des Botanischen Gartens Chenshan, geplant von den Münchner Büros Valentien + Valentien und Straub + Thurmayr. Die Bauten wurden in einen „bandartigen Gartenring" integriert, eingebettet in die geschwungenen Landschaftslinien. Die Architekten erklären: „Mit ihren im Grund- wie Aufriss dynamischen Formen und der wechselnden Materialität zwischen Beton als Träger der Landschaftsebene und Glas als transparenter Füllung fügen sie sich wie selbstverständlich in den Duktus der Landschaftsarchitektur ein." Empfangsgebäude und Besucherzentrum an der Südseite des Geländes beherbergen Informations- und Ausstellungsbereiche sowie Verwaltungsräume. Neben dem Forschungszentrum im Norden planten die Architekten im Nordosten mehrere Gewächshäuser entlang des Shen-Jing-He-Kanals. In einem alten Steinbruch wurde ein Freilufttheater realisiert. Apartments und Gästehäuser für Forscher und Gäste liegen in den Wiesen südlich vom Zentrum des Parks. Den Architekten zufolge hat der Botanische Garten Chenshan „Vorbildcharakter für die Nutzung erneuerbarer Energien und intelligenter, ressourcenschonender Klimakonzepte", doch bereits der Botanische Garten an sich ist unbedingt dem Schutz und der Erforschung der Natur gewidmet.

Le centre d'accueil, les serres et le bâtiment de recherches créés par Auer+Weber sont situés sur les 202 ha du Jardin botanique de Chenshan, aménagé par l'agence munichoise d'architectes paysagistes Valentien+Valentien et Straub-Thurmayr. Les bâtiments sont intégrés à un « anneau de jardins » dans le parc, lui-même niché dans un paysage vallonné. Les architectes expliquent : « Ce sont les formes et la disposition dynamiques des bâtiments qui intègrent l'architecture au paysage et à son design, ainsi que l'alternance des matériaux entre le béton, élément porteur du paysage, et le verre, qui bouche en quelque sorte les ouvertures dans l'anneau. » Du côté sud du parc, le centre d'accueil des visiteurs comprend un espace pédagogique, un espace d'exposition et un espace administratif de bureaux. Le centre de recherches est situé au nord et les architectes ont placé une série de serres au nord-est, à proximité du canal Shen Jing He. Un amphithéâtre en plein air occupe une ancienne carrière. Des immeubles d'appartements et des villas destinés aux chercheurs et aux invités sont disposés dans les prairies au sud du parc. Pour les architectes, le Jardin botanique de Chenshan « se veut un exemple de l'utilisation des énergies renouvelables et d'une conception climatique intelligente pour économiser les ressources », d'autant plus que le thème du jardin botanique en soi implique forcément la protection et l'étude de la nature.

Above, night lighting of the green-houses gives them an almost unreal appearance. Right page, the 18 000-square-meter research building.

Bei nächtlicher Beleuchtung (oben) wirken die Gewächshäuser fast unwirklich. Auf der rechten Seite das 18 000 m² große Forschungsgebäude.

Ci-dessus, l'éclairage nocturne des serres les fait paraître presque irréelles. Page de droite, le bâtiment de 18 000 m² consacré à la recherche.

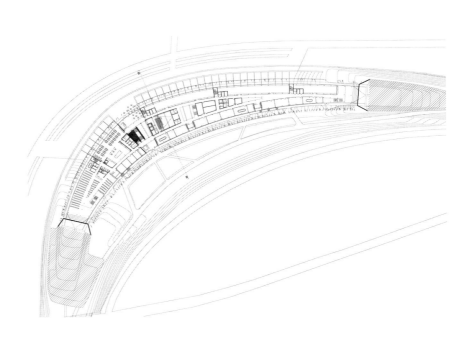

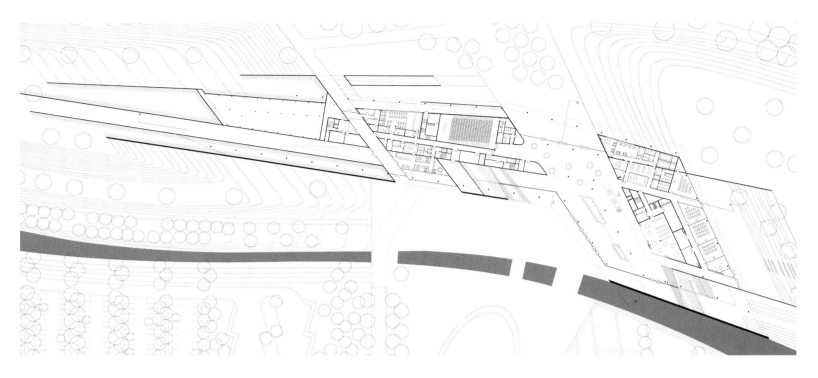

A plan and images of the visitor center or reception building show its more rectilinear forms, inserted nonetheless into the landscape.

Ein Grundriss und Aufnahmen des Besucherzentrums bzw. Empfangs-gebäudes zeigen eine geradlinige Architektur, die sich dennoch in die Landschaft fügt.

Le plan et les images du centre d'accueil ou bâtiment de la réception montrent ses formes plus rectilignes, mais pas moins bien insérées dans le paysage pour autant.

Over 20 000 square meters in area, the visitor center has a fully glazed façade, but is also sliced into the earth as can be seen in the section drawings below.

Das Besucherzentrum mit mehr als 20 000 m² Nutzfläche hat eine Glas-fassade, ist jedoch auch in den Boden eingelassen, wie die Quer-schnitte unten illustrieren.

Le centre d'accueil d'une surface de plus de 20 000 m² dispose d'une façade entièrement vitrée, mais une tranche en est aussi enterrée, comme on le voit sur les schémas en coupe ci-dessous.

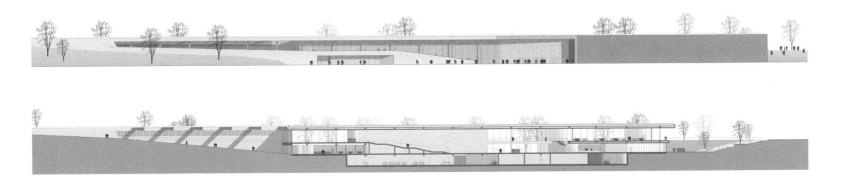

PIETA-LINDA AUTTILA

Pieta-Linda Auttila
NoMad Productions

Tel: +358 503 622 465
E-mail: pietalinda@hotmail.com

PIETA-LINDA AUTTILA was born in 1974 in Tampere, Finland. She received a Master's degree as a spatial designer and interior architect from the University of Art and Design (Helsinki, 2009). She was the coordinator of an "artistically rich and multicultural workshop" (Studio, Helsinki, 2005–07). She worked for Arkkitehtiruutu Oy (Lahti, Finland, 2007) and Stratakissaravuo Architects (Rethymno, Crete, 2008), before designing the Wisa Wooden Design Hotel (Helsinki, 2009, published here).

PIETA-LINDA AUTTILA wurde 1974 in Tampere in Finnland geboren. Sie erhielt ihren Master als Raumgestalterin und Innenarchitektin an der Kunst- und Designschule der Aalto-Universität in Helsinki (2009). Sie war die Koordinatorin einer „künstlerisch reichen, multikulturellen Werkstatt" (Studio, Helsinki, 2005–07). Auttila arbeitete für die Büros Arkkitehtiruutu Oy (Lahti, Finnland, 2007) und Stratakissaravuo Architects (Rethymnon, Kreta, 2008), bevor sie das Wisa Wooden Design Hotel (Helsinki, 2009, hier vorgestellt) plante.

PIETA-LINDA AUTTILA, née en 1974 à Tampere (Finlande), a obtenu son M.A. en design d'espace et architecture d'intérieur à l'Université d'art et de design d'Helsinki (2009). Elle a été coordinatrice d'un « atelier polyculturel d'une grande richesse artistique », le Studio (Helsinki, 2005–07), et a travaillé pour les agences Arkkitehtiruutu Oy (Lahti, Finlande, 2007) et Stratakissaravuo Architects (Rethymno, Crète, 2008), avant de concevoir le Wisa Wooden Design Hotel (Helsinki, 2009, publié ici).

WISA WOODEN DESIGN HOTEL

Helsinki, Finland, 2009

Address: Valkosaari, Helsinki, Finland, +358 20 414 7021
Area: 80 m². Client: UPM Kymmene. Cost: not disclosed

Pieta-Linda Auttila was chosen to design the **WISA WOODEN DESIGN HOTEL** through a 2009 competition organized by UPM, an energy, pulp, paper, and engineered materials company that employs 23 000 people worldwide. Participants in the competition were given just 24 hours to design "a bold and iconic work from Finnish pine and spruce." The Wisa Wooden Design Hotel is set at the northern point of Valkosaari Island in Helsinki's Southern Harbor. According to the firm: "Despite its name, the Wisa Wooden Design Hotel wasn't designed for public use, yet the building will offer facilities for a sleepover. The Wisa Wooden Design Hotel is meant to be noticed and admired." The designer states: "I wanted to blow the wooden block in pieces from the middle. By bending the block, I forced the slats to a new form that offers a contrast to the original shape, the block. Thus the solid shape becomes partly transparent, and the strictly geometrical shape becomes organic. The interior space is secondary as the partly sheltered patio takes the leading role."

Pieta-Linda Auttila erhielt den Auftrag zur Planung des **WISA WOODEN DESIGN HOTELS** durch einen Wettbewerb, der 2009 von UPM ausgeschrieben wurde, einer Energie, Zellstoff, Papier und Baumaterialien produzierenden Firma, die weltweit 23 000 Mitarbeiter hat. Den Teilnehmern des Wettbewerbs wurden nur 24 Stunden gewährt, um „ein gewagtes und einprägsames Bauwerk aus finnischer Kiefer und Fichte" zu entwerfen. Das Wisa Wooden Design Hotel steht an der Nordspitze der Insel Valkosaari im Südhafen von Helsinki. Wie die Firma mitteilt: „Das Wisa Wooden Design Hotel ist, seiner Bezeichnung zum Trotz, nicht zur öffentlichen Nutzung bestimmt; dennoch bietet das Gebäude auch Übernachtungsmöglichkeiten an. Das Wisa Wooden Design Hotel soll beachtet und bewundert werden." Die Architektin erklärt: „Ich wollte den hölzernen Block, von der Mitte ausgehend, in Stücke zerlegen. Durch Biegen des Blocks zwang ich die Latten in eine neue Form, die einen Gegensatz zum Original darstellt. Dadurch wird die geschlossene Form teilweise transparent und die streng geometrische Form organisch. Der Innenraum wird sekundär, weil der teilüberdachte Patio die führende Rolle übernimmt."

Pieta-Linda Auttila a été sélectionnée pour concevoir le **WISA WOODEN DESIGN HOTEL** à l'issue d'un concours organisé par UPM, entreprise de production d'énergie, de pulpe de papier, de papier et de matériaux de transformation qui emploie 23 000 personnes dans le monde. Les participants n'avaient disposé que de vingt-quatre heures pour concevoir « une réalisation audacieuse et iconique en pin et épicéa de Finlande ». L'hôtel est situé à la pointe nord de l'île de Valkosaari dans le port sud d'Helsinki. Selon l'entreprise : « Malgré son nom, cet hôtel n'a pas été conçu pour un usage public, mais pourra néanmoins accueillir des personnes pour la nuit. Il a été conçu pour être vu et admiré. » Pour la designer : « Je voulais faire exploser un bloc de bois à partir de son centre. En le cintrant, j'ai forcé les lattes à prendre une forme contrastant avec le volume d'origine. Ainsi un solide est devenu en partie transparent et une forme strictement géométrique est devenue organique. L'espace intérieur est secondaire, le patio en partie protégé joue le premier rôle. »

The Wisa Wooden Design Hotel is a very small, experimental structure intended to show the kind of things that can be done in such circumstances with wood. Elevations (below) show the adaptation of the structure to the terrain.

Das Wisa Wooden Design Hotel ist ein sehr kleines, experimentelles Gebäude, das beweisen soll, was sich unter derartigen Umständen aus Holz machen lässt. Die Ansichten (unten) zeigen die Anpassung des Bauwerks an das Gelände.

Le Wisa Wooden Design Hotel est une très petite construction expérimentale destinée à montrer ce que l'on peut faire avec du bois dans des circonstances particulières. Les élévations (ci-dessous) illustrent l'adaptation de la structure au terrain.

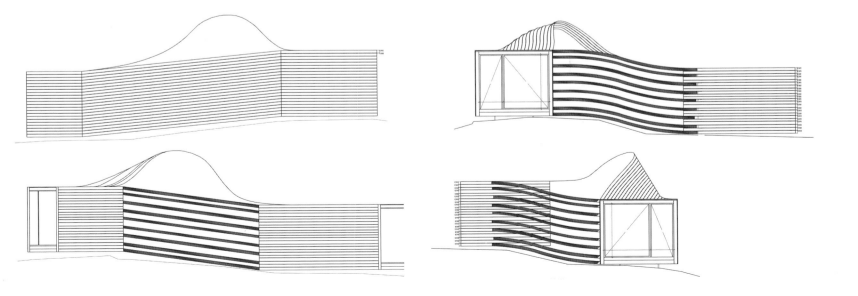

The central, freely curving form of
the hotel makes use of open slats in
a sculptural pattern that reveal views
of the water.

*Die zentrale, frei gekrümmte Form
des Hotels entsteht durch Latten in
plastischer Anordnung, durch die sich
Ausblicke zum Wasser eröffnen.*

*La forme centrale libre organise en
une mise en scène sculpturale le
déploiement des lattes de bois qui,
par moments, permettent de découvrir des vues du fleuve.*

BALMORI ASSOCIATES

Balmori Associates
833 Washington Street, 2nd Floor
New York, NY 10014
USA

Tel: +1 212 431 9191
Fax: +1 212 431 8616
E-mail: info@balmori.com
Web: www.balmori.com

DIANA BALMORI was born in Gijón, Spain, and attended the Undergraduate Architecture Program at the University of Tucumán (Argentina, 1949–52), before studying at the University of California at Los Angeles (1968–70, B.A.; 1970–75, Ph.D. in Urban History). She was a partner for Landscape and Urban Design with Cesar Pelli & Associates (New Haven, 1981–90). She is the founding principal of Balmori Associates created in 1990 in New Haven, with an office in New York since 2001. In 2006, Diana Balmori was appointed a Senior Fellow in Garden and Landscape Studies at Dumbarton Oaks in Washington, D.C., and is serving her second term on the US Commission of Fine Arts. She has served as a jury member for the Bilbao Jardín 2009 garden festival. Her recent built work includes MPPAT (Master Plan for Public Administrative Town, Sejong, Korea, 2007); Duke University Master Plan (with Cesar Pelli & Associates, Durham, North Carolina, USA, 2008); the Garden That Climbs the Stairs (Bilbao, Spain, 2009, published here); Botanical Research Institute of Texas (BRIT, Fort Worth, USA, 2011); Campa de los Ingleses (Bilbao, 2011); and Plaza Euskadi (Bilbao, 2011). According to the firm's own description: "Through research, collaboration, and innovation, Balmori Associates explore and expand the boundaries between nature and structure."

DIANA BALMORI ist in Gijón, Spanien, geboren und studierte von 1949 bis 1952 Architektur an der Universität von Tucumán in Argentinien. Sie setzte ihre Studien an der University of California in Los Angeles fort (1968–70, B.A., 1970–75, Promotion in Stadtgeschichte). Sie war als Partnerin im Büro Cesar Pelli & Associates (New Haven, 1981–90) für Garten- und Landschaftsplanung tätig und gründete 1990 ihr eigenes Büro Balmori Associates in New Haven, das seit 2001 auch in New York ansässig ist. 2006 wurde Diana Balmori Senior Fellow für den Studiengang Garten und Landschaft in Dumbarton Oaks in Washington, D. C., und ist zum zweiten Mal Mitglied der US Commission of Fine Arts. Beim Gartenfestival Bilbao Jardín 2009 fungierte sie als Jurymitglied. Zu ihren neuesten Arbeiten gehören der MPPAT (Masterplan für das Verwaltungsviertel von Sejong, Korea, 2007), der Masterplan für die Duke University (mit Cesar Pelli & Associates, Durham, North Carolina, USA, 2008), der Garten, der die Treppe hinaufwächst (Bilbao, Spanien, 2009, hier vorgestellt), das Botanische Forschungsinstitut von Texas (BRIT, Fort Worth, USA, 2011), der Park Campa de los Ingleses (Bilbao, 2011) und die Plaza Euskadi (Bilbao, 2011). Das Büro beschreibt seine Arbeitsweise wie folgt: „Durch Recherchen, Zusammenarbeit sowie innovative Ansätze sondiert Balmori Associates die Grenzen zwischen Natur und Struktur und erweitert sie."

DIANA BALMORI, née à Gijón (Espagne), a suivi le programme de préparation aux études d'architecture de l'université de Tucumán (Argentine, 1949–52), avant d'étudier à l'université de Californie à Los Angeles (1968–70, B.A. ; 1970–75, Ph.D. en histoire urbaine). Elle a été partenaire pour l'urbanisme et le paysage chez Cesar Pelli & Associates (New Haven, 1981–90). Elle dirige l'agence Balmori Associates qu'elle a fondée en 1990 à New Haven et qui possède un bureau à New York depuis 2001. En 2006, elle a été nommée senior fellow en études du paysage à l'institut de Dumbarton Oaks, à Washington, et siège pour la seconde fois à la Commission américaine des beaux-arts. Elle a été membre du jury du festival Bilbao Jardín 2009. Parmi ses réalisations récentes : le plan directeur de la ville administrative à Sejong (MPPAT, Sejong, Corée, 2007) ; le plan directeur de l'université Duke (avec Cesar Pelli & Associates, Durham, Caroline du Nord, 2008) ; The Garden That Climbs the Stairs (Bilbao, 2009, publié ici) ; le Botanical Research Institute of Texas (BRIT, Fort Worth, Texas, 2011) ; le parc Campa de los Ingleses (Bilbao, 2011) et la Plaza Euskadi (Bilbao, 2011). « Par la recherche, la collaboration et l'innovation, Balmori Associates explore et repousse les limites entre nature et structure », précise le descriptif de l'agence.

THE GARDEN
THAT CLIMBS THE STAIRS

Bilbao, Spain, 2009

Address: Isozaki Atea, Ensanche, Bilbao, Spain. Area: 80 m²
Client: II International Competition: Bilbao Jardin 2009 and Fundación Bilbao 700
Cost: €12 000

With its curvilinear planters arcing across the geometric and mineral area of the square and stairs, the Garden That Climbs the Stairs introduces nature to an otherwise quite arid space.

Mit den geschwungenen Pflanzkübeln, die quer über den geometrisch gestalteten steinernen Platz und die Treppen führen, bringt der Garten, der die Treppe hinaufwächst, Natur in einen sonst recht faden Freiraum.

Par ses jardinières curvilignes qui « poussent » dans l'univers géométrique et minéral de la place et des escaliers, ce « Jardin qui monte les escaliers » introduit la nature dans un environnement par ailleurs assez aride.

Making use of Cor-ten steel, the planters assume a slightly irregular profile as they "climb" the steps, giving passersby something to look at, smell, and comment about.

Die Pflanzkübel aus Corten-Stahl verändern in dem Maß, wie sie die Treppe „emporsteigen", ein bisschen ihr Profil, sodass die Passanten etwas zum Hinschauen, zum Riechen und natürlich auch zum Kommentieren haben.

Alors qu'elles « montent » les escaliers, ces jardinières en acier Corten au profil assez irrégulier donnent aux passants matière à regarder, sentir et commenter.

As a member of the jury for the second Bilbao Jardín festival (2009), Diana Balmori was invited to create a garden in the city. The location she chose is a stairway located between two 83-meter-high towers by Arata Isozaki (Isozaki Atea, 2004–08). These steps lead to Santiago Calatrava's bridge over the Nervión River (Campo Volantin Footbridge, 1990–97). Balmori sought to create numerous contrasts in this small garden: between red flowers, green grass, and gray paving, for example. The firm states: "The garden climbs the stairs, running in undulating lines of different textures and colors. Envisioned as a dynamic urban space, it moves in time and with the seasons. Its lush planting cascades down as though the garden was flowing or melting, bleeding the colors into each other. In one gesture, it narrates a story of land-scape taking over and expanding over the public space and architecture, therefore transforming the way that the stairs and the space is perceived and read by the user." The garden is one of several projects by Balmori Associates in Bilbao that include the Abandoibarra Master Plan (competition winner, 1997), Plaza Euskadi (2011), and Campa de los Ingleses (2011).

Als Mitglied der Jury für das zweite Gartenfestival von Bilbao (2009) wurde Diana Balmori eingeladen, einen Garten mitten in der Stadt zu realisieren. Sie ent-schied sich für eine Treppenanlage zwischen zwei 83 m hohen Hochhäusern von Arata Isozaki (die Isozaki Atea, 2004–08). Die Treppe führt zu Santiago Calatravas Brü-cke über den Nervión (die Fußgängerbrücke Campo Volantin, 1990–97). Balmori hat in diesem kleinen Garten zahlreiche starke Kontraste geschaffen, z. B. rote Blumen, grünes Gras und graues Pflaster. Das Büro sagt dazu: „Der Garten steigt die Treppen in geschwungenen Linien mit unterschiedlichen Texturen und Farben hinauf. Er ist als dynamischer urbaner Raum gedacht und ändert sich mit der Zeit und den Jahreszeiten. Die üppige Bepflanzung fließt wie eine Kaskade die Treppe hinunter, dabei ver-schmelzen die Farben miteinander. Mit einer einzigen Geste erzählt dieser Garten, wie Landschaft ‚an die Macht kommt' und sich über den öffentlichen Raum und die Architektur ausbreitet. So verändert sich bei dem Nutzer die Art, wie er die Treppe und den Freiraum wahrnimmt." Dieser Garten ist eines von mehreren Projekten, die das Büro Balmori Associates in Bilbao realisiert hat. Dazu gehören auch der Masterplan für Abandoibarra (Wettbewerbssieger 1997), die Plaza Euskadi (2011) und der Park Campa de los Ingleses (2011).

Membre du jury du second festival Bilbao Jardín en 2009, Diana Balmori a été invitée à y créer un jardin. Elle a choisi un lieu particulier : un grand escalier entre deux tours de 83 m de haut dues à Arata Isozaki (Isozaki Atea, 2004–08). Il conduit au pont jeté par Santiago Calatrava sur le Nervión (passerelle de Campo Volantin, 1990–97). Balmori a cherché à multiplier les contrastes, par exemple entre les fleurs rouges, l'herbe verte et le pavement gris : « Le jardin monte les escaliers en formant des vagues de différentes textures et couleurs. Conçu comme un espace urbain dynamique, il change avec le temps et les saisons. Ses plantations luxuriantes retombent en cascade comme si le jardin coulait sur les marches ou se fondait avec elles, les couleurs débordant les unes sur les autres. Dans ce geste, il raconte l'histoire d'un paysage qui se développe et prend le dessus sur l'espace public et l'architecture, transformant ainsi la façon dont l'escalier et l'espace sont perçus par leurs usagers. » Ce jardin fait partie d'un ensemble de projets de Balmori Associates à Bilbao, dont le plan directeur d'Abandoibarra (concours remporté, 1997), la Plaza Euskadi (2011) et le parc Campa de Los Ingleses (2011).

The drawing of the work (below) shows its protean forms. The adaptation to the rising stair gives the installation an even more organic appearance and dynamism than it might have had on a uniformly flat surface.

Die Zeichnung (unten) zeigt deutlich die fließenden Formen. Die Anpassung an den Treppenlauf lässt diese Installation noch organischer und dynamischer wirken, als dies auf einer ebenen Fläche der Fall gewesen wäre.

Le dessin (ci-dessous) montre la qualité protéiforme du projet. Son adaptation aux escaliers lui donne un aspect encore plus organique et un dynamisme que cette installation n'aurait pas eu sur une surface uniformément plane.

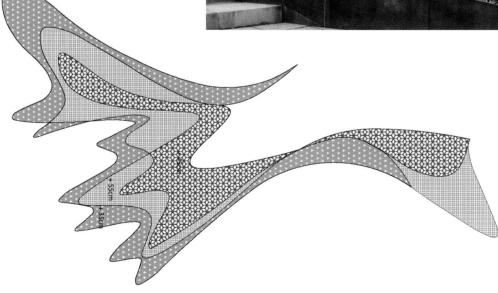

SHIGERU BAN

Shigeru Ban Architects / 5–2–4 Matsubara / Setagaya-ku
Tokyo 156–0043 / Japan
Tel: +81 3 3324 6760 / Fax: +81 3 3324 6789
E-mail: tokyo@shigerubanarchitects.com
Web: www.shigerubanarchitects.com

Born in 1957 in Tokyo, **SHIGERU BAN** studied at SCI-Arc from 1977 to 1980. He then attended the Cooper Union School of Architecture, where he studied under John Hejduk (1980–82). He worked in the office of Arata Isozaki (1982–83), before founding his own firm in Tokyo in 1985. His work includes numerous exhibition designs (such as those for the Alvar Aalto show at the Axis Gallery, Tokyo, 1986). His buildings include the Odawara Pavilion (Kanagawa, 1990); the Paper Gallery (Tokyo, 1994); the Paper House (Lake Yamanaka, 1995); and the Paper Church (Takatori, Hyogo, 1995), all in Japan. He has also designed ephemeral structures such as his Paper Refugee Shelter made with plastic sheets and paper tubes for the United Nations High Commissioner for Refugees (UNHCR). He designed the Japanese Pavilion at Expo 2000 in Hanover. He installed his Paper Temporary Studio on top of the Centre Pompidou in Paris to work on the new Centre Pompidou-Metz (Metz, France, 2006–10). Other recent work includes the Papertainer Museum (Seoul Olympic Park, Songpa-Gu, South Korea, 2003–06, published here); the Nomadic Museum (New York, New York, USA, 2004–05; Santa Monica, California, USA, 2005–06; Tokyo, Japan, 2007, also published here); the Nicolas G. Hayek Center (Tokyo, 2005–07); the Takatori Church (Kobe, Hyogo, 2005–07), the last two in Japan; and the disaster relief Post-Tsunami Rehabilitation Houses (Kirinda, Hambantota, Sri Lanka, 2005–07). Recent work includes Hanegi Forest Annex (Setagaya, Tokyo, 2004); Mul(ti)houses (Mulhouse, France, 2001–05); and the Metal Shutter Houses on West 19th Street in New York (New York, 2009).

Der 1957 in Tokio geborene **SHIGERU BAN** studierte von 1977 bis 1980 am Southern California Institute of Architecture (SCI-Arc) und anschließend bis 1982 bei John Hejduk an der Cooper Union School of Architecture. Bevor er 1985 in Tokio ein eigenes Büro gründete, arbeitete er bei Arata Isozaki (1982–83). Zu seinen Werken zählen viele Ausstellungsarchitekturen (u. a. Alvar Aalto in der Galerie Axis, Tokio, 1986) und u. a. folgende Bauwerke: der Odawara-Pavillon (Kanagawa, 1990), eine Galerie aus Papier (Tokio, 1994), ein Haus aus Papier (Yamanaka-See, 1995) und eine Kirche aus Papier (Takatori, Hyogo, 1995), alle in Japan. Er hat auch temporäre Bauten geplant, z. B. für den Hohen Flüchtlingskommissar der Vereinten Nationen (UNHCR) einen Schutzbau für Flüchtlinge, der aus Plastikfolie und Papprohren besteht. Er entwarf den japanischen Pavillon für die Expo 2000 in Hannover und installierte auf dem Centre Pompidou in Paris aus Papier sein temporäres Atelier, um dort am neuen Centre Pompidou-Metz (Metz, 2006–10, hier vorgestellt) zu arbeiten. Zu seinen neueren Werken zählen das Papertainer Museum (Olympiapark Seoul, Songpa-Gu, Südkorea, 2003–06), das Nomadic Museum (New York, 2004–05; Santa Monica, Kalifornien, 2005–06; Tokio, 2007, ebenfalls hier vorgestellt), das Nicolas G. Hayek Center (Tokio, 2005–07), die Kirche in Takatori (Kobe, Hyogo, 2005–07), beide in Japan, sowie Einrichtungen für die Katastrophenhilfe nach der Tsunami-Katastrophe (Kirinda, Hambantota, Sri Lanka, 2005–07). Neuere Bauwerke sind auch ein Anbau im Hanegi-Wald (Setagaya, Tokio, 2004), die Mul(ti)houses (Mulhouse, Frankreich, 2001–05) und das Metal Shutter House in der West 19th Street in New York (2009).

Né en 1957 à Tokyo, **SHIGERU BAN** a étudié au SCI-Arc de 1977 à 1980 et à l'École d'architecture de la Cooper Union, auprès de John Hejduk (1980–82). Il a travaillé dans l'agence d'Arata Isozaki (1982–83), avant de fonder la sienne à Tokyo en 1985. Son œuvre comprend de nombreuses installations d'expositions (Alvar Aalto Show à la galerie Axis, Tokyo, 1986) et des bâtiments comme le pavillon Odawara (Kanagawa, 1990) ; une Galerie de papier (Tokyo, 1994) ; une Maison de papier (lac Yamanaka, 1995) et une Église de papier (Takatori, Hyogo, 1995), tous au Japon. Il a également conçu des structures éphémères comme son Abri en papier pour réfugiés fait de film plastique et tubes de carton pour le Haut Commissariat des Nations Unies pour les réfugiés (UNHCR). Il a dessiné le Pavillon japonais pour Expo 2000 à Hanovre. Son atelier temporaire en tubes de carton a été installé au sommet du Centre Pompidou à Paris, annexe de son agence pendant le chantier du nouveau Centre Pompidou-Metz (Metz, France, 2006–10), publié ici. Parmi ses autres réalisations récentes : le musée Papertainer (Parc olympique de Séoul, Songpa-Gu, Corée-du-Sud, 2003–06) ; le Musée nomade (New York, 2004–05; Santa Monica, Californie, 2005–06; Tokyo, 2007, également publié ici) ; le Centre Nicolas G. Hayek (Tokyo, 2005–07) ; l'église de Takatori (Kobe, Hyogo, 2005–07) et les Maisons de la reconstruction après le tsunami (Kirinda, Hambantota, Sri Lanka, 2005–07) ; l'Annexe de la forêt d'Hanegi (Setagaya, Tokyo, 2004) ; les Mul(ti)houses (Mulhouse, France, 2001–05) et les Metal Shutter Houses sur la 19e Rue Ouest à New York (2009).

PAPERTAINER MUSEUM

Seoul Olympic Park, Songpa-Gu, South Korea, 2003–06

Floor area: 3454 m². Client: Designhouse Inc
Cost: not disclosed
Team: Shigeru Ban Architects + KACI International (Kyeong-Sik Yoon, Principal)

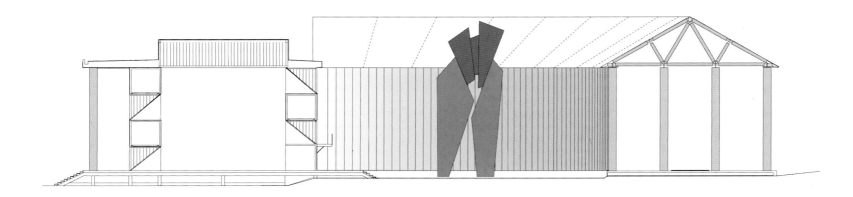

This unusual project involves the combination of two of Shigeru Ban's favorite construction elements—structural paper tubes and used shipping containers—both of which represent a significant contribution to the reduction of the overall ecological impact of such a structure. Ban had already designed a temporary art exhibition facility with these elements (Nomadic Museum, Pier 54, New York, 2005). Composed of a colonnaded, rectangular container structure ten meters high and a semicircular "Paper Gallery" enclosing an arc-shaped inner courtyard, this was a temporary exhibition pavilion for the celebration of the 30th anniversary of the Korean publisher Designhouse. The forested 14 214-square-meter site is located in the Olympic Park of Seoul. The first "container wall" was intended for exhibition booths, while the second housed office and storage areas. The alternating placement of the containers, with regular voids, animated the main façade, while the paper tube colonnade in front of the structure lent it a gravitas that it might have lacked given the use of such industrial materials. The semicircular Paper Gallery was made of two walls composed of 75-centimeter-diameter paper tube poles, with a roof truss made of 30-centimeter paper tubes.

Dieses ungewöhnliche Projekt kombinierte zwei bevorzugte Bauelemente des Architekten – Röhren aus Papier und gebrauchte Schiffscontainer. Beide tragen entscheidend dazu bei, die ökologische Auswirkung eines solchen Bauwerks zu reduzieren. Ban hatte aus denselben Elementen schon einmal eine temporäre Kunsthalle errichtet (Nomadic Museum, Pier 54, New York, 2005). Der zum 30. Geburtstag des koreanischen Verlags Designhouse realisierte temporäre Ausstellungsraum bestand aus einer 10 m hohen, mit Säulen umstandenen rechteckigen Containerkonstruktion und einer halbkreisförmigen „Papiergalerie", die einen bogenförmigen Innenhof umschloss. Das bewaldete 14 214 m² große Grundstück liegt im Olympiapark von Seoul. Die erste „Containerwand" war für Ausstellungsräume vorgesehen, in der zweiten befanden sich Büro- und Lagerräume. Die rhythmische Anordnung der Container mit regelmäßigen Aussparungen belebte die Hauptfassade. Zugleich verliehen die vorgelagerten Kolonnaden aus Papierröhren dem Bau eine Würde, die er wegen der industriellen Baumaterialien sonst wohl nicht gehabt hätte. Die halbrunde Papiergalerie bestand aus zwei Wänden, die wiederum aus Papierröhren mit 75 cm Durchmesser konstruiert waren. Seinen Abschluss fand das Ganze mit einem Dachstuhl aus Papierröhren mit 30 cm Durchmesser.

Cet étonnant projet combine deux des matériaux de construction favoris de Shigeru Ban, les tubes de carton et les conteneurs de transport qui, tous deux, représentent une contribution significative à la réduction de l'impact écologique global de ce bâtiment. Ban avait antérieurement conçu des installations d'expositions temporaires à partir d'éléments semblables (Musée nomade, Pier 54, New York, 2005). Ce pavillon temporaire, doté d'une structure composée de conteneurs rectangulaires empilés sur 10 m de haut et d'une « Galerie de papier » semi-circulaire fermant une cour intérieure en demi-cercle, a été construit pour la célébration du trentième anniversaire de la maison d'édition coréenne Designhouse. Son terrain boisé de 14 214 m² se trouve dans le Parc olympique de Séoul. Le premier « mur de conteneurs » servait aux guichets d'entrée, le second abritait bureaux et stockages. La disposition alternée de conteneurs et de vides réguliers animait la façade principale, tandis que la colonnade en tubes de carton lui donnait une *gravitas* qui ne devait *a priori* rien à ce type de matériaux industriels. La Galerie de papier, semi-circulaire, était faite de deux colonnades de piliers de carton de 75 cm de diamètre sur lesquelles venait se poser une ferme de charpente en tubes de carton de 30 cm de diamètre.

The Papertainer Museum, as its name implies, employs both paper tube columns and shipping containers—two elements that Shigeru Ban has employed with success in the past few years.

Das Papertainer Museum besteht, wie schon der Name andeutet, aus Papierröhren und Schiffscontainern – zwei Elemente, die Shigeru Ban in den vergangenen Jahren immer wieder erfolgreich eingesetzt hat.

Ce musée, comme son nom l'indique, utilise à la fois des tubes de carton et des conteneurs d'expédition, deux éléments utilisés avec succès par Shigeru Ban depuis plusieurs années.

Shigeru Ban's mastery of the use of paper tubes as structural elements in his architecture is visible in this image of the columns and beams that support this building.

Shigeru Bans meisterhafter Einsatz von Papierröhren als konstruktives Element zeigt sich auf dieser Aufnahme von Säulen und Trägern, die den Bau stützen.

La maîtrise dans l'utilisation des tubes de carton comme éléments structurels se constate dans cette image de colonnes et de poutres qui soutiennent le bâtiment.

The stunning form of the Papertainer Museum has a processional or voluntarily repetitive rhythm that lends it grandeur precisely because industrial elements are used.

Die atemberaubende formale Gestaltung des Papertainer Museum ist von feierlichem, bewusst von Wiederholungen geprägtem Rhythmus. Die daraus entstehende Erhabenheit bildet einen Kontrapunkt zu den industriellen Bauelementen.

La forme étonnante du musée Papertainer suit un rythme processionnel ou volontairement répétitif qui confère une certaine grandeur à cette utilisation d'éléments industriels.

NOMADIC MUSEUM

New York, 2004–05; Santa Monica, 2005–06; Tokyo, 2007

Area: 4180 m². Client: Ashes and Snow, LLC
Cost: not disclosed

The Nomadic Museum was a 4180-square-meter structure intended to house "Ashes and Snow," an exhibition of large-scale photographs by Gregory Colbert, on view in New York from March 5 to June 6, 2005. It was re-created subsequently in Santa Monica, California, and in Tokyo. No less than 205 meters long, the 16-meter-high rectangular building was made up essentially of steel shipping containers and paper tubes made from recycled paper, with inner and outer waterproof membranes and coated with a waterproof sealant. Located on Pier 54 on Manhattan's Lower West Side, the building had a central 3.6-meter-wide wooden walkway, composed of recycled scaffolding planks, lined on either side with river stones. The overall impression of this structure was not unlike that of a temple, or, as the architect wrote: "The simple triangular gable design of the roof structure and ceremonial, columnar interior walkway of the museum echo the atmosphere of a classical church." The first building to be made from shipping containers in New York, the Nomadic Museum is an intriguing effort to employ recyclable materials to create a large-scale structure. Despite the rather difficult access to the site and high entrance fee, many New Yorkers went to visit Ban's museum, perhaps more intrigued by its spectacular outer and interior forms than by the theatrical photographs of Colbert.

Das Nomadic Museum war ein 4180 m² großes Bauwerk, das für die Ausstellung „Ashes and Snow" des Fotografen Gregory Colbert gebaut wurde, die zwischen dem 5. März und 6. Juni 2005 großformatige Fotografien in New York präsentierte. Anschließend wurde der Bau in Santa Monica, Kalifornien, sowie in Tokio wieder errichtet. Das nicht weniger als 205 m lange, 16 m hohe, rechteckige Gebäude bestand in erster Linie aus Stahlcontainern und Pappröhren aus recyceltem Papier. Wasserfest versiegelte Membrane wurden innen und außen am Bau installiert, der außerdem mit einem wasserfesten Dichtungsmittel beschichtet wurde. Durch das am Pier 54 in der Lower Westside von Manhattan gelegene Museum zog sich ein mittig verlaufender, 3,6 m breiter hölzerner Laufsteg aus recycelten Gerüstplanken, der rechts und links von einem Bett aus Flusssteinen gesäumt wurde. Der Gesamteindruck des Baus war dem eines Tempels nicht unähnlich, oder, wie der Architekt schrieb: „Der schlichte Dreiecksgiebel der Dachkonstruktion und der feierliche, säulengesäumte Gang im Museum erinnern atmosphärisch an klassische Kirchenbauten." Das Nomadic Museum war das erste Gebäude aus Schiffscontainern in New York und faszinierte mit seinem Bemühen, bei einem Bau dieser Größenordnung recyclingfähige Materialien zu verwenden. Trotz der eher schweren Erreichbarkeit des Standorts und des hohen Eintrittspreises besuchten viele New Yorker Bans Museum, vielleicht sogar mehr vom spektakulären Außen- und Innenbau angezogen als von den dramatischen Fotografien Colberts.

Ce Musée nomade est une structure de 4180 m² conçue pour l'exposition de photographies grand format de Gregory Colbert intitulée « Cendres et neige », organisée en 2005 à New York. Il fut remonté par la suite à Santa Monica (Californie) et à Tokyo. De 205 m de long sur 16 de haut, cette construction rectangulaire se composait essentiellement de conteneurs de transport en acier, de tubes de carton en papier recyclé et d'une couverture étanche à membrane intérieure et extérieure hydrofuge à joint d'étanchéité. Installée sur le Pier 54 dans le quartier du Lower West Side à Manhattan, la structure s'organisait autour d'une allée centrale de 3,6 m de large faite de planches d'échafaudage recyclées et bordée de chaque côté par des galets. L'impression générale était proche de celle d'un temple, ou comme l'architecte l'a écrit : « La simple forme à pignon de la structure de couverture et l'allée aux colonnes de connotation cérémonielle à l'intérieur rappelaient l'atmosphère d'une église classique. » Première construction en conteneurs réalisée à New York, le Musée nomade est un essai original d'utilisation de matériaux recyclables pour une construction d'importantes dimensions. Malgré un accès au site assez difficile et un prix d'entrée élevé, de nombreux New-Yorkais ont visité le musée de Ban, peut-être plus intrigués par ses formes spectaculaires que par les photographies théâtrales de Colbert.

Built with shipping containers and paper tubes, the Nomadic Museum is seen here in its New York dockside setting (above), in Tokyo (below), and in Santa Monica (left page).

Das aus Containern und Pappröhren konstruierte Nomadic Museum hier an seinen Standorten an einem Pier in New York (oben), in Tokio (unten) sowie in Santa Monica (linke Seite).

Construit avec des conteneurs maritimes et des tubes en carton, le Musée nomade est ici photographié sur les docks de New York (en haut), à Tokyo (en bas) et à Santa Monica (page de gauche).

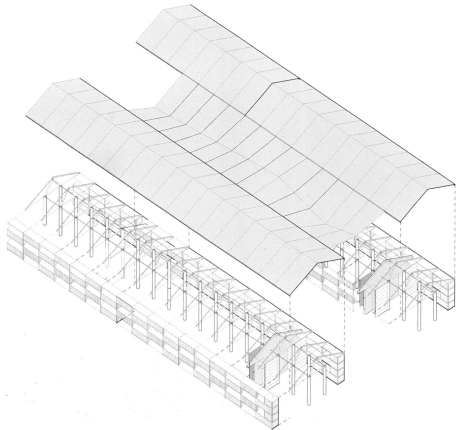

Although the Nomadic Museum was extremely simple, and repetitive in its structural principles, the vast interior space with its controlled natural lightning and central wooden walkway immediately took on the appearance of a temple-like space.

Obwohl das Nomadic Museum ein extrem einfaches Gebäude mit einer repetitiven Struktur war, strahlte der riesige Innenraum mit dem kontrol-lierten Einfall von Tageslicht und dem hölzernen Mittelgang eine sakrale Atmosphäre aus.

De principe structurel extrêmement simple et répétitif, le Musée nomade offre un vaste volume intérieur à l'éclairage naturel maîtrisé, doté d'une allée centrale en bois qui évoque l'image d'un temple.

CHARLES BARCLAY

Charles Barclay Architects
74 Josephine Avenue
London SW2 2LA
UK

Tel: +44 20 86 74 00 37
Fax: +44 20 86 83 96 96
E-mail: cba@cbarchitects.co.uk
Web: www.cbarchitects.co.uk

CHARLES BARCLAY was born in London in 1962. He graduated from North London University (now Metropolitan) in 1994 and created Charles Barclay Architects in 1996. He worked previously for Rick Mather, Mark Guard, and John Winter in London, for Peter Eisenman in New York, and for Sarvodaya in Sri Lanka. Charles Barclay writes about architecture and design, and is a guest critic at Metropolitan University's Department of Architecture. The work of Charles Barclay Architects ranges from houses to remodeling of inner London schools. Their highest-profile commission to date is the Kielder Observatory, won in competition in 2005 and completed in May 2008 (Kielder, Northumberland, UK, published here). Ongoing projects include the Grafton and Vittoria Schools (Islington, London, UK); a Ranch House (Buenos Aires, Argentina); and an African Eco-House (Entebbe, Uganda).

CHARLES BARCLAY wurde 1962 in London geboren. Nach seinem Abschluss an der North London University (heute London Metropolitan University) im Jahr 1994 gründete er 1996 Charles Barclay Architects. Zuvor hatte er bereits für die in London ansässigen Architekturbüros von Rick Mather, Mark Guard und John Winter gearbeitet sowie für Peter Eisenman in New York und für Sarvodaya in Sri Lanka. Charles Barclay betätigt sich auch als Autor zu Architektur- und Designthemen und ist Gastkritiker am Department of Architecture der Metropolitan University. Die Projektbandbreite von Charles Barclay Architects reicht von Wohnhausentwürfen bis hin zur Modernisierung von Londoner Schulen. Die bis dato größte Aufmerksamkeit erlangte das Büro mit seinem Entwurf für das Kielder Observatory, das als Siegerbeitrag aus einem im Jahr 2005 entschiedenen internationalen Wettbewerb hervorgegangen war und im Mai 2008 fertiggestellt wurde (Kielder, Northumberland, Großbritannien, hier vorgestellt). Zu den gegenwärtigen Projekten des Büros gehören zwei Schulumbauten in London (Grafton School und Vittoria School, Islington, Großbritannien), ein Ranchhaus in Buenos Aires (Argentinien) und ein Öko-Haus in Entebbe (Uganda).

CHARLES BARCLAY, né à Londres en 1962, est diplômé de la North London University (aujourd'hui Metropolitan University) en 1994 et a fondé Charles Barclay Architects en 1996. Auparavant, il avait travaillé pour Rick Mather, Mark Guard et John Winter à Londres, pour Peter Eisenman à New York et pour Sarvodaya au Sri Lanka. Il écrit sur l'architecture et le design, et est critique invité au département d'Architecture de la Metropolitan University. Son travail couvre aussi bien des maisons individuelles que la rénovation d'écoles londoniennes. Son projet le plus remarqué à cette date a été l'Observatoire de Kielder, remporté à l'issue d'un concours en 2005 et achevé en mai 2008 (Kielder, Northumberland, GB, publié ici). Parmi ses projets en cours figurent les écoles Grafton et Vittoria (Islington, Londres) ; une maison de ranch (Buenos Aires, Argentine) et une écomaison en Afrique (Entebbe, Uganda).

KIELDER OBSERVATORY

Kielder, Northumberland, UK, 2008

Address: Kielder, Northumberland NE48 1ER, UK, +44 78 05 63 84 69, www.kielderobservatory.org
Area: 235 m². Client: Forestry Commission. Cost: €450 000

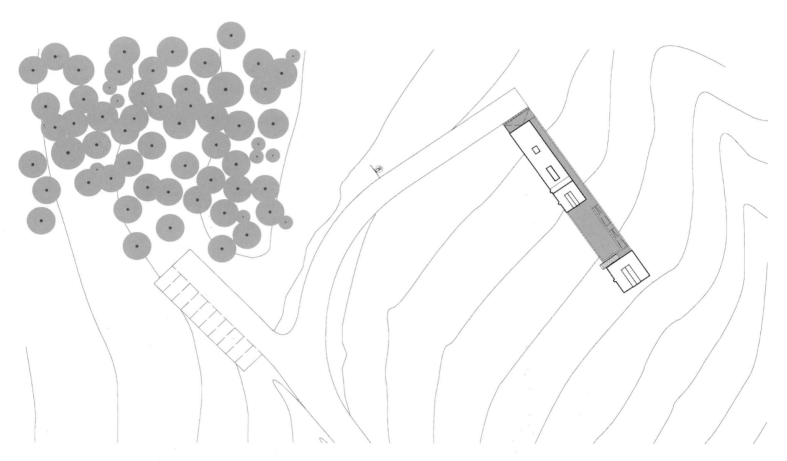

Charles Barclay Architects won the 2005 international competition with over 230 entries to build an astronomical **OBSERVATORY IN THE KIELDER WATER AND FOREST PARK** in Northumberland near the Scottish border. This commission is part of an ongoing initiative entitled "Art and Architecture at Kielder" that has seen the construction of other small structures in the park, such as James Turrell's *Kielder Skyspace*. The program called for a structure intended to house two telescopes with a view of the southern sky and a room for amateurs or scientific research. An open deck joining the two telescopes allows all-comers to set up their own equipment for "star-gazing events." The building is designed to be removed from the site after 25 years with minimal damage to the ground. "We wanted the experience of being on the observatory to feel like being on a vessel at sea in this rough, open landscape, with an amazing array of stars overhead," states the architect. Siberian larch was used for its "low-carbon" profile and to make a concerted contrast with high-tech observatories. A 2.5kW wind turbine and photovoltaic panels provide energy.

2005 gewannen Charles Barclay Architects den international ausgeschriebenen Wettbewerb mit mehr als 230 Beiträgen für den Bau einer **STERNWARTE IM WATER AND FOREST PARK VON KIELDER** in Northumberland, nahe der Grenze zu Schottland. Die Ausschreibung erfolgte im Rahmen der seit 1999 bestehenden Initiative „Art and Architecture at Kielder", durch die bereits einige kleinere Projekte wie etwa James Turrells *Kielder Skyspace* in dem Naturpark realisiert wurden. Verlangt war ein Gebäudeentwurf, der die Aufstellung von zwei Teleskopen zur Beobachtung des Südhimmels sowie einen für die Nutzung von Hobbyastronomen wie von Forschern gedachten Raum berücksichtigen sollte. Zwischen den beiden Aufbauten für die Teleskope befindet sich eine Plattform, auf der jeder Besucher seine eigene Ausrüstung zur Sternenbeobachtung aufstellen kann. Die gesamte Konstruktion ist so angelegt, dass sie nach 25 Jahren wieder abgebaut werden kann, ohne nennenswerte Spuren zu hinterlassen. „Unsere Idee war, dass man sich beim Besuch des Observatoriums in der rauen weiten Landschaft fühlen sollte, als sei man – Abertausende von Sternen über sich – an Bord eines Schiffes auf dem Meer", erklärt der Architekt. Um den Bau möglichst ressourcenschonend zu errichten, wurden sibirische Lärchen verwendet, die zugleich für einen bewussten visuellen Kontrast zu den üblichen Hightech-Observatorien sorgt. Die benötigte Energie wird mithilfe einer 2,5-KW-Windturbine und einer Solarstromanlage erzeugt.

Charles Barclay Architects a remporté, parmi 230 participants, le concours international organisé en 2005 pour la construction d'un **OBSERVATOIRE ASTRONOMIQUE DANS LE KIELDER WATER AND FOREST PARK** (Northumberland), près de la frontière écossaise. Cette commande fait partie d'un programme en cours de développement intitulé « Art et architecture à Kielder » qui est à l'origine de la présence d'autres petites constructions comme le *Kielder Skyspace* de James Turrell. La demande portait sur une structure contenant deux télescopes et une salle pour chercheurs, amateurs ou scientifiques. Une terrasse relie les deux télescopes et permet aux astronomes de disposer leur propre équipement pour leurs séances d'observation des étoiles. Le bâtiment est conçu pour être démonté dans vingt-cinq ans, en laissant le minimum de traces au sol. « Nous voulions que les utilisateurs de l'observatoire aient le sentiment de se trouver dans un navire en pleine mer au milieu de ce paysage naturel, tourmenté et ouvert, sous une étonnante voûte étoilée », explique l'architecte. Le mélèze de Sibérie a été choisi pour sa faible empreinte carbone et pour renforcer le contraste avec les observatoires d'allure plus généralement high-tech. Une éolienne de 2,5 kW et des panneaux photovoltaïques fournissent l'énergie nécessaire.

The long, thin wooden structure is set on progressively higher pilotis in order to maintain its horizontality on the sloping site.

Um die Abschüssigkeit des Geländes auszugleichen, wurde die lange schmale Holzkonstruktion auf unterschiedlich lange Pfeiler gesetzt.

La longue et fine construction en bois repose sur des pilotis de plus en plus hauts qui compensent la pente du terrain.

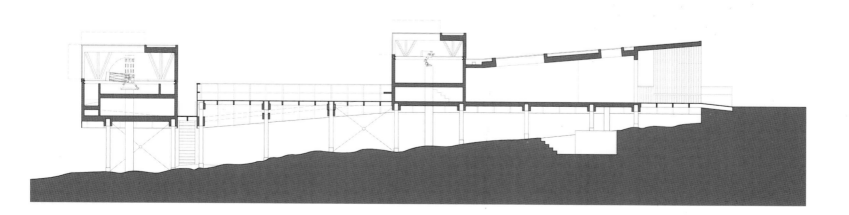

Above, Charles Barclay's sketch of the structure as seen from the opposite angle of the photo below. The wooden structure blends in with its beige setting in these pictures taken shortly after construction.

Die obige Zeichnung des Architekten und das Foto unten zeigen das Bauwerk aus entgegengesetzten Winkeln. Die Aufnahmen entstanden kurz nach der Errichtung des Baus und zeigen den farblichen Einklang von Holz und sandfarbenem Untergrund.

Ci-dessus, un croquis de l'architecte représente l'observatoire sous un angle opposé de celui de la photographie ci-dessous. Habillée de bois, la construction se fond dans le cadre terreux de ces images de fin de chantier.

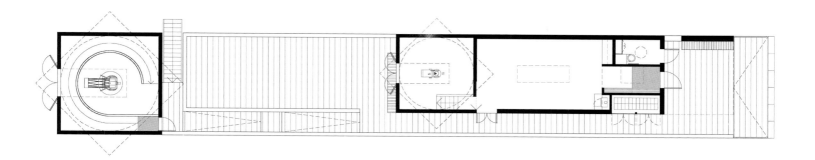

The simple, rectangular floor plan seen above culminates in the square observatory space visible in the photo above (and left on the plan).

Der einfache, rechteckige Grundriss oben hat seinen Höhepunkt in dem quadratischen Beobachtungsraum (auf dem Foto oben und auf der Grundrisszeichnung links).

La simplicité du plan rectangulaire culmine dans la forme carrée de l'observatoire (à gauche sur le plan et photo ci-dessus).

BARLINDHAUG CONSULT AS

Barlindhaug Consult AS
Sjølundveien 2
9291 Tromsø
Norway

Tel: +47 77 62 26 00
Fax: +47 77 62 26 99
E-mail: peter.w.soderman@barlindhaug.no
Web: www.barlindhaug.no

The chief architect of this project was **PETER WILHELM SØDERMAN**, who works with the firm Barlindhaug Consult AS in Tromsø, Norway. He was born in Vasa, Finland, in 1960, and received his M.Arch degree from the Helsinki University of Technology in 1990. From 1985 to the present, he has worked on public and private projects with Marja & Kari Kyyhkynen Architects, Vasa, Finland; Nyréns Architecture, Stockholm, Sweden; Anderssen+Fremming Architects, Tynset and Hamar, Norway; Hille Melbye architects and HRTB architects, both Oslo, Norway; Sigurd Hamran architects, Tromsø; Contur Architects, Tromsø; and, most recently, Barlindhaug Consult AS, Tromsø. Recent projects by Peter Søderman include the Reinen Elementary School (Tromsø, 2002); Først og fremst Housing Project (Hammerfest, 2004); Vestre Mortensnes Housing Project (Tromsø, 2004); Breivang High School (Tromsø, 2005); and the Svalbard Global Seed Vault (Longyearbyen, Svalbard, 2007–08, published here), all in Norway. Barlindhaug Consult AS provides engineering services to the Norwegian and international markets. The company's scope of services includes engineering and construction, Arctic technology, energy conservation planning, and impact assessments.

Leitender Architekt des Projekts war **PETER WILHELM SØDERMAN** vom Büro Barlindhaug Consult AS in Tromsø, Norwegen. Er wurde 1960 in Vasa, Finnland, geboren und erhielt seinen M.Arch. 1990 an der Technischen Universität Helsinki. Seit 1985 arbeitet er an öffentlichen und privaten Projekten, u.a. für Marja & Kari Kyyhkynen Architekten, Vasa, Finnland, für Nyréns Architecture, Stockholm, für Anderssen + Fremming Architekten, Tynset und Hamar, Norwegen, für die Osloer Hille + Melbye Architekten und HRTB Architekten, für Sigurd Hamran Architekten und Contur Architekten sowie für Barlindhaug Consult AS, alle Tromsø. Zu den jüngeren Projekten von Peter Søderman zählen die Grundschule Reinen (Tromsø, 2002), die Wohnanlagen Først og fremst (Hammerfest, 2004) und Vestre Mortensnes (Tromsø, 2004), die Breivang-Schule (Tromsø, 2005) sowie der Svalbard Global Seed Vault (Longyearbyen, Spitzbergen, 2007–08, hier vorgestellt), alle in Norwegen. Barlindhaug Consult AS bietet ingenieurtechnische Dienstleistungen für den norwegischen und internationalen Markt an. Das Leistungsspektrum der Firma umfasst technische Planung und Bauausführung, arktische Technologie, Planung von Energiesparmaßnahmen und Umweltverträglichkeitsprüfungen.

PETER WILHELM SØDERMAN, architecte responsable du projet de Svalbard, travaille pour l'agence norvégienne Barlindhaug Consult AS installée à Tromsø. Né à Vasa, Finlande, en 1960, il est architecte diplômé de l'université de Technologie d'Helsinki (1990). De 1985 à aujourd'hui, il a travaillé sur des projets tant privés que publics avec Marja & Kari Kyyhkynen Architects, à Vasa, Finlande; Nyréns Architecture, Stockholm, Suède; Anderssen+Fremming Architects, Tynset et Hamar, Norvège; Hille+Melbye Architects et HRTB Architects à Oslo, Norvège; Sigurd Hamran Architects, Tromsø; Contur Architects, Tromsø, et, plus récemment, Barlindhaug Consult AS. Parmi ses réalisations récentes figurent l'école élémentaire de Reinen (Tromsø, 2002); les logements Først og fremst (Hammerfest, 2004) et Vestre Mortensnes (Tromsø, 2004); le collège Breivang (Tromsø, 2005) et le Svalbard Global Seed Vault (Longyearbyen, Svalbard, 2007–08, publié ici). Barlindhaug Consult AS est une agence d'ingénierie qui intervient aussi bien en Norvège qu'à l'international. Elle propose des services dans les domaines de la construction, de la technologie arctique, de l'énergie et des études d'impact.

SVALBARD GLOBAL SEED VAULT

Longyearbyen, Svalbard, Norway, 2007–08

*Site area: 1720 m². Client: Statsbygg, Norwegian Ministry of Government Administration and Reform
Cost: $880 000. Team: Peter W. Søderman, Louis Lunde, Trond Hansen (Architects),
Sverre Barlindhaug (Engineer)*

The long, rectangular form of the entrance to the Seed Vault is highlighted by a glittering work imagined by the artist Dyveke Sanne.

Die gestreckte Rechtecksform des Eingangs zum Seed Vault wird von einem glitzernden Kunstwerk der Künstlerin Dyveke Sanne hervorgehoben.

Le volume rectangulaire allongé de l'entrée du Seed Vault est signalé par une œuvre scintillante de l'artiste Dyveke Sanne.

Located on a remote island in the Arctic Circle, the **SVALBARD GLOBAL SEED VAULT** was designed to conserve 100 million seeds of 268 000 plants originating in 100 different countries, making the largest collection of food crop seeds anywhere in the world. As the Norwegian government's declaration on the occasion of the opening of the vault in February 2008 read: "The seed vault is part of an unprecedented effort to protect the planet's rapidly diminishing biodiversity. The diversity of our crops is essential for food production, yet it is being lost." This "fail-safe" facility, dug deep into the frozen rock of an Arctic mountain, is intended to secure for centuries, or longer, seeds representing every important crop variety available in the world today. As well as protecting against the daily loss of diversity, the vault could also prove indispensable for restarting agricultural production at the regional or global level in the wake of a natural or man-made disaster. Even in the worst-case scenarios of global warming, the vault rooms will remain naturally frozen for up to 200 years. The Global Crop Diversity Trust (www.croptrust.org) is providing support for the ongoing operations of the vault, which has the capacity to store up to 4.5 million samples or some two billion seeds. The vault consists in three secure rooms located at the end of a 125-meter-long tunnel blasted out of the mountain site. The seeds are stored at a temperature of -18°C in foil pouches, allowing some samples to be usable for as long as 2000 years or more. The artist Dyveke Sanne and KORO, the Norwegian agency overseeing art in public spaces, created a work made of reflective steel, mirrors, and prisms that "acts as a beacon, reflecting polar light in the summer months."

Der **GLOBAL SEED VAULT** liegt auf Spitzbergen, einer entlegenen Insel am Polarkreis, und wurde realisiert, um 100 Millionen Samen von 268 000 Nutzpflanzen aus 100 verschiedenen Ländern einlagern zu können – die größte Sammlung von Nutzpflanzensaatgut weltweit. Anlässlich der Einweihung der Einrichtung im Februar 2008 erklärte die norwegische Regierung: „Der Saatguttresor ist Teil einer nie da gewesenen Anstrengung, die rasch schwindende Biodiversität dieses Planeten zu erhalten. Die Vielfalt unserer Nutzpflanzen ist unerlässlich für unsere Nahrungsmittelproduktion, und doch verlieren wir sie." Diese tief in den stets eiskalten Felsen eines arktischen Bergs geschlagene Sicherheitseinrichtung soll das Saatgut sämtlicher bedeutender, heute weltweit existierender Nutzpflanzenarten jahrhundertelang, wenn nicht gar länger, erhalten. Doch der Tresor ist nicht nur eine Sicherung gegen den täglich wachsenden Verlust an Biodiversität, er könnte sich auch als notwendig erweisen, sollte es je nötig sein, die landwirtschaftliche Produktion regional oder global nach einer von der Natur oder dem Menschen verschuldeten Katastrophe wieder aufzunehmen. Selbst bei Eintreten der denkbar schlechtesten Umstände hinsichtlich der Erderwärmung dürften die Tresorräume noch bis zu 200 Jahre lang Minustemperaturen aufweisen. Der Global Crop Diversity Trust (www.croptrust.org) unterstützt den aktuellen Betrieb des Tresors, dessen Kapazität auf die Lagerung von bis zu 4,5 Millionen Musterspezies oder etwa 2 Milliarden Samen angelegt ist. Der Tresor besteht aus drei Sicherheitsräumen am Ende eines 125 m langen Tunnels, der in den Berg hineingesprengt wurde. Das Saatgut wird bei einer Temperatur von −18 °C in Folie verpackt gelagert, was erlaubt, die Proben bis zu 2000 Jahre oder länger nutzbar zu erhalten. In Kooperation mit der norwegischen Behörde für Kunst im öffentlichen Raum, KORO, konnte die Künstlerin Dyveke Sanne eine Arbeit aus Spiegelstahl, Spiegeln und Prismen realisieren, die „wie ein Leuchtfeuer wirkt und das polare Licht in den Sommermonaten reflektiert".

Implanté sur une île lointaine de l'intérieur du Cercle arctique, le **SVALBARD GLOBAL SEED VAULT** (Caveau international de conservation de semences de Svalbard) a été conçu pour la conservation de 100 millions de semences de 268 000 plantes alimentaires originaires de 100 pays différents ce qui en fait la plus importante collection de ce type dans le monde. La déclaration du gouvernement norvégien, publiée à l'occasion de l'inauguration des installations en 2008, précisait : « Ce caveau de semences fait partie d'un effort sans précédent pour protéger la planète de la diminution rapide de la diversité. Celle-ci qui est essentielle pour la production d'aliments est en cours d'appauvrissement dramatique. » Ces installations à toute épreuve, creusées dans la roche gelée d'une montagne de l'Arctique, devraient protéger pour des siècles ou plus des semences représentant toutes les variétés végétales exploitables importantes existant dans le monde. Leur contenu pourrait se révéler indispensable pour le redémarrage de productions agricoles au niveau régional ou global à la suite de désastres naturels ou provoqués par l'homme. Même dans le pire des scenarii de réchauffement global, les salles devraient rester naturellement gelées pendant au moins deux cents ans. Le Global Crop Diversity Trust (www.croptrust.org) finance les opérations qui consistent à engranger plus de 4,5 millions d'échantillons et quelque 2 milliards de semences. Le caveau se compose de trois salles de sécurité à l'extrémité d'un tunnel de 125 m de long creusé à l'explosif dans la montagne. Les semences sont stockées à -18 °C dans des emballages spéciaux. L'artiste Dyveke Sanne et l'agence norvégienne KORO en charge de l'installation d'œuvres d'art dans des lieux publics ont créé, à l'entrée, une œuvre en acier réfléchissant, miroirs et prises, qui « agit comme un phare, reflétant la lumière polaire pendant les mois d'été ».

The architecture of the Seed Vault is as simple as its function—to provide a protected environment for the seeds of the world, potentially a key to the survival of the human race in the case of some future catastrophe.

Die Architektur des Seed Vault ist ebenso einfach wie sein Zweck – er dient als Schutzraum für Saatgut aus aller Welt – im Falle zukünftiger Katastrophen ein potenzieller Schlüssel zum Überleben der Menschheit.

L'architecture du Seed Vault est aussi simple que sa fonction : offrir un environnement protégé à la conservation de semences venues du monde entier, pour la survie de la race humaine en cas de future catastrophe.

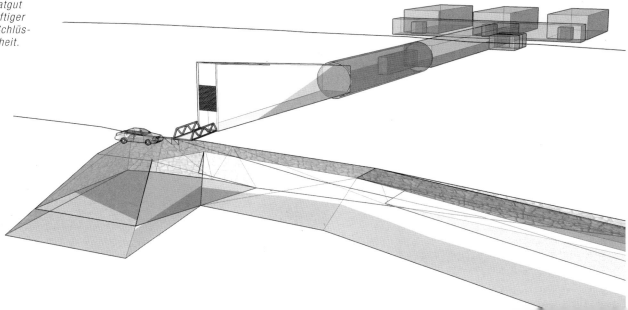

The vault burrows deep into a mountain to ensure the stability of the collections in terms of temperature, even if global warming should begin to change exterior conditions.

Der Seed Vault reicht tief in den Berg hinein, wohin er verlegt wurde, um Temperaturstabilität für die Bestände selbst bei Veränderung der äußeren klimatischen Gegebenheiten durch die globale Erwärmung zu gewährleisten.

Le caveau est creusé au plus profond de la montagne pour garantir la constance thermique de la collection de semences, même si le réchauffement climatique doit entraîner la modification des conditions extérieures.

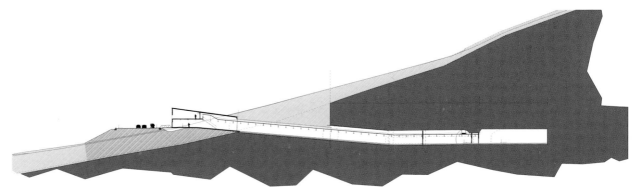

Above, vials and pouches containing seeds and the stacked sample collections.

Oben Behälter und Beutel mit Saatgut, unten die gestapelten Lagerbestände.

Ci-dessus, flacons et sachets contenant les semences. Ci-dessous, le stockage des collections.

SEBASTIAN BERGNE

Sebastian Bergne Ltd
2 Ingate Place
London SW8 3NS
UK

Tel: + 44 20 76 22 33 33
E-mail: mail@sebastianbergne.com
Web: www.sebastianbergne.com

Born in 1966, the industrial designer **SEBASTIAN BERGNE** traveled with his family from the Middle East to Asia and the Mediterranean. After graduating from the Royal College of Art (London, UK, 1990), he established his London studio the same year, and had a second in Bologna (Italy, 2000–07). Sebastian Bergne has worked with a variety of clients including Authentics, DeBeers, Driade, Epson, Sassoon, Tefal, and MUJI. His work is included in permanent collections such as those of the Museum of Modern Art (New York) and the Design Museum (London). He has been a Visiting Professor at the Royal College of Art and other institutions. His work includes the "Corker" Corkscrew (Edition Nouveaux Objets, 2006); "Ice Cream Machine" for Dinner by Heston Blumenthal (produced by Mike Smith Studios, 2010); "Enjoy" Kitchen utensils, 90% recycled PET (Tefal, 2010); "Natura" Cookware Range—100% recycled aluminum (Tefal, Tolix, 2010); "ColourWare" Plate Compositions (with Sophie Smallhorn, own edition, 2011); "Monthly Measure" Calendar and Ruler (Atelier d'exercices, 2011); "Flap" Domestic Desk (Tolix, 2012); and the "Curl" Table Lamp with tunable white light (Luceplan Spa, 2012). His only architectural work is the LEGO Greenhouse (London, UK, 2011, published here).

Produktdesigner **SEBASTIAN BERGNE**, geboren 1966, reiste mit seiner Familie aus dem Nahen Osten nach Asien und in den Mittelmeerraum. Nach seinem Studienabschluss am Royal College of Art (London, 1990) gründete er noch im selben Jahr ein Büro in London, gefolgt von einem zweiten in Bologna (2000–07). Bergne arbeitete für so unterschiedliche Auftraggeber wie Authentics, DeBeers, Driade, Epson, Sassoon, Tefal und MUJI. Seine Entwürfe sind in Sammlungen des Museum of Modern Art (New York) und dem Design Museum (London) vertreten. Er hat als Gastprofessor am Royal College of Art und anderen Institutionen gelehrt. Zu seinen Entwürfen zählen der Korkenzieher „Corker" (Edition Nouveaux Objets, 2006), die „Ice Cream Machine" für Dinner by Heston Blumenthal (Produktion: Mike Smith Studios, 2010), die Küchenutensilien „Enjoy" aus 90 % recyceltem PET (Tefal, 2010), die Topfserie „Natura" aus 100 % recyceltem Aluminum (Tefal, 2010), die Tellerkombination „ColourWare" (mit Sophie Smallhorn, eigene Edition, 2011), Kalender und Lineal „Monthly Measure" (Atelier d'exercices, 2011), der Sekretär „Flap" (Tolix, 2012) und die Tischleuchte „Curl" mit regulierbarem weißem Licht (Luceplan Spa, 2012). Sein einziges Architekturprojekt ist das LEGO Greenhouse (London, 2011, hier vorgestellt).

Né en 1966, le designer industriel **SEBASTIAN BERGNE** a parcouru en famille le Moyen-Orient, l'Asie et la Méditerranée. Diplômé du Royal College of Art (Londres, 1990), il a ouvert son agence londonienne la même année, puis une deuxième à Bologne (Italie, 2000–07). Il a travaillé avec des clients très divers, parmi lesquels Authentics, DeBeers, Driade, Epson, Sassoon, Tefal et MUJI. Ses œuvres figurent dans des collections permanentes, notamment celles du Musée d'art moderne de New York et du Musée du design de Londres. Il est actuellement professeur associé au Royal College of Art. Ses travaux comprennent : le tire-bouchon « Corker » (Édition Nouveaux objets, 2006) ; la « machine à glace » pour le restaurant Dinner by Heston Blumenthal (production Mike Smith Studios, 2010) ; les instruments de cuisine « Enjoy » en PET recyclé à 90 % (Tefal, 2010) ; la batterie de cuisine « Natura », 100 % aluminium recyclé (Tefal, Tolix, 2010) ; les compositions d'assiettes « ColourWare » (avec Sophie Smallhorn, édition propre, 2011) ; le calendrier et la règle « Monthly Measure » (Atelier d'exercices, 2011) ; le bureau « Flap » (Tolix, 2012) et la lampe de bureau « Curl » à lumière blanche réglable (Luceplan Spa, 2012). La serre en LEGO (Londres, 2011, publiée ici) est sa seule réalisation architecturale.

LEGO GREENHOUSE
Covent Garden, London, UK, 2011

Area: 5 m². Cost: not disclosed
Client: Covent Garden, LEGO & London Design Festival

A sketch and photos show the Lego Greenhouse in its setting. Hardly large enough to be considered as "architecture," the structure plays on the ambiguity of Lego and the presence of nature in this mineral square.

Skizze und Aufnahmen zeigen das Lego Greenhouse in seinem Kontext. Die Konstruktion, kaum groß genug, um als „Architektur" verstanden zu werden, spielt mit der Mehrdeutigkeit von Legosteinen und Natur auf dem von Stein dominierten Platz.

Le croquis et les photos montrent la serre en Lego dans son environnement. Tout juste assez grande pour pouvoir être considérée comme « architecturale », la structure joue sur l'ambiguïté des briques Lego et la présence de nature dans un décor minéral.

LEGO commissioned Sebastian Berne to create a public installation using approximately 100 000 of the firm's trademark transparent and brown plastic bricks. His **LEGO GREENHOUSE** was displayed in Covent Garden from 15 to 25 September 2011. The structure was effectively an operating greenhouse built entirely in LEGO, with real plants. The designer explains, "Its pitched roof references reflect the architecture that surrounds it, while the plants inside bring nature back to this area once famous for its garden trade." In fact, his own explanation of the project is the best description of his aims, "As with the majority of my work, I enjoy taking a material or process and pushing the boundary of what can be done with it. This time we have created an interesting juxtaposition of a natural environment growing in an almost digital, mass-produced LEGO structure… In my work, I love to make something special from the ordinary, and I hope that's what has happened here. It's an everyday function, made of a material we know, in an ordinary environment, but together they make something extraordinary, and I think it is going to be quite magical." Glowing in the dark, the LEGO Greenhouse was part of the London Design Festival 2011.

Im Auftrag von LEGO realisierte Sebastian Bergne eine Installation im öffentlichen Raum aus rd. 100 000 transparenten und braunen der berühmten Plastiksteine der Firma. Sein **LEGO GREENHOUSE** war vom 15. bis 25. September 2011 in Covent Garden zu sehen. Die Konstruktion war ein funktionales Gewächshaus mit echten Pflanzen, vollständig aus Legosteinen realisiert. Der Designer erklärt: „Das Giebeldach greift die bauliche Umgebung auf, während die Pflanzen Natur in einen Stadtteil zurückbringen, der früher für den Handel mit Pflanzen berühmt war." Was ihn motiviert, verdeutlicht seine Projektbeschreibung: „Wie bei den meisten Entwürfen reizt es mich, ein Material oder einen Fertigungsprozess aufzugreifen und an dessen Grenzen zu gehen. Hier kam es zu einem faszinierenden Kontrast zwischen einem natürlichen Umfeld und dem fast digital anmutenden Haus aus massengefertigten Legosteinen, in dem es wächst … Mit meiner Arbeit möchte ich das Alltägliche zum Besonderen machen – ich hoffe, das ist hier gelungen. Ein alltägliches funktionales Objekt aus vertrauten Materialien, in einem gewöhnlichen Umfeld, doch im Zusammenspiel etwas Besonderes. Das wird sicher eine ganz eigene Magie haben." Das nachts beleuchtete LEGO Greenhouse war ein Beitrag zum London Design Festival 2011.

LEGO a confié à Sebastian Bergne la création d'une installation publique qui utilise environ 100 000 des briques de plastique transparentes et marron qui sont la marque déposée de l'entreprise. La **SERRE LEGO** a été exposée à Covent Garden du 15 au 25 septembre 2011. C'est une vraie serre en état de marche, construite entièrement en LEGO, avec de vraies plantes à l'intérieur. Le designer explique que « le toit en pente reflète l'architecture autour de la serre, tandis que les plantes à l'intérieur ramènent la nature sur cette place qui était autrefois connue pour ses commerces de jardinage ». Mais c'est l'explication qu'il donne lui-même du projet qui décrit le mieux ses objectifs : « Comme dans la plupart de mes travaux, j'aime partir d'un matériau ou d'un processus et repousser les limites de ce qui peut en être fait. Cette fois, nous avons créé une juxtaposition intéressante d'un environnement naturel qui se développe dans une structure en LEGO issue d'une fabrication en série presque numérique… Dans mon travail, j'adore créer quelque chose de spécial à partir de l'ordinaire, et j'espère que c'est le cas ici. La serre a une fonction courante, elle est faite d'un matériau que nous connaissons bien, et placée dans un environnement ordinaire, mais l'ensemble crée quelque chose d'extraordinaire, et je pense même magique. » Éclairée et brillant la nuit, la serre LEGO a participé au Festival de design de Londres en 2011.

The transparency of the LEGO Green-house contrasts with the opacity of the buildings around it. It does not disturb passersby but surely makes them wonder why it is there.

Die Transparenz des LEGO Green-house kontrastiert mit der Geschlossenheit der Nachbarbauten. Es stört die Passanten nicht, wirft aber zweifellos die Frage auf, was es an diesem Ort zu suchen hat.

La transparence de la serre LEGO contraste avec l'opacité des bâtiments dont elle est entourée. Les passants ne sont pas réellement troublés mais se demandent certainement ce qu'elle fait là.

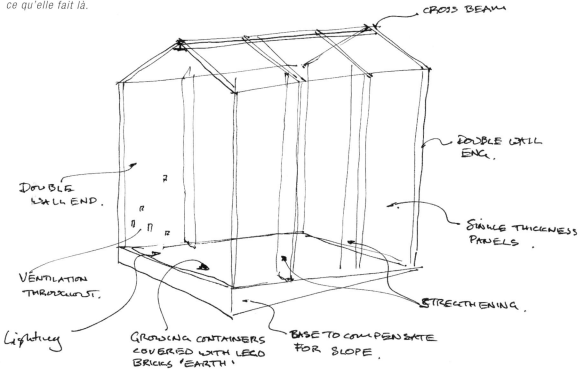

BIG

BIG
Bjarke Ingels Group
Nørrebrogade 66d, 2nd Floor
2200 Copenhagen N
Denmark

Tel: +45 72 21 72 27 / Fax: +45 35 12 72 27
E-mail: big@big.dk / Web: www.big.dk

BJARKE INGELS was born in 1974 in Copenhagen. He graduated from the Royal Academy of Arts School of Architecture (Copenhagen, 1999) and attended the ETSAB School of Architecture (Barcelona). He created his own office in 2005 under the name Bjarke Ingels Group (BIG), after having cofounded PLOT Architects in 2001 and collaborated with Rem Koolhaas at OMA (Rotterdam). In 2004 he was awarded the Golden Lion at the Venice Biennale for the Stavanger Concert House. One of his latest completed projects, the Mountain (Copenhagen, Denmark, 2006–08, published here), has received numerous awards including the World Architecture Festival Housing Award, Forum Aid Award, and the MIPIM Residential Development Award. **JAKOB LANGE** is an Associate of BIG and has been collaborating with Bjarke Ingels since 2003. He was born in 1978 in Odense, Denmark, and also attended the Royal Academy of Arts School of Architecture. He was the project leader for The Mountain. BIG is now led by eight partners and has also opened an office in New York. The firm designed the Danish Expo Pavilion (Shanghai, China, 2010); the Superkilen Master Plan (Copenhagen, Denmark, 2011); Shenzhen International Energy Mansion (Shenzhen, China, 2013); the Danish Maritime Museum (Elsinore, Denmark, 2013); the Faroe Islands Education Center (Thorshavn, Faroe Islands, Denmark, 2014); the Amager Bakke Waste-to-Energy Plant (Copenhagen, Denmark, 2009–); Tallinn Town Hall (Estonia); and the National Library of Astana (Kazakhstan).

BJARKE INGELS wurde 1974 in Kopenhagen geboren. Er schloss sein Studium an der Architekturfakultät der Königlichen Akademie der Künste ab (Kopenhagen, 1999) und besuchte die Architekturfakultät der ETSAB in Barcelona. 2005 gründete er sein eigenes Büro Bjarke Ingels Group (BIG), nachdem er 2001 PLOT Architects mitbegründet und Projekte mit Rem Koolhaas/OMA (Rotterdam) realisiert hatte. Für seinen Entwurf des Konzerthauses in Stavanger erhielt er 2004 auf der Biennale in Venedig den Goldenen Löwen. Eines seiner aktuellsten fertiggestellten Projekte, Mountain (Kopenhagen, Dänemark, 2006–08, hier vorgestellt) wurde mit zahlreichen Preisen ausgezeichnet, darunter dem World Architecture Festival Housing Award, dem Forum Aid Award und dem MIPIM Residential Development Award. **JAKOB LANGE** gehört zu den Partnern von BIG und arbeitet seit 2003 mit Ingels zusammen. Lange, geboren 1978 in Odense, besuchte ebenfalls die Architekturschule der Königlich Dänischen Kunstakademie. Für Mountain übernahm Lange die Projektleitung. BIG hat inzwischen acht Partner und unterhält ein Büro in New York. Das Team entwarf den Dänischen Pavillon für die Expo 2010 (Schanghai, China), den Masterplan für Superkilen (Kopenhagen, Dänemark, 2011), das Internationale Energiezentrum in Shenzhen (Shenzhen, China, 2013), das Dänische Schifffahrtsmuseum (Helsingør, Dänemark, 2013), das Bildungszentrum der Färöer-Inseln (Thorshavn, Färöer-Inseln, Dänemark, 2014), das Müllheizkraftwerk Amager Bakke (Kopenhagen, Dänemark, seit 2009), das Rathaus in Tallinn (Estland) sowie die Nationalbibliothek in Astana (Kasachstan).

BJARKE INGELS est né en 1974 à Copenhague. Diplômé de l'École d'architecture de l'Académie royale des beaux-arts (Copenhague, 1999), il a également suivi les cours de l'École d'architecture ETSAB (Barcelone). Il a ouvert son cabinet en 2005 sous le nom Bjarke Ingels Group (BIG) après avoir participé à la fondation de PLOT Architects en 2001 et collaboré avec Rem Koolhaas à OMA (Rotterdam). Il a reçu le Lion d'or 2004 à la Biennale de Venise pour la salle de concerts de Stavanger. L'un de ses derniers projets réalisés, The Mountain (Copenhague, 2006–08, publié ici), a reçu plusieurs récompenses dont le prix logement du World Architecture Festival, le prix Forum Aid et le prix MIPIM développement résidentiel. **JAKOB LANGE** est l'un des associés de BIG et collabore avec Bjarke Ingels depuis 2003. Né en 1978 à Odense (Danemark), il a également étudié à l'École d'architecture de l'Académie royale des arts de Copenhague. Il a été architecte de projet pour The Mountain. BIG est actuellement dirigé par huit partenaires et a ouvert un bureau à New York. L'agence a conçu le Pavillon danois pour l'Exposition universelle de Shanghai (Shanghai, 2010) ; le plan directeur du site Superkilen (Copenhague, 2011) ; la Shenzhen International Energy Mansion (Shenzhen, Chine, 2013) ; le Musée maritime danois (Elseneur, Danemark, 2013) ; le Centre éducatif des îles Féroé (Thorshavn, îles Féroé, Danemark, 2014) ; le Centre de transformation des déchets en énergie d'Amager Bakke (Copenhague, 2009–) ; l'hôtel de ville de Tallinn (Estonie) et la bibliothèque nationale d'Astana (Kazakhstan).

THE MOUNTAIN
Copenhagen, Denmark, 2006–08

Address: Ørestads Boulevard 55, 2300 Copenhagen, Denmark
Area: 33 000 m². Client: Høpfner A/S, Danish Oil Company A/S. Cost: €36 million
Collaboration: Jakob Lange (Project Architect), JDS

"How do you combine the splendors of the suburban backyard with the social intensity of urban density?" ask the architects. Their response is based in part on a program that called for two-thirds of the space in the building to be devoted to parking (480 spots) and just one-third to living (80 apartments). They decided to use the parking garages as a base on which to build terraced housing, creating a "symbiotic" relationship between the two elements. With a sloping elevator and ceiling heights that rise to 16 meters in certain places, even the garage is an architectural experience. The garden terraces that flow over the building provide the architects with the suburban lifestyle that they had aimed for while retaining urban density. A watering system ensures the survival of the balcony plants, while only a glass door separates each apartment from its terrace. Perforated aluminum plates are used for cladding on the north and west façades, allowing light and air into the parking areas. The perforations in the façade are intended to "form a huge reproduction of Mount Everest."

„Wie kombiniert man die Annehmlichkeiten eines Reihenhausgartens mit der sozialen Intensität städtischer Dichte?", lautete bei diesem Projekt die Ausgangsfrage der Architekten. Die Lösung fiel wie folgt aus: Zwei Drittel des gesamten Gebäudevolumens sollten von einem Parkhaus (mit 480 Plätzen) und nur ein Drittel von Wohnraum eingenommen werden. In symbiotischer Beziehung zwischen den beiden Elementen war der Parkbereich als Fundament gedacht, auf dem in treppenförmiger Stufung 80 Apartments aufgesetzt werden sollten. Ein diagonal verlaufender Aufzug und bis zu 16 m hohe Decken machen hier selbst die Benutzung eines Parkhauses zu einem architektonischen Erlebnis. Die kaskadenartige Anlage von Bungalows und Gartenterrassen erfüllt die geforderte Verquickung von suburbanem Wohnstil und dichtem urbanen Nebeneinander. Ein spezielles Bewässerungssystem sorgt für eine ausreichende Wasserversorgung der begrünten Terrassen – ein Schritt durch die Glastür, schon steht man im eigenen blühenden Garten. Die Nord- und die Westfassade des Baus sind mit perforierten Aluminiumplatten verkleidet, durch die Licht und frische Luft in den Parkhausbereich gelangen. Zugleich hält die Fassadenperforation ein metaphorisches Element bereit, fügen sich die Löcher doch zu einer „riesigen Reproduktion des Mount Everest" zusammen.

« Comment combiner les splendeurs de la cour de la maison de banlieue et l'intensité sociale de la densité urbaine ? » se sont demandés les architectes. Leur réponse consiste en partie en un programme qui réserve les deux tiers de l'espace construit aux parkings (480 emplacements) et un tiers seulement aux logements (80 appartements). Ils ont décidé de se servir des parkings comme d'une base sur laquelle édifier des appartements en terrasses en créant une relation « symbiotique » entre les deux éléments. En dehors de l'ascenseur incliné et des hauteurs de plafond qui atteignent jusqu'à 16 m à certains endroits, le garage devient lui aussi une nouvelle expérience architecturale. Les terrasses-jardins qui cascadent en façade offrent ce style de vie de banlieue que les architectes souhaitaient tout en conservant un certain sentiment de densité urbaine. Un système d'arrosage assure la survie des plantations et l'appartement n'est séparé de sa terrasse que par une porte de verre. Des plaques d'aluminium perforé habillent les façades nord et ouest, laissent entrer un éclairage naturel et permettent l'aération du parking. Les perforations des façades dessinent une « énorme reproduction de l'Everest ».

Despite the fundamental regularity of its units, as seen in the drawing (right), the complex assumes something of an organic aspect due to the angling and irregular external outline of the whole.

Trotz der streng einheitlichen Ausführung der einzelnen Bungalows, deutlich erkennbar auf der Zeichnung rechts, bekommt die Anlage durch ihren komplexen, vielwinkeligen Umriss etwas Organisches.

Malgré le plan régulier des appartements, le complexe n'en présente pas moins un aspect organique provoqué par son inclinaison en gradins et son profil extérieur irrégulier (dessin à droite).

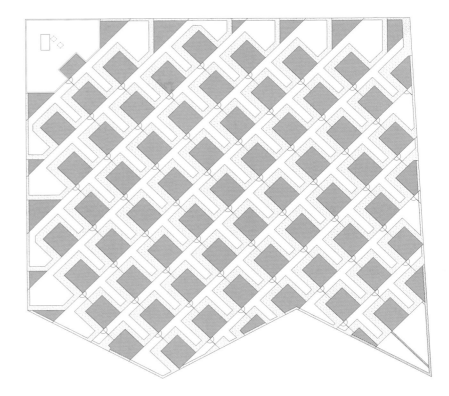

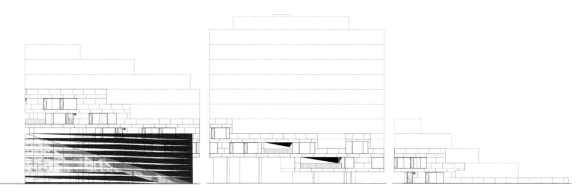

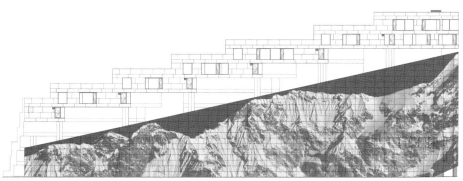

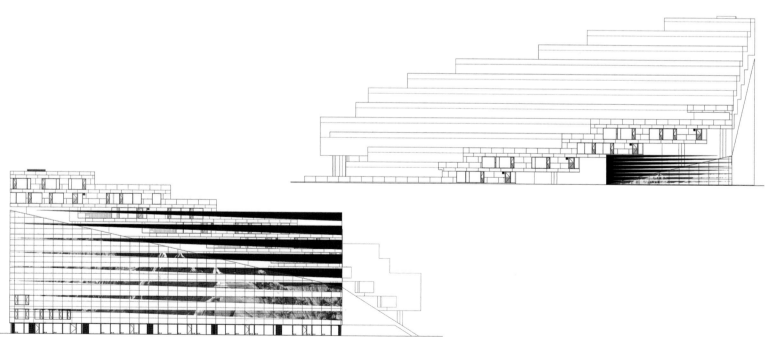

A liberal use of wood and latticework surfaces contributes to the "natural" aspect of the project, in contrast with the substantive rectangular volumes revealed by the elevations seen here.

Die großzügige Verwendung von Holz zur Wand- und Bodenverschalung unterstützt den „Naturaspekt" des Projekts und bildet ein Gegengewicht zur bestimmenden Rechtwinkeligkeit, die in den Aufrissen oben deutlich wird.

La généreuse utilisation du bois et de lattis de bois contribue à donner au projet un aspect « naturel » qui contraste avec l'importance de ses volumes parallélépipédiques (élévations ci-dessus).

PATRICK BLANC

Patrick Blanc

E-mail: info@murvegetalpatrickblanc.com
Web: www.verticalgardenpatrickblanc.com

Born in Paris, France, in 1953, **PATRICK BLANC** received his doctorate in Botany in 1989 (Docteur d'Etat ès Sciences, Université Pierre et Marie Curie, Paris VI). He does research on the comparative growth rates of plants and their capacity to adapt to extreme environments at the CNRS (Laboratoire d'Ecologie, Brunoy, since 1982). He has published more than 50 articles in scientific journals since 1977. He currently teaches at the University of Paris VI, and has patented his system of "mur végétal," or vertical gardens. Recent vertical gardens installed by Patrick Blanc include those at the European Parliament (Brussels, Belgium, 2006); the CaixaForum (Madrid, 2006–07, published here); a concert hall in Taipei (Taiwan, 2007); the Plaza de España (in collaboration with Herzog & de Meuron; Santa Cruz de Tenerife, Canary Islands, Spain, 2008; page 156); and the Museum of Natural History in Toulouse (France, 2008). He also installed works at Jean Nouvel's Cartier Foundation (1998) and the Quai Branly Museum (2004), both in Paris. His work was named one of the "50 Best Inventions of the Year" by Time magazine (2009). Current work includes the Max Juvénal Bridge (Aix-en-Provence, France, 2008); Orchid Waltz, National Theater Concert Hall (Taipei, 2009); Green Office (Meudon, France, 2011); Drew School (San Francisco, USA, 2011); and Tower One Central Park (Sydney, Australia, 2013).

PATRICK BLANC wurde 1953 in Paris geboren. 1989 promovierte er in Botanik (Docteur d'Etat ès Sciences, Université Pierre et Marie Curie, Paris VI). Seit 1982 forscht er am CNRS (Laboratoire d'Écologie, Brunoy) über die relativen Wachstumsraten von Pflanzen und ihre Fähigkeit, sich an extreme Umweltbedingungen anzupassen. Seit 1977 hat er über 50 Artikel in Fachzeitschriften veröffentlicht. Derzeit lehrt er an der Universität Paris VI. Sein System der „mur végétal", des vertikalen Gartens, hat er patentieren lassen. Seine neuesten vertikalen Gärten hat Patrick Blanc am Europäischen Parlament in Brüssel angelegt (2006), am CaixaForum (Madrid, 2006–07, hier vorgestellt), in einer Konzerthalle in Taipeh (Taiwan, 2007), an der Plaza de España (in Zusammenarbeit mit Herzog & de Meuron in Santa Cruz de Tenerife, Kanarische Inseln, 2008) und beim Museum für Naturgeschichte in Toulouse (2008). Er hat ebenfalls Arbeiten für die Fondation Cartier von Jean Nouvel (1998) und beim Musée du Quai Branly (2004) realisiert, die sich beide in Paris befinden. Seine Arbeiten wurden 2009 vom „Time Magazine" zu den „50 besten Erfindungen des Jahres" gewählt. Zu seinen neuesten Arbeiten zählen die Max-Juvénal-Brücke (Aix-en-Provence, Frankreich, 2008), Orchid Waltz im Konzertsaal des Nationaltheaters von Taipeh (2009), das Green Office (Meudon, Frankreich, 2011), die Drew School (San Francisco, 2011) und der Tower One Central Park (Sydney, 2013).

Né à Paris en 1953, **PATRICK BLANC** est docteur en botanique (doctorat d'État ès sciences de l'université Pierre et Marie Curie, Paris VI, 1989). Depuis 1982, il effectue des recherches sur les taux de croissance comparés des plantes et leur capacité à s'adapter à des environnements extrêmes, au Laboratoire d'écologie du CNRS à Brunoy. Il a publié plus de 50 articles scientifiques depuis 1977. Il enseigne actuellement à l'université de Paris VI et a breveté son système de « mur végétal », ou jardin vertical. Parmi les lieux qui ont accueilli ses récents jardins verticaux figurent le Parlement européen (Bruxelles, 2006) ; le CaixaForum (Madrid, 2006–07, publié ici) ; une salle de concert à Taipei (Taiwan, 2007) ; la Plaza de España, en collaboration avec Herzog & de Meuron (Santa Cruz de Tenerife, îles Canaries, 2008, page 156) ; le Muséum d'histoire naturelle de Toulouse (2008) et deux réalisations parisiennes de Jean Nouvel : la Fondation Cartier (1998) et le musée du quai Branly (2004). Son travail a été retenu parmi les « 50 meilleures inventions de l'année » du magazine Time en 2009. Ses projets actuels : le pont Max Juvénal (Aix-en-Provence, 2008) ; Orchid Waltz, dans la salle de concert du Théâtre national de Taipei (2009) ; l'immeuble de bureaux Green Office (Meudon, 2011) ; la Drew School (San Francisco, 2011) et la Tower One Central Park (Sydney, 2013).

CAIXAFORUM VERTICAL GARDEN

Madrid, Spain, 2006–07

Floor area: 600 m²
Client: Obra Social Fundacion La Caixa, Madrid
Cost: €400 000

Patrick Blanc's vertical garden is located next to to the entrance of the CaixaForum designed by the Swiss architects Herzog & de Meuron, but on a neighboring structure.

Patrick Blancs vertikaler Garten befindet sich unmittelbar neben dem Eingang des CaixaForum, einem Bau der Schweizer Architekten Herzog & de Meuron, jedoch an einem benachbarten Gebäude.

Le jardin vertical de Patrick Blanc est implanté à côté de l'entrée du Caixa-Forum des architectes suisses Herzog & de Meuron, mais sur un bâtiment voisin.

Patrick Blanc's **CAIXAFORUM VERTICAL GARDEN** is located next to to the entrance of a new exhibition building designed by Herzog & de Meuron located close to the Prado in Madrid. The former Mediodía Power Station, an 1899 brick structure, was lifted off the ground by the Swiss architects, allowing for an entrance below its restored façades. A small, sloping square leads down to the Paseo del Prado, and it is here that Blanc's wall of plants and flowers rises on the façade of a neighboring building. Patrick Blanc explains the principles behind his realizations by asking a question: "Do plants need soil?" It turns out that they don't and that a combination of water with minerals dissolved in it is sufficient for their growth. Nor need roots damage walls if the plants are constantly provided with the minerals and water they need. The Madrid installation is 24 meters high and contains 15 000 plants of 250 different species. "The garden is a dialogue with the botanical garden on the street and adjacent to the Prado," according to the architect Jacques Herzog. "We love to make new things, to experiment with materials and create a very unusual encounter between the rough and the natural, the smooth and the artificial, to incorporate nature so there can be the smell of a garden where you would not expect it."

Patrick Blancs **VERTIKALER GARTEN AM CAIXAFORUM** befindet sich unmittelbar neben dem Eingang des neuen, von Herzog & de Meuron entworfenen Ausstellungszentrums unweit des Prado in Madrid. Das ehemalige Mediodía-Elektrizitätswerk, ein Backsteinbau von 1899, wurde von den Schweizer Architekten vom Boden gelöst und angehoben, wodurch unterhalb der restaurierten Fassaden ein Eingangsbereich entstand. Ein kleiner, leicht abschüssiger Platz führt zum Paseo del Prado, wo Blancs Wand aus Grün- und Blühpflanzen an der Fassade eines benachbarten Gebäudes emporklettert. Patrick Blanc erklärt die Prinzipien seiner Projekte mit einer Frage: „Brauchen Pflanzen Erde?" Wie sich herausstellt, ist dies nicht der Fall. Eine Kombination aus Wasser und Minerallösung reicht, um Wachstum zu ermöglichen. Auch schädigen die Wurzeln das Mauerwerk nicht zwangsläufig, vorausgesetzt, sie werden mit der nötigen Menge an Mineralien und Wasser versorgt. Die Madrider Installation ist 24 m hoch und besteht aus 15 000 Pflanzen von 250 verschiedenen Arten. „Der Garten tritt in einen Dialog mit dem an der Straße gelegenen Botanischen Garten neben dem Prado", erläutert der Architekt Jacques Herzog. „Wir schaffen gern Neues, experimentieren mit Materialien und schaffen ungewöhnliche Dialoge zwischen Rauem und Natürlichem, Glattem und Künstlichem, um die Natur einzubinden, sodass man dem Duft eines Gartens begegnet, wo man ihn nicht erwartet."

Le **JARDIN VERTICAL DU CAIXAFORUM** de Patrick Blanc est installé à côté de l'entrée de ce lieu d'exposition conçu par Herzog & de Meuron à proximité du musée du Prado à Madrid. L'ancienne centrale électrique de Mediodía, une construction en brique datant de 1899, a été littéralement soulevée par les architectes suisses pour former une entrée sous ses façades restaurées. Une petite place en pente mène au Paseo del Prado, et c'est ici que s'élève, sur la façade d'un immeuble voisin, le jardin de plantes et de fleurs de Blanc. Celui-ci explique les principes de cette réalisation en posant une question : « Les plantes ont-elles besoin du sol ? » Il se trouve qu'elles peuvent s'en passer et qu'une combinaison d'eau et de minéraux peut assurer leur croissance. Leurs racines n'endommagent pas les façades si elles reçoivent continuellement l'eau et les minéraux dont elles ont besoin. L'installation de Madrid mesure 24 m de haut et contient 15 000 plantes de 250 espèces différentes. « Ce jardin est un dialogue avec le Jardin botanique qui s'étend de l'autre côté de la rue, adjacent au Prado », précise Jacques Herzog. « Nous aimons faire des choses nouvelles, expérimenter les matériaux et créer des rencontres très inhabituelles entre le brut et le naturel, le doux et l'artificiel, intégrer la nature de telle façon que l'on sente les odeurs d'un jardin là où vous ne les attendiez pas. »

BOHLIN CYWINSKI JACKSON

*Bohlin Cywinski Jackson
8 West Market Street, Suite 1200, Wilkes-Barre, PA 18701, USA
Tel: +1 570 825 8756 / Fax: +1 570 825 3744
E-mail: info_request@bcj.com / Web: www.bcj.com*

BOHLIN CYWINSKI JACKSON was founded in 1965 by Peter Bohlin and Richard Powell in Wilkes-Barre, Pennsylvania. Peter Bohlin received a B.Arch degree from Rensselaer Polytechnic Institute (1959), and an M.Arch degree from Cranbrook Academy of Art (1961). Today the principals of the firm are Peter Bohlin, Jon Jackson, Frank Grauman, William Loose, Cornelius Reid, Karl Backus, Gregory Mottola, Roxanne Sherbeck, and Robert Miller and Raymond Calabro. The firm has additional offices in Pittsburgh, Philadelphia, Seattle, and San Francisco. In 1994, the practice received the Architecture Firm Award from the American Institute of Architects. Significant work includes the Pacific Rim Estate (Medina, Washington, 1997, joint venture with Cutler Anderson Architects); Headquarters for Pixar Animation Studios (Emeryville, California, 2001); and the Liberty Bell Center Independence National Historical Park (Philadelphia, Pennsylvania, 2003). In 2005, they completed the Ballard Library and Neighborhood Service Center (Seattle, Washington), listed by the AIA as one of the "Top Ten Green Buildings" for that year, and a couple of years later the two projects published here: Grand Teton Discovery and Visitor Center, Moose Junction (Grand Teton National Park, Wyoming, 2007) and Combs Point Residence (Finger Lakes Region, New York, 2007). Current work includes the Trinity College Master Plan (Hartford, Connecticut, 2008); Williams College Faculty Buildings and Library (Williamstown, Massachusetts, 2008 and 2012); California Institute of Technology Chemistry Building (Pasadena, California, 2010); Peace Arch US Port of Entry (Blaine, Washington, 2012), all in the USA, and retail stores for Apple Inc. in various locations worldwide.

Das Büro **BOHLIN CYWINSKI JACKSON** wurde 1965 von Peter Bohlin und Richard Powell in Wilkes-Barre, Pennsylvania, gegründet. Peter Bohlin machte seinen B.Arch. in Architektur am Rensselaer Polytechnic Institute (1959) und den M.Arch. an der Cranbrook Academy of Art (1961). Die gegenwärtigen Chefs sind Peter Bohlin, Jon Jackson, Frank Grauman, William Loose, Cornelius Reid, Karl Backus, Gregory Mottola, Roxanne Sherbeck, Robert Miller und Raymond Calabro. Die Firma hat weitere Büros in Pittsburgh, Philadelphia, Seattle und San Francisco. 1994 erhielt das Büro den Architecture Firm Award vom American Institute of Architects (AIA). Zu seinen bedeutenden Bauwerken gehören der Pacific Rim Estate (Medina, Washington, 1997, als Joint Venture mit Cutler Anderson Architects), der Hauptsitz der Pixar Animation Studios (Emeryville, Kalifornien, 2001) sowie das Liberty Bell Center im Independence National Historical Park (Philadelphia, Pennsylvania, 2003). 2005 wurden die Ballard Library und das Neighborhood Service Center (Seattle, Washington) fertiggestellt, die das AIA in die Top-Ten-Liste der „Green Buildings" des Jahres aufnahm, und zwei Jahre später die beiden hier veröffentlichten Projekte: das Grand Teton Discovery and Visitor Center, Moose Junction (Grand Teton National Park, Wyoming, 2007) und das Wohnhaus Combs Point (Finger Lakes Region, New York, 2007). Zu den jüngeren Arbeiten des Büros gehören der Masterplan für das Trinity College (Hartford, Connecticut, 2008), Fakultätsbauten und Bibliothek des Williams College (Williamstown, Massachusetts, 2008 und 2012), das Chemistry Building am California Institute of Technology (Pasadena, Kalifornien, 2010), der Peace Arch US Port of Entry (Blaine, Washington, 2012), alle in den USA, sowie Ladengeschäfte für Apple an verschiedenen Orten weltweit.

L'agence **BOHLIN CYWINSKI JACKSON** a été fondée en 1965 par Peter Bohlin et Richard Powell à Wilkes-Barre (Pennsylvanie). Peter Bohlin est reçu son diplôme B.Arch. du Rensselaer Polytechnic Institute (1959) et son M.Arch. de la Cranbrook Academy of Art (1961). Les associés actuels sont Peter Bohlin, Jon Jackson, Frank Grauman, William Loose, Cornelius Reid, Karl Backus, Gregory Mottola, Roxanne Sherbeck, Robert Miller et Raymond Calabro. L'agence possède des bureaux à Pittsburgh, Philadelphie, Seattle et San Francisco. En 1994, elle a reçu le prix de l'Agence d'architecture de l'American Institute of Architects. Parmi ses réalisations les plus significatives : le Pacific Rim Estate (Medina, Washington, 1997, avec Cutler Anderson Architects) ; le siège des Pixar Animation Studios (Emeryville, Californie, 2001) et le Liberty Bell Center dans l'Independence National Historical Park (Philadelphie, Pennsylvanie, 2003). En 2005, ils ont achevé la bibliothèque Ballard et un centre de services de quartier (Seattle, Washington) désigné par l'AIA comme une « des dix grandes constructions vertes » de l'année, et deux ans plus tard deux projets publiés ici : centre d'informations des visiteurs de Grand Teton (Moose Junction, Parc national de Grand Teton, Wyoming, 2007) et la résidence Combs Point (Finger Lakes Region, New York, 2007). Plus récemment ils ont réalisé le plan directeur de Trinity College (Hartford, Connecticut, 2008) ; les bâtiments de la faculté et la bibliothèque du Williams College (Williamstown, Massachusetts, 2008 et 2012) ; le bâtiment de la chimie du California Institute of Technology (Pasadena, Californie, 2010) ; l'Arche de la paix, port d'entrée américain (Blaine, Washington, 2012), tous aux États-Unis, et plusieurs magasins Apple dans le monde.

GRAND TETON DISCOVERY AND VISITOR CENTER

Moose Junction, Grand Teton National Park, Wyoming, USA, 2007

Address: about 800 meters west of Moose Junction, Moose, Grand Teton National Park, Wyoming,
+1 307 739 3300, www.grand.teton.national-park.com
Area: 1812 m². Client: National Park Service, Grand Teton National Park Foundation,
Grand Teton Association. Cost: not disclosed

The low, but spectecular forms of the Center seem to respond to the natural setting.

Die niedrigen, aber eindrucksvollen Formen des Zentrums scheinen auf die natürliche Umgebung Bezug zu nehmen.

Les formes surbaissées mais spectaculaires du centre semblent répondre à son cadre naturel.

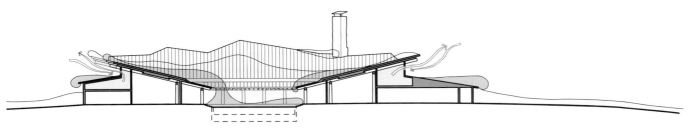

This building was made with log timber frames and laminated wood beams harvested from sustainably grown forests. The architects state: "The logs tell us of themselves, they remind us of great northern forests; the sounds, the smells, the soft touch of the earth. The milled timbers tell us of the nature of wood, its grain, how it is cut and planed." Board-formed concrete walls used for exterior walls, because of the presence of deep snowfalls, also show the trace of wood, although cedar siding is also used. An exposed concrete floor honed to reveal its aggregate and an upward looking window wall add more modern touches, but the presence of nature is so overwhelming on this site that visitors need not look far to see and sense it.

Dieses Gebäude wurde mit einer Rahmenkonstruktion aus Baumstämmen und verleimten Holzbalken errichtet, die aus nachhaltig bewirtschafteten Wäldern stammen. Die Architekten erklären: „Die Baumstämme erzählen uns ihre Geschichte, sie erinnern uns an die großen Wälder des Nordens, deren Geräusche, Gerüche, ihren weichen Boden. Die zurechtgesägten Balken sprechen von der Natur des Holzes, seiner Maserung, wie es geschnitten und gehobelt wird." Wegen der heftigen Schneefälle bestehen die Außenwände aus Beton, der die Spuren der Schalbretter zeigt, wenngleich auch Verkleidung aus Zedernholz verwendet wurde. Der geschliffene Boden aus Sichtbeton, der seine Körnung zeigt, und die schräg stehende Fensterwand setzen weitere moderne Akzente, aber die Präsenz der Natur auf diesem Gelände ist so überwältigend, dass sie den Besucher jederzeit bewusst ist.

Ce bâtiment repose entièrement sur une ossature en grumes et poutres de bois lamellé issu de forêts d'exploitation durable. Pour les architectes : « Ces grumes nous parlent d'elles-mêmes, elles nous rappellent les grandes forêts nordiques, les sons, les odeurs, la douceur de la terre au toucher. Les bois travaillés nous parlent de la nature du bois, de son grain, de la façon dont il a été coupé et débité. » Les murs en béton nécessaires pour protéger le centre des importantes chutes de neige ont également conservé la trace de leur coffrage de bois. Ailleurs, on trouve aussi des bardages en cèdre. Un sol en béton brut sablé pour montrer sa composition et un mur de fenêtres regardant vers le ciel font partie des quelques touches plus modernes, mais la présence de la nature reste si forte que les visiteurs n'ont pas à se rendre plus loin pour la voir et la sentir.

Seen from the exterior, the Center seems very much at home in its wildnerness setting, its warm interiors contrasting with the rather cold landscape seen in the image above.

Von außen fügt sich das Center wie selbstverständlich in die unberührte Landschaft ein. Das warme Interieur ist ein deutlicher Kontrast zur winterlichen Umgebung oben im Bild.

Vu de l'extérieur, le Centre semble parfaitement à sa place dans le décor désertique, ses intérieurs chaleureux contrastant avec le paysage plutôt froid qu'on voit sur la photo du haut.

The interiors of the center continue the overall use of wood, though the floors are made of concrete. Full-height glazing allows visitors to see the surrounding mountains.

Auch im Inneren des Zentrums wurde überall Holz verwendet; die Böden sind allerdings aus Beton. Die geschosshohe Verglasung bietet den Besuchern Aussicht auf die Berge der Umgebung.

Le bois est aussi présent à l'intérieur, mais les sols sont en béton. De grands murs de verre permettent de voir les montagnes environnantes.

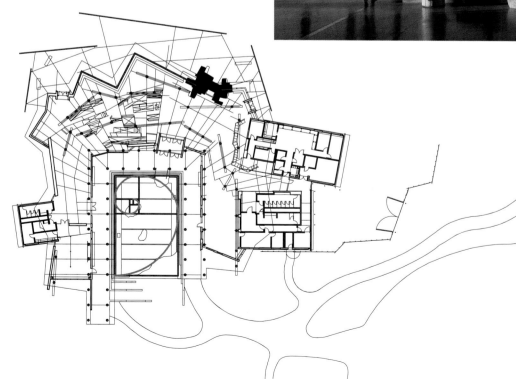

A plan (left) shows how the angled articulation of the structure, combined with generous glazing, allows visitors to take in the full breadth and scope of views of the park.

Ein Grundriss (links) illustriert die schiefwinklige Gliederung des Komplexes. Großzügige Verglasung bietet den Besuchern Panoramablicke in den Nationalpark.

Le plan (à gauche) montre comment la structure anguleuse du bâtiment, associée au généreux vitrage, offre aux visiteurs des vues du parc dans toute sa large étendue.

COMBS POINT RESIDENCE

Finger Lakes Region, New York, USA, 2007

Address: not disclosed
Area: 502 m² (main house); 130 m² (guesthouse). Client: Wendell and Kim Weeks
Cost: not disclosed

This residence was conceived as a "string of structures" formed essentially by the main house, office, and guesthouse. This string is drawn out between a lakefront and a valley waterfall. Circulation is organized along the southern glass wall, while an elevated exterior walkway also brings together the elements of the complex. Douglas fir glulam post and beams were used as structural elements. The woods used are Forest Stewardship Council (FSC) certified, with such choices as formaldehyde-free plywood figuring in the choice of the architects for environmental reasons. Gently lifted off the ground, with their broad glazing and generous wood surfaces, the elements of the **COMBS POINT RESIDENCE** take full advantage of the natural setting while disturbing the environment as little as possible.

Dieses Wohnhaus wurde als Aneinanderreihung von Gebäuden konzipiert, die sich aus Haupthaus, Bürobau und Gästetrakt zusammensetzt. Diese Reihe erstreckt sich zwischen dem Seeufer und einem Tal mit Wasserfall. Die Erschließung erfolgt entlang der südlichen Glaswand; ein erhöht angebrachter Außengang verbindet ebenfalls die einzelnen Elemente des Komplexes. Ein Ständerbau aus Douglasien-Brettschichtholz bildet die Konstruktion. Die verwendeten Hölzer sind vom Forest Stewardship Council (FSC) zertifiziert; die Architekten entschieden sich aus Rücksicht auf die Umwelt für formaldehydfreies Sperrholz. Die leicht vom Boden abgehobenen Bauten des **HAUSES COMBS POINT** fügen sich mit ihren großen Glas- und Holzflächen bestens in ihr natürliches Umfeld ein und belasten die Umwelt so wenig wie möglich.

Cette résidence est un « chapelet de structures » constitué par la maison principale, un bureau et une maison d'amis. Il s'étire entre le lac et une cascade dans une vallée. La circulation s'organise au sud le long d'un mur de verre. Une passerelle en bois suspendue réunit les divers composants de l'ensemble. L'ossature est à poteaux et poutres en lamellé-collé de pin de Douglas. Pour des raisons environnementales, les bois retenus sont certifiés par le FSC (Forest Stewardship Council), en particulier des contreplaqués sans formaldéhyde. Légèrement surélevés du sol, bénéficiant de généreux vitrages et d'importantes parois de bois, les différents composants de la **RÉSIDENCE COMBS POINT** profitent pleinement de leur cadre naturel et exercent un impact environnemental minimum.

The site drawing to the right shows
the insertion of the string-like form of
the residence in its natural setting.

*Der Lageplan rechts zeigt, wie sich
die Bauten hintereinander in ihre
natürliche Umgebung einfügen.*

*Un dessin du site, à droite, montre
l'insertion du plan en chapelet de la
résidence dans son cadre naturel.*

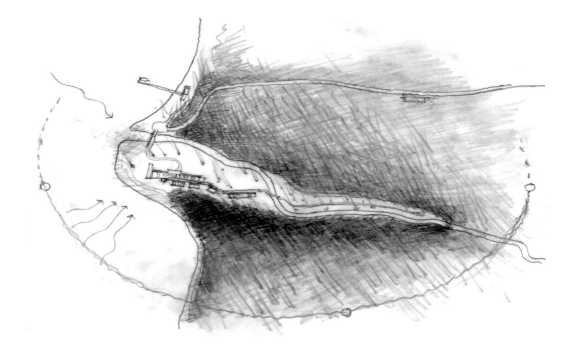

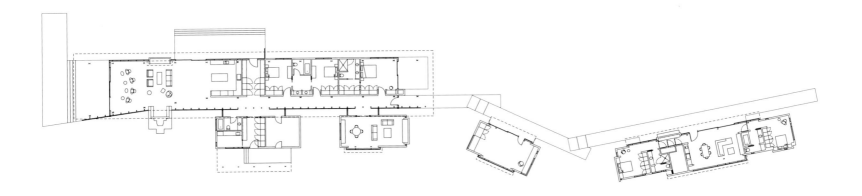

The long, low succession of volumes is inserted into a forest environment, with generous glazing emphasizing the connection with nature.

Die lange, niedrige Folge der Bauten ist in eine bewaldete Umgebung gesetzt; die großzügige Verglasung betont die Verbindung zur Natur.

La longue succession des petites constructions basses s'insère dans un environnement boisé. Le généreux vitrage met en valeur la connexion avec la nature.

A wooden walkway links the different parts of the residence, while such elements as the angled roof seen above break the sensation of strict rectangular volumes.

Ein hölzerner Weg verbindet die verschiedenen Teile des Komplexes, während bestimmte Elemente wie das oben sichtbare, abgewinkelte Dach die Wirkung der streng rechteckigen Volumen aufbrechen.

Une allée en bois relie les différentes parties de la résidence. Des éléments comme le toit à contre-pente, ci-dessus, rompt le sentiment de volumes strictement rectangulaires.

Full-height glazing offers astonishing views of the nearby lake. Sparse furnishing fits well into the architectural environment.

Die geschosshohe Verglasung bietet erstaunliche Ausblicke auf den nahe gelegenen See. Die sparsame Möblierung passt sich gut in das architektonische Umfeld ein.

Le vitrage toute hauteur offre des vues étonnantes sur le lac proche. Peu abondant, le mobilier est bien adapté à son environnement architectural.

As the drawing below shows, the upward angle of the roof is calculated in places to allow sunlight to penetrate into the interiors.

Aus der Zeichnung unten lässt sich ablesen, dass das abgewinkelte Dach so ausgebildet wurde, um mehr Sonnenlicht in die Innenräume einzulassen.

Comme le montre le dessin ci-dessous, la pente du toit est calculée pour permettre aux rayons du soleil de pénétrer jusqu'à l'intérieur des maisons.

VINCENT CALLEBAUT ARCHITECTURES

Vincent Callebaut Architectures
119 rue Manin
75019 Paris
France

Tel: +33 1 42 45 11 10
E-mail: vincent@callebaut.org
Web: www.vincent.callebaut.org

VINCENT CALLEBAUT was born in 1977 in Belgium. He graduated from the Institut Victor Horta in Brussels in 2000, where he received the René Serrure Prize for the best diploma project, a proposal for the "Metamuseum of Arts and Civilizations, Quai Branly." He worked as an intern in the offices of Odile Decq and Massimiliano Fuksas in Paris, before opening his own firm in Brussels and Paris. He has collaborated with Jakob + MacFarlane, Claude Vasconi, and Jacques Rougerie. Callebaut seeks to contribute to a "new Ecopolis via 'parasitical' strategies for an investigative architecture, mixing biology with information and communications technologies." His projects (all unbuilt) include Underwater Venice of Beirut, a Master Plan for Martyrs' Square (Beirut, 2004); Fractured Monolith, Hotel and Congress Center (Brussels, 2004); Eye of the Storm, a performing arts center for Seoul (South Korea, 2005); Red Baobab, a project for the New National Library in Prague (2006); as well as Anti-Smog (Paris, 2007); and Perfumed Jungle (Hong Kong, 2007), the last two published here.

VINCENT CALLEBAUT wurde 1977 in Belgien geboren. Sein Studium schloss er 2000 am Institut Victor Horta in Brüssel ab, wo er mit dem René-Serrure-Preis für das beste Diplomprojekt ausgezeichnet wurde, seinen Entwurf „Metamuseum of Arts and Civilizations, Quai Branly". Er war als Praktikant in den Büros von Odile Decq und Massimiliano Fuksas in Paris tätig, bevor er sein eigenes Büro mit Sitz in Brüssel und Paris gründete. Er kooperierte mit Jakob + MacFarlane, Claude Vasconi und Jacques Rougerie. Callebaut geht es darum, zu einer „neuen Ökopolis beizutragen", und zwar „durch ‚parasitäre' Strategien für eine investigative Architektur, in der sich Biologie, Informations- und Kommunikationstechnologien miteinander verbinden". Zu seinen (sämtlich ungebauten) Projekten zählen u.a. ein Unterwasser-Venedig in Beirut, ein Masterplan für einen Märtyrerplatz (Beirut, 2004), das Hotel- und Kongresszentrum Fractured Monolith (Brüssel, 2004), Eye of the Storm, ein Zentrum für darstellende Künste in Seoul (Südkorea, 2005), Red Baobab, ein Projekt für die Neue Nationalbibliothek in Prag (2006), sowie seine Projekte Anti-Smog (Paris, 2007) und Perfumed Jungle (Hongkong, 2007), beide hier vorgestellt.

VINCENT CALLEBAUT, né en 1977 en Belgique, est diplômé de l'Institut Victor Horta à Bruxelles en 2000, qui lui a accordé le prix René Serrure pour le meilleur projet de diplôme avec son « Metamuseum des arts et civilisations, quai Branly ». Il a été stagiaire chez Odile Decq et Massimiliano Fuksas à Paris, avant d'ouvrir sa propre agence à Bruxelles et Paris. Il a collaboré avec Jakob + MacFarlane, Claude Vasconi et Jacques Rougerie. Callebaut cherche à contribuer à la création d'une « nouvelle Ecopolis *via* des stratégies "parasitaires" d'architecture de recherche, mêlant biologie et technologies de l'information et de la communication ». Ses projets (aucun réalisé pour l'instant) comprennent Underwater Venice of Beyrouth, un plan directeur pour la place des Martyrs (Beyrouth, 2004) ; Fractured Monolith, centre hôtelier et de congrès (Bruxelles, 2004) ; Eye of the Storm, un centre pour les arts de la scène à Séoul (Corée-du-Sud, 2005) ; Red Baobab, projet pour la Bibliothèque nationale de Prague (2006), ainsi qu'Anti-Smog (Paris, 2007) et Jungle parfumée (Hong Kong, 2007), ces deux derniers publiés dans ces pages.

ANTI-SMOG

Paris, France, 2007

Floor area: 2065 m². Client: City of Paris
Cost: not disclosed

The architect describes **ANTI-SMOG** as an "Innovation Center in Sustainable Development" to be located near the Canal de l'Ourcq in the 19th arrondissement of Paris. The complex would make use of "all available renewable energy forms to fight against the Parisian smog." Two distinct museum structures would produce more energy than they consume—the Solar Drop with a superstructure covered in polyester fiber and 250 square meters of photovoltaic cells, and the Wind Tower, a "helical structure incrusted with wind machines." The Solar Drop would be covered with a layer of titanium dioxide (TiO2) in the form of anatase, "which, by reacting to ultraviolet rays, allows the reduction of air pollution." Planted arches would allow the collection of rainwater for the complex. As Callebaut describes it: "Below this thermo-regulating solar roof, there is a huge exhibition and meeting room organized around a central garden, a phyto-purified aquatic lagoon. It is a didactic place dedicated to new ecological urbanities and renewable energies." The Wind Tower, 45 meters tall, would be topped by a suspended garden with spectacular views of the city. The architect imagines that it might be used to house the "Vélib" bicycles, introduced to Paris by its mayor, or solar cars, in a silo configuration. "This," says Vincent Callebaut, "is a play project, an urban and truly living graft. In osmosis with its surroundings, it is an architecture that interacts with its surroundings in climatic, chemical, kinetic, and social ways to better reduce the ecological footprint in the urban area."

Der Architekt beschreibt **ANTI-SMOG** als „Innovationsprojekt für nachhaltige Entwicklung", das in der Nähe des Canal de l'Ourcq im 19. Arrondissement von Paris angesiedelt sein soll. Der Komplex soll „alle verfügbaren Formen erneuerbarer Energien nutzen, um den Pariser Smog zu bekämpfen". Zwei separate Museumsbauten würden mehr Energie produzieren als sie verbrauchen – der sogenannte Solar Drop mit einem Überbau aus Polyesterfaser und 250 m² Solarmodulen sowie der Wind Tower, eine „mit Windrädern besetzte Helixkonstruktion". Der Solar Drop würde mit einer Anatasmodifikation von Titandioxid (TiO₂) überzogen werden, „das dank seiner Reaktion mit ultravioletter Strahlung Luftverschmutzung reduzieren" würde. Begrünte Bögen würden Regen für den Komplex sammeln. Callebaut beschreibt sein Projekt wie folgt: „Unter dem wärmeregulierenden Solardach befindet sich ein riesiger Ausstellungs- und Konferenzraum, der um einen zentral angelegten Garten mit einem Teich organisiert ist, dessen Wasser biologisch geklärt wird. Es ist ein didaktischer Ort, der sich mit neuen ökologischen Urbanitäten und erneuerbaren Energien auseinandersetzt." Der 45 m hohe Wind Tower soll oben mit einem hängenden Garten abschließen, der beeindruckende Ausblicke über die Stadt bieten würde. Der Architekt hofft, hier auch die vom Pariser Bürgermeister eingeführten „Vélib"-Fahrräder oder solarbetriebene Autos unterzubringen. Laut Vincent Callebaut handelt es sich um „eine Projektspielerei, ein urbanes und wahrhaft lebendiges Transplantat. Es ist eine Architektur, die in einer Form von Osmose mit ihrem Umfeld in klimatischer, chemischer, kinetischer und sozialer Weise interagiert, um den ökologischen Fußabdruck in der Stadt wirksamer zu reduzieren."

L'architecte présente **ANTI-SMOG** comme un « prototype didactique d'expérimentations écologiques » qui pourrait être installé près du canal de l'Ourcq dans le XIXᵉ arrondissement de Paris. Ce complexe utiliserait « toutes les formes disponibles d'énergies renouvelables pour combattre le *smog* parisien ». Deux structures muséales distinctes devraient produire davantage d'énergie qu'elles n'en consomment : la *Solar drop* dont la superstructure est recouverte de fibre de polyester et de 250 m² de cellules photovoltaïques, et la *Wind Tower*, une « structure hélicoïdale incrustée de turbines à vent ». La *Solar Drop* serait recouverte d'une couche de dioxyde de titane (TiO₂) sous forme d'anatase « qui, en réagissant aux rayons ultraviolets, permet de réduire la pollution de l'air ». Des arches plantées permettraient de collecter l'eau de pluie réutilisée par le complexe. « Sous cette couverture solaire thermorégulatrice, se trouve une énorme salle d'expositions et de réunions organisée autour d'un jardin central, un lagon aquatique phyto-épuré. C'est un lieu didactique consacré aux nouvelles urbanités écologiques et aux énergies renouvelables. » La *Wind Tower*, de 45 m de haut, serait surmontée d'un jardin suspendu offrant de superbes vues sur la ville. L'architecte a aussi imaginé abriter les « Vélib' » ou des voitures à énergie solaire dans une configuration de silo. « Il s'agit, précise Callebaut, d'un projet ludique, une greffe urbaine et vivante. En osmose avec son milieu, c'est une architecture qui interagit complètement avec son contexte qu'il soit climatique, chimique, cinétique ou social pour mieux réduire notre empreinte écologique en milieu urbain. »

The Anti-Smog complex takes the idea of the "green" building a step further than usual: the architect proposes to reduce ambient pollution rather than simply taking care not to contribute to energy waste.

Der Anti-Smog-Komplex spinnt das Konzept „grüner" Bauten ein Stück weiter: Der Architekt plant, Umweltverschmutzung aktiv zu reduzieren, statt lediglich Energieverschwendung zu vermeiden.

En proposant de diminuer concrètement la pollution ambiante plutôt que de simplement ne pas contribuer au gaspillage de l'énergie, le complexe Anti-Smog fait progresser le concept de bâtiment « vert ».

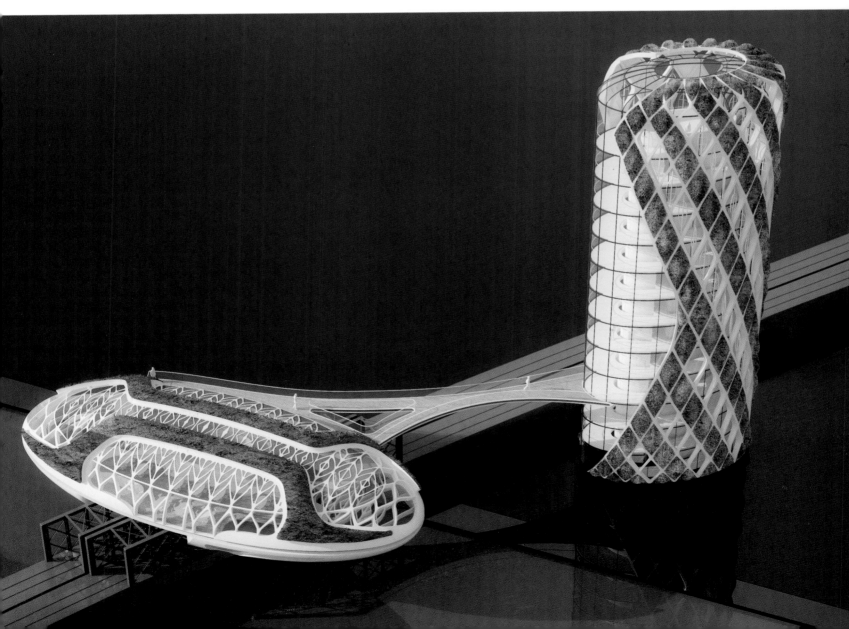

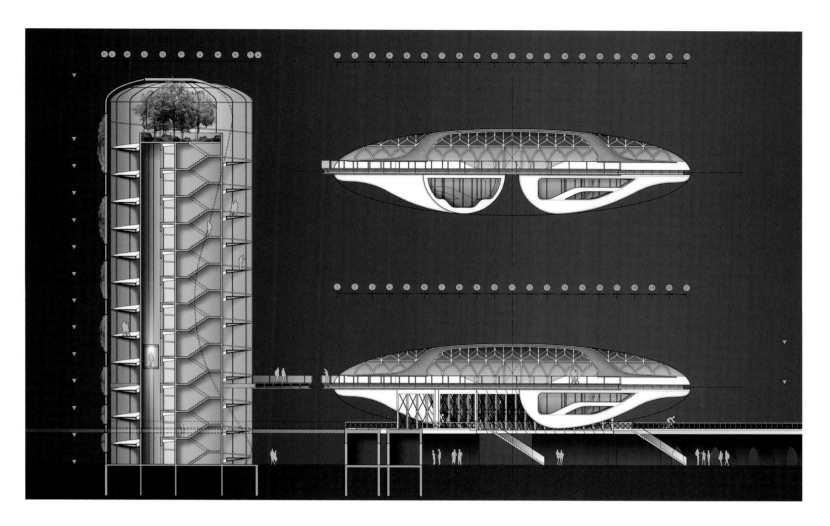

The rather futuristic forms proposed by Vincent Callebaut confirm the visionary aspect of his design. Light and open space are grafted onto the existing, less modern environment.

Die vergleichsweise futuristischen Formen von Vincent Callebauts Entwurf betonen seinen visionären Ansatz. Helle und offene Räume werden in das weniger moderne Umfeld eingeschrieben.

Les formes futuristes proposées par Vincent Callebaut confirment l'aspect visionnaire de son projet. L'espace ouvert et lumineux se greffe sur un environnement moins moderne.

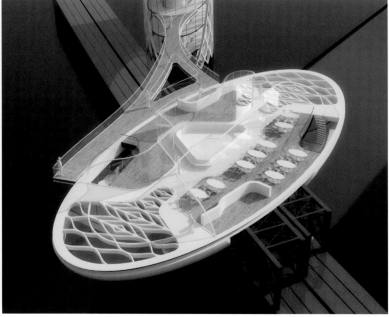

PERFUMED JUNGLE

Hong Kong, China, 2007

Site area: 2.7 km². Client: City of Hong Kong
Cost: not disclosed. Collaboration: Vincent Callebaut, Arnaud Martinez, Maguy Delrieu

This is a "Master Plan for the Eco-Design of the Central Waterfront of the Business District of Hong Kong." The architect explains: "Hong Kong is one of the more populated territories in the world with a density of 30 000 inhabitants per square kilometer. To respond to this overpopulation, the 'Urban Jungle' proposes to re-tame nature and to widen the territory of the ultra-contemporary city." Any new built spaces would be self-sufficient, producing more energies and biodiversity than they consume. A "mesh of irregular cells" brings water into the entire new district, forming open-air swimming pools, marinas, new quays, or lagoons for biological purification. "In front of the skyline of the Kowloon peninsula," says Callebaut, "a true cascade of aquatic and vegetable terraces like the ones of a rice terrace are laid out on this fifth façade. This new topography, without any wall, thus without any limit, is not only meant to be inhabited by the citizens of Hong Kong, but is also designed to be infiltrated, crossed and printed by the numerous species of the fauna and local flora or in migration that will come to install themselves." The towers the architect proposes are modeled on arborescent development and have fishnet skin "closed on a random basis with cushions of substrate and vegetable fertilizers enabling the development of luxuriant vegetation."

Das Projekt ist ein „Masterplan für die ökologische Gestaltung des zentralen Uferabschnitts im Geschäftsviertel von Hongkong". Der Architekt führt aus: „Hongkong zählt mit 30 000 Bewohnern pro Quadratkilometer zu den am dichtesten bevölkerten Gegenden der Welt. Um dieser Überbevölkerung entgegenzutreten, geht es dem ‚urbanen Dschungel' darum, die Natur aufs Neue zu zähmen und neues Territorium für eine ultra-zeitgenössische Stadt zu erschließen." Sämtliche Neubauten wären autark und würden mehr Energie und Biodiversität produzieren, als sie verbrauchen. Ein „Geflecht aus unregelmäßigen Zellen" würde Wasser in das gesamte neue Stadtviertel holen, aus denen Freibäder, Jachthäfen, neue Kaianlagen oder Lagunen für biologische Wasseraufbereitung entstehen könnten. „Vor der Skyline der Halbinsel Kowloon", beschreibt Callebaut, „würde eine Kaskade von wassergefüllten oder mit Gemüsekulturen bepflanzten Terrassen, ähnlich wie Reisterrassen, entstehen, die die gesamte fünfte Fassade überziehen würden. Diese neue Art von Topografie, die ohne Mauer und somit ohne Begrenzung auskommt, soll nicht nur von den Bürgern Hongkongs bewohnt werden, sondern ist auch daraufhin angelegt, von den verschiedenen Arten regionaler oder vorbeiziehender Flora und Fauna, die sich hier niederlassen, erobert, passiert und geprägt zu werden." Die vom Architekten geplanten Hochhausbauten basieren auf Wachstumsmodellen von Bäumen und sind mit einer fischnetzartigen Haut überzogen, „die nach dem Zufallsprinzip mit Kissen aus Substrat und Gemüsedünger gefüllt werden, um eine üppige Vegetation anzuregen".

Il s'agit ici d'un « plan directeur pour l'écoconception de la partie centrale du front de mer du quartier d'affaires de Hong Kong ». L'architecte explique : « Avec une densité de 30 000 habitants au km², Hong Kong est l'un des territoires les plus peuplés du monde. Pour répondre à cette surpopulation, la "Jungle urbaine" propose de redomestiquer la nature et d'agrandir le territoire de la cité ultra-contemporaine. » Toute nouvelle construction devrait être autosuffisante et produire plus d'énergie et de biodiversité qu'elle n'en consomme. Une « résille de cellules irrégulières » fournit l'eau au quartier tout entier, formant des piscines en plein air, des marinas, de nouveaux quais ou des lagons d'épuration biologique. « Face au panorama de la péninsule de Kowloon, explique Callebaut, une vraie cascade de terrasses aquatiques et végétalisées, comme celle des cultures rizicoles, est disposée sur cette cinquième façade. Cette topographie nouvelle, sans mur, et donc sans la moindre limite, est non seulement pensée pour les habitants de la ville, mais aussi pour être infiltrée, parcourue et appropriée par les nombreuses espèces de la faune et de la flore locale ou en migration qui viendront s'y installer. » Les tours proposées par l'architecte sont modelées sur des développements de type arborescent et présentent une peau en filet « posée sur une base aléatoire avec des coussins de substrats et d'engrais permettant le développement d'une végétation luxuriante ».

The Perfumed Jungle is presented with vast open spaces that might almost give the impression that these towers need not have a precise function, yet they would produce both energy and biodiversity.

Der Perfumed Jungle präsentiert sich mit riesigen Freiflächen, wodurch beinahe der Eindruck entsteht, die Türme hätten keine spezielle Funktion. Tatsächlich sollen sie Energie erzeugen und Biodiversität schaffen.

La « Jungle parfumée » se présente comme de vastes espaces ouverts donnant l'impression que ces tours n'ont pas de fonction précise, or elles produisent de l'énergie et défendent la biodiversité.

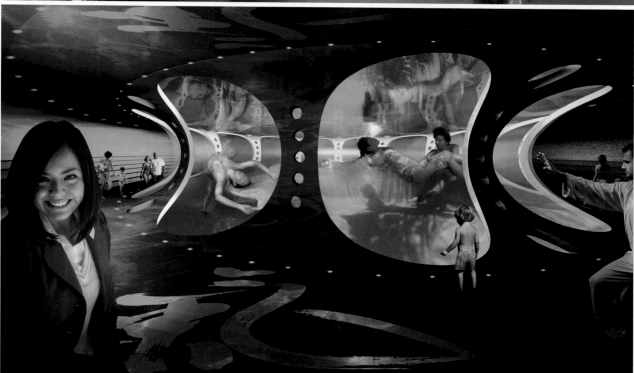

Callebaut's fantastic environment seems to suggest that architecture could become an integral part of a living environment.

Callebauts fantastische Umwelt scheint geradezu nahezulegen, dass Architektur integraler Bestandteil des gesamten Lebensraums werden könnte.

L'environnement fantastique imaginé par Callebaut suggère que l'architecture pourrait devenir partie intégrante d'un environnement vivant.

CARNEY LOGAN BURKE ARCHITECTS

Carney Logan Burke Architects
215 South King Street
Jackson, Wyoming 83001
USA

Tel: +1 307 733 4000
Fax: +1 307 733 1147
E-mail: design@clbarchitects.com
Web: www.clbarchitects.com

JOHN CARNEY is the founding principal of Carney Logan Burke. He completed his M.Arch degree at the Graduate School of Design at Harvard in 1977. He worked from that date until 1983 with Metz Train and Youngren (Chicago and Denver) before creating his own firm, John Carney & Associates in 1983. Beginning in 1990 he was a partner at Urban Design Group. In 1992, he moved to Jackson Hole, Wyoming, to establish the predecessor of his current firm. **ERIC LOGAN** graduated with an M.Arch degree from Arizona State University in 1991, and moved to Denver to work as an apprentice with Urban Design Group. He joined Carney Architects in 1995, and became a partner in 2006 when the name of the firm was changed to Carney Logan Burke Architects. **KEVIN BURKE** was born in New Hampshire, graduating from the School of Architecture at Roger Williams University in 1990, joining Carney Architects in 1999, and becoming a partner in the new firm in 2006. The work of the firm includes the Laurance S. Rockefeller Preserve (Grand Teton National Park, Moose, Wyoming, 2007, published here); Four Seasons Hotel & Private Residences (Denver, Colorado, 2010); Home Ranch Welcome Center (Jackson, Wyoming, 2011); Butte Residential Compound (Jackson, Wyoming, 2012); and the Central Wyoming College, Health & Science Center (Riverton, Wyoming, 2013), all in the USA.

JOHN CARNEY ist Gründungspartner von Carney Logan Burke. Seinen M.Arch. absolvierte er 1977 an der Harvard Graduate School of Design. Anschließend arbeitete er bis 1983 bei Metz Train and Youngren (Chicago und Denver), im selben Jahr folgte die Gründung seines Büros John Carney & Associates. Ab 1990 war er Partner bei Urban Design Group. 1992 zog er nach Jackson Hole, Wyoming, wo er den Vorgänger seines heutigen Büros gründet. **ERIC LOGAN** machte seinen M.Arch. 1991 an der Arizona State University und zog nach Denver, wo er als Assistent bei Urban Design Group arbeitete. 1995 schloss er sich Carney Architects an und wurde 2006 Partner, als das Büro sich den Namen Carney Logan Burke Architects gab. **KEVIN BURKE,** geboren in New Hampshire, schloss sein Studium 1990 an der Architekturfakultät der Roger Williams University ab, ist seit 1999 bei Carney Architects tätig und wurde 2006 Partner des neuen Büros. Zu den Projekten des Teams zählen: Laurance S. Rockefeller Preserve (Grand Teton National Park, Moose, Wyoming, 2007, hier vorgestellt), Four Seasons Hotel mit privaten Gästehäusern (Denver, Colorado, 2010), Home Ranch Welcome Center (Jackson, Wyoming, 2011), Familienanwesen Butte (Jackson, Wyoming, 2012) sowie das Zentrum für Medizin und Naturwissenschaften am Central Wyoming College (Riverton, Wyoming, 2013), alle in den USA.

JOHN CARNEY est le directeur fondateur de Carney Logan Burke. Il a obtenu son M.Arch à la GSD de Harvard en 1977 et a travaillé dès lors jusqu'en 1983 avec Metz Train and Youngren (Chicago et Denver) avant d'ouvrir sa propre société, John Carney & Associates, en 1983. Il est partenaire du groupe Urban Design depuis 1990. Il a déménagé en 1992 à Jackson Hole, dans le Wyoming, pour monter l'agence qui a précédé son agence actuelle. **ERIC LOGAN** a obtenu son M.Arch à l'université d'Arizona en 1991 et est ensuite venu s'installer à Denver pour effectuer son apprentissage dans le groupe Urban Design. Il a rejoint Carney Architects en 1995 et en est devenu l'un des partenaires en 2006 lorsque l'agence a été rebaptisée Carney Logan Burke Architects. **KEVIN BURKE** est né dans le New Hampshire, il est diplômé de l'école d'architecture de l'université Roger Williams (1990), a rejoint Carney Architects en 1999 et est devenu l'un des partenaires de la nouvelle société en 2006. Leurs réalisations comprennent : la réserve Laurance S. Rockefeller (parc national du Grand Teton, Moose, Wyoming, 2007, publiée ici) ; l'hôtel et résidences privées Four Seasons (Denver, Colorado, 2010) ; le centre d'accueil Home Ranch (Jackson, Wyoming, 2011) ; le complexe résidentiel Butte (Jackson, Wyoming, 2012) et le Centre médical et scientifique du Central Wyoming College (Riverton, Wyoming, 2013), toutes aux États-Unis.

LAURANCE S. ROCKEFELLER PRESERVE

Grand Teton National Park, Moose, Wyoming, USA, 2007

Area: 957 m². Client: Grand Teton National Park (end user)
Cost: not disclosed

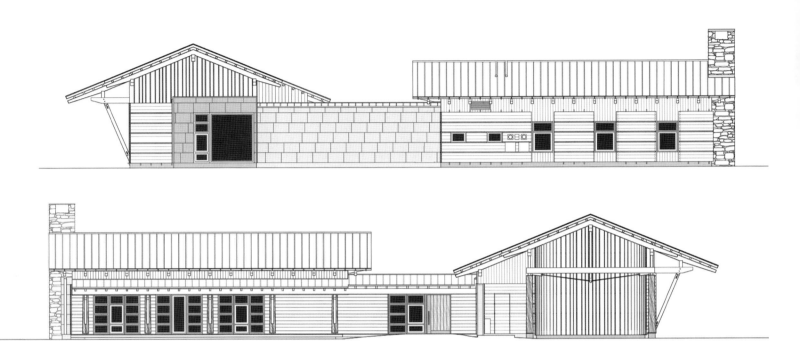

This project started with a gift from Laurance S. Rockefeller to the American people of a 445-hectare "inholding" in Grand Teton National Park that had been a family retreat. The scheme for the preserve involved removing approximately 35 family buildings from the tract of land and creating a network of trails and an interpretive center for the public. The center was the first LEED Platinum-rated building in the National Park Service and in Wyoming. The architects explain that the "very simple L-shaped concept with gabled forms and deep overhangs evolved into a 'chapel to nature' in a clearing at the edge of the woods. The building program includes a welcome and orientation area, exhibit galleries and a resource library room." Wood, stone, and zinc paneling in natural tones were chosen for their durability and connection to the site and region, while inside similar materials were used with more refined surfaces and finishes. A ground source heat pump, photovoltaic panels, and natural ventilation contribute to the reduction of energy use. The timber-frame and insulated-concrete-form structure, employs FSC-certified lumber for over 69% of all wood products used. Materials with high recycled contents were used wherever possible and 24% of total building materials were sourced from within 500 miles of the project.

Eine Schenkung war der Anlass für dieses Projekt: Laurance S. Rockefeller hatte ein 445 ha großes Privatgrundstück im Grand-Teton-Nationalpark, das von seiner Familie als Feriendomizil genutzt wurde, dem amerikanischen Staat überschrieben. Für die Realisierung des Naturschutzgebiets mussten zunächst 35 Bestandsbauten der Familie weichen und ein Wegenetz sowie ein Informationszentrum für Besucher angelegt werden. Das Zentrum erhielt als erster Bau Wyomings und des National Park Service ein LEED-Zertifikat in Platin. Die Architekten erklären: „Die sehr schlichte L-förmige Anlage mit teilweise weit heruntergezogenen Giebeldächern entwickelte sich zu einer ‚der Natur geweihten Kapelle' auf einer Lichtung am Waldrand. Das Programm umfasst einen Empfangs- und Informationsbereich, Ausstellungsflächen und eine Bibliothek." Wegen ihrer Witterungsbeständigkeit und als Verbindungselemente zu Umfeld und Region kamen Holz, Stein und Zinkblech in naturnahen Tönen zum Einsatz; innen wurden ähnliche Materialien mit aufwendigerer Oberflächenbehandlung verarbeitet. Eine Erdwärmepumpe, Solarmodule und natürliche Belüftung tragen zur Senkung des Energiebedarfs bei. Der Holzrahmen- und Betonformsteinbau wurde zu 69 % mit vom FSC zertifiziertem Holz realisiert. Soweit möglich wurden Materialien mit hohem Recyclinganteil verbaut; 24 % aller Baustoffe stammen aus Quellen im Umkreis von 800 km.

Le projet a commencé par le don de Laurance S. Rockefeller au peuple américain d'une « réserve privée » de 445 ha qui avait auparavant été une retraite familiale, située dans le parc national du Grand Teton. Le concept de la réserve impliquait de supprimer environ 35 bâtiments familiaux du terrain pour créer un réseau de sentiers et un centre d'information du public. Le centre a été la première construction certifiée LEED platine de l'Administration des parcs nationaux et du Wyoming. Les architectes expliquent que « le concept très simple en forme de L aux architectures à pignons et profonds surplombs a évolué vers une "chapelle consacrée à la nature" dans une clairière à l'orée de la forêt. Le programme de construction comprenait un espace d'accueil et d'orientation, des galeries d'expositions et une salle de documentation et bibliothèque ». Les panneaux de bois, pierre et zinc aux teintes naturelles ont été choisis pour leur durabilité et leur lien avec le site et la région, on retrouve des matériaux similaires à l'intérieur avec des surfaces et finitions plus raffinées. Une pompe à chaleur géothermique, des panneaux photovoltaïques et la ventilation naturelle contribuent à réduire la consommation d'énergie. Le bois certifié FSC représente plus de 69 % de tout le bois utilisé dans la structure à charpente en bois et forme de béton isolée. Des matériaux largement recyclables ont été utilisés à chaque fois que c'était possible et 24 % des matériaux de construction ont été produits dans un rayon de 800 km autour du projet.

Elevation drawings show the simplicity of the design, well adapted to its national park setting.

Aufrisse zeigen den schlichten Entwurf, der gut auf sein Umfeld im Nationalpark zugeschnitten wurde.

Les plans en élévation montrent la simplicité du design, bien adapté au décor du parc national.

Broad overhangs protect the areas near the structure, which otherwise shows the same straightforward, unencumbered forms seen in the drawings.

Das teilweise weit hinuntergezogene Dach schützt umlaufende Zonen am Bau, der auf der Aufnahme ebenso geradlinig und unverstellt wirkt wie auf den Zeichnungen.

De larges surplombs protègent les alentours de la structure qui affiche sinon les formes simples et sans fioritures qu'on voit sur les schémas.

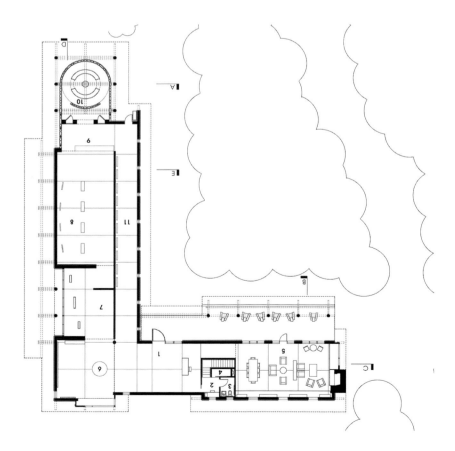

A floor plan reveals the L-shaped design in its entirety. Above, a wooden bridge designed by the architects crosses a stream.

Der Grundriss zeigt die gesamte L-förmige Anlage. Eine von den Architekten geplante Brücke quert einen Fluss (oben).

Le plan révèle la forme en L de l'ensemble dans son intégralité. Ci-dessus, un pont en bois conçu par les architectes traverse un cours d'eau.

The broad, open interior features large-screen displays that alternate with generous, real windows that frame views of the natural setting.

Im weiten offenen Innenraum wechseln große Displays sich mit großzügigen Fenstern ab, die Ausblicke in die natürliche Landschaft bieten.

Le vaste espace intérieur ouvert propose des projections sur grands écrans qui alternent avec les fenêtres aux dimensions généreuses encadrant le décor naturel.

CARTER + BURTON ARCHITECTURE

Carter + Burton Architecture PLC
11 West Main Street
Berryville, VA 22611
USA

Tel: +1 540 955 1644
Fax: +1 540 955 0410
E-mail: info@carterburton.com
Web: www.carterburton.com

PAGE CARTER attended the University of Virginia (1975–79), and the Harvard University Graduate School of Design, where she obtained her M.Arch degree in 1987. She worked in several offices in Boston, Cambridge, Houston (Skidmore, Owings & Merrill), and Baltimore (RTKL), before founding Carter + Burton Architecture. **JIM BURTON** received a B.A. in Architecture from Mississippi State University (1990) and studied Civil Engineering and Art at Longwood College (1979–81). He worked in several firms in Tennessee and Virginia (1987–99), before forming Carter + Burton in 1999. Their work includes the Studio Loggerheads (Clarke County, Virginia, 1997); the Matoaka (Clarke County, Virginia, 1999); the schematic design for the Nakashima Peace Chapel Exhibit (Washington D.C., 2001); the Healthy House (Warren County, Virginia, 2003); the Kampschroer-Yoon (Arlington, Virginia, 2006); the Yoga Studio (Clarke County, Virginia, LEED Gold certified 2007); the Shenandoah Retreat (Warren County, Virginia, 2001–07, published here); the Boxhead (Clarke County, Virginia, 2008); and the Patsy Cline Museum (Winchester, Virginia, in design), all in the USA.

PAGE CARTER studierte an der University of Virginia (1975–79) und der Harvard University Graduate School of Design, wo sie 1987 mit einem M.Arch. abschloss. Sie war in verschiedenen Büros in Boston, Cambridge, Houston (Skidmore, Owings & Merrill) und Baltimore (RTKL) tätig, bevor sie Carter + Burton Architecture gründete. **JIM BURTON** schloss sein Architekturstudium an der Mississippi State University mit einem B.A. ab (1990) und studierte Bauingenieurwesen und Kunst am Longwood College (1979–81). Vor der Gründung von Carter + Burton (1999) arbeitete er in verschiedenen Büros in Tennessee und Virginia (1987–99). Zu den Projekten des Teams zählen u. a. das Studio Loggerheads (Clarke County, Virginia, 1997), das Haus Matoaka (Clarke County, Virginia, 1999), ein Vorentwurf für die Nakashima-Peace-Chapel-Ausstellung (Washington, D. C., 2001), das Healthy House (Warren County, Virginia, 2003), das Haus Kampschroer-Yoon (Arlington, Virginia, 2006), ein Yoga-Studio (Clarke County, Virginia – LEED-Gold-Zertifikat 2007), der Shenandoah Retreat (Warren County, Virginia, 2001–07, hier vorgestellt), das Haus Boxhead (Clarke County, Virginia, 2008) sowie das Patsy Cline Museum (Winchester, Virginia, im Entwurf), alle in den USA.

PAGE CARTER a étudié à l'université de Virginie (1975–79) et à la Graduate School of Design de Harvard, où elle a obtenu son M.Arch en 1987. Elle a travaillé pour plusieurs agences de Boston, Cambridge, Houston (Skidmore, Owings & Merrill) et Baltimore (RTKL), avant de fonder Carter + Burton Architecture. **JIM BURTON**, diplômé d'un B.A. en architecture de l'université du Mississippi (1990), a étudié l'art et l'ingénierie civile à Longwood College (1979–81). Il a travaillé dans plusieurs agences du Tennessee et de Virginie (1987–99), avant la création de Carter + Burton en 1999. Parmi leurs réalisations : le Studio Loggerheads (comté de Clarke, Virginie, 1997) ; la maison Matoaka (comté de Clarke, Virginie, 1999) ; un projet pour l'exposition de la chapelle de la paix de Nakashima (Washington DC, 2001) ; la Healthy House (comté de Warren, Virginie, 2003) ; la maison Kampschroer-Yoon (Arlington, Virginie, 2006) ; le Yoga Studio (comté de Clarke, Virginie, certifié LEED or 2007) ; la Shenandoah Retreat (comté de Warren, Virginie, 2001–07, publiée ici) ; la maison Boxhead (comté de Clarke, Virginie, 2008) et le Patsy Cline Museum (Winchester, Virginie, en cours d'étude), toutes aux États-Unis.

SHENANDOAH RETREAT

Warren County, Virginia, USA, 2001–07

Floor area: 261 m². Clients: Roxanne Fischer and Donald Orlic. Cost: not disclosed
Design Team: Will Harrison, Ted Singer, Michelle Timberlake

The clients for the **SHENANDOAH RETREAT** are two scientists who work for the National Institutes of Health. Roxanne Fischer explains that their choice of Carter + Burton was related to a desire to get away from the locally popular Colonial-style houses. "Our tastes are for architecture that is not as decorative, and as scientists we appreciate clean, organized spaces." Located on a 10-hectare site on the North Fork of the Shenandoah River, the house sits in a small clearing in the forest allowing for views of the Blue Ridge Mountains. The clients also wanted ample wall space for their art collection. The two-bedroom house has a passive solar design strategy with a geothermal heat pump and radiant floor heating. Custom-built storage and furniture was integrated with modern furnishings to achieve a "minimalist aesthetic." The retreat is composed of a series of smaller forms, including a four-story tower. The tower, meant to be used as a vertical gallery for the art collection with a custom-designed lighting system, is an organizing element in the design separating the private and public spaces. The main rooms face south and have angled glass walls for "optimal solar exposure, and solid north walls to provide a thermal barrier against winter wind." A lower level houses a large family room and guest suite with glass doors opening onto a terrace. A wood and concrete deck connects the kitchen to a porch pavilion.

Auftraggeber für den **SHENANDOAH RETREAT** sind zwei für die National Institutes of Health tätige Wissenschaftler. Roxanne Fischer begründet die Wahl von Carter + Burton mit dem Wunsch, sich von den in der Region so populären Häusern im Kolonialstil abzusetzen. „Uns gefällt Architektur, die nicht allzu ornamental ist, und als Wissenschaftler wissen wir klare, gut organisierte Räume zu schätzen." Das Haus liegt auf einem 10 ha großen Grundstück am nördlichen Arm des Shenandoah River auf einer kleinen Waldlichtung mit Aussicht auf die Blue Ridge Mountains. Die Bauherren wünschten sich ausreichend Wandfläche für ihre Kunstsammlung. Das Haus mit zwei Schlafzimmern verfügt über ein Solarenergiesystem sowie eine Erdwärmepumpe und eine Fußbodenheizung. Das moderne Mobiliar wurde mit maßgefertigten Einbaumöbeln kombiniert, um eine „minimalistische Ästhetik" zu schaffen. Das Haus besteht aus verschiedenen kleineren Baukörpern und einem viergeschossigen Turm. Der Turm mit seinem speziell angefertigten Lichtsystem wird als vertikale Galerie für die Kunstsammlung genutzt und trägt zugleich zur Raumorganisation bei, indem er Privat- und Gemeinschaftsbereiche voneinander trennt. Die Haupträume sind nach Süden ausgerichtet und haben schräge Glasfronten für „optimalen Sonnenlichteinfall und massive Nordwände zum Schutz vor dem Winterwind". Im unteren Geschoss befinden sich ein großes Wohnzimmer und ein Gästebereich mit Glastüren, die sich zu einer Terrasse öffnen. Eine Plattform aus Holz und Beton verbindet die Küche mit einem Verandapavillon.

Les clients de cette **« RETRAITE DE SHENANDOAH »** sont deux scientifiques qui travaillent pour l'Institut national de la santé. Roxanne Fisher a expliqué que le choix de l'agence Carter + Burton tenait au désir de s'écarter du style « colonial » apprécié localement. « Nos goûts vont à une architecture qui n'est pas décorative et en tant que scientifiques, nous apprécions les espaces nets et organisés. » La maison, implantée dans une petite clairière sur un terrain de 10 ha au bord de la branche nord de la Shenandoah River, bénéficie de vues sur les Blue Ridge Mountains. Les Fisher souhaitaient également de grands espaces muraux pour présenter leur collection d'art. La maison dotée de deux chambres à coucher est équipée d'installations solaires passives à pompe à chaleur géothermique et chauffage radiant par le sol. Les rangements et le mobilier fabriqués sur mesure sont intégrés à des meubles modernes dans une approche esthétique minimaliste. La maison se compose de plusieurs volumes, dont une tour de quatre niveaux qui devrait servir de galerie verticale pour la collection d'art, éclairée par un système de luminaires spécialement conçus. Elle est un élément d'organisation du plan et sépare les espaces privés de ceux de réception. Les pièces principales, face au sud, sont fermées par des murs de verre inclinés pour « optimiser l'exposition solaire tandis que les murs nord aveugles font office de barrière thermique conte le vent d'hiver ». Le niveau inférieur comprend un grand séjour familial et une suite pour invités dont les portes vitrées ouvrent sur une terrasse. Une plate-forme en bois et béton réunit la cuisine au pavillon du porche d'entrée.

The floor plan of the house, right, corresponds in its spirit and linear articulation to the photographed elevations seen opposite.

Im Etagengrundriss des Hauses (rechts) spiegeln sich Stimmung und lineare Gliederung der fotografierten Ansichten (rechte Seite) wider.

Le plan au sol de la maison, à droite, correspond dans son esprit et son articulation linéaire aux élévations photographiées ci-contre.

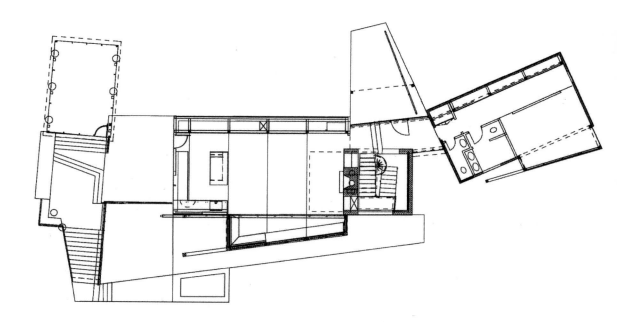

A section drawing shows calculations
related to the penetration of the
sun into the house. Below, a double-
height living space with a cantilevered
balcony.

*Eine Schnittzeichnung illustriert die
Berechnungen zum Sonneneinfall in
den Bau. Unten der doppelgeschos-
sige Wohnraum mit auskragendem
Balkon.*

*Ce plan de coupe montre les angles
de pénétration du soleil dans la maison. Ci-dessous, un espace de séjour
double hauteur à balcon intérieur en
porte-à-faux.*

The outdoor wooden deck, above, is sheltered between two volumes but allows generous views on the natural environment and hills in the distance.

Die Holzterrasse (oben) liegt geschützt zwischen zwei Baukörpern und erlaubt dennoch weite Ausblicke in die Umgebung und auf die Berge im Hintergrund.

La terrasse en bois ci-dessus est protégée entre deux volumes et offre de généreuses perspectives sur l'environnement naturel et les collines dans le lointain.

MARCO CASAGRANDE

Casagrande Laboratory
PL 14, 10210 Inkoo
Finland

Tel: +358 50 308 91 66
E-mail: info@clab.fi
Web: www.clab.fi

Born in 1971 in Turku, Finland, **MARCO CASAGRANDE** attended the Helsinki University of Technology, Department of Architecture. He worked in the office of Casagrande & Rintala (1998–2003) and has been the principal of the Casagrande Laboratory since 2003. His work includes Floating Sauna (Rosendal, Norway, 2002); Treasure Hill (Taipei, Taiwan, 2003); Post-Industrial Fleet (Venice Biennale, Italy, 2004); 7-Eleven Sauna (Taipei, Taiwan, 2007); Chen House (Sanjhih, Taiwan, 2007–08, published here); Guandu River City (Taipei, Taiwan, 2009); and the Bug Dome (Shenzhen and Hong Kong Bi-City Biennale of Architecture/Urbanism, Shenzhen, China, 2009). He is currently working on a new university of architecture and urbanism in Taipei. Marco Casagrande says that a ruin emerges when something "man-made has become part of nature. I am looking forward," he says, "to designing ruins."

Der 1971 in Turku, Finnland, geborene **MARCO CASAGRANDE** studierte Architektur an der Technischen Universität Helsinki. Er arbeitete im Büro Casagrande & Rintala (1998–2003) und leitet seit 2003 die Firma Casagrande Laboratory. Zu seinen Arbeiten zählen die Floating Sauna (Rosendal, Norwegen, 2002), Treasure Hill (Taipeh, Taiwan, 2003), Post-Industrial Fleet (Biennale von Venedig, 2004), die 7-Eleven Sauna (Taipeh, Taiwan, 2007), das Haus Chen (Sanjhih, Taiwan, 2007–08, hier vorgestellt), die Guandu River City (Taipeh, Taiwan, 2009) und der Bug Dome (Shenzhen and Hong Kong Bi-City Biennale of Architecture/Urbanism, Shenzhen, China, 2009). Gegenwärtig plant er eine neue Universität für Architektur und Städtebau in Taipeh. Marco Casagrande sagt, dass eine Ruine entstehe, wenn etwas „von Menschen Gemachtes Teil der Natur wird. Ich freue mich darauf", sagt er, „Ruinen zu entwerfen."

Né en 1971 à Turku (Finlande), **MARCO CASAGRANDE** a fait ses études au département d'Architecture de l'Université de technologie d'Helsinki. Après avoir créé l'agence Casagrande & Rintala (1998–2003), il dirige depuis 2003 Casagrande Laboratory. Parmi ses réalisations : un sauna flottant (Rosendal, Norvège, 2002) ; la restauration de Treasure Hill (Taipei, Taïwan, 2003) ; le projet de Flotte postindustrielle (Biennale de Venise, 2004) ; le sauna 7-Eleven (Taipei, Taïwan, 2007) ; la maison Chen (Sanjhih, Taïwan, 2007–08, publiée ici) ; la Guandu River City (Taipei, Taïwan, 2009) et le Bug Dome (Biennale d'architecture/urbanisme Bi-City de Shenzhen et Hong Kong, Shenzhen, Chine, 2009). Il travaille actuellement à un projet de nouvelle université d'architecture et d'urbanisme pour Taipei. Marco Casagrande explique qu'une ruine apparaît lorsque « quelque chose réalisé par l'homme vient à faire partie de la nature… Je cherche, dit-il, à concevoir des ruines ».

CHEN HOUSE

Sanjhih, Taipei, Taiwan, 2007–08

Address: not disclosed
Area: 62 m². Client: Chen family. Cost: not disclosed

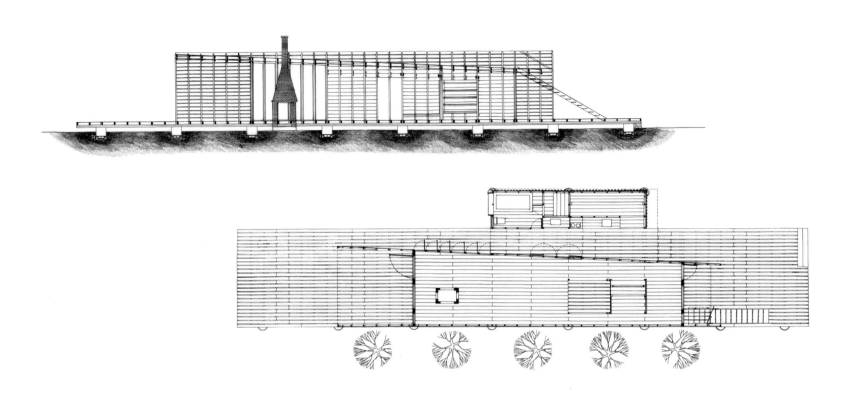

This house, made of mahogany and concrete, is set on 3890 square meters of farmland in the Datun Mountains. It is set up off the ground to allow for occasional flooding conditions and has a total footprint of 138 square meters. The site is also subject to typhoon or even earthquake conditions. The slatted design is intended to capture cooling breezes in warm months, while a fireplace is used for winter heating. With its extended wooden deck, the house offers an easy transition between interior and exterior. Marco Casagrande states: "The house is not strong or heavy—it is weak and flexible. It is also not closing the environment out, but designed to give farmers a needed shelter." He quotes a short poem called "Iron" by Bertolt Brecht (1898–1956) that can readily be applied to this design: "In a dream last night, I saw a great storm. It seized the scaffolding. It tore the cross-clasps, the iron ones, down. But what was made of wood, swayed and remained."

Dieses Wohnhaus aus Mahagoni und Beton steht auf einem 3890 m² großen landwirtschaftlichen Gelände in den Datun-Bergen. Es ist aufgeständert, um es vor gelegentlich vorkommenden Überschwemmungen zu sichern, und hat eine Gesamtgrundfläche von 138 m². Das Gebiet ist auch durch Taifune und sogar durch Erdbeben gefährdet. Die Gestaltung mit Holzlatten dient dazu, im Sommer kühlende Winde einzulassen; ein Kamin sorgt für Wärme im Winter. Die große Holzterrasse bietet fließende Übergänge zwischen Innen- und Außenbereichen. Marco Casagrande erklärt: „Das Haus ist nicht fest oder schwer – es ist schwach und flexibel. Es schließt auch seine Umgebung nicht aus, sondern dient dazu, Bauern den notwendigen Schutz zu gewähren." Er zitiert ein kurzes Gedicht von Bertolt Brecht (1898–1956) mit dem Titel „Eisen", das auf diesen Entwurf zutreffen könnte: „Im Traum heute Nacht/Sah ich einen großen Sturm./Ins Baugerüst griff er/Den Bauschragen riss er/Den eisernen, abwärts./Doch was da aus Holz war/Bog sich und blieb."

Cette maison en béton et acajou a été construite sur un terrain agricole de 3890 m² dans les montagnes Datun. D'une emprise au sol de 138 m², elle est surélevée par rapport au sol pour la protéger des inondations éventuelles. La région est également soumise à des typhons ou des tremblements de terre. La façade en lattis permet de capter les brises rafraîchissantes pendant la saison chaude. Une cheminée est prévue pour l'hiver. Tout autour de la maison, une terrasse en bois assure la transition entre l'intérieur et l'extérieur. Selon Marco Casagrande : « Cette maison n'est ni massive ni lourde, elle est légère et flexible. Elle ne se ferme pas par rapport à son environnement mais est conçue pour offrir aux fermiers un abri nécessaire. » Il cite un bref poème de Bertolt Brecht (1898–1956) intitulé « Fer » qui pourrait s'appliquer à ce projet : « La nuit dernière, dans un rêve, j'ai vu une grande tempête. Elle s'en est prise à l'échafaudage. Elle a arraché les croisillons, qui étaient en fer. Mais ce qui était en bois a oscillé, mais résisté. »

The house has a decidedly temporary feeling to it, perhaps inspired as much by shipping containers as by more traditional wooden structures.

Das Haus macht einen eindeutig temporären Eindruck; der Entwurf wurde wohl von Transportcontainern ebenso wie von traditionellen Holzkonstruktionen beeinflusst.

L'aspect de la maison semble décidément temporaire, effet peut-être dû à son inspiration qui vient davantage des conteneurs d'expédition que des constructions en bois traditionnelles.

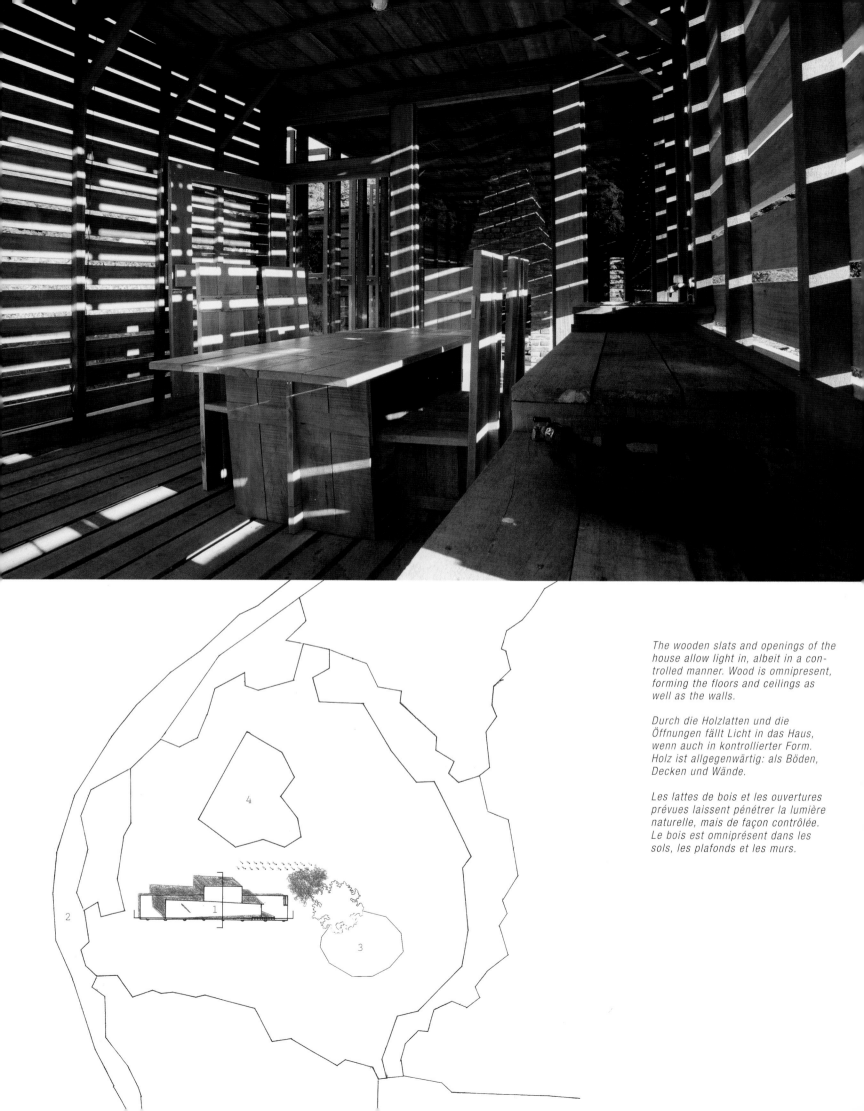

The wooden slats and openings of the house allow light in, albeit in a controlled manner. Wood is omnipresent, forming the floors and ceilings as well as the walls.

Durch die Holzlatten und die Öffnungen fällt Licht in das Haus, wenn auch in kontrollierter Form. Holz ist allgegenwärtig: als Böden, Decken und Wände.

Les lattes de bois et les ouvertures prévues laissent pénétrer la lumière naturelle, mais de façon contrôlée. Le bois est omniprésent dans les sols, les plafonds et les murs.

The interior is as sparsely furnished
as might be expected. Although
electrical light is provided for, it too
is minimal.

Innen ist das Haus erwartungsgemäß
sparsam möbliert. Elektrisches Licht
ist zwar vorhanden, wird aber auch
sparsam eingesetzt.

L'intérieur est aussi peu abondamment meublé que l'on pouvait s'y
attendre. L'éclairage électrique est
lui aussi minimal.

CASEY BROWN

Casey Brown Architecture
Level 1, 63 William Street
East Sydney, NSW 2010
Australia

Tel: +61 2 9360 7977
Fax: +61 2 9360 2123
E-mail: cb@caseybrown.com.au
Web: www.caseybrown.com.au

ROBERT BROWN received his degrees in architecture from the University of New South Wales (1976 and 1979) and from Columbia University Graduate School of Architecture in New York (1992–93). He worked with Fisher Lucas Architects in Sydney (1976), Julian Harrap Architects in London (1983), and the Heritage Council NSW (1984–86), before creating Dawson Brown Partnership (1986–89), Dawson Brown + Ackert Architecture (1989–92), and Dawson Brown Architecture (1993–2004). In 2004, he created the firm Casey Brown with partner **CAROLINE CASEY**. The James-Robertson House (Great Mackerel Beach, Sydney, NSW, 2001–03) won a 2004 Residential Architecture Award from the Royal Australian Institute of Architects (NSW Chapter). Recent projects include the Sastrugi Ski Lodge (Thredbo, NSW, 2000); Graigee Lee House (Palm Beach, Sydney, NSW, 2001); and the Bungan Beach House (Bungan Beach, Sydney, NSW, 2003). More recently, they have completed the Permanent Camping House (Mudgee, NSW, 2007, published here); the Stanwell Park House (Stanwell Park Beach, Sydney, NSW, 2007); and Eagles Rest Winery (Hunter Valley, NSW, 2010), all in Australia.

ROBERT BRAUN machte seine Abschlüsse in Architektur an der University of New South Wales (1976 und 1979) und dem Graduiertenkolleg für Architektur an der Columbia University in New York (1992–93). Er arbeitete für Fisher Lucas Architects in Sydney (1976), Julian Harrap Architects in London (1983) und das Heritage Council NSW (1984–86), bevor er die Büros Dawson Brown Partnership (1986–89), Dawson Brown + Ackert Architecture (1989–92) und Dawson Brown Architecture (1993 bis 2004) gründete. 2004 schließlich eröffnete er mit **CAROLINE CASEY** als Partnerin das Büro Casey Brown. Das James-Robertson House (Great Mackerel Beach, Sydney, NSW, 2001–03) wurde 2004 mit dem Preis für Wohnhausarchitektur des Royal Australian Institute of Architects (Abteilung New South Wales) ausgezeichnet. Weitere Projekte sind die Sastrugi Ski Lodge (Thredbo, NSW, 2000), das Graigee Lee House (Palm Beach, Sydney, NSW, 2001) sowie das Bungan Beach House (Bungan Beach, Sydney, 2003). Danach wurden das Hausprojekt Permanent Camping (Mudgee, NSW, 2007, hier vorgestellt), das Stanwell Park House (Stanwell Park Beach, Sydney, 2007) und das Weingut Eagles Rest (Hunter Valley, NSW, 2010) fertiggestellt, alle in Australien.

ROBERT BRAUN est diplômé en architecture de l'université de Nouvelle-Galles-du-Sud (1976 et 1979) et de l'École supérieure d'architecture de l'université Columbia à New York (1992–93). Il a travaillé avec les agences Fisher Lucas Architects à Sydney (1976), Julian Harrap Architects à Londres (1983) et pour l'Heritage Council NSW (1984–86), avant de fonder le Dawson Brown Partnership (1986–89), Dawson Brown + Ackert Architecture (1989–92) et Dawson Brown Architecture (1993–2004). En 2004, il crée l'agence Casey Brown avec **CAROLINE CASEY**. La maison James-Robertson (Great Mackerel Beach, Sydney, NGS, 2001–03) a remporté le prix de l'architecture résidentielle du Royal Australian Institute of Architects (section de Nouvelle-Galles-du-Sud). Parmi leurs projets récents : le chalet de ski Sastrugi (Thredbo, NGS, 2000), la maison Graigee Lee (Palm Beach, Sydney, NGS, 2001), et la maison de plage de Bungan Beach (Sydney, NGS, 2003), la Maison de camping permanent (Mudgee, NGS, 2007, publiée ici), la maison de Stanwell Park (Stanwell Park Beach, Sydney, NGS, 2007), et le chais d'Eagles Rest (Hunter Valley, NGS, 2010), le tout en Australie.

PERMANENT CAMPING
Mudgee, NSW, Australia, 2007

Area: 18 m². Client: not disclosed. Cost: not disclosed
Collaboration: Hernan Alvarez (Project Architect),
Jeffrey Broadfield (Builder)

This tiny house is located on a mountain site in a sheep station in central western New South Wales. The panoramic view from the house reaches hundreds of kilometers around the site. The two-story, copper-clad structure has a very small three by three meter footprint, and has sides that open to provide verandas to the north, east, and west. The sides close entirely to protect the house from bush fires. Recycled ironbark (eucalyptus) is used inside the house, which contains a sleeping loft and kitchen with a wood-fired stove. The roof collects rainfall and a toilet is located outside. Heavy insulation protects residents from both cold wind and daytime heat. Because of the extreme isolation of its location, the house was entirely prefabricated in Sydney and transported on site.

Das winzige Haus liegt auf einem Hügel mitten auf einer Schaffarm im Herzen von New South Wales. Der Panoramablick vom Haus reicht Hunderte von Kilometer weit in das Umland. Der zweigeschossige kupferverkleidete Bau hat eine ungewöhnlich kleine Grundfläche von 3 x 4 m und lässt sich nach Norden, Osten und Westen öffnen, sodass kleine Veranden entstehen. Die Seiten lassen sich vollständig schließen, um das Haus vor Buschfeuern zu schützen. Im Innern, in dem es ein Podest mit Bett und eine Küche mit Holzofen gibt, kam recyceltes Ironbark-Holz (eine Eukalyptusart) zum Einsatz. Über das Dach wird Regenwasser gesammelt, draußen befindet sich ein separates Außen-WC. Dank starker Dämmung sind die Bewohner vor kalten Winden ebenso wie vor der tagsüber herrschenden Hitze geschützt. Aufgrund der extrem isolierten Lage des Grundstücks wurde das gesamte Haus in Syndey vorgefertigt und zum Standort transportiert.

Cette minuscule maison est située dans les montagnes de Nouvelle-Galles-du-Sud, au cœur d'alpages pour brebis. La vue panoramique que l'on a de ses ouvertures porte sur des centaines de kilomètres. La construction — deux niveaux habillés de cuivre — n'occupe qu'une emprise au sol de 3 x 3 m. Ses côtés s'ouvrent pour former des vérandas au nord, à l'est et à l'ouest. Ces côtés se referment entièrement pour protéger la maison des incendies naturels. L'intérieur, qui contient une pièce pour dormir et une cuisine à cuisinière à bois, est habillé d'écorce d'eucalyptus recyclé. La toiture collecte l'eau de pluie et les toilettes sont extérieures. Une épaisse couche d'isolant protège des vents froids et de la chaleur diurne. Du fait de son isolement extrême, l'ensemble a été entièrement préfabriqué à Sydney et transporté sur place.

With its very small area and protective cladding, the house might almost appear to be a military surveillance point. Sitting lightly on the ground, this is architecture that speaks clearly to environmental concerns.

Mit seiner besonders kleinen Grundfläche und der schützenden Verkleidung wirkt das Haus fast wie ein militärischer Wachturm. Das leicht über den Boden erhobene Haus ist Architektur, die deutlich von Umweltbewusstsein zeugt.

Par sa petite taille et son habillage de protection, la maison pourrait presque faire penser à une tour de guet. Reposant à peine sur le sol, elle exprime clairement dans son architecture ses préoccupations environnementales.

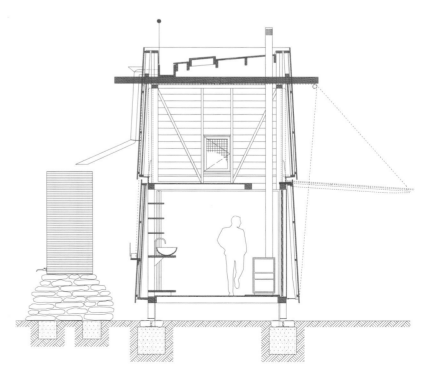

A square plan makes way for generous open space when the outer shutters of the house are raised. A woodburning stove provides warmth in the dry surroundings.

Der quadratische Grundriss wird zum großzügigen, offenen Raum, sobald die äußeren Fensterläden des Hauses aufgeklappt sind. Inmitten der dürren Landschaft sorgt ein Holzofen für Wärme.

Le plan de forme carré dégage un généreux volume ouvert quand les volets extérieurs sont relevés. Le poêle à bois apporte un peu de chaleur dans cet environnement sauvage.

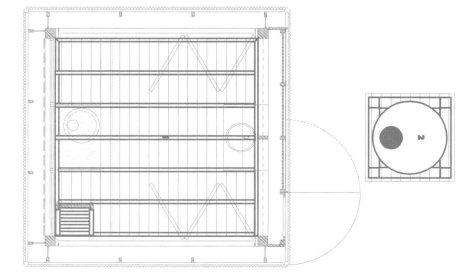

The spartan upper-level living spaces are covered in wood slats, echoing the rather blank and protected appearance of the little house in its closed mode.

Der spartanische Wohnbereich im Obergeschoss ist holzvertäfelt und greift die eher schmucklose und schützende Optik des kleinen Hauses im geschlossenen Zustand auf.

Les pièces de style spartiate de l'étage sont doublées d'un lattis de bois. Leur aspect refermé fait écho au style assez neutre et défensif de cette petite maison.

EDWARD CULLINAN

Cullinan Studio
5 Baldwin Terrace
London N1 7RU
UK

Tel: +44 20 77 04 19 75
Fax: +44 20 73 54 27 39
E-mail: eca@ecarch.co.uk
Web: www.cullinanstudio.com

Born in London, UK, in 1931, **EDWARD CULLINAN** was educated at Cambridge (1951–54), the Architectural Association in London, and Berkeley (1954–56). He worked for Denys Lasdun (1958–65), where he designed the student residences at the University of East Anglia, before setting up his own practice in 1959 and starting teaching at Cambridge in 1965. He established Edward Cullinan Architects as a co-operative in 1965; the practice then changed name in November 2012 to Cullinan Studio. Recent work of the firm includes the Downland Gridshell (Singleton, 2000–02, published here); the International Digital Laboratory (University of Warwick, Coventry, 2007–08); the New Herbarium, Library, Art and Archives Wing of the Royal Botanic Gardens (Kew, London, 2007–09); the Stonebridge Hillside Hub (Brent, 2007–09); the John Hope Gateway, Royal Botanic Garden (Edinburgh, Scotland, 2007–09); the New Library and IT Centre, Fitzwilliam College (Cambridge, 2008–09); the BFI Master Film Store (Gaydon, Warwickshire, 2010–11), and a Maggie's Cancer Caring Centre (Freeman Hospital, Newcastle, 2012–13), all in the UK. Current work includes a Maggie's Cancer Caring Centre (Freeman Hospital, Newcastle, 2012–13).

EDWARD CULLINAN, geboren 1931 in London, studierte in Cambridge (1951–54), an der Architectural Association in London sowie in Berkeley (1954–56). Er arbeitete bei Denys Lasdun (1958–65), für dessen Büro er die Studentenwohnheime der University of East Anglia entwarf, ehe er 1959 sein eigenes Büro gründete und 1965 begann, in Cambridge zu lehren. 1965 gründete er Edward Cullinan Architects als Kooperative; seit November 2012 firmiert das Büro als Cullinan Studio. Jüngere Projekte sind u. a. Downland Gridshell (Singleton, 2000–02, hier vorgestellt), das International Digital Laboratory (Universität Warwick, Coventry, 2007–08), das Neue Herbarium sowie der Bibliotheks-, Kunst- und Archivflügel im Königlichen Botanischen Garten (Kew, London, 2007–09), der Stonebridge Hillside Hub (Brent, 2007–09), der John Hope Gateway im Königlichen Botanischen Garten (Edinburgh, 2007–09), das neue Bibliotheks- und Computerzentrum am Fitzwilliam College (Cambridge, 2008 bis 2009) sowie der BFI Master Film Store (Gaydon, Warwickshire, 2010–11), alle in Großbritannien. Zu den aktuellen Projekten des Studios zählt auch ein Maggie's Cancer Caring Centre (Freeman Hospital, Newcastle, 2012–13).

Né à Londres en 1931, **EDWARD CULLINAN** a fait ses études à Cambridge (1951–54), à l'Architectural Association de Londres et à Berkeley (1954–56). Il a travaillé pour Denys Lasdun (1958–65) et a conçu les résidences étudiantes de l'université d'East Anglia avant de monter son agence en 1959 et de commencer à enseigner à Cambridge en 1965. Il a ouvert Edward Cullinan Architects sous forme de coopérative en 1965, l'agence a ensuite été rebaptisée Cullinan Studio en novembre 2012. Ses réalisations récentes comprennent le Downland Gridshell (Singleton, 2000–02, publié ici) ; le Laboratoire numérique international (université de Warwick, Coventry, 2007–08) ; le nouvel herbarium, la bibliothèque, l'aile Art et les archives des jardins botaniques royaux (Kew, Londres, 2007–09) ; le centre Stonebridge Hillside Hub (Brent, 2007–09) ; le centre John Hope Gateway du Jardin botanique royal (Édimbourg, 2007–09) ; la nouvelle bibliothèque et le centre TI du Fitzwilliam College (Cambridge, 2008–09) et l'entrepôt de films du BFI (Gaydon, Warwickshire, 2010–11) et un centre Maggie's de soins des cancéreux (hôpital Freeman, Newcastle, 2012–13), toutes au Royaume-Uni. Ses projets actuels comprennent un centre Maggie's de soins des cancéreux (hôpital Freeman, Newcastle, 2012–13).

DOWNLAND GRIDSHELL

Singleton, UK, 2000–02

Area: 1200 m² (floor). Client: Weald & Downland Open Air Museum
Cost: £1.5 milion

The Weald and Downland Museum acts primarily to restore and rebuild traditional timber-framed buildings. The institution required two new spaces: a climate-controlled storage area for its collection of historic artifacts, and a large open space in which to conserve and repair the museum's collection of buildings. The response they found was the Gridshell, "a three-domed oak lattice structure, which was a collaboration between Edward Cullinan Architects, Buro Happold Engineers and the Green Oak Carpentry Company." The two-story structure has a 500 m² lower level (the Artifacts Store) in a 10 x 50 m configuration, and 700 m² above, with a 10.5 meter maximum height on the upper level, which is used for timber framing. As the architects say, "This is a rural building for the 21st century." Sophisticated computer modeling techniques, as well as physical models were used to determine how the complex structure would be designed and erected. Untreated timber floors, ample natural light and use of thermal mass in the soil to control temperature show the architects' concern with sustainability. Six tons of oak was used in what is described as the "first all-timber gridshell in the world," with a doubly curved 48-meter-long roof. A special node connector was designed for the structure and subsequently patented. Another unusual aspect of the construction was the use of a flexible scaffold that was progressively reduced in height, lowering the grid into its final shape. Short-listed for England's Stirling Prize, the **DOWNLAND GRIDSHELL** demonstrates the unusual innovative methods and capacities of its architects.

Die Hauptaufgabe des Weald and Downland Museum, eines Freilichtmuseums, besteht in der Restaurierung und Rekonstruktion traditioneller Holzfachwerkbauten. Das Institut benötigte zwei neue Räume: einen klimatisierten Lagerraum für seine Sammlung historischer Artefakte sowie einen großflächigen, offenen Raum für Konservierungs- und Restaurierungsarbeiten. Diese sind nun in der „Gridshell" untergebracht, einer dreifach überkuppelten Gitterkonstruktion aus Eichenholz, ein Gemeinschaftswerk von Edward Cullinan Architects, Buro Happold Engineers und der Green Oak Carpentry Company. Der zweigeschossige Bau verfügt über ein 500 m² umfassendes Untergeschoss von 10 x 50 m zur Lagerung der Artefakte und ein 700 m² großes Obergeschoss mit einer maximalen Deckenhöhe von 10,5 m, das zum Bau von Holzrahmen genutzt wird. Den Architekten zufolge handelt es sich hier um „ein ländliches Gebäude für das 21. Jahrhundert". Um zu entscheiden, wie der komplexe Bau entworfen und realisiert werden könne, bediente man sich komplizierter Computerprogramme und realer Modelle. Unbehandelte Holzböden, viel Tageslicht und die Nutzung von thermischer Masse im Boden zur Regelung der Temperatur zeugen vom Interesse der Architekten an nachhaltigen Lösungen. Für die, wie es heißt, „erste Ganzholzrasterschale der Welt", eine doppelt gekrümmte, 48 m lange Überdachung, wurden 6 t Eichenholz verbaut. Für die Konstruktion wurde eine spezielle Knotenverbindung entwickelt und anschließend zum Patent angemeldet. Ein weiterer ungewöhnlicher Aspekt der Konstruktion besteht in der Verwendung eines flexiblen Gerüsts, dessen Höhe schrittweise reduziert wurde, während man das Raster auf seine endgültige Form absenkte. Die **DOWNLAND GRIDSHELL** kam auf die Auswahlliste für den britischen Stirling Prize; sie veranschaulicht die ungewöhnlich innovativen Methoden und Fähigkeiten der Architekten.

Le Weald and Downland Museum est une institution dédiée à la restauration et au remontage de constructions traditionnelles à ossature en bois. Il avait besoin d'un nouveau bâtiment de stockage climatisé pour ses objets historiques et d'un vaste volume ouvert où réparer et conserver sa collection d'ossatures. La réponse est le Gridshall, « structure en treillis de chêne à trois dômes, fruit d'une collaboration entre Edward Cullinan Architects, Buro Happold Engineers et la Green Oak Carpentry Company ». Il se compose d'un niveau inférieur de 500 m² (l'Artifacts Store) de 10 x 50 m et d'un niveau supérieur de 700 m² de 10,5 m de haut au maximum pour les ossatures en bois. Comme le précise l'architecte : « Il s'agit d'un bâtiment rural pour le XXIᵉ siècle. » Des techniques de modélisation informatique sophistiquées ainsi que des maquettes ont servi à établir les plans et la construction de cette structure complexe. Les sols en bois brut, un généreux éclairage naturel et l'utilisation de la masse thermique du sol pour contrôler la température montrent le souci de développement durable de l'architecte. Six tonnes de chêne ont permis d'ériger « la première coque à structure au monde en treillis tout en bois », à toiture à double courbe de 48 m de long. Une pièce de connexion spécifique a été dessinée et brevetée. Un autre aspect intéressant de ce projet est le recours à un échafaudage souple dont la hauteur a été progressivement réduite, jusqu'à la forme finale. Nominé pour le prix Stirling britannique, le **DOWNLAND GRIDSHELL** est une brillante démonstration des méthodes et des capacités novatrices de ses architectes.

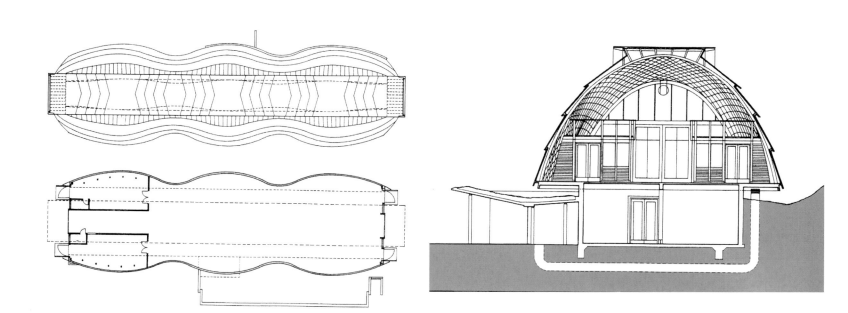

The layered, curving appearance of the building is unusual to say the least. Despite its very modern structural solution, it retains something of the handmade feeling of earlier rural buildings.

Die geschwungene Schuppenoptik des Baus ist mehr als ungewöhnlich. Trotz modernster Konstruktionsmethoden hat das Gebäude die handwerkliche Aura früher ländlicher Architekturformen.

L'aspect du bâtiment aux courbes stratifiées est pour le moins inhabituel. Malgré la solution très moderne adoptée pour la structure, il conserve en partie l'impression de fait main des anciens bâtiments ruraux.

The undulating form of the Gridshell and its layered design obviously make it fit into its natural setting more readily than a Modernist geometric form.

Die geschwungenen Formen des Gridshell und seine schuppenförmige Optik tragen zweifellos dazu bei, dass sich das Gebäude selbstverständlicher in die Landschaft fügt als ein geometrischer moderner Bau.

La forme ondulée du « Downland Gridshell » et sa conception en strates lui permis de s'adapter plus facilement à son cadre naturel qu'une forme géométrique moderniste n'aurait pu le faire.

DECOI ARCHITECTS

Mark Goulthorpe
Associate Professor, MIT, 77 Massachusetts Avenue, Cambridge, MA 02143, USA
Tel: +1 617 852 3527 / E-mail: mg_decoi@mit.edu / Web: www.hyposurface.org
http://web.mit.edu/mg_decoi/www/miran

dECOi is a small architectural/design practice that looks to open the boundaries of conventional practice through a fresh and exploratory approach to design. **MARK GOULTHORPE**, born in Kent, UK, and educated in Liverpool and in Oregon, established dECOi in 1991 after having worked for four years in the office of Richard Meier in New York. dECOi was awarded the prestigious international FEIDAD Digital Design Award in 2002 and again in 2004, and was invited to the *Architecture of the Non-Standard Manifesto* exhibition at the Centre Pompidou in Paris in 2003. Mark Goulthorpe was a unit master intermediate, unit 2, at the Architectural Association (London, 1995–96), and is currently teaching advanced digital design at MIT. dECOi's work ranges from pure design and artwork to interior design, architecture, and urbanism. Projects include the Chan (Origin) House (Kuala Lumpur, 1995); Missoni Showroom (Paris, France, 1996); Swiss Re Headquarters (technical/design studies for Foster & Partners, London, UK, 1998); Dietrich House (London, UK, 2000); Glapyros House (Paris, France, 2001); Bankside ECOmorph, addition of a penthouse to the top of a tower (South Bank, London, UK, 2004/2007–); and One Main (Cambridge, Massachusetts, USA, 2009, published here). Art and research works include Aegis HypoSurface, dynamically reconfigurable, interactive architectural surface (Birmingham, UK, 2000); Excideuil Folly, parametric 3D-glyphting (Excideuil, France, 2001); IMTS HypoSurface, the frontispiece for the International Manufacturers Technology Show (Chicago, USA; 2006); and "Enchanted," a choreographed event in which HypoSurface was used to take further the protocols of the interactive systems with a multi-disciplinary team (Chicago, USA, 2008).

dECOi ist ein kleines Architektur- und Designbüro, das die Grenzen der konventionellen Praxis durch neuartiges Vorgehen und Forschungsarbeit überwinden will. Der im britischen Kent geborene **MARK GOULTHORPE** studierte in Liverpool und Oregon und gründete dECOi 1991, nachdem er vier Jahre im Büro von Richard Meier in New York gearbeitet hatte. dECOi erhielt 2002 und 2004 den renommierten internationalen FEIDAD Digital Design Award und war 2003 zur Ausstellung *Architecture of the Non-Standard Manifesto* im Centre Pompidou in Paris eingeladen. Mark Goulthorpe war Unit Master Intermediate, Unit 2, an der Architectural Association (London, 1995–96); gegenwärtig lehrt er Advanced Digital Design am Massachusetts Institute of Technology (MIT). Die Tätigkeit von dECOi reicht von reinem Design und künstlerischer Gestaltung über Innenausstattung bis zu Architektur und Städtebau. Zu den Projekten zählen das Haus Chan (Origin) in Kuala Lumpur (1995), der Showroom von Missoni in Paris (1996), die Hauptverwaltung Swiss Re (technische und Entwurfsstudien für Foster & Partners, London, 1998), das Haus Dietrich (London, 2000), das Haus Glapyros (Paris, 2001), Bankside ECOmorph, Erweiterung eines Hochhauses durch ein Penthouse (South Bank, London, 2004 und seit 2007) und One Main (Cambridge, Massachusetts, 2009, hier vorgestellt). Zu den künstlerischen und Forschungsarbeiten gehören Aegis HypoSurface, eine dynamisch veränderbare, interaktive Architekturfläche (Birmingham, 2000), Excideuil Folly, ein parametrischer 3-D-Entwurf (Excideuil, Frankreich, 2001), IMTS HypoSurface, das Eingangsportal für die International Manufacturers Technology Show (Chicago, 2006), sowie „Enchanted", ein choreografiertes Event, bei dem HypoSurface dazu verwendet wurde, um die Anwendungsmöglichkeiten der interaktiven Systeme mit einem interdisziplinären Team weiterzuentwickeln (Chicago, 2008).

dECOi est une petite agence d'architecture et de design qui cherche à dépasser les limites de la pratique conventionnelle par une approche fraîche et exploratoire du processus de conception. **MARK GOULTHORPE**, né dans le Kent (GB) et élevé à Liverpool et dans l'Oregon, a fondé dECOi en 1991 après avoir travaillé quatre ans pour Richard Meier à New York. dECOi a reçu le prestigieux prix international FEIDAD de la conception numérique en 2002 et de nouveau en 2004 et a été invité à l'exposition « Architectures non standard » organisée par le Centre Pompidou à Paris en 2003. Mark Goulthorpe a été Unit Master Intermediate, pour l'Unité 2 à l'Architectural Association (Londres, 1995–96) et enseigne actuellement la conception numérique avancée au Massachusetts Institute of Technology (MIT). Les interventions de dECOi vont de la pure conception et du travail artistique à l'aménagement intérieur, l'architecture et l'urbanisme. Parmi ses projets et réalisations figurent : la maison Chan (Origin) (Kuala Lumpur, 1995) ; le showroom Missoni (Paris, 1996) ; le siège de Swiss Re (études de conception et études techniques pour Foster & Partners, Londres, 1998) ; la maison Dietrich (Londres, 2000) ; la maison Glapyros (Paris, 2001) ; Bankside ECOmorph, adjonction d'un penthouse au sommet d'une tour (South Bank, Londres, 2004/2007–) et One Main (Cambridge, Massachusetts, 2009, publié ici). Parmi les réalisations artistiques et de recherche de l'agence figurent : Aegis HypoSurface, une surface architecturale interactive reconfigurable dynamiquement (Birmingham, GB, 2000) ; le projet Excideuil Folly, parametric 3D glyphting (Excideuil, France, 2001) ; IMTS HypoSurface, frontispice pour l'International Manufacturers Technology Show (Chicago, 2006) et « Enchanted », une manifestation chorégraphiée au cours de laquelle une HypoSurface servait de base au développement de protocoles de systèmes interactifs par une équipe multidisciplinaire (Chicago, 2008).

ONE MAIN

Cambridge, Massachusetts, USA, 2009

Address: One Main Street, Cambridge, Massachusetts, USA
Area: 1000 m². Client: not disclosed. Cost: not disclosed
Collaboration: Raphael Crespin (Project Architect)

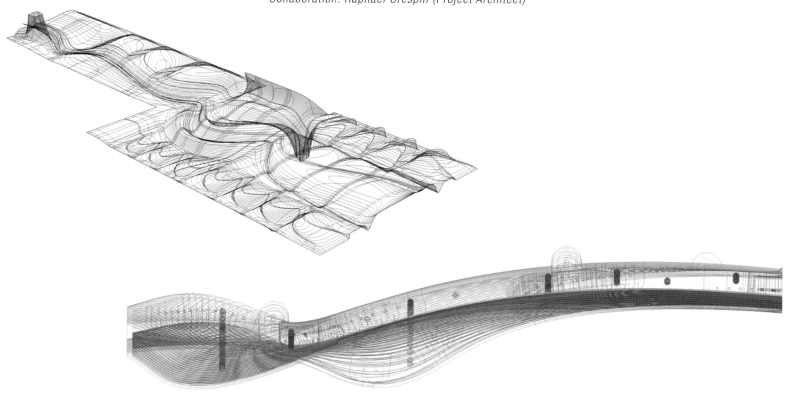

Located at One Main Street in Cambridge, this is an office refurbishment project that "relentlessly deploys numeric command machining of sustainable plywood to evidence the versatility and efficiency available via CAD-CAM design-build processes." Mark Goulthorpe has long defended the qualities of computer-driven design and manufacturing and in this instance he gives form to his concept of a "seamless and non-standard protocol of customized fabrication." His point is that these tools can be used to create a unique environment that is not dependent on "old-fashioned" industrial manufacturing procedures. And in this instance wood is the main element. Goulthorpe concludes: "In a material sense, the project assumes a radical environmental agenda, using a sustainable and carbon-absorbing raw material (forested spruce), translated efficiently into refined and functional elements via dexterous, low-energy digital tooling."

Bei diesem Projekt handelt es sich um die Modernisierung eines an der Main Street in Cambridge gelegenen Bürogebäudes, bei der „durch ausschließlich computergesteuerte Bearbeitung von nachhaltig gewonnenem Sperrholz die mit den Planungs- und Ausführungsverfahren CAD-CAM erzielbare vielseitige Anwendbarkeit und Effizienz bewiesen werden sollen". Mark Goulthorpe setzt sich schon seit langer Zeit für computergesteuertes Entwerfen und Produzieren ein, und in diesem Fall verleiht er seinem Konzept des „durchgehenden und nicht standardisierten Verfahrens individueller Fabrikation" eine sichtbare Gestalt. Seiner Meinung nach können diese Instrumente dazu genutzt werden, eine einzigartige Umwelt zu gestalten, die nicht auf „altmodischen" industriellen Produktionsverfahren beruht. Und im vorliegenden Fall ist Holz das Hauptelement dafür. Goulthorpe erklärt abschließend: „In materieller Hinsicht ist dieses Projekt radikal umweltfreundlich, weil es ein nachhaltiges und Kohlenstoff absorbierendes Rohmaterial (Fichte aus bewirtschafteten Wäldern) mittels geeigneter digitaler Low-Energy-Instrumente effizient in veredelte funktionale Elemente verwandelt."

Cette rénovation de bureaux situés 1, Main Street à Cambridge « déploie implacablement des processus d'usinage à commande numérique de contreplaqués de qualité durable pour faire apparaître la versatilité et les qualités offertes par les processus de conception et de réalisation par CAO-FAO ». Mark Goulthorpe a longtemps défendu cette orientation et donne ici forme à un concept de « protocole continu de fabrication sur mesure non-standard ». Son argument est que ces outils peuvent servir à créer des environnements uniques, qui ne dépendent pas des processus de fabrication industrielle « démodés ». « Le bois est ici l'élément principal. Au sens matériel, le projet s'est fixé un objectif environnemental radical, par l'utilisation d'un matériau brut durable et absorbeur de CO_2 (épicéa d'exploitation rationnelle), transformé avec efficacité en éléments fonctionnels raffinés par des outils numériques habiles à faible consommation d'énergie », conclut Goulthorpe.

As is usually the case in his work, Mark Goulthorpe of dECOi has used sophisticated computer modeling and manufacturing to conceive this space.

Wie üblich hat sich Mark Goulthorpe von dECOi ausgefeilter Computermodelle und Produktionsmethoden für die Gestaltung dieser Räume bedient.

Comme la plupart du temps, Mark Goulthorpe de l'agence dECOi a utilisé des techniques de modélisation et de fabrication sophistiquées pour concevoir cet espace.

Interior perspectives show that the overall design has also been applied to the furnishings. Within the relatively straightforward space, the architect adds unexpected elements.

Die Innenansichten zeigen, dass in die Gesamtplanung auch die Möblierung einbezogen war. In den relativ klaren Raum hat der Architekt unerwartete Elemente eingefügt.

Ces vues intérieures montrent que la conception de l'ensemble a également été appliquée au mobilier. Dans cet espace relativement classique, l'architecte a inséré des éléments inattendus.

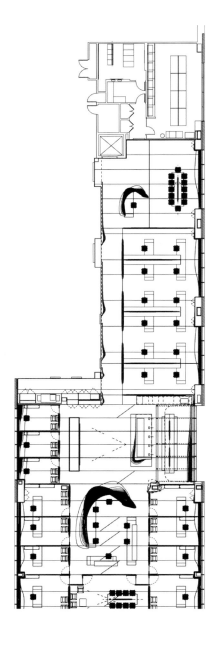

The detailing and furniture design are a product of the fully computer-oriented work of Mark Goulthorpe, allying wood with the most contemporary techniques.

Detailgestaltung und Möblierung sind das Produkt der vollständig computerorientierten Arbeit von Mark Goulthorpe, der Holz mit modernsten Techniken verbindet.

Les finitions et le mobilier sont des productions caractéristiques du travail de Mark Goulthorpe, entièrement orienté vers les techniques numériques les plus modernes auxquelles il associe le bois.

DILLER SCOFIDIO + RENFRO

Diller Scofidio + Renfro
601 West 26th Street, Suite 1815
New York, NY 10001
USA

Tel: +1 212 260 7971 / Fax: +1 212 260 7924
E-mail: disco@dsrny.com / Web: www.dsrny.com

ELIZABETH DILLER was born in Łódź, Poland, in 1954. She received her B.Arch degree from Cooper Union School of Architecture in 1979 and is a Professor of Architecture at Princeton University. **RICARDO SCOFIDIO** was born in New York in 1935. He graduated from Cooper Union School of Architecture and Columbia University, and is now Professor Emeritus of Architecture at Cooper Union. **CHARLES RENFRO** was born in Baytown, Texas, in 1964. He graduated from Rice University and Columbia University. Diller + Scofidio was founded in 1979 and Renfro became a Partner in 2004. According to their own description: "DS+R is a collaborative, interdisciplinary studio involved in architecture, the visual arts, and the performing arts." They completed the Brasserie Restaurant in the Seagram Building (New York, 2000); the Viewing Platforms at Ground Zero in Manhattan (New York, 2001); the Blur Building (Expo 02, Yverdon-les-Bains, Switzerland, 2002); and the Institute of Contemporary Art in Boston (Massachusetts, 2006). Recently completed projects include the Lincoln Center Redevelopment Project in New York, including the expansion of the Juilliard School of Music (2009), the renovation of Alice Tully Hall (2009), public spaces throughout the campus, and the Hypar Pavilion Lawn (2011, published here); the conversion of the High Line, a 2.4-kilometer stretch of elevated railroad, into a New York City park (Phase 1, 2009; Phase 2, 2011); and the Creative Arts Center at Brown University (Providence, Rhode Island, 2011), all in the USA unless stated otherwise.

ELIZABETH DILLER wurde 1954 in Łódź, Polen, geboren. 1979 machte sie ihren Bachelor in Architektur an der Cooper Union School of Architecture und ist derzeit Professorin für Architektur an der Princeton University. **RICARDO SCOFIDIO** wurde 1935 in New York geboren. Er schloss seine Studien an der Cooper Union School of Architecture und an der Columbia University ab und ist heute emeritierter Professor für Architektur an der Cooper Union. **CHARLES RENFRO** wurde 1964 in Baytown, Texas, geboren. Er studierte an der Rice und der Columbia University. Das Büro Diller + Scofidio wurde 1979 gegründet, Renfro kam als Partner 2004 hinzu. Das Büro beschreibt seine Tätigkeit wie folgt: „DS + R ist ein interdisziplinär zusammenarbeitendes Büro, das sich mit Architektur, bildender und darstellender Kunst beschäftigt." Zu den von DS + R ausgeführten Projekten gehören das Brasserie-Restaurant im Seagram Building (New York, 2000), die Aussichtsplattformen am Ground Zero in Manhattan (2001), das Blur Building (Expo 02, Yverdon-les-Bains, Schweiz, 2002) und das Institute of Contemporary Art in Boston (2006). Zu den neueren abgeschlossenen Projekten zählen die Sanierung des Lincoln Center for the Performing Arts in New York, zu dem auch der Erweiterungsbau der Juilliard School of Music (2009) gehört, und die Renovierung der Alice Tully Hall (2009). Hinzu kamen öffentliche Freiräume auf dem gesamten Campus des Lincoln Center for the Performing Arts und die Rasenfläche auf dem Hypar Pavilion (2011, hier vorgestellt), außerdem die Umwandlung der High Line, einer 2,4 Kilometer langen ehemaligen Hochbahnstrecke, in einen Park mitten in New York City (Bauabschnitt 1, 2009, Bauabschnitt 2, 2011) und das Creative Arts Center an der Brown University (Providence, Rhode Island, 2011), alle in den USA, sofern nicht anders angegeben.

Née à Łódź (Pologne) en 1954, **ELIZABETH DILLER** est titulaire d'un B.Arch. de l'École d'architecture de la Cooper Union (1979). Elle est professeur d'architecture à l'université de Princeton. **RICARDO SCOFIDIO**, né à New York en 1935, est diplômé de l'École d'architecture de la Cooper Union et de l'université Columbia. Il est aujourd'hui professeur émérite d'architecture à la Cooper Union. **CHARLES RENFRO**, né à Baytown (Texas) en 1964, est diplômé de l'université Rice et de l'université Columbia. Renfro a rejoint en 2004 l'agence Diller + Scofidio, fondée en 1979. Ils se décrivent ainsi : « DS+R est une agence interdisciplinaire collaborative qui se consacre à l'architecture, aux arts visuels et aux arts du spectacle. » Elle a réalisé, entre autres, le restaurant Brasserie du Seagram Building (New York, 2000) ; la plateforme d'observation de Ground Zero à Manhattan (2001) ; le Blur Building de l'Exposition nationale suisse de 2002 (Yverdon-les-Bains) et l'Institute of Contemporary Art de Boston (Massachusetts, 2006). Parmi ses projets récents aux États-Unis figurent : le projet de redéveloppement du Lincoln Center à New York, comprenant l'extension de la Juilliard School of Music (2009), la rénovation de l'Alice Tully Hall (2009), divers espaces publics et la Hypar Pavilion Lawn (2011, publiée ici) ; la transformation en parc de la High Line à New York, une section de voie ferrée suspendue de 2,4 km (Phase 1, 2009 ; Phase 2, 2011) et le Creative Arts Center de l'université Brown (Providence, Rhode Island, 2011).

HYPAR PAVILION LAWN

New York, New York, USA, 2011

Address: 142 West 65th Street, New York, NY 10023, USA
Area: 670 m². Client: Lincoln Center for the Performing Arts. Cost: not disclosed
Collaboration: FXFowle (Executive Architect), Ove Arup & Partners (Structural & MEP Engineers),
Mathews Nielsen Landscape Architects (Landscape Architect)

As part of their ongoing Lincoln Center for the Performing Arts Redevelopment project, Diller Scofidio + Renfro designed "a twisting lawn that acts as an occupiable grass roof over a glass pavilion restaurant." The **HYPAR LAWN** is located in Lincoln Center's North Plaza and is oriented away from the noise of the city "to create a bucolic urbanism." The geometry of the lawn directly corresponds to the contoured wood ceiling of the restaurant below, framing views to the plaza and the street. A tall fescue mixed with Kentucky bluegrass was chosen for the lawn because of its durability. The increased thermal mass of the grass roof dramatically reduces the mechanical loads of the restaurant below. Water is drained through the structural columns underneath the lawn surface.

Für das noch nicht abgeschlossene Sanierungsprojekt des Lincoln Center for the Performing Arts hat das Büro Diller Scofidio + Renfro eine „in sich gewundene, schräge Rasenfläche entworfen, die als benutzbares Rasendach auf einem verglasten Pavillon mit Restaurant dient". Der **HYPAR LAWN** befindet sich an der North Plaza des Lincoln Centers. Er liegt vom Lärm der Stadt abgewendet, um eine Atmosphäre des „bukolischen Urbanismus" zu schaffen. Die Gestalt der Rasenfläche folgt den Konturen der Holzdecke des darunter befindlichen Restaurants und bietet Ausblicke auf die Plaza und die Straße. Aus Gründen der Widerstandsfähigkeit wurde als Rasen eine Mischung aus hohem Schwingelgras (Festuca) und Wiesenrispengras (Poa pratensis) gewählt. Dank der thermischen Eigenschaften des Rasendachs wird im darunterliegenden Restaurant der Energiebedarf deutlich reduziert. Das Wasser wird durch die tragenden Stützen unterhalb der Rasenfläche abgeleitet.

Dans le cadre du projet (en cours) de redéveloppement du Lincoln Center, l'agence Diller Scofidio + Renfro a conçu une « pelouse inclinée praticable servant de toiture à un pavillon de verre qui abrite un restaurant ». L'**HYPAR LAWN** est située sur la place nord du Lincoln Center, à l'écart du bruit de la ville, pour « créer un urbanisme bucolique ». Le plan de la pelouse correspond exactement à celui du plafond en bois du restaurant qu'elle couvre et offre différentes vues sur la place et la rue. L'herbe est un mélange de fétuque élevée et de pâturin des prés, tous deux choisis pour leur résistance. La masse thermique élevée du toit végétalisé réduit de façon spectaculaire les besoins mécaniques du restaurant en matière d'énergie. L'eau de pluie est drainée par des colonnes structurelles installées sous la surface de la pelouse.

Above, the tilted, grass-covered roof is placed above the restaurant and opposite a reflecting pond with a work by Henry Moore placed at its center.

Oben das geneigte Rasendach auf dem Restaurant und davor eine spiegelnde Wasserfläche mit einer Skulptur von Henry Moore in der Mitte.

Ci-dessus, la toiture inclinée semée de gazon recouvre le restaurant. Devant, le bassin est animé en son centre par une œuvre d'Henry Moore.

The lawn adds readily usable leisure space to an otherwise rather strict and largely mineral square. The grass roof also, of course, serves to reduce energy requirements for the restaurant.

Die Rasenfläche bietet einen weiteren, gut nutzbaren Erholungsraum in einer sonst mit ihrem Plattenbelag ziemlich strengen Platzanlage. Das Rasendach reduziert zudem den Energiebedarf des Restaurants.

La pelouse offre un espace de détente parfaitement utilisable à l'intérieur d'une place aux contours assez stricts et à l'esprit minéral. La toiture végétalisée permet de réduire la consommation énergétique du restaurant.

VLADIMIR DJUROVIC

Vladimir Djurovic Landscape Architecture (VDLA)
Villa Rizk
Broumana
Lebanon

Tel: +961 4 862 444/555
Fax: +961 4 862 462
E-mail: info@vladimirdjurovic.com
Web: www.vladimirdjurovic.com

VLADIMIR DJUROVIC was born to a Serb father and a Lebanese mother in 1967. He received a degree in Horticulture from Reading University in England in 1989 and his M.A. in Landscape Architecture from the University of Georgia in 1992, after having worked at EDAW in Atlanta. Vladimir Djurovic Landscape Architecture (VDLA) was created in 1995 in Beirut, Lebanon. The office has participated in and won several international competitions, such as Freedom Park South Africa (2003). They have completed numerous private residences in Lebanon, including the F House (with Nabil Gholam; Dahr El Sawan, 2000–04). The firm won a 2008 Award of Honor in the residential design category from the American Society of Landscape Architects (ASLA) for its Bassil Mountain Escape project in Faqra (Lebanon). After the work on the award-winning Samir Kassir Square (Beirut, 2004, published here), current work includes the landscaping of the Wynford Drive site in Toronto (Canada) to accommodate the Aga Khan Museum by Fumihiko Maki and the Ismaili Centre by Charles Correa. VDLA won the international competition for this design in 2006. Other current work includes the Salame Residence (Faqra, Lebanon, 2009); Beirut Marina (Solidere, BCD, Lebanon; architect: Steven Holl); Beirut Terraces (Solidere, BCD, Lebanon; architect: Herzog & de Meuron); 3 Beirut (Solidere, BCD, Lebanon; architect: Foster + Partners); and the Hariri Memorial Garden (Beirut, 2005–11).

VLADIMIR DJUROVIC wurde 1967 als Sohn eines serbischen Vaters und einer libanesischen Mutter geboren. 1989 schloss er sein Studium mit einem Hochschulabschluss in Gartenbau an der Universität Reading in England ab. 1992, nachdem er im Büro EDAW in Atlanta gearbeitet hatte, machte er seinen Master in Landschaftsarchitektur an der Universität von Georgia. 1995 gründete er in Beirut im Libanon sein Büro Vladimir Djurovic Landscape Architecture (VDLA). Das Büro hat an verschiedenen internationalen Wettbewerben teilgenommen und sie gewonnen, wie z. B. 2003 beim Freedom Park in Pretoria, Südafrika. Zu den Projekten des Büros gehören zahlreiche Aufträge für den privaten Wohnungsbau im Libanon, u. a. das Haus F (mit Nabil Gholam, Dahr El Sawan, 2000–04). 2008 gewann das Büro für sein Projekt Bassil Mountain Escape in Faqra, Libanon, den Ehrenpreis der American Society of Landscape Architects (ASLA) in der Kategorie Wohnhausdesign. Nach dem preisgekrönten Entwurf für den Samir-Kassir-Platz (Beirut, 2004, hier vorgestellt) arbeitete Djurovic an der Landschaftsgestaltung des Wynford-Drive-Geländes in Toronto, Kanada, auf dem das von Fumihiko Maki entworfene Aga-Khan-Museum sowie das Ismaili Centre von Charles Correa errichtet werden. Das Büro VDLA gewann 2006 den internationalen Wettbewerb für diesen Entwurf. Weitere Projekte im Libanon sind das Wohnhaus Salame (Faqra, 2009), der Jachthafen von Beirut (Solidere, BCD, Architekt: Steven Holl), die Beirut Terraces (Solidere, BCD, Architekt: Herzog & de Meuron), 3 Beirut (Solidere, BCD, Architekt: Foster + Partners) und die Gedenkstätte Hariri Memorial Garden (Beirut, 2005–11).

VLADIMIR DJUROVIC, né d'un père serbe et d'une mère libanaise en 1967, est titulaire d'un diplôme d'horticulture de l'université de Reading (GB, 1989). Il a obtenu un M.A. en architecture du paysage à l'université de Géorgie (1992) après avoir travaillé dans l'agence EDAW à Atlanta. L'agence Vladimir Djurovic Landscape Architecture (VDLA) a été fondée en 1995 à Beyrouth. Elle a remporté plusieurs concours internationaux, dont celui du Freedom Park en Afrique du Sud (2003), et a réalisé de nombreuses résidences privées au Liban, dont la F House (Dahr El Sawan, 2000–04, avec Nabil Gholam). En 2008, elle a reçu le prix d'honneur dans la catégorie « projets résidentiels » de l'American Society of Landscape Architects (ASLA) pour la retraite de montagne Bassil à Faqra, au Liban. Après avoir remporté un prix pour la place Samir Kassir (Beyrouth, 2004, publiée ici), l'agence travaille actuellement sur les aménagements paysagers du site de Wynford Drive à Toronto (Canada), qui regroupe le musée de l'Aga Khan de Fumihiko Maki et l'Ismaili Centre de Charles Correa. VDLA en avait remporté le concours international en 2006. Parmi ses autres projets figurent la Salame Residence (Faqra, Liban, 2009) ; la marina de Beyrouth (Solidere, BCD, Liban, architecte : Steven Holl) ; Beirut Terraces (Solidere, BCD, Liban, architectes : Herzog & de Meuron) ; 3 Beirut (Solidere, BCD, Liban, architectes : Foster + Partners) et le jardin-mémorial Hariri (Beyrouth, 2005–11).

SAMIR KASSIR SQUARE

Beirut, Lebanon, 2004

Site area: 815 m². Client: Solidere (Société Libanaise de Développement et Reconstruction)
Cost: $322 000. Collaboration: Vladimir Djurovic (Principal), Paul De Mar Yousef (Design Architect),
Salim Kanaan (Project Architect)

Vladimir Djurovic has a decidedly minimalist style in his gardens and **SAMIR KASSIR SQUARE** is no exception. Located in the recently redeveloped Beirut Central District, the small park was conceived around two existing ficus trees that had somehow managed to survive the violence that wracked Beirut for years. "The challenge of this project," says Djurovic, "was to create a quiet refuge on a limited piece of land surrounded by buildings, while addressing the prominent street frontage that it occupies. In essence, to become a small escape dedicated to the city and its people." A raised "water mirror" is a central feature of the square, faced by a 20-meter-long solid stone bench. This project was a winner of the 2007 Aga Khan Award for Architecture. The jury citation reads: "The Samir Kassir Square is a restrained and serene urban public space that skillfully handles the conditions and infrastructure of its location in a city that has undergone rapid redevelopment. The Award will go to Vladimir Djurovic, the pre-eminent landscape architect working in Lebanon today."

Vladimir Djurovics Gärten zeichnen sich durch einen minimalistischen Stil aus, und der **SAMIR-KASSIR-PLATZ** ist keine Ausnahme. Der im sanierten Zentrum von Beirut gelegene Park wurde um zwei Feigenbäume herum geplant, die erstaunlicherweise die jahrelang in Beirut wütende Gewalt überstanden haben. Djurovic zufolge lag „die Herausforderung des Projekts darin, einen Zufluchtsort auf einem engen, von Gebäuden umstandenen Grundstück zu schaffen und dabei die prominente Straßenfront des Platzes zu gestalten; im Grunde sollte es ein kleiner Zufluchtsort für die Stadt und ihre Bewohner werden". Ein erhöhter „Wasser-Spiegel" ist zentraler Blickpunkt des Platzes, der von einer 20 m langen Steinbank flankiert wird. Das Projekt wurde 2007 mit dem Aga-Khan-Preis für Architektur ausgezeichnet. Die Jury merkte an: „Der Samir-Kassir-Platz ist ein zurückgenommener und heiterer öffentlicher Platz, der gekonnt mit den Bedingungen und der Infrastruktur seines Standorts in einer Stadt umgeht, die sich rasch verändert hat. Der Preis geht an Vladimir Djurovic, den herausragendsten heute im Libanon praktizierenden Landschaftsarchitekten."

Le style des jardins de Vladimir Djurovic est résolument minimaliste et la **PLACE SAMIR-KASSIR** n'y fait pas exception. Situé dans le centre récemment reconstruit de Beyrouth, ce petit square a été conçu autour de deux ficus sauvés des violences qui dévastèrent la ville pendant des années. « Le défi de ce projet, explique Djurovic, était de créer un refuge sur une parcelle de terrain de dimensions limitées et entourée d'immeubles, tout en traitant son importante façade sur rue. Fondamentalement, l'idée était de réaliser un lieu dédié à la ville et à ses habitants. » Un « miroir d'eau » surélevé est l'élément central du projet, face à un banc de pierre massive de 20 m de long. Ce projet a remporté le prix d'architecture Aga Khan 2007. La citation du jury précisait : « La place Samir-Kassir est un espace public limité et serein qui s'adapte avec talent aux conditions et à l'infrastructure de sa situation dans une ville qui connaît un développement rapide. Le prix ira à Vladimir Djurovic, le plus éminent architecte paysagiste œuvrant actuellement au Liban. »

A central feature of the square are two ficus trees that symbolize the continuity of the place, in spite of all the events that have marked the history of Beirut in recent years.

Zentrale Elemente des Platzes sind zwei Feigenbäume – Symbol der Kontinuität des Ortes, allen Ereignissen zum Trotz, die die Geschichte Beiruts in den vergangenen Jahren geprägt haben.

Une des caractéristiques importantes de ce square est la présence de deux anciens ficus qui symbolisent la permanence du lieu, malgré les événements rècents qui ont marqué l'histoire de Beyrouth.

Vladimir Djurovic carefully juxtaposes different materials and textures, combining stone with water and trees, as these images show.

Mit Bedacht stellt Vladimir Djurovic kontrastierende Materialien und Texturen einander gegenüber, kombiniert Stein mit Wasser und Bäumen, wie diese Bilder zeigen.

Vladimir Djurovic a juxtaposé avec finesse différents matériaux et textures en assemblant pierre, eau et arbres.

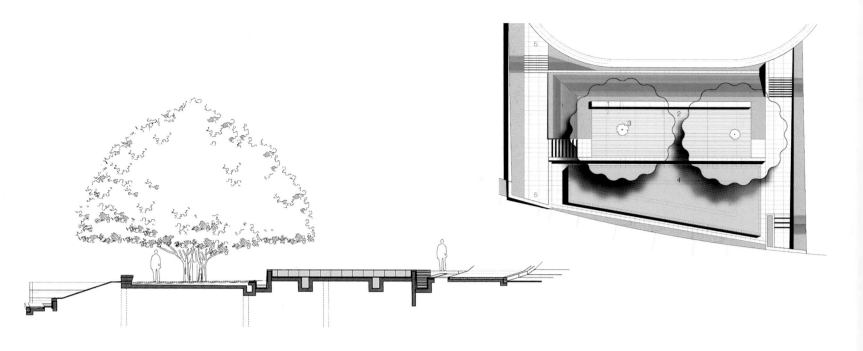

Dominated by its two old trees, the square uses the sound of water to create a haven of peace in the middle of the city.

Der von den zwei Bäumen beherrschte Platz wird dank des plätschernden Wassers zum friedlichen Zufluchtsort mitten in der Stadt.

Dominé par ses deux vieux arbres, le jardin profite du bruit de l'eau, créant un havre de paix au cœur de la ville.

La Baronia House

DRN ARCHITECTS

dRN Architects
Isidora Goyenechea 3200
Santiago
Chile

Tel: +56 2 231 4114
E-mail: contacto@drn.cl
Web: www.drn.cl

dRN Architects was established in 2005 by **NICOLÁS DEL RÍO** and **MAX NÚÑEZ** in Santiago, Chile. Born in Santiago in 1975, Nicolás del Río studied at the Universidad Católica de Chile, obtaining his degree in 2001. He also studied at the Politecnico di Milano (Italy, 1998–99) and obtained a Master's degree in Sustainable Design from Oxford Brookes University, UK, in 2010. Since 2005 he has taught a first-year design studio at the Universidad Andrés Bello (Santiago). Born in Santiago in 1976, Max Núñez received his M.Arch degree from the Universidad Católica de Chile in 2004 and an M.Arch degree from Columbia University, New York, in 2010. He also studied prior to that at the Politecnico di Milano (1998–99). Since 2005 he has taught a second-year design studio at the Universidad Andrés Bello in Santiago. Their work includes the Skibox (Portillo, 2006); Mountain Refuge Chalet C6 (Portillo, 2006); Mountain Refuge Chalet C7 (Portillo, 2008); Beach House (Cerro Tacna, 2008); Los Canteros Mountain Refuge (Farellones, 2008); Beach House (Cachagua, 2009); La Baronia House (Quintero, V Region, 2009, published here); and the House at Punta Chilen (Chiloé Island, X Region, 2009, also published here), all in Chile.

Das Büro dRN Architects wurde 2005 von **NICOLÁS DEL RÍO** und **MAX NÚÑEZ** in Santiago de Chile gegründet. Der 1975 in Santiago geborene Nicolás del Río studierte an der Universidad Católica de Chile, wo er 2001 seinen Abschluss machte, außerdem am Politecnico di Milano (Italien, 1998–99); den Master in nachhaltigem Entwerfen erwarb er 2010 an der Brookes University im britischen Oxford. Seit 2005 unterrichtet er den Anfängerkurs in Entwerfen an der Universidad Andrés Bello (Santiago). Max Núñez, 1976 in Santiago geboren, machte 2004 seinen M.Arch. an der Universidad Católica de Chile sowie 2010 einen M.Arch. an der Columbia University, New York. Davor studierte er auch am Politecnico di Milano (1998–99). Seit 2005 unterrichtet er den zweiten Kurs im Entwerfen an der Universidad Andrés Bello in Santiago. Zu den Bauten des Büros zählen die Skibox (Portillo, 2006), die Berghütte Chalet C6 (Portillo, 2006), die Berghütte Chalet C7 (Portillo, 2008), ein Ferienhaus in Cerro Tacna (2008), die Berghütte Los Canteros (Farellones, 2008), ein Ferienhaus in Cachagua (2009), das Wohnhaus La Baronia (Quintero, V. Region, 2009, hier vorgestellt) und ein Wohnhaus in Punta Chilen (Insel Chiloé, X. Region, 2009, ebenfalls hier vorgestellt), alle in Chile.

L'agence dRN Architects a été fondée en 2005 par **NICOLÁS DEL RÍO** et **MAX NÚÑEZ** à Santiago du Chili. Né à Santiago en 1975, Nicolás del Río a étudié à l'Université catholique du Chili, dont il est diplômé (2001), au Politecnico de Milan (1998–99), et a obtenu un mastère en conception durable de l'université Brookes à Oxford (GB) en 2010. Depuis 2005, il enseigne en première année d'atelier de conception à l'université Andrés Bello (Santiago). Né à Santiago en 1976, Max Núñez a passé son diplôme d'architecture à l'Université catholique du Chili en 2004 et avait étudié précédemment au Politecnico de Milan (1998–99). Depuis 2005, il enseigne en seconde année d'atelier de conception à l'université Andrés Bello de Santiago. Parmi leurs réalisations, toutes au Chili : la Skibox (Portillo, 2006) ; le refuge de montagne C6 (Portillo, 2006) ; le refuge de montagne C7 (Portillo, 2008) ; une maison de plage (Cerro Tacna, 2008) ; le refuge de montagne de Los Canteros (Farellones, 2008) ; une maison de plage (Cachagua, 2009) ; la maison La Baronia (Quintero, Vᵉ Région, 2009, publiée ici) et la maison de Punta Chilen (île de Chiloé, Xᵉ Région, 2009, également publiée ici).

LA BARONIA HOUSE

Quintero, Valparaíso, Chile, 2009

Address: not disclosed
Area: 150 m². Client: not disclosed. Cost: not disclosed

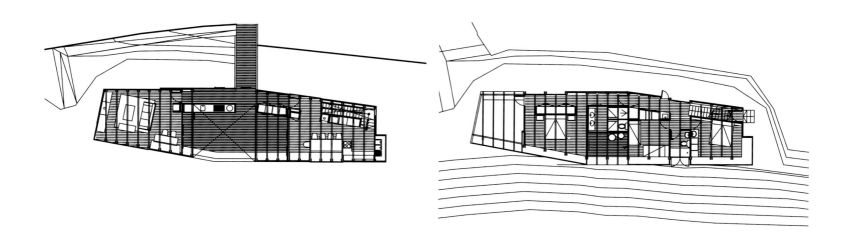

Dominating the coastline, the house has ample glazed surfaces. The light bridge that leads to the entrance affirms the maritime vocabulary employed.

Das die Küste dominierende Haus hat reichlich verglaste Flächen. Die leichte Erschließungsbrücke unterstreicht die Anwendung eines maritimen Vokabulars.

Dominant le littoral, la maison possède de généreuses surfaces vitrées. La passerelle légère qui conduit à l'entrée confirme le vocabulaire maritime utilisé par l'architecte.

Set up above the shore, the house has something of the appearance of a beached ship in the image to the left. Drawings show the slightly angled forms.

Das Foto links zeigt, dass das hoch über dem Ufer stehende Haus einem gestrandeten Schiff ähnelt. An den Zeichnungen sind seine etwas eckigen Formen ablesbar.

Implantée au-dessus de la côte, la maison fait un peu penser à un bateau échoué (image de gauche). Les plans donnent le détail de sa forme légèrement inclinée.

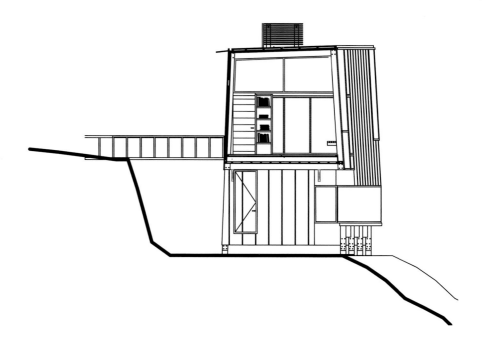

This unusual residence sits on a hill above the ocean in an exposed position. The architects took this location as the theme for their design in some sense, noting that the "corroding power of the salty breeze coming from the Pacific Ocean can wear out an unprotected structure in a short period of time. Here the breaking waves are not a romantic vision of nature but a very crude reality of the temporal condition of architecture." Their solution was to cover a good part of the house in pre-weathered Cor-ten steel while allowing views to the ocean through generous glazed surfaces. The interior of the structure is made of bolted wooden frames, and is intended to be flexible enough to be converted to different uses over time. Thus the surface of this house is harder and stronger than its interior, an inversion of the usual relation between skin and structure.

Dieses ungewöhnliche Wohnhaus steht exponiert auf einem Berg hoch über dem Ozean. Die Architekten wählten diesen Standort in gewisser Weise als Thema für ihren Entwurf und erwähnen: „Die starke Korrosion kann durch die salzhaltigen Winde vom Pazifischen Ozean ein ungeschütztes Bauwerk in kurzer Zeit zerstören. Hier ist die Brandung keine romantische Naturerscheinung, sondern harte Realität im Hinblick auf die Lebensdauer eines Gebäudes." Ihre Lösung bestand darin, einen Großteil des Hauses mit Corten-Stahl zu verkleiden, aber den Ausblick zum Ozean durch großzügige Verglasung freizugeben. Die innen liegende, verschraubte Holzkonstruktion soll flexibel genug sein, um sich später veränderter Nutzung anpassen zu lassen. So ist die Außenfläche des Hauses härter und widerstandsfähiger als sein innen liegendes Tragwerk – eine Umkehr des üblichen Verhältnisses zwischen Außenhaut und Konstruktion.

Cette curieuse maison implantée sur la crête d'une falaise au-dessus de l'océan occupe une position très exposée. En un sens, les architectes ont pris ce lieu pour thème, notant que « le pouvoir de corrosion de la brise de mer salée venant de l'océan Pacifique peut venir à bout d'une construction non protégée en une brève période de temps ». La solution choisie a été d'habiller une bonne partie de la maison d'acier Corten prépatiné, ce qui permet par ailleurs d'ouvrir de grandes baies vitrées vers l'océan. L'ossature est en poutres de bois boulonnées, système assez flexible pour prévoir des évolutions de la maison dans le futur. La « surface » est donc plus dure et plus solide que l'intérieur, inversion de la relation habituelle entre peau et structure.

Broad windows wrap around a bed-room, providing dramatic views of the ocean in the wood-framed structure.

Große Fenster umgeben einen Schlaf-raum und bieten aus der Holzrahmen-konstruktion dramatische Ausblicke auf den Ozean.

Un bandeau de fenêtres devant l'ossature en bois entoure une des chambres qui bénéficie ainsi de vues spectaculaires sur l'océan.

Bathroom and dining areas are also open to waterside views. A drawing shows the slightly cantilevered form of the house and its insertion into the sharply sloped site.

Auch das Bad und der Essbereich öffnen sich zu Ausblicken auf das Wasser. Eine Zeichnung zeigt die leicht auskragende Form des Hauses und seine Einfügung in das steile Hanggrundstück.

Comme les coins-repas, la salle de bains ouvre également sur l'océan. Un dessin montre le léger porte-à-faux de la maison et son insertion dans la pente marquée.

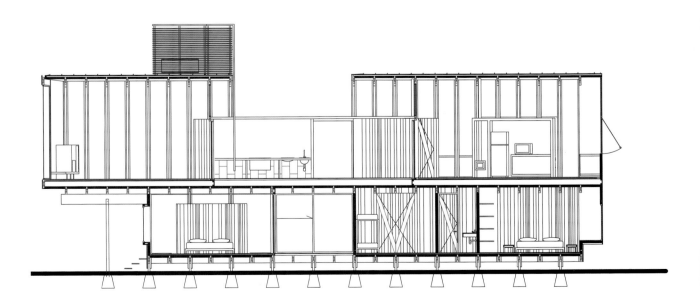

HOUSE AT PUNTA CHILEN

Chiloé Island, Lake District, Chile, 2009

Address: not disclosed
Area: 276 m². Client: not disclosed. Cost: not disclosed

Chiloé is a large island located off the coast of Chile. This house is set at the tip of a peninsula on a site that offers residents a 360° view. The Andes and no less than eight volcanoes can be seen in the distance. The architects state: "A rhythmic repetition of columns on the first floor carries the structure to the perimeter and generates changing shadows on the interiors. The oblique shape of the Cor-ten steel roof on the second floor defines an irregular perimeter opposed to the flat line of the horizon." Within its protective shell of steel and glass, the interior of the house is entirely clad in wood, again generating a contrast between the skin or shell of the architecture and its gentler interior.

Chiloé ist eine große, der Küste von Chile vorgelagerte Insel. Dieses Haus steht dort an der Spitze einer Halbinsel auf einem Grundstück, das den Bewohnern einen Rundblick von 360 Grad bietet. In der Ferne sind die Anden und nicht weniger als acht Vulkane zu sehen. Die Architekten erklären: „Eine rhythmische Wiederholung der Stützen im Erdgeschoss führt um das ganze Gebäude und erzeugt wechselnde Schatten im Innern. Die schräge Form des Dachs aus Corten-Stahl auf dem Obergeschoss erzeugt einen unregelmäßigen Umriss im Gegensatz zur flachen Linie des Horizonts." Innerhalb seiner schützenden Hülle aus Stahl und Glas ist das Haus vollkommen mit Holz verkleidet, wodurch wiederum ein Gegensatz zwischen Haut oder Hülle des Gebäudes und seinem freundlicheren Innern entsteht.

Chiloé est une grande île qui fait face à la côte du Chili. La maison s'élève à l'extrémité d'une péninsule et offre une vue panoramique à 360°. On peut apercevoir dans le lointain les Andes et pas moins de huit volcans. « La répétition rythmique des colonnes au rez-de-chaussée, qui soutiennent la construction dans son périmètre génère un jeu d'ombres mouvantes à l'intérieur. La forme en oblique du toit en acier Corten dessine un tracé irrégulier qui s'oppose à la ligne de l'horizon », expliquent les architectes. Protégé par cette coque de verre et d'acier, l'intérieur entièrement habillé de bois provoque un contraste entre la rigueur vigoureuse de l'extérieur et l'aspect plus chaleureux de l'intérieur.

Both generously glazed, the two levels of the house as seen from this angle form a base with a lighter, perched element placed above.

In diesem Blickwinkel bilden die beiden großzügig verglasten Ebenen des Hauses eine Basis für ein daraufgesetztes, leichteres Element.

Tous deux généreusement vitrés, les deux niveaux de la maison vus sous cet angle semblent former le socle d'un élément perché plus léger.

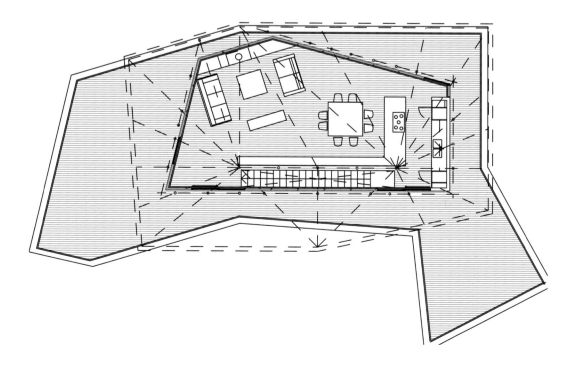

The upper-level deck and the sloped roof take on unexpected forms and the entire house offers a broad view of the water.

Die Terrasse auf der oberen Ebene und das geneigte Dach zeigen unge- wöhnliche Formen; das ganze Haus ist zum Wasser hin weit geöffnet.

La terrasse du niveau supérieur et les versants de la toiture prennent des formes inattendues. La maison toute entière offre de vastes panoramas de l'océan.

With its full-height glazing contrasting with the wooden ceiling and floor,
the house appears to be entirely open
to its natural surroundings.

*Mit seiner geschosshohen Verglasung
im Gegensatz zu den hölzernen
Decken und Böden erscheint das
Haus vollkommen zu seiner natürlichen Umgebung geöffnet.*

À travers ses murs entièrement
vitrés, qui contrastent avec les sols
et les plafonds en bois, la maison
semble s'ouvrir entièrement vers
son cadre naturel.

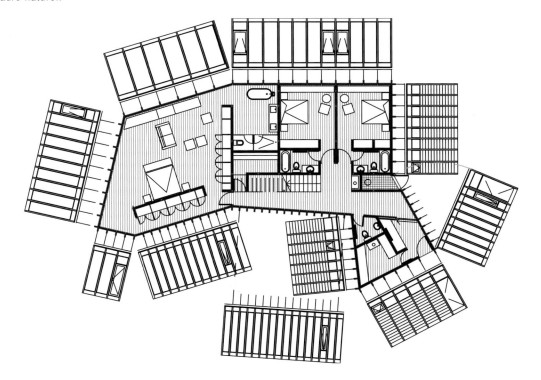

Even the bathroom and bathtub have
fully glazed windows with views to
the water.

Sogar aus dem Badezimmer und der
Wanne hat man durch die großen
Glasfenster Ausblicke auf das Wasser.

Même la salle de bains possède un
mur entièrement vitré qui donne sur
l'océan.

Aside from the metallic supports
and railings, the house makes a
broad use of wood, from the floors
to the underside of the roof.

Abgesehen von den Metallstützen
und -geländern wurde im Haus
überwiegend Holz verwendet, von
den Böden bis zur Dachunterseite.

Mis à part les piliers métalliques et
les rampes, la maison utilise essentiellement le bois pour les sols ou les
sous-faces de la toiture.

DUMAY + FONES + VERGARA

Dumay + Fones + Vergara Architects
Ernesto Pinto Lagarrigue 156 Of. F
Barrio Bellavista
8420492 Santiago
Chile

Tel: +56 2 735 0417
Fax: +56 2 735 0417
E-mail: contacto@ftres.cl
Web: www.ftres.cl

ALEJANDRO DUMAY CLARO was born in Santiago, Chile, in 1977. **NICOLÁS FONES CLARO** was also born in Santiago in 1977, as was **FRANCISCO VERGARA ARTHUR**. They all graduated from the Faculty of Architecture of Mayor University (Santiago, 2002). In 2005, they created their own firm, F3, recently renamed to Dumay + Fones + Vergara. Their work, either collective or individual, includes the Lake Rupanco House (2005); the moveable Minga House (2005); the Hotel Equidomos (Pisco Elqui, 2005); the María Pinto House (María Pinto, 2006); the Fuente Nueva Chapel (Lake Rupanco, 2006, published here); and the Emilia Tellez Building (Santiago, 2006), all in Chile.

ALEJANDRO DUMAY CLARO wurde ebenso wie **NICOLÁS FONES CLARO** und **FRANCISCO VERGARA ARTHUR** 1977 in Santiago de Chile geboren. Alle drei beendeten 2002 ihr Studium an der Architekturfakultät der Universidad Mayor in Santiago. 2005 gründeten sie ihr eigenes Büro, F3, das kürzlich in Dumay + Fones + Vergara umbenannt wurde. Zu ihren individuellen oder gemeinsamen Arbeiten zählen das Haus am Rupanco-See (2005), das mobile Haus Minga (2005), das Hotel Equidomos (Pisco Elqui, 2005), ein Haus in María Pinto (2006), die Kapelle Fuente Nueva (Rupanco-See, 2006, hier vorgestellt) und das Edificio Emilia Tellez (Santiago, 2006), alle in Chile.

ALEJANDRO DUMAY CLARO est né à Santiago du Chili en 1977, comme **NICOLÁS FONES CLARO** et **FRANCISCO VERGARA ARTHUR**. Tous trois sont diplômés de la faculté d'architecture de l'université Mayor (Santiago, 2002). En 2005, ils ont créé leur agence, F3, qui a récemment pris le nom de Dumay + Fones + Vergara. Toutes au Chili, leurs réalisations, collectives ou individuelles, comprennent : la maison du lac Rupanco (2005) ; la maison mobile Minga (2005) ; l'hôtel Equidomos (Pisco Elqui, 2005) ; la maison à María Pinto (María Pinto, 2006) ; la chapelle de Fuente Nueva (Lac Rupanco, 2006, publiée ici) et l'immeuble Emilia Tellez (Santiago, 2006).

FUENTE NUEVA CHAPEL

Lake Rupanco, Lake District, Chile, 2006

Area: 21 m². Client: not disclosed
Cost: not disclosed

Located in southern Chile, this project is set on a three-hectare site near Lake Rupanco. The austere chapel with a capacity for twelve people was built with simple materials at a low cost. The architects conceived of it "as a totality without differentiation of structural elements (walls, ceilings, windows)." Impregnated pine paneling is used on the exteriors, while, according to the architects, "inside, the image of the altar is provided by the landscape itself, the lake and the mountains; this defines the orientation of the volume and its direction." A shrine and two niches for sculptures designed by the owner are set in the north façade. A terrace forms the entrance to the chapel and somewhat expands its presence within the natural setting.

Dieser Bau steht auf einem 3 ha großen Gelände am Rupanco-See im Süden Chiles. Die in nüchterner Form gestaltete Kapelle, die zwölf Personen fasst, wurde zu geringen Kosten aus einfachen Materialien errichtet. Die Architekten konzipierten sie „als Gesamtform ohne Differenzierung der Konstruktionselemente (Wände, Decken, Fenster)". Für die Außenwände wurden Paneele aus imprägniertem Kiefernholz verwendet, während, laut Aussage der Architekten, „innen die Ansicht des Altars von der Landschaft, dem See und den Bergen gebildet wird. Diese bestimmen auch die Orientierung des Gebäudes und seine Stellung." Ein Schrein und zwei Nischen für vom Besitzer gestaltete Skulpturen befinden sich an der Nordseite. Eine Terrasse bildet den Eingang zur Kapelle und erweitert ein wenig ihre Präsenz innerhalb des natürlichen Umfelds.

Cette chapelle est érigée sur un terrain de 3 ha près du lac Rupanco situé dans le sud du Chili. Cette petite construction austère d'une capacité de douze personnes a été réalisée avec un budget modeste et des matériaux simples. Les architectes l'ont conçue comme « une totalité, sans différenciation entre les éléments structurels (murs, plafonds, fenêtres) ». L'extérieur est en panneaux de pin imprégné tandis que, « à l'intérieur, l'image du mur de l'autel est fournie par le paysage même, le lac et les montagnes, ce qui définit l'orientation du volume ». Un petit autel et deux niches pour des sculptures dessinées par le propriétaire ont été prévus dans la façade nord. L'entrée est signalée par une terrasse qui renforce encore la présence de l'édifice dans son cadre naturel.

The use of solid wood in this exceptional setting makes the chapel quite unusual, despite the use of a form that is apparently quite "ordinary."

Die Anwendung von Massivholz an diesem besonderen Standort macht die Kapelle außergewöhnlich, trotz ihrer scheinbar „gewöhnlichen" Form.

Le recours au bois massif dans ce cadre exceptionnel fait l'originalité de cette chapelle malgré sa forme apparemment classique.

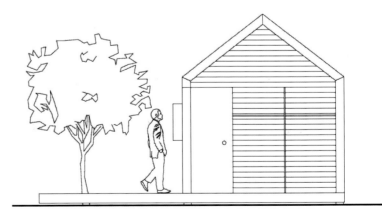

Drawings of the structure and the photo to the left show its scale and simple design.

Die Zeichnungen vom Gebäude und das Foto links lassen Maßstab und die schlichte Gestaltung erkennen.

Les dessins et la photo de gauche montrent l'échelle et la simplicité de ce projet.

The notched entrance to the chapel, with the simple bell, emphasizes the austerity of the structure and signals its function.

Der zurückgesetzte Eingang zur Kapelle und die schlichte Glocke betonen die Strenge des Gebäudes und verweisen auf seine Funktion.

La découpe de l'entrée de la chapelle et sa petite cloche font ressortir l'austérité de la construction tout en signalant sa fonction.

Closer views show that the planks used in the platform continue right over the walls and roof of the chapel, leaving room for protruding windows.

Bei näherer Betrachtung zeigt sich, dass die für die Plattform verwendeten Bretter sich über die Wände und das Dach der Kapelle fortsetzen und Platz für vorkragende Fenster lassen.

Des vues rapprochées montrent que les planches de la terrasse sont dans l'alignement précis de celles des murs et de la toiture de la chapelle, ne s'interrompant que pour les avancées des fenêtres.

ECOSISTEMA URBANO

Ecosistema Urbano Arquitectos
Estanislao Figueras 6
Madrid 28008
Spain

Tel/Fax: +34 915 59 16 01
E-mail: info@ecosistemaurbano.com
Web: www.ecosistemaurbano.com

ECOSISTEMA URBANO was created in 2000 by Belinda Tato, born in Madrid in 1971, who studied at the ETSA of Madrid (1999) and the Bartlett School of Architecture, London (1996), and Jose Luis Vallejo, born in Bilbao in 1971, who also studied at the ETSAM (1999) and Bartlett School (1996). Currently the team is involved in research projects concerning the future of city design that they call "eco-techno-logical cities," financed by the Spanish Ministry of Industry. They are working on several urban proposals for different Spanish municipalities (in the spirit of the Ecoboulevard of Vallecas in Madrid, Spain, 2006, published here). One of their projects, Air Tree – Madrid Pavilion Public Space, represented Madrid at Shanghai Expo 2010 in China. They have also worked on an Internet network (ecosistemaurbano.org, 2007–10); Ecópolis Plaza, Rivas Vaciamadrid (Madrid, Spain, 2009–10); and are currently developing Stortorget, the main public square of Hamar in Norway ("DreamHamar," 2011–).

Gegründet wurde **ECOSISTEMA URBANO** 2000 von Belinda Tato, geboren 1971 in Madrid, Studium an der ETSA Madrid (1999) und der Bartlett School of Architecture, London (1996), sowie von Jose Luis Vallejo, geboren 1971 in Bilbao, Studium ebenfalls an der ETSAM (1999) und der Bartlett School (1996). Derzeit ist das Team beteiligt an Forschungsprojekten zur Zukunft der Stadtplanung – sogenannter „öko-techno-logischer Städte" –, gefördert vom spanischen Ministerium für Industrie. Das Büro arbeitet an einer Reihe von Stadtplanungsentwürfen für verschiedene spanische Gemeinden (wie den Ecoboulevard in Vallecas, Madrid, 2006, hier vorgestellt). Ein Projekt des Büros – Air Tree, Pavillon der Stadt Madrid – vertrat Madrid auf der Expo 2010 in Schanghai. Das Team entwickelte außerdem ein Internet-Netzwerk (<ecosistemaurbano.org>, 2007–10), entwarf die Ecópolis Plaza, Rivas Vaciamadrid (Madrid, 2009–10) und arbeitet aktuell an einem Entwurf für den Stortorget, den alten Marktplatz in Hamar in Norwegen („DreamHamar", seit 2011).

ECOSISTEMA URBANO a été fondé en 2000 par Belinda Tato, née à Madrid en 1971 où elle a étudié à l'ETSA (1999), après l'École d'architecture Bartlett de Londres (1996), et Jose Luis Vallejo, né à Bilbao en 1971, qui a également étudié à l'ETSAM (1999) et à l'École Bartlett (1996). L'équipe participe actuellement à des projets de recherche sur l'avenir du design urbain baptisés « eco-techno-logical cities » et financés par le ministère espagnol de l'Industrie. Ils travaillent à plusieurs projets urbains pour différentes municipalités en Espagne (dans l'esprit de l'Écoboulevard de Vallecas à Madrid, 2006, publié ici), l'un d'entre eux – Árbol de Aire, l'Arbre d'air, Madrid, pavillon de l'Espace public – a représenté Madrid à l'Expo de Shanghai 2010. Ils ont également collaboré à un réseau Internet (ecosistemaurbano.org, 2007–10) ; à Ecópolis Plaza, Rivas Vaciamadrid (Madrid, 2009–10) et sont en train de développer Stortorget, la principale place de Hamar, en Norvège (« DreamHamar », 2011–).

ECOBOULEVARD OF VALLECAS

Madrid, Spain, 2006

Site area: 22 500 m²
Client: Empresa Municipal de Vivienda y Suelo de Madrid
Cost: € 2.6 million

According to the architects: "The proposal for the **ECOBOULEVARD OF VALLECAS** can be defined as an operation of urban recycling that consists of the installation of three socially revitalizing air trees placed in the existing urban pattern, the densification of trees within their existing concourse, the reduction and asymmetric disposition of the traffic routes…" The "air trees," powered with photovoltaic cells, are considered "temporary prostheses," to be dismantled, "leaving remaining spaces that resemble forest clearings." The architects were selected through a competition with a social and environmental program intended to improve daily life in the area. The "air trees" occupy space that should eventually be populated with mature real trees and are intended as gathering places. The "air trees" contain a system that uses water vapor with power generated by the photovoltaic cells to create a space that is "8° to 10ºC cooler than the rest of the street in summer."

Die Architekten erklären: „Der Entwurf für den **ECOBOULEVARD IN VALLECAS** lässt sich als urbane Recyclingoperation definieren, bei der drei sozial stimulierende ‚Luftbäume' in ein bestehendes urbanes Raster integriert werden, sowie als Steigerung der Baumdichte in ihrer unmittelbaren Umgebung und zugleich als Reduzierung und asymmetrische Verschiebung der Verkehrswege …" Die mit Solarzellen betriebenen „Luftbäume" sind als „temporäre Prothesen" gedacht, die letztendlich wieder abgebaut werden und „Räume entstehen lassen, die an Waldlichtungen erinnern". Den Zuschlag erhielten die Architekten im Rahmen eines sozial und umweltpolitisch orientierten Wettbewerbs, dessen Ziel es war, den Alltag im Stadtviertel zu verbessern. Die „Luftbäume" besetzen Flächen, auf denen später große Bäume gepflanzt werden sollen, und dienen als Treffpunkte. Die Bäume sind mit Solarzellen zur Stromerzeugung und einem Wasserzerstäubungssystem ausgestattet. So entsteht ein Ort, der „im Sommer 8 bis 10 ºC kühler ist als der übrige Teil der Straße".

« La proposition de l'**ECOBOULEVARD DE VALLECAS** peut se définir comme une opération de recyclage urbain qui consiste en l'installation de trois "arbres d'air" insérés dans le tissu urbain, censés dynamiser les relations sociales. Ils s'accompagnent d'une densification des plantations d'arbres existantes, ainsi que d'une réduction et d'une implantation en asymétrie des axes de circulation… », expliquent les architectes. Ces « arbres d'air », alimentés par des cellules photovoltaïques, sont considérés comme des « prothèses temporaires » prévues pour être ultérieurement démantelées « en laissant les espaces subsistants ressembler à des clairières en forêt ». Les architectes ont été retenus, après concours, sur un programme social et environnemental destiné à améliorer la vie quotidienne du quartier. Les « arbres d'air » occupent un espace qui sera sans doute planté ultérieurement d'arbres venus à maturité, et deviendra un lieu public agréable. Ils contiennent un système de diffusion de vapeur d'eau dont l'énergie est fournie par des cellules photovoltaïques pour créer un volume dont la température est de « 8 à 10 °C plus basse que le reste de la rue en été ».

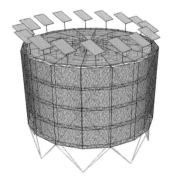
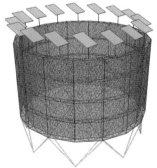

The sculptural installations of Ecosistema Urbano are arrayed in the central area of an avenue, providing islands of coolness and greenery in the dry city of Madrid.

Die skulpturalen Installationen von Ecosistema Urbano sind auf der Mittelachse einer Allee angeordnet und schaffen kühle, grüne Inseln inmitten der Trockenheit von Madrid.

Les installations sculpturales d'Ecosistema Urbano se répartissent le long de la zone centrale du boulevard. Ils constituent des îlots de fraîcheur et de verdure dans l'air sec de Madrid.

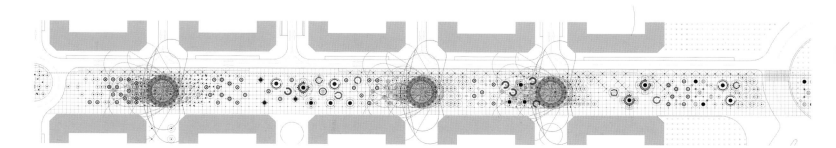

The round volumes of the pavilions house nothing but vegetation and serve no "real" purpose in the usual sense of architecture. They might thus be compared to ecological sculptures.

In den runden Baukörpern der Pavillons sind ausschließlich Pflanzen untergebracht, sie dienen keinem „wirklichen" Zweck im üblichen architektonischen Sinn. Man könnte sie also als ökologische Skulpturen verstehen.

Les volumes circulaires des pavillons n'abritent que de la végétation mais ne répondent à aucun objectif concret en termes d'architecture. On pourrait les comparer à des sculptures écologiques.

Another pavilion borrows its formal vocabulary from industrial architecture, but like the others is lifted off the ground, making it function like a tree or perhaps a wind chimney.

Ein weiterer Pavillon orientiert sich formal an industrieller Architektur, ist jedoch wie die übrigen über dem Boden aufgeständert und „funktioniert" am ehesten wie ein Baum oder Windturm.

Un autre pavillon emprunte son vocabulaire à l'architecture industrielle. Comme les autres, il est surélevé par rapport au sol, et opère comme un arbre, ou une cheminée à vent.

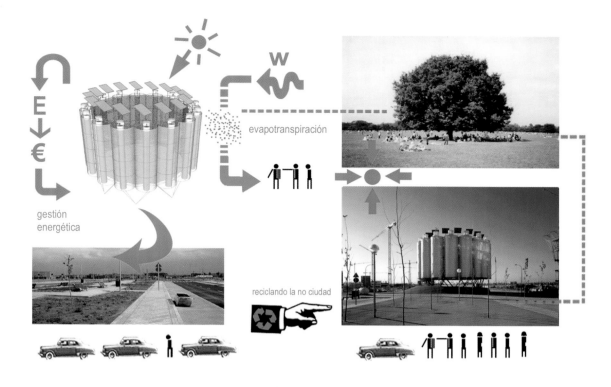

evapotranspiración

gestión energética

reciclando la no ciudad

FERCABER

SHUHEI ENDO

Shuhei Endo Architecture Institute
2–14–5 Tenma
Kita-ku
Osaka 530–0043
Japan

Tel: +81 6 6354 7456
Fax: +81 6 6354 7457
E-mail: endo@paramodern.com
Web: www.paramodern.com

Born in Shiga Prefecture, Japan, in 1960, **SHUHEI ENDO** obtained his Master's degree from the Kyoto City University of Art in 1986. He worked after that with the architect Osamu Ishii and established his own firm, the Shuhei Endo Architecture Institute, in 1988. His work has been widely published and he has received numerous prizes, including the Andrea Palladio International Prize in Italy (1993). He is currently Professor at the Graduate School of Architecture, Kobe University. His work includes Slowtecture S (Maihara, Shiga, 2002); Growtecture S (Osaka, 2002); Springtecture B (Biwa-cho, Shiga, 2002); Bubbletecture M (Maihara, Shiga, 2003); Rooftecture C (Taishi, Hyogo, 2003); Rooftecture H (Kamigori, Hyogo, 2004); and Bubbletecture O (Maruoka, Fukui, 2004). Along with Bubbletecture H (Sayo-cho, Hyogo, 2006–07, published here), he completed Slowtecture M (Miki-city, Hygo) and Rooftecture M's (Habikino City, Osaka) in 2007, all in Japan.

SHUHEI ENDO wurde 1960 in der japanischen Präfektur Shiga geboren. Nach seinem Masterabschluss an der Städtischen Kunsthochschule Kyoto im Jahr 1986 arbeitete er zunächst für den Architekten Osamu Ishii. 1988 gründete er seine eigenes Büro, das Shuhei Endo Architecture Institute. Endo hat zahlreiche Publikationen veröffentlicht und ist vielfach ausgezeichnet worden, u. a. mit dem Premio internazionale di architettura Andrea Palladio (1993). Gegenwärtig lehrt Endo als Professor an der Graduiertenfakultät für Architektur der Universität Kobe. Zu Endos realisierten Projekten gehören Slowtecture S (Maihara, Shiga, 2002), Growtecture S (Osaka, 2002), Springtecture B (Biwa-cho, Shiga, 2002), Bubbletecture M (Maihara, Shiga, 2003), Rooftecture C (Taishi, Hyogo, 2003), Rooftecture H (Kamigori, Hyogo, 2004) und Bubbletecture O (Maruoka, Fukui, 2004). Parallel zu Bubbletecture H (Sayo-cho, Hyogo, 2006–07, hier vorgestellt) entstanden 2007 Slowtecture M (Miki-city, Hygo, Japan) und Rooftecture M's (Habikino City, Osaka), alle Projekte in Japan.

Né dans la préfecture de Shiga au Japon en 1960, **SHUHEI ENDO** a obtenu son M.Arch de l'Université des arts de Tokyo en 1986. Il a ensuite travaillé pour l'architecte Osamu Ishii et fondé sa propre agence, Shuhei Endo Architecture Institute, en 1988. Son œuvre a été largement publiée et a reçu de nombreuses distinctions, dont le prix Andrea Palladio International en Italie (1993). Il enseigne actuellement à l'École supérieure d'architecture de l'université de Kobé. Parmi ses réalisations : Slowtecture S (Maihara, Shiga, 2002) ; Growtecture S (Osaka, 2002) ; Springtecture B (Biwa-cho, Shiga, 2002) ; Bubbletecture M (Maihara, Shiga, 2003) ; Rooftecture C (Taishi, Hyogo, 2003) ; Rooftecture H (Kamigori, Hyogo, 2004) et Bubbletecture O (Maruoka, Fukui, 2004). Parallèlement à Bubbletecture H (Sayo-cho, Hyogo, 2006–07, publiée ici), il a achevé Slowtecture M (Miki-city, Hygo) et Rooftecture M's (Habikino City, Osaka) en 2007.

BUBBLETECTURE H

Sayo-cho, Hyogo, Japan, 2006–07

Address: 679-5148, 1-chome, Hikarityou, Sayo, Sayo-gun 330-3, Hyogo, Japan,
+81 79 158 20 65, www.eco-hyogo.jp/taikenkan/
Area: 968 m². Client: Hyogo Prefecture. Cost: not disclosed

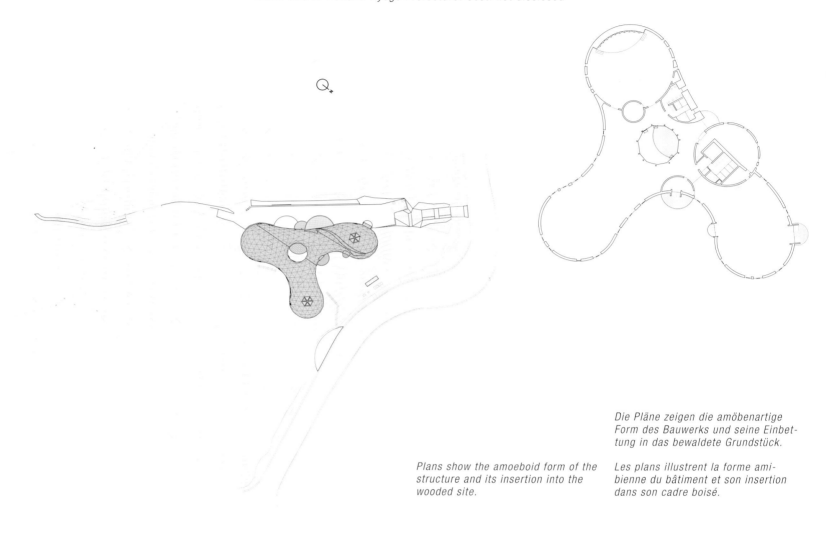

Die Pläne zeigen die amöbenartige Form des Bauwerks und seine Einbettung in das bewaldete Grundstück.

Plans show the amoeboid form of the structure and its insertion into the wooded site.

Les plans illustrent la forme amibienne du bâtiment et son insertion dans son cadre boisé.

This is a one-story structure located on a 5000-square-meter site in a mountainous region some two hours from Osaka. The program includes the education of adults and children on environmental issues and advances in "green" technology. Set on a steep slope near a forest, the structure was designed to have the minimum possible impact on the environment. A three-dimensional truss structure in Japanese cypress is covered with 1.2-millimeter-thick weather-resistant Cor-ten steel that does not rust after the initial finishing process. The roof was designed to allow the growth of mosses. A waiting room and office are included in the structure, as well as the public exhibition or teaching space. The architect stresses that this unusual form is directly related to the program and also to his desire to protect the site as much as possible during and after construction.

Endos eingeschossiger Kuppelbau namens Bubbletecture H liegt auf einem 5000 m² großen Grundstück in einer bergigen Region zwei Fahrtstunden außerhalb von Osaka. Genutzt wird das Gebäude u. a. für Lehrveranstaltungen, in denen Erwachsene und Kinder mit „grünen Technologien" vertraut gemacht werden. Der Architekt hat bei seinem Entwurf darauf geachtet, dass der auf einem steil abfallenden Gelände in unmittelbarer Waldnähe errichtete Bau die Natur so wenig wie möglich beeinträchtigt. Er entwickelte eine dreidimensionale Trägerstruktur aus japanischem Zypressenholz, die mit 1,2 mm dicken Stahlplatten mit ähnlichen Eigenschaften wie Cor-ten-Stahl umhüllt wurde, die nach der Bewitterung nicht weiter rosten können. Dafür kann und soll auf dem Dach Moos anwachsen. Neben dem für Bildungsveranstaltungen und öffentliche Ausstellungen genutzten Raum umfasst das Gebäude außerdem einen Aufenthaltsraum und ein Büro. Wie der Architekt betont, hat sich die ungewöhnliche Form einerseits unmittelbar aus dem Nutzungskonzept ergeben, andererseits aus seinem Wunsch, das Gelände während und nach dem Bau so weit wie möglich zu schonen.

Cette construction d'un seul niveau a été édifiée sur un terrain de 5000 m² dans une région montagneuse à deux heures d'Osaka. Le programme portait sur un centre de formation d'adultes et d'enfants aux enjeux environnementaux et aux progrès des technologies « vertes ». Implanté sur un terrain très incliné à proximité d'une forêt, le projet a été conçu pour exercer le plus faible impact possible sur l'environnement. La structure porteuse tridimensionnelle en cyprès du Japon est recouverte d'une tôle d'acier de type Corten de 1,2 mm d'épaisseur dont l'oxydation se stabilise rapidement. Le toit a été conçu pour permettre la croissance de mousse. On trouve à l'intérieur du bâtiment une salle d'attente, un bureau, un espace destiné à l'enseignement et une salle d'expositions. L'architecte précise que la forme inhabituelle est une conséquence directe du programme et aussi de son désir de protéger le site autant que possible, aussi bien en cours du chantier qu'après.

Seen from ground level, the design seems to have a relation to the geodesic domes of Buckminster Fuller, albeit covered in this instance with pre-oxidized Cor-ten steel.

Vom Boden aus gesehen scheint der Entwurf eine gewisse Verwandtschaft zu den geodätischen Kuppeln Buckminster Fullers zu besitzen, wobei Endos Werk mit einer Hülle aus voroxidiertem Stahl versehen ist.

Vus du sol, ces dômes semblent proches de ceux de Buckminster Fuller, mais sont en fait recouverts de panneaux en acier Corten.

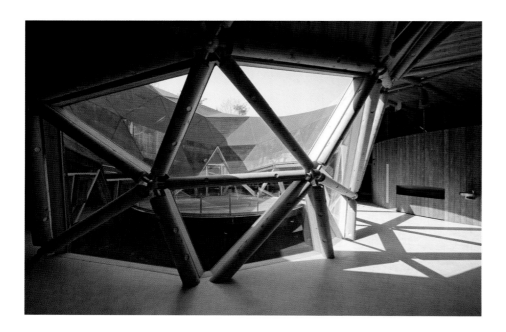

The bulbous forms of Endo's design are unexpected and surely make no effort to be fashionable in any traditional sense. Triangular windows bring natural light into this metal tent.

Die ungewöhnliche Knollenform ist sicherlich nicht darauf angelegt, im traditionellen Sinne „schick" zu sein. Durch dreieckige Fenster fällt Tageslicht in den metallenen Polyeder ein.

Les formes bulbeuses et inattendues du projet d'Endo ne font aucun effort pour être à la mode au sens traditionnel du terme. Des fenêtres triangulaires éclairent l'intérieur de cette tente de métal.

The triangulated space frame used to support the building allows the architect to create a column-free interior space. Elevations show how it fits into its hilly site.

Die Verwendung eines aus vielen einzelnen Dreiecken zusammengesetzten Raumfachwerks ermöglichte es dem Architekten, einen säulenfreien Innenraum zu schaffen. Die Aufrisse zeigen die Einbettung des Gebildes in das abschüssige Gelände.

La structure porteuse tridimensionnelle a permis à l'architecte de créer un volume intérieur sans colonne. Les élévations montrent la manière dont elle est adaptée au terrain.

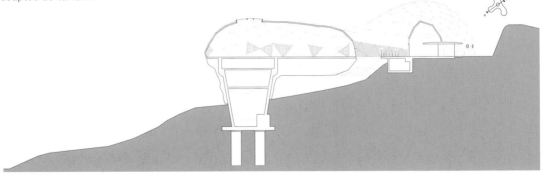

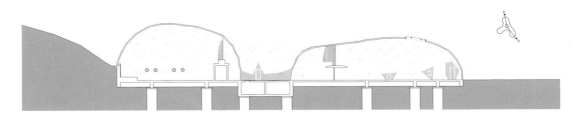

ETH-STUDIO MONTE ROSA /
BEARTH & DEPLAZES

ETH-Studio Monte Rosa, Faculty of Architecture, ETH Zurich
Wolfgang-Pauli-Str. 15
8093 Zurich
Switzerland

Tel: +41 44 633 36 10
Fax: +41 44 633 11 49
E-mail: baumgartner@arch.ethz.ch
Web: www.deplazes.arch.ethz.ch

Born in 1960 in Chur, Switzerland, **ANDREA DEPLAZES** graduated from the ETH Zurich in 1988. He cofounded the office Bearth & Deplazes in 1995 with **VALENTIN BEARTH.** He has been a professor of architecture and construction at the ETH Zurich since 1997. The Faculty of Architecture at the ETH Zurich is one of the largest and most highly reputed architecture schools in the world. In the summer of 2003 Andrea Deplazes was asked by Meinrad Eberle, the project manager for the 150th Anniversary Jubilee of the ETH Zurich to work on the development of a new hut for the Monte Rosa, near Zermatt (2008–09, published here). Over a period of four semesters, students in the **ETH-STUDIO MONTE ROSA** worked on several designs for the structure, settling on a "rock crystal" form. The project was developed as an interdisciplinary collaboration between the ETH Zurich, the Swiss Alpine Club (SAC), industry, and experts in construction in extreme environments.

ANDREA DEPLAZES, geboren 1960 in Chur in der Schweiz, beendete 1988 sein Studium an der ETH Zürich. Mit **VALENTIN BEARTH** gründete er 1995 das Büro Bearth & Deplazes. Seit 1997 ist er Professor für Architektur und Konstruktion an der ETH Zürich. Die Architekturfakultät der ETH Zürich ist eine der größten und renommiertesten Architekturschulen der Welt. Im Sommer 2003 wurde Andrea Deplazes von Meinrad Eberle, dem Manager der 150-Jahr-Feier der ETH Zürich, aufgefordert, an der Planung einer neuen Berghütte für den Monte Rosa bei Zermatt (2008–09, hier vorgestellt) mitzuarbeiten. Über einen Zeitraum von vier Semestern arbeiteten Studenten im **ETH-STUDIO MONTE ROSA** an mehreren Entwürfen für das Gebäude und entschieden sich für die Form eines „Bergkristalls". Das Projekt wurde in interdisziplinärer Zusammenarbeit von der ETH Zürich, dem Schweizer Alpen-Club (SAC), der Industrie und Experten für das Bauen an extremen Standorten entwickelt.

Né en 1960 à Chur, en Suisse, **ANDREA DEPLAZES** est diplômé de l'ETH (Zurich, 1988). En 1995, il fonde avec **VALENTIN BEARTH** l'agence Bearth & Deplazes, et enseigne l'architecture et la construction à l'ETH à Zurich depuis 1997. La faculté d'architecture de l'ETH est un des plus grands et plus réputés centres d'enseignement de l'architecture dans le monde. À l'occasion du 150ᵉ anniversaire de l'école en 2003, Meinrad Eberle, responsable de ce jubilé, a demandé à Andrea Deplazes de réfléchir à un nouveau refuge sur le mont Rose près de Zermatt (2008–09, publié ici). Pendant quatre semestres, les étudiants du **ETH-STUDIO MONTE ROSA** ont travaillé sur plusieurs projets et se sont arrêtés sur une forme en « cristal de roche ». La mise au point du projet a été l'objet d'une collaboration interdisciplinaire entre l'ETH Zurich, le Club alpin suisse, des entreprises et des experts spécialisés dans la construction en environnements extrêmes.

NEW MONTE ROSA HUT SAC

Zermatt, Switzerland, 2008–09

Address: "Untere Plattje" between the Monte Rosa and the Grenz Glacier (coordinates 629.146 / 089.553),
2883.50 m a.s.l., Zermatt, Valais, Switzerland, +41 27 967 21 15, www.neuemonterosahuette.ch
Area: 1154 m². Client: Swiss Alpine Club SAC. Cost: €4.3 million
Collaboration: Andrea Deplazes, Marcel Baumgartner (Project Manager),
Kai Hellat, Daniel Ladner

The **MONTE ROSA HUT**, owned by the Swiss Alpine Club, is a mountain hut located at the base of the Monte Rosa at an altitude of 2883 meters. It is the starting point for climbers trying to reach the Monte Rosa and other nearby peaks. The first hut was built on this site in 1895. The participants in the project analyzed the energy consumption of the original hut to see how they could improve the environmental impact of the new building. CO_2 emissions of the new structure are three times lower than those of the previous building, and 90 percent of its energy needs are provided by sunlight. Lead-acid accumulators provide power even during low sunlight periods. Construction materials brought up to the site by no less than 3000 helicopter lifts were selected for minimum environmental impact, and they can all be recovered from the site at the moment of demolition. Numerically controlled manufacturing methods were used to allow the creation of unique structural and cladding elements. The basic internal structure of the hut, which is set on a stainless-steel foundation, is made of wood, while the external shell is in aluminum.

Die **MONTE-ROSA-HÜTTE** des Schweizer Alpen-Clubs ist eine Berghütte in 2883 m Höhe am Fuß des Monte Rosa. Sie ist der Ausgangspunkt für Bergsteiger auf den Monte Rosa und die Gipfel der benachbarten Berge. Die erste Hütte wurde 1895 auf diesem Gelände errichtet. Die an diesem Projekt Beteiligten untersuchten den Energiebedarf der alten Hütte, um festzustellen, wie die Auswirkungen des Neubaus auf die Umwelt verringert werden könnten. Die CO_2-Emissionen der neuen Hütte sind dreimal niedriger als die des Altbaus, und 90 % ihres Energiebedarfs werden durch Sonnenlicht gedeckt. Bleisäure-Batterien liefern Strom auch in Perioden geringer Sonneneinstrahlung. Die mit nicht weniger als 3000 Helikopterflügen angelieferten Baumaterialien wurden nach dem Grad ihrer Umwelteinwirkung ausgewählt und können alle bei Abriss des Gebäudes wiederverwendet werden. Computergesteuerte Produktionsmethoden ermöglichten die Herstellung besonderer Konstruktions- und Verkleidungselemente. Das innen liegende Tragwerk der Hütte, die auf einem Edelstahlfundament steht, ist aus Holz, die Außenhülle aus Aluminium.

Le **REFUGE DU MONT ROSE**, propriété du Club alpin suisse, est situé à la base du mont, à 2883 m d'altitude. C'est le point de départ pour les alpinistes vers le mont Rose et d'autres sommets. Un premier refuge avait été construit en 1895. Les participants au projet ont analysé la consommation d'énergie de cette première construction pour voir comment ils pourraient améliorer l'impact environnemental de la nouvelle. Les émissions de CO_2 sont maintenant trois fois inférieures à celle du précédent refuge et 90 % de ses besoins énergétiques sont remplis par la lumière solaire. Des accumulateurs plomb-acide fournissent l'énergie pendant les périodes de faible intensité lumineuse. Les matériaux de construction livrés sur le site par pas moins de 3000 rotations d'hélicoptère, ont été sélectionnés pour leur impact environnemental minimal. Ils pourront tous être récupérés en cas de démolition. Des processus d'usinage à commande numérique ont été utilisés pour les éléments d'habillage de dimensions uniques. La structure interne de ce refuge est en bois, recouvert d'aluminium à l'extérieur, le tout reposant sur des fondations en acier inoxydable.

Set in the range of mountains near the Matterhorn, the Monte Rosa Hut is just barely visible in the image to the left.

Auf dem Foto links ist die Monte-Rosa-Hütte in der Bergkette am Matterhorn kaum zu erkennen.

Le refuge du mont Rose est à peine visible dans le majestueux panorama de la chaîne de montagnes du mont Cervin.

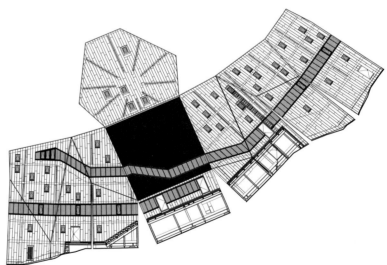

A topographical site plan, an "unfolded" drawing of the structure, and detail images above show how the use of wood is integrated into an extremely modern structure.

Ein topografischer Lageplan, eine „entfaltete" Zeichnung des Gebäudes und Detailfotos (oben) zeigen, wie das Material Holz in ein extrem modernes Bauwerk integriert wurde.

Le plan de la topographie du terrain, une représentation « dépliée » de la construction et les images de détails ci-dessus montrent comment le bois a été intégré dans cette construction extrêmement moderne.

The structure of the cabin is in wood, as are the interiors. Drawings show the floor plan and demonstrate how the building is anchored into its site.

Das Tragwerk der Hütte ist aus Holz, ebenso die Innenausstattung. Die Zeichnungen zeigen den Grundriss und die Einfügung des Bauwerks in das Gelände.

L'ossature est en bois, de même que les aménagements intérieurs. Les dessins montrent le plan au sol et l'ancrage du bâtiment dans son terrain.

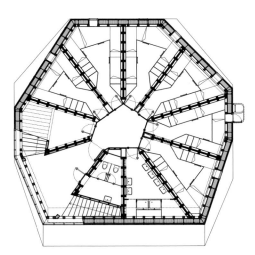

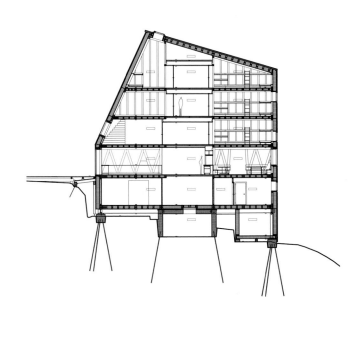

FELIX-DELUBAC

FELIX-DELUBAC architectes
7 Rue Moncey
75009 Paris
France

Tel: +33 1 49 70 04 62
E-mail: contact@felix-delubac-architectes.com
Web: www.felix-delubac-architectes.com

CHRISTIAN FÉLIX was born in 1972 in Cholet, France. He obtained his diploma as an architect from the École d'architecture de Paris-Villemin in 1999 and went to work in the office of Christian Hauvette in Paris. **LAETITIA DELUBAC** was born in 1975 in Paris and also obtained her degree at Paris-Villemin (1999). She worked with Valode & Pistre and Christian Hauvette before the creation of their firm. Their work includes the Ecolodge (Siwa, Egypt, 2006–07, published here); Ferdinand apartment (Paris, 2008); Laboratories for the CNRS and the Cemagref (with Christian Hauvette, Lyon, 2009); and two projects that are still in progress, the Washington apartment (Paris, 2010–); and a Passive House built with wood and a thatched roof (Normandy, 2010–), all in France unless stated otherwise.

CHRISTIAN FÉLIX wurde 1972 in Cholet, Frankreich, geboren. 1999 absolvierte er sein Diplom an der École d'architecture de Paris-Villemin und arbeitete anschließend im Büro von Christian Hauvette in Paris. **LAETITIA DELUBAC** wurde 1975 in Paris geboren, auch sie machte ihren Abschluss in Paris-Villemin (1999). Vor der Gründung des gemeinsamen Büros arbeitete sie bei Valode & Pistre und Christian Hauvette. Zu ihren Entwürfen zählen die Ecolodge (Siwa, Ägypten, 2006–07, hier vorgestellt), das Apartment Ferdinand (Paris, 2008), Labors für das CNRS und Cemagref (mit Christian Hauvette, Lyon, 2009) sowie zwei Projekte in Planung, das Apartment Washington (Paris, seit 2010) und ein Holz-Passivhaus mit Reetdach (Normandie, seit 2010), alle in Frankreich, sofern nicht anders angegeben.

CHRISTIAN FÉLIX, né en 1972 à Cholet (France), est diplômé de l'École d'architecture de Paris-Villemin (1999) et a travaillé chez Christian Hauvette à Paris. **LAETITIA DELUBAC**, née en 1975 à Paris, est diplômée du même établissement (1999). Elle a travaillé chez Valode & Pistre et Christian Hauvette. Parmi les réalisations de leur agence figurent l'Ecolodge (Siwa, Égypte, 2006–07, publiée ici) ; l'appartement Ferdinand (Paris, 2008) ; des laboratoires pour le CNRS et le Cemagref (avec Christian Hauvette, Lyon, 2009) et deux projets en cours : l'appartement Washington (Paris, 2010–) et une maison passive en bois à toit de chaume (Normandie, 2010–).

ECOLODGE

Siwa, Egypt, 2006–07

Area: 390 m². Client: not disclosed. Cost: not disclosed

The sketch and the covered seating area with a view on the water (below) demonstrate the relative simplicity of the design, blending with a sense of local materials and traditions.

Die Skizze und der überdachte Sitzbereich mit Blick aufs Wasser (unten) unterstreichen die Schlichtheit des Entwurfs, der von Gespür für lokale Materialien und Traditionen zeugt.

Le croquis et le séjour extérieur en bordure du lac (ci-dessous) illustrent la simplicité relative du projet qui fait appel à un sens certain des matériaux et des traditions locaux.

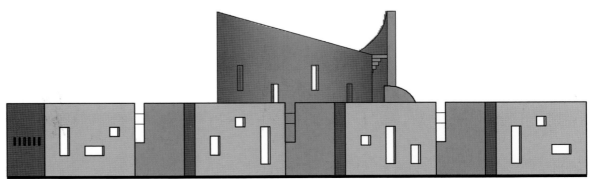

A drawing showing the emerging central volume and the image above with the colonnaded patio and basin again bring out the relation of the design to the regional use of courtyards in a similar vein.

Eine Zeichnung zeigt den aufragenden zentralen Baukörper, die Aufnahme oben den säulengesäumten Innenhof mit Wasserbecken. Beide belegen einmal mehr den Bezug des Entwurfs zu regionalen Bauformen mit ähnlichen Hofanlagen.

Élévation de façade montrant la manière dont le volume central semble jaillir. Au-dessus, le patio à péristyle et le bassin rappellent eux aussi des pratiques architecturales régionales.

The retreat and guesthouse in the desert is located on the peninsula of the Siwa Oasis on a 35 x 35-meter site. The architects state: "We have chosen to dilate the project in order to cover the plot completely. This allows us to provide as many patios as guest rooms, a closed courtyard, and garden; so many quiet places facing the desert." Four different façades offer four different points of view. The living room to the north opens onto a pergola that looks over the salt lake. Guest rooms on the west look out at the Adrere Amellal, while the southern façade with the staff quarters has minimal openings. The garden and swimming pool are located to the west. Walls are made of kershef, a local material made from mud, sand, and sun-dried salt. No electricity is used in the house, while a wind tower with a viewing terrace contains the owner's suite.

Das Feriendomizil und Gästehaus liegt auf einem 35 x 35 m großen Grundstück in der Wüste, auf der Halbinsel der Siwa-Oase. Die Architekten führen aus: „Wir haben uns entschieden, das Projekt zu erweitern, um die Gesamtfläche des Grundstücks vollständig zu nutzen. Das erlaubte uns, für jedes Gästezimmer eigene Terrassen anzulegen, einen geschlossenen Innenhof und einen Garten und damit eine Vielzahl stiller Orte mit Blick auf die Wüste." Vier verschiedene Fassaden bieten vier verschiedene Ansichten. Der nach Norden gelegene Wohnraum öffnet sich zu einer Pergola und überblickt den Salzsee. Die westlichen Gästezimmer haben Blick auf Adrere Amellal, während die Südfassade, hinter der die Personalräume liegen, nur minimale Öffnungen hat. Garten und Swimmingpool liegen nach Westen hin. Die Wände bestehen aus *kershef*, einem regionaltypischen Baumaterial aus Lehm, Sand und sonnengetrocknetem Salz. Im gesamten Haus gibt es keinen Strom, die Räume des Hausherrn mit Aussichtsterrasse liegen in einem Windfängerturm.

Cette maison d'hôtes dans le désert se trouve sur la péninsule de l'oasis de Siwa. Elle occupe un terrain de 35 x 35 m. « Nous avons choisi de dilater le projet afin d'occuper la totalité de la parcelle, expliquent les architectes, ce qui nous a permis de créer un patio par chambres d'hôtes, une cour fermée et un jardin, autant de lieux tranquilles face au désert. » Les quatre façades différenciées offrent quatre points de vue différents. Le séjour au nord ouvre sur une pergola qui donne sur le lac salé. Les chambres d'hôtes situées à l'ouest regardent vers la butte calcaire de l'Adrere Amellal tandis que la façade sud, derrière laquelle se trouvent les installations pour le personnel, ne possède que peu d'ouvertures. Le jardin et la piscine sont à l'ouest. La tour du vent soutenant une terrasse d'observation abrite la suite du propriétaire. Les murs sont en *kershef*, matériau de la région fait de boue, de sable et de sel séchés au soleil. L'Ecolodge n'utilise pas d'électricité.

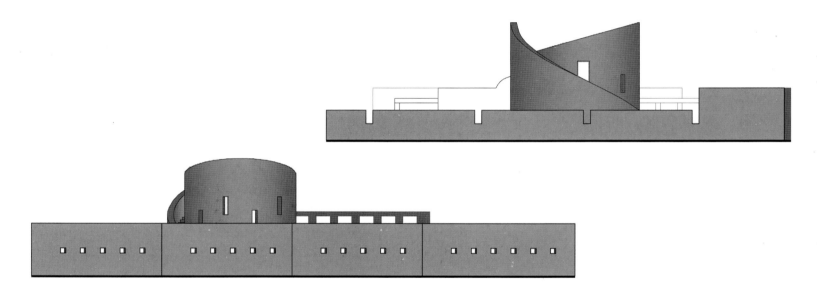

A plan (right) shows the angled, largely rectilinear forms of the design, centered on the circular, spiraling central element. Covered passages and numerous courtyards fill the allotted site, making use of materials that are typical in more rural Egyptian settings.

Der Grundriss rechts illustriert die schiefwinkligen, zumeist linearen Formen des Entwurfs, in dessen Zentrum ein spiralförmig-runder Baukörper steht. Laubengänge und Innenhöfe ziehen sich durch das gesamte Grundstück. Gearbeitet wurde mit Materialien, die typisch für ländlichere Gegenden Ägyptens sind.

Le plan de droite montre la répartition des chambres implantées en biais autour de l'élément central en spirale. Les différentes parties sont reliées par de nombreuses cours et passages couverts. Les matériaux sont typiques de l'Égypte rurale.

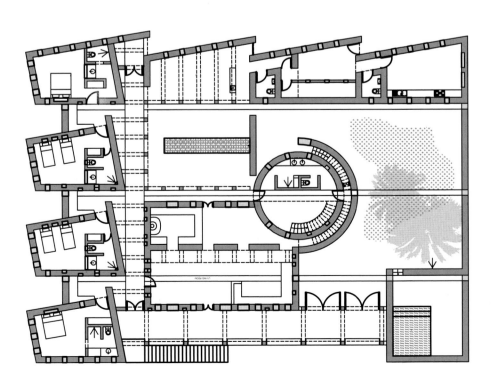

Shaded interior spaces provide comfortable refuge from the heat of the desert. Materials such as rope, earthen walls, and wooden furniture complement the natural aspect of the architecture.

Schattige Innenräume sind ein angenehmer Rückzugsort vor der Hitze der Wüste. Materialien wie Seile, Lehmwände oder Holzmöbel unterstreichen den natürlichen Charakter der Architektur.

Des espaces intérieurs abrités permettent de se protéger de la chaleur du désert. Les matériaux comme la terre des murs, le bois des meubles ou la corde participent à l'aspect naturel de cette architecture.

A dining area and pool on this page reflect the atmosphere of protected comfort that the architects have fashioned using simple and largely ecologically sensitive materials.

Essbereich und Pool auf dieser Seite sind Beispiele für den geschützten Komfort, den die Architekten mit schlichten und vorwiegend ökologischen Materialien geschaffen haben.

La salle à manger et la piscine sur cette page reflètent une atmosphère de confort protecteur que les architectes ont su créer en recourant à des matériaux simples et en grande partie écologiques.

FLOAT

Float Architectural Research and Design
Erin Moore
Architecture Department
University of Oregon
210 Lawrence Hall
1206 University of Oregon
Eugene, OR 97403
USA

Tel: +1 520 400 2900
E-mail: erin@floatarch.com
Web: www.floatwork.com

Erin Moore graduated from Smith College, Northampton, Massachusetts (1996) and received her M.Arch degree from the University of California, Berkeley (2003). She worked with Van Der Ryn Architects (Sausalito, California, 2002–03), Ibarra Rosano Design Architects (Tucson, 2003–05), and Line and Space Architects in Tucson (2005–06), before founding **FLOAT** Architectural Research and Design, where she has been the principal since 2006. She is an Assistant Professor in the Architecture Department of the University of Oregon since 2008. Her work includes Floodspace, research and design (ongoing, in collaboration with Simi Hoque Ph.D., Massachusetts Institute of Technology); Rainette Verte, a studio in Bordeaux (France; design in development); the Watershed (Willamette Valley, Oregon, 2006–07, published here); and CEK Cabin (Tenakee Springs, Alaska, remodel, 2008).

Erin Moore graduierte am Smith College, Northampton, Massachusetts (1996) und erhielt ihren M. Arch. an der University of California-Berkeley (2003). Sie arbeitete für Van Der Ryn Architects (Sausalito, Kalifornien, 2002–03), Ibarra Rosano Design Architects (Tucson, 2003–05) und Line and Space Architects in Tucson (2005 bis 2006), bevor sie das Büro **FLOAT** Architectural Research and Design gründete, dessen Chefin sie seit 2006 ist. Seit 2008 ist sie Dozentin an der Fakultät für Architektur der Universität Oregon. Zu ihren Projekten zählen Floodspace, Forschung und Gestaltung (eine Kooperation mit Simi Hoque Ph. D., Massachusetts Institute of Technology), Rainette Verte, ein Studio in Bordeaux (Frankreich, Entwurf in der Entwicklung), Watershed (Willamette Valley, Oregon, 2006–07, hier vorgestellt) sowie CEK Cabin (Tenakee Springs, Alaska, Umbau, 2008).

Erin Moore, diplômée de Smith College, Northampton, Massachusetts, en 1996, a obtenu son M.Arch de l'université de Californie-Berkeley en 2003. Elle a travaillé avec Van Der Ryn Architects à Sausalito, Californie, de 2002 à 2003, Ibarra Rosano Design Architects à Tucson de 2003 à 2005, et Line and Space Architects à Tucson de 2005 à 2006, avant de fonder **FLOAT** Architectural Research and Design, qu'elle dirige depuis 2006. Elle est professeur assistante au département d'Architecture de l'université de l'Oregon depuis 2008. Parmi ses réalisations : Floodspace, recherche et projet (en cours, en collaboration avec Simi Hoque Ph.D., Massachusetts Institute of Technology) ; Rainette Verte, un studio à Bordeaux (France – en cours) ; le Watershed (Willamette Valley, Oregon, 2006–07, publié ici) et la CEK Cabin (Tenakee Springs, Alaska, rénovation, 2008).

WATERSHED

Willamette Valley, Oregon, USA, 2006–07

Area: 6.5 m². Client: not disclosed
Cost: not disclosed

This writing studio for a philosophy professor and nature writer (the mother of Erin Moore) is a project intended to "engage architecture with ecology." The first request of the client was to be able to hear rain falling on the roof of the structure. Located in the watershed of the Marys River, the structure is designed to make visitors aware of local plant and animal life—for example with small tunnels beneath the Watershed that encourage reptiles and amphibians to come into view. A water collection basin serves as a front step, but also attracts birds and deer. Built without road access, without electricity on site, and without significant excavation, the structure is both removable and recyclable. The Watershed was built with poured-on-site concrete foundation piers, topped by a steel frame. Cedar planks are bolted to the frame and can be individually removed and replaced.

Bei dieser Schreibwerkstatt für eine Philosophieprofessorin und Naturschriftstellerin (Erin Moores Mutter) geht es um „die Verbindung von Architektur und Ökologie". Erste Vorgabe der Auftraggeberin war der Wunsch, den Regen auf das Hausdach fallen hören zu können. Das Häuschen liegt an der Wasserscheide des Marys River und soll Besuchern die Pflanzen- und Tierwelt der Gegend vor Augen führen – etwa durch kleine Tunnel unter dem Watershed, die Reptilien und Amphibien anlocken. Ein Wasserbecken dient als Eingangsstufe und zieht zugleich Vögel und Wild an. Der Bau hat keinen Zufahrtsweg, keine Stromanschlüsse und wurde ohne substanziellen Erdaushub realisiert, ist demontierbar und recycelbar. Gebaut wurde die Hütte mit vor Ort gegossenen Gründungspfeilern aus Beton, auf die ein Stahlrahmen gesetzt wurde. Zedernholzbohlen wurden auf den Rahmen geschraubt. Sie lassen sich einzeln entfernen und austauschen.

Ce petit studio pour une femme professeur de philosophie et écrivain sur le thème de la nature (mère d'Erin Moore) est un projet qui veut « intégrer l'architecture à l'écologie ». La première demande de la cliente était d'entendre la pluie tomber sur le toit. Située dans le bassin hydrographique de la Marys River, la construction prend en compte les plantes et la vie animale. Par exemple, de petits tunnels ont été prévus sous la maison pour les reptiles et les amphibiens. Le bassin de collecte des eaux sert de seuil, mais attire aussi les oiseaux et les daims qui viennent y boire. Construit sans voie d'accès ni branchement à l'électricité et sans que le sol ait été creusé significativement, cette maisonnette est à la fois déplaçable et recyclable. Son ossature en acier s'appuie sur des pieux en béton coulé sur place. Les planches de cèdre vissées sur l'ossature peuvent être facilement démontées et remplacées.

The Watershed can be seen as a
minimal form of shelter in a natural
environment. Aside from its four
small concrete foundation piers, the
house actually sits above the earth.

Das Watershed-Projekt lässt sich als
ein aufs Minimum reduzierter Schutzraum in der Landschaft verstehen.
Abgesehen von den vier kleinen
Gründungspfeilern aus Beton schwebt
das Haus über dem Boden.

Le Watershed peut s'interpréter
comme une forme d'abri minimal
isolé dans son environnement naturel. En dehors de ses quatre petits
pieux de fondation en béton, la maison est littéralement posée sur le sol.

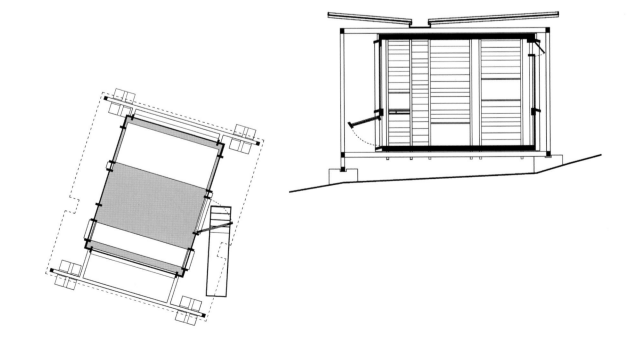

An observation point as much as a residence, the Watershed provides for generous views of the terrain, and the careful collection of rainwater (right).

Egal, ob man Watershed als Haus oder als Beobachtungsstation versteht, – es bietet rundum einen Ausblick ins Gelände. Auch Regenwasser wird hier gesammelt (rechte Seite).

Point d'observation aussi bien qu'habitation, le Watershed offre des vues généreuses sur la campagne et récupère avec soin l'eau de pluie (à droite).

NORMAN FOSTER

Foster + Partners
Riverside Three, 22 Hester Road
London SW11 4AN, UK

Tel: +44 20 77 38 04 55 / Fax: +44 20 77 38 11 07
E-mail: info@fosterandpartners.com
Web: www.fosterandpartners.com

Born in Manchester, UK, in 1935, **NORMAN FOSTER** studied architecture and city planning at Manchester University (1961). He was awarded a Henry Fellowship to Yale University, where he received his M.Arch degree and met Richard Rogers, with whom he created Team 4. He received the RIBA Gold Medal for Architecture (1983). He was knighted in 1990 and was honored with a Life Peerage in 1999. The American Institute of Architects granted him their Gold Medal for Architecture in 1994 and he was awarded the Pritzker Prize in 1999. Lord Norman Foster has notably built the IBM Pilot Head Office (Cosham, UK, 1970–71); Sainsbury Center for Visual Arts and Crescent Wing, University of East Anglia (Norwich, UK, 1976–77; 1989–91); Hong Kong and Shanghai Banking Corporation Headquarters (Hong Kong, 1981–86); Stansted Airport (Stansted, UK, 1987–91); the Commerzbank Headquarters (Frankfurt, 1994–97); Chek Lap Kok Airport (Hong Kong, 1995–98); the new German Parliament, Reichstag (Berlin, 1995–99); British Museum Redevelopment (London, 1997–2000); Millennium Bridge (London, 1996–2002); Petronas University of Technology (Seri Iskandar, Malaysia, 1999–2004); Chesa Futura (St. Moritz, Switzerland, 2000–04, published here); Millau Viaduct (Millau, France, 1993–2005); and Wembley Stadium (London, 1996–2006). More recent work includes Beijing Airport (China, 2003–08); Faustino Winery (Ribera del Duero, Spain, 2007–10); Masdar Institute (Abu Dhabi, UAE, 2008–10, also published here); Sperone Westwater (New York, 2009–10); Spaceport America (New Mexico, USA, 2009–12); and the master plan for the West Kowloon Cultural District (Hong Kong, 2009–).

NORMAN FOSTER wurde 1935 in Manchester geboren, wo er später Architektur und Stadtplanung studierte (1961). Ein Henry Fellowship ermöglichte ihm das Studium in Yale, wo er seinen M. Arch. absolvierte und Richard Rogers begegnete, mit dem er das Büro Team 4 gründete. Er wurde mit der RIBA-Goldmedaille für Architektur ausgezeichnet (1983), 1990 zum Ritter geschlagen und 1999 in den lebenslangen Adelsstand erhoben. 1994 verlieh ihm das American Institute of Architects die Goldmedaille für Architektur, 1999 erhielt er den Pritzker-Preis. Zu Lord Norman Fosters besonders hervozuhebenden Bauten zählen: der IBM-Hauptsitz in Cosham (Cosham, GB, 1970–71), das Sainsbury Center for Visual Arts und der Crescent Wing, Universität von East Anglia (Norwich, GB, 1976–77, 1989–91), der Hauptsitz der Hong Kong and Shanghai Banking Corporation (Hongkong, 1981–86), der Flughafen Stansted (GB, 1987–91), der Hauptsitz der Commerzbank (Frankfurt/Main, 1994 bis 1997), der Flughafen Chek Lap Kok (Hongkong, 1995–98), der Umbau des Reichstags (Berlin, 1995–99), der Umbau des British Museum (London, 1997–2000), die Millennium Bridge (London, 1996–2002), die Technische Universität Petronas (Seri Iskandar, Malaysia, 1999–2004), Chesa Futura (St. Moritz, Schweiz, 2000–04, hier vorgestellt), das Viadukt von Millau (Millau, Frankreich, 1993–2005) und das Wembley-Stadion (London, 1996–2006). Aktuelle Projekte sind der Flughafen Peking (2003–08), das Weingut Faustino (Ribera del Duero, Spanien, 2007–10), das Masdar Institute (Abu Dhabi, VAE, 2008–10, ebenfalls hier vorgestellt), Sperone Westwater (New York, 2009–10), der Spaceport America (New Mexico, USA, 2009–12) sowie der Masterplan für den Kulturbezirk in West Kowloon (Hongkong, seit 2009).

Né à Manchester en 1935, **NORMAN FOSTER** a étudié l'architecture et l'urbanisme à l'université de Manchester (1961). Il a bénéficié d'une bourse d'études Henry Fellowship pour l'université Yale où il a obtenu son M.Arch. et rencontré Richard Rogers avec lequel il a créé l'agence Team 4. Titulaire de la médaille d'or du RIBA en 1983, il a été anobli en 1990 et fait pair à vie en 1999. L'American Institute of Architects lui a accordé sa médaille d'or en 1994 et il a reçu le prix Pritzker en 1999. Lord Foster a construit en particulier : le siège pilote d'IBM (Cosham, GB, 1970–71) ; le Sainsbury Center for Visual Arts and Crescent Wing de l'université d'East Anglia (Norwich, GB, 1976–77 ; 1989–91) ; le siège de la Hong Kong and Shanghai Banking Corporation (Hong-Kong, 1981–86) ; l'aéroport de Stansted (1987–91) ; le siège de la Commerzbank à Francfort (Allemagne, 1994–97) ; l'aéroport de Chek Lap Kok (Hong-Kong, 1995–98) ; le Parlement allemand, le Reichstag (Berlin, 1995–99) ; les nouveaux aménagements du British Museum (Londres, 1997–2000) ; le pont du Millennium (Londres, 1996–2002) ; l'Université de technologie Petronas (Seri Iskandar, Malaisie, 1998–2004) ; Chesa Futura (Saint-Moritz, Suisse, 2000–04, publié ici) ; le viaduc de Millau (Millau, France, 1993–2005) et le stade de Wembley (Londres, 1996–2006). Plus récemment, il a réalisé l'aéroport de Pékin (2003–08) ; les chais Faustino (Ribera del Duero, Espagne, 2007–10) ; l'Institut Masdar (Abou Dhabi, EAU, 2008–10, également publié ici) ; la galerie Sperone Westwater (New York, 2009–10) ; le Spaceport America (Nouveau Mexique, 2009–12) et le plan directeur du quartier culturel de West Kowloon (Hong-Kong, 2009–).

CHESA FUTURA

St. Moritz, Switzerland, 2000–04

*Area: 4650 m². Client: SISA Immobilien AG
Cost: not disclosed*

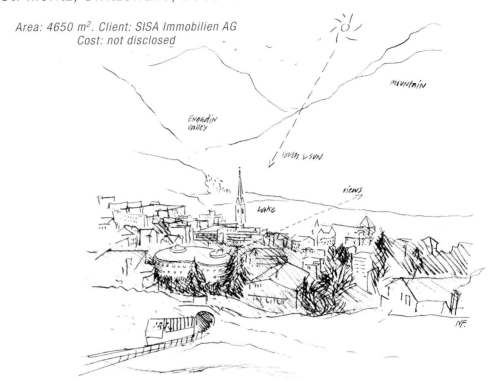

A sketch by the architect, right, shows his careful consideration of the town below, the view, and the incidence of sunlight on the structure. Below and right, photos of the completed building.

Eine Skizze des Architekten (rechts) belegt, wie sorgfältig der Ort im Tal, der Ausblick sowie der Lichteinfall auf das Gebäude berücksichtigt wurden. Unten und rechte Seite Aufnahmen des fertiggestellten Baus.

À droite, ce croquis de l'architecte témoigne de sa prise en compte attentive de la ville en contrebas, de la vue et de l'incidence du soleil sur la structure. Ci-dessous et à droite, photos du bâtiment terminé.

This three-story 4650 m² apartment building is intended to combine local tradition and the most recent computer-assisted design. Wooden shingles are often used as roofing in the Swiss mountains, but here the architect has covered the entire, rather unusually shaped structure with larch shingles. As always, Norman Foster emphasizes the environmental aspects of his work, insisting for example that "timber is a renewable resource; the trees absorb carbon dioxide as they grow; felling older trees reinforces the foresting practice of harvesting to encourage regeneration; and by using locally cut timber, little energy is consumed in its transportation." The bubble-like form allows for panoramic views on the southern side over St. Moritz and toward the lake, as well as exposure to the sun, which is sought after in the cold winter months in this location. The northern façade of the building is more closed. In another bow to local building traditions, the building is lifted off the ground on eight pilotis, although there is an underground level for car parking, storage, and heating facilities. The idea of lifting farm buildings off the ground in Switzerland was devised to keep pests out of storage buildings, but also to preserve the wood from prolonged exposure to moisture. Foster's "house of the future" did not need to relate to such ancient preoccupations, but clearly he wanted to make reference to the past of Swiss architecture while pointing in new directions. As the office statement has it, "Taken overall, **CHESA FUTURA** might be regarded as a mini manifesto for architecture, not just here but in other parts of the world. Contrary to the pattern of sprawl that disfigures the edges of so many expanding communities, it shows how new buildings can be inserted into the existing grain at increased densities, while sustaining indigenous building techniques and preserving the natural environment."

Bei diesem dreigeschossigen, 4650 m² umfassenden Apartmenthaus sollten heimische Traditionen mit dem neuesten, computergestützten Entwurfsverfahren kombiniert werden. In den Schweizer Bergen deckt man häufig die Dächer mit Holzschindeln, aber hier verkleidete der Architekt den gesamten, eher ungewöhnlich geformten Bau mit Schindeln aus Lärchenholz. Wie stets unterstreicht Norman Foster die umweltrelevanten Aspekte seiner Arbeit, indem er beispielsweise ausführt, dass „Nutzholz ein erneuerbarer Rohstoff ist, die Bäume nehmen während ihres Wachstums Kohlenstoff auf. Wenn man ältere Bäume fällt, unterstützt man das forstwirtschaftliche Verfahren, demzufolge Holz geschlagen wird, um die Regeneration zu fördern, und wenn man vor Ort gefälltes Holz verwendet, wird für dessen Transport nur wenig Energie verbraucht." Die wie aufgeblasen wirkende Form des Hauses gestattet auf der Südseite Rundblicke über St. Moritz und zum See hin ebenso wie größtmögliche Sonneneinstrahlung, ein an diesem Ort in den kalten Wintermonaten begehrter Vorteil. Die Nordfassade des Hauses wirkt geschlossener. Auch der Umstand, dass der Bau durch acht Piloten über den Boden angehoben ist, verweist auf lokale Bautraditionen. Darüber hinaus gibt es ein Untergeschoss mit Parkplätzen, in dem auch Lagerräume und die Heizanlage untergebracht sind. Die Idee, Bauernhöfe in der Schweiz nicht direkt auf den Erdboden zu stellen, kam auf, um Ungeziefer von den gelagerten Vorräten fernzuhalten und auch, um das Holz vor der im Boden enthaltenen Feuchtigkeit zu schützen. Fosters „Haus der Zukunft" resultierte nicht aus solchen uralten Notwendigkeiten, sondern soll einen Bezug zur Vergangenheit der schweizerischen Architektur herstellen, während es neue Richtungen aufzeigt. Wie es im Exposé des Büros heißt, könnte **CHESA FUTURA** insgesamt als Architekturmanifest en miniature betrachtet werden, und zwar nicht nur für die Schweiz, sondern auch für andere Teile der Welt. Im Gegensatz zu den baulichen Wucherungen, die die Ränder so vieler wachsender Städte verschandeln, zeigt es, wie neue Bauten zur Verdichtung in bestehende Strukturen eingefügt und gleichzeitig heimische Bauverfahren erhalten werden sowie die umgebende Natur geschont wird.

Cet immeuble de logements de 4650 m² associe des traditions locales et les logiciels de CAO les plus récents. Si les bardeaux sont souvent utilisés en toiture dans les montagnes suisses, l'architecte en a recouvert ici la totalité de la forme assez inhabituelle de son immeuble. Comme toujours, Norman Foster insiste sur les aspects environnementaux de son travail, par exemple sur le fait que « le bois est une ressource renouvelable ; les arbres absorbent le dioxyde de carbone au cours de leur pousse. Exploiter les arbres à maturité fait partie des bonnes pratiques sylvicoles en encourageant la régénération des forêts. En utilisant des bois locaux, la quantité d'énergie nécessaire à leur transport est réduite ». La forme en bulle permet d'obtenir des vues panoramiques sur la partie sud de Saint-Moritz et le lac ainsi qu'une généreuse exposition au soleil, toujours recherchée dans cette station de montagne. La façade nord est plus fermée. Autre clin d'œil aux traditions locales de construction, l'immeuble est surélevé sur huit pilotis, bien que le parking, des pièces de rangement et les équipements de chauffage se trouvent en sous-sol. Cette surélévation se justifiait historiquement pour protéger les greniers des animaux nuisibles, mais également pour protéger le bois d'une exposition prolongée à l'humidité du sol. La « maison du futur » de Foster ne répond bien évidemment pas à ce genre de préoccupation mais l'architecte a voulu cette référence au passé tout en indiquant de nouvelles orientations. **CHESA FUTURA**, comme l'explique la présentation de l'agence, peut être considérée comme un mini-manifeste d'architecture, non seulement pour la Suisse mais pour d'autres parties du monde. Contrairement au mouvement d'extension urbanistique qui défigure les abords de tant de villes et de villages, elle montre que de nouvelles constructions plus denses peuvent être insérées dans le tissu urbain tout en conservant des techniques de constructions locales et en préservant l'environnement.

A drawing shows the enveloping, curved forms of the buildings with its two main cores.

Die Zeichnung zeigt die geschwungene Gebäudehülle sowie die beiden Hauptgebäudekerne.

Schéma des formes courbes et enveloppantes des bâtiments avec leurs deux noyaux principaux.

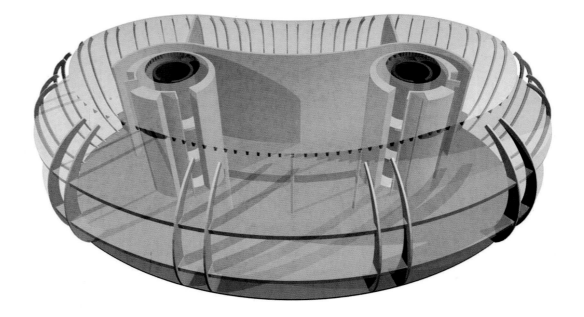

Larch turns gray when exposed to the elements and, in this instance, the building will tend to "disappear" into its environment as it ages. Views of the surrounding mountains are framed by the building.

Lärchenholz wird witterungsbedingt grau, was hier dazu führt, dass der Bau mit zunehmendem Alter in seinem Umfeld „verschwinden" wird. Der Bau rahmt den Blick in die Berge.

Le mélèze devient gris lorsqu'il est exposé aux intempéries, de sorte qu'ici, le bâtiment aura tendance à « s'effacer » dans le décor en vieillissant. Les vues des montagnes environnantes sont encadrées par le bâtiment.

MASDAR INSTITUTE
Abu Dhabi, UAE, 2008–10 (Phase 1A)

*Area: 14 000 m² (Phase 1A). Client: Mubadala Development Company.
Cost: not disclosed. Collaboration: PHA Consult (Sustainability MEP Engineer),
Adams Kara Taylor (Structural Engineer)*

The Masdar City Master Plan, developed by Foster + Partners, calls for the creation of a prototypical sustainable city in Abu Dhabi. The **MASDAR INSTITUTE** is the first part of the scheme to be realized, and is intended to provide context for the entire program. As the architects describe the ecological aspects of the institute: "The buildings are oriented to provide optimum shade and reduce cooling loads, and shaded colonnades at podium level exploit the benefits of exposed thermal mass. Façades are designed to respond to their orientation, and photovoltaic installations on every roof are combined with carefully positioned photovoltaic panels to shade streets and buildings. Cooling air currents are channeled through the public spaces using a contemporary interpretation of the region's traditional wind towers. The public spaces are further cooled by green landscaping and water to provide evaporative cooling." The complex includes laboratories, residences, and accompanying spaces.

Der von Foster + Partners entwickelte Masterplan für Masdar City sieht vor, den Prototyp einer nachhaltigen Stadt in Abu Dhabi zu realisieren. Das **MASDAR INS-TITUTE** ist Teil des ersten Bauabschnitts und soll zugleich den Kontext für das gesamte Programm vorgeben. Die Architekten beschreiben die ökologischen Eigenschaften des Instituts: „Die Gebäude wurden nach optimaler Schattennutzung und mit Blick auf die Reduzierung des Kühlaufwands ausgerichtet; schattige Kolonnaden im Sockelgeschoss profitieren von der Wärmespeicherkapazität des Baus. Die Fassaden wurden entsprechend ihrer Ausrichtung geplant; Fotovoltaikanlagen auf allen Dächern wurden kombiniert mit Solarpaneelen, die so positioniert wurden, dass sie Straßen und Gebäude beschatten. Dank einer zeitgenössischen Interpretation regionaltypischer, traditioneller Windfängertürme werden kühlende Luftströme erzeugt, die zur Kühlung der öffentlichen Bereiche beitragen. Zusätzliche Kühlung erfahren die öffentlichen Bereiche durch Begrünung und Wasser und die dadurch entstehende Verdunstungskühlung." Zum Komplex gehören Labors, Wohneinheiten und ergänzende Einrichtungen.

Conçu par Foster + Partners, le plan directeur de la ville de Masdar dessinait le prototype d'une ville durable à Abou Dhabi. L'**INSTITUT MASDAR** qui représente la première partie de ce projet fournit un contexte de référence à l'ensemble du programme. « Les bâtiments sont orientés pour offrir le maximum d'ombre et réduire le gain solaire. Des colonnades qui apportent de l'ombre au niveau du podium bénéficient de la mise en exposition de leur masse thermique. Les façades sont conçues en fonction de leur orientation et sur chaque toit des équipements photovoltaïques sont alimentés par des panneaux photovoltaïques positionnés avec soin pour donner de l'ombre sur les rues et les bâtiments. Les courants d'air frais sont canalisés dans les espaces publics grâce à une version contemporaine des tours à vent traditionnelles locales. Les espaces publics sont également climatisés par des aménagements paysagers et des plans d'eau qui apportent une évaporation rafraichissante », expliquent les architectes. Le complexe comprend des laboratoires, des logements et leurs espaces attenants.

The complex stands out from its desert surroundings with an appearance that might be likened to that of a fortress. Right page, an internal street provides shelter from the sun and a contrast of materials.

Der Komplex hebt sich wie eine Festung von der Wüstenlandschaft ab. Eine interne Passage (rechte Seite) bietet Schutz vor der Sonne und ein kontrastreiches Spiel verschiedener Materialien.

Le complexe se détache sur le désert qui l'entoure par son apparence qui pourrait être comparée à celle d'une forteresse. Page de droite, un passage interne abrite du soleil et permet un contraste entre matériaux.

The architect alternates materials and forms to create a city-like interior environment, with protection and relief from the Gulf sun remaining a priority. Below, a section drawing of the entire complex.

Durch den Einsatz verschiedener Materialien und Formen schafft der Architekt eine überdachte Stadtlandschaft. Der Schutz vor der Sonne hat am Golf oberste Priorität. Unten ein Querschnitt des Gesamtkomplexes.

L'architecte alterne les matériaux et les formes pour créer un environnement intérieur urbain où la protection et l'atténuation du soleil du Golfe restent une priorité. Ci-dessous, schéma en coupe du complexe dans son ensemble.

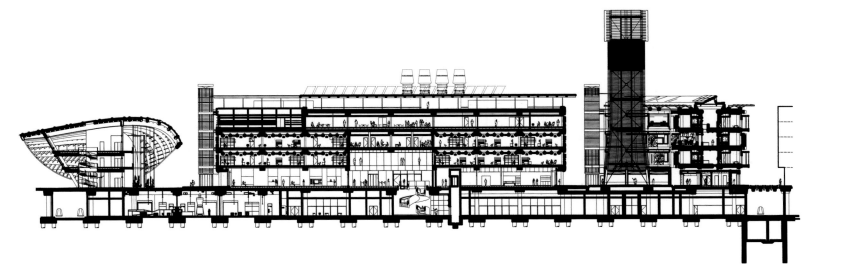

FRANK O. GEHRY

Gehry Partners, LLP
12541 Beatrice Street
Los Angeles, CA 90066
USA

Tel: +1 310 482 3000 / Fax: +1 310 482 3006
E-mail: info@foga.com / Web: www.foga.com

Born in Toronto, Canada, in 1929, **FRANK GEHRY** studied at the University of Southern California, Los Angeles (1949–54), and at Harvard (1956–57). Principal of Frank O. Gehry and Associates, Inc., Los Angeles, since 1962, he received the Pritzker Prize in 1989. His early work in California included the redesign of his own house, and the construction of a number of others such as the Norton Residence (Venice, 1984) and the Schnabel Residence (Brentwood, 1989). His first foreign projects included Festival Disney (Marne-la-Vallée, France, 1988–92), and the Guggenheim Bilbao (Spain, 1991–97), which is felt by some to be one of the most significant buildings of the late 20th century. Other work includes the DG Bank Headquarters (Berlin, Germany, 2001); the Fisher Center for the Performing Arts at Bard College (Annandale-on-Hudson, New York, USA, 2003); and the Walt Disney Concert Hall (Los Angeles, USA, 2003). More recent work includes a Maggie's Centre (Dundee, Scotland, 1999–2003); the Jay Pritzker Pavilion in Millennium Park (Chicago, USA, 2004); the Hotel at the Marques de Riscal winery (Elciego, Spain, 1999–2007); his first New York building, the InterActiveCorp Headquarters (New York, New York, USA, 2003–07); an extension of the Art Gallery of Ontario (Toronto, Canada, 2000–08); the Serpentine Gallery Pavilion (London, UK, 2008, published here); Cleveland Clinic Lou Ruvo Center for Brain Health (Las Vegas, Nevada, USA, 2005–10); and Orchestral Academy (Miami, Florida, USA, 2003–11). He is currently working on the Louis Vuitton Foundation for Creation in the Bois de Boulogne in Paris, France, and the Dwight D. Eisenhower Memorial in Washington, D.C., USA.

FRANK GEHRY wurde 1929 in Toronto, Kanada, geboren und studierte an der University of Southern California, Los Angeles (1949–51), sowie in Harvard (1956–57). Seit 1962 ist Gehry Direktor von Frank O. Gehry and Associates, Inc., in Los Angeles. 1989 wurde er mit dem Pritzker-Preis ausgezeichnet. Zu seinem Frühwerk in Kalifornien zählen der Umbau seines eigenen Hauses und der Bau mehrerer Wohnhäuser, darunter die Norton Residence (Venice, 1984) und die Schnabel Residence (Brentwood, 1989). Zu seinen ersten Projekten im Ausland gehören sein Bau für Festival Disney (Marne-la-Vallée, Frankreich, 1988–92) und das Guggenheim-Museum Bilbao (Spanien, 1991–97), das viele für eines der bedeutendsten Bauwerke des späten 20. Jahrhunderts halten. Andere Arbeiten sind u. a. die DG-Bank-Zentrale in Berlin (2001), das Fisher Center für darstellende Künste am Bard College (Annandale-on-Hudson, New York, 2003) und die Walt Disney Concert Hall (Los Angeles, 2003). Zu seinen jüngeren Arbeiten zählen Maggie's Centre (Dundee, Schottland, 1999–2003), der Jay-Pritzker-Pavillon im Millennium-Park in Chicago (2004), das Hotel am Weingut Marques de Riscal (Elciego, Spanien, 1999–2007), Gehrys erster Bau in New York, die Zentrale von InterActiveCorp an der West 19th Street in Manhattan (2003–07), die Erweiterung der Art Gallery of Ontario (Toronto, 2000–08), der Serpentine-Sommerpavillon (London, 2008, hier vorgestellt), das Lou Ruvo Center for Brain Health der Cleveland Clinic (Las Vegas, 2005–10) sowie die Orchestral Academy (Miami, 2003–11). Gegenwärtig arbeitet er an der Fondation Louis Vuitton pour la Création im Bois de Boulogne in Paris sowie dem Dwight D. Eisenhower Memorial in Washington, D. C.

Né à Toronto, Canada, en 1929, **FRANK GEHRY** étudie à l'USC (University of Southern California) à Los Angeles (1949–51) puis à Harvard (1956–57). Il dirige l'agence Frank O. Gehry and Associates, Inc., Los Angeles, depuis 1962, et a reçu en 1989 le prix Pritzker. Ses premiers travaux en Californie comprennent la restructuration de sa propre maison et la construction d'un certain nombre de maisons dont la résidence Norton (Venice, 1984) et la résidence Schnabel (Brentwood, 1989). Ses premières réalisations à l'étranger furent le Festival Disney (Disney Village, Marne-la-Vallée, France, 1988–92) et le musée Guggenheim Bilbao (Espagne, 1991–97) jugé par beaucoup comme l'un des plus importants bâtiments de la fin du XXᵉ siècle. Parmi ses projets remarqués figurent également le siège de la DG Bank (Berlin, 2001) ; le Fisher Center for the Performing Arts à Bard College (Annandale-on-Hudson, New York, 2003) et le Walt Disney Concert Hall (Los Angeles, 2003). Plus récemment, il a réalisé le Maggie's Centre (Dundee, Écosse, 1999–2003) ; le pavillon Jay Pritzker dans le Millennium Park (Chicago, 2004) ; l'hôtel du domaine viticole Marques de Riscal (Elciego, Espagne, 1999–2007) ; son premier immeuble à New York, le siège d'InterActiveCorp (New York, 2003–07) ; une extension de la galerie d'art de l'Ontario (Toronto, 2000–08) ; le pavillon de la Serpentine Gallery (Londres, 2008, publié ici) ; le Centre de santé mentale Lou Ruvo de la Cleveland Clinic (Las Vegas, Nevada, 2005–10) et l'Orchestral Academy (Miami, Floride, 2003–11). Il travaille actuellement sur le projet de la fondation Louis Vuitton pour la création dans le Bois de Boulogne à Paris et le mémorial Dwight D. Eisenhower à Washington.

SERPENTINE GALLERY PAVILION

London, UK, 2008

Area: 526 m². Client: Serpentine Gallery
Cost: not disclosed

The 2008 Serpentine Summer Pavilion was a timber structure "which act[ed] as an urban street connecting the park with the permanent gallery building." Glass canopies hanging inside the structure provided shade and protected visitors from rain. It was intended as a place for live performances with a capacity of about 275 spectators. Gehry explains: "The interplay between the exoskeleton of timber planks and the multiple glazed roof surfaces invokes imagery of striped park tent structures and catapults, capturing the visual energy of a place created from the juxtaposition of random elements." The relationship of the project to music was clearly in the mind of the architect when he designed the pavilion. Gehry explained that "the idea of a concert platform in the Serpentine Pavilion gave me the reason for the way it grew. Once that was settled in my mind and we dealt with that as a primary issue, then I also realized that it could work for a lot more things, such as lectures and all the other events in the program. I did pick classical music as the priority, knowing that once you developed something with that priority then it would easily have multiple uses for all the other things, because they were much less difficult to accomplish. The classical music element was the most difficult thing to achieve with this kind of structure." The 2008 Serpentine Summer Pavilion was sold and has now been installed at Château La Coste near Aix-en-Provence, France, where it is due to be used for musical events, and where Frank Gehry is due to realize another structure in the near future.

Der Serpentine-Sommerpavillon 2008 war eine Holzkonstruktion, die „wie eine öffentliche Straße funktioniert[e] und den Park und das Galeriegebäude" verband. Abgehängte Dachsegmente aus Glas spendeten Schatten und schützten die Besucher vor Regen. Hier sollten Live-Veranstaltungen für bis zu 275 Zuschauer stattfinden. Gehry führt aus: „Das Zusammenspiel zwischen dem Außenskelett aus Holzbindern und einer Vielzahl gläserner Dachsegmente erinnert an gestreifte Gartenzelte oder an Katapulte und visualisiert die Energie eines Ortes, der aus den Gegensätzen willkürlicher Elemente geboren wurde." Offenkundig beschäftigte den Architekten bei der Planung der musikalische Aspekt des Pavillons. Gehry erklärte: „Die Idee einer Plattform für Konzerte im Serpentine-Pavillon gab mir den Anstoß für die weitere Entwicklung. Sobald wir dieses Anliegen mit Priorität behandelten, merkte ich, dass sich dieser Ansatz auch für vieles andere eignen könnte, etwa für Vorträge und alle übrigen Veranstaltungen des Programms. Für mich hatte die klassische Musik oberste Priorität, weil ich wusste, dass etwas, das man mit Blick auf einen bestimmten Primärzweck entwickelt, auch für vieles andere nutzbar ist, das leichter zu realisieren ist. Und bei einer solchen Konstruktion war es am schwierigsten, dem funktionalen Aspekt ‚klassische' Musik gerecht zu werden." Der Serpentine-Sommerpavillon 2008 wurde verkauft und steht inzwischen am Château La Coste bei Aix-en-Provence, wo er für Konzerte genutzt werden soll. Frank Gehry wird dort in naher Zukunft einen weiteren Bau realisieren.

Le pavillon de l'été 2008 de la Serpentine Gallery était une structure en bois « qui agi[ssai]t comme une artère urbaine allant du parc au bâtiment permanent de la galerie. » Des verrières suspendues à l'intérieur apportaient de l'ombre et protégeaient les visiteurs de la pluie. Le pavillon était conçu pour accueillir des performances en direct avec une capacité de 275 places environ. Gehry explique : « L'interaction entre l'exosquelette de planches et les multiples surfaces vitrées du toit évoque l'image de tentes rayées et de catapultes, captant l'énergie visuelle d'un lieu créé à partir de la juxtaposition d'éléments aléatoires. » L'architecte avait manifestement en tête le lien du projet avec la musique lorsqu'il a conçu le pavillon. Gehry a déclaré que « l'idée d'une plate-forme de concert dans le pavillon de la Serpentine m'a fourni le motif de sa croissance. Une fois que les choses ont été bien claires dans mon esprit et que nous en avons parlé comme d'une première possibilité, j'ai réalisé que je pouvais aussi prévoir bien plus, notamment les conférences et autres événements du programme. J'ai choisi la musique classique en priorité, en sachant qu'après avoir développé un projet avec cette priorité, je trouverais facilement des usages multiples pour tout le reste, car il s'agit de choses bien moins difficiles à réaliser. L'élément de musique classique a été le plus difficile à réaliser avec ce type de structure ». Le pavillon 2008 de la Serpentine Gallery a été vendu et est désormais installé au château La Coste, près d'Aix-en-Provence, où il doit servir à des manifestations musicales et où Frank Gehry doit réaliser une autre structure très prochainement.

Seen from the angle of the main axis of the Serpentine Gallery, the Gehry Pavilion takes on the air of a triumphal, asymmetric arch. The pavilion projects an image of suspended lightness that the architect's work does not always seek to achieve.

Entlang der zentralen Blickachse der Serpentine Gallery präsentiert sich der Gehry-Pavillon wie ein asymmetrischer Triumphbogen. Der Pavillon ist von einer schwebenden Leichtigkeit, die der Architekt in seinem Werk durchaus nicht immer anstrebt.

Vu depuis l'angle du principal axe de la Serpentine Gallery, le pavillon de Gehry prend l'allure d'un arc de triomphe asymétrique. Il projette une image de légèreté en suspension que le travail de l'architecte ne cherche pas toujours à concrétiser.

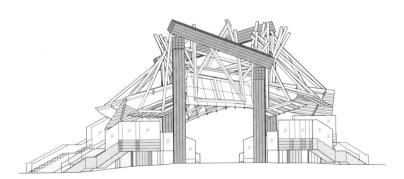
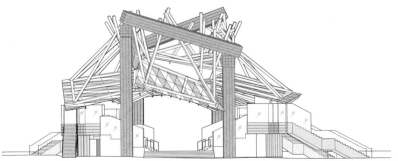

The partially covered open space beneath the dramatically angled glass and wood canopy allows a full and free program to take place on the lawn in front of the Serpentine.

Der teilüberdachte offene Bereich unter der dramatisch verkanteten Glas- und Holzkonstruktion ermöglicht kostenfreie Veranstaltungen auf dem Rasen vor der Galerie.

L'espace ouvert en partie couvert sous l'auvent de verre et bois extra-ordinairement anguleux permet à un programme complet d'être exécuté librement sur l'herbe devant la Serpentine Gallery.

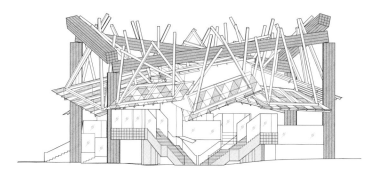

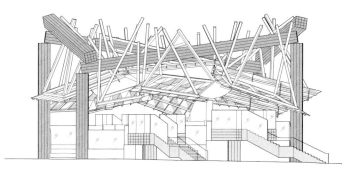

The suspended planes forming the roof of the pavilion hang high above the performance and seating space. Elevations of the pavilion from various angles give an impression of a complex accumulation of wooden or glass elements.

Die abgehängten Dachsegmente des Pavillons schweben hoch über dem Bühnen- und Publikumsbereich. Aufrisse des Pavillons aus verschiedenen Blickwinkeln vermitteln einen Eindruck von der Komplexität der kombinierten Holz- und Glaselemente.

Les plans suspendus formant le toit sont accrochés haut au-dessus de l'espace réservé aux performances et au public. Les élévations du pavillon sous différents angles donnent l'impression d'une accumulation complexe d'éléments en bois ou verre.

GLAVOVIC STUDIO

Glavovic Studio Inc.
724 NE 3rd Avenue
Fort Lauderdale, FL 33304
USA

Tel: +1 954 524 5728
Fax: +1 954 524 5729
E-mail: info@glavovicstudio.com
Web: www.glavovicstudio.com

MARGI NOTHARD was born in 1963 in Harare, Zimbabwe. She attended the University of Kwa Zulu-Natal in Durban as an undergraduate. She received her M.Arch degree from the Southern California Institute of Architecture (SCI-Arc) in 1992. Margi Nothard is the president and design principal of Glavovic Studio Inc. The firm's work includes the Girls' Club (Fort Lauderdale, 2007); Young Circle ArtsPark (Hollywood, Florida, 2003–07, published here); the Museum of ArtINSU: Art Plaza (Fort Lauderdale, 2011); and Young @ Art / Broward County Children's Museum and Reading Center Project (Davie, Florida, 2012), all in the USA.

MARGI NOTHARD wurde 1963 in Harare, Simbabwe, geboren. Sie studierte zuerst an der Universität von Kwazulu-Natal in Durban und machte 1992 ihren Master in Architektur am Southern California Institute of Architecture (SCI-Arc). Margi Nothard ist Firmenchefin und leitende Entwurfsarchitektin des Büros Glavovic Studio Inc. Zu den Arbeiten des Büros gehören die Sammlung Girls' Club (Fort Lauderdale, 2007), der ArtsPark mit Kunstinstallationen im Stadtteil Young Circle (Hollywood, Florida, 2003–07, hier vorgestellt), das Museum of ArtINSU: Art Plaza (Fort Lauderdale, 2011) und das Young @ Art/Broward County Children's Museum and Reading Center Project – Kindermuseum und Lesezentrum (Davie, Florida, 2012), alle in den USA.

MARGI NOTHARD, née en 1963 à Harare au Zimbabwe, a étudié à l'université de KwaZulu-Natal à Durban. Elle a obtenu son M.Arch. à l'Institut d'architecture de Californie du Sud (SCI-Arc, 1992). Elle est présidente et responsable de la conception de Glavovic Studio Inc. Aux États-Unis, l'agence a réalisé, entre autres, le Girls' Club (Fort Lauderdale, Floride, 2007) ; le Young Circle ArtsPark (Hollywood, Floride, 2003–07, publié ici) ; le Musée d'artINSU: Art Plaza (Fort Lauderdale, Floride, 2011) et le Young @ Art Children's Museum/Broward County Library (Davie, Floride, 2012).

YOUNG CIRCLE ARTSPARK

Hollywood, Florida, USA, 2003–07

Address: One Young Circle, Hollywood Boulevard at US1, Hollywood, FL 33020, USA, +1 954 921 3520
Area: 4 hectares (park); 1300 m² (pavilion). Client: City of Hollywood. Cost: $13 million (Phase I); $26 million overall
Collaboration: Marvin Scharf, IBI Group (Executive Architect)

One challenge of this site is that it is located in the center of Hollywood and is surrounded by a 4-5 lane one-way federal highway (US 1) with multiple cross entries. The architectural program was divided into two main buildings (Performing Arts and Visual Arts). The landscaping is based on an emerging spiral that becomes a cantilevered canopy. The flat center of the park was raised to provide variety, and to accommodate trees. The architect states: "Materials such as poured-in-place concrete connect the buildings to the earth and reinforce their emergence. These built structures then pierce the sky with metal and wood panels providing a counterpoint to the landscaped earth. The tree and building canopy are one with the blue sky. Art as environment, art as light, art as sound, and art as architecture."

Eine Herausforderung bei diesem Gelände ist seine Lage: mitten im Stadtzentrum von Hollywood und von der vier- bis fünfspurigen Bundesstraße US 1 mit zahlreichen Einmündungen umgeben. Das Raumprogramm wurde auf zwei Hauptgebäude verteilt (darstellende und bildende Künste). Die Landschaftsgestaltung basiert auf einer sich in die Höhe schraubenden Spirale, die zu einem ausladenden Baldachin wird. Das flache Zentrum des Parks wurde mit Erde aufgeschüttet, um das Gelände lebendiger zu gestalten und um Bäume pflanzen zu können. Die Architektin sagt dazu: „Mit Materialien wie Ortbeton werden die Gebäude mit der Erde verbunden und ihr Erscheinen betont. Diese gebauten Strukturen durchdringen dann mit Metall- und Holzpaneelen den Himmel und bilden einen Kontrapunkt zu der landschaftlich gestalteten Erdoberfläche. Der Baum- und Gebäudebaldachin vereinigt sich mit dem blauen Himmel. Kunst als Umfeld, Kunst als Licht, Kunst als Klang und Kunst als Architektur."

L'un des défis posés par ce terrain du centre d'Hollywood était d'être un immense rond-point encerclé par l'autoroute fédérale US 1 de quatre à cinq voies. Le programme architectural a été réparti en deux bâtiments principaux (arts du spectacle et arts visuels). L'aménagement paysager repose sur une spirale qui se termine en un auvent en porte-à-faux. La partie centrale a été surélevée pour donner davantage de variété au relief, puis plantée d'arbres. « Des matériaux comme le béton coulé sur site ancrent les bâtiments dans le sol et renforcent l'impression d'émergence. Ces constructions pointent ensuite vers le ciel leurs panneaux de métal et de bois qui viennent en contrepoint du sol aménagé. Les arbres et l'auvent ne font qu'un avec le ciel. L'art comme environnement, l'art comme lumière, l'art comme son et l'art comme architecture. »

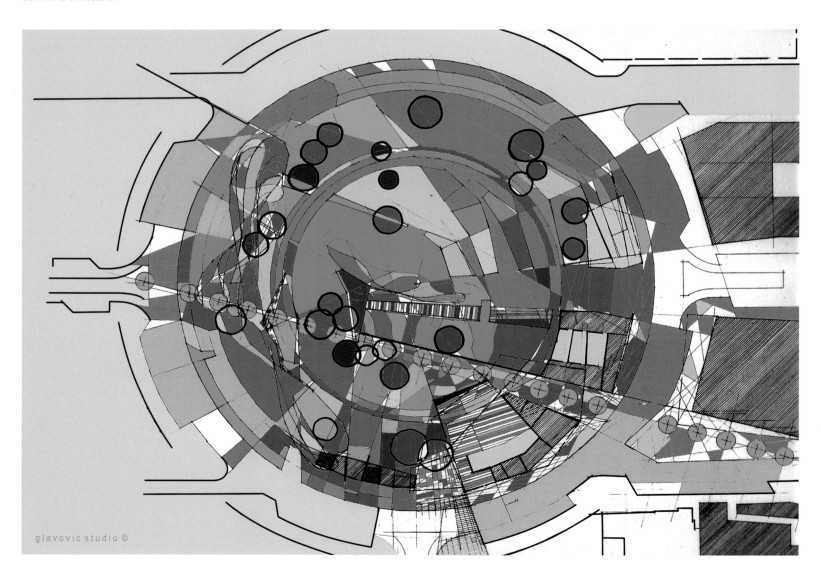

glavovic studio ©

The unusual round form of the park is visible both in the overall image and the plan on the left, which also gives an indication of the planting and the use of the space. A building in the park is seen on the right.

Die ungewöhnliche Kreisform des Parks kann man sowohl auf der Luftaufnahme als auch auf dem Grundriss links erkennen, der auch Angaben zur Bepflanzung und Nutzung der verschiedenen Freiräume enthält. Rechts ein Gebäude in diesem Park.

L'étonnant plan circulaire du parc, vu dans le plan à gauche et l'image ci-dessus, précise les plantations et l'utilisation de l'espace. À droite, un des bâtiments édifiés à l'intérieur du parc.

The design is uncluttered and color-ful. The designs on the ground echo the angled architecture of the arts centers that are the main architec-tural feature of the park.

Das Design ist schlicht und farben-froh. Die Muster auf dem Boden neh-men die Linienführung der winkelför-migen Architektur der Kunstzentren auf, der größten Gebäude im Park.

La composition est dégagée et colo-rée. Les parterres font écho à l'archi-tecture des centres d'art, principaux éléments architecturals du parc.

Night lighting allows the park spaces to be used beyond the more usual day periods. On the whole, the outlines of the park forms and the planting are simple and efficient.

Wegen der nächtlichen Beleuchtung kann der Park auch bei Dunkelheit genutzt werden. Insgesamt sind die Konturen der Parkgestaltung und die Bepflanzung einfach und rationell.

L'éclairage nocturne permet d'utiliser les lieux au-delà des horaires habituels. Les formes construites et les plantations se répondent de façon simple et efficace.

NICHOLAS GRIMSHAW

57 Clerkenwell Road, London EC1M 5NG, UK
Tel: +44 207 291 4141
E-mail: communications@grimshaw-architects.com
Web: www.grimshaw-architects.com

A 1965 graduate of the Architectural Association (AA), **NICHOLAS GRIMSHAW** was born in 1939 in London. He created the firm Nicholas Grimshaw and Partners Ltd. in 1980, now known as Grimshaw. His numerous industrial/corporate/commercial structures include those built for Herman Miller in Bath (1976); BMW at Bracknell (1980); the furniture maker Vitra (Weil am Rhein, Germany, 1981); and the Financial Times in London (1988). He also built the British Pavilion at the 1992 Universal Exhibition in Seville. One of his most visible works is the former International Terminal of Waterloo Station (London, 1988–93). Grimshaw currently employs over 200 people with offices in London, New York, and Melbourne. Andrew Whalley, a partner in the firm, was educated at the Mackintosh School of Architecture (B.Arch, 1984) and at the AA in London (1986). Vincent Chang, also a partner, received his degrees at the Cambridge University School of Architecture (1988, 1991). Buildings include the Rolls Royce Manufacturing Plant and Head Office (West Sussex, UK, 2003); Zurich Airport (Zurich, Switzerland, 2003 and 2004); Sankei Nishi-Umeda Building (Osaka, Japan, 2004); the Eden Project (St Austell, UK, 1998–2005, published here); University College London New Engineering Building (London, UK, 2005); Southern Cross Station (Melbourne, Australia, 2002–06); Caixa Galicia Arts Foundation (A Coruña, Spain, 2006); University College London Cancer Institute, Paul O'Gorman Building (London, UK, 2007); Dubai Tower (design 2007); Amsterdam Bijlmer ArenA Station (Amsterdam, The Netherlands, 2002–07); Horno 3, Museo Del Acero (Monterrey, Mexico, 2006–07); London School of Economics New Academic Building (London, UK, 2004–08); and the Experimental Media and Performing Arts Center (EMPAC) (Troy, New York, USA, 2004–08).

NICHOLAS GRIMSHAW, 1939 in London geboren, schloss sein Studium 1965 an der dortigen Architectural Association (AA) ab. 1980 gründete er sein Büro Nicholas Grimshaw and Partners Ltd., heute bekannt als Grimshaw. Zu seinen zahllosen Fabrik-, Büro- und Gewerbebauten zählen Projekte für Herman Miller in Bath (1976), BMW in Bracknell (1980), den Möbelhersteller Vitra (Weil am Rhein, Deutschland, 1981) und die *Financial Times* in London (1988). Grimshaw realisierte auch den britischen Pavillon auf der Weltausstellung 1992 in Sevilla. Eine seiner bekanntesten Arbeiten ist das ehemalige Internationale Terminal an der Waterloo Station (London, 1988–93). Grimshaw beschäftigt derzeit rund 200 Mitarbeiter in seinen Büros in London, New York und Melbourne. Andrew Whalley, einer der Partner des Büros, studierte an der Mackintosh School of Architecture (B.Arch., 1984) und der AA in London (1986). Vincent Chang, ebenfalls Partner, machte seine Abschlüsse an der Architekturfakultät in Cambridge (1988, 1991). Zu den Bauten des Büros zählen die Werksanlagen und die Geschäftszentrale von Rolls Royce (West Sussex, GB, 2003), der Flughafen Zürich (2003 und 2004), das Sankei Nishi-Umeda Building (Osaka, Japan, 2004), die neue Fakultät für Bauingenieurwesen am University College London (2005), die Southern Cross Station (Melbourne, Australien, 2002–06), die Kunststiftung Caixa Galicia (A Coruña, Spanien, 2006), das Paul O'Gorman Building des Krebszentrums am University College London (2007), der Dubai Tower (Entwurf 2007), der Bahnhof Bijlmer ArenA (Amsterdam, 2002–07), Horno 3 am Museo del Acero (Monterrey, Mexiko, 2006–07), das New Academic Building an der London School of Economics (London, 2004–08) sowie das Zentrum für experimentelle Medien und darstellende Künste (EMPAC) in Troy (New York, 2004–08).

Diplômé de l'Architectural Association (AA) en 1965, **NICHOLAS GRIMSHAW** est né en 1939 à Londres. Il fonde l'agence Nicholas Grimshaw and Partners Ltd. en 1980, maintenant connue sous le nom Grimshaw. Ses nombreux bâtiments industriels, de bureaux, ou commerciaux incluent ceux construits pour Herman Miller à Bath (1976) ; BMW à Bracknell (1980) ; le fabricant de meubles Vitra (Weil-am-Rhein, Allemagne, 1981) et le Financial Times, à Londres, en 1988. Il a également construit le Pavillon britannique de l'Exposition universelle de 1992 à Séville. Une de ses réalisations les plus connues est l'ancien terminal international la gare de Waterloo (Londres, 1988–93). Grimshaw emploie une équipe de 200 personnes dans ses bureaux de Londres, New York et Melbourne. Andrew Whalley, un associé de l'agence, a étudié à l'École d'architecture Mackintosh de Glasgow (B.Arch, 1984) et à l'AA de Londres (1986). Vincent Chang, également associé, est diplômé de l'École d'architecture de l'université de Cambridge (1988, 1991). Leurs projets réalisés incluent l'usine de fabrication et le siège de Rolls Royce (West Sussex, Royaume-Uni, 2003) ; l'aéroport de Zurich (Zurich, 2003 et 2004) ; l'immeuble Sankei Nishi-Umeda (Osaka, Japon, 2004) ; l'Eden Project (Saint Austell, 1998–2005, publié ici) ; le nouveau bâtiment de l'ingénieurie au University College de Londres (2005) ; la gare de Southern Cross (Melbourne, 2002–06) ; la fondation artistique Caixa Galicia (La Corogne, Espagne, 2006) ; le bâtiment Paul O'Gorman, pour l'Institut du cancer du University College de Londres (UCL Cancer Institute 2007) ; la Dubai Tower (projet conçu en 2007) ; la gare Amsterdam Bijlmer ArenA (Amsterdam, 2002–07) ; Horno 3, le musée de l'Acier (Monterrey, Mexique, 2006–07) ; le nouveau bâtiment universitaire de la London School of Economics (Londres, 2004–08) et l'Experimental Media and Performing Arts Center (EMPAC) (Troy, New York, 2004–08).

THE EDEN PROJECT
St Austell, UK, 1998–2005

Area: Biomes and Link Building: 23 000 m²; Dry Tropics Biome, Education Center,
and Visitor Gateway: 14 890 m², Eden Foundation: 1800 m². Client: Eden Project Ltd.
Cost: Biomes and Link Building: £57 million; Dry Tropics Biome, Education Center, and Visitor Gateway: £9 million;
Eden Foundation: £2,3 million

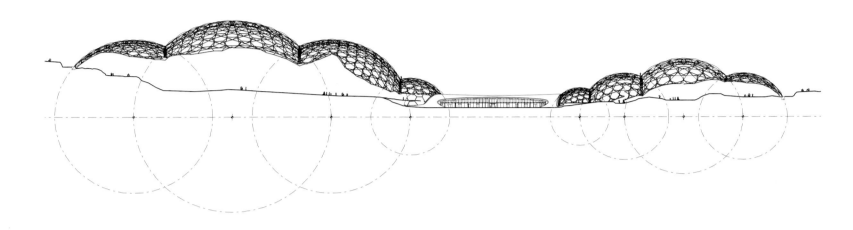

This very unusual project is intended as a "showcase for global bio-diversity and human dependence upon plants." The first phase, completed in 2001, was made up of 23 000 m² of "linked, climate-controlled transparent capsules (biomes) set in a design landscape." The budget for this project, which made use of the same consultants who worked on Grimshaw's very successful Waterloo International Terminal, was £57 million. Although its objectives might be considered as more far-reaching, this scheme does bring to mind the Yamanashi Museum of Fruit designed by Itsuko Hasegawa in Japan, which is also made up of a series of greenhouse structures. The domes in St Austell are to be based on lightweight structures with the highest possible volume vis-à-vis their surface. The cladding is made up of "optically clear air inflated foil (ETFE or Ethylene Tetra Fluoro Ethylene) pillows." The whole is intended to "give the impression of a biomorphic organism." As the architects say, "The final scheme represents the perfect fulfillment of Buckminster Fuller's vision—the maximum enclosed volume within the minimal surface area." The Visitor Center, opened on May 15, 2000, is "primarily an educational facility, housing multimedia exhibits that introduce the aims and objectives of the project. It curves dramatically, complementing the contours of the quarry." Intended for 645 000 visitors a year, the **EDEN PROJECT** attracted 1.956 million in its first year of operation. The Eden Foundation building, built to an entirely PVC-free specification, is a 1800 m² structure with a contract value of £2.5 million and was completed in 2002.

Dieses außergewöhnliche Projekt ist gedacht als „Schaukasten der weltweiten biologischen Vielfalt und der menschlichen Abhängigkeit von Pflanzen". Der 2001 fertiggestellte, erste Abschnitt besteht aus 23 000 m² „miteinander verbundener, klimatisierter, transparenter Kuppeln, sogenannte Biomes, die in eine gestaltete Landschaft eingefügt sind". Das Budget für dieses Projekt, zu dem die gleichen Berater herangezogen wurden, wie zu Grimshaws äußerst gelungenem International Terminal am Bahnhof Waterloo, betrug 57 Millionen Pfund. Obgleich die Zielsetzung hier sehr viel umfassender ist, erinnert die Anlage doch an das von Itsuko Hasegawa entworfene Yamanashi Museum of Fruit, das ebenfalls aus einer Abfolge von Gewächshausbauten besteht. Die Kuppeln in St. Austell basieren auf Leichtbaukonstruktionen mit dem im Verhältnis zu ihrer Oberfläche größtmöglichen Rauminhalt. Die Verkleidung besteht aus „durchsichtigen, luftgefüllten Folienkissen (ETFE oder Ethylentetrafluorethylen)". Das Ganze soll „den Eindruck eines biomorphen Organismus" hervorrufen. Der Architekt erläutert: „Der endgültige Entwurf stellt die perfekte Erfüllung von Buckminster Fullers Vision dar – maximaler Rauminhalt bei minimaler Oberfläche." Bei dem am 15. Mai 2000 eröffneten Besucherzentrum „handelt es sich in erster Linie um eine Lehreinrichtung mit multimedialen Exponaten, die in die Ziele des Projekts einführen. Seine spektakulär geschwungene und gerundete Architektur passt sich den Umrisslinien der ehemaligen Kaolingrube an. Das für 645 000 Besucher pro Jahr ausgelegte **EDEN-PROJEKT** zog im ersten Jahr nach seiner Eröffnung 1,956 Millionen Menschen an. Das 2002 fertig gewordene, 2,5 Millionen Pfund teure Gebäude der Eden Foundation kommt gänzlich ohne die Verwendung von PVC aus und umfasst 1800 m².

Ce très curieux projet se veut « une vitrine de la biodiversité globale et de la dépendance de l'homme par rapport aux plantes ». Sa première phase, achevée en 2001, se compose de 23 000 m² de « capsules transparentes » (biomes) interconnectées, à microclimat contrôlé, implantées dans un paysage aménagé. Le budget de ce projet, qui a fait appel aux mêmes consultants que ceux qui avaient collaboré avec Grimshaw au Terminal international de Waterloo, s'est élevé à 57 millions de livres. Bien que ces objectifs puissent sembler très éloignés, cette entreprise rappelle le Musée du fruit de Yamanashi, conçu par Itsuko Hasegawa au Japon, également composé d'une série de serres. Les dômes de Saint Austell sont faites de structures légères offrant le plus grand volume possible par rapport à leur surface. L'habillage est en « oreillers en film optiquement transparent (en ETFE ou éthylène tétra fluoro éthylène) gonflé ». L'ensemble donne « l'impression d'un organisme biomorphique ». Pour l'architecte : « La réalisation finale représente l'accomplissement parfait de la vision de Buckminster Fuller, le plus grand volume clos possible sous la surface couvrante la plus réduite possible. » Le Centre d'accueil des visiteurs, ouvert le 15 mai 2000, est « essentiellement un centre éducatif abritant des présentations multimédias qui expliquent les buts et objectifs du projet. Sa courbure spectaculaire se fond dans les contours de la carrière. » Prévu pour 645 000 visiteurs annuels, le **PROJET EDEN** en a attiré près de 2 millions la première année. Le bâtiment de la Eden Foundation, construit selon un programme entièrement sans PVC, est une construction de 1800 m² de 2,5 millions de livres, achevée en 2002.

Fitting into the landscape of Bodelva Pit, the architecture calls on high technology that fully respects the environment. The very large volume of the PVC-free domes is, in fact, the result of imagined spherical shapes.

Die Architektur – Hochtechnologie, die die Umwelt schont – schmiegt sich in die Landschaft der ehemaligen Bodelva Kaolingrube. Die mächtigen PVC-freien Kuppeln sind Teilsegmente gedachter Kugeln.

Au cœur du paysage de Bodelva Pit, l'architecture fait appel à une haute technologie qui respecte parfaitement l'environnement. Le volume imposant des dômes sans PVC est en fait la traduction de formes sphériques imaginaires.

The faceted domes of the complex glow like an unreal form of life. The Foundation Building, with its series of 10 propped softwood beams, oriented towards the pit, is seen below, left.

Die facettierten Kuppeln des Komplexes leuchten wie unwirkliche Lebensformen. Das Gebäude der Eden Foundation mit zehn schiefen, zur Grube orientierten Weichholzstützen ist unten links zu sehen.

Les dômes à facettes du complexe luisent d'une forme irréelle de vie. On voit ci-dessous à gauche le bâtiment de la fondation et ses séries de 10 poutres en bois tendre étayées, en direction de la fosse.

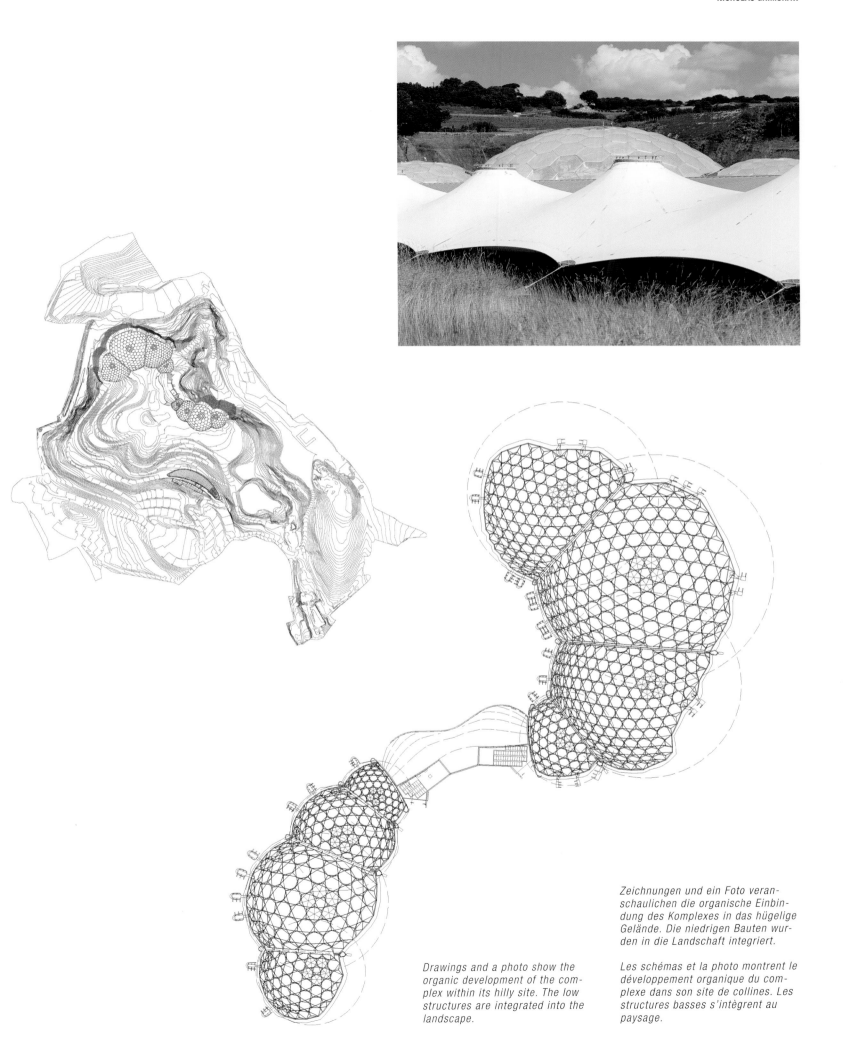

Drawings and a photo show the organic development of the complex within its hilly site. The low structures are integrated into the landscape.

Zeichnungen und ein Foto veranschaulichen die organische Einbindung des Komplexes in das hügelige Gelände. Die niedrigen Bauten wurden in die Landschaft integriert.

Les schémas et la photo montrent le développement organique du complexe dans son site de collines. Les structures basses s'intègrent au paysage.

GUSTAFSON GUTHRIE NICHOL

Gustafson Guthrie Nichol Ltd
Pier 55, Floor 3
1101 Alaskan Way
Seattle, WA 98101
USA

Tel: +1 206 903 6802
Fax: +1 206 903 6804
E-mail: contact@ggnltd.com
Web: www.ggnltd.com

KATHRYN GUSTAFSON was born in 1951 in the US. She attended the University of Washington (Seattle, 1970), the Fashion Institute of Technology (New York, 1971), and the École Nationale Supérieure du Paysage (Versailles, France, 1979). Gustafson Porter Ltd was founded in 1997 by Kathryn Gustafson and Neil Porter. In 1999, Gustafson, with partners **JENNIFER GUTHRIE** and **SHANNON NICHOL**, established the practice Gustafson Guthrie Nichol Ltd in Seattle. Aside from Towards Paradise (Venice Architecture Biennale, Venice, Italy, 2008), the firm has completed the Lurie Garden in Millennium Park (Chicago, Illinois, 2004, published here); and the Kogod Courtyard at the Smithsonian Institution (Washington, D.C., 2005–07, also published here). Current work includes CityCenterDC, a mixed-use project being developed with Foster + Partners (Washington, D.C., 2010–); the Bill and Melinda Gates Foundation Campus (Seattle, 2011); and the Smithsonian National Museum of African American History and Culture gardens (Washington, D.C., 2015).

KATHRYN GUSTAFSON wurde 1951 in den Vereinigten Staaten geboren. 1970 studierte sie an der University of Washington (Seattle), ab 1971 am Fashion Institute of Technology an der State University of New York, wo sie ihren Abschluss im Fach Modedesign machte. Danach ging sie nach Paris und studierte Landschaftsarchitektur an der École nationale supérieure du paysage (Versailles) und machte dort 1979 ihr Diplom. Das Büro Gustafson Porter Ltd wurde 1997 von Kathryn Gustafson und Neil Porter gegründet. 1999 gründete Gustafson gemeinsam mit ihren Büropartnerinnen **JENNIFER GUTHRIE** und **SHANNON NICHOL** das Büro Gustafson Guthrie Nichol Ltd in Seattle. Neben dem Projekt „Towards Paradise" für die Architekturbiennale Venedig 2008 hat das Büro 2004 den Lurie Garden im Millennium Park in Chicago, Illinois ausgeführt (hier vorgestellt) sowie den Kogod Courtyard, einen Innenhof im Gebäude der Smithsonian Institution (Washington, D.C., 2005–07, ebenfalls hier vorgestellt). Zu den im Bau befindlichen Projekten gehören das CityCenterDC, ein Projekt für eine Mischnutzung, das gemeinsam mit dem Büro Foster + Partners (Washington, D.C., seit 2010) geplant wird, sowie der Bill and Melinda Gates Foundation Campus (Seattle, 2011) und die Gartenanlage des Smithsonian National Museum of African American History and Culture (Washington, D.C.), die 2015 fertiggestellt werden soll.

KATHRYN GUSTAFSON, née aux États-Unis en 1951, a étudié à l'université de Washington (Seattle, 1970), à l'Institut des technologies de la mode (New York, 1971) et à l'École nationale supérieure du paysage (Versailles, 1979). L'agence Gustafson Porter Ltd a été fondée en 1997 par Kathryn Gustafson et Neil Porter. En 1999, Gustafson et ses associés, **JENNIFER GUTHRIE** et **SHANNON NICHOL**, ont fondé l'agence Gustafson Guthrie Nichol Ltd à Seattle. En dehors de *Towards Paradise* (Biennale d'architecture de Venise, 2008), l'agence a réalisé le Lurie Garden dans le Millennium Park (Chicago, Illinois, 2004, publié ici) et la Kogod Courtyard à la Smithsonian Institution (Washington, 2005–07, également publiée ici). Elle travaille actuellement sur les projets suivants aux États-Unis : CityCenterDC, projet immobilier mixte en collaboration avec Foster + Partners (Washington, 2010–) ; le campus de la Bill and Melinda Gates Foundation (Seattle, 2011) et les jardins du Smithsonian National Museum of African American History and Culture (Washington, 2015).

LURIE GARDEN

Chicago, Illinois, USA, 2004

Address: Monroe Street and Columbus Drive, Chicago, IL 60601, USA, www.luriegarden.org
Area: 12 629 m². Client: Millennium Park. Cost: not disclosed
Collaboration: Piet Oudolf (Plantsman), Robert Israel (Conceptual Reviewer)

The **LURIE GARDEN** is situated on the roof of the Lakefront Millennium Parking Garage in Chicago's Millennium Park. The site is between the band shell designed by Frank O. Gehry and a renovation of the Art Institute of Chicago by Renzo Piano. Millennium Park is part of Grant Park and the Lurie Garden "continues the precedent of Grant Park's 'rooms' with treed enclosures, perimeter circulation, and axial views; it expresses these qualities in forms that are distinct to the garden's special site and context." A large hedge encloses the garden from the north and west. The land forms within the garden were created using lightweight geofoam due to weight restrictions on the garage roof. Although the garden is manifestly urban in its site and surroundings, its artificial aspects are by no means visible. It is, rather, an attractive public space that has been designed to accommodate large crowds exiting nearby concerts. Its modernity sits well with the architectural environment and particularly in the presence of works by Frank Gehry and Renzo Piano. Limestone from a local midwestern quarry is used for curbing, stone stairs, stair landings, wall coping, and wall cladding in the interior of the garden. Flamed granite is used as paving and wall veneer in the water feature and the Dark Plate area.

Der **LURIE GARDEN** ist auf dem Dach des Parkhauses Lakefront Millenium im Millenium Park von Chicago angelegt worden. Das Gelände befindet sich zwischen der von Frank O. Gehry entworfenen Konzertmuschel und dem von Renzo Piano renovierten Flügel des Art Institute of Chicago. Der Millennium Park gehört zum Grant Park, und im Lurie Garden „finden die Gartenräume des Grant Park mit den von Bäumen umschlossenen Bereichen, den am Rand geführten Wegeverbindungen und den Sichtachsen ihre Fortsetzung. Die neue Gartenanlage drückt diese Qualitäten in einer Formensprache aus, die das besondere Gelände und den Kontext des Gartens hervorhebt." Eine große Hecke begrenzt den Garten an der Nord- und Westseite. Die Geländemodulation im Garten ist mit leichtem EPS-Hartschaum (Geofoam) gestaltet, um den Gewichtsbeschränkungen auf dem Parkhausdach Rechnung zu tragen. Auch wenn es sich aufgrund der Lage und der Umgebung um einen ausgesprochen urbanen Garten handelt, so bleibt doch seine Künstlichkeit verborgen. Der Garten ist ein attraktiver öffentlicher Freiraum, der so geplant ist, dass er große Menschenmengen aufnehmen kann, die von den benachbarten Konzerten kommen. Seine Modernität passt gut zu dem architektonischen Umfeld, besonders zu den Arbeiten von Frank O. Gehry und Renzo Piano. Kalkstein aus einem örtlichen Steinbruch im Mittelwesten wurde für die Randsteine, Natursteintreppen, Podeste, die Verkleidung der Mauern und die Mauerkronen im Garten verwendet. Geflammter Granit wurde als Bodenpflaster und Mauerverblendung beim Wasserspiel und im Bereich der Dark Plate verwendet.

Le **LURIE GARDEN** a été aménagé sur la toiture du parking Lakefront Millennium Parking Garage, dans le Millennium Park à Chicago, entre l'auditorium en plein air signé Frank O. Gehry et l'aile du Chicago Art Institute rénovée par Renzo Piano. Le Millennium Park fait partie du Grant Park et le Lurie Garden « reprend le précédent créé par ce parc de "pièces" entourées d'arbres, de circulation périmétrique et de vues en perspective. Il exprime cette spécificité par des formes adaptées aux caractéristiques du site et du contexte ». Une importante haie protège le jardin au nord et à l'ouest. De légers vallonnements ont été créés en Géofoam légère pour éviter de trop alourdir la toiture du parking. Même si le site et l'environnement de ce jardin sont résolument urbains, ses aspects artificiels restent invisibles. C'est un lieu public attractif, conçu pour accueillir des visiteurs en grand nombre, comme les spectateurs des concerts de plein air, par exemple. Sa modernité s'intègre bien à son environnement architectural et en particulier aux réalisations de Gehry et de Piano. Les bordures, les escaliers, les paliers, les couronnements et le parement des murs sont en pierre calcaire du Midwest. Le pavement et l'habillement des fontaines et du Dark Plate sont en granit flammé.

As seen against the Chicago skyline (left page) or in the plan and "aerial" view on this page, the garden quite literally brings a breath of fresh air and natural color to the otherwise metallic and mineral urban environment.

Vor dem Hintergrund der Skyline von Chicago (linke Seite), aber auch auf dem Grundriss und der „Luftaufnahme" auf dieser Seite erkennt man, dass der Garten fast im wörtlichen Sinn eine frische Brise und natürliche Farben in ein ansonsten von Stahl und Stein geprägtes urbanes Umfeld bringt.

Devant le panorama urbain de Chicago (page de gauche) ou dans le plan et la vue « aérienne » de cette page, le jardin apporte un peu de fraîcheur et de couleurs naturelles dans un environnement minéral et métallique.

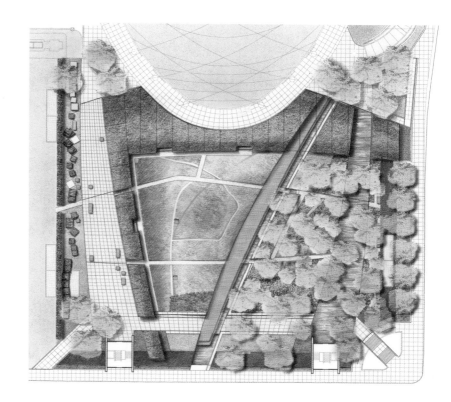

The convivial atmosphere of the park is visible in these images, which give little hint that the park was created on the rooftop of a parking area. Frank O. Gehry's band shell is visible in the image above.

Auf diesen Bildern spürt man die heitere und gesellige Atmosphäre des Parks, und man denkt nicht, dass er auf dem Dach eines Parkhauses angelegt wurde. Auf dem Bild oben ist im Hintergrund die Konzertmuschel von Frank O. Gehry zu erkennen.

L'atmosphère conviviale du parc, qui se sent dans ces images, ne laisse rien deviner de son aménagement sur la toiture d'un parking. En haut à gauche, la scène d'orchestre créée par Frank O. Gehry.

Though the landscape created by the designers in this place is essentially "artificial" as opposed to being "natural," its dense planting and flowers, as seen in the image above, give a very definite impression of allowing the natural world to take its rightful place in the city.

Auch wenn der von den Planern geschaffene Gartenraum durch und durch „künstlich" ist, als Gegensatz zu „natürlich", so vermittelt die dichte Bepflanzung den Eindruck, als würde die Natur den ihr rechtmäßig zustehenden Platz in der Stadt einnehmen, wie man auf dem Bild oben erkennt.

Si le paysage créé est essentiellement « artificiel » – par opposition à « naturel » –, la densité des plantations, comme le montre l'image ci-dessus, donne l'impression que le monde naturel a retrouvé la place qui lui revenait.

ROBERT AND ARLENE KOGOD COURTYARD
Washington, D.C., USA, 2005–07

Address: 8th and F Streets, NW, Donald W. Reynolds Center, Washington, D.C. 20001, USA
Area: 2601 m². Client: The Smithsonian Institution. Cost: not disclosed
Collaboration: Foster + Partners (Design Architects)

The **KOGOD COURTYARD** is a new public space in the center of the historic United States Patent Office building. Called the Donald Reynolds Center, the structure houses the Smithsonian American Art Museum and National Portrait Gallery. Enclosed by a glass canopy, the courtyard receives museum goers or formal events for up to 1000 people. A central water feature runs the length of the space. The landscaping work is intended as a "link between the historic building and the new roof." Large stone planters with 7.5-meter-high canopy trees are used to define a central space in the courtyard. The designers state: "The planting concept for the Robert and Arlene Kogod Courtyard reinforces the overall design concept. The temperate palette of evergreen trees and shrubs complement and distinguish the existing architecture of the courtyard with their variations in scale, form, and texture as well as the symmetry or asymmetry of their arrangement." Architectural lighting is part of the project, allowing the space to be equally attractive after nightfall. Granite pavers with a flamed finish contrasts with honed white marble cladding on the planters. The design architects for the overall project are Foster + Partners.

Der **KOGOD COURTYARD** ist ein neuer öffentlicher Innenhof in dem historischen Gebäude des US-Patentamts. Das heutige Donald Reynolds Center beherbergt das Smithsonian Museum für amerikanische Kunst und die Nationale Porträtgalerie. Der Innenhof wird von einem Glasdach geschlossen, sodass sich hier die Museumsbesucher bewegen können oder auch Veranstaltungen für bis zu 1000 Personen stattfinden können. Eine zentrale Wasserinstallation wird durch die gesamte Länge des Raums geführt. Der landschaftsgestalterische Entwurf soll als „Verbindung zwischen dem historischen Gebäude und dem neuen Dach wirken". Steintröge, die mit 7,5 m hohen großkronigen Bäumen bepflanzt sind, definieren den zentralen Raum in diesem Innenhof. Die Planer bemerken dazu: „Die Bepflanzung des Robert and Arlene Kogod Courtyard betont das gesamte Entwurfskonzept. Die gemäßigten Farben der immergrünen Bäume und Gehölze, ihre unterschiedlichen Größen, Formen und Texturen sowie ihre symmetrische oder asymmetrische Anordnung vervollständigen die vorhandene Architektur und betonen sie." Die Beleuchtung, mit der die Architektur in Szene gesetzt wird, ist Teil des Projekts und trägt zur Attraktivität dieses Raums nach Einbruch der Dunkelheit bei. Geflammte Granitplatten als Bodenbelag kontrastieren mit der geschliffenen weißen Marmorverkleidung der Pflanztröge. Entwurfsplaner für das Gesamtprojekt ist das Büro Foster + Partners.

La **KOGOD COURTYARD** est un nouvel espace public créé au centre du siège historique de l'administration des brevets des États-Unis. Appelé Donald Reynolds Center, ce bâtiment abrite aujourd'hui le Smithsonian American Art Museum et la National Portrait Gallery. Abritée par un auvent de verre, la cour accueille les visiteurs des musées et le public de diverses manifestations (jusqu'à 1000 participants). Un bassin central occupe toute la longueur de l'espace. L'aménagement paysager est conçu pour faire le « lien entre le bâtiment historique et la nouvelle verrière ». D'importantes jardinières de pierre plantées d'arbres de plus de 7 m de haut entourent l'espace central. Les paysagistes précisent : « Le concept des plantations renforce celui de l'ensemble. La palette discrète d'arbres et de buissons à feuilles persistantes complète et anime l'architecture existante de la cour par des variations d'échelle, de forme et de texture, ainsi que par la symétrie ou l'asymétrie des implantations. » L'éclairage architectural fait partie intégrante de ce projet, afin de rendre le lieu tout aussi attractif en nocturne. Un pavement de granit flammé contraste avec le parement en marbre blanc veiné des jardinières. L'agence d'architecture responsable de l'ensemble du projet était Foster + Partners.

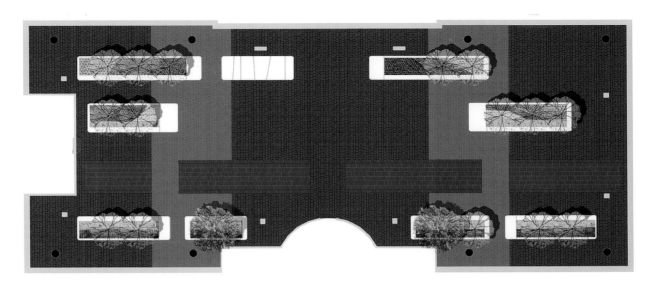

Within the walls of the Neoclassical Smithsonian American Art Museum and National Portrait Gallery, Gustafson Guthrie Nichol have created garden spaces that are placed, in the image below, under a light, curving skylight structure.

Das Büro Gustafson Guthrie Nichol hat im Innenhof des klassizistischen Gebäudekomplexes des Smithsonian Museum für amerikanische Kunst und der Nationalen Porträtgalerie unter einer leichten, gewellten Oberlichtkonstruktion Gartenräume geschaffen.

C'est sous une immense verrière ondulée tendue entre les murs du Smithsonian American Art Museum et de la National Portrait Gallery de style néoclassique que l'agence Gustafson Guthrie Nichol a créé ce jardin.

The natural presence in the building is, of course, circumscribed by the need for visitors to be able to circulate freely, but the designers have found an appropriate balance between the presence of trees and shrubs with the mineral passageways required.

Die Natur innerhalb des Gebäudes ist natürlich eingeschränkt, damit sich die Besucher frei bewegen können, aber die Planer haben ein ausgewogenes Verhältnis der Bäume und Kleingehölze zu den geforderten Wegeverbindungen mit ihren Plattenbelägen gefunden.

La présence de la nature dans le bâtiment est conditionnée par la liberté de déplacement des visiteurs, mais les architectes ont trouvé un équilibre harmonieux dans l'implantation des jardinières d'arbres et de fleurs et les allées dallées de pierre.

Whether in daylight or after sunset, the spaces designed by Gustafson Guthrie Nichol make full use of lighting, as seen in the image of the stone planter and bench (right). A central water feature animates the space (below).

Ob bei Tag oder nach Sonnenunter-gang, die von Gustafson Guthrie Nichol entworfenen Gartenräume werden durch das Licht in Szene gesetzt, wie man auf dem Bild mit dem Pflanztrog und der Bank (rechts) sehen kann. Ein Wasserbecken belebt die Mitte des Raums (unten).

De jour comme de nuit, les espaces conçus par Gustafson Guthrie Nichol utilisent toutes les ressources de l'éclairage naturel et artificiel, comme le montrent ces images d'une jardinière de pierre et de son banc (à droite). Un bassin anime une partie de l'espace (ci-dessous).

HEBERLE MAYER

Heberle Mayer
Büro für Architektur & Städtebau
Karl-Marx-Allee 81
10243 Berlin
Germany

Tel: +49 30 20 63 47 70
Fax: +49 30 20 63 47 80
E-mail: post@heberle-mayer.de
Web: www.heberle-mayer.de

MARTIN HEBERLE was born in 1967 in Tübingen, Germany. He studied architecture beginning in 1989, obtaining his diploma from the TU Berlin in 1996. From 1997 to 2000, he worked in the office of Barkow Leibinger Architects. He began his partnership with Christof Mayer in 2000. **CHRISTOF MAYER** was born in 1967 in Wangen im Allgäu, Germany. From 1989 to 1998, he studied architecture in Berlin and London, receiving his diploma from the TU Berlin in 1998. He was one of the founders of raumlaborberlin (1999). Raumlaborberlin is a group of architects and urban designers based in Berlin who work in "various interdisciplinary teams that investigate strategies for urban renewal." They have experimented in urban design and planning, architecture, interactive environments, research, and the design of public space and art installations. The work of Heberle Mayer (Büro für Architektur & Städtebau) includes: IHP, the construction of a new roof over the existing roller sports facility at the Poststadion (Tiergarten, Berlin, 2009–10); U6 (Berlin, 2009–10, published here); W44, the rehabilitation, modernization and expansion of EFH (Frohnau, Berlin, 2009–10); SWY, a new detached house (Treptow, Berlin, 2013–14); and PAU8, an office building (Lichterfelde, Berlin, 2013–14), all in Germany.

MARTIN HEBERLE wurde 1967 in Tübingen geboren. Sein Architekturstudium, das er 1989 aufnahm, schloss er 1996 mit Diplom an der TU Berlin ab. Von 1997 bis 2000 war er für Barkow Leibinger Architekten tätig. Seit 2000 praktiziert er in Partnerschaft mit Christof Mayer. **CHRISTOF MAYER** wurde 1969 in Wangen im Allgäu geboren. Er studierte von 1989 bis 1998 Architektur in Berlin und London. Sein Diplom schloss er 1998 an der TU Berlin ab. 1999 war Mayer Mitbegründer von raumlaborberlin, einer Gruppe Berliner Architekten und Stadtplaner, die in „verschiedenen interdisziplinären Teams Strategien für städtebauliche Erneuerung entwickeln". Experimentierfelder der Gruppe sind Stadtplanung, Architektur, interaktive Räume, Forschung, die Gestaltung von öffentlichem Raum sowie Kunstinstallationen. Zu den Arbeiten von Heberle Mayer (Büro für Architektur & Städtebau) gehören u. a. IHP, der Neubau eines Dachs für die Rollschuhbahn im Poststadion (Tiergarten, Berlin, 2009 bis 2010), U6 (Berlin, 2009–10, hier vorgestellt), W44, die Sanierung, Modernisierung und Erweiterung eines Einfamilienhauses (Frohnau, Berlin, 2009–10), SWY, ein frei stehendes Wohnhaus (Treptow, Berlin, 2013–14) sowie das Bürogebäude PAU8 (Lichterfelde, Berlin, 2013–14).

MARTIN HEBERLE est né en 1967 à Tübingen, en Allemagne. Il a fait des études d'architecture à partir de 1989 et a obtenu son diplôme à l'Université technique (TU) de Berlin en 1996. De 1997 à 2000, il a travaillé dans l'agence Barkow Leibinger Architects. Le partenariat avec **CHRISTOF MAYER** a commencé en 2000. Ce dernier est né en 1967 à Wangen im Allgäu, en Allemagne. De 1989 à 1998, il a fait des études d'architecture à Berlin et Londres et a obtenu son diplôme à la TU de Berlin en 1998. Il est l'un des fondateurs de raumlaborberlin (1999), Un groupe d'architectes et d'urbanistes basé à Berlin qui travaille en « diverses équipes interdisciplinaires explorant des stratégies de renouvellement urbain ». Ils se sont ainsi essayés à l'urbanisme et la planification, l'architecture, les environnements interactifs, la recherche et la conception d'espaces publics et d'installations artistiques. Les réalisations de Heberle Mayer (Büro für Architektur & Städtebau) comprennent : IHP, un nouveau toit pour le centre de sports sur roulettes du Poststadion (Tiergarten, Berlin, 2009–10) ; U6 (Berlin, 2009–10, publié ici) ; W44, la rénovation, modernisation et extension d'EFH (Frohnau, Berlin, 2009–10) ; SWY, une maison individuelle (Treptow, Berlin, 2013–14) et PAU8, un immeuble de bureaux (Lichterfelde, Berlin, 2013–14), toutes en Allemagne.

U6 BERLIN PENTHOUSE

Berlin, Germany, 2009–10

Area: 135 m². Client: Vera Tollmann, Christian von Barries
Cost: €70 000

Working in collaboration with his clients, architect Christof Mayer proposed to create an open-plan apartment starting with a Filclair kit greenhouse that he placed on the roof of an industrial building in Berlin. The concept is related to a greenhouse that the French architects Lacaton & Vassal proposed for Documenta 12 in Kassel (2007). Disagreement with Documenta director Roger Buergel led the French pair to withdraw their names from the project, which was nonetheless seen by Mayer's clients. They obtained a 30-year lease on rooftop space. The architect explains: "The planning and approval by the authorities proved to be a problem. After much back and forth and a series of constraints (do not build over the entire width of the roof, south wall to be built-up as a fire wall, all interior walls to be constructed from lightweight concrete blocks), the backpack-structure passed the building regulations." Although this concept might well be used elsewhere at relatively low cost, the architect points out that it is not easy to find owners who are willing to rent rooftop space.

Gemeinsam mit den Auftraggebern entwickelte Christof Mayer ein offenes Wohnkonzept, das mit einem Filclair-Gewächshaus auf dem Dach eines Berliner Gewerbebaus realisiert werden konnte. Der Entwurf nimmt Bezug auf ein Gewächshaus, das die französischen Architekten Lacaton & Vassal für die documenta 12 (2007) in Kassel geplant hatten. Unstimmigkeiten mit dem damaligen künstlerischen Leiter der documenta, Roger Buergel, veranlassten das französische Team, sich von ihrem Projekt zu distanzieren, das Mayers Berliner Auftraggeber zuvor noch gesehen hatten. Sie sicherten sich einen 30-jährigen Pachtvertrag auf einem Dach. Die Architekten erklären: „Planung und Baugenehmigung erwiesen sich als problematisch. Nach langem Hin und Her und einer Reihe von Auflagen (keine Bebauung der gesamten Dachbreite, Südwand als Brandmauer zu errichten, sämtliche Innenwände aus Leichtbetonsteinen zu bauen) wurde die Huckepackkonstruktion schließlich genehmigt." Obwohl sich das Konzept auch an anderen Standorten kostengünstig realisieren ließe, weisen die Architekten daraufhin, dass es schwierig sei, Bauherren zu finden, die Dachflächen pachten würden.

En collaboration avec ses clients, l'architecte Christof Mayer a suggéré de créer un appartement sans cloisons à partir d'une serre en kit Filclair qu'il a placée sur le toit d'un immeuble industriel de Berlin. Le projet fait référence à une serre proposée par les architectes français Lacaton & Vassal pour la Documenta 12 à Kassel (2007). À la suite d'un différend avec le directeur de la Documenta Roger Buergel, les Français ont retiré leurs noms du projet qui a néanmoins été vu par les clients de Mayer. Ils ont obtenu un bail de 30 ans pour un espace sur un toit. L'architecte explique : « La planification et le permis des autorités se sont avérés problématiques. Après maints allers et retours et la multiplication des contraintes (ne pas construire sur toute la largeur du toit, bâtir le mur sud comme mur pare-feu, toutes les parois intérieures en blocs de béton légers), la structure de survie a fini par respecter les règlementations en matière de construction. » C'est pourquoi, même si le concept peut parfaitement être utilisé ailleurs à un coût relativement faible, l'architecte souligne la difficulté de trouver des propriétaires acceptant de louer des espaces sur les toits.

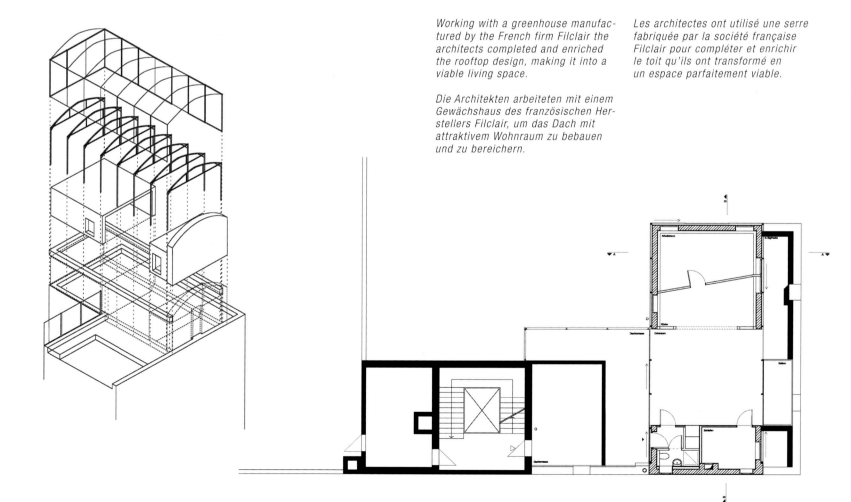

Working with a greenhouse manufactured by the French firm Filclair the architects completed and enriched the rooftop design, making it into a viable living space.

Die Architekten arbeiteten mit einem Gewächshaus des französischen Herstellers Filclair, um das Dach mit attraktivem Wohnraum zu bebauen und zu bereichern.

Les architectes ont utilisé une serre fabriquée par la société française Filclair pour compléter et enrichir le toit qu'ils ont transformé en un espace parfaitement viable.

Sunshades and bright, generous spaces characterize the interiors. As the plans to the left show, the basic forms of the structure are rectangular, with a long, arched roof.

Geprägt wird das Interieur von hellen, großzügigen Räumen und Sonnenblenden. Wie die Grundrisse auf der linken Seite belegen, ist die Grundform des Baus ein langes Rechteck mit einem Tonnendach.

L'intérieur est marqué par des paresoleil et des espaces clairs et généreux. Comme on le voit sur le plan à gauche, les formes de base de l'ensemble sont rectangulaires avec un long toit voûté.

ANNA HERINGER
AND EIKE ROSWAG

Roswag & Jankowski Architekten
Lehrter Str. 57 Haus 4
10557 Berlin
Germany

Tel: +49 30 89 73 37 73
Fax: +49 30 89 73 37 72
E-mail: kontakt@werk-a.de
Web: www.werk-a.de

ANNA HERINGER was born in 1977 in Rosenheim, Germany. She studied Architecture at the University of Linz in Austria (1999–2004) and is currently a Visiting Professor at the University of Stuttgart. She is also working on the BASEhabitat studio for building in developing countries at the University of Art and Design in Linz. She has been involved in rural development work with the NGOs Shanti and Dipshikha since 1997. **EIKE ROSWAG** was born in 1969 in Gießen, Germany. He obtained his Dipl.-Ing. Architecture degree from the Technical University in Berlin (1992–2000). He worked as a partner of ZRS Architekten Ingenieure in Berlin, beginning in 2003 on projects using earth as a building material. From 2003 to 2004 he worked on the design and construction of a rammed-earth house near Berlin (Ihlow House). Since 2006 he has been a partner of Roswag & Jankowski Architekten in Berlin and has taught at the Technical University there. Heringer and Roswag worked together on the Handmade School published here (Rudrapur, Dinajpur, Bangladesh, 2005), a recipient of the 2007 Aga Khan Award for Architecture.

ANNA HERINGER wurde 1977 in Rosenheim geboren. Sie studierte Architektur an der Kunstuniversität Linz in Österreich (1999–2004) und ist derzeit Gast-professorin an der Universität Stuttgart. An der Kunstuniversität Linz ist sie zudem am Projekt BASEhabitat beteiligt, das sich mit Architektur in Entwicklungsländern befasst. Seit 1997 engagiert sie sich für ländliche Entwicklungsprojekte der Nichtregierungsorganisationen Shanti und Dipshikha. **EIKE ROSWAG** wurde 1969 in Gießen geboren. Er schloss sein Architekturstudium an der Technischen Universität Berlin (1992–2000) als Diplom-Ingenieur ab. Er arbeitete als Partner bei ZRS Architekten Ingenieure in Berlin und begann 2003, Erde als Baumaterial bei seinen Projekten zu nutzen. 2003 bis 2004 arbeitete er am Entwurf und Bau eines Stampflehmhauses in der Nähe von Berlin (Haus Ihlow). Seit 2006 ist er Partner bei Roswag & Jankowski Architekten in Berlin und unterrichtet an der dortigen Technischen Universität. Heringer und Roswag realisierten gemeinsam die hier vorgestellte Handmade School (Rudrapur, Dinajpur, Bangladesch, 2005), die 2007 mit dem Aga-Khan-Preis für Architektur ausgezeichnet wurde.

ANNA HERINGER, née en 1977 à Rosenheim, Allemagne, a étudié l'architecture à l'université de Linz (Autriche, 1999–2004) et est actuellement professeur invitée à l'université de Stuttgart. Elle travaille également au studio BASEhabitat de l'Université des arts et du design industriel de Linz, lequel conçoit des bâtiments pour les pays en voie de développement. Elle s'implique dans des projets de développement rural avec les ONG Shanti et Dipshikha depuis 1997. **EIKE ROSWAG**, né en 1969 à Gießen, Allemagne, est architecte diplômé de l'Université technique de Berlin (1992–2000). Il a travaillé comme associé pour ZRS Architekten Inge-nieure à Berlin, à partir de 2003, sur des projets utilisant la terre comme matériau de construction. En 2003–04, il a travaillé à la conception et la construction d'une maison en béton de terre près de Berlin (maison Ihlow). Depuis 2006, il est l'un des associés de Roswag & Jankowski Architekten à Berlin où il enseigne à l'Université technique. Heringer et Roswag ont collaboré sur le projet de la Handmade School publiée ici (Rudrapur, Dinajpur, Bangladesh, 2005) qui a reçu le prix Aga Khan d'architecture en 2007.

HANDMADE SCHOOL

Rudrapur, Dinajpur, Bangladesh, 2005

Floor area: 325 m². Client: Dipshikha/METI, Bangladesh. Cost: €25 000
Collaboration: Anna Heringer and Eike Roswag

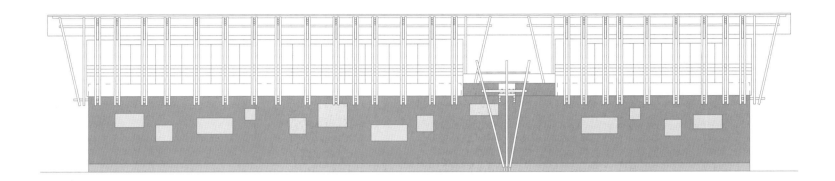

"We believe that architecture is more than simply shelter. It is intimately connected with the creation of identity and self-confidence. And this is the basis of sustainable development," declare Anna Heringer and Eike Roswag. Their school made of earth and bamboo was built for and with the Modern Education and Training Institute (METI) and its NGO mother organization, Dipshikha, in 2005 in Rudrapur in northern Bangladesh. The project was undertaken in cooperation with Shanti Bangladesh and the Papal Children's Mission (PMK). The ground floor of the structure has thick earth walls, while the upper story, where colorful saris are stretched on the ceiling, is made of bamboo. Three classrooms and six organically shaped "caves" are located on the ground floor, and two large, flexible class areas are on the upper floor. No less than 12 500 bamboo strips were used to make the porous façades of the upper level. Made with the assistance of 25 local laborers, the structure makes use of traditional building techniques with "technical improvements." The school is used by 168 children. The jury citation of the 2007 Aga Khan Award for Architecture given to the **HANDMADE SCHOOL** reads: "This joyous and elegant two-story primary school in rural Bangladesh has emerged from a deep understanding of local materials and a heartfelt connection to the local community. Its innovation lies in the adaptation of traditional methods and materials of construction to create light-filled celebratory spaces, as well as informal spaces for children. Earthbound materials, such as loam and straw, are combined with lighter elements like bamboo sticks and nylon lashing to shape a built form that addresses sustainability in construction in an exemplary manner."

„Wir glauben, dass Architektur mehr ist als nur ein Obdach. Sie ist eng verknüpft mit der Bildung von Identität und Selbstbewusstsein. Und sie ist Grundlage einer nachhaltigen Entwicklung", erklären Anna Heringer und Eike Roswag. Ihre Schule aus Bambus und Lehm wurde 2005 für das Modern Education and Training Institute (METI) und dessen NGO-Mutterorganisation Dipshikha in Rudrapur in Nord-Bangladesch erbaut. Das Projekt entstand in Kooperation mit Shanti Bangladesch und dem Päpstlichen Missionswerk der Kinder (PMK). Das Erdgeschoss des Baus hat massive Lehmmauern, während das obere Stockwerk, in dem bunte Saris unter der Decke hängen, aus Bambus gefertigt wurde. Im Erdgeschoss liegen drei Klassenzimmer und sechs organisch geformte „Höhlen", im Obergeschoss befinden sich zwei große flexible Schulräume. Die lichtdurchlässigen Fassaden des Obergeschosses wurden aus 12 500 Bambusstäben gefertigt. Der mithilfe von 25 ortsansässigen Arbeitern errichtete Bau bedient sich regionaler Bautechniken, die „technisch optimiert" wurden. Die Schule wird von 168 Kindern genutzt. In der Begründung der Jury des Aga-Khan-Preises für Architektur, den die **HANDMADE SCHOOL** 2007 erhielt, heißt es: „Die fröhliche und elegante zweistöckige Grundschule im ländlichen Bangladesch entstand aus einem tiefen Verständnis für regionale Materialien und einer zutiefst empfundenen Bindung an die örtliche Gemeinschaft. Ihre Neuheit liegt in der Abwandlung traditioneller Baumethoden und -materialien, um lichterfüllte, festliche und informelle Räume für Kinder zu schaffen. Erdverbundene Materialien wie Lehm und Stroh wurden mit leichteren Materialien wie Bambusstäben und Nylonseilen kombiniert, um einen Raum zu gestalten, der nachhaltiges Bauen exemplarisch umsetzt."

« Nous pensons que l'architecture doit être davantage qu'un simple abri. Elle est intimement liée à la création d'une identité et de la confiance en soi. C'est la base du développement durable », expliquent Anna Heringer et Eike Roswag. Leur école en terre et bambou a été édifiée pour l'Institut moderne d'éducation et de formation (METI) et son organisation non gouvernementale mère, Dipshikha, en 2005 à Rudrapur dans le nord du Bangladesh. Le projet a été initié en coopération avec Shanti Bangladesh et la mission papale pour l'enfance (PMK). Le rez-de-chaussée du bâtiment présente d'épais murs de terre tandis que l'étage, au plafond duquel pendent des saris de couleurs vives, est en bambou. Trois salles de classe et six « cavernes » de forme organique se trouvent au rez-de-chaussée et deux grandes salles d'utilisation souple à l'étage. 12 500 lattes de bambou ont été utilisées pour la façade du niveau supérieur. Mené avec l'aide de 25 paysans locaux, le chantier a fait appel à des techniques traditionnelles « techniquement améliorées ». La **HANDMADE SCHOOL** reçoit 168 enfants. La citation du jury du prix Aga Khan d'architecture 2007 précisait : « Cette élégante école de deux niveaux dans le Bangladesh rural est le résultat d'une profonde compréhension des matériaux locaux ainsi que d'un rapport sincère avec les populations locales. Son innovation réside dans son adaptation aux méthodes et aux matériaux de constructions traditionnels pour créer d'agréables espaces lumineux ainsi que des espaces informels pour les enfants. Les matériaux issus de la terre, tels que le limon et la paille, sont combinés avec des éléments plus légers tels que les branches de bambou et les cordes de nylon pour réaliser une construction dont la durabilité est exemplaire. »

Originality in architecture may well have to do with first anchoring a structure in local tradition and materials and then making it modern through details in design and construction.	*Originalität in der Architektur hat sicherlich viel damit zu tun, zunächst lokale Traditionen und Materialien zu berücksichtigen und erst dann durch gestalterische und bauliche Details modern zu interpretieren.*	*Souvent en architecture l'originalité tient à l'ancrage du projet dans les traditions et les matériaux locaux. L'apport de la modernité s'affirme alors dans les détails de conception et de construction.*

The flow of light and air through the building is obvious in these images. Nor does an emphasis on simple local materials give any sense that the building was made on a restricted budget.

Die Bilder veranschaulichen, wie Licht und Luft ungehindert durch das Gebäude strömen. Die einfachen lokalen Baumaterialien lassen dennoch nicht ahnen, dass das Budget für dieses Projekt knapp war.

Les flots d'air et de lumière qui pénètrent dans l'école sont évidents sur ces images. L'accent mis sur des matériaux locaux simples ne trahit en rien la faiblesse du budget de construction.

STEVEN HOLL

*Steven Holl Architects, P.C.
450 West 31st Street, 11th floor
New York, NY 10001, USA*

*Tel: +1 212 629 7262 / Fax: +1 212 629 7312
E-mail: nyc@stevenholl.com / Web: www.stevenholl.com*

Born in 1947 in Bremerton, Washington, **STEVEN HOLL** obtained his B.Arch degree from the University of Washington (1970). He studied in Rome and at the Architectural Association in London (1976). He opened his own office in New York in 1976. Holl has taught at the University of Washington, Syracuse University, and, since 1981, at Columbia University. His notable buildings include Void Space / Hinged Space Housing (Nexus World, Fukuoka, Japan, 1991); Stretto House (Dallas, Texas, 1992); Chapel of Saint Ignatius, Seattle University (Seattle, Washington, 1997); and an extension to the Cranbrook Institute of Science (Bloomfield Hills, Michigan, 1999). Winner of the 1998 Alvar Aalto Medal, Steven Holl's more recent work includes the Turbulence House in New Mexico for the artist Richard Tuttle (2005); the Pratt Institute Higgins Hall Center Insertion (Brooklyn, New York, 2005); and the New Residence at the Swiss Embassy (Washington, D.C., 2006) all in the USA unless stated otherwise. He recently won the competition (2009) for the Glasgow School of Art (Glasgow, UK), and completed an expansion and renovation of the Nelson-Atkins Museum of Art (Kansas City, Missouri, USA, 1999–2007); Linked Hybrid (Beijing, 2003–09); the Knut Hamsun Center (Hamarøy, Norway, 2006–09); HEART: Herning Museum of Contemporary Art (Herning, Denmark, 2007–09, published here); and the Vanke Center / Horizontal Skyscraper (Shenzhen, China, 2008–09, also published here), which won the 2011 AIA Honor Award for Architecture. Current projects include Cité de l'Océan et du Surf (Biarritz, France, 2005–10, with Solange Fabião); the Nanjing Museum of Art and Architecture (China, 2008–10); Shan-Shui Hangzhou (master plan, Hangzhou, China, 2010–); and the Hangzhou Music Museum (Hangzhou, China, 2010–).

STEVEN HOLL wurde 1947 in Bremerton, Washington, geboren. 1970 schloss er sein Studium an der University of Washington mit dem B.Arch. ab. Danach studierte er in Rom und an der Architectural Association in London (1976). 1976 gründete er sein Büro in New York. Holl lehrte an der University of Washington und der Syracuse University sowie seit 1981 an der Columbia University. Zu seinen Projekten zählen die Wohnanlage Void Space/Hinged Space (Nexus World, Fukuoka, Japan, 1991), das Stretto House (Dallas, Texas, 1992), die Kapelle St. Ignatius, Seattle University (Seattle, Washington, 1997), und ein Erweiterungsbau des Cranbrook Institute of Science (Bloomfield Hills, Michigan, 1999). 1998 wurde Holl mit der Alvar-Aalto-Medaille ausgezeichnet. Zu seinen neueren Bauwerken gehören das Turbulence House in New Mexico für den Künstler Richard Tuttle (2005), die Erweiterung des Pratt Institute Higgins Hall Center (Brooklyn, New York, 2005) und die neue Residenz der Schweizer Botschaft (Washington, D.C., 2006). 2009 gewann er den Wettbewerb für die Erweiterung der Glasgow School of Art (Glasgow, Schottland), und er vollendete einen Anbau und die Renovierung des Nelson-Atkins Museum of Art (Kansas City, Missouri, USA, 1999–2007), außerdem die Wohnanlage Linked Hybrid (Peking, 2003 bis 2009), das Knut Hamsun Center (Hamarøy, Norwegen, 2006–09), das HEART: Herning Museum of Contemporary Art (Herning, Dänemark, 2007–09, hier vorgestellt) und das Vanke Center/Horizontal Skyscraper (Shenzhen, China, 2008–09, ebenfalls hier vorgestellt), ein Projekt, für das er 2011 den Ehrenpreis für Architektur des American Institute of Architects (AIA) erhielt. Zu seinen laufenden Projekten zählen die Cité de l'Océan et du Surf (Biarritz, Frankreich, 2005–10, mit Solange Fabião), das Nanjing Museum of Art and Architecture (China, 2008–10), der Masterplan für Shan-Shui Hangzhou (China, seit 2010) und das Hangzhou Music Museum (seit 2010).

Né en 1947 à Bremerton (Washington), **STEVEN HOLL** a obtenu son B.Arch. à l'université de Washington (1970) et étudié à Rome et à l'AA à Londres (1976). Il ouvre une agence à New York en 1976. Il a enseigné à l'université de Washington, à l'université de Syracuse et, depuis 1981, à l'université Columbia. Parmi ses réalisations les plus notables : les immeubles de logements Void Space/Hinged Space (Nexus World, Fukuoka, Japon, 1991) ; la Stretto House (Dallas, Texas, 1992) ; la chapelle de Saint-Ignace, université de Seattle (Seattle, Washington, 1997) et une extension du Cranbrook Institute of Science (Bloomfield Hills, Michigan, 1999). Il est titulaire de la médaille Alvar Aalto 1998. Parmi ses réalisations plus récentes : la Turbulence House pour l'artiste Richard Tuttle (Nouveau-Mexique, 2005) ; le Higgins Hall du Pratt Institute (Brooklyn, New York, 2005) et la nouvelle résidence de l'ambassade de Suisse (Washington, 2006). Il a récemment remporté le concours (2009) pour la Glasgow School of Art (Glasgow, GB) et a achevé une extension et la rénovation du Nelson-Atkins Museum of Art (Kansas City, Missouri, 1999–2007). Il a aussi réalisé le complexe résidentiel Linked Hybrid (Pékin, 2003–09) ; le Centre Knut Hamsun (Hamarøy, Norvège, 2006–09) ; le HEART Herning Museum of Contemporary Art (Herning, Danemark, 2007–09, publié ici) et le Vanke Center/Horizontal Skyscraper (Shenzhen, Chine, 2008–09, publié ici), qui lui a valu le prix d'honneur d'architecture de l'AIA en 2011. Plus récemment : la Cité de l'océan et du surf (Biarritz, 2005–10, avec Solange Fabião) ; le Musée d'art et d'architecture de Nankin (Chine, 2008–10) ; le plan directeur de Shan-Shui Hangzhou (Hangzhou, Chine, 2010–) et le Musée de la musique de Hangzhou (2010–).

VANKE CENTER / HORIZONTAL SKYSCRAPER

Shenzhen, China, 2008–09

Address: Neihuan Road, Vanke Center, Dameisha, Yantian District, Shenzhen 518083, China
Area: 120 445 m² (building), 52 000 m² (landscape area)
Client: Shenzhen Vanke Real Estate Co. Cost: not disclosed

As seen from certain angles, the complex appears to be an assembly of different buildings. Though cladding varies, however, the entire very large building is part of a single complex.

Aus bestimmten Blickwinkeln wirkt der Komplex wie ein Ensemble aus verschiedenen Gebäuden. Trotz der unterschiedlichen Fassadenverkleidungen ist es aber ein einziger Gesamtkomplex.

Vu sous certains angles, le complexe donne l'impression d'un assemblage de différentes constructions d'habillages variés, qui constituent en réalité un seul bâtiment.

In the drawing to the right, the idea of the "horizontal skyscraper" is made clear. The office, residential, and hotel spaces are grouped in different parts of the building, which is supported on large pillars.

Auf der Zeichnung rechts wird der Gedanke des „horizontalen Hochhauses" deutlich. Büros, Wohnungen und das Hotel sind in unterschiedlichen Teilen des auf großen Stützen ruhenden Gebäudes zusammengefasst.

Le dessin de droite, illustre le concept de « gratte-ciel horizontal ». Les bureaux, les logements et l'hôtel sont installés dans différentes parties de l'immeuble qui repose sur d'énormes piliers.

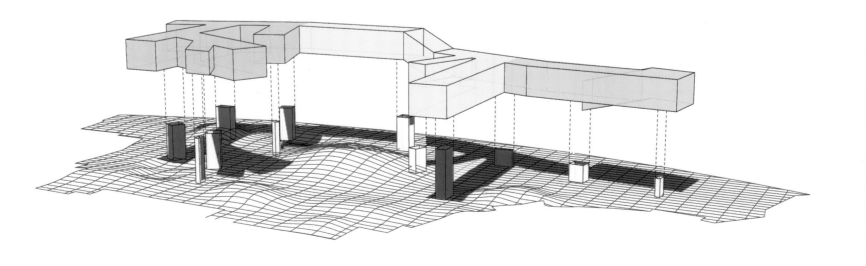

It is with some pride that Steven Holl describes this mixed-use complex as a **"HORIZONTAL SKYSCRAPER"** that is as long as the Empire State Building is tall. The Vanke Center includes hotel space, offices for the Vanke Company, serviced apartments, and a public park. While Holl's Linked Hybrid (Beijing, 2003–09) emphasizes a certain verticality, the Vanke Center is mainly about horizontal lines inserted into a tropical landscape. In fact, the landscape contains a conference center, and, under mounds, a 500-seat auditorium and restaurants. The office explains: "The building appears as if it were once floating on a higher sea that has now subsided, leaving the structure propped up high on eight legs. The decision to float one large structure right under the 35-meter height limit, instead of several smaller structures each catering to a specific program, generates the largest possible green space open to the public on the ground level." The landscape component of the project is also one element of the environmental strategy of Steven Holl because its ponds, fed by a gray-water system, serve to cool the air. Solar panels are used as well as local materials such as bamboo.

Steven Holl beschreibt diesen Gebäudekomplex mit einem gewissen Stolz als **„HORIZONTALEN WOLKENKRATZER"**, der so lang ist, wie das Empire State Building hoch ist. Zum Vanke Center gehören ein Hotel, Büros für die Firma Vanke Company, ein Aparthotel und ein öffentlicher Park. Holls Projekt Linked Hybrid hat noch eine gewisse Vertikalität. Beim Vanke Center herrschen horizontale Linien vor, die in eine tropische Landschaft eingefügt sind. Auf dem Gelände befinden sich ein Konferenzzentrum und unter künstlichen Hügeln verborgen ein Auditorium mit 500 Sitzplätzen sowie Restaurants. Das Büro erklärt: „Das Gebäude wirkt, als wäre es früher einmal auf einem höheren Wasserspiegel geschwommen, und nun sieht man den auf acht Stützen gesetzten Gebäudekomplex. Die Entscheidung, ein großes Gebäude über dem Erdboden schweben zu lassen und dabei knapp unter der vorgeschriebenen Grenze von 35 m Höhe zu bleiben, anstatt mehrere kleine Gebäude zu errichten, hat zur Folge, dass ein größtmöglicher öffentlicher Freiraum entsteht." Die Freiraumgestaltung gehört zur Umweltstrategie von Steven Holl, denn die dort angelegten Teiche werden mit Grauwasser gespeist und dienen dazu, die Luft zu kühlen. Solarzellen kommen ebenso zum Einsatz wie ortstypische Baumaterialien, z. B. Bambus.

Steven Holl présente avec fierté ce complexe immobilier mixte comme un **« GRATTE-CIEL HORIZONTAL »** aussi long que l'Empire State Building est haut. Le Vanke Center regroupe un hôtel, des bureaux de la Vanke Company, des appartements en résidence et un parc public. Si le Linked Hybrid de Holl (Pékin, 2003–09) mettait l'accent sur une certaine verticalité, le Vanke Center joue essentiellement de son horizontalité, insérée dans un paysage de type tropical. Les aménagements paysagers abritent également un centre de conférences, des restaurants et un auditorium de 500 places. Selon le descriptif : « On pourrait imaginer que l'immeuble a longtemps flotté sur une mer aujourd'hui disparue, qui, en se retirant, l'aurait laissé reposer sur le fond sur huit grands pieds. La décision de faire "flotter" l'immeuble juste sous la limite de hauteur autorisée de 35 m, plutôt que d'opter pour plusieurs constructions autonomes plus basses consacrées chacune à un programme différent, a permis d'accroître au maximum la surface des espaces verts ouverts au public. » La partie paysagère du projet relève de la stratégie environnementale de l'architecte, les bassins, alimentés par les eaux grises, servant à rafraîchir l'air. Des panneaux solaires et des matériaux naturels locaux comme le bambou sont également utilisés.

Steven Holl has shown a consistent interest in the landscaping around his buildings. Planting adds to the continuity of the whole and relieves the appearance of density that would otherwise have dominated.

Steven Holl hat sich schon immer für die Landschaftsgestaltung an seinen Gebäuden interessiert. Pflanzen tragen zur Kontinuität des Ganzen bei und mildern die Massigkeit der Baukörper, die sonst dominieren würden.

Steven Holl manifeste un intérêt de longue date pour les aménagements paysagers de ses réalisations. Les plantations contribuent à la continuité de l'ensemble et allègent l'impression de densité qu'un tel projet aurait pu susciter.

At the same time as the architecture appears to rise from the earth or to enter it, the planting rises up on the roof of the building, as seen in the image above, right. Below, an overall plan of the complex.

So wie die Architektur sich von der Erde zu lösen scheint oder in sie eindringt, erobern sich die Pflanzen das Dach des Gebäudes, wie man auf dem Bild oben rechts erkennen kann. Unten: Gesamtplan des Komplexes.

L'architecture semble sortir du sol ou y plonger, d'autant plus que les plantations recouvrent la toiture (en haut à droite). Ci-dessous, plan général du complexe.

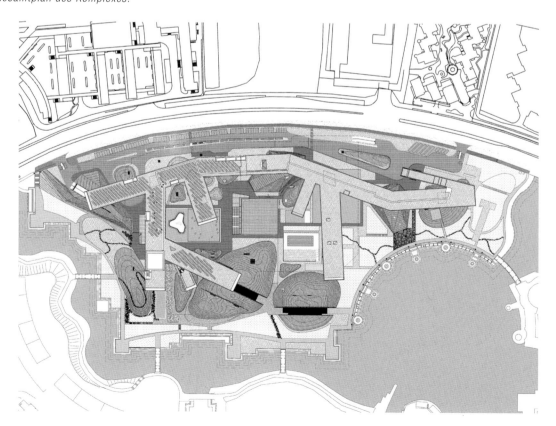

Though major elements of the design, such as the suspended blocks seen above, are perfectly rectilinear, the architect uses color and natural forms to soften the mass of the building.

Die prägnanten Entwurfselemente, wie die aufgeständerten Gebäudeblöcke oben, sind alle streng rechteckig. Um der Masse der Gebäude ihre Dominanz zu nehmen, verwendet der Architekt Farbe und eine aus der Natur entlehnte Formensprache.

Alors que les principaux éléments du projet, comme les blocs suspendus vus ci-dessus, sont de plan parfaitement rectiligne, l'architecte a utilisé des formes et des couleurs naturelles pour adoucir la masse de l'ensemble.

Suspended stairs and passageways, and some irregular forms, connect and enliven the spaces within the "horizontal skyscraper."

Frei schwebende Treppen und Stege sowie unregelmäßige Formen verbinden und beleben die Freiräume in diesem „horizontalen Wolkenkratzer".

Des escaliers, des passages suspendus et quelques formes libres, relient et animent les espaces interstitiels de ce « gratte-ciel horizontal ».

HEART: HERNING MUSEUM OF CONTEMPORARY ART

Herning, Denmark, 2007–09

Address: Birk Centerpark 8, 7400 Herning, Denmark, +45 9712 1033, www.heartmus.com
Area: 5600 m². Client: Herning Center of the Arts. Cost: not disclosed

Here, as in other projects, Steven Holl contrasts the crisp forms of the architecture with the presence of rounded lines in the earth and a basin set in the grass around the museum.

Steven Holl setzt hier, wie auch bei anderen Projekten, auf den Kontrast zwischen der spröden, streng linearen Architektur des Museums und den umgebenden gerundeten Erdformen sowie dem in die Rasenfläche eingelassenen Wasserbecken.

Ici, comme dans d'autres projets, Steven Holl fait contraster les formes tendues caractéristiques de son architecture avec des éléments plus doux comme les terrassements ou le bassin entouré de pelouses devant le musée.

This center combines visual arts and music through the **HERNING MUSEUM OF CONTEMPORARY ART**, the MidWest Ensemble, and the Socle du Monde. The intention of Steven Holl was to "fuse landscape and architecture" in a single-story structure that includes temporary exhibition galleries, a 150-seat auditorium, museum, rehearsal rooms, restaurant, library, and offices. The museum features a collection of 46 works by Piero Manzoni and has an ongoing interest in textiles, given the fact that the corporate sponsor (Herning) is a shirt manufacturer. Steven Holl states that the "roof geometry resembles a collection of shirt sleeves laid over the gallery spaces: the curved roofs bring balanced natural light to the galleries. The loose edges of the plan offer spaces for the café, auditorium, lobby, and offices." Orthogonal gallery spaces are conceived as "treasure boxes." The unusual surface of the building's exterior adds interest, as the architect explains: "Truck tarps were inserted into the white concrete formwork to yield a fabric texture to the building's exterior walls." The scheme features a 3700-square-meter "bermed landscape of grass mounds and pools" that conceals parking and service areas.

Das **HERNING MUSEUM OF CONTEMPORARY ART** verbindet mit dem MidWest Ensemble und dem Socle du Monde die visuellen Künste mit der Musik. Steven Holls Ziel war es, durch einen eingeschossigen Baukörper, in dem Räume für Wechselausstellungen, ein Auditorium mit 150 Sitzplätzen, ein Museum, Übungsräume, ein Restaurant, eine Bibliothek und Büros untergebracht sind, „die Landschaft und die Architektur miteinander zu verschmelzen". Das Museum besitzt 46 Werke von Piero Manzoni und ist besonders an Textilien interessiert, zumal der Hauptsponsor Herning Hemden produziert. Holl merkt an, dass „die Geometrie des Dachs an Hemdenärmel erinnert, die über die Ausstellungsräume gehängt sind: Durch die geschwungenen Dächer gelangt diffuses Tageslicht in die Ausstellungsräume. Die freien Ecken im Grundriss bieten Platz für das Café, das Auditorium, die Eingangshalle und die Büros." Die rechtwinkligen Ausstellungsräume sind als „Schatztruhen" gedacht. Die ungewöhnliche Fassade macht den Bau besonders interessant. Holl erklärt: „In die weiße Betonschalung sind Fahrzeugplanen eingelegt worden, um den Außenfassaden eine textile Struktur zu verleihen." Eine 3700 m² große Gartenanlage mit Wasserbecken und Rasenwellen verbirgt die Parkplätze und Dienstleistungsbereiche.

Ce centre allie arts visuels et musique grâce au **HERNING MUSEUM OF CONTEMPORARY ART**, au Ensemble MidWest et au Socle du Monde. L'intention de Steven Holl était ici de « fusionner le paysage et l'architecture » dans une construction d'un seul niveau avec galeries d'expositions temporaires, auditorium de 150 places, musée, salles de répétition, restaurant, bibliothèque et bureaux. Le musée présente notamment une collection de 46 œuvres de Piero Manzoni et cultive un intérêt pour les textiles (le mécène, Herning, est un fabricant de chemises). Steven Holl explique que « la géométrie des toitures fait penser à des manches de chemises repliées sur les volumes des galeries : les toits incurvés permettent de capter un éclairage naturel équilibré, orienté vers les galeries. Les parties en projection accueillent un café, l'auditorium, le hall d'entrée et des bureaux ». Les galeries orthogonales sont conçues comme des « coffrets à bijoux ». Le traitement de surface des murs extérieurs est étonnant : « Des bâches de camion glissées dans les coffrages du béton blanc ont donné aux murs un aspect textile. » Le projet comprend aussi un « paysage de bermes, de monticules gazonnés et de bassins » qui s'étend sur 3700 m² et dissimule parkings et installations techniques.

In an aerial view of the building, it is evident that its own lines prolong and reinforce the landscaping, making it appear to be at the nexus of the forces that surround it.

Auf der Luftaufnahme des Gebäudes wird deutlich, dass seine Linienführung in der Landschaft eine Antwort findet und die Freiraumgestaltung zu einer wichtigen Verbindung wird.

Vue aérienne du bâtiment montrant comment ses axes prolongent et renforcent les aménagements paysagers, semblant les placer ainsi au cœur du réseau de forces qui l'entoure.

The rounded forms that project from
the museum into the landscape can
be seen in these images, together
with the rectangular basin.

*Auf diesen Bildern kann man die
gerundeten Formen, die von dem
Museum in die Landschaft streben,
gut erkennen, ebenso das rechteckige
Wasserbecken.*

*Des avancées en partie arrondies se
projettent du musée vers le paysage
en bordure d'un grand bassin
rectangulaire.*

HOTSON BAKKER BONIFACE HADEN

Hotson Bakker Boniface Haden architects + urbanistes
406–611 Alexander Street
Vancouver, BC, V6A 1E1
Canada

Tel: +1 604 255 1169
Fax: +1 604 255 1790
E-mail: design@hbbharc.com

HOTSON BAKKER BONIFACE HADEN has long been involved in what they call "sustainable city-shaping," for example in the progressive adaptive reuse and urbanism of Vancouver's Granville Island. Their Capers building in Vancouver was the first commercial application of geothermal technology in western Canada. The firm has recently completed the campus plan and academic buildings for the new Quest University in Squamish, British Columbia, Canada, where sustainable design "infuses the site planning, the building design, and the curriculum." Further, in contrast with some other approaches to green architecture, HBBH "believes in the importance of making buildings 'visibly green' as a means of fostering public knowledge about key environmental issues, such as greenhouse gas emissions, and the significant role buildings play in global environmental health." Bruce Haden, the partner in charge of the Nk'Mip project published here (Osoyoos, British Columbia, Canada, 2004–06), grew up in Kingston, Ontario, and studied architecture at the University of Waterloo, receiving his M.Arch degree from the University of British Columbia. He has been involved in a number of projects that concern native Indian tribes, as can be seen in his work with Haida Gwaii and bands in the Northwest Territories.

Das Büro **HOTSON BAKKER BONIFACE HADEN** engagiert sich schon lange für „nachhaltige Stadtgestaltung", etwa mit Projekten wie der fortschrittlichen, flexiblen Umnutzung und Stadtplanung der zu Vancouver gehörenden Granville-Insel. Das Capers Building in Vancouver war das erste kommerzielle Bauprojekt in Westkanada mit Erdwärmetechnik. Kürzlich stellte das Team Lehrgebäude für die neue Quest University in Squamish, British Columbia, Kanada, fertig, bei denen nachhaltiges Design „die Planung des Geländes, den baulichen Entwurf und den Lehrplan" beeinflusst. Im Gegensatz zu anderen Ansätzen ist HBBH „überzeugt, dass es entscheidend ist, Bauten ‚sichtbar grün' zu gestalten, um der Öffentlichkeit Schlüsselfragen des Umweltschutzes zu vermitteln, etwa Wissen über Treibhausgase und die bedeutende Rolle, die Bauten für die Gesundheit unseres Planeten spielen". Bruce Haden, verantwortlich für das hier vorgestellte Nk'Mip-Projekt (Osoyoos, British Columbia, Kanada, 2004–06), wuchs in Kingston, Ontario, auf, studierte Architektur an der Universität Waterloo und erwarb seinen M.Arch. an der Universität von British Columbia. Er war an zahlreichen Projekten für heimische Indianerstämme beteiligt, wie seine Arbeit mit Haida Gwaii und verschiedenen Stammesgruppierungen in den Northwest Territories zeigt.

L'agence **HOTSON BAKKER BONIFACE HADEN** s'est longtemps intéressée à ce qu'elle appelle « la mise en forme durable des villes », par exemple dans la démarche de réutilisation progressive adaptée pour l'urbanisme de Granville Island à Vancouver. Son immeuble Capers Building à Vancouver est la première application des technologies géothermiques dans l'ouest du Canada. Elle a récemment réalisé le plan du campus ainsi que les bâtiments universitaires de la nouvelle université Quest à Squamish, Colombie britannique, Canada, pour laquelle la conception durable « touche l'ensemble de la planification, la conception des bâtiments et le cours des études ». De plus, à la différence de certaines approches de l'architecture verte, HBBH « croit en l'importance de constructions visiblement "vertes" pour promouvoir la prise de conscience par le public d'enjeux environnementaux clés, comme les conséquences des gaz à effet de serre, et le rôle significatif du bâti dans la santé globale de l'environnement ». Bruce Haden, associé en charge du projet Nk'Mip publié ici (Osoyoos, Colombie britannique, Canada, 2004–06), a grandi à Kingston, Ontario, et a étudié l'architecture à l'université de Waterloo. Il a obtenu son diplôme M.Arch à l'université de Colombie britannique. Il a travaillé sur un certain nombre de projets concernant les tribus indiennes, comme le montre son travail dans les Haida Gwaii et pour les tribus des territoires du Nord-Ouest.

NK'MIP DESERT CULTURAL CENTRE

Osoyoos, British Columbia, Canada, 2004–06

Floor area: 1115 m². Client: Osoyoos Indian Band. Cost: $2.9 million
Project Architect: Brady Dunlop

Hotson Bakker Boniface Haden was hired by the Osoyoos Indian Band to master plan the Nk'Mip Desert Cultural Centre's 81-hectare site, part of a new resort that includes a winery, an 18-hole golf course with clubhouse, and tourist accommodations. The site is located at the far northern end of the American deserts that extend southward to the Sonoran Desert in Mexico. In an unusual climate for Canada, summer temperatures can rise as high as 40°C and fall to -18°C in winter. The program of the center includes indoor and outdoor exhibition spaces, a theater, gift shop, administrative offices, rattlesnake research facilities, and 50 kilometers of hiking trails. The green features of the project include its main rammed-earth wall, its orientation and choice of site, radiant heating and cooling based on ceiling and floor slabs, a habitable green roof, water-use management, and support for endangered species research. Bluestain pine was used for the cladding because an infestation of pine beetles in British Columbia led to an excess of this type of tree. The center's earthen wall—80 meters long, 5.5 meters high, and 60 centimeters thick—is the largest rammed-earth wall in North America. Made from local soil mixed with concrete, it retains warmth in winter and cools the building in summer.

Die Gruppe der Osoyoos-Indianer beauftragte Hotson Bakker Boniface Haden mit der Erstellung des Masterplans für das 81 ha große Gelände des Nk'Mip Desert Cultural Centre, das Teil eines neuen Erholungsgebiets ist und zu dem auch ein Weingut, ein 18-Loch-Golfplatz mit Klubhaus und Touristenunterkünfte gehören. Das Gelände markiert das nördliche Ende der amerikanischen Wüstengegenden, die sich nach Süden bis zur Sonora-Wüste in Mexiko ziehen. In einem für Kanada ungewöhnlichen Klima können die Temperaturen hier auf 40 °C steigen und im Winter auf bis zu −18 °C fallen. Das Programm des Zentrums umfasst Ausstellungsbereiche im Innen- und Außenraum, ein Theater, einen Souvenirladen, Verwaltungsbüros, eine Klapperschlangen-Forschungsstation und insgesamt 50 km Wanderwege. Grüne Merkmale des Projekts sind u. a. die große Hauptmauer aus Stampflehm einschließlich ihrer Standortwahl und Ausrichtung sowie eine in Decken- und Bodenpaneele integrierte Strahlungsheizung und -kühlung, ein begehbares begrüntes Dach, Wassersparsysteme und schließlich das Engagement für die Erforschung bedrohter Arten. Für die Holzverkleidung wählte man Küstenkiefer, da eine Käferepidemie in British Columbia zu Bauholzüberschuss geführt hatte. Die Mauer des Zentrums – 80 m lang, 5,5 m hoch und 60 cm stark – ist die größte Stampflehmmauer Nordamerikas. Die aus einer Mischung aus regionaler Erde und Beton gefertigte Mauer dient im Winter als Wärmespeicher und kühlt das Gebäude im Sommer.

L'agence Hotson Bakker Boniface Haden a été engagée par les Indiens Osoyoos pour réaliser le plan directeur du Centre du patrimoine du désert de Nk'Mip, site de 81 ha qui fait partie de nouvelles installations touristiques comprenant un chai, un golf de 18 trous avec *club-house* et des hébergements pour visiteurs. Le lieu se trouve à l'extrémité nord des grandes étendues désertiques américaines qui partent du désert de Sonora au Mexique. Inhabituelles pour le Canada, les températures d'été peuvent s'élever jusqu'à 40 °C et descendre jusqu'à -18 °C en hiver. Le programme du centre comprend des espaces d'expositions couverts et en plein air, un auditorium, une boutique de cadeaux, des bureaux administratifs, un centre de recherche sur les serpents à sonnettes et 50 km de pistes de randonnée. Les aspects durables du projet comprennent le mur principal en béton de terre, l'orientation et le choix de l'emplacement, le chauffage et le rafraîchissement radiant par les sols et les plafonds, un toit végétalisé habitable, la gestion de l'eau et le soutien à la recherche sur les espèces en voie de disparition. On a utilisé un bardage en pin Bluestain très abondant, car le pin local est infesté de parasites. Le mur de terre du bâtiment du Centre – 80 m de long, 5,5 m de haut et 60 cm d'épaisseur – est le plus grand mur en béton de terre jamais monté en Amérique du Nord. Réalisé en terre locale mélangée à du béton, il retient la chaleur en hiver et conserve la fraîcheur en été.

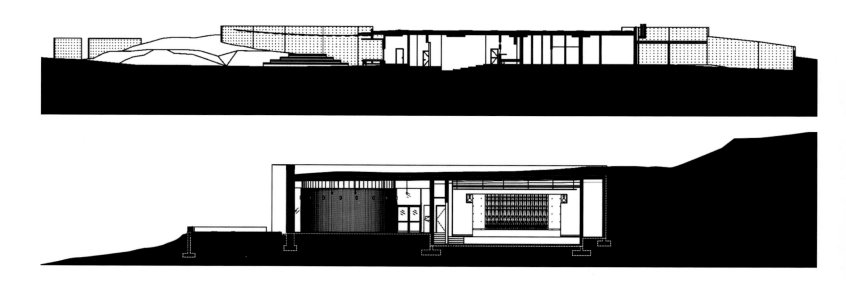

The basic structure is inserted into the hillside and fronted by the strong rammed-earth wall.

Das schlichte Gebäude wurde in den Abhang hineingebaut und liegt hinter einer mächtigen Stampflehmmauer.

La structure de base est insérée dans le flanc de la colline et comme bloquée par un puissant mur de terre.

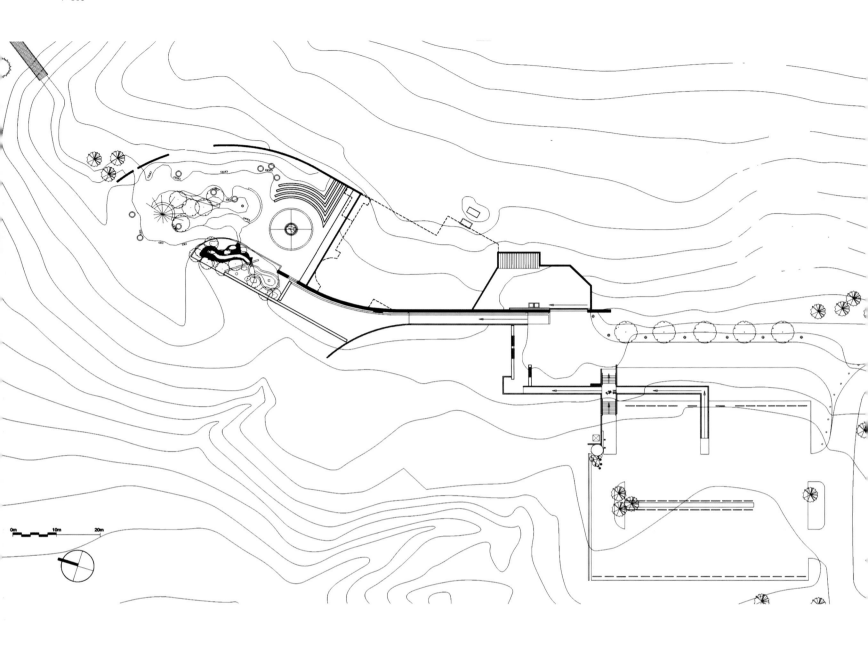

0m 10m 20m

The layered effect of the rammed-earth wall makes it blend into its natural setting, as the site plan with its topographic lines (above) shows from a different perspective. Right, Indian heritage.

Dank ihres Schichteffekts verschmilzt die Stampflehmmauer geradezu mit ihrem Umfeld, wie auch der topografische Geländeplan (oben) aus einer anderen Perspektive deutlich macht. Rechts indianische Artefakte.

L'effet de stratification du mur de terre l'intègre encore mieux dans son cadre naturel, comme le plan du site et les courbes de niveaux (ci-dessus) le montrent sous une perspective différente. À droite, témoignage de la tradition indienne.

The modern volumes of the center lie behind its long visible wall, as seen in the plan below.

Die modernen Baukörper des Centers liegen hinter der lang gestreckten, nach außen hin sichtbaren Mauer, wie der Grundriss unten zeigt.

Comme le montre le plan ci-dessous, les volumes modernes qui composent le centre sont protégés par le long mur de terre.

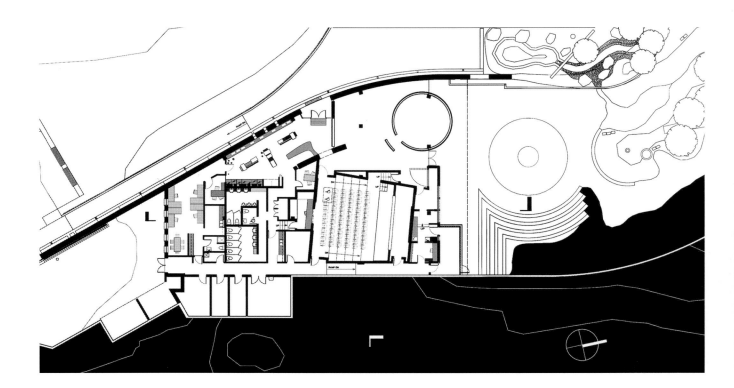

A sense of earthy solidity pervades
the architecture and makes it contex-
tual without any sense of pastiche.

Die Architektur ist von erdiger Boden-
ständigkeit und dabei kontextuell,
ohne je zur Nachahmung zu werden.

Cette architecture qui diffuse un
sentiment de grande solidité maté-
rielle joue le contexte sans tomber
pour autant dans le pastiche.

HWKN (HOLLWICH KUSHNER)

HWKN (Hollwich Kushner)
281 5th Avenue
New York, NY 10016
USA

Tel: + 1 646 461 6307
E-mail: press@hwkn.com
Web: www.hwkn.com

MATTHIAS HOLLWICH is a registered European Architect, cofounder and principal of Hollwich Kushner (HWKN), and cofounder of Architizer.com. Before starting his own firms he worked at OMA (Rotterdam), Eisenman Architects (New York), and Diller+Scofidio (New York). He is currently a Visiting Professor at the University of Pennsylvania, where he initiated New Aging, an international conference on aging and architecture, held in the fall of 2010. **MARC KUSHNER** is a partner in Hollwich Kushner and cofounder and CEO of Architizer.com. After graduating from Harvard's Graduate School of Design he worked with J Mayer H Architects in Berlin and Lewis Tsurumaki Lewis (LTL) in New York. In 2009 Hollwich and his partners founded Architizer.com, the "first crowd-sourced database for architecture online." Architizer remains the fastest growing platform for architecture online. Marc Kushner teaches at Columbia University's Graduate School of Architecture, Planning and Preservation, and lectures on the topic of social media and architecture. Their work includes Aging in Africa (Ivory Coast, 2008); Mini Rooftop (New York, NY, 2008); Il laboratorio del gelato (New York, NY, 2010); Uniqlo Cubes (New York, NY, 2011); and Wendy, MoMA PS1 (Long Island City, Queens, NY, 2012, published here). Their ongoing work includes 18 Park (Jersey City, NJ, 2013); Fire Island Pines Pavilion (Fire Island Pines, NY, 2013); and the Jerusalem Academy of Music and Dance (Jerusalem, Israel, 2013).

MATTHIAS HOLLWICH ist europäischer Architekt, Gründer und Direktor von Hollwich Kushner (HWKN) und Mitbegründer von Architizer.com. Zuvor arbeitete er für OMA (Rotterdam), Eisenman Architects sowie Diller + Scofidio (New York). Er ist Gastprofessor an der University of Pennsylvania, wo er im Herbst 2010 die internationale Konferenz „New Aging" zum Thema Altern und Architektur initiierte. **MARC KUSHNER** ist Partner bei Hollwich Kushner und Mitbegründer und Geschäftsführer von Architizer. Nach seinem Abschluss an der Harvard GSD arbeitete er zunächst für J. Mayer H. Architects in Berlin und Lewis Tsurumaki Lewis (LTL) in New York. 2009 gründeten Hollwich und seine Partner Architizer.com, die „erste Crowdsourcing-basierte Onlinedatenbank für Architektur". Architizer ist die derzeit am schnellsten wachsende Onlineplattform für Architektur. Marc Kushner ist Dozent am Graduiertenkolleg für Architektur, Stadtplanung und Denkmalschutz an der Columbia University und hält Vorträge zu den Themen Soziale Medien und Architektur. Zu ihren Projekten zählen Aging in Africa (Elfenbeinküste, 2008), Mini Rooftop (New York, 2008), Il laboratorio del gelato (New York, 2010), Uniqlo Cubes (New York, 2011) und Wendy für das MoMA PS1 (Long Island City, Queens, New York, 2012, hier vorgestellt). Zu ihren laufenden Projekten gehören 18 Park (Jersey City, New Jersey, 2013), der Fire Island Pines Pavilion (Fire Island Pines, New York, 2013) und die Akademie für Musik und Tanz in Jerusalem (Israel, 2013).

MATTHIAS HOLLWICH est un architecte européen, cofondateur de Hollwich Kushner (HWKN), dont il est aussi le directeur, et cofondateur d'Architizer.com. Avant de créer ses entreprises, il a travaillé à OMA (Rotterdam), Eisenman Architects et Diller+Scofidio (New York). Il est actuellement professeur associé à l'université de Pennsylvanie où il a lancé un congrès international sur le vieillissement et l'architecture « New Aging », qui a eu lieu à l'automne 2010. **MARC KUSHNER** est partenaire de Hollwich Kushner, cofondateur et CEO d'Architizer.com. Après avoir obtenu son diplôme à la GSD à Harvard, il a travaillé avec J. Mayer H Architects à Berlin et Lewis Tsurumaki Lewis (LTL) à New York. En 2009, Hollwich et ses partenaires ont fondé Architizer.com, la « première banque de données ouverte en ligne d'architecture ». Architizer est encore aujourd'hui la plate-forme d'architecture en ligne à la croissance la plus rapide. Marc Kushner enseigne à l'École supérieure d'architecture, urbanisme et conservation de l'université Columbia et donne des cours sur les médias sociaux et l'architecture. Les réalisations de HWKN comprennent la maison de retraite Aging in Africa (Côte d'Ivoire, 2008) ; Mini Rooftop (New York, 2008) ; la boutique Il laboratario del gelato (New York, 2010) ; les Uniqlo Cubes (New York, 2011) et Wendy (MoMA PS1, Long Island City, Queens, New York, 2012, publié ici). Parmi leurs travaux en cours : l'immeuble 18 Park (Jersey City, New Jersey, 2013) ; le pavillon Fire Island Pines (Fire Island Pines, New York, 2013) et l'Académie de musique et de danse de Jérusalem (Jérusalem, Israël, 2013).

WENDY

MoMA PS1, Long Island City, Queens, NY, USA, 2012

Area: 93 m². Client: MoMA PS1
Cost: not disclosed

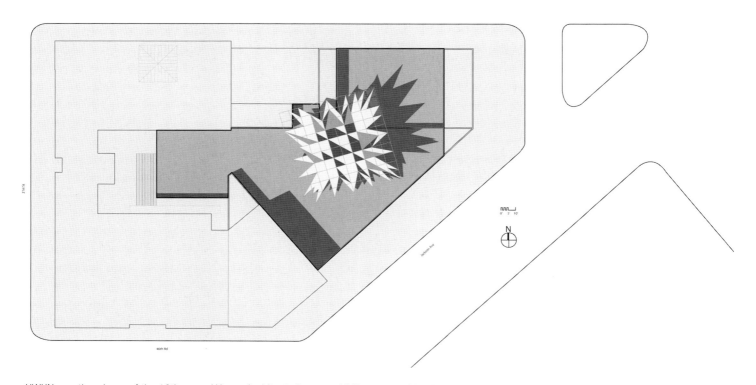

HWKN was the winner of the 13th annual Young Architects Program (YAP) sponsored by the Museum of Modern Art and MoMA PS1 in Queens. Participating architects are asked to create a temporary, outdoor installation at MoMA PS1 that provides shade, seating, and water. The architects must also work within guidelines that address environmental issues, including sustainability and recycling. Opened to the public on July 1, 2012, their pavilion, called **WENDY**, was made of fabric treated with a titanium oxide (TiO_2) nanofilm to neutralize airborne pollutants. According to HWKN: "During the summer of 2012, Wendy will clean the air to an equivalent of taking 260 cars off the road." Scaffolding was employed to form the 17 x 17 x 14-meter spiked structure. Its arms spray mist to cool visitors and play recorded music. When asked why the structure is called Wendy, Matthias Hollwich responds: "She is a storm that innovates architecture with new ideas of sustainability—and every storm has a name. It breaks down the barrier between architecture and people—it is not just about good-looking buildings—for us it is about personality."

HWKN gewann den Wettbewerb des 13. Young Architects Program (YAP), finanziert vom Museum of Modern Art und dem MoMA PS1 in Queens. Aufgabe der Architekten war es, eine temporäre Installation für den Außenbereich des MoMA PS1 zu entwerfen, die Schatten spenden sowie Sitzgelegenheiten und Wasser zur Verfügung stellen sollte. Darüber hinaus gab es umweltspezifische Vorgaben wie Nachhaltigkeit und Recycling. Der am 1. Juli 2012 eröffnete Pavillon **WENDY** war mit Textil bespannt; seine Haut war mit Titanoxid(TiO_2)-Nanofilm beschichtet und neutralisierte so Feinstaubpartikel in der Luft. HWKN erklären: „Im Sommer 2012 wird Wendy eine Verbesserung der Luftqualität erreichen, die quasi 260 Fahrzeuge von der Straße holt." Die 17 x 17 x 14 m große Sternkonstruktion wurde aus Gerüststangen gebaut. Die strahlenförmigen Arme versprühen feinen Wassernebel zur Kühlung der Besucher; hier sind außerdem Musikboxen installiert. Auf die Frage, wie es zum Namen Wendy kam, antwortet Matthias Hollwich: „Sie ist ein Wirbelsturm, der die Architektur mit Ideen zur Nachhaltigkeit erneuert – jeder Wirbelsturm hat einen Namen. Sie reißt die Mauern zwischen Architektur und den Menschen ein – uns geht es nicht einfach darum, dass Bauten gut aussehen – uns geht es um ihre Persönlichkeit."

HWKN a remporté le 13ᵉ concours annuel du programme « Jeunes architectes » (YAP) parrainé par le Musée d'art moderne de New York et le MoMA PS1 dans le Queens. Il s'agit pour les architectes participants de créer une installation extérieure temporaire pour le MoMA PS1 qui dispense ombre, eau et possibilité de s'asseoir. Ils doivent également respecter des directives en matière d'environnement, notamment en ce qui concerne la durabilité et le recyclage. Ouvert au public le 1ᵉʳ juillet 2012, le pavillon baptisé **WENDY** est en textile recouvert d'un film de nanoparticules d'oxyde de titanium (TiO_2) qui neutralise les polluants atmosphériques. D'après HWKN : « Au cours de l'été 2012, Wendy éliminera de l'air l'équivalent de la pollution émise par 260 voitures. » La structure aux pointes de 17 x 17 x 14 m a été formée à l'aide d'échafaudages. Ses branches diffusent une brume rafraîchit les visiteurs et de la musique. À la question de l'origine du nom Wendy, Matthias Hollwich répond que « c'est un ouragan qui renouvelle l'architecture avec une nouvelle idée de la durabilité – et les ouragans ont toujours un nom. Elle fait tomber la barrière qui sépare l'architecture des gens – car il ne s'agit pas seulement de construire des bâtiments qui ont belle allure, pour nous, c'est une question de personnalité ».

The spiked forms of Wendy are seen in the site drawing above and the photos on the right page. With its scaffolding frame, the structure looks something like a controlled (blue) explosion.

Die sternförmige Konstruktion von Wendy ist auf dem Lageplan oben und den Aufnahmen rechts zu erkennen. In dem Rahmengestell aus Gerüststangen wirkt der Bau wie eine kontrollierte (blaue) Explosion.

On voit sur le plan du site ci-dessus et les photos ci-contre la forme et les pointes de Wendy. Avec son cadre d'échafaudages, la construction fait penser à une explosion (bleue) contrôlée.

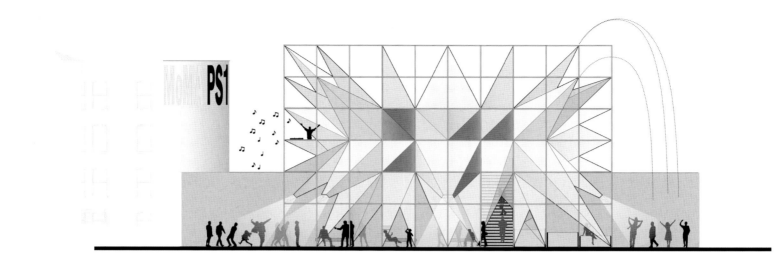

An elevation drawing and a photo with a crowd give a better idea of the scale of the structure and its placement near the PS1 building.

Ein Aufriss und eine Aufnahme mit Besuchern vermitteln eine bessere Vorstellung von der Größe der Konstruktion und ihrer Platzierung neben dem PS1-Gebäude.

Le schéma en élévation et la photo avec la foule donnent une meilleure idée de la taille de la construction et de son emplacement à côté du bâtiment du PS1.

Seen from within, Wendy resolves itself into a light fabric form, less architecture than sculpted space.

Von innen gesehen löst sich Wendy zu einer leichten Textilkonstruktion auf, weniger Architektur als geformter Raum.

Vue de l'intérieur, Wendy se réduit à une forme légère de tissu, relevant moins de l'architecture que de l'espace sculpté.

IROJE KHM ARCHITECTS

IROJE KHM Architects
1805 Gardentower Building
98–78 Unni-dong, Jongro-gu
Seoul 110–795
South Korea

Tel: +82 2 766 1928
Fax: +82 2 766 1929
E-mail: iroman@unitel.co.kr
Web: www.irojekhm.com

HYOMAN KIM is the principal of IROJE KHM Architects. He graduated from the Department of Architecture of DanKook University (Seoul, 1978). Since 2004 he has been a Professor at the Graduate School of Architecture, KyongGi University (Seoul) and at the Department of Architecture of DanKook University (now located in Yongin). His work includes Lim Geo Dang (Go Yang, 2001, published here); Hye Ro Hun (Gwangju, 2005, also published here); Purple Whale (Paju Book City, Gyeounggi-do, 2008); Island House (Gapyung-gun, Gyeounggi-do, 2007–09); Purple Hill House (Youngin, Gyeounggi-do, 2009); and BuYeonDang House (SungNam, Gyeounggi-do, 2009). Ongoing work includes the PyeongChang Institute for Buddhism (PyeongChangGun, GangWonDo, 2009–), and Green Hill Village (Seoul, 2009–), all in South Korea. "Concept is an ideal and abstract thought," says HyoMan Kim. "The concept does not hold value until the concept is embodied into a concrete building in reality."

HYOMAN KIM ist Chef der Firma IROJE KHM Architects. Er studierte Architektur an der DanKook University (Seoul, 1978). Seit 2004 hat er eine Professur an der Graduate School of Architecture der KyongGi University (Seoul) sowie an der Architekturabteilung der DanKook University (jetzt in Yongin). Zu seinen Bauwerken zählen das Haus Lim Geo Dang (Go Yang, 2001, hier vorgestellt), das Haus Hye Ro Hun (Gwangju, 2005, ebenfalls hier vorgestellt), Purple Whale (Paju Book City, Gyeounggi-do, 2008), Island House (Gapyung-gun, Gyeounggi-do, 2007–09), das Haus Purple Hill (Youngin, Gyeounggi-do, 2009) und das Haus BuYeonDang (SungNam, Gyeounggi-do, 2009). Zu seinen aktuellen Arbeiten gehören das PyeongChang Institute for Buddhism (PyeongChangGun, GangWonDo, seit 2009) und das Green Hill Village (Seoul, seit 2009), alle in Südkorea. „Das Konzept ist ein idealer und abstrakter Gedanke", sagt HyoMan Kim. „Das Konzept hat keinerlei Bedeutung, bevor es in einem konkreten Gebäude realisiert wurde."

HYOMAN KIM, diplômé du département d'Architecture de l'université DanKook (Séoul, 1978), dirige l'agence IROJE KHM. Depuis 2004, il est également professeur à l'École supérieure d'architecture de l'université KyongGi (Séoul) et au département d'Architecture de l'université DanKook (aujourd'hui relocalisée à Yongin). Parmi ses réalisations, toutes en Corée-du-Sud, figurent la maison Lim Geo Dang (Go Yang, 2001, publiée ici) ; la maison Hye Ro Hun (Gwangju, 2005, également publiée ici) ; le bâtiment industriel de la Baleine pourpre (Purple Whale, Paju Book, Gyeounggi-do, 2008) ; la Maison-île (Island House, Gapyung-gun, Gyeounggi-do, 2007–09) ; la maison de la Colline pourpre (Purple Hill House, Youngin, Gyeounggi-do, 2009) et la maison BuYeonDang (SungNam, Gyeounggi-do, 2009). Il travaille actuellement sur les projets de l'Institut du bouddhisme de PyeongChang (PyeongChangGun, GangWonDo, 2009–) et le village de la Colline verte (Green Hill Village, Séoul, 2009–). « Le concept est un idéal, une pensée abstraite », écrit HyoMan Kim : « Le concept n'a pas de valeur tant qu'il ne s'incarne pas dans une construction concrète, réelle. »

LIM GEO DANG

Go Yang, South Korea, 2001

Address: JangHangDong, IlSan, Go Yang, South Korea
Area: 108 m². Client: Jong Gi Lim. Cost: $176 000

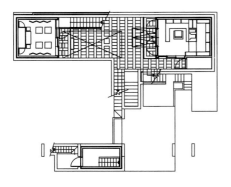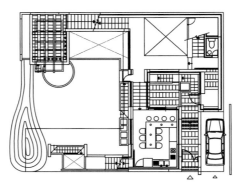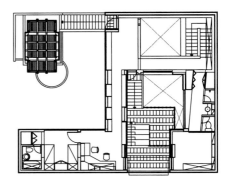

The basic square form of the plan is notched to create a partially enclosed courtyard, as seen in the drawings above and the photo below.

Die Grundform des Quadrats ist aufgebrochen, um einen teilumschlossenen Innenhof zu bilden, wie die Pläne oben und das Foto unten zeigen.

Le plan essentiellement carré est entaillé pour créer une cour en partie fermée, comme le montrent les dessins ci-dessus et la photo ci-dessous.

The architect makes a powerful and unexpected combination of a concrete base and a wooden upper volume.

Dem Architekten ist eine eindrucksvolle und ungewöhnliche Kombination aus einem Betonsockel und dem darauf gesetzten Volumen aus Holz gelungen.

L'architecte a réussi la combinaison inattendue et frappante d'un socle en béton et d'un volume supérieur en bois.

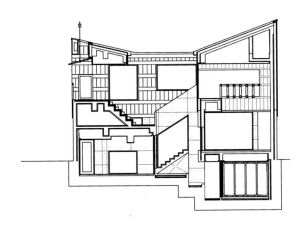

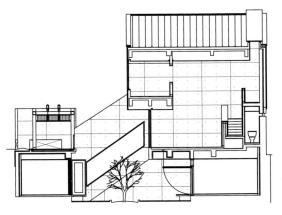

The clients for this small house were authors and publishers who asked for a building that was "traditional but modern." The site of the residence measures just 231 square meters. The architect responded to this request, stating: "The spatial design concept set for this small house was based on its dramatic circulation, which was characteristic of traditional architecture in Korea. The circulation of ancient Korea continues infinitely in space, overlapping and penetrating asymmetrically, and, finally, producing several picturesque frames relating nature and building." A "madang" or traditional inner courtyard is included in the design. Only the living and dining spaces are located at ground level to allow for the largest possible courtyard. The bedroom area above is a pilotis structure, with space beneath that is also a type of courtyard. Using sublimated ideas about traditional wooden architecture in particular, the architect has sought to "read this inheritance in modern language."

Die Auftraggeber dieses kleinen Hauses waren Autoren und Verleger, die sich ein „traditionelles, aber modernes" Gebäude wünschten. Das Grundstück des Wohnhauses misst nur 231 m². Der Architekt erklärt zu diesem Wunsch: „Das Raumkonzept für dieses kleine Wohnhaus basiert auf seinen ungewöhnlichen Verbindungswegen, die für die traditionelle Architektur in Korea charakteristisch sind. Die Verbindungswege im antiken Korea führten in die Unendlichkeit des Raums, überschnitten und durchdrangen sich asymmetrisch und bildeten schließlich mehrere pittoreske Rahmen, die Natur und Gebäude in Beziehung zueinander setzten." Ein „Madang" oder traditioneller Innenhof ist auch in diesem Haus enthalten. Im Erdgeschoss liegen nur der Wohn- und Essbereich, um Raum für den größtmöglichen Innenhof zu gewinnen. Die Schlafräume darüber befinden sich in einer aufgeständerten Konstruktion; darunter entsteht ebenfalls eine Art Innenhof. Der Architekt hat versucht, „dieses Erbe in eine moderne Sprache zu übersetzen", indem er traditionelle Vorstellungen vor allem über Holzarchitektur übernahm.

Les clients – auteurs et éditeurs – avaient demandé à l'architecte de leur concevoir une maison « traditionnelle mais moderne » sur un petit terrain de 231 m². HyoMan, qui a répondu à leur demande, explique que « le concept spatial mis au point pour cette petite maison s'appuie sur un spectaculaire système de circulation, caractéristique de l'architecture traditionnelle coréenne. Dans l'ancienne Corée, la circulation se poursuit à l'infini dans l'espace. Elle s'entrecroise, pénètre l'espace asymétriquement pour, finalement, produire plusieurs modes de relations pittoresques entre la nature et le bâti ». Le projet a intégré un *madang* ou cour intérieure traditionnelle. Seuls le séjour et la zone des repas occupent le rez-de-chaussée pour laisser à la cour le maximum de surface. Le niveau des chambres, sous lequel un autre espace sert également de cour, est monté sur pilotis. Par l'utilisation des principes subliminaux de l'architecture traditionnelle, en particulier en bois, l'architecte a recherché « une lecture de cet héritage à travers un langage moderne ».

The relatively cold concrete surfaces are contrasted with the warmer wood. Both materials are present inside and outside the house.

Die relativ kalt wirkenden Betonflächen stehen in Kontrast zum wärmeren Holz. Beide Materialien sind im Haus innen und außen präsent.

Contraste entre les plans en béton relativement froids et la chaleur du bois. Les deux matériaux se retrouvent à l'intérieur et à l'extérieur de la maison.

HYE RO HUN

Gwangju, South Korea, 2005

*Address: Ilgok-dong, Bukgu, Gwangju, South Korea
Area: 169 m². Client: Hyung Sub Sim. Cost: $351 000
Collaboration: SuMi Jung*

The architect uses rectilinear volumes but makes them "collide" in unexpected ways, generating relatively complex spaces.

Der Architekt verwendet rechtwinklige Formen, die er auf ungewöhnliche Weise „kollidieren" lässt und dadurch relativ komplexe Räume erzeugt.

L'architecte utilise des volumes simples qu'il fait entrer en « collision » de manière inattendue pour créer des espaces relativement complexes.

Wood covers the nearly symmetrical towers that stand above the concrete and glass base.

Holz überzieht die fast symmetrischen Türme, die auf einer Basis aus Beton und Glas stehen.

Les tours presque symétriques qui s'élèvent d'une base en béton et verre sont bardées de bois.

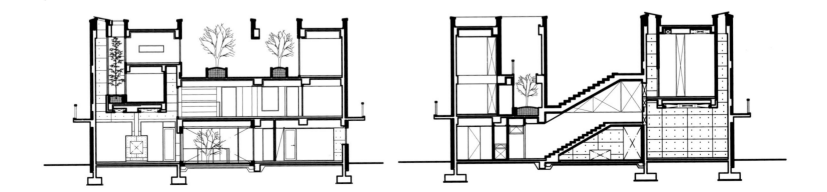

This house is set at the limit between an urban environment and that of the mountains. Both landscapes are taken into account by the design. The designer describes the entrance walkway as an "architectural canyon." Two wooden boxes contain duplex rooms that are laid on a landscaped architectural mass that contains the nine-meter-high living room with an overhead natural light source and dining room. One box contains the double-height master bedroom and study room and another box contains two bedrooms and study rooms for two children. The exterior finish of the house is in exposed concrete and red cedar, while exposed concrete, lacquer, and plywood are employed in the interior. The architect states that he has willfully made the continuity of space, both vertical and horizontal, the theme of his work here.

Dieses Haus steht an der Grenze zwischen städtischer Bebauung und gebirgiger Umgebung. Der Entwurf bezieht beide Landschaften ein. Der Architekt beschreibt den Erschließungsweg als „architektonischen Canyon". Zwei Holzkisten enthalten Räume auf verschiedenen Ebenen in einer Architekturlandschaft, die auch den 9 m hohen Wohnraum mit einem Oberlicht als natürliche Lichtquelle sowie den Essraum enthält. In einer der Kisten befinden sich der doppelgeschosshohe Schlafraum und das Arbeitszimmer der Bauherren, in der anderen zwei Schlaf- und Arbeitszimmer für die beiden Kinder. Die Außenwände des Hauses bestehen aus Sichtbeton und Rotzeder, wobei im Innenraum Sichtbeton, Lack und Sperrholz zur Anwendung kamen. Der Architekt erklärt, dass er dabei bewusst den vertikalen und horizontalen Raumfluss zum Thema seines Entwurfs gemacht habe.

Cette maison est implantée entre une zone urbaine et une région de montagnes, deux types de paysages qui ont été pris en compte dans le projet. L'architecte compare l'allée d'entrée à un « canyon architectural ». Les deux boîtes habillées de bois contenant les pièces en duplex reposent sur une base paysagée occupée par un séjour de 9 m de haut à éclairage zénithal et par la salle à manger. Une des boîtes accueille la chambre principale double hauteur et un bureau, et l'autre deux chambres et des bureaux pour les deux enfants. Les façades sont en béton brut et cèdre rouge tandis qu'à l'intérieur règnent le béton brut, le contreplaqué et la laque. L'architecte précise que le thème de ce projet est la continuité de l'espace, à la fois verticale et horizontale.

Throughout the composition, wood and concrete clash and blend, attracting attention to the similarities of the materials as well as their overt differences.

Im gesamten Entwurf treffen Holz und Beton aufeinander und verbinden sich; sie machen auf die Verwandtschaft dieser Materialien wie auch ihre Unterschiede aufmerksam.

Le bois et le béton se fondent ou se heurtent dans l'ensemble de la composition en attirant l'attention sur les similarités et les contrastes des matériaux.

A potted tree between the two wooden "towers" contrasts with the rather strict and austere lines of the architecture.

Der Baum zwischen den beiden hölzernen „Türmen" bildet einen Gegensatz zu den ansonsten recht strengen Umrissen der Architektur.

Un arbre en pot placé entre les deux « tours » de bois apporte une note contrastée par rapport aux lignes assez strictes, voire austères, de l'architecture.

JUNYA ISHIGAMI

junya.ishigami+associates
3–18–12, Roppongi
Minato-ku
Tokyo 106–0032
Japan

Tel: +81 3 6277 6642
E-mail: ii@jnyi.jp
Web: www.jnyi.jp

JUNYA ISHIGAMI was born in Kanagawa, Japan, in 1974. He studied at the Tokyo National University of Fine Arts and Music in the Architecture Department, graduating in 2000. He worked in the office of Kazuyo Sejima & Associates (now SANAA) from 2000 to 2004, establishing Junya Ishigami + Associates in 2004. Given his age, his list of projects is not long, but he has designed a number of tables, including one 9.5 meters long and 3 millimeters thick made of prestressed steel, and a project for the Hotel Kaiyo and housing (2007). Aside from the Kanagawa Institute of Technology KAIT workshop (Japan, 2007–08), he has designed a New York store for Yohji Yamamoto (USA, 2008) in the so-called Meatpacking District, and participated in the 2008 Venice Architecture Biennale (Greenhouses for the Japanese Pavilion, Venice, Italy, published here). Despite his limited number of completed works Junya Ishigami has emerged as one of the more significant young Japanese architects.

JUNYA ISHIGAMI wurde 1974 in Kanagawa, Japan, geboren. Er studierte an der Fakultät für Architektur der Staatlichen Kunst- und Musikhochschule Tokio, wo er 2000 seinen Abschluss machte. Zwischen 2000 und 2004 arbeitete er für Kazuyo Sejima & Associates (inzwischen SANAA) und gründete 2004 sein Büro Junya Ishigami + Associates. Angesichts seines Alters ist seine Projektliste nicht lang, doch hat Ishigami bereits mehrere Tische entworfen, darunter den 9,5 m langen „Table" aus 3 mm starkem Spannstahl, sowie ein Projekt für die Hotel- und Wohnanlage Kaiyo (2007). Neben dem Werkstattgebäude für das Kanagawa Institute of Technology (KAIT; Japan, 2007–08) gestaltete er einen Yohji Yamamoto Store im New Yorker Meatpacking District (2008) und war 2008 auf der Architekturbiennale in Venedig vertreten (Gewächshäuser für den japanischen Pavillon, hier vorgestellt). Trotz der geringen Anzahl gebauter Projekte, hat sich Junya Ishigami als einer der maßgeblichen jungen japanischen Architekten etabliert.

JUNYA ISHIGAMI, né en 1974 à Kanagawa au Japon, a étudié au département d'Architecture de l'Université nationale des beaux-arts et de musique de Tokyo, dont il est sorti diplômé en 2000. Il a travaillé chez Kazuyo Sejima & Associates (aujourd'hui SANAA) de 2000 à 2004 et a créé l'agence Junya Ishigami + Associates en 2004. Son jeune âge explique que sa liste de réalisations ne soit pas très longue, mais il a dessiné un certain nombre de tables, dont une de 9,5 m de long et 3 mm d'épaisseur en acier précontraint (Table), et un projet pour l'hôtel Kaiyo et des logements (2007). En dehors d'installations pour l'Institut de technologie Kanagawa (2007–08), il a conçu le magasin new-yorkais du couturier japonais Yohji Yamamoto (2008) dans le quartier du Meatpacking. Il a participé à la Biennale d'architecture de Venise en 2008 (serres pour le pavillon japonais, publiées ici). Malgré ce nombre limité de projets achevés, Ishigami apparaît comme l'un des jeunes architectes japonais les plus prometteurs.

GREENHOUSES, JAPANESE PAVILION

Venice Architecture Biennale, Venice, Italy, 2008

*Area: 20 m², 6 m², 11 m², 6 m². Client: The Japan Foundation. Cost: not disclosed
Collaboration: Taro Igarashi (Commissioner), Hideaki Ohba (Botanist),
Jun Sato (Structural Engineer)*

For the 2008 Venice Architecture Biennale, Junya Ishigami designed a series of small glass greenhouses that he set around the building in the *giardini*. Each of the greenhouses was conceived as an actual building, pushing the limits of structural soundness thanks to sophisticated calculations. His intention was to suggest "the future possibilities of architecture." Ishigami also refers to Joseph Paxton's Crystal Palace at the Great Exhibition in London (1851), which took the form of a greenhouse. Ishigami worked with the botanist Hideaki Ohba, who carefully selected varieties of plants that at first seemed to be native to the environment, but in fact represent a "slight disturbance in the landscape of the park." Wooden furniture was placed in the garden, suggesting the ambiguity or more precisely "simultaneity" of interior and exterior space, while the inside of the pavilion itself was essentially empty except for delicate drawings on the white walls.

Für die Architekturbiennale 2008 in Venedig entwarf Junya Ishigami eine Reihe kleinerer Gewächshäuser, die er rund um den Pavillon in den Giardini platzierte. Jedes Gewächshaus war als eigenständiger Bau konzipiert und dank ausgeklügelter Berechnungen eben gerade in der Lage, stabil aufrecht zu stehen. Seine Absicht war es, „künftige Möglichkeiten der Architektur" aufzuzeigen. Zugleich nimmt Ishigami auf Joseph Paxtons Kristallpalast Bezug, der 1851 zur Londoner Weltausstellung erbaut worden und ebenfalls wie ein Gewächshaus angelegt war. Ishigami arbeitete mit dem Botaniker Hideaki Ohba zusammen, der sorgsam Pflanzen auswählte, die zunächst einheimisch wirkten, tatsächlich aber „eine subtile Störung der Parklandschaft" darstellten. Außerdem wurden im Garten Holzmöbel aufgestellt, eine Anspielung auf die Mehrdeutigkeit, oder vielmehr „Simultaneität", von Innen- und Außenraum. Die Innenräume des Pavillons selbst waren bis auf wenige zarte Zeichnungen an den weißen Wänden so gut wie leer.

Junya Ishigami a conçu pour la Biennale de Venise 2008 une série de petites serres en verre disposées autour du pavillon japonais dans les Giardini. Chacune a été conçue comme une vraie construction, dont la stabilité a fait l'objet de calculs sophistiqués. Son intention était de suggérer « les possibilités futures de l'architecture ». Ishigami se réfère également au Crystal Palace construit par Joseph Paxton pour la grande exposition de Londres (1851), qui était aussi en forme de serre. Il a travaillé avec le botaniste Hideaki Ohba qui a sélectionné méticuleusement différentes plantes apparemment natives du lieu, mais qui, en fait, représentent un « léger dérangement dans le paysage du parc ». Le mobilier de bois a été disposé dans les jardins pour suggérer une ambiguïté, ou plus précisément une « simultanéité », entre l'intérieur et l'extérieur, tandis que l'intérieur du pavillon lui-même reste essentiellement vide, à part quelques délicats dessins sur ses murs blancs.

At first glance, the vegetation contained in Ishigami's greenhouses appears to be indigenous, but on closer examination reveals itself to be more exotic.

Die auf den ersten Blick einheimisch wirkenden Pflanzen in Ishigamis Gewächshäusern erweisen sich bei näherem Hinsehen als exotischere Gattungen.

À première vue, la végétation contenue dans les serres d'Ishigami semble indigène, mais elle est en fait plutôt exotique.

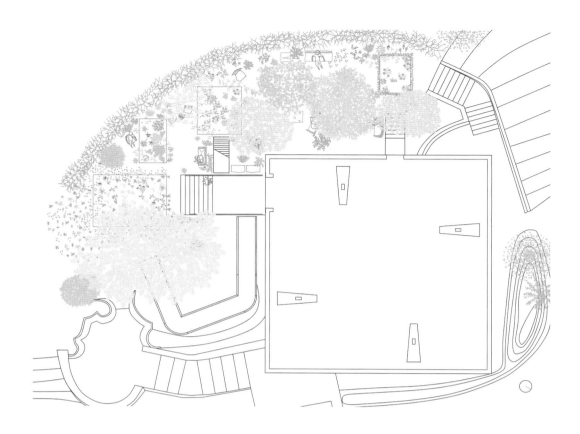

The inside space almost looks white in these images, but the walls are covered with delicate drawings. Below, a drawing of the outdoor structures in their natural setting.

Auch im Innern des Pavillons, der auf den Fotos fast weiß wirkt, erkennt man erst auf den zweiten Blick die ungemein feinen Wandzeichnungen. Unten eine Zeichnung der von Bäumen umstandenen Gewächshäuser.

Bien que l'espace intérieur semble presque blanc sur ces reproductions, les murs sont en fait recouverts de délicats dessins. Ci-dessous, une représentation des serres dans leur cadre naturel.

JACKSON CLEMENTS BURROWS

Jackson Clements Burrows Pty Ltd. Architects
One Harwood Place
Melbourne, Victoria 3000
Australia

Tel: +61 3 9654 6227
Fax: +61 3 9654 6195
E-mail: jacksonclementsburrows@jcba.com.au
Web: www.jcba.com.au

TIM JACKSON was born in San Francisco, USA, in 1964. He worked in the office of Denton Corker Marshall before joining his father's practice (Daryl Jackson Architects), and then running his own firm between 1993 and 1998. In Australia he was the project director for the Abito Apartments (Fitzroy, Victoria) that won the 2007 Royal Australian Institute of Architects Architecture Award for Multi-Residential Housing. He also worked on the Kew House (Kew, Victoria, 2004; RAIA Award for Residential Architecture). **JONATHAN CLEMENTS** was born in 1971 in Melbourne, Australia. He received his B.Arch degree from Deakin University and worked prior to the formation of Jackson Clements Burrows in 1998 with Daryl Jackson. Projects he has been involved with at Jackson Clements Burrows include Cape Schanck House (Cape Schanck, Victoria, 2006, published here) and Pier Point Apartments (Geelong, Victoria, 2006–). **GRAHAM BURROWS** was born in 1971 in Johannesburg, South Africa. He studied at the University of Melbourne and was employed prior to 1998 in the office of Daryl Jackson. Projects he has run for Jackson Clements Burrows include the Separation Creek Residence (Separation Creek, Victoria, 2007) and the Saint Kilda Foreshore Promenade Development in Melbourne (2008). Other recent work by Jackson Clements Burrows includes the Trojan House (Melbourne, Victoria, 2005) and the Hue Apartments, a multi-residential project with 29 apartments (Richmond, Melbourne, 2007), all in Australia.

TIM JACKSON wurde 1964 in San Francisco geboren. Er arbeitete bei Denton Corker Marshall und trat danach in das Büro seines Vaters (Daryl Jackson Architects) ein. Von 1993 bis 1998 leitete er ein eigenes Büro. In Australien war er Projektleiter für die Abito Apartments (Fitzroy, Victoria), die 2007 vom Royal Australian Institute of Architects (RAIA) mit dem Architekturpreis für Mehrfamilienhäuser ausgezeichnet wurden. Er war auch am Wohnhaus in Kew (Kew, Victoria, 2004, RAIA Award for Residential Architecture) beteiligt. **JONATHAN CLEMENTS** wurde 1971 in Melbourne, Australien, geboren. Er erwarb seinen B.Arch. an der Deakin University und arbeitete vor der Gründung von Jackson Clements Burrows im Jahr 1998 bei Daryl Jackson. Bei Jackson Clements Burrows war er an folgenden Projekten beteiligt: einem Wohnhaus in Cape Schanck (Cape Schanck, Victoria, 2006, hier vorgestellt) und den Pier Point Apartments (Geelong, Victoria, seit 2006). **GRAHAM BURROWS** wurde 1971 in Johannesburg, Südafrika, geboren und studierte an der University of Melbourne. Bis 1998 war er im Büro Daryl Jackson angestellt. Zu seinen Projekten für Jackson Clements Burrows gehören ein Wohnhaus in Separation Creek (Victoria, 2007) und die Uferbebauung Saint Kilda in Melbourne (2008). Weitere aktuelle Arbeiten von Jackson Clements Burrows sind das Trojan House (Melbourne, Victoria, 2005) und der Mehrfamilienkomplex Hue mit 29 Wohnungen (Richmond, Melbourne, 2007).

TIM JACKSON, né à San Francisco en 1964, a travaillé pour Denton Corker Marshall avant de rejoindre l'agence de son père (Daryl Jackson Architects) puis de fonder et diriger la sienne (1993–98). Il a été en charge du projet des Abito Apartments (Fitzroy, Victoria) qui a remporté le prix d'architecture du logement collectif 2007 du Royal Australian Institute of Architects. Il a également travaillé sur le projet de la maison Kew (Kew, Victoria, 2004; prix d'architecture résidentielle du RAIA). **JONATHAN CLEMENTS**, né en 1971 à Melbourne, a obtenu son B.Arch. de l'université Deakin et a travaillé avec Daryl Jackson avant la création de Jackson Clements Burrows en 1998. Parmi les projets auxquels il a participé chez Jackson Clements Burrows figurent la maison du cap Schanck (Victoria, 2006, publiée ici) et l'immeuble de logements de Pier Point (Geelong, Victoria, 2006–). **GRAHAM BURROWS**, né en 1971 à Johannesburg (Afrique du Sud), a étudié à l'université de Melbourne et travaillé chez Daryl Jackson avant 1998. Pour Jackson Clements Burrows, il a dirigé les projets de la résidence à Separation Creek (Victoria, 2007) et la promenade de front de mer de Saint Kilda à Melbourne (2008). Parmi les récentes réalisations de Jackson Clements Burrows figurent la maison de Troie (Melbourne, Victoria, 2005) et les Hue Apartments, projet multirésidentiel de 29 appartements (Richmond, Melbourne, 2007).

CAPE SCHANCK HOUSE

Cape Schanck, Victoria, Australia, 2006

Floor area: 350 m². Client: not disclosed. Cost: not disclosed
Collaboration: Jon Clements, Tim Jackson, Graham Burrows,
Kim Stapleton, George Fortey, Brett Nixon

The area in which this house is located is characterized by grass-covered dunes and dense brush. The architects found a hollowed and burned log on the site on the occasion of their first visit and used the metaphor of the log for their design. They compare the base of the house to the surrounding dunes—views of the house are concealed by a wall or screen fence on approach, allowing a broad vision of the surrounding countryside over the deck and pool only from the point of entry. The upper level, inspired by the log, contains a kitchen, dining and living areas, a garage, and laundry room. Another upper-level area contains the master bedroom and a study. These main areas are finished in black-stained spotted gum hardwood cladding, confirming the burnt log analogy. Interiors for this house, destined for a retired couple and their extended family, were also designed by the architects. Considerable attention was paid to passive energy strategies including the orientation of the house and shading. Well water is used for the swimming pool and rainwater for household use.

Die Gegend, in der das Haus liegt, wird von grasbewachsenen Dünen und dichtem Buschland dominiert. Bei ihrem ersten Besuch fanden die Architekten einen ausgehöhlten, verkohlten Holzstumpf auf dem Grundstück, den sie als Metapher in ihren Entwurf einfließen ließen. Sie vergleichen das Fundament des Hauses mit den Dünen – der Blick auf das Haus selbst wird bei der Anfahrt durch eine Mauer bzw. einen Zaun verstellt, ein Panoramablick auf die landschaftliche Umgebung über die Terrasse und den Pool hinweg ist nur vom Eingangsbereich aus möglich. In der oberen, vom Holzstumpf inspirierten Ebene des Hauses befinden sich Küche, Ess- und Wohnbereiche, eine Garage und ein Hauswirtschaftsraum. Ein weiteres Obergeschoss beherbergt das Hauptschlafzimmer und ein Arbeitszimmer. Diese Bereiche sind mit Spotted-Gum-Hartholz (einer Eukalyptusart) vertäfelt, was die Analogie zum verkohlten Holzstumpf unterstreicht. Auch die Inneneinrichtung dieses Domizils für ein pensioniertes Paar und seine große Familie wurde von den Architekten entworfen. Besonderen Wert legte man auf einen passiven Energiehaushalt, der u. a. durch die Orientierung des Hauses und Sonnenschutzstrategien erreicht wurde. Quellwasser speist den Pool, für den Hausverbrauch wird Regenwasser gesammelt.

L'environnement de cette maison se caractérise par des dunes couvertes d'herbes et de buissons. Lors de leur première visite, les architectes avaient trouvé sur le terrain une bûche creuse et calcinée et en ont utilisé la métaphore dans leur projet. Ils assimilent la base de la maison aux dunes environnantes. La vue sur la maison est dissimulée aux passants par un mur ou un écran, qui ne permet de découvrir la campagne environnante, par-delà la terrasse et la piscine, que de l'entrée. Le niveau supérieur, qui rappelle une bûche, contient la cuisine, les zones de séjour et de repas, un garage et une lingerie. L'autre niveau supérieur regroupe la chambre principale et un bureau. Ces parties principales sont parées de bois dur (gommier tacheté) teint en noir, ce qui renforce l'analogie avec la bûche. L'intérieur de cette maison, destinée à un couple de retraités et à leur famille élargie, a également été conçu par l'agence. Une attention considérable a été portée aux stratégies d'utilisation de l'énergie passive comme l'orientation de la maison et la protection solaire. L'eau d'un puits sert à alimenter la piscine et la pluie est récupérée pour les usages domestiques.

With its dramatic cantilevered form and one boxlike volume set up on stilts, the Cape Schanck House has an immediately recognizable profile.

Mit seinem dramatisch auskragenden Baukörper und einem auf Stelzen gesetzten kubischen Volumen hat das Cape Schanck House ein unverwechselbares Profil.

Le volume en porte-à-faux et la boîte sur pilotis assurent à la maison du cap Schanck un profil immédiatement identifiable.

The kitchen (above) is designed in black and white in cut-out forms that recall the architecture of the house. Below, plans for the two levels.

Die Küche (oben) ist schwarzweiß gehalten, wirkt wie ausgeschnitten und greift die Architektur des Hauses auf. Unten die Grundrisse zweier Ebenen.

La cuisine (ci-dessus) se compose de volumes découpées noir et blanc qui rappellent l'architecture de la maison. Ci-dessous, plans des deux niveaux.

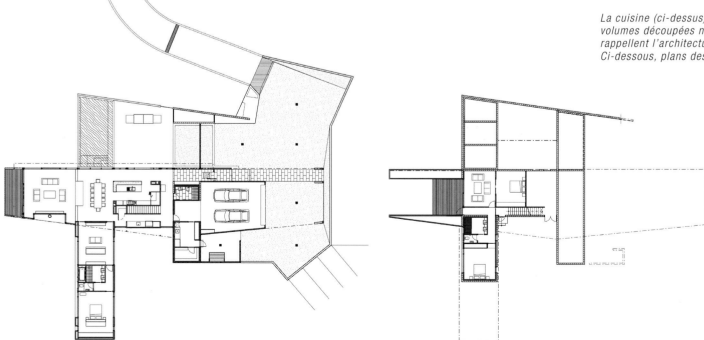

A section of the house shows its overhang on the sloped site. The projecting volumes allow for spectacular views on the neighboring area.

Ein Aufriss des Hauses veranschaulicht den Überhang über das abschüssige Grundstück. Dank der auskragenden Volumina bieten sich spektakuläre Ausblicke.

La coupe de la maison montre un important porte-à-faux au-dessus de la pente du terrain. Les volumes en projection offrent des vues spectaculaires sur la nature avoisinante.

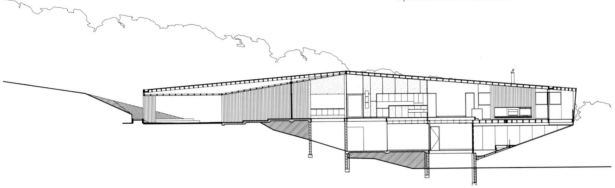

CHRIS JACOBS

Chris Jacobs
United Future, 8500 Steller Drive, Building 5
Culver City, CA 90232, USA
Tel: +1 310 280 7778 / E-mail: chris@unitedfuture.com
Web: www.unitedfuture.com

CHRIS JACOBS is the cofounder and Executive Creative Director of United Future, a design firm founded in 2005. The goal of the company "is to create cross-culture, cross-platform solutions that unite people and business processes through the use of transparent-technology ideologies." He worked previously as a Creative Director with Equus (Singapore, 2002) and Lemon Asia (Hong Kong). Jacobs has also worked as an independent consultant for companies such as SAP, Time Warner, and Universal Music. He attended the Art College Center of Design (1991–95) and is thus not an architect. He explains: "I've always had a love of architecture, and have designed a few homes while working in the field professionally. My true loves are industrial design and graphic design, with an emphasis on interface design and usability for Internet applications. I always felt that a good designer can design anything, from a shower curtain ring to a movie poster to an automobile. I've always pushed myself to be multidisciplined in a multitude of fields, including typography, digital illustration, 3D, interface usability, etc. Because of my love of industrial design, I forced myself to learn Rhino3D. When I was tasked to design a Vertical Farm (published here), I worked around the clock and designed it in one sitting (using Rhino3D), with the idea that this structure had to be stackable and modular. I then had it remodeled in 3D Studio Max by Dean Fowler with further detail design assistance by Rolf Mohr, an architect we work with on occasion."

CHRIS JACOBS ist Mitbegründer und leitender Creative Director von United Future, einem 2005 gegründeten Designbüro. Ziel der Agentur ist es, „kultur- und grundsatzübergreifende Lösungen zu finden, die Menschen und Geschäftsprozesse durch eine transparente technische Weltanschauung verbinden". Zuvor war er als Creative Director für Equus (Singapur, 2002) und Lemon Asia (Hongkong) tätig. Darüber hinaus war Jacobs als freier Berater für Firmen wie SAP, Time Warner und Universal Music aktiv. Er studierte am Art College Center of Design (1991–95) und ist somit kein Architekt. Er erklärt: „Ich hatte schon immer eine Leidenschaft für Architektur und habe während meiner beruflichen Tätigkeit in diesem Bereich auch einige Häuser entworfen. Doch meine wahre Leidenschaft ist das Produkt- und Grafikdesign, mit einem Schwerpunkt auf Interfacedesign und dessen Umsetzung für Internetanwendungen. Ich war schon immer der Meinung, dass ein guter Designer alles gestalten kann, von Ringen für Duschvorhänge über Kinoplakate bis hin zu Autos. Ich habe mich immer bemüht, multidisziplinär in einer ganzen Bandbreite von Bereichen arbeiten zu können, etwa in der Typografie, der digitalen Illustration, in 3D, benutzerfreundlichen Interfaces etc. Wegen meiner Leidenschaft für Produktdesign war ich gezwungen, mir Rhino3D zu erschließen. Als ich den Auftrag erhielt, einen vertikalen Bauernhof (hier vorgestellt) zu entwerfen, arbeitete ich rund um die Uhr und entwarf das Projekt (mit Rhino3D) in einem Zug. Die Idee war, dass die Konstruktion stapelbar und modular sein sollte. Schließlich musste der Entwurf von Dean Fowler mit 3D Studio Max neu modelliert werden, weitere Unterstützung beim Entwurf von Details kam von Rolf Mohr, einem Architekten, mit dem wir gelegentlich zusammenarbeiten."

CHRIS JACOBS est cofondateur et directeur de création de United Future, une agence de design créée en 2005. L'objectif de cette société est de « trouver des solutions trans-cultures, trans-plates-formes qui réunissent des personnes et des processus économiques à travers l'utilisation d'idéologies de technologies transparentes ». Il a été précédemment directeur de création d'Equus (Singapour, 2002) et de Lemon Asia (Hong Kong). Jacobs a également été consultant indépendant pour des entreprises comme SAP, Time Warner et Universal Music. Il a étudié au Art College Center of Design (1991–95) et n'est donc pas un architecte. Il explique ainsi : « J'ai toujours éprouvé un grand amour pour l'architecture et j'ai dessiné quelques maisons pendant que je travaillais professionnellement dans ce secteur. J'aime surtout le design industriel et le design graphique, avec un accent sur la conception d'interfaces et leur utilisation dans les applications Internet. J'ai toujours pensé qu'un bon designer pouvait tout concevoir, d'un anneau de rideau de douche à une affiche de film ou une automobile. Je me suis toujours efforcé d'être multidisciplinaire dans une multitude de domaines, dont la typographie, l'illustration numérique, la 3D, la convivialité des interfaces, etc. Dans cette passion pour le design industriel, je me suis forcé à apprendre le logiciel Rhino3D. Lorsque l'on m'a demandé de concevoir une Ferme verticale (publiée ici), j'ai travaillé 24/24 h et je l'ai conçue en une fois (avec Rhino3D), sur l'idée que cette structure devait être modulaire et empilable. Puis je l'ai fait retravailler en 3D Studio Max par Dean Fowler avec l'assistance en conception de détail de Rolf Mohr, un architecte avec lequel nous travaillons occasionnellement. »

VERTICAL FARM

Harlem, New York, New York, USA, 2007

Floor area: not disclosed. Client: Chris Jacobs. Cost: $200 million
Collaboration: Rolf Mohr

The concept behind this research project is that of bringing an actual farming space to the core of inner cities, from Los Angeles to New York, where Chris Jacobs imagines installing it in Harlem. Jacobs says: "Close your eyes; now imagine 30 stories of contemporary architecture designed to show off the real green with floor-to-ceiling windows, specialized equipment—solar panels everywhere. Put it next to a freeway; make it a 24-hour operation glowing brightly from the inside. A beacon of green technology. Would this technologically advanced 'greenscraper' spawn a new type of Agro-tourism?" Despite dreaming of such a project on a very large scale, Jacobs admits that "a two-story hydroponic structure atop a multistory affordable housing project might be the most pragmatic way to start." Chris Jacobs has thought through the potential for such a structure in the United States, where venture capital or philanthropic foundations might be persuaded to participate in the cost, with the goal of bringing jobs and fresh produce to America's underprivileged inner cities.

Das Konzept dieses Forschungsprojekts war es, eine reale Landwirtschaftsfläche in das Zentrum von Großstädten zu integrieren – von Los Angeles oder New York, wo Chris Jacobs sie an einen fiktiven Standort in Harlem verlegte. Jacobs führt aus: „Schließ deine Augen und stell dir ein 30-stöckiges zeitgenössisches Gebäude vor, das gebaut wurde, um echtes Grün zu präsentieren, mit geschosshohen Fenstern, spezieller technischer Ausstattung – überall Solarmodule. Stell es dir direkt neben einer Stadtautobahn vor, lass es als 24-Stunden-Fabrik hell von innen leuchten. Ein Leuchtfeuer grüner Technologie. Könnte dieser technisch anspruchsvolle ‚Greenscraper' zu einer neuen Art von Agro-Tourismus führen?" Trotz seiner Träume von einem Projekt in monumentaler Größenordnung räumt Jacobs ein, dass „eine zweistöckige Hydrokultur-Konstruktion auf einem mehrstöckigen Gebäude mit subventionierten Sozialbauwohnungen zu Anfang wohl der pragmatischere Weg wäre". Chris Jacobs hat die Chancen für ein solches Bauwerk in den USA sehr wohl durchdacht: Möglicherweise ließen sich Risikokapitalgeber und karitative Stiftungen überzeugen, Kosten zu übernehmen, um neue Arbeitsplätze zu schaffen und frisches Obst und Gemüse in die unterprivilegierten Innenstädte Amerikas zu bringen.

Le concept de ce projet de recherche est d'installer de vrais espaces agricoles au cœur des villes, de Los Angeles à New York où Jacobs imagine son implantation à Harlem. « Fermez les yeux et imaginez trente étages d'architecture contemporaine conçus pour montrer cette verdure authentique à travers des baies toute hauteur, des équipements spécialisés, y compris des panneaux solaires dans tous les sens. Placez-le tout près d'une autoroute, faites qu'on le voit de jour comme de nuit, brillamment éclairé de l'intérieur. Un concentré spectaculaire de technologie verte ! Ce "gratte-vert" de haute technologie ne pourrait-il pas lancer un nouveau type d'agrotourisme ? » Tout en rêvant à ce projet à très grande échelle, Jacobs admet qu'« une structure hydroponique de deux niveaux au sommet d'un immeuble de logements accessibles à tous pourrait être un point de départ plus pragmatique ». Il a réfléchi au potentiel d'une structure de ce type aux États-Unis, où les investisseurs et les fondations philanthropiques pourraient être convaincus de participer au coût de l'opération dans le but de créer des emplois et de fournir des produits frais aux habitants défavorisés des centres des villes.

Chris Jacobs addresses the question of just how agriculture might well enter the urban environment in a coherent way, assisted by an intelligent use of architecture.

Chris Jacobs setzt sich mit der Frage auseinander, wie sich Landwirtschaft dank intelligenter Architektur schlüssig in ein urbanes Umfeld integrieren lässt.

Chris Jacobs traite le problème de l'introduction éventuelle de l'agriculture dans un cadre urbain de manière cohérente, aidé par une mise en œuvre intelligente de l'architecture.

CREDITS

Kyu Sung Woo, Putney 672
dECOi Architects, Cambridge 170

Bohlin Cywinski Jackson, Finger Lakes Region 120

wHY Architecture, Grand Rapids 654

Gustafson Guthrie Nichol, Chicago 272

Johnsen Schmaling Architects, Green Lake 384

Bohlin Cywinski Jackson, Grand Teton National Park 114
Carney Logan Burke Architects, Grand Teton National Park 138

Hotson Bakker Boniface Haden, Osoyoos 304

Nic Lehoux and Jacqueline Darjes, Point Roberts 446

Float, Willamette Valley 236

Renzo Piano, San Francisco 556

Shigeru Ban, Santa Monica 80
Glavovic Studio, Hollywood 260
Office dA, Los Angeles 518

Ken Smith, Santa Fe 606

Carter + Burton Architecture, Warren County 144
Gustafson Guthrie Nichol, Washington, D.C. 278
KieranTimberlake, Washington, D.C. 410

Perkins+Will, Atlanta 544

Raymond Jungles, Coconut Grove 396

dRN Architects, Quintero, Valparaíso 188
Alberto Mozó, Santiago de Chile 486
WMR, Los Arcos 660

Dumay + Fones + Vergara, Lake Rupanco 202

dRN Architects, Chiloé Island 188

Germán del Sol, Puerto Natales 620

70F, Almere 18
MIII architecten, Hoorn 460
Koen van Velsen, Hilversum 648

Charles Barclay, Kielder 84

Sebastian Bergne, London 98
Frank O. Gehry, London 254

Edward Cullinan, Singleton 164

Nicholas Grimshaw, St. Austell 266

Balmori Associates, Bilbao 68

Patrick Blanc, Madrid 110
Ecosistema Urbano, Madrid 208
selgascano, Madrid 594

Victor Neves, Esposende 500

selgascano, Mérida 602

80 Shigeru Ban, New York
178 Diller Scofidio + Renfro, New York
320 HWKN (Hollwich Kushner), Long Island City
344 Chris Jacobs, Harlem
354 James Corner Field Operations /
Diller Scofidio + Renfro, New York
424 Kengo Kuma, New Canaan
644 Michael Van Valkenburgh, New Haven
678 WORK Architecture Company,
Long Island City

416 Mathias Klotz, Punta del Este
528 Carlos Ott, José Ignacio, Maldonado

90 **Barlindhaug Consult AS**, Longyearbyen

54 **Auer+Weber+Assoziierte**, Shanghai
478 **Morphosis**, Shanghai
492 **Neri & Hu**, Shanghai
686 **Zhu Xiaofeng Scenic Architecture**, Qingpu

582 **Saunders & Wilhelmsen**, Hardanger Fjord
366 **Jensen & Skodvin Architects**, Tautra Island
374 **Jensen & Skodvin Architects**, Gudbrandsjuvet
562 **PUSHAK**, Måsøy 562
440 **Lassila Hirvilammi Architects**, Kärsämäki
576 **SARC Architects**, Joensuu
378 **Emma Johansson and Timo Leiviskä**, Mikkeli
62 **Pieta-Linda Auttila**, Helsinki
300 **Steven Holl**, Herning
104 **BIG**, Copenhagen
404 **Kempe Thill**, Rostock
282 **Heberle Mayer**, Berlin
32 **AFF**, Tellerhäuser
588 **SeARCH**, Rheden
390 **Françoise-Hélène Jourda**, Herne
44 **Aldinger Architekten**, Stuttgart
612 **Werner Sobek**, Tieringen

74 **Shigeru Ban**, Seoul
320 **IROJE KHM Architects**, Go Yang
326 **IROJE KHM Architects**, Gwangju
464 **Ken Sungjin Min**, Gangwon-do
548 **Dominique Perrault**, Seoul

568 **Hiroshi Sambuichi**, Inujima
216 **Shuhei Endo**, Sayo-cho

182 **Vladimir Djurovic**, Beirut
Li Xiaodong, Lijiang 454

80 **Shigeru Ban**, Tokyo
506 **Nikken Sekkei**, Tokyo

228 **FELIX-DELUBAC**, Siwa
250 **Norman Foster**, Abu Dhabi

430 **Kengo Kuma**, Yusuhara

150 **Marco Casagrande**, Sanjhih
536 **Sergio Palleroni**, Taipei

470 **MODUS**, Bressanone
640 **Matteo Thun**, Lana, Merano

132 **Vincent Callebaut Architectures**, Hong Kong
294 **Steven Holl**, Shenzhen

12 **24H Architecture**, Chiang Mai

286 **Anna Heringer and Eike Roswag**, Rudrapur

48 **Emilio Ambasz**, Venice-Mestre
330 **Junya Ishigami**, Venice

626 **Studio Mumbai**, Nandgaon

244 **Norman Foster**, St. Moritz
512 **Rolf Karl Nimmrichter**, Dietlikon

Effan Adhiwira, Badung 24

222 **ETHStudio Monte Rosa / Bearth & Deplazes**, Zermatt

158 **Casey Brown**, Mudgee

434 **Lacaton & Vassal**, Mulhouse

Jackson Clements Burrows, Cape Schank 338
Taylor Cullity Lethlean, Cranbourne 634

38 **Agence Babylone**, Saclay
126 **Vincent Callebaut Architectures**, Paris

100 CONTEMPORARY
GREEN
BUILDINGS

IMPRINT

PROJECT MANAGEMENT
Florian Kobler and
Inga Hallsson, Cologne

COLLABORATION
Harrient Graham, Turin

PRODUCTION
Ute Wachendorf, Cologne

DESIGN
Sense/Net Art Direction,
Andy Disl and Birgit
Eichwede, Cologne
www.sense-net.net

GERMAN TRANSLATION
Caroline Behlen, Berlin;
Christiane Court, Frankfurt;
Karin Haag, Vienna;

Kristina Brigitta Köper,
Berlin; Nora von Mühlendahl,
Ludwigsburg; Laila Neubert-
Mader, Ettlingen; Annette
Wiethüchter, Berlin; Holger
Wölfle, Berlin

FRENCH TRANSLATION
Jacques Bosser, Montesquiou
Claire Debard, Freiburg

PRINTED IN CHINA
ISBN 978–3–8365–4191–6

Philip Jodidio

100 CONTEMPORARY
GREEN
BUILDINGS

100 Zeitgenössische Grüne Bauten
100 Bâtiments Verts Contemporains

VOL 2

TASCHEN

CONTENT VOLUME I

INTRODUCTION Einleitung/Introduction **6**

24H ARCHITECTURE Panyaden School *Chiang Mai* **12**
70F Petting Farm *Almere* **18**
EFFAN ADHIWIRA Green School *Badung* **24**
AFF "Hutznhaisl" *Tellerhäuser* **32**
AGENCE BABYLONE Active Nature *Saclay* **38**
ALDINGER ARCHITEKTEN Cafeteria and Day Care Center, Waldorf School *Stuttgart* **44**
EMILIO AMBASZ Ospedale dell'Angelo *Venice-Mestre* **48**
AUER+WEBER+ASSOZIIERTE Buildings in Chenshan Botanical Garden *Shanghai* **54**
PIETA-LINDA AUTTILA Wisa Wooden Design Hotel *Helsinki* **62**
BALMORI ASSOCIATES The Garden That Climbs the Stairs *Bilbao* **68**
SHIGERU BAN Papertainer Museum *Seoul* / Nomadic Museum *New York; Santa Monica; Tokyo* **74**
CHARLES BARCLAY Kielder Observatory *Kielder* **84**
BARLINDHAUG CONSULT AS Svalbard Global Seed Vault *Longyearbyen* **90**
SEBASTIAN BERGNE LEGO Greenhouse *London* **98**
BIG The Mountain *Copenhagen* **104**
PATRICK BLANC CaixaForum Vertical Garden *Madrid* **110**
BOHLIN CYWINSKI JACKSON Grand Teton Discovery and Visitor Center *Grand Teton National Park* /
Combs Point Residence *Finger Lakes Region* **114**
VINCENT CALLEBAUT ARCHITECTURES Anti-Smog *Paris* / Perfumed Jungle *Hong Kong* **126**
CARNEY LOGAN BURKE ARCHITECTS Laurance S. Rockefeller Preserve *Grand Teton National Park* **138**
CARTER + BURTON ARCHITECTURE Shenandoah Retreat *Warren County* **144**
MARCO CASAGRANDE Chen House *Sanjhih* **150**
CASEY BROWN Permanent Camping *Mudgee* **158**
EDWARD CULLINAN Downland Gridshell *Singleton* **164**
DECOI ARCHITECTS One Main *Cambridge* **170**
DILLER SCOFIDIO + RENFRO Hypar Pavilion Lawn *New York* **178**
VLADIMIR DJUROVIC Samir Kassir Square *Beirut* **182**
DRN ARCHITECTS La Baronia House *Quintero* / House at Punta Chilen *Chiloé Island* **188**
DUMAY + FONES + VERGARA Fuente Nueva Chapel *Lake Rupanco* **202**
ECOSISTEMA URBANO Ecoboulevard of Vallecas *Madrid* **208**
SHUHEI ENDO Bubbletecture H *Sayo-cho* **216**
ETH-STUDIO MONTE ROSA / BEARTH & DEPLAZES New Monte Rosa Hut SAC *Zermatt* **222**
FELIX-DELUBAC Ecolodge *Siwa* **228**
FLOAT Watershed *Willamette Valley* **236**
NORMAN FOSTER Chesa Futura *St. Moritz* / Masdar Institute *Abu Dhabi* **244**
FRANK O. GEHRY Serpentine Gallery Pavilion *London* **254**
GLAVOVIC STUDIO Young Circle ArtsPark *Hollywood* **260**
NICHOLAS GRIMSHAW The Eden Project *St. Austell* **266**
GUSTAFSON GUTHRIE NICHOL Lurie Garden *Chicago* / Robert and Arlene Kogod Courtyard *Washington, D.C.* **272**
HEBERLE MAYER U6 Berlin Penthouse *Berlin* **282**
ANNA HERINGER AND EIKE ROSWAG Handmade School *Rudrapur* **286**
STEVEN HOLL Vanke Center / Horizontal Skyscraper *Shenzhen* /
HEART: Herning Museum of Contemporary Art *Herning* **292**
HOTSON BAKKER BONIFACE HADEN Nk'Mip Desert Cultural Center *Osoyoos* **304**
HWKN (HOLLWICH KUSHNER) Wendy *Long Island City* **320**
IROJE KHM ARCHITECTS Lim Geo Dang *Go Yang* / Hye Ro Hun *Gwangju* **320**
JUNYA ISHIGAMI Greenhouses, Japanese Pavilion *Venice* **330**
JACKSON CLEMENTS BURROWS Cape Schanck House *Cape Schanck* **338**
CHRIS JACOBS Vertical Farm *Harlem* **344**

CREDITS **348**

CONTENT VOLUME II

JAMES CORNER FIELD OPERATIONS /   The High Line *New York* **354**
DILLER SCOFIDIO + RENFRO
MICHAEL JANTZEN   Homestead House **362**
JENSEN & SKODVIN ARCHITECTS   Tautra Maria Convent *Tautra Island* / Juvet Landscape Hotel *Gudbrandsjuvet* **366**
EMMA JOHANSSON AND TIMO LEIVISKÄ   Anttolanhovi Art and Design Villas *Mikkeli* **378**
JOHNSEN SCHMALING ARCHITECTS   Camouflage House *Green Lake* **384**
FRANÇOISE-HÉLÈNE JOURDA   Mont-Cenis Academy and Municipal District Center *Herne* **390**
RAYMOND JUNGLES   Coconut Grove *Coconut Grove* **396**
KEMPE THILL   Hedge Building *Rostock* **404**
KIERANTIMBERLAKE   Sidwell Friends Middle School *Washington, D.C.* **410**
MATHIAS KLOTZ   La Roca House *Punta del Este* **416**
KENGO KUMA   Glass Wood House *New Canaan* / Yusuhara Marché *Yusuhara* **424**
LACATON & VASSAL   Social Housing, Cité Manifeste *Mulhouse* **434**
LASSILA HIRVILAMMI ARCHITECTS   Kärsämäki Church *Kärsämäki* **440**
NIC LEHOUX AND JACQUELINE DARJES   The Lilypad *Point Roberts* **446**
LI XIAODONG   Yuhu Elementary School *Lijiang* **454**
MIII ARCHITECTEN   Environmental Education Center *Hoorn* **460**
KEN SUNGJIN MIN   Kumgang Ananti Golf & Spa Resort *Gangwon-do* **464**
MODUS   Damiani Holz & Ko Headquarters *Bressanone* **470**
MORPHOSIS   Giant Interactive Group Corporate Headquarters *Shanghai* **478**
ALBERTO MOZÓ   BIP Computer Office and Shop *Santiago de Chile* **486**
NERI & HU   The Waterhouse at South Bund *Shanghai* **492**
VICTOR NEVES   Reorganization of the Riverside of Esposende *Esposende* **500**
NIKKEN SEKKEI   Sony City Osaki *Tokyo* **506**
ROLF KARL NIMMRICHTER   S House *Dietlikon* **512**
OFFICE DA   Helios House *Los Angeles* **518**
CARLOS OTT   Playa Vik *Faro José Ignacio* **528**
SERGIO PALLERONI   Zhong Xiao Boulevard Urban Ecological Corridor *Taipei* **536**
PERKINS+WILL   1315 Peachtree Street *Atlanta* **544**
DOMINIQUE PERRAULT   Ewha Womans University *Seoul* **548**
RENZO PIANO   Renovation and Expansion of the California Academy of Sciences *San Francisco* **556**
PUSHAK   Lillefjord *Måsøy* **562**
HIROSHI SAMBUICHI   Inujima Art Project Seirensho *Inujima* **568**
SARC ARCHITECTS   Metla, Finnish Forest Research Institute *Joensuu* **576**
SAUNDERS & WILHELMSEN   Summer House *Hardanger Fjord* **582**
SEARCH   Posbank Tea Pavilion *Rheden* **588**
SELGASCANO   Studio in the Woods *Madrid* / Mérida Factory Youth Movement *Mérida* **594**
KEN SMITH   Santa Fe Railyard Park and Plaza *Santa Fe* **606**
WERNER SOBEK   H16 *Tieringen* **612**
GERMÁN DEL SOL   Hotel Remota *Puerto Natales* **620**
STUDIO MUMBAI   Palmyra House *Nandgaon* **626**
TAYLOR CULLITY LETHLEAN   Royal Botanic Gardens *Cranbourne* **634**
MATTEO THUN   Vigilius Mountain Resort *Lana* **640**
MICHAEL VAN VALKENBURGH   Connecticut Water Treatment Facility *New Haven* **644**
KOEN VAN VELSEN   Media Authority Building *Hilversum* **648**
WHY ARCHITECTURE   Grand Rapids Art Museum *Grand Rapids* **654**
WMR   Till House *Los Arcos* / Mandakovic House *Los Arcos* **660**
KYU SUNG WOO   Putney Mountain House *Putney* **672**
WORK ARCHITECTURE COMPANY   Public Farm 1 *Long Island City* **678**
ZHU XIAOFENG SCENIC ARCHITECTURE   The Green Pine Garden *Qingpu* **686**

INDEX **692**
CREDITS **696**

JAMES CORNER FIELD OPERATIONS / DILLER SCOFIDIO + RENFRO

James Corner Field Operations
475 10th Avenue, 10th floor, New York, NY 10018, USA
Tel: +1 212 433 1450 / Fax: +1 212 433 1451
E-mail: info@fieldoperations.net / Web: www.fieldoperations.net

Diller Scofidio + Renfro
601 West 26th Street, Suite 1815, New York, NY 10001, USA
Tel: +1 212 260 7971 / Fax: +1 212 260 7924
E-mail: disco@dsrny.com / Web: www.dsrny.com

JAMES CORNER FIELD OPERATIONS is an interdisciplinary design firm based in New York City. Corner is founder and Director of JCFO and is also Chair of the Department of Landscape Architecture at the University of Pennsylvania School of Design. He was educated at Manchester Metropolitan University, UK (B.A. in Landscape Architecture with first class honors), and the University of Pennsylvania (M.L.A./U.D.). Lisa Tziona Switkin is an associate partner and project leader for the High Line at JCFO with a B.A. in Urban Planning from the University of Illinois and an M.L.A. from the University of Pennsylvania. **DILLER SCOFIDIO + RENFRO** is an interdisciplinary firm based in New York City. Elizabeth Diller is Professor of Architecture at Princeton University; Ricardo Scofidio is Professor Emeritus of Architecture at the Cooper Union in New York; and Charles Renfro has served as a Visiting Professor at Rice University, Columbia University, and Parsons The New School for Design. Matthew Johnson, a Senior Associate at DS+R and project leader for the High Line, is a native of Michigan. He is a graduate of the University of Michigan and holds an M.Arch from Princeton University. The team is primarily involved in thematically driven experimental works that take the form of architectural commissions, temporary installations and permanent site-specific installations, multimedia theater, electronic media, and print.

JAMES CORNER FIELD OPERATIONS ist ein interdisziplinär arbeitendes Büro in New York City. James Corner ist Gründer und Direktor des Büros und Inhaber des Lehrstuhls für Landschaftsarchitektur an der University of Pennsylvania School of Design. Er hat an der Manchester Metropolitan University in Großbritannien seinen Bachelor in Landschaftsarchitektur mit Auszeichnung bestanden, dann hat er an der University of Pennsylvania sein Studium als Master in Landschaftsarchitektur und Stadtplanung abgeschlossen. Lisa Tziona Switkin ist Büropartnerin und Projektleiterin für das Projekt High Line im Büro JCFO. Sie hat ihren Bachelor in Stadtplanung an der University of Illinois gemacht und ihren Master in Landschaftsarchitektur an der University of Pennsylvania. **DILLER SCOFIDIO + RENFRO** ist ein ebenfalls interdisziplinär arbeitendes Büro in New York City. Elizabeth Diller ist Professorin für Architektur an der Princeton University, Ricardo Scofidio ist Professor emeritus für Architektur an der Cooper Union in New York, und Charles Renfro war Gastprofessor an der Rice University und der Columbia University sowie Parsons The New School for Design. Matthew Johnson, einer der Teilhaber des Büros DS + R und Projektleiter von High Line, stammt aus Michigan. Er hat seinen Studienabschluss an der University of Michigan gemacht und seinen Master an der Princeton University. Das Team beschäftigt sich vorwiegend mit experimentellen Aufträgen aus den Bereichen Architektur, temporäre und ständige ortsspezifische Installationen, Multimediatheater, elektronische und Druckmedien.

JAMES CORNER FIELD OPERATIONS est une agence interdisciplinaire new-yorkaise fondée et dirigée par James Corner, architecte paysagiste et urbaniste. Également président et professeur du département d'Architecture du paysage à l'École de design de l'université de Pennsylvanie, il a fait ses études à la Manchester Metropolitan University (B.A. d'architecture du paysage, avec les honneurs), Royaume-Uni, et à l'université de Pennsylvanie (M.L.A/U.D.). Lisa Tziona Switkin, directrice associée de JCFO et directrice de projet pour la High Line (2011, publiée ici), est titulaire d'un B.A. d'urbanisme de l'université de l'Illinois et d'un M.L.A. de l'université de Pennsylvanie. **DILLER SCOFIDIO + RENFRO** est une agence interdisciplinaire basée à New York. Elizabeth Diller est professeur d'architecture à l'université de Princeton, Ricardo Scofidio professeur émérite d'architecture à la Cooper Union à New York et Charles Renfro professeur invité aux universités Rice et Columbia, ainsi qu'à la Parsons New School for Design. Originaire du Michigan, Matthew Johnson, associé senior chez DS+R et directeur de projet pour la High Line, est diplômé de l'université du Michigan et titulaire d'un M.Arch. de l'université de Princeton. Leurs recherches essentiellement thématiques et expérimentales prennent la forme de commandes architecturales, d'installations temporaires, d'installations permanentes adaptées au site, de théâtre multimédia, de médias électroniques et de publications.

THE HIGH LINE

New York, New York, USA, 2009 (Phase I), 2011 (Phase II)—ongoing

Address: West Side of Manhattan, from Gansevoort Street to West 34th Street,
between 10th and 11th Avenues, New York City, USA, +1 212 206 9922, www.thehighline.org.
Length: 2.4 km. Client: City of New York, Friends of the High Line
Cost: $156 million (Phases I and II). Collaboration: Piet Oudolf, Craig Schwitter (Principal, Buro Happold),
Joseph F. Tortorella (Vice President, Robert Silman Associates),
Herve Descottes (Principal, L'Observatoire International)

The designers and architects who worked on the High Line had the clear challenge to make creative use of an abandoned elevated rail line in lower Manhattan. Their solution has revitalized the area and created a new park space.

Die besondere Herausforderung für die Planer und Architekten bestand darin, für diesen brachliegenden Hochbahngleiskörper mitten in Lower Manhattan eine kreative Nutzung zu finden. Ihre Lösung hat das gesamte Stadtviertel neu belebt und einen neuen Park entstehen lassen.

Les designers et les architectes ayant travaillé sur le projet de la High Line dans le bas de Manhattan devaient répondre au défi de trouver une réutilisation créative de cette voie ferrée suspendue abandonnée. Leur projet a revitalisé le quartier et offert à New York un nouvel espace vert.

The High Line has offered new green areas to both residents and tourists, but also served to incite a good deal of construction and renovation along the path of the rail spur.

Die High Line bietet neue Grünräume sowohl für die Anwohner als auch für Touristen. Infolge des neuen Parks wurden entlang der ehemaligen Bahnstrecke viele Sanierungen vorgenommen, und es entstanden Neubauten.

La High Line qui offre de nouveaux espaces verts aux résidents et aux touristes, a entraîné le développement de nombreux projets de construction et de rénovation le long de son tracé.

THE HIGH LINE is a public park constructed on an elevated railway running about 2.4 kilometers from Gansevoort Street in the Meatpacking District to West 34th Street on Manhattan's West Side. The West Side Improvement Project, including the High Line, was built because of the number of accidents involving the street-level railroad crossing of trains, and was put into effect in 1929. Intended to avoid the negative effects of subway lines over crowded streets, the High Line cuts through the center of city blocks. Increasing truck traffic led to the demolition of parts of the High Line in the 1960s and a halt to train operations in 1980. Despite efforts to demolish the remaining structure to allow new construction, a good part of the High Line survived and a group called Friends of the High Line, created in 1999, eventually convinced authorities to renovate it rather than to allow its destruction. James Corner Field Operations, Diller Scofidio + Renfro, Piet Oudolf, and a number of other parties have participated in a collective project for the High Line to renovate and bring new life to a disused part of the city. As they say: "Inspired by the melancholic, unruly beauty of the High Line where nature has reclaimed a once vital piece of urban infrastructure, the team retools this industrial conveyance into a postindustrial instrument of leisure, life, and growth. By changing the rules of engagement between plant life and pedestrians, our strategy of agri-tecture combines organic and building materials into a blend of changing proportions that accommodate the wild, the cultivated, the intimate, and the hyper-social."

THE HIGH LINE ist ein öffentlicher, etwa 2,4 km langer Park, der auf einer ehemaligen Hochbahntrasse zwischen der Gansevoort Street im Stadtviertel Meatpacking District und der West 34th Street auf der West Side von Manhattan angelegt ist. Das Projekt zur Verbesserung der Infrastruktur der West Side, zu dem auch der Bau der High Line gehörte, entstand im Jahr 1929. Die High Line wurde damals gebaut, da es zahlreiche Unfälle gegeben hatte, weil die Züge die Straßen niveaugleich querten. Mit der High Line sollte die negative Wirkung von Schienenverkehr auf beengten Straßenräumen vermieden werden, und so wurde die Schneise für die High Line mitten durch die Blockbebauung des Viertels geschlagen. Aufgrund des wachsenden Lkw-Verkehrs wurde in den 1960er-Jahren die High Line teilweise abgebrochen und der Zugverkehr 1980 ganz eingestellt. Trotz aller Versuche, die Reste der Bahntrasse abzureißen und etwas Neues zu bauen, hat die High Line überlebt. Einer 1999 gegründeten Initiative, den Friends of the High Line, gelang es, die Behörden davon zu überzeugen, die Trasse zu sanieren statt sie abzubrechen. James Corner Field Operations, Diller Scofidio + Renfro, Piet Oudolf und andere Teams haben an dem Gemeinschaftsprojekt zur Sanierung der High Line mitgearbeitet, damit diesem vernachlässigten Teil der Stadt zu neuem Leben verholfen wird. Die Planer kommentieren: „Wir haben uns von der melancholischen, spröden Schönheit der High Line anregen lassen, wo sich die Natur ein Stück ehemals vitaler, urbaner Infrastruktur zurückerobert hat. Unser Team verwandelt den Gleiskörper in eine postindustrielle Freizeitlandschaft, die mit Leben und mit Wachstum erfüllt ist. Indem wir die Regeln der Beziehungen zwischen dem Pflanzenleben und den Fußgängern verändert haben, verbindet unsere Strategie der Agri-Tektur organische und künstliche Werkstoffe, sodass eine abwechslungsreiche Mischung aus wilden, naturnahen Bereichen, Pflanzenkulturen sowie intimen und hypersozialen Abschnitten entsteht."

Le parc public de **LA HIGH LINE** a été aménagé sur une ancienne voie ferrée surélevée d'environ 2,4 km de long entre la rue Gansevoort, dans le quartier de Meatpacking, et la 34e Rue Ouest, dans le West Side de Manhattan. Le projet d'amélioration du West Side, comprenant la High Line, avait été mis en œuvre en 1929 pour réduire le nombre d'accidents aux passages à niveau. La ligne traversait même des « blocs » du centre-ville pour limiter certains effets négatifs des voies suspendues au-dessus de rues encombrées. L'augmentation de la circulation des camions a entraîné la démolition de certaines parties de la High Line dans les années 1960 et la fin de l'exploitation de la voie en 1980. Malgré plusieurs tentatives de la détruire totalement pour faire place à de nouvelles constructions, une bonne partie des voies subsistait encore et, en 1999, une association des amis de la High Line a été créée et a fini par convaincre les autorités municipales de la rénover plutôt que de la détruire. James Corner Field Operations, Diller Scofidio + Renfro, Piet Oudolf et un certain nombre d'autres participants ont préparé un projet collectif de rénovation de la ligne et de revitalisation de ce quartier en déshérence : « Inspirée par la beauté originale et mélancolique de la High Line, où la nature avait repris ses droits sur un élément d'infrastructure urbaine jadis vital, l'équipe a transformé cet équipement industriel en outil post-industriel de loisirs, de vie et de croissance. En modifiant les règles des rapports entre la vie végétale et les piétons, notre stratégie d'agri-tecture combine éléments organiques et matériaux de construction selon des proportions variées, adaptées au caractère sauvage de la nature, aux plantes cultivées, à l'intime et à l'hypersocial. »

In some places, the original rails are left in place to give an indication of the original function of the elevated platform. The High Line connects frequently to the street level (above).

An einigen Orten hat man die Originalgleise einfach belassen, um auf die ursprüngliche Funktion der erhöhten Plattform hinzuweisen. Die High Line ist an vielen Stellen mit dem Straßenniveau verbunden (oben).

Des rails ont été laissés en place à certains endroits pour rappeler la fonction d'origine de ce jardin suspendu. La High line est fréquemment reliée au niveau de la rue (ci-dessus).

Walkways and benches are, of course, part of the scheme that allows walkers to view the essentially industrial architecture of the area from a new vantage point.

Fußwege und Bänke gehören natürlich auch zu dem Entwurf. So können Fußgänger die Industriearchitektur, die dieses Viertel prägt, aus einem neuen Blickwinkel betrachten.

L'aménagement des allées et les bancs font partie du projet, permettant aux promeneurs d'apercevoir l'architecture essentiellement industrielle du quartier sous un nouvel angle.

MICHAEL JANTZEN

Michael Jantzen
1031 Highlands Plaza Drive West
Suite 519W
St. Louis, MO 63110
USA

Tel: +1 310 989 1897
E-mail: info@michaeljantzen.com
Web: www.michaeljantzen.com

Born in 1948, **MICHAEL JANTZEN** received a B.F.A. degree from Southern Illinois University (Edwardsville, Illinois, 1971). He received an M.F.A. degree with a major in Multimedia from Washington University (Saint Louis, Missouri, 1973). Jantzen was then hired by Washington University's School of Fine Arts and by the School of Architecture to teach studio courses as a Visiting Professor. In 1975, one of his first solar houses was featured in numerous national and international magazines. Over the next ten years, he continued to design and build energy-efficient structures with an emphasis on modular high-tech housing systems. In 1997, he was awarded a grant from Art Center College of Design Digital Media Department to develop ideas for an interface between media and architecture. In 1998, Jantzen created a conceptual house called the Malibu Video Beach House, and Elements, an interactive digital media theme park. From 1999 to 2001, he designed and built the M House, "a modular, re-locatable, environmentally responsive, alternative housing system." Since then, Jantzen has worked with various companies as a consultant to develop experimental design projects. Recent work includes Desert Winds Eco-Spa (2008), a concept design for a wellness spa that generates all of its energy from the wind and sun; Sun Rays Pavilion (2009), a concept design for a large solar-powered pavilion; and Homestead House (2009, published here).

MICHAEL JANTZEN wurde 1948 geboren und erhielt seinen B.F.A. 1971 an der Southern Illinois University (Edwardsville, Illinois). Seinen M.F.A. machte er 1973 mit dem Hauptfach Multimedia an der Washington University (Saint Louis, Missouri, 1973). Im Anschluss erhielt Jantzen einen Lehrauftrag an den Fakultäten für bildende Kunst und Architektur der Washington University und leitete dort Studiokurse als Gastprofessor. 1975 wurde eines seiner ersten Solarhäuser in zahlreichen nationalen und internationalen Zeitschriften publiziert. Im Lauf der folgenden zehn Jahre entwarf und errichtete er weitere energieeffiziente Bauten, wobei er sich auf hochtechnisierte Modulhäuser spezialisierte. 1997 erhielt er ein Forschungsstipendium der Abteilung für digitale Medien des Art Center College of Design, um Ideen für eine Schnittstelle zwischen Medien und Architektur zu entwickeln. 1998 entwarf Jantzen ein Konzepthaus, das Malibu Video Beach House, und Elements, einen interaktiven, digitalen Medienfreizeitpark. Zwischen 1999 und 2001 entwarf und baute er das M House, „ein modulares, umzugsfähiges, umweltsensibles, alternatives Wohnbausystem". Seither arbeitet Jantzen für verschiedene Firmen als Berater und entwickelt experimentelle Designprojekte. Jüngere Projekte sind u. a. das Desert Winds Eco-Spa (2008), ein Konzeptentwurf für ein Wellnesszentrum, das seinen gesamten Strombedarf aus Wind- und Solarenergie bezieht, Sun Rays Pavilion (2009), ein Konzept für einen großen, mit Solarenergie betriebenen Pavillon, sowie das Homestead House (2009, hier vorgestellt).

Né en 1948, **MICHAEL JANTZEN** a obtenu son B.F.A. de la Southern Illinois University (Edwardsville, Illinois, 1971) et son M.F.A. spécialisé en multimédia de l'université Washington (Saint Louis, Missouri, 1973). L'École des beaux-arts et l'École d'architecture de l'université Washington lui ont ensuite offert de devenir professeur d'atelier invité. En 1975, l'une de ses premières maisons solaires a été publiée dans de nombreux magazines nationaux et internationaux. Au cours des dix années suivantes, il a conçu et réalisé des constructions écologiques autour de systèmes modulaires de haute technologie. En 1997, il a obtenu une bourse du département de conception de médias numériques de l'Art Center pour développer ses idées sur une interface entre médias et architecture. En 1998, il a créé une maison conceptuelle appelée la Malibu Video Beach House, et Elements, un parc à thème sur les médias numériques interactifs. De 1999 à 2001, il a conçu et construit la maison M, « système d'habitation modulaire, transportable, écologique ». Depuis, il a travaillé comme consultant sur de nombreux projets expérimentaux. Parmi ses réalisations récentes : le Desert Winds Eco-Spa (2008), le concept d'un spa qui génère l'énergie dont il a besoin à partir des vents et du soleil ; Sun Rays, un grand pavillon à énergie solaire (2009) et la Homestead House (2009, publiée ici).

HOMESTEAD HOUSE

2009

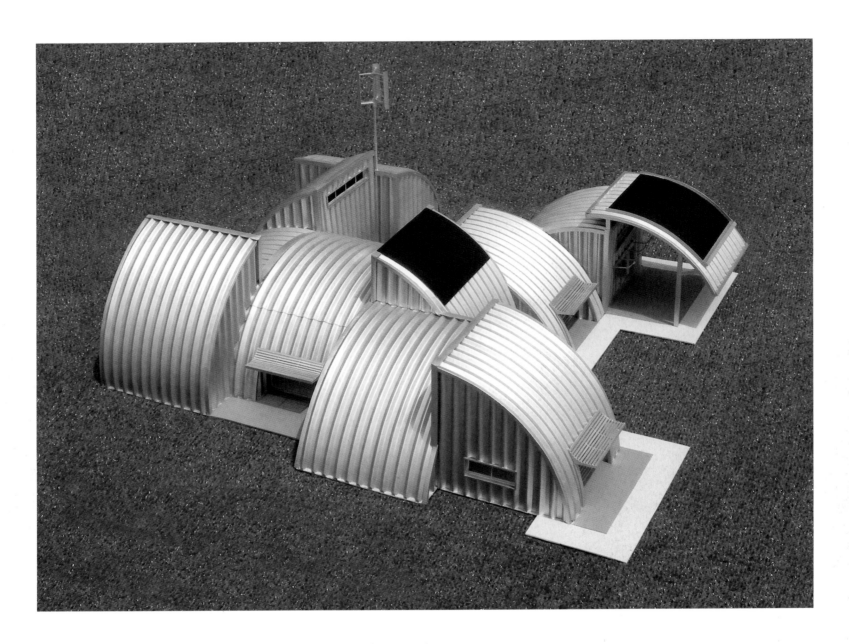

For this project, Michael Jantzen looked into "readily available agricultural building components in the creation of alternative housing systems." The house makes use of commercially available steel, and a "prefabricated, modular, high-strength, low-cost, arch building system normally used for agricultural purposes." Using simple tools, the recyclable steel sheets can be bolted together, which can also be dismounted easily. The system allows modules to be assembled in various ways. A lighter interior structure is imagined that can be filled with pulped newspaper for insulation. Photovoltaic cells, a small wind turbine, passive solar heating, and rainwater collection are all envisaged for energy independence.

Für dieses Projekt griff Michael Jantzen auf „leicht erhältliche Baukomponenten zurück, mit denen sich alternative Wohnbauprojekte realisieren lassen". Das Haus nutzt handelsübliche Stahlprofile sowie ein „vorgefertigtes, modulares, sehr belastbares und kostengünstiges Bogensystem, das üblicherweise in der Landwirtschaft Verwendung findet". Mithilfe einfacher Werkzeuge lassen sich die recyclingfähigen Stahlbleche verschrauben und ebenso leicht wieder demontieren. Das System erlaubt es, die Module auf verschiedene Weise zusammenzusetzen. Für den Innenausbau ist eine leichtere Konstruktion vorgesehen, die mit zerfasertem Zeitungspapier gedämmt werden kann. Fotovoltaikzellen, ein kleiner Windgenerator, eine Solarheizung und Regenwassernutzung sollen für energetische Unabhängigkeit sorgen.

Pour réaliser ce projet, Michael Jantzen a recherché « des éléments de constructions agricoles facilement disponibles pour créer un système d'habitat alternatif ». La maison est donc en acier et fait appel à « un système constructif en arcs préfabriqués, modulaires à haute résistance et de coût peu élevé, souvent utilisé dans les exploitations agricoles ». Les tôles d'acier recyclées sont vissées à l'aide d'outils simples et peuvent donc se démonter aisément. Le système permet d'assembler les modules de diverses façons. Une structure intérieure plus légère est isolée thermiquement de l'extérieur par de la pulpe de papier. Des cellules photovoltaïques, une petite éolienne, un chauffage solaire passif et la collecte des eaux de pluie devraient assurer une certaine indépendance énergétique.

JENSEN & SKODVIN ARCHITECTS

Jensen & Skodvin Arkitektkontor AS
Sinsenveien 4D
0572 Oslo
Norway

Tel: +47 22 99 48 99
Fax: +47 22 99 48 88
E-mail: office@jsa.no
Web: www.jsa.no

JENSEN & SKODVIN was established in 1995 by Jan Olav Jensen and Børre Skodvin. The firm currently has nine architects. Born in 1959, Jan Olav Jensen received his degree from the Oslo School of Architecture in 1985. He has been a Professor at the Oslo School of Design and Architecture since 2004. He was the Kenzo Tange Visiting Critic at Harvard University (1998) and won a 1998 Aga Khan Award for Architecture for the Lepers Hospital in Chopda Taluka, India. Børre Skodvin was born in 1960 and received his degree from the Oslo School of Architecture in 1988. He has been a teacher at the Oslo School of Design and Architecture since 1998. Their built work includes the Storo Metro Station (Oslo, 2003); headquarters and exhibition space for the Norwegian Design Council (Oslo, 2004); Sinsen Metro Station (Oslo, 2005); a Multipurpose City Block (Oslo, 2005); the Tautra Maria Convent (Tautra Island, 2004–06, published here); and a thermal bath, therapy center, and hotel (Bad Gleichenberg, Austria, 2005–07). They have worked recently on the Gudbrandsjuvet Tourist project, viewing platforms, and bridges (Gudbrandsjuvet, Norway 2008); Giørtz Summer House (Valldal, 2008); and the Juvet Landscape Hotel (Gudbrandsjuvet, 2007–09, also published here), all in Norway unless stated otherwise. Ongoing work includes a plan for a new town in south Oslo (2005–15).

JENSEN & SKODVIN wurde 1995 von Jan Olav Jensen und Børre Skodvin gegründet. Derzeit beschäftigt das Büro neun Architekten. Olav Jensen, geboren 1959, schloss sein Studium 1985 an der Architektur- und Designhochschule Oslo ab, wo er seit 2004 als Professor tätig ist. Er war Kenzo-Tange-Gastkritiker in Harvard (1998) und wurde 1998 für das Leprakrankenhaus in Chopda Taluka, Indien, mit dem Aga-Khan-Preis für Architektur ausgezeichnet. Børre Skodvin wurde 1960 geboren und schloss sein Studium 1988 an der Architektur- und Designhochschule Oslo ab, wo er seit 1998 lehrt. Zu ihren realisierten Projekten zählen die Metrostation Storo (Oslo, 2003), die Zentrale und ein Ausstellungsraum für den Norwegischen Designverband (Oslo, 2004), die Metrostation Sinsen (Oslo, 2005), ein Gebäude mit gemischter Nutzung (Oslo, 2005), das Marienkloster Tautra (Insel Tautra, 2004–06, hier vorgestellt) sowie das Heilbad, Therapiezentrum und Hotel Bad Gleichenberg (Österreich, 2005–07). In letzter Zeit arbeitete das Büro an Aussichtsplattformen und Brücken für das Tourismusprojekt Gudbrandsjuvet (Gudbrandsjuvet, Norwegen 2008), dem Giørtz Sommerhaus (Valldal, 2008) und dem Juvet Landscape Hotel (Gudbrandsjuvet, 2007–09, ebenfalls hier vorgestellt), alle in Norwegen, sofern nicht anders angegeben. Laufende Projekte sind u. a. ein neues Stadtzentrum in Süd-Oslo (2005–15).

L'agence **JENSEN & SKODVIN** a été fondée en 1995 par Jan Olav Jensen et Børre Skodvin. Elle emploie aujourd'hui neuf architectes. Né en 1959, Olav Jensen est diplômé de l'École d'architecture d'Oslo (1985). Il est professeur à l'École de design et d'architecture d'Oslo depuis 2004. Il a été critique invité à la chaire Kenzo Tange à Harvard (1998) et a remporté le prix Aga Khan d'architecture 1988 pour l'hôpital de lépreux de Chopda Taluka, en Inde. Børre Skodvin, né en 1960, est également diplômé de l'École d'architecture d'Oslo (1988). Il est enseignant à l'École de design et d'architecture d'Oslo depuis 1998. Parmi leurs réalisations : la station de métro Storo (Oslo, 2003) ; le siège et l'espace d'expositions du Conseil norvégien du design (Oslo, 2004) ; la station de métro Sinsen (Oslo, 2005) ; un bloc urbain mixte (Oslo, 2005) ; le couvent de Tautra Maria (île de Tautra, 2004–06, publié ici) et des bains, un centre thérapeutique et un hôtel à Bad Gleichenberg (Autriche, 2005–07). Ils ont récemment travaillé sur le projet touristique du Gudbrandsjuvet comprenant des plates-formes d'observation et des ponts (Gudbrandsjuvet, Norvège, 2008) ; la Maison d'été Giørtz (Valldal, 2008) ; le Juvet Landscape Hotel (Gudbrandsjuvet, 2007–09, publié ici) et un plan pour une ville nouvelle au sud d'Oslo (2005–15).

TAUTRA MARIA CONVENT

Tautra Island, Norway, 2004–06

Floor area: 2000 m². Client: Cistercian nuns, Mississippi Abbey
Cost: €6 million. Collaboration: Jan Olav Jensen, Børre Skodvin, Siri Moseng,
Torstein Koch, Kaja Poulsen, Torunn Golberg, Martin Draleke, AnneLise Bjerkan
Landscape Architects: the nuns

This structure is situated on Tautra Island in the Trondheimsfjord, a 130-kilometer-long inlet of the Norwegian Sea, in the central west part of the country. It is a new monastery for 18 Cistercian nuns, including a small church and the production facilities required for the nuns to make a living. Only ruins remained of a Cistercian monastery founded on the island 800 years ago. "One of our first ideas," say the architects, "was to create a low building with a series of gardens, giving light and creating a sense of privacy and exclusion, while at the same time opening up for some of the spectacular views across the fjord, as, for instance, in the refectory (the dining hall), where the nuns all sit at the same side of the table, like in Da Vinci's *Last Supper*, looking silently through the glass wall toward the sea and the mountains on the other side." By analyzing the daily routine of the nuns, the architects were able to eliminate approximately 30 percent of the original program, most notably by removing corridors. The final plan consists of a system of different-sized rooms connected in the corners and with seven gardens between them. The architects conclude, "The nuns have been very active clients and have planned the landscaping and fencing around the convent and inside the seven gardens themselves, with the help of professionals from the local congregation."

Das Marienkloster Tautra befindet sich auf der gleichnamigen Insel im 130 km langen Trondheimsfjord in Mittelnorwegen. Die neue Anlage wird von 18 Zisterzienserinnen genutzt und umfasst eine kleine Kirche sowie eine Reihe von Werkstätten, in denen die Schwestern ihren Lebensunterhalt besorgen. Von dem vor 800 Jahren auf der Insel gegründeten Zisterzienserkloster sind heute nur noch Ruinen vorhanden. „Gleich zu Anfang hatten wir die Idee", so die Architekten, „ein niedriges Gebäude mit einer Reihe von Gärten zu entwerfen, das einen Charakter von Intimität und Abgeschiedenheit haben, aber zugleich von verschiedenen Punkten aus eine spektakuläre Aussicht über den Fjord eröffnen sollte, etwa vom Refektorium (dem Speisesaal) aus. Bei den Mahlzeiten sitzen die Nonnen nebeneinander an einer Seite der Tafel, wie in Leonardo da Vincis *Letztem Abendmahl,* und können durch die Glaswand still auf das Wasser und die sich auf der anderen Seite erhebenden Berge hinausschauen." Indem sich die Architekten ein genaues Bild vom Tagesablauf der Nonnen machten, konnten sie die ursprünglichen Planungen um ein knappes Drittel straffen, vor allem durch das Weglassen der Flure. Der endgültige Entwurf besteht aus einem System von verschieden großen und an ihren Ecken miteinander verbundenen Räumen, zwischen denen sieben Gärten angelegt sind. Die Architekten vergessen nicht darauf hinzuweisen, dass ihre „Auftraggeberinnen sich intensiv an den Planungen beteiligt haben. Unterstützt von professionellen Kräften aus der Gemeinde, übernahmen die Schwestern die Gestaltung der Gärten und des Außenbereichs und entwarfen die Umzäunung des Klosters."

Ce bâtiment se trouve sur l'île de Tautra dans le fjord de Trondheim (130 km de long), au centre de sa côte ouest. Il s'agit d'un nouveau monastère conçu pour 18 sœurs cisterciennes comprenant une petite église et les équipements nécessaires à une existence en partie autarcique. Il ne restait sur le site que les ruines d'un monastère cistercien fondé 80 ans plus tôt. « Une de nos premières idées, expliquent les architectes, a été de créer un bâtiment bas et une succession de jardins pour apporter de la lumière et donner un sentiment d'intimité et de vie à l'écart, tout en prévoyant des perspectives spectaculaires sur le fjord, comme, par exemple, dans le réfectoire. Les religieuses sont toutes assises du même côté de la table, comme dans la *Cène* de Vinci, et regardent en silence à travers le mur de verre la mer et les montagnes. » En analysant le rituel quotidien des nones, les architectes ont pu éliminer environ 30 % du programme initial, en particulier en supprimant des couloirs. Le plan définitif se compose d'un système de salles de dimensions diverses réunies par leurs angles et séparées par sept jardins. « Les sœurs ont été des clientes très actives et se sont chargées des jardins et des barrières autour du couvent et dans les jardins avec l'aide d'artisans de la communauté locale. »

The convent benefits from an exceptional natural setting. Its somewhat irregular appearance allows it to blend in with its environment, while providing a modern home and place of contemplation and worship.

Das Kloster liegt inmitten einer beeindruckenden Naturkulisse. Dank seiner „ungeordneten" Erscheinung fügt es sich ganz in die Landschaft ein und erweist sich zugleich als moderne Lebensstätte und Ort der Andacht.

Le couvent bénéficie d'un cadre naturel exceptionnel. Son plan, légèrement irrégulier, lui permet de se fondre dans son environnement, tout en remplissant ses fonctions liturgiques et de logement modernes.

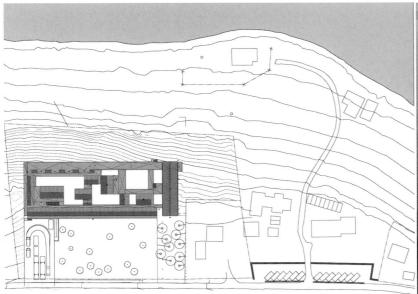

A light, glazed wooden design permits views of nature and the inner courtyards. Though largely rectilinear, the architecture achieves an "organic" presence in this location.

Durch die Verglasung der hellen Holzkonstruktion kann man in die Innenhöfe und die Natur hinausblicken. Obgleich fast vollständig rechtwinklig angelegt, besitzt die Architektur eine „organische" Anmutung.

La construction légère en bois offre des vues sur la nature et les cours intérieures. Bien qu'en grande partie rectiligne, l'architecture n'en évoque pas moins une présence organique.

Above, the dining area of the nuns enables them to sit side by side, looking out at the natural setting. This communion with nature is visible elsewhere in the convent as well.

Im Speiseraum sitzen die Schwestern nebeneinander und schauen von der Tafel hinaus in die Natur. Auch an anderen Stellen des Klosters wurde auf die Gemeinschaft mit der Natur Wert gelegt.

Ci-dessus, le réfectoire des nonnes. Elles sont assises côte à côte, face au paysage. Cette communion avec la nature est également visible dans d'autres parties du couvent.

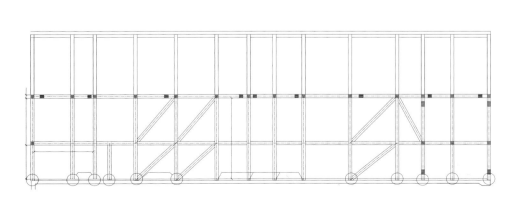
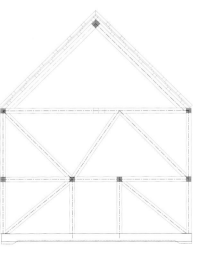

The largest open space within the
convent is this 200-square-meter
chapel with its webbed wooden roof,
open to natural light.

Der größte offene Raum des Klosters
ist die 200 m² große Kapelle mit
ihrem vielfach verstrebten Holzdach,
durch das natürliches Licht herein-
fällt.

Le plus vaste espace ouvert du
couvent est cette chapelle de 200 m²
à la charpente complexe, mais
ouverte sur le ciel.

JUVET LANDSCAPE HOTEL

Gudbrandsjuvet, Norway, 2007–09

Address: Alstad, 6210 Valldal, Norway, +47 95 03 20 10, www.juvet.com
Area: 800 m². Client: Knut Slinning. Cost: €1 million

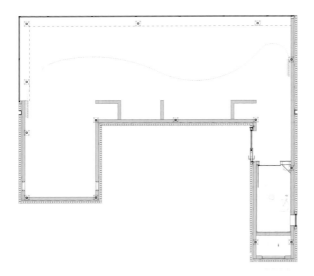

Sitting lightly in their natural setting, the pavilions that form the hotel are geometrically shaped and amply glazed.

Die Pavillons des Hotels greifen kaum in die landschaftliche Umgebung ein, sind geometrisch gestaltet und groß-zügig verglast.

L'hôtel se compose de pavillons de formes géométriques largement vitrées, délicatement déposés dans leur cadre naturel.

The **JUVET LANDSCAPE HOTEL** is located in northwestern Norway. Tourists are drawn here by a spectacular waterfall in a gorge near the Gudbrandsjuvet road. The client, Knut Slinning, is a local resident. The idea of the Juvet Landscape Hotel emerged as an opportunity to take advantage of the scenery with minimal architectural intervention. This approach permitted the architects to build in locations that would otherwise be prohibited for reasons of conservation. Instead of a conventional hotel, with guest rooms grouped together in one large building, the Landscape Hotel distributes rooms throughout the terrain as small individual houses. Through careful orientation, each room gets its own view of the landscape, and no room looks out at another. The rooms are built in massive wood with just 50 millimeters of exterior insulation, and are intended for summer use only. Each building rests on a set of 40-millimeter steel rods drilled into the rock, thus leaving the existing topography and vegetation almost untouched. The architects state: "Today's concern for sustainability in architecture focuses almost exclusively on reduced energy consumption in production and operation. We think that conservation of topography is another aspect of sustainability which deserves attention."

Das **JUVET LANDSCAPE HOTEL** liegt im Nordwesten Norwegens. Touristen kommen vor allem wegen des spektakulären Wasserfalls in die Gudbrandsjuvet-Schlucht. Bauherr Knut Slinning lebt selbst in der Gegend. Die Idee zum Juvet Landscape Hotel entstand aus dem Wunsch heraus, die landschaftliche Lage bei einem minimalen architektonischen Eingriff optimal zu nutzen. Dieser Ansatz erlaubte den Architekten, an Orten zu bauen, wo dies aus Naturschutzgründen sonst nicht möglich gewesen wäre. Statt die Zimmer wie bei einem konventionellen Hotel in einem großen Haupthaus zu bündeln, verteilen sie sich beim Landscape Hotel über mehrere kleine, frei stehende Häuser im gesamten Gelände. Dank sorgfältiger Ausrichtung hat jedes Zimmer Ausblick in die Landschaft, jedoch keinen Sichtkontakt zu den übrigen Zimmern. Die Häuser wurden aus Massivholz gebaut, sind lediglich außen mit einer 50 mm starken Dämmung versehen und als Sommerhäuser konzipiert. Alle Bauten sind auf 40 mm starken Stahlstangen aufgeständert, die in den felsigen Untergrund gebohrt wurden, sodass Topografie und Vegetation weitgehend unberührt blieben. Die Architekten erklären: „Bemühungen um Nachhaltigkeit in der Architektur konzentrieren sich fast ausschließlich auf die Reduzierung des Energieverbrauchs bei Fertigung und Nutzung. Wir sind der Ansicht, dass der Schutz der Topografie ein weiterer Aspekt von Nachhaltigkeit ist, der Aufmerksamkeit verdient."

Le **JUVET LANDSCAPE HOTEL**, qui appartient à un habitant de la région, Knut Slinning, se trouve dans le nord-ouest de la Norvège. Les touristes viennent admirer une cascade spectaculaire dans une gorge à proximité de la route de Gudbrandsjuvet. L'idée de cet hôtel est de profiter du spectacle de la nature, mais en minimisant l'intervention architecturale. Cette approche a permis aux architectes de construire sur des terrains qui auraient pu leur être interdits pour des raisons de conservation. Refusant le schéma conventionnel de l'hôtel regroupant des chambres dans un seul grand bâtiment, ils les ont réparties sur le terrain comme de petites maisons individuelles. Une orientation étudiée offre à chacune une vue sur le paysage et aucune ne peut voir les autres. Les constructions sont en bois massif doublé d'une couche d'isolant de 50 mm épaisseur. Elles ne servent qu'en été. Chaque unité repose sur des pilotis d'acier de 40 mm de diamètre forés dans le rocher, ce qui permet de ne pratiquement pas toucher à la topographie et à la végétation. « Les préoccupations actuelles de durabilité en architecture se concentrent presque exclusivement sur la réduction de la consommation d'énergie dans la consommation, la production et le fonctionnement. Nous pensons que conserver la topographie est un autre aspect de la durabilité qui mérite notre attention », commentent les architectes.

The full-height glazing and undisturbed natural setting almost give clients the impression that they are really in the midst of nature, even as they sit in a protected environment.

Dank der deckenhohen Verglasung und der naturbelassenen Umgebung haben die Gäste fast den Eindruck, draußen in der Natur zu sein, statt in einem geschützten Raum zu sitzen.

Le vitrage toute hauteur et le cadre naturel laissé intact donnent presque aux clients l'impression se trouver au milieu de la nature, même s'ils sont dans un environnement protégé.

EMMA JOHANSSON AND TIMO LEIVISKÄ

Arkkitehtitoimisto Emma Johansson
Kaikukuja 1 h 100
00530 Helsinki
Finland

Arkkitehtitoimisto Timo Leiviskä
Kajaanintie 36, 5 C 44
90130 Oulu
Finland

Tel: +358 50 372 27 43
E-mail: emma.johansson@oulu.fi
Web: www.emmajohansson.fi

Tel: +358 50 530 35 48
E-mail: timo.leiviska@gmail.com
Web: www.timoleiviska.webs.com

EMMA JOHANSSON was born in 1985 in Turku, Finland. She studied architecture at the University of Oulu (2004–2012). She created her own office, Arkkitehtitoimisto Emma Johansson Oy, in 2007. Her work includes the Anttolanhovi Lakeside Villas (Mikkeli, 2007–08, published here); a mobile dwelling consisting of small units destined to the Finnish archipelago area (2009–11); and a Sustainable Wooden Village (Pudasjärvi, in collaboration with Kristian Järvi, 2009–12), all in Finland. **TIMO LEIVISKÄ** was born in 1981 in Oulu, Finland. He studied architecture at the University of Oulu and at the Faculty of Architecture of the University of Porto, Portugal (2005–06). His office, Arkkitehtitoimisto Timo Leiviskä Oy, was founded in 2007. His work includes the Anttolanhovi Hillside Villas (Mikkeli, 2007–08, published here); a villa in Pulolanka (2009–10); and a villa in Kuhmo (2010–12), all in Finland.

EMMA JOHANSSON wurde 1985 in Turku, Finnland, geboren. Sie studierte von 2004 bis 2012 Architektur an der Universität von Oulu. 2007 eröffnete sie ihr eigenes Büro, Arkkitehtitoimisto Emma Johansson Oy. Zu ihren Arbeiten zählen die Anttolanhovi-Seevillen (Mikkeli, 2007–08, hier vorgestellt), eine mobile, aus kleinen Elementen bestehende Wohneinheit, gedacht für die finnische Seenlandschaft (2009–11), sowie ein nachhaltig gebautes Dorf aus Holz (Pudasjärvi, in Zusammenarbeit mit Kristian Järvi, 2009–12), alle in Finnland. **TIMO LEIVISKÄ** wurde 1981 im finnischen Oulu geboren. Er studierte Architektur an der Universität von Oulu und war 2005 bis 2006 Student der Architekturfakultät der Universität Porto (Portugal). Sein Büro, Arkkitehtitoimisto Timo Leiviskä Oy, gründete er 2007. Zu seinen Arbeiten gehören die Anttolanhovi-Bergvillen (Mikkeli, 2007–08, hier vorgestellt), eine Villa (Pulolanka, 2009–10) sowie eine weitere Villa (Kuhmo, 2010–12), alle in Finnland.

EMMA JOHANSSON, née en 1985 à Turku (Finlande), a étudié l'architecture à l'université d'Oulu (Finlande, 2004–2012). Elle a créé son agence, Arkkitehtitoimisto Emma Johansson Oy, en 2007. Parmi ses réalisations : les villas Anttolanhovi côté lac (Mikkeli, 2007–08, publiées ici) ; un logement mobile composé de petites unités pour l'archipel de Finlande (2009–11) et un village durable en bois (Pudasjärvi, en collaboration avec Kristian Järvi, 2009–12). **TIMO LEIVISKÄ**, né en 1981 à Oulu, a étudié l'architecture à l'université d'Oulu et à la faculté d'architecture de l'université de Porto (Portugal, 2005–06). Son agence, Arkkitehtitoimisto Timo Leiviskä Oy, a été fondée en 2007. Parmi ses réalisations, toutes en Finlande, les villas Anttolanhovi côté colline (Mikkeli, 2007–08, publiées ici) ; une villa à Pulolanka (2009–10) et une villa à Kuhmo (2010–12).

ANTTOLANHOVI ART AND DESIGN VILLAS

Mikkeli, Finland, 2007–08

Address: Hovintie 224, Mikkeli, Finland, +358 207 57 52 38, www.anttolanhovi.fi
Area: 132 m² (Lakeside Villas); 180 m² (Hillside Villas)
Client: Anttolanhovi Hotel. Cost: not disclosed

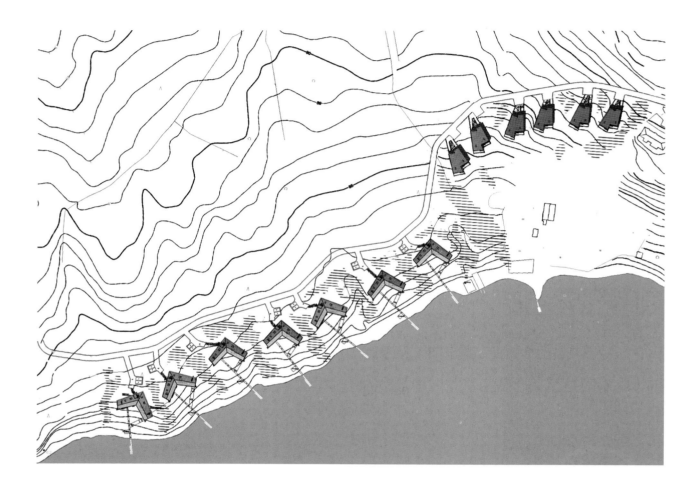

Designed by Emma Johansson (Lakeside Villas) and Timo Leiviskä (Hillside Villas), the **ANTTOLANHOVI ART AND DESIGN VILLAS** have their own saunas, open fireplaces, and hotel services. Each villa is associated with an artist who has contributed to the house. The artists for the Art and Design Villas are Kari Cavén, Kaarina Kaikkonen, Marika Mäkelä, Teemu Saukkonen, Hanna Vahvaselkä, Rauha Mäkilä, Antti Keitilä, Johanna Ilvessalo, and Jussi Tiainen (the photographer who took the photos for this entry). They are designed to have as small an "ecological footprint" as possible. They are built with natural materials, principally timber. The wall cladding is either Finnish birch or Finnish spruce, while the floors are made of natural stone. Linen, cotton, and wool have been used for all indoor textiles. The Lakeside Villas, situated about 25 meters from the Saimaa lakeshore, have a lounge, kitchen, and three bedrooms. The Hillside Villas are semidetached structures measuring 103 square meters on one side and 77 square meters on the other, with a total of five bedrooms for each pair of structures. They are 70 meters from the lakeshore.

Die von Emma Johansson (Seevillen) und Timo Leiviskä (Bergvillen) geplanten **ANTTOLANHOVI ART AND DESIGN VILLAS** haben eigene Saunen, offene Kamine und erhalten Dienstleistungen vom Hotel. Jede Villa ist mit einem Künstler verbunden, der zu ihrer Ausstattung beigetragen hat. Beteiligt waren die Künstler Kari Cavén, Kaarina Kaikkonen, Marika Mäkelä, Teemu Saukkonen, Hanna Vahvaselkä, Rauha Mäkilä, Antti Keitilä, Johanna Ilvessalo und Jussi Tiainen (der Fotograf, der die Bilder für dieses Buch aufgenommen hat). Die Häuser haben die bestmögliche Ökobilanz; sie wurden aus natürlichen Materialien, vorwiegend aus Holz, errichtet. Die Wandverkleidung besteht aus einheimischer Birke bzw. Fichte, während die Böden aus Naturstein sind. Im Innern sind alle Textilien aus Leinen, Baumwolle oder Wolle. Die Seevillen stehen etwa 25 m vom Ufer des Saimaa-Sees entfernt; sie enthalten jeweils einen Aufenthaltsraum, eine Küche und drei Schlafräume. Die Bergvillen sind Doppelhäuser mit je 103 m² bzw. 77 m² Grundfläche und zusammen fünf Schlafräumen. Sie stehen 70 m vom Seeufer entfernt.

Conçues par Emma Johansson (villas côté lac) et Timo Leiviskä (villas côté colline), les **VILLAS D'ART ET DE DESIGN D'ANTTOLANHOVI** possèdent des saunas, des cheminées ouvertes et bénéficient de services hôteliers. Chacune est associée au nom d'un artiste qui a contribué à son aménagement : Kari Cavén, Kaarina Kaikkonen, Marika Mäkelä, Teemu Saukkonen, Hanna Vahvaselkä, Rauha Mäkilä, Antti Keitilä, Johanna Ilvessalo et Jussi Tiainen (le photographe auteur des photos reproduites ici). Elles ont été conçues de façon à exercer la plus faible empreinte écologique possible et sont construites en matériaux naturels, principalement du bois. L'habillage des murs est soit en bouleau de Finlande soit en épicéa de Finlande et les sols sont en pierre naturelle. À l'intérieur, les tissus retenus sont en lin, coton ou laine. Les villas côté lac, situé à 25 m environ de la rive du lac de Saimaa possèdent un salon, une cuisine et trois chambres. Celles côté colline, à 70 m du lac sont des villas doubles de 103 et 77 m² comptant 5 chambres par paire.

The site plan on the left page shows the Lakeside and Hillside Villas in their respective locations. Above, the Hillside Villas.

Der Lageplan auf der linken Seite zeigt die Standorte der See- und der Bergvillen. Oben: die Bergvillen.

Le plan du terrain (page de gauche) montre les deux ensembles de villas – côté lac et côté collines – dans leur situation respective. En haut les villas côté collines.

Below, two images of the Lakeside Villas designed by Emma Johansson, with their partially covered terraces and generous use of wood.

Zwei Fotos der von Emma Johansson entworfenen Seevillen mit ihren teilüberdachten Terrassen und der großzügigen Verwendung von Holz.

Ci-dessous, deux images des villas côté lac, en grande partie en bois et conçues par Emma Johansson. Leurs terrasses sont en partie couvertes.

Plans of the Hillside Villas and an interior view of one of the Lakeside Villas.

Grundrisse der Bergvillen und eine
Innenaufnahme einer Seevilla.

Des plans des villas côté colline et
la vue intérieure d'une des villas
côté lac.

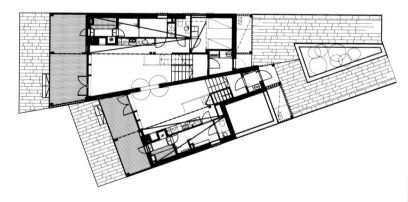

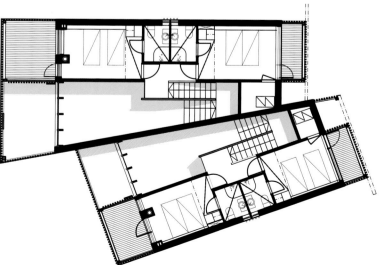

Drawings of the Lakeside Villas showing their low, open V-form and insertion into the wooded setting.

Die Zeichnungen der Seevillen zeigen deren flache, offene V-Form sowie ihre Einfügung in die bewaldete Umgebung.

Représentations de villas côté lac montrant leur forme surbaissée et leur toit à pente asymétrique, et de leur insertion dans leur environnement boisé.

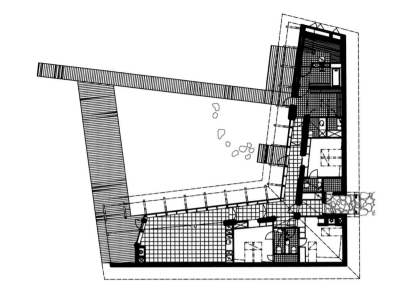

Two interior views of these houses are seen above.

Zwei Innenansichten der oben dargestellten Häuser.

Deux vues intérieures des maisons.

JOHNSEN SCHMALING ARCHITECTS

Johnsen Schmaling Architects
1699 North Astor Street
Milwaukee, WI 53202
USA

Tel: +1 414 287 9000 / Fax: +1 414 287 9025
E-mail: info@johnsenschmaling.com
Web: www.johnsenschmaling.com

BRIAN JOHNSEN received his M.Arch degree from the University of Wisconsin in Milwaukee in 1997. He was a cofounder of Johnsen Schmaling Architects in 2003. **SEBASTIAN SCHMALING** received his M.Arch from the Harvard GSD in 2002. Schmaling, originally from Berlin, had previously attended the University of Wisconsin, where he received another M.Arch degree (1996), and the Technische Universität Berlin, Germany (Vordiplom, Diplom-Ingenieur 1994). He was a cofounder of the firm in 2003 with Brian Johnsen. Their work includes the Storewall corporate headquarters (Milwaukee, 2005); the Camouflage House (Green Lake, 2005–06, published here); the Blatz Milwaukee, transformation of a former downtown brewery (2006); Celeste 1218, an "urban loft" (Milwaukee, 2007); the Downtown Bar (Milwaukee, 2007–08); and the Ferrous House, a bar and lounge (Spring Prairie, 2007–08). More recently they have worked on the Blur Loft (Milwaukee, 2009); OS House, a sustainable residence (Racine, 2009–10); Studio for a Composer (Spring Prairie, 2011); Stacked Cabin (Muscoda, 2011); Topo House (Blue Mounds, 2012), all in Wisconsin; and Mountain Retreat (Big Sky, Montana, 2013), all in the USA.

BRIAN JOHNSEN absolvierte seinen M.Arch. 1997 an der University of Wisconsin in Milwaukee. 2003 war er Mitbegründer von Johnsen Schmaling Architects. **SEBASTIAN SCHMALING** absolvierte seinen M.Arch. 2002 an der Harvard GSD. Schmaling, ursprünglich aus Berlin, hatte zunächst an der University of Wisconsin studiert, wo er ebenfalls mit einem M.Arch. abschloss (1996), sowie an der Technischen Universität Berlin (Vordiplom, Diplom-Ingenieur 1994). 2003 gründete er mit Brian Johnsen das gemeinsame Büro. Zu ihren Projekten zählen die Firmenzentrale von Storewall (Milwaukee, 2005), das Camouflage House (Green Lake, 2005–06, hier vorgestellt), Blatz Milwaukee, Umbau einer ehemaligen Brauerei (2006), Celeste 1218, ein „urbanes Loft" (Milwaukee, 2007), die Downtown Bar (Milwaukee, 2007–08) und das Ferrous House, Bar und Lounge (Spring Prairie, 2007–08). In jüngerer Zeit arbeitete das Büro am Blur Loft (Milwaukee, 2009), dem OS House, einem nachhaltigen Einfamilienhaus (Racine, 2009–10), dem Studio für einen Komponisten (Spring Prairie, 2011), der Stacked Cabin (Muscoda, 2011), dem Topo House (Blue Mounds, 2012), alle in Wisconsin, sowie dem Mountain Retreat (Big Sky, Montana, 2013), alle in den USA.

BRIAN JOHNSEN a obtenu son M.Arch. à l'université du Wisconsin de Milwaukee en 1997. Il a été l'un des cofondateurs de Johnsen Schmaling Architects en 2003 avec **SEBASTIAN SCHMALING**. Ce dernier a obtenu son M.Arch. à la Harvard GSD en 2002. Originaire de Berlin, il avait auparavant suivi les cours de l'université du Wisconsin où il a obtenu un autre M.Arch. (1996) et de l'Université technique de Berlin (examen intermédiaire, diplôme d'ingénieur en 1994). Leurs réalisations comprennent le Storewall, siège de société (Milwaukee, 2005) ; la Camouflage House (Green Lake, 2005–06, publiée ici) ; le Blatz, la transformation d'une ancienne brasserie du centre-ville de Milwaukee (2006) ; Celeste 1218, un « loft urbain » (Milwaukee, 2007) ; le bar Downtown (Milwaukee, 2007–08) et la Ferrous House, un bar et lounge (Spring Prairie, 2007–08). Plus récemment, ils ont travaillé au Blur Loft (Milwaukee, 2009) ; à la OS House, une résidence durable (Racine, 2009–10) ; à un studio pour compositeur (Spring Prairie, 2011) ; à la petite maison Stacked Cabin (Muscoda, 2011) ; à la Topo House (Blue Mounds, 2012), projets tous situés dans le Wisconsin, et à la Mountain Retreat (Big Sky, Montana, 2013), tous aux États-Unis.

CAMOUFLAGE HOUSE

Green Lake, Wisconsin, USA, 2005–06

Floor area: 232 m²
Clients: John Geiger and Kathy Murkowski
Cost: not disclosed

A decomposed or sublimated photo of the forest in fall is the basis for the irregular, alternating panel design that marks the main façade of a house that is carefully inserted into its natural setting.

Eine dekonstruierte Aufnahme von Herbstwald ist die Grundlage für das unregelmäßige Muster aus Paneelen, das die Hauptfassade kennzeichnet. Das Haus selbst wurde einfühlsam in die Landschaft integriert.

Une photographie pixellisée ou sublimée de la forêt en automne est à la base de la composition alternée des panneaux de la façade principale insérée avec soin dans son cadre naturel.

The **CAMOUFLAGE HOUSE** is located on a steep lake bluff and is set into the hillside. The rectangular layout of the house contrasts with a complex system of façade layers made up of solids and voids—glass panels and walls—that "express its ambition to assimilate with its surroundings." Untreated cedar cladding is combined with colored Prodema wood veneer panels for the exterior wall surfaces. An open breezeway connects a garage to the linear, two-story house itself. A partially covered balcony offers views of the lake. Bedrooms are located on the lower level with a terrace extending the length of the house. The kitchen, dining and living spaces are formed as an open space on the upper level, with a screened porch available for the warmer months. The architects state, "The inside of the house, while unapologetically contemporary, continues Wisconsin's long history of lake cottage architecture, which has traditionally featured exposed timber construction, interior wood siding, combined living and dining halls centered around a (Cor-ten steel) fireplace, and a limited palette of natural materials." Colored concrete floors affirm the contemporary nature of the interior design—as does, in a different way, the use of sustainable materials throughout.

Das **CAMOUFLAGE HOUSE** liegt am Steilufer eines Sees und wurde in die Anhöhe hinein gebaut. Der rechteckige Grundriss des Hauses kontrastiert mit einem komplexen System mehrerer Fassadenschichten aus Leere und Masse – Glaspaneelen und Wänden – die „das Ziel zum Ausdruck bringen, es mit der Umgebung zu verschmelzen". Für die Verkleidung der Außenwände wurde unbehandeltes Zedernholz mit farbigen Furnierplatten von Prodema kombiniert. Ein überdachter Weg verbindet die Garage mit dem geradlinigen zweigeschossigen Haus. Von einem teilüberdachten Balkon bietet sich der Blick auf den See. Die Schlafzimmer liegen in der unteren Etage, wo sich eine Terrasse über die gesamte Länge des Hauses erstreckt. Küchen-, Ess- und Wohnbereiche in der oberen Etage sind als offener Raum gestaltet. Hier steht für die Sommermonate auch eine geschützte Veranda zur Verfügung. Die Architekten erklären: „Das Innere des Hauses knüpft trotz seines offensichtlich zeitgenössischen Stils an die lange Geschichte der Ferienhausarchitektur an den Seen Wisconsins an, mit ihren traditionell freiliegenden Fachwerkkonstruktionen, holzvertäfelten Innenräumen, kombinierten Wohn- und Essbereichen, die sich um einen Kamin (hier aus Cor-Ten-Stahl) gruppieren und einer begrenzten Palette natürlicher Materialien." Farbig gestrichene Betonfußböden unterstreichen das Zeitgenössische der Innenarchitektur – ebenso wie es, wenn auch auf andere Weise, die durchweg verwendeten, umweltfreundlichen Baumaterialien tun.

La **MAISON « CAMOUFLAGE »**, accrochée à la rive escarpée d'un lac, est encastrée dans le flanc d'une colline. Son plan rectangulaire contraste avec le système stratifié complexe des façades composées de pleins et de vides – murs et panneaux de verre –, qui « expriment l'ambition de s'assimiler à son environnement ». Pour l'extérieur, le bardage en cèdre brut se combine à des panneaux en bois de Prodema coloré et vernis. Un passage couvert mais ouvert relie le garage à la maison d'aspect linéaire composée de deux niveaux. Un balcon en partie couvert donne sur le lac. Les chambres sont situées au niveau inférieur, et donnent sur une terrasse qui court tout le long du bâtiment. Les zones de cuisine, de repas et de séjour forment un espace ouvert au niveau supérieur et bénéficient d'un porche protégé par des écrans pour les mois les plus chauds. Selon l'architecte : « L'intérieur de la maison, bien que résolument contemporain, poursuit la longue histoire de l'architecture des cottages de bords de lac du Wisconsin qui fait traditionnellement appel à la construction en poutres apparentes, aux intérieurs habillés de bois, avec le séjour et la salle à manger regroupés autour d'une cheminée (ici en acier Corten) et une palette limitée de matériaux naturels. » Les sols en béton coloré affirment la nature contemporaine du projet de même que, d'une façon différente, l'utilisation de matériaux recyclables dans toute la maison.

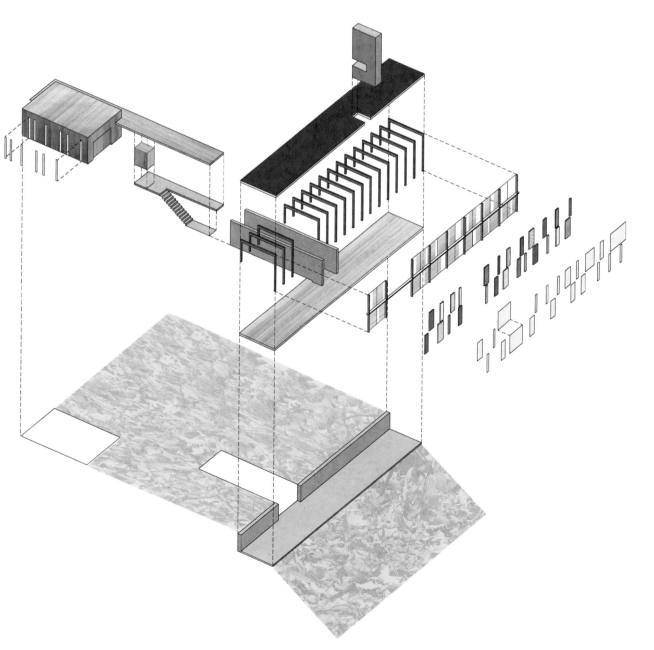

A drawing shows the composition of the house with its partially sloped site and lake views accentuated above by floor-to-ceiling glazing.

Eine Zeichnung veranschaulicht das Zusammenspiel des Hauses mit dem teilweise abschüssigen Grundstück. Die deckenhohe Verglasung (oben) bringt die Aussicht zur Geltung.

Le dessin montre la composition de la maison sur son terrain en pente. Ci-dessus, les vues sur le lac sont mises en valeur par les vitrages toute hauteur.

FRANÇOISE-HÉLÈNE JOURDA

*Jourda Architectes Paris
1 Cité de Paradis
75010 Paris
France*

*Tel: +33 1 55 28 82 20
Fax: +33 1 55 28 85 18
E-mail: archi@jourda-architectes.com
Web: www.jourda-architectes.com*

Born in 1955, **FRANÇOISE-HÉLÈNE JOURDA** received her diploma as an architect in 1979. She has taught at the École d'architecture in Lyon, at the University of Architecture in Oslo, at the University of Minnesota, and at the Technical University of Kassel in Germany. She has worked most notably on the Law Courts of Melun (France, 1994); Futuroscope and Entertainment Center (Krefeld, Germany, 1996); a park and housing area with a 13 000-square-meter greenhouse (Potsdam, Germany, 1997); the Clinique de l'Europe (Lyon, France, 1998); the Mont-Cenis Academy and Municipal District Center (Herne, Germany, 1992–99, published here); and the Decathlon Store in Hanover (Germany, 1999), which served as the French Pavilion for Expo 2000. More recently she completed offices and an apartment building (Vienna, Austria, 2004–05); and social housing (Châtelet, Rouen, France, 2009–12). She was Commissioner of the French Pavilion at the 2004 Venice Architecture Biennale, where the theme was "Sustainable Metamorphoses." In October 2007, she completed a report on sustainable development in construction at the request of the Minister of Ecology and Sustainable Development, Jean-Louis Borloo.

FRANÇOISE-HÉLÈNE JOURDA, 1955 geboren, machte 1979 ihr Diplom in Architektur. Sie lehrte an der École d'architecture in Lyon, der Architekturhochschule in Oslo, der University of Minnesota und der Technischen Universität Kassel. Zu ihren wichtigsten Projekten gehören der Gerichtshof von Melun, Frankreich (1994), das Futuroscope and Entertainment Center in Krefeld (1996), eine Park- und Wohnhausanlage mit einem 13 000 m² großen Gewächshaus in Potsdam (1997), das Hôpital de l'Europe in Lyon (1998), die Akademie Mont-Cenis (Herne, 1992–99, hier vorgestellt) und die Decathlon-Niederlassung in Hannover (1999), die als französischer Pavillon für die Expo 2000 diente. In jüngerer Zeit realisierte sie ein Büro- und Apartmenthaus (Wien, 2004–05) sowie sozialen Wohnungsbau (Châtelet, Rouen, 2009–12). Sie war die Beauftragte des französischen Pavillons auf der Architekturbiennale in Venedig 2004 unter dem Thema „Nachhaltige Metamorphosen". Im Oktober 2007 erstellte sie eine Untersuchung zu nachhaltiger Entwicklung in der Bauindustrie im Auftrag des französischen Ministers für Umwelt und nachhaltige Entwicklung, Jean-Louis Borloo.

Née en 1955, **FRANÇOISE-HÉLÈNE JOURDA** a obtenu son diplôme d'architecte en 1979. Elle a enseigné à l'École d'architecture de Lyon, l'université d'architecture d'Oslo, l'université du Minnesota et l'université technique de Kassel, en Allemagne. Elle a travaillé notamment au palais de justice de Melun (1994) ; au Futuroscope et centre de loisirs (Krefeld, Allemagne, 1996) ; à un parc et ensemble résidentiel comportant une serre de 13 000 m² (Potsdam, Allemagne, 1997) ; à la clinique de l'Europe (Lyon, 1998) ; à l'Académie du Mont-Cenis et Centre municipal de district (Herne, Allemagne, 1992–99, publié ici) et au magasin Decathlon de Hanovre (Allemagne, 1999) qui a servi de Pavillon français à l'Expo 2000. Plus récemment, elle a réalisé des bureaux et un immeuble d'habitations (Vienne, Autriche, 2004–05) et des logements sociaux (Châtelet, Rouen, 2009–12). Elle a été commissaire du Pavillon français à la Biennale d'architecture de Venise 2004 dont le thème était « métamorphoses durables ». En octobre 2007, elle a rédigé un rapport sur le développement durable dans la construction à la demande du ministre de l'Écologie et du développement durable, Jean-Louis Borloo.

MONT-CENIS ACADEMY
AND MUNICIPAL DISTRICT CENTER

Herne, Germany, 1992–99

Floor area: 7100 m² (total interior: 11 700 m²). Client: EMC Mont-Cenis
Landscape: Latz, Riehl und Schulz, Kassel. Cost: DM 100 million

The IBA Emscher Park International Building Exhibition consists of more than 100 renovation, architectural, and landscaping projects spread over an area of approximately 800 km² in the Ruhr region. Set in a former coal-mining area, the **MONT-CENIS ACADEMY**, originally intended as a training center for government employees, consists of a library, a social welfare center and a community center. The 168-meter-long building, essentially a timber "shed" with a glass skin, was designed with ecological concerns in mind by Jourda & Perraudin Architectes, Jourda Architectes, HHS Planer + Architekten BDA. The roof of the structure includes a 10 000 m² array of photovoltaic cells intended to amply cover the building's electrical needs. Methane gas released from the former mining zones is recycled to generate electricity, which can be stored in an on-site battery plant. The architect designed the wooden furniture.

Die Internationale Bauausstellung (IBA) Emscher Park besteht aus mehr als 100 über eine Fläche von ca. 800 km² im Ruhrgebiet verteilten Projekten der Renovierung, Architektur und Landschaftsgestaltung. Die **AKADEMIE MONT-CENIS**, eine Fortbildungsakademie des Landes Nordrhein-Westfalen auf dem Areal einer ehemaligen Zeche, umfasst außerdem eine Bibliothek, einen Bürgersaal und ein Stadtteilbüro. Das 168 m lange Gebäude, das aussieht wie ein „Holzschuppen" mit einer Glashaut, wurde nach ökologischen Gesichtspunkten von der Architektengemeinschaft Jourda & Perraudin Architectes, Jourda Architectes, HHS Planer + Architekten BDA geplant. Das Dach des Gebäudes enthält auf einer Fläche von insgesamt 10 000 m² Fotovoltaikzellen, die den Energiebedarf des Komplexes decken sollen. Aus der ehemaligen Zeche gewonnenes Grubengas wird für die Elektrizitätsgewinnung aufbereitet und in einer vor Ort installierten Batteriespeicheranlage gespeichert. Die Inneneinrichtung aus Holz wurde von der Architektin entworfen.

L'Exposition internationale d'architecture (IBA) Emscher Park regroupe plus de 100 projets de rénovation, d'architecture et d'aménagements paysagers répartis sur un secteur de 800 km² dans la région de la Ruhr. Implantée dans une ancienne zone minière, l'**ACADÉMIE DU MONT-CENIS** qui était au départ un centre de formation pour les fonctionnaires fédéraux, comprend une bibliothèque, un centre social et un centre communautaire. Le bâtiment de 168 m de long – un shed en bois à peau de verre – a été conçu par Jourda & Perraudin Architectes, Jourda Architectes, HHS Planer + Architekten BDA dans un esprit écologique. Le toit est équipé d'un réseau de 10 000 m² de cellules photovoltaïques qui devraient amplement couvrir les besoins énergétiques. Le gaz de méthane récupéré dans les anciennes mines est recyclé pour produire de l'électricité qui peut être accumulée dans une installation in situ. L'architecte a conçu le mobilier en bois.

Various architectural metaphors are used here including references to the industrial shed, or to large greenhouses. Rough wood columns, green plants and water within the confines of the building symbolize the ecological concerns of the architects.

Form und Konstruktion der Akademie erinnern an einen Industriebau oder ein Gewächshaus. Unten rechts: Im Innern symbolisieren Stützen aus roh bearbeitetem Holz, Grünpflanzen und Wasserbecken das ökologische Anliegen der Architekten.

Diverses métaphores architecturales rappelent des entrepôts industriels et des serres. En bas à droite : colonnes de bois brut, plantes vertes et présence de l'eau à l'intérieur du bâtiment reflètent les préoccupations écologiques des architectes.

Within the shelter of the simple
outside shed, pavilions house a hotel, the activities of the academy,
a casino, and a municipal center.

Die schlichte Außenhülle umgibt eine
Reihe von Pavillons, in denen ein
Hotel, die Arbeitsräume der Akademie, ein Casino und ein Stadtteilzent-
rum untergebracht sind.

A l'abri de cette vaste serre, des
pavillons abritent un hôtel, les activités de l'académie et un centre
municipal.

RAYMOND JUNGLES

Raymond Jungles, Inc.
242 SW 5th Street
Miami, FL 33130
USA

Tel/Fax: +1 305 858 6777
E-mail: raymond@raymondjungles.com
Web: www.raymondjungles.com

RAYMOND JUNGLES was born in Omaha, Nebraska, in 1956. He received a Bachelor of Landscape Architecture degree from the University of Florida (1981) and founded Raymond Jungles, Inc. in 1982. Raymond Jungles cites Roberto Burle Marx, the famous Brazilian garden designer, as his "favorite artist." The two men met in 1979 when Burle Marx came to lecture at the University of Florida. His recent work includes Coconut Grove, Florida Garden (Coconut Grove, Florida, 2003–09, published here); the Key West Botanical Garden (Key West, Florida, 2009); the Brazilian Garden at Naples Botanical Garden (Naples, Florida, 2009); the Golden Rock Inn (Nevis, West Indies, 2009); 1111 Lincoln Road (Miami Beach, Florida, 2009); and Brazilian Modern, New York Botanical Garden Orchid Show (Bronx, New York, 2009). Current work includes the Miami Beach Botanical Garden Redesign (Miami Beach, Florida, 2011); and the New World Symphony Campus Expansion (Miami Beach, 2011), all in the USA unless stated otherwise.

RAYMOND JUNGLES wurde 1956 in Omaha, Nebraska, geboren. Er machte 1981 seinen Bachelor in Landschaftsarchitektur an der University of Florida und gründete 1982 sein Büro Raymond Jungles, Inc. Raymond Jungles bezeichnet Roberto Burle Marx, den berühmten brasilianischen Gartenplaner, als seinen „Lieblings-künstler". Die beiden Männer trafen sich 1979, als Burle Marx an der University of Florida einen Vortrag hielt. Zu den neueren Projekten von Jungles gehören der Garten des Wohnhauses Coconut Grove in Florida Garden (Coconut Grove, Florida, 2003–09, hier vorgestellt), der Botanische Garten von Key West (Florida, 2009), der Brasilia-nische Garten im Botanischen Garten von Naples (Florida, 2009), der Garten des Golden Rock Inn auf der zu den Kleinen Antillen gehörenden Insel Nevis (2009), die Gar-tengestaltung 1111 Lincoln Road (Miami Beach, Florida, 2009) und die Orchideenschau Brasilian Modern im Botanischen Garten von New York (Bronx, 2009). Zu seinen aktuellen Arbeiten in den USA zählen die Neuplanung des Botanischen Gartens in Miami Beach (Florida, 2011) und die Gartenanlagen des Erweiterungsbaus des Campus der New World Symphony (Miami Beach, 2011).

RAYMOND JUNGLES, né à Omaha (Nebraska) en 1956, est titulaire d'un B.A. d'architecture du paysage de l'université de Floride (1981) et a fondé Raymond Jungles, Inc. en 1982. Roberto Burle Marx, le célèbre concepteur brésilien de jardins, est son « artiste favori », qu'il avait rencontré en 1979, lorsque le paysagiste était venu donner une conférence à l'université de Floride. Parmi ses réalisations récentes (aux États-Unis, sauf mention contraire) : Coconut Grove, Florida Garden (Coconut Grove, Floride, 2003–09, publié ici) ; le jardin botanique de Key West (Key West, Floride, 2009) ; le jardin brésilien du jardin botanique de Naples (Naples, Floride, 2009) ; la Golden Rock Inn (Niévès, Saint-Christophe-et-Niévès, 2009) ; 1111 Lincoln Road (Miami Beach, Floride, 2009) et le « Brazilian Modern », exposition d'orchidées du jar-din botanique de New York (Bronx, New York, 2009). Parmi ses dernières réalisations aux États-Unis : la restructuration du jardin botanique de Miami Beach (Miami Beach, Floride, 2011) et l'extension du campus du New World Symphony (Miami Beach, 2011).

COCONUT GROVE

Florida Garden, Coconut Grove, Florida, USA, 2003–09

*Area: 1.36 hectares. Client: not disclosed. Cost: not disclosed
Collaboration: Alison Spear, Proun Space Studio,
John Bennett and Gustavo Bonevardi*

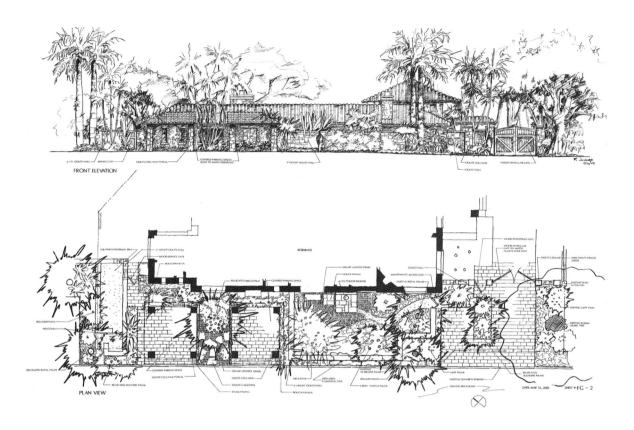

Raymond Jungles worked for six years on the grounds of this family compound. A large 80-year-old East Indian Banyan tree marks a ridge on the property, straddling three residential lots. The owner acquired 11 other properties and razed four residential structures in the course of the project, allowing for extra garden areas. The designers state: "From their first meeting, the design group decided the unifying elements for the entire site would be landforms and sculptural spaces, defined with monolithic slabs of oolite limestone. More than 500 cubic yards (382 cubic meters), which represents 80% of the stone used, was excavated on site. More than 800 indigenous, habitat-producing trees, including more than 500 palms, cycads from around the world, and fragrant flowering trees and shrubs enhance the well-balanced spaces, imparting a provocative sense of variety."

Raymond Jungles hat sechs Jahre auf dem Grundstück dieses Familienbesitzes gearbeitet. Ein großer, 80 Jahre alter, ursprünglich aus Ostindien stammender Banyanbaum wächst auf dem höchsten Punkt des Grundstücks, das in drei Parzellen unterteilt ist. Der Besitzer kaufte elf weitere Grundstücke hinzu und riss im Lauf der Bauarbeiten vier Wohnhäuser ab, um Platz für weitere Gartenbereiche zu erhalten. Die Planer merken an: „Schon beim ersten Treffen hat das Entwurfsteam beschlossen, das gesamte Gelände durch eine Modulierung der Landschaft und durch skulptural gestaltete Freiräume zu vereinheitlichen, die mit monolithischen Platten aus Kalkoolith gestaltet werden. Mehr als 382 m³ Naturstein, das sind 80 % des verwendeten Materials, sind vor Ort gebrochen worden. Mehr als 800 heimische Bäume haben hier ihren neuen Standort gefunden, u. a. mehr als 500 Palmen. Palmfarne (Cycadales) aus allen Regionen der Welt, Bäume und Gehölze mit duftenden Blüten sind die Anziehungspunkte der ausgewogenen Freiräume und vermitteln ein Gefühl von Vielfalt."

Raymond Jungles a travaillé six ans sur les plans de ce domaine familial. Un important banian d'Inde orientale, vieux de 80 ans, marque une butte sur la propriété et détermine trois parcelles résidentielles. Au cours du projet, le propriétaire a acquis onze autres propriétés et rasé quatre maisons pour agrandir ses jardins. « Dès notre première réunion, le groupe chargé de la conception a décidé que les éléments unificateurs du site seraient des mouvements de terrain et des espaces sculpturaux définis par des dalles monolithiques de calcaire oolithique. Plus de 382 m³ de pierre – soit 80 % du total utilisé – ont été trouvés sur place. Plus de 800 arbres de la région, dont plus de 500 palmiers, fougères du monde entier, arbres et buissons à fleurs odorantes, animent ces espaces bien équilibrés en imposant un sentiment provoquant de variété », explique l'architecte.

Above, an elevation drawing showing the residence and a plan of the grounds located near the house. To the right, the house and swimming pool, surrounded by the essentially tropical vegetation.

Oben, Ansicht des Wohnhauses und Lageplan der unmittelbar an das Haus angrenzenden Gartenbereiche. Das Wohnhaus mit dem Swimmingpool (rechts) ist vorwiegend von tropischer Vegetation umgeben.

Ci-dessus, dessin d'élévation de la résidence et plan des jardins. À droite, la maison et sa piscine, noyées dans une végétation de nature essentiellement tropicale.

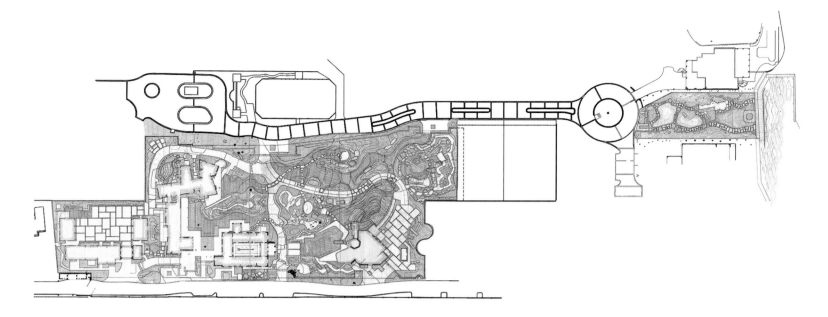

Above, a plan of the entire compound showing both the various structures and the paths that lead residents through the garden. Below, a more modern house and pool in the grounds.

Der Gesamtplan des Anwesens (oben) zeigt neben den Gebäuden auch die Wege, auf denen die Bewohner durch den Garten geleitet werden. Unten, ein modernes Haus mit Pool auf dem Gelände des Anwesens.

Ci-dessus, plan d'ensemble de la propriété montrant à la fois les différentes constructions et les allées qui sillonnent le jardin. Ci-dessous, toujours dans la même propriété, une maison moderne et sa piscine.

The landscape architect varies both the nature of the vegetation and its height, giving great variety to the treatment of the outside areas.

Der Landschaftsarchitekt spielt mit der Art und mit der Höhe der Vegetation, sodass die Außenbereiche sehr vielfältig gestaltet sind.

Les variations dans la nature des plantations et leur hauteur ont permis une grande variété de traitements.

Mature trees, in good part palms in this image, alternate with lower shrubs and tropical plants near the grass.

Alte Bäume, auf diesem Bild vor allem Palmen, wechseln sich mit niedrigen Gehölzen und tropischen Pflanzen ab.

De grands arbres adultes, surtout des palmiers, alternent avec des arbustes et des plantes tropicales basses.

The extent of the property and its different types of architecture allow Raymond Jungles to create an entire environment of plants and basins that make the domain into a place apart from its surroundings.

Angesichts der Größe des Anwesens und der unterschiedlichen Architekturen konnte Raymond Jungles hier eine ganze Welt von Pflanzen und Wasserbecken schaffen, die das Gelände in einen von seiner Umgebung völlig abgeschiedenen Ort verwandeln.

L'étendue de la propriété et la variété des types d'architecture ont permis à Raymond Jungles de créer un environnement de plantes et de bassins qui singularise ce domaine dans son environnement.

KEMPE THILL

Atelier Kempe Thill Architects and Planners
Van Nelleweg 8065, Building 8
3044 BC Rotterdam
The Netherlands

Tel: +31 10 750 37 07
Fax: +31 10 750 36 97
E-mail: info@atelierkempethill.com
Web: www.atelierkempethill.com

ANDRÉ KEMPE was born in 1968 in Freiberg, in former East Germany. He attended the Technical University in Dresden (1990–96) and undertook Urban Studies thereafter in Paris (1993–94) and in Tokyo (1994). He worked in the offices of Frits van Dongen (Amsterdam, 1996–97) and Karelse van der Meer (Rotterdam, 1997–2000), before cofounding Atelier Kempe Thill in Rotterdam (2000). **OLIVER THILL** was born in 1971 in Karl-Marx-Stadt (today Chemnitz), in former East Germany. He also attended the Technical University in Dresden (1990–96) before undertaking similar Urban Studies in Paris and Tokyo. He worked in the office of Frits van Dongen (1996–97) and DKV (Rotterdam, 1997–2000), before joining Kempe in the creation of their firm in 2000. Kempe Thill is specialized in public projects, housing, and urban planning. They seek to create "architecture that is neutral and inexpensive, as well as enjoyable and innovative." Their projects include the Hedge Building (Rostock, Germany, 2003, published here); a museum in Veenhuizen (2005–08); a housing estate (Zwolle, 2005–08); the Railwayline Building (Rotterdam, 2007–); Eco Housing (Tienen, Belgium, 2007–); the Confucius Tower (Amsterdam, 2008–); and the Drug Addict's Hotel (Amsterdam, 2008–), all in the Netherlands unless stated otherwise.

ANDRÉ KEMPE wurde 1968 in Freiberg, DDR, geboren. Er besuchte die Technische Universität Dresden (1990–96) und studierte Städtebau in Paris (1993–94) und Tokio (1994). Er arbeitete für Frits van Dongen (Amsterdam, 1996–97) und Karelse van der Meer (Rotterdam, 1997–2000), bevor er in Rotterdam das Atelier Kempe Thill mitbegründete (2000). **OLIVER THILL** wurde 1971 in Karl-Marx-Stadt (heute Chemnitz) geboren. Auch er besuchte die Technische Universität Dresden (1990–96), bevor er sich ähnlichen Studien wie Kempe in Paris und Tokio widmete. Er arbeitete für Frits van Dongen (1996–97) und DKV (Rotterdam, 1997–2000), bevor er mit André Kempe 2000 das gemeinsame Büro gründete. Kempe Thill ist auf öffentliche Bauten, Wohnungsbau und Stadtplanung spezialisiert. Ihr Ziel ist es, „Architektur zu gestalten, die sowohl neutral und erschwinglich als auch angenehm und innovativ ist". Zu ihren Projekten zählen u. a. der niederländische Pavillon für die Internationale Gartenbauausstellung in Rostock, das Hedge Building (2003, hier vorgestellt), ein Museum in Veenhuizen (2005–08), ein Sozialbauprojekt in Zwolle (2005–08), die Umnutzung von Gleisunterbauten (Rotterdam, seit 2007), ein Ökohausprojekt (Tienen, Belgien, seit 2007), der Confucius-Turm (Amsterdam, seit 2008) sowie eine Unterkunft für Drogenabhängige (Amsterdam, seit 2008), alle in den Niederlanden, sofern nicht anders vermerkt.

ANDRÉ KEMPE, né en 1968 à Freiberg, dans l'ex-Allemagne de l'Est, a étudié à l'Université polytechnique de Dresde (1990–96) et effectué des études d'urbanisme à Paris (1993–94) et Tokyo (1994). Il a travaillé dans les agences de Frits van Dongen (Amsterdam, 1996–97) et de Karelse van der Meer (Rotterdam, 1997–2000), avant de fonder l'Atelier Kempe Thill à Rotterdam (2000). **OLIVER THILL**, né en 1971 à Karl-Marx-Stadt (aujourd'hui Chemnitz), ex-Allemagne de l'Est, a également étudié à l'Université polytechnique de Dresde (1990–96) et effectué les mêmes études d'urbanisme à Paris et Tokyo. Il a travaillé dans les agences de Frits van Dongen (1996–97) et DKV (Rotterdam, 1997–2000), avant de rejoindre Kempe pour créer ensemble leur agence en 2000. Kempe Thill est spécialisée dans les projets publics, le logement et l'urbanisme. Elle cherche à créer « architecture neutre et inexpressive, mais en même temps novatrice et agréable à vivre ». Parmi leurs réalisations : le Hedge Building (Rostock, Allemagne, 2003, publié ici) ; un musée à Veenhuizen (Pays-Bas, 2005–08) ; un ensemble de logements (Pays-Bas, Zwolle, 2005–08) ; l'immeuble de la gare (Rotterdam, 2007–) ; des logements écologiques (Tirlemont, Belgique, 2007–) ; la tour Confucius (Amsterdam, 2008–) et l'hôtel Drug Addict's (Amsterdam, 2008–).

HEDGE BUILDING

Rostock, Germany, 2003

Floor area: 200 m². Client: IBC Hillegom/NL. Cost: €400 000
Collaboration: André Kempe, Cornelia Sailer, Ruud Smeelen, Oliver Thill, Takashi Nakamura
Landscape Architect: Niek Roozen, Weesp, NL

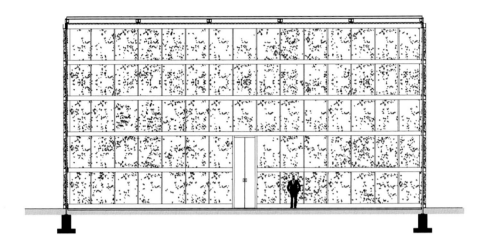

This building served as the Dutch Pavilion at the IGA international garden exhibition in Rostock, Germany, and is now used as a cultural building by the city of Rostock. As the architects write: "The project demonstrates the logic and rationality of Dutch agriculture and unearths surprisingly romantic qualities within its limited conditions." The so-called smart screen, an ivy hedge grown in Dutch greenhouses in sections 1.2 x 1.8 meters in size, can be assembled in sections. Described by the architects as a pergola, the structure is outfitted precisely to allow these smart screens to be used as 10-meter-high green walls. A screen made of translucent plastic covers the interior. The architects insist on the "neutral" aspect of the design, which allows it to be used for different functions. They also insist on the ambiguity thus created between interior and exterior. "The result is a game played between inside and outside," they say. "The light from above makes the space feel like an interior, while the light entering through the hedges gives the space the character of an exterior space. What's more, the gentle sway of the leaves and their shadows enhances the perception of the space."

Der als niederländischer Pavillon auf der Internationalen Gartenbauausstellung (IGA) in Rostock realisierte Bau dient inzwischen als städtische Kultureinrichtung. Die Architekten schreiben: „Das Projekt veranschaulicht die Logik und Rationalität der niederländischen Landwirtschaft und entfaltet im Rahmen seiner begrenzten Möglichkeiten erstaunlich romantische Qualitäten." Der *smart screen*, eine in niederländischen Gewächshäusern in 1,2 x 1,8 m großen Segmenten gezogene Efeuhecke lässt sich aus Einzelteilen montieren. Die von den Architekten als Pergola bezeichnete Konstruktion ermöglicht es, diese *smart screens* zu 10 m hohen grünen Mauern aufzurichten. Eine transparente Kunststoffdecke schützt den Raum. Besonders wichtig ist den Architekten die „Neutralität" des Entwurfs, der eine Nutzung für unterschiedlichste Zwecke erlaubt. Darüber hinaus betonen sie die Mehrdeutigkeit von innen und außen: „Auf diese Weise ergibt sich ein Spiel zwischen Innen- und Außenraum. Durch die Belichtung von oben wirkt der Raum wie ein Innenraum, dabei verleiht das Licht, das seitlich durch die Hecken fällt, dem Inneren etwas von einem Außenraum. Hinzu kommt, dass das zarte Rascheln der Blätter und ihr Schattenspiel das Raumempfinden verstärken."

Ce bâtiment a été le Pavillon néerlandais pour l'exposition internationale de jardins IGA à Rostock en Allemagne où il sert maintenant de centre culturel. Comme le précise l'architecte : « Ce projet démontre la logique et la rationalité de l'agriculture néerlandaise et révèle des qualités étonnamment romantiques dans ses conditions de vie limitée. » L'ainsi nommé « écran intelligent », composé de haies de lierre venant de serres néerlandaises par section de 1,2 x 1,8 m, a été assemblé. Cette structure, présentée par les architectes comme une pergola, a été montée avec précision pour créer des murs verts de 10 m de haut. Un écran en plastique translucide vert recouvre l'intérieur. Les architectes insistent sur l'aspect « neutre » de cette installation, ce qui lui permet de remplir différentes fonctions et de créer une ambiguïté entre l'intérieur et l'extérieur. « C'est finalement un jeu entre l'intérieur et l'extérieur, disent-ils, la lumière tombant du haut donne l'impression que l'on se trouve à l'intérieur, tandis que celle qui pénètre par les haies donne à l'espace le caractère de salon extérieur. De plus, le léger balancement des feuilles et de leurs ombres accroît la perception de cet espace. »

The Hedge Building is almost more of a cage than it is a building, with its high walls filled out with an ivy screen. Here vegetation and architecture are united.

Das Hedge Building ist mit seinen hohen Wänden aus Efeurankgittern fast mehr Käfig als Gebäude. Hier finden Vegetation und Architektur zu einer Einheit.

Le Hedge Building est autant une cage qu'un bâtiment. Ses hautes parois sont recouvertes de lierre : union de l'architecture et de la végétation.

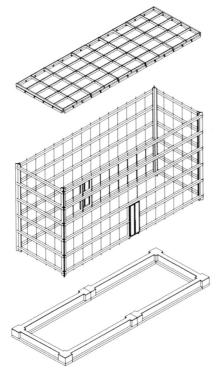

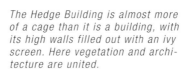

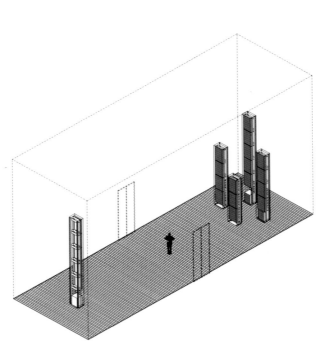

KIERANTIMBERLAKE

*KieranTimberlake
420 North 20th Street
Philadelphia, PA 19130
USA
Tel: +1 215 922 6600 / Fax: +1 215 922 4680
E-mail: kta@kierantimberlake.com
Web: www.kierantimberlake.com*

Founded in Philadelphia in 1984 by Stephen Kieran and James Timberlake, **KIERANTIMBERLAKE** comprises a staff of 60. Kieran graduated from Yale University and got his M.Arch from the University of Pennsylvania. Timberlake graduated from the University of Detroit before receiving his M.Arch from the University of Pennsylvania. The firm's projects include programming, planning, and design of all types of new structures and their interiors; and the renovation, reuse, and conservation of existing structures. KieranTimberlake has received over 80 design awards, including the 2008 Architecture Firm Award from the American Institute of Architects. In 2003 the firm developed SmartWrap: The Building Envelope of the Future, a mass customizable, high-performance building façade that was initially exhibited at the Smithsonian Institution, Cooper-Hewitt National Design Museum. Structures completed in 2007 include the Sculpture Building Gallery, Yale University (New Haven, Connecticut), and the Suzanne Roberts Theatre, Philadelphia Theatre Company (Philadelphia, Pennsylvania). Buildings by KieranTimberlake completed in 2008 include the Sidwell Friends Middle School (Washington, D.C., 2005–06, published here); and the Multi-Faith Center and Houghton Memorial Chapel Restoration, Wellesley College (Wellesley, Massachusetts). Currently in design are the Northwest Campus Student Housing, University of California (Los Angeles, California); the Center City Building, University of North Carolina at Charlotte (Charlotte, North Carolina); and the Morse and Stiles Colleges, Yale University (New Haven, Connecticut), all in the USA.

KIERANTIMBERLAKE wurde 1984 von Stephen Kieran und James Timberlake in Philadelphia gegründet und hat 60 Mitarbeiter. Kieran schloss sein Studium in Yale ab und erwarb seinen M.Arch. an der University of Pennsylvania. Timberlake machte seinen Abschluss an der University of Detroit und absolvierte seinen M.Arch. ebenfalls an der University of Pennsylvania. Das Büro befasst sich mit Programmentwicklung, Planung und Gestaltung von Neubauten aller Art und deren Innenraumgestaltung sowie der Sanierung, Umnutzung und Erhaltung von Altbauten. KieranTimberlake erhielt über 80 Designpreise, darunter den Architecture Firm Award 2008 des American Institute of Architects. 2003 entwickelte das Büro SmartWrap, die Gebäudehülle der Zukunft, eine technisch ausgeklügelte Gebäudefassade, die maßgeschneidert, aber in Massenfertigung hergestellt werden kann und erstmals im Cooper-Hewitt National Design Museum der Smithsonian Institution präsentiert wurde. Zu den 2007 realisierten Bauten zählen u. a. die Sculpture Building Gallery an der Yale University (New Haven, Connecticut) sowie das Suzanne Roberts Theatre für die Philadelphia Theatre Company (Philadelphia, Pennsylvania). 2008 wurden folgende Bauten bezugsfertig: die Sidwell Friends Middle School (Washington D. C., 2005–06, hier vorgestellt) sowie das Multi-Faith Center und die Sanierung der Houghton Memorial Chapel am Wellesley College (Wellesley, Massachusetts). In Planung sind ein Studentenwohnheim für den Northwest-Campus der University of California (Los Angeles), das Center City Building der University of North Carolina (Charlotte, North Carolina) sowie das Morse und das Stiles College, Yale University (New Haven, Connecticut), alle in den USA.

Fondée à Philadelphie en 1984 par Stephen Kieran et James Timberlake, l'agence **KIERANTIMBERLAKE** emploie 60 collaborateurs. Kieran est diplômé de Yale et a obtenu son M.Arch. de l'université de Pennsylvanie. Timberlake, diplômé de l'université de Detroit, a également obtenu un M.Arch. de l'université de Pennsylvanie. L'agence se consacre à la programmation, l'urbanisme et la conception de tous types de constructions et à leurs aménagements intérieurs ainsi qu'à la rénovation, la réutilisation et la restauration de bâtiments existants. KieranTimberlake a reçu plus de 80 prix, dont celui de l'agence 2008 de l'Institut américain des architectes. En 2003, l'agence a créé SmartWrap, « L'enveloppe du bâtiment du futur », façade préfabriquée personnalisable à hautes performances qui a été présentée pour la première fois au Cooper-Hewitt National Design Museum à Washington. Parmi leurs réalisations : la Sculpture Building Gallery de l'université Yale (New Haven, Connecticut) et le théâtre Suzanne Roberts de la Philadelphia Theatre Company (Philadelphie, Pennsylvanie). Parmi leurs projets achevés très récemment : le collège de Sidwell Friends (Washington DC, 2005–06, publié ici) et la restauration du Centre œcuménique et du Houghton Memorial Chapel du Wellesley College (Wellesley, Massachusetts). Ils travaillent actuellement à divers projets : logements pour étudiants du Northwest Campus, université de Californie (Los Angeles, Californie) ; le Center City Building de l'université de Caroline du Nord (Charlotte, Caroline du Nord) et les Morse et Stiles Colleges, université Yale (New Haven, Connecticut), tous au États-Unis.

SIDWELL FRIENDS MIDDLE SCHOOL

Washington, D.C., USA, 2005–06

Floor area: 3623 m² (addition); 3112 m² (renovation)
Client: Sidwell Friends School. Cost: $21.5 million
Collaboration: Andropogon Associates (Landscape), CVM Engineers (Structural Engineers),
Bruce E. Brooks & Associates (Mechanical Engineers)

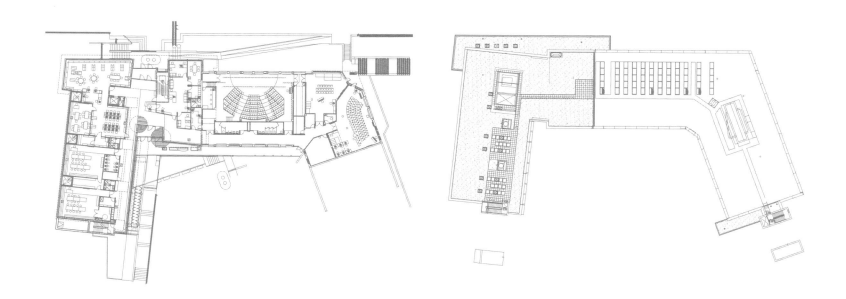

The architects have developed a master plan for this Quaker independent school that places a strong emphasis on environmental responsibility. A new building adds 3623 square meters to the existing facility. The building was awarded a LEED Platinum rating, the highest level of certification attainable from the USGBC, and it is the first school of its type in the United States to receive such a rating. Exterior sunscreens, and classrooms that place an emphasis on natural lighting, are part of the environmental strategy. Occupancy sensors and automatic dimmers reduce electricity consumption. Exterior walls of the addition and the third floor of the existing building are clad in recycled wood from red cedar fermentation barrels. Operable windows encourage the use of natural ventilation. Solar chimneys are designed for mechanically assisted natural ventilation to minimize the need for artificial cooling. A "wetland" zone integrated into the landscaping recycles building wastewater for future "gray water" use, thus reducing water consumption from municipal sources by 94%. A "vegetated roof" collects rainwater, and photovoltaic panels generate 5% of electrical requirements.

Für diese freie Quäkerschule entwickelten die Architekten einen Masterplan, der besonderen Wert auf ökologische Verantwortung legt. Ein Neubau erweitert die bestehende Schuleinrichtung um 3623 m². Das Gebäude wurde als erste Schule in den Vereinigten Staaten mit einer LEED-Platinmedaille ausgezeichnet, der höchstmöglichen Zertifizierungsstufe des USGBC. Teil des ökologischen Konzepts sind Sonnenschutzvorrichtungen an der Außenfassade und den Klassenräumen, die besonders auf natürliche Belichtung hin ausgelegt sind. Infrarotsensoren und automatische Dimmer reduzieren den Stromverbrauch. Die Außenmauern des Anbaus und der dritte Stock des Altbaus wurden mit Holz von recycelten Fässern aus Riesenlebensbaum verblendet. Fenster, die sich öffnen lassen, fördern die natürliche Belüftung. Zusätzlich wurden Solarkamine installiert, um die mechanische natürliche Belüftung zu unterstützen und den Bedarf an künstlicher Kühlung zu minimieren. Ein in das Gelände integriertes „Feuchtgebiet" soll Brauchwasser aus den Gebäuden aufbereiten, um das „Grauwasser" in Zukunft nutzen zu können, wodurch sich der Wasserbedarf aus städtischen Quellen um 94 % senken lässt. Ein begrüntes Dach sammelt Regenwasser, Solarzellen generieren 5 % des Strombedarfs.

Les architectes ont conçu pour cette école quaker un plan qui met un fort accent sur la responsabilité environnementale. Le nouveau bâtiment de 3623 m² complète des installations existantes. Il a reçu la certification LEED Platine, le plus haut niveau accordé par l'USGBC, et est la première école de ce type aux États-Unis à le recevoir. Les écrans extérieurs et les salles de classe qui bénéficient fortement de l'éclairage naturel relèvent de la stratégie environnementale retenue. Des capteurs d'occupation des locaux et des rhéostats automatiques réduisent la consommation d'électricité. Les murs extérieurs du nouveau bâtiment et le troisième niveau des constructions existantes sont habillés de bois recyclé venant de barriques de fermentation en cèdre rouge. Des fenêtres ouvrables encouragent le recours à la ventilation naturelle. Des cheminées solaires facilitent mécaniquement les flux d'air pour réduire les besoins en climatisation. Une zone de lagunage a été intégrée dans les aménagements paysagers pour recycler les eaux usées, ce qui réduit la consommation de l'eau du réseau municipal de 94 %. Un toit végétalisé recueille l'eau de pluie et des panneaux photovoltaïques produisent 5 % de l'électricité consommée.

The addition to this prestigious school by the architects provides a large efficient volume with a clear emphasis on environmental concerns.

Der Anbau an die renommierte Schule ist ein großer, effizienter Baukörper, der ausdrücklich ökologische Belange berücksichtigt.

L'extension de cette prestigieuse école est un vaste volume efficacement conçu qui met clairement l'accent sur ses ambitions écologiques.

Rooftop planters allow young students to be educated not only about plants but also about environmental concerns and ways to address them.

Pflanzkübel auf dem Dach erlauben nicht nur, die Schüler an Pflanzen heranzuführen, sondern ebenso an Umweltfragen und Möglichkeiten, wie man diesen gerecht werden kann.

Les jardinières du toit permettent aux élèves d'être sensibilisés non seulement à la culture des plantes mais aussi aux préoccupations environnementales et aux façons d'y répondre.

The bright, open classrooms seem
very much in harmony with banks
of solar arrays seen to the right.

*Die hellen offenen Klassenzimmer
scheinen hervorragend mit den auf-
gereihten Solarmodulen auf dem
Dach (rechts) zu harmonieren.*

*Les salles de cours largement ouvertes
paraissent en harmonie avec les
installations de panneaux solaires
(à droite).*

MATHIAS KLOTZ

Mathias Klotz
Los Colonos 0411
Providencia, Santiago
Chile

Tel: +56 2 233 6613 / Fax: +56 2 232 2479
E-mail: estudio@mathiasklotz.com
Web: www.mathiasklotz.com

MATHIAS KLOTZ was born in 1965 in Viña del Mar, Chile. He received his architecture degree from the Pontificia Universidad Católica de Chile in 1991. He created his own office in Santiago the same year. He has taught at several Chilean universities and was Director of the School of Architecture of the Universidad Diego Portales in Santiago (2001–03). Recent work includes the Casa Viejo (Santiago, 2001); the Smol Building (Concepción, 2001); the Faculty of Health, Diego Portales University (Santiago, 2004); the remodeling of the Cerro San Luis House (Santiago, 2004); the Ocho al Cubo House (Marbella, Zapallar, 2005); La Roca House (Punta del Este, Uruguay, 2006, published here); the Techos House (Nahuel Huapi Lake, Patagonia, Argentina, 2006–07); the 11 Mujeres House (Cachagua, 2007); 20 one-family houses in La Dehesa (Santiago); and the Buildings Department San Isidro (Buenos Aires, Argentina), all in Chile unless stated otherwise. Mathias Klotz has received numerous awards for sustainable design including Green Good Design awards in 2010 for the La Roca House, and for the Nicanor Parra Library of the Diego Portales University (Santiago, 2010–11), plus a 2011 Holcim Award for the same building.

MATHIAS KLOTZ wurde 1965 in Viña del Mar, Chile, geboren. Er schloss sein Architekturstudium 1991 an der Pontificia Universidad Católica de Chile ab. Sein eigenes Büro gründete er im gleichen Jahr in Santiago. Klotz hat an verschiedenen Universitäten Chiles gelehrt und war Dekan der Architekturfakultät der Universidad Diego Portales in Santiago (2001–03). Zu seinen neueren Projekten zählen u. a. die Casa Viejo (Santiago, 2001), das Geschäftszentrum Smol (Concepción, 2001), die Fakultät für Gesundheitswissenschaften an der Universidad Diego Portales (Santiago, 2004), der Umbau der Casa Cerro San Luis (Santiago, 2004), die Casa Ocho al Cubo (Marbella, Zapallar, 2005), die Casa La Roca (Punta del Este, Uruguay, 2006, hier vorgestellt), die Casa Techos (Nahuel-Huapi-See, Patagonien, Argentinien, 2006–07), die Casa 11 Mujeres (Cachagua, 2007), 20 Einfamilienhäuser in La Dehesa (Santiago) sowie die Baubehörde in San Isidro (Buenos Aires, Argentinien), alle in Chile, sofern nicht anders vermerkt. Für seine nachhaltige Architektur wurde Mathias Klotz mit zahlreichen Preisen ausgezeichnet, darunter 2010 mit dem Preis für Green Good Design für die Casa La Roca und die Bibliothek Nicanor Parra an der Universidad Diego Portales (Santiago, 2010–11) sowie 2011 mit einem Holcim-Preis für dasselbe Projekt.

MATHIAS KLOTZ est né en 1965 à Viña del Mar, au Chili. Il a obtenu son diplôme d'architecture à l'Université catholique pontificale du Chili en 1991 et a créé son agence à Santiago la même année. Il a enseigné dans plusieurs universités chiliennes et a dirigé l'École d'architecture de l'université Diego Portales de Santiago (2001–03). Ses réalisations récentes comptent la Casa Viejo (Santiago, 2001) ; le bâtiment Smol (Concepción, 2001) ; la faculté des sciences de la santé de l'université Diego Portales (Santiago, 2004) ; le réaménagement de la Casa Cerro San Luis (Santiago, 2004) ; la Casa Ocho al Cubo (Marbella, Zapallar, 2005) : la Casa La Roca (Punta del Este, Uruguay, 2006, publiée ici) ; la Casa Techos (lac Nahuel Huapi, Patagonie, Argentine, 2006–07) ; la Casa 11 Mujeres (Cachagua, 2007) ; 20 maisons individuelles à La Dehesa (Santiago) et le service de la construction de San Isidro (Buenos Aires), toutes au Chili sauf si précisé. Mathias Klotz a reçu de nombreux prix pour ses créations durables, notamment en 2010 le prix de design Green Good pour la Casa La Roca et la bibliothèque Nicanor Parra de l'université Diego Portales (Santiago, 2010–11) et en 2011 un prix Holcim pour le même bâtiment.

LA ROCA HOUSE
Punta del Este, Uruguay, 2006

Address: Punta de José Ignacio, 80 kilometers north of Punta del Este, Uruguay
Area: 300 m². Client: not disclosed. Cost: not disclosed
Collaboration: Baltasar Sánchez, Carolina Pedroni

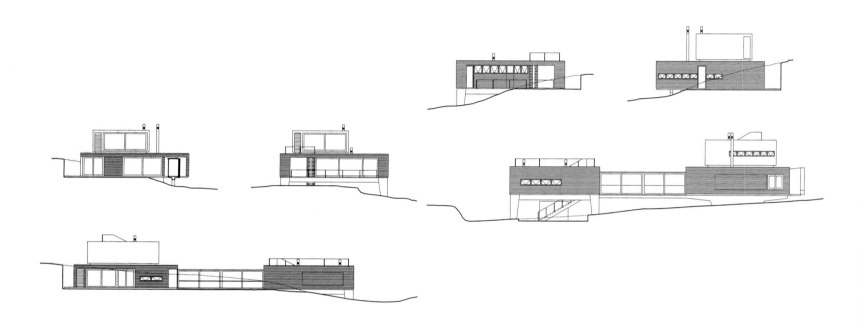

The exact location of this house is the village of José Ignacio, 80 kilometers north of Punta del Este on the Atlantic coast of Uruguay. The "public" and "private" spaces of the house are divided into two boxes of the same height with patios beneath and between the boxes. The architect states: "**LA ROCA HOUSE** is defined through a sequence of spaces, almost square in plan, which run entering from the most public to the most intimate, crossing terraces, patios, exterior, intermediate, and interior spaces and arriving finally at the master bedroom." Natural ventilation obviates the need for air conditioning, while roof gardens shield the roofs of the boxes from heat gain. Gray water from the house is recycled for garden irrigation. Ipe wood and exposed concrete are the most obvious material elements employed in the architectural design.

Der genaue Standort dieses Wohnhauses ist das Dorf José Ignacio, 80 km nördlich von Punta del Este an der Atlantikküste von Uruguay. Die „öffentlichen" und „privaten" Bereiche des Hauses sind in zwei gleich hohe Kisten mit Patios darunter und dazwischen aufgeteilt. Der Architekt erklärt: „Das **HAUS LA ROCA** besteht aus einer Folge von – im Grundriss fast quadratischen – Räumen. Sie führt, vom Eingang ausgehend, über die weitgehend öffentlichen bis zu den absolut intimen Bereichen, über Terrassen, Patios, Außen-, Zwischen- und Innenräume und endet schließlich im Elternschlafzimmer." Die natürliche Belüftung macht eine Klimaanlage überflüssig; Dachgärten verhindern, dass die Dächer der Kisten sich aufheizen. Das Brauchwasser des Hauses wird zur Bewässerung des Gartens wiederaufbereitet. Ipe-Holz und Sichtbeton sind die bestimmenden Materialien für diesen Entwurf.

Cette maison est située dans le village de José Ignacio, à 80 km au nord de Punta del Este sur la côte atlantique de l'Uruguay. Les parties « privées » et « publiques » se répartissent en deux boîtes de même hauteur. Des patios sont aménagés sous et entre ces deux éléments. « La **CASA LA ROCA** se définit comme une séquence d'espaces suivant un plan presque carré, qui va de l'entrée et de la partie la plus publique jusqu'à la plus intime en franchissant des terrasses, des patios, l'extérieur, des espaces intermédiaires et intérieurs pour arriver finalement à la chambre principale », explique l'architecte. La ventilation naturelle rend la climatisation inutile et la végétalisation des toitures protège l'intérieur du gain thermique. Les eaux usées sont recyclées pour l'irrigation des jardins. Les matériaux utilisés les plus visibles sont le béton et le bois d'ipé.

Made of wood and concrete, the house is designed with a rectilinear vocabulary as the drawings above show. It is low and open to the ocean.

Das aus Holz und Beton errichtete Haus folgt einem rechtwinkligen Vokabular, wie die Zeichnungen oben beweisen. Es ist niedrig und zum Ozean offen.

Construite en bois et béton, la maison entièrement ouverte sur l'océan utilise un vocabulaire de lignes droites étirées, comme le montrent les dessins ci-dessus.

Opposite page: A bedroom offers a spectacular view of the terraces and the ocean beyond.

Gegenüberliegende Seite: Aus einem Schlafraum bietet sich eine spektakuläre Aussicht auf die Terrassen und den Ozean.

Page opposée : une des chambres bénéficie d'une vue spectaculaire sur les terrasses de l'océan.

Wooden terraces allow the residents to take in the view without going onto the beach directly. The design of these elements is open and simple.

Die hölzernen Terrassen bieten den Bewohnern Aussicht, ohne dass sie zum Strand hinuntergehen müssten. Die Elemente sind offen und einfach gestaltet.

De dessin très simple, les terrasses en bois permettent aux habitants de bénéficier de la vue sans devoir se rendre à la plage.

Plans of the house show the way it is
composed with square elements.

*Die Grundrisse des Hauses zeigen,
wie der Bau aus quadratischen Modu-
len zusammengesetzt ist.*

*Les plans de la maison illustrent sa
composition à partir d'éléments de
forme carrée.*

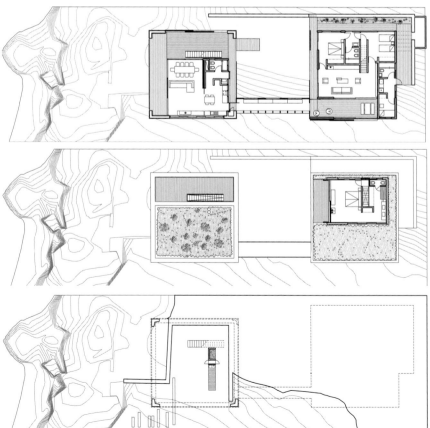

KENGO KUMA

Kengo Kuma & Associates
2–24–8 Minami Aoyama
Minato-ku
Tokyo 107–0062
Japan

Tel: +81 3 3401 7721
Fax: +81 3 3401 7778
E-mail: kuma@ba2.so-net.ne.jp
Web: www.kkaa.co.jp

Born in 1954 in Kanagawa, Japan, **KENGO KUMA** graduated in 1979 from the University of Tokyo with an M.Arch degree. In 1985–86 he received an Asian Cultural Council Fellowship Grant and was a Visiting Scholar at Columbia University. In 1987 he established the Spatial Design Studio, and in 1991 he created Kengo Kuma & Associates. His work includes the Karuizawa Resort Hotel (Karuizawa, 1993); Kiro-san Observatory (Ehime, 1994); Atami Guesthouse, a guesthouse for Bandai Corp (Atami, 1992–95); the Japanese Pavilion for the Venice Biennale (Venice, Italy, 1995); Tomioka Lakewood Golf Club Clubhouse (Tomioka, 1993–96); and Toyoma Noh-Theater (Miyagi, 1995–96). He has also completed the Great (Bamboo) Wall Guesthouse (Beijing, China, 2002); One Omotesando (Tokyo, 2003); LVMH Osaka (2004); the Nagasaki Prefecture Art Museum (2005); and the Zhongtai Box, Z58 building (Shanghai, China, 2003–06). Recent work includes the Steel House (Bunkyo-ku, Tokyo, 2005–07); Sakenohana (London, UK, 2007); Tiffany Ginza (Tokyo, 2008); Nezu Museum (Tokyo, 2007–09); Museum of Kanayama (Ota City, Gunma, 2009); Glass Wood House (New Canaan, Connecticut, USA, 2007–10, published here); Yusuhara Marché (Yusuhara, Kochi, 2009–10, also published here); and the GC Prostho Museum Research Center, Torii Matsu Machi (Aichi, 2009–10), all in Japan unless stated otherwise.

KENGO KUMA wurde 1954 in Kanagawa, Japan, geboren und schloss sein Studium an der Universität Tokio 1979 mit einem M.Arch. ab. 1985 bis 1986 erhielt er ein Stipendium des Asian Cultural Council und war Gastdozent an der Columbia University. 1987 gründete er das Büro Spatial Design Studio, 1991 folgte die Gründung von Kengo Kuma & Associates. Sein Werk umfasst das Hotel Karuizawa (Karuizawa, 1993), das Planetarium Kiro-san (Ehime, 1994), das Atami-Gästehaus für Bandai (Atami, 1992–95), den japanischen Pavillon für die Biennale in Venedig (1995), das Tomioka Lakewood Golfclubhaus (Tomioka, 1993–96) und das No-Theater in Toyoma (Miyagi, 1995–96). Darüber hinaus realisierte er das Great (Bamboo) Wall Guest House (Peking, China, 2002), One Omotesando (Tokio, 2003), LVMH Osaka (2004), das Kunstmuseum der Präfektur Nagasaki (2005) sowie die Zhongtai Box, Z58 (Schanghai, China, 2003–06). Jüngere Projekte sind u. a. das Steel House (Bunkyo-ku, Tokio, 2005–07), Sakenohana (London, 2007), Tiffany Ginza (Tokio, 2008), das Nezu Museum (Tokio, 2007–09), das Museum von Kanayama (Ota City, Gunma, 2009), das Glass Wood House (New Canaan, Connecticut, 2007–10, hier vorgestellt), Yusuhara Marché (Yusuhara, Kochi, 2009–10, ebenfalls hier vorgestellt) sowie das Forschungszentrum des GC Prostho Museum, Torii Matsu Machi (Aichi, 2009–10).

Né en 1954 à Kanagawa (Japon), **KENGO KUMA** est diplômé d'architecture de l'université de Tokyo (1979). En 1985–86, il bénéficie d'une bourse de l'Asian Cultural Council et devient chercheur invité à l'université Columbia. En 1987, il crée le Spatial Design Studio et, en 1991, Kengo Kuma & Associates. Parmi ses réalisations : l'hôtel de vacances Karuizawa (Karuizawa, 1993) ; l'observatoire Kiro-san (Ehime, 1994) ; la maison d'hôtes d'Atami pour Bandai Corp (Atami, 1992–95) ; le Pavillon japonais pour la Biennale de Venise 1995 ; le club-house du golf du lac de Tomioka (Tomioka, 1993–96) et le théâtre de nô Toyoma (Miyagi, 1995–96). Il a également réalisé la maison d'hôte de la Grande Muraille de bambou (Pékin, 2002) ; l'immeuble One Omotesando (Tokyo, 2003) ; l'immeuble LVMH Osaka (2004) ; le Musée d'art de la préfecture de Nagasaki (2005) et l'immeuble Zhongtai Box, Z58 (Shanghai, 2003–06). Plus récemment, il a construit la Maison en acier (Bunkyo-ku, Tokyo, 2005–07) ; le restaurant Sakenohana (Londres, 2007) ; l'immeuble Tiffany Ginza (Tokyo, 2008) ; le musée Nezu (Tokyo, 2007–09) ; le musée de Kanayama (Ota, Gunma, 2009) ; la Maison en bois et verre (New Canaan, Connecticut, 2007–10, publiée ici) ; le marché de Yusuhara (Yusuhara, Kochi, 2009–10, également publié ici) et le centre de recherches du musée GC Prostho, Torii Matsu Machi (Aichi, 2009–10).

GLASS WOOD HOUSE

New Canaan, Connecticut, USA, 2007–10

Area: 830 m². Client: not disclosed. Cost: not disclosed
Collaboration: Yuki Ikeguchi, Satoshi Sano

This project involved the renovation of a house designed by Philip Johnson in 1956 and the construction of a new house on the site. The original structure is described by Kengo Kuma as a "symmetric glass box standing alone in a forest." "Philip Johnson's house stands alone," says Kuma, "so we proposed the L-shaped plan in which the new building hitched onto the old one, in order to present a new relation between nature and the architecture." The new structure has 7.6 x 15.2-centimeter flat steel bar pillars and a wooden roof. "We created a major change in the existing house," says the architect, "by getting rid of the symmetry and covering the exterior with wooden louvers, so that the architecture would gain more 'intimacy.'" In Kengo Kuma's terms the result is to create a sort of "intimate" or "mild" transparency that supercedes the "isolated" transparency conceived in the 1950s.

Neben der Sanierung eines Philip-Johnson-Baus von 1956 umfasst das Projekt auch den Neubau eines Wohnhauses auf demselben Grundstück. Den Bestandsbau beschreibt Kengo Kuma als „symmetrische Glasbox, isoliert in einem Wald platziert". Kuma erklärt: „Philip Johnsons Haus ist frei stehend, weshalb wir einen L-förmigen Grundriss entwickelten. Der Neubau schließt an den älteren Bau an, sodass ein neues Verhältnis zwischen Natur und Architektur entsteht." Der Neubau hat ein Holzdach und Stützen aus 7,6 x 15,2 cm starken Stahlträgern. „Beim Altbau nahmen wir eine wesentliche Veränderung vor", berichtet der Architekt, „indem wir uns von der Symmetrie verabschiedeten und den Bau außen mit hölzernen Sonnenschutzblenden versahen, sodass die Architektur mehr ‚Intimität' gewann." Kengo Kuma zufolge ist das Ergebnis eine „intime" bzw. „abgemilderte" Transparenz, die die „isolierte" Transparenz der 1950er-Jahre ablöst.

Ce projet comprenait la rénovation d'une maison conçue par Philip Johnson en 1956 et la construction d'une nouvelle résidence sur le même terrain. La construction d'origine est présentée par Kengo Kuma comme « une boîte de verre symétrique isolée dans la forêt ». « La maison de Philip Johnson est isolée, explique-t-il, ainsi avons-nous proposé un plan en L dans lequel la construction nouvelle s'accroche à l'ancienne pour créer une relation nouvelle entre la nature et l'architecture. » La nouvelle construction qui repose sur des piliers en acier de 7,6 x 15,2 cm de section est recouverte d'une toiture en bois. « Nous avons apporté un changement majeur à la maison existante en supprimant la symétrie et en recouvrant les façades de volets de bois pour que l'architecture gagne en "intimité". » Kengo Kuma explique également avoir créé une sorte de transparence « intime » ou « douce » qui remplace la transparence « isolée » des années 1950.

Kengo Kuma is a master of lightness and integration of modern architecture into a natural setting, as is evident here, far from his native Japan.

Kengo Kuma ist ein Meister der Leichtigkeit und der Einbindung moderner Architektur in eine Landschaft. Das wird auch hier deutlich, fernab seines Heimatlands Japan.

Kengo Kuma est un orfèvre en matière de légèreté et d'intégration de formes contemporaines dans un cadre naturel, comme il le montre ici, loin de son Japon natal.

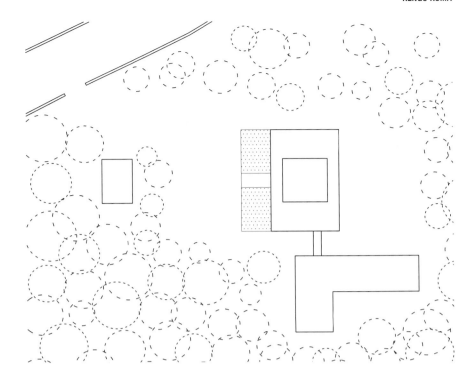

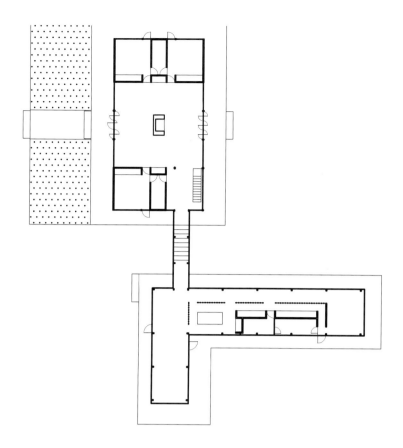

Plans show the strictly geometric design, but images demonstrate the extreme lightness of the structure—a fact that allows it to sit in the natural setting without disturbing it.

Während Grundrisse die strenge Geometrie des Entwurfs belegen, zeugen Aufnahmen von der auffälligen Leichtigkeit des Baus – ihr ist es zu verdanken, dass das Haus in der Landschaft liegt, ohne sie zu stören.

Ces plans illustrent la géométrie rigoureuse du projet dont les images expriment l'extrême légèreté qui lui permet de s'intégrer avec délicatesse dans son cadre naturel sans le perturber.

In the image above, or in the one on the right, the forest penetrates the house in a visual sense, and the building floats above the sloping site.

Auf der Ansicht oben und auch rechts scheint der Wald das Haus ganz zu durchdringen. Es schwebt geradezu über dem Hanggrundstück.

Dans l'image ci-dessus ou celle de droite, la forêt semble pénétrer visu-ellement dans la maison en suspen-sion au-dessus de la pente du terrain.

YUSUHARA MARCHÉ

Yusuhara, Kochi, Japan, 2009–10

*Address: 1196–1 Yusuhara, Takaoka-gun, Kochi, Japan
Area: 1132 m². Cost: not disclosed. Client: Tomio Yano, Mayor of Yusuhara
Collaboration: Kazuhiko Miyazawa, Suguru Watanabe*

Though this building is rather substantial in its apparent mass, the architect alleviates the feeling of weight with full glazing on the ground floor. A site plan (left) shows how the building fits into the dense town pattern.

Obwohl der Bau von der Masse her substanziell wirkt, gelingt es dem Architekten, diesen Eindruck durch geschosshohe Verglasung im Parterre aufzulockern. Ein Lageplan (links) illustriert, wie sich das Gebäude in die dichte städtische Bebauung fügt.

Bien que ce bâtiment soit de dimensions assez importantes, l'architecte a allégé le sentiment éventuel de massivité en vitrant entièrement le rez-de-chaussée. Un plan (à gauche) montre comment le projet s'est adapté à la densité de son environnement urbain.

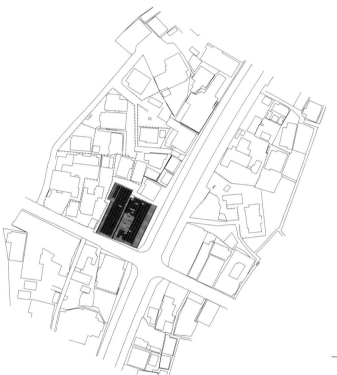

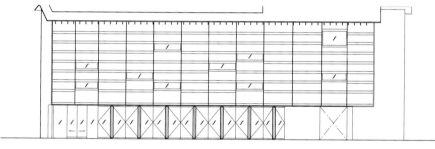

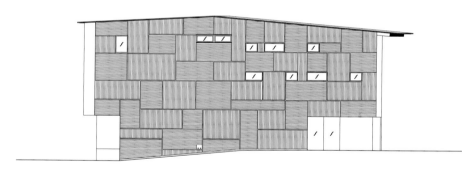

This is a market selling local products coupled with a small 15-room hotel. Yusuhara is a town of 3900 people located in the mountains. The architect employed thatching in deference to regional traditions. Glass marks the front entrance, with straw modules in the "unprecedented" form of a curtain wall bound to the structure. Cedar logs are used inside with irregular bark peeling. Kengo Kuma states: "Using rough-textured materials, such as thatch and logs, we tried to create new characteristics for Yusuhara."

In diesem Marktgebäude zum Verkauf lokaler Produkte ist auch ein kleines Hotel mit 15 Zimmern untergebracht. Yusuhara ist eine Kleinstadt mit 3900 Einwohnern und liegt in den Bergen. In Anlehnung an regionale Bautraditionen arbeitete der Architekt mit einer Reetdachtechnik. Der Haupteingang wird von Glas dominiert, während Strohmodule in Form eines „nie dagewesenen" Curtainwall vor der Fassade angebracht wurden. Im Innern des Baus kamen Zedernholzstämme mit teilweise entfernter Rinde zum Einsatz. Kengo Kuma erklärt: „Indem wir Materialien mit rauen Oberflächen nutzten, wie etwa Reet und Holzstämme, versuchten wir, neue Besonderheiten in Yusuhara einzuführen."

Ce petit marché de produits locaux couplé à un hôtel de 15 chambres été construit à Yusuhara, ville de 3900 habitants située dans une région montagneuse. L'architecte a utilisé le chaume par respect des traditions régionales. La façade d'entrée est néanmoins en verre surmontée de panneaux modulaires en chaume qui forment un mur-rideau « sans précédent ». À l'intérieur, on remarque des grumes de cèdre grossièrement équarries. Pour Kengo Kuma : « En utilisant des matériaux de texture brute, comme le chaume et les grumes, nous avons voulu donner à Yusuhara un nouveau caractère architectural. »

By using flattened blocks of thatched straw, the architect both calls on local materials and yet makes his materials modern through their form and accumulation.

Durch den Einsatz von gepressten Reetballen nimmt der Architekt Bezug auf lokale Baumaterialien, gibt diesen jedoch durch ihre formale Gestaltung und Bündelung ein modernes Gesicht.

L'architecte utilise des panneaux de chaume, matériau local qu'il modernise aussi bien dans sa façon de l'utiliser que par son accumulation.

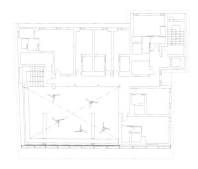

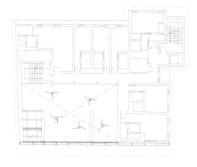

Wood is used inside the building, including these treelike columns and the rough wood ceiling. Modernity is thus firmly balanced with a natural or rural ambiance. To the right, one of the 15 hotel rooms in the building.

Im Innern des Gebäudes wurde Holz verarbeitet, etwa in Form von baumähnlichen Stützen und unbehandeltem Holz an der Decke. So entsteht ein gelungenes Gleichgewicht zwischen Moderne und natürlichem bzw. ländlichem Ambiente. Rechts eines der 15 Hotelzimmer.

Le bois brut est très présent à l'intérieur, comme dans les colonnes en forme d'arbre ou le plafond. La modernité du projet n'empêche pas une ambiance de nature ou de ruralité. À droite, l'une des 15 chambres de l'hôtel.

The image above and the section drawing showing the building's structure both emphasize the intelligent mixture of very contemporary materials and the rougher presence of numerous wooden elements.

Das Bild oben und der Querschnitt der Gebäudekonstruktion rechts unterstreichen die ausgesprochen intelligente Kombination zeitgenössischer Materialien und zahlreicher Elemente aus Holz.

La photographie ci-dessus et le dessin de coupe montrant la structure du bâtiment mettent en évidence l'intelligent mélange de matériaux contemporains et de multiples éléments en bois.

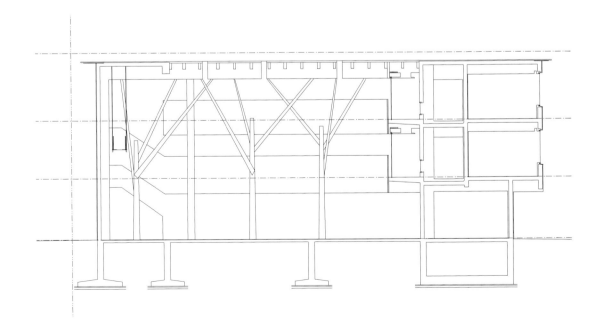

LACATON & VASSAL

Lacaton & Vassal
206 Rue La Fayette
75010 Paris

Tel: +33 1 47 23 49 09
Fax: +33 1 47 23 49 17
E-mail: lacaton.vassal@wanadoo.fr
Web: www.lacatonvassal.com

ANNE LACATON was born in 1955 in Saint-Pardoux-la-Rivière, France. She studied at the École d'architecture de Bordeaux (1980) and received a DESS degree in Urbanism in Bordeaux in 1984. **JEAN-PHILIPPE VASSAL** was born in 1954 in Casablanca, Morocco. He received his diploma from the École d'architecture de Bordeaux (1980) and worked as an architect and city planner in Niger from 1980 to 1985. Notable projects include the Café of the Architektur Zentrum in Vienna (Austria, 2001); the renovation of the Palais de Tokyo, a location for contemporary art in Paris (2002); and 14 low-cost residences at the Cité Manifeste in Mulhouse (2005, published here). They have also completed houses in the Dordogne region (1997); in Lège Cap Ferret (1998); and in Coutras (2000). More recent work includes the School of Architecture (Nantes, 2009); 23 dwellings (Trignac, 2010, under construction); renovation and transformation of the Tour Bois le Prêtre – Druot (Paris, 2011); and Phase II of the Palais de Tokyo renovation (2012). They are working on the FRAC Nord-Pas de Calais (Dunkerque, 2013), all in France unless stated otherwise.

ANNE LACATON wurde 1955 in Saint-Pardoux-la-Rivière, Frankreich, geboren. Sie studierte an der École d'architecture de Bordeaux (1980) und absolvierte ihr DESS-Diplom in Urbanistik 1984 in Bordeaux. **JEAN-PHILIPPE VASSAL** wurde 1954 in Casablanca, Marokko, geboren. Er machte sein Diplom an der École d'architecture de Bordeaux (1980) und war von 1980 bis 1985 als Architekt und Stadtplaner im Niger tätig. Wichtige Projekte sind u. a. das Café und Restaurant im Architekturzentrum Wien (2001), die Sanierung des Palais de Tokyo, Museum für zeitgenössische Kunst in Paris (2002), und 14 soziale Wohnbauten in der Cité Manifeste in Mulhouse (2005, hier vorgestellt). Darüber hinaus realisierte das Büro Häuser in der Dordogne (1997), in Lège Cap Ferret (1998) sowie in Coutras (2000). Neuere Projekte sind die Hochschule für Architektur (Nantes, 2009), 23 Wohnungen (Trignac, 2010, im Bau), Sanierung und Umbau des Tour Bois le Prêtre – Druot (Paris, 2011) sowie der zweite Bauabschnitt der Sanierung des Palais de Tokyo (2012). Aktuell in Arbeit ist das FRAC Nord-Pas de Calais (Dunkerque, 2013), alle in Frankreich soweit nicht anders vermerkt.

ANNE LACATON est née en 1955 à Saint-Pardoux-la-Rivière (France). Elle a fait ses études à l'École d'architecture de Bordeaux (1980) et a obtenu un DESS en urbanisme à Bordeaux en 1984. **JEAN-PHILIPPE VASSAL** est né en 1954 à Casablanca. Il est diplômé de l'École d'architecture de Bordeaux (1980) et a travaillé au Niger en tant qu'architecte et urbaniste de 1980 à 1985. Leurs projets les plus remarquables comprennent notamment le café de l'Architektur Zentrum de Vienne (Autriche, 2001) ; la rénovation du Palais de Tokyo, un centre d'art contemporain à Paris (2002) et 14 résidences à loyer modéré à la Cité Manifeste de Mulhouse (2005, publié ici). Ils ont aussi réalisé des maisons en Dordogne (1997), à Lège-Cap-Ferret (1998) et à Coutras (2000). Parmi leurs projets plus récents figurent l'École d'architecture (Nantes, 2009) ; 23 logements (Trignac, 2010 – en construction) ; la rénovation et transformation de la tour Bois le Prêtre – Druot (Paris, 2011) et la phase II de la rénovation du Palais de Tokyo (2012), tous en France sauf si spécifié. Ils travaillent actuellement à la FRAC Nord-Pas de Calais (Dunkerque, 2013).

SOCIAL HOUSING, CITÉ MANIFESTE

Mulhouse, France, 2005

Area: 14 residences, 2262 m² including garages and winter gardens,
ranging from 175 m² to 102 m² each. Client: SOMCO, Mulhouse
Cost: €1.05 million (€75 000 per house excluding taxes)

This welfare housing program includes a total of 61 residences, of which 14 were designed by Lacaton & Vassal. The other architects were Jean Nouvel, Poitevin & Raynaud, Lewis + Block, and Shigeru Ban working with Jean de Gastines. The site was the former location of a textile plant. For Lacaton & Vassal, known for their minimalist or even rough style, a primary goal was to provide quality housing with the limited budget allotted. They started by creating "a simple, efficient and economical envelope and structure, that permitted us to define a maximum volume and floor area, with surprising and contrasted spaces." The ground floor is made of reinforced concrete with a height of more than three meters. The facades are largely glazed and can be opened. A galvanized steel greenhouse with clear polycarbonate panels was placed on this base—partially insulated and heated—with other sections intended for use as winter gardens. Ventilation is achieved by façade design that allows for half of the surfaces to be opened. Despite this surprising solution, the architects assure that an efficient control of temperature and comfort has been achieved. Each of the apartments crosses through the volume and is divided into two levels.

Der Komplex besteht aus insgesamt 61 Sozialwohnungen, von denen Lacaton & Vassal 14 entwarfen. Weitere Architekten waren Jean Nouvel, Poitevin & Raynaud, Lewis + Block sowie Shigeru Ban mit Jean de Gastines. Das ehemalige Industriegelände wurde früher von einem Textilunternehmen genutzt. Oberste Priorität für Lacaton & Vassal – bekannt für ihren minimalistischen, mitunter rauen Stil – war die Realisierung qualitätvollen Wohnraums im definierten Budgetrahmen. Ausgangspunkt des Entwurfs war „eine schlichte, effiziente und ökonomische Gebäudehülle und Konstruktionsform, die erlaubt, mit ungewöhnlichen, kontrastreichen Räumen maximales Volumen und Nutzfläche zu realisieren." Das Erdgeschoss aus Stahlbeton hat eine Raumhöhe von mehr als 3 m; die Fassaden sind weitgehend verglast und lassen sich öffnen. Auf dem Sockelgeschoss sitzt eine teilweise gedämmte und beheizbare Gewächshauskonstruktion aus verzinktem Stahl und klaren Polycarbonatplatten. Teile des Aufbaus lassen sich als Wintergarten nutzen. Durchlüftung wird durch Fassaden gewährleistet, die sich bis zur Hälfte ihrer Gesamtfläche öffnen lassen. Trotz dieser ungewöhnlichen Lösung garantiert die Planung effiziente Temperierung und angenehmen Wohnkomfort. Alle Einheiten erstrecken sich durch die gesamte Tiefe des Baus und wurden als Maisonettewohnungen angelegt.

Ce programme de logements sociaux sur le site d'une ancienne usine textile comprend 61 logements dont 14 ont été conçus par Lacaton & Vassal, les autres architectes étant Jean Nouvel, Poitevin & Raynaud, Lewis + Block et Shigeru Ban associé à Jean de Gastines. Le site était celui d'une ancienne usine textile. Pour Lacaton & Vassal, connus pour leur style minimaliste voire brut, l'objectif essentiel était d'offrir une réelle qualité de logement dans le cadre d'un budget limité. Ils ont commencé par créer « une enveloppe et une structure simples, efficaces et économiques permettant d'obtenir le maximum de volume et de surface au sol, pour des espaces contrastés et surprenants ». Le rez-de-chaussée en béton armé bénéficie d'une hauteur sous plafond de 3 m. Les façades sont largement vitrées et peuvent s'ouvrir. Une serre en acier galvanisé à vitrage en panneaux de polycarbonate a été posée sur cette base – en partie isolée et chauffée – d'autres sections étant utilisées comme jardins d'hiver. La ventilation est facilitée par la possibilité d'ouvrir à moitié la façade largement vitrée. En dépit de cette surprenante solution, les architectes assurent avoir obtenu un confort et un contrôle de température satisfaisants. Chaque appartement s'étend sur tout le volume et se répartit sur deux niveaux.

What appears at first glance to be industrial architecture on the closer inspection affords pleasant, airy spaces. Left page, an aerial view, and, below, a plan of the complex.

Was auf den ersten Blick wie Industriearchitektur wirkt, erweist sich auf den zweiten Blick als angenehm offener Wohnraum. Links eine Luftaufnahme, unten ein Grundriss des Komplexes.

Ce qui semble à première vue une architecture industrielle offre des espaces agréables et aérés quand on y regarde de plus près. Page de gauche, une vue aérienne et ci-dessous, un plan du complexe.

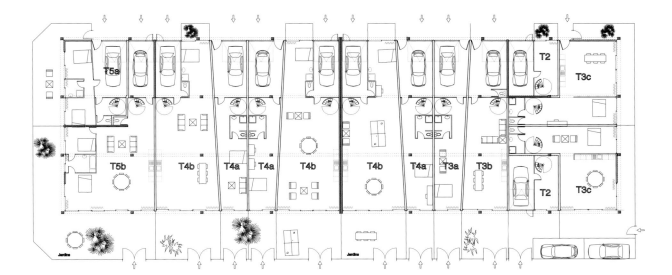

Given the often gray skies of Mulhouse, the ample openings translate into year-round light, which is more than a traditional configuration would have allowed.

Da der Himmel über Mulhouse oft grau ist, bedeutet die großflächige Verglasung ganzjährigen Tageslichteinfall, was traditionelle Konfigurationen nicht erlaubt hätten.

Avec le ciel souvent gris de Mulhouse, les larges ouvertures se traduisent par de la lumière toute l'année, ce qu'une configuration traditionnelle ne permettrait pas.

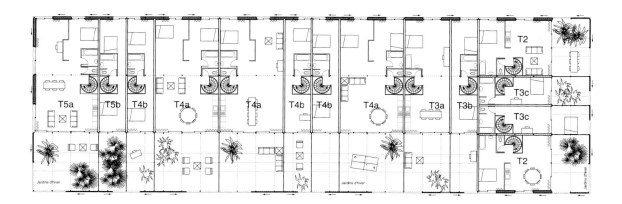

The outdoor terraces feature a re-
tractable shading system. An interior,
such as the one seen here, appears
relatively dark, with light coming
essentially from the terrace.

Die Terrassen wurden mit bewegli-
chen Markisen ausgestattet. Innenräume wie oben im Bild wirken vergleichsweise dunkel: Licht fällt in
erster Linie von der Terrasse ein.

La terrasse est équipée d'un système
d'ombrage rétractable. L'intérieur,
comme ici, semble plutôt sombre car
la lumière vient essentiellement de la
terrasse.

LASSILA HIRVILAMMI ARCHITECTS

Lassila Hirvilammi Architects Ltd.
Hakalankatu 10 B
60100 Seinäjoki
Finland

Tel/Fax: +358 6 4141 225
E-mail: info@lh-ark.fi
Web: www.lassilahirvilammi.fi

LASSILA HIRVILAMMI was founded in Oulu, Finland, in 2001 as Lassila Mannberg Architects. In 2004, the office moved to Seinäjoki, a small town located in southern Ostrobothnia known for the library, Lakeuden Risti Church, and central administrative buildings designed by Alvar Aalto. The office works on a variety of different projects, including churches, office buildings, housing, private residences, interior design, and renovations. The principal is Anssi Lassila, born in 1973; Teemu Hirvilammi was born in 1974. Their work includes the Kärsämäki Church (Kärsämäki, 1999–2004, published here) and the Klaukkala Church and Parish Center (Klaukkala, 2005). Their recent work includes the Frami D-Block, a 7000-square-meter extension to the Seinäjoki Technology Center Frami (a joint venture with architects Lahdelma Mahlamäki Ltd., 2007–09); the Maakunta-aukio housing and commercial building (Seinäjoki, 2005–); and the Kuokkala Church (a joint venture with Luonti Ltd., Jyväskylä, 2005–10), all in Finland.

2001 gründete sich im finnischen Oulu das Architekturbüro Lassila Mannberg Architects, aus dem später **LASSILA HIRVILAMMI** hervorgegangen ist. 2004 zog das Büro nach Seinäjoki, einer kleinen Stadt im südlichen Ostbottnien, die durch ihre von Alvar Aalto entworfenen Gebäude – eine Bibliothek, die Kirche Lakeuden Risti und städtische Verwaltungsgebäude – bekannt geworden ist. Das Büro wird von Anssi Lassila, geboren 1973, geführt; Teemu Hirvilammi wurde 1974 geboren. Zusammen arbeiten sie an einer Vielzahl unterschiedlicher Projekte, darunter Kirchen, Bürogebäude, Wohnanlagen und Privathäuser sowie Innendesign und Renovierungen. Neben der hier vorgestellten neuen Kirche von Kärsämäki (1999–2004) gehören auch eine Kirche und das Gemeindezentrum in Klaukkula (2005) zu ihren Bauten. Zu den neueren Projekten von Lassila und Hirvilammi gehören u. a. der Frami Block D, eine 7000 m² große Erweiterung des Technologiezentrums Frami in Seinäjoki (in Zusammenarbeit mit dem Architekturbüro Lahdelma Mahlamäki Ltd., 2007–09), das Wohn- und Geschäftshaus Maakunta-aukio in Seinäjoki (seit 2005) und die Kuokkala-Kirche in Jyväskylä (in Zusammenarbeit mit Luonti Ltd., 2005–10).

L'agence **LASSILA HIRVILAMMI** a été fondée en 2001 à Oulu, en Finlande, sous la dénomination initiale de Lassila Mannberg Architects. En 2004, elle s'est installée à Seinäjoki, petite ville du Sud de l'Ostrobothnie connue pour sa bibliothèque, l'église de Lakeuden Risti et les bâtiments de l'administration centrale conçus par Alvar Aalto. L'agence travaille sur des projets variés : églises, immeubles de bureaux, logements, résidences privées, architecture intérieure et rénovation. L'agence est dirigée par Anssi Lassila, né en 1973 ; Teemu Hirvilammi est né en 1974. Parmi leurs réalisations, toutes en Finlande : l'église de Kärsämäki (1999–2004, publiée ici) et l'église et centre paroissial de Klaukkala (2005). Ils travaillent actuellement sur le projet de Frami D-Block, une extension de 7000 m² du centre de technologie Frami de Seinäjoki (en collaboration avec les architectes Lahdelma Mahlamäki Ltd., 2007–09) ; l'immeuble de logements et de commerces Maakunta-aukio (Seinäjoki, 2005–) et l'église de Kuokkala (en collaboration avec Luonti Ltd., Jyväskylä, 2005–10).

KÄRSÄMÄKI CHURCH

Kärsämäki, Finland, 1999–2004

Floor area: 200 m²
Client: Parish of Kärsämäki. Cost: €1 million

The first church in the parish of Kärsämäki was completed in 1765 and demolished in 1841. In 1998, the municipality decided to rebuild the old church, without any clear idea of the original appearance of the building. So it was decided, instead, to create a modern building using traditional 18th-century methods, and the project of Lassila Hirvilammi was chosen through a competition. The building has two essential elements, a log "core" and a black tarred and shingle-clad "cloak." The architects have tried "to generate an atmosphere of archaic simplicity and optimal weather resistance." Vestibules, a vestry, and a storeroom are housed in the space between the "cloak" and the church itself. There is no fixed seating in the church and even the altar is movable. There is no electricity or heating in the church either, and lighting during the day is through a skylight, whereas candle lanterns light the space at night. The hand-sawn logs used for the frame were cut in forests owned by the parish and transported partly with the aid of horses. The notched corner joints were carved with axes, handsaws, and chisels. The 50 000 shingles used for roofing and cladding were made of hand-split aspen dipped in tar, just as the 70 000 nails used in the process were hand-forged. Though the goal was to use old methods, the net result is both beautiful and ecologically responsible.

Die 1765 gebaute erste Kirche der Gemeinde Kärsämäki wurde im Jahr 1841 abgerissen. 1998 entschied die Gemeindeverwaltung, die alte Kirche wiederauferstehen zu lassen, allerdings ohne eine genaue Vorstellung davon zu haben, wie das Original genau ausgesehen hat. Daher entschloss man sich, mithilfe traditioneller Baumethoden aus dem 18. Jahrhundert ein neues Gebäude zu errichten. Der über einen Wettbewerb ausgewählte Vorschlag von Lassila Hirvilammi sah zwei wesentliche Bestandteile vor, einen „Kern" aus Holz und eine schwarz geteerte Schindelverkleidung als „Mantel". Dabei haben die Architekten versucht, „eine Atmosphäre von archaischer Einfachheit bei gleichzeitig optimaler Wetterfestigkeit zu erzeugen". Zwischen dem „Mantel" und dem eigentlichen Kirchenraum wurden ein Vestibül, eine Sakristei und ein Lagerraum eingefügt. Im Kirchenraum verzichtete man auf fest installierte Sitzbänke, sogar der Altar lässt sich verschieben. Auch Elektrizität und Heizung gibt es nicht, die Raumbeleuchtung erfolgt tagsüber durch ein Oberlicht und abends mit Kerzenlicht. Die handgesägten Baumstämme für das Tragwerk wurden in gemeindeeigenen Forsten geschlagen und teilweise mithilfe von Pferden transportiert. Die genuteten Verbindungseckpunkte der Planken wurden mit Äxten, Handsägen und Beiteln zurechtgearbeitet. Für die Dachdeckung wurden 50 000 Schindeln per Hand aus Espenholz gespleißt und mit Teer überzogen, und auch die insgesamt 70 000 verwendeten Nägel sind allesamt handgeschmiedet. Ging es zunächst darum, auf alte Baumethoden zurückzugreifen, ist das Gesamtergebnis nun ebenso reizvoll wie umweltbewusst.

La première église de la paroisse de Kärsämäki a été édifiée en 1765 et démolie en 1841. En 1998, la municipalité décida de la reconstruire sans idée précise de l'apparence initiale de l'édifice. On opta pour une construction à l'aide des méthodes traditionnelles du XVIIIᵉ siècle et le projet de Lassila Hirvilammi a été choisi à l'issue d'un concours. Les architectes ont essayé de « susciter une atmosphère de simplicité archaïque et de résistance optimale au passage du temps. » Les vestibules, un vestiaire et une salle de rangement occupent l'espace entre le « manteau » et l'église elle-même. Aucun siège n'est fixe et l'autel lui-même est mobile. L'église n'est ni électrifiée ni chauffée. L'éclairage diurne est assuré par une verrière tandis que des lanternes à chandelles sont utilisées la nuit. Les poutres en bois juste scié qui ont servi à l'ossature proviennent des forêts de la paroisse et ont été en partie transportées à l'aide de chevaux. Les jointures d'angles en encoche ont été travaillées à l'aide de haches, de scies manuelles et de ciseaux. Les 50 000 shingles de la toiture et de parement sont en peuplier fendu à la main, et goudronnés. Les 70 000 clous ont été forgés à la main. Si le but était surtout d'utiliser des méthodes anciennes, le résultat est à la fois superbe et écologique.

The simple shingle siding of the church corresponds to its bucolic natural setting.

Die Außenwandverkleidung der Kirche aus Schindeln passt gut zu ihrem idyllischen Standort in der Natur.

Le parement en simples shingles de l'église répond à son cadre naturel bucolique.

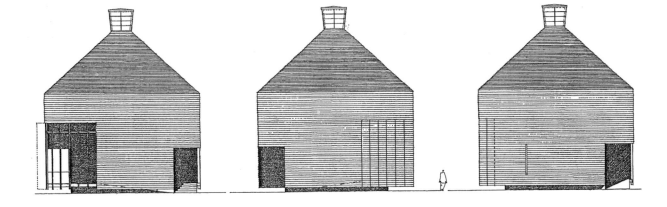

The interior, as simple as and clad in wood like the exterior, offers a soaring space with light coming from openings in the roof.

Das Kircheninnere, ebenso schlicht und wie die Außenseite vollständig mit Holz verschalt, bildet einen hoch aufragenden Raum, der sein Licht durch Öffnungen im Dach erhält.

L'intérieur, aussi simple que l'extérieur et également habillé de bois, n'en offre pas moins un volume élancé. La lumière vient d'ouvertures pratiquées dans la toiture.

The plan of the church is made up of squares, as can be seen from the drawings below.

Wie in den unteren Zeichnungen zu sehen ist, setzt sich der Grundriss der Kirche aus mehreren Quadraten zusammen.

Le plan de l'église se compose de carrés comme le montrent les dessins ci-dessous.

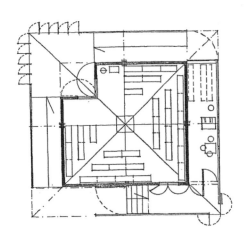
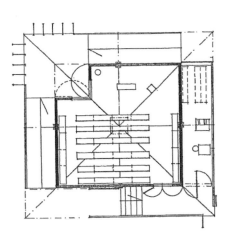
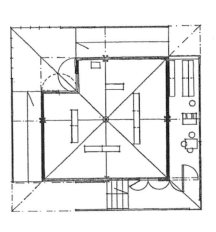

NIC LEHOUX
AND JACQUELINE DARJES

Nic Lehoux Photography
557 West 17th Avenue
Vancouver BC V5Z1T6
Canada

Tel: +1 866 599 2774
E-Mail: nic@niclehoux.com
Web: www.niclehoux.com

NIC LEHOUX was born in 1968 in Quebec, Canada. His presence in this book is unusual in that he does not have a background as an architect, but rather as a photographer, a profession for which he did not receive formal training aside from an apprenticeship. Lehoux has focused more specifically on architectural photography, subsequent to a decision at the age of 19 not to pursue a career as an architect. **JACQUELINE DARJES** was born in 1972 in Regina, Canada. She runs Nic Lehoux Architectural Photography. Lehoux's interest in contemporary architecture has clearly led him to imagine that he could actually build a small house, which he did for the first time, together with Jacqueline Darjes, with the Lilypad (Point Roberts, Washington, USA, 2008–09, published here and photographed by Nic Lehoux).

NIC LEHOUX wurde 1968 in Quebec, Kanada, geboren. Seine Aufnahme in das vorliegende Buch ist ungewöhnlich, da er kein studierter Architekt ist, sondern vielmehr Fotograf, wofür er, außer einer Lehre, auch keine professionelle Ausbildung absolvierte. Lehoux hat sich auf Architekturfotografie spezialisiert, nachdem er im Alter von 19 Jahren beschlossen hatte, auf eine Laufbahn als Architekt zu verzichten. **JACQUELINE DARJES** wurde 1972 in Regina, Kanada, geboren. Sie leitet die Firma Nic Lehoux Architectural Photography. Lehoux war aufgrund seines Interesses an moderner Architektur der Meinung, dass er auch selbst ein kleines Haus bauen könnte: Als erstes Projekt realisierte er, zusammen mit Jacqueline Darjes, das Lilypad (Point Roberts, Washington, USA, 2008–09, hier veröffentlicht mit Fotografien von Nic Lehoux).

NIC LEHOUX est né en 1968 à Québec. Sa présence dans cet ouvrage peut surprendre puisqu'il n'a pas suivi de formation d'architecte mais est photographe, profession pour laquelle il n'a d'ailleurs pas suivi d'enseignement formel en dehors d'un apprentissage. Il s'est plus spécifiquement orienté vers la photographie d'architecture, après avoir renoncé à l'âge de 19 ans à poursuivre des études d'architecte. **JACQUELINE DARJES** est née en 1972 à Regina au Canada. Elle gère le studio Nic Lehoux Architectural Photography. L'intérêt de Lehoux pour l'architecture contemporaine l'a amené à penser qu'il pouvait se construire une petite maison, la Lilypad, ce qu'il a fait avec Jacqueline Darjes (Point Roberts, Washington, 2008–09, publiée ici et photographiée par Nic Lehoux).

THE LILYPAD

Point Roberts, Washington, USA, 2008–09

Address: 936 Claire Lane, Point Roberts, Washington, USA
Area: 24 m². Client: Nic Lehoux and Jacqueline Darjes. Cost: $4500
Collaboration: Jacqueline Darjes (interiors)

The basic structure of this house, set on a forested site amongst 400-year-old Douglas fir trees and western red cedar, measures just 16 square meters, plus an upper loft of eight square meters. It was built entirely by the two designers themselves, off the power grid and wholly of wood, above a 30-square-meter cedar deck lifted off the ground with sonotubes. The idea that this deck "floats" above the earth justifies the **LILYPAD** name. The house has recycled 80-year-old Douglas fir windows. The structure was built between November 2008 and October 2009. Glulam beams that support the upper loft were recovered from a construction site. The interior of this simple but convivial house is whitewashed. The actual construction cost was just $3000 or a total of $4500 including the decking.

Die Grundkonstruktion dieses Hauses auf einem mit 400 Jahre alten Douglastannen und amerikanischen Rotzedern bestandenen Grundstück misst nur 16 m², zuzüglich eines Lofts von 8 m². Der ganze Bau wurde von den Planern selbst errichtet, fern vom Energieversorgungsnetz und nur aus Holz, auf einer 30 m² großen Plattform aus Zedernholz, die auf Sonotube-Baurohren über dem Erdboden steht. Die Vorstellung, dass diese Plattform über der Erde schwebt, rechtfertigt den Namen **LILYPAD** (Seerosenblatt). Für das Haus wurden 80 Jahre alte Fenster aus Douglastanne wiederverwendet. Die Errichtung des Gebäudes dauerte von November 2008 bis Oktober 2009. Die das Loft tragenden, verleimten Holzbalken wurden von einer anderen Baustelle übernommen. Die Innenwände dieses schlichten, aber wohnlichen Hauses sind gekalkt. Die Baukosten betrugen nur 3000 US-Dollar, einschließlich der Plattform 4500 US-Dollar.

Cette petite maison de 16 m² au sol (plus une mezzanine de 8 m²) a été construite au milieu d'une forêt de sapins de Douglas et de cèdres rouges vieux de quatre siècles. Elle a été entièrement réalisée par ses deux concepteurs. À l'écart du réseau d'électricité, elle est totalement en bois, posée sur une terrasse de 30 m² surélevée du sol par des tubes de coffrage de poteaux. L'idée de cette terrasse « flottant » au-dessus du sol éclaire le nom retenu de **LILYPAD** (feuille de nénuphar). Les fenêtres de récupération en pin de Douglas sont vieilles de 80 ans. La construction a duré de novembre 2008 à octobre 2009. Les poutres en lamellé-collé qui soutiennent la mezzanine ont été récupérées sur un chantier. L'intérieur de cette maison simple mais conviviale est blanchi à la chaux. La construction a coûté 3000 $, ou 4500 en comptant la terrasse.

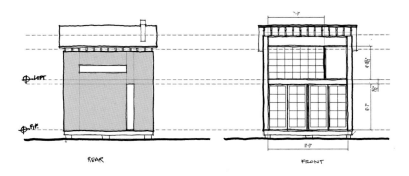

REAR   FRONT

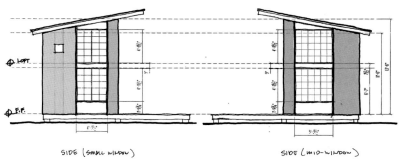

SIDE (SMALL WINDOW)   SIDE (MID-WINDOW)

The elevations above make it clear that the Lilypad is indeed quite small, although the photographer's images show how open the space is.

Die Ansichten oben zeigen, dass das Lilypad wirklich sehr klein ist, auch wenn die Fotos die Offenheit der Räume bezeugen.

Les coupes montrent les faibles dimensions de la Lilypad, même si les photographies accentuent l'ampleur du volume intérieur.

The placement of a bed on an upper mezzanine with the rest of the space open on two levels gives the house a more voluminous feeling than its actual floor area would imply.

Weil das Bett ins obere Zwischengeschoss gestellt wurde, wobei der restliche Raum über die volle Höhe offen geblieben ist, wirkt das Haus geräumiger, als die tatsächliche Flächengröße vermuten ließe.

L'implantation du lit en mezzanine et le reste du volume ouvert sur toute sa hauteur, donnent une impression d'espace plus importante que la surface au sol ne pouvait le laisser penser.

The Lilypad is something of a "do-it-yourself" project since neither of the participants are professional architects.

Lilypad ist eine Art „Do-it-yourself"-Projekt, da keiner der Beteiligten ausgebildeter Architekt ist.

La Lilypad est un peu une maison de bricoleurs puisque ni l'un ni l'autre de ses créateurs n'est architecte.

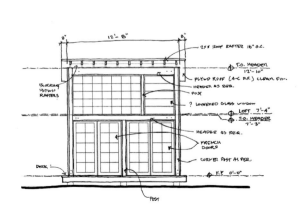

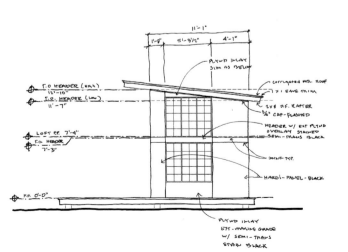

LI XIAODONG

Li Xiaodong Atelier
School of Architecture 224
Beijing 100084
China

Tel: +86 139 0100 9654
Fax: +86 10 6277 0314
E-mail: xd-li@tsinghua.edu.cn
Web: www.lixiaodong.net

LI XIAODONG graduated from the School of Architecture at Tsinghua University in Beijing in 1984 and received his Ph.D. at the School of Architecture, Delft University of Technology (1989–93). He is currently the Chair Professor of the Architecture program at the School of Architecture, Tsinghua University. He is a practicing architect, educator, and researcher on architecture. Li Xiaodong's design ranges from interior architecture to urban spaces. His Yuhu Elementary School and Community Center (Lijiang, China, 2003–04, published here) was widely praised and published and his Bridge School in Xiashi (Fujian, China, 2008–09) was the winner of the 2009 AR Emerging Architecture Award and winner of a 2010 Aga Khan Award for Architecture.

LI XIAODONG schloss sein Architekturstudium 1984 an der Universität Tsinghua in Peking ab und promovierte an der Architekturfakultät der Technischen Universität Delft (1989–93). Gegenwärtig ist er leitender Professor der Studiengangs Architektur an der Universität Tsinghua. Er ist praktizierender Architekt, Lehrer und Wissenschaftler. Li Xiaodongs Entwürfe reichen von Innenarchitektur bis hin zu urbanen Räumen. Großes Lob erntete seine Grundschule mit Gemeindezentrum in Yuhu (Lijiang, China, 2003–04, hier vorgestellt), die weithin publiziert wurde. Seine Brückenschule in Xiashi (Fujian, China, 2008–09) wurde 2009 mit dem AR Award für neue Architektur und 2010 mit einem Aga-Khan-Preis für Architektur ausgezeichnet.

LI XIAODONG, diplômé de l'École d'architecture de l'université Tsinghua à Pékin en 1984 et docteur de l'École d'architecture de l'Université de technologie de Delft (1989–93), est actuellement professeur titulaire du programme d'architecture de l'université Tsinghua. Il est architecte praticien, enseignant et chercheur en architecture. Il intervient aussi bien en architecture intérieure qu'en urbanisme. Son école élémentaire et centre communal de Yuhu (Lijiang, Chine, 2003–04, publiée ici) a été saluée et largement publiée et son école-pont à Xiashi (Fujian, Chine, 2008–09) a remporté le prix 2009 de l'architecture émergeante de l'Architectural Review et un prix Aga Khan pour l'architecture en 2010.

YUHU ELEMENTARY SCHOOL

Lijiang, Yunnan, China, 2003–04

Area: 800 m². Client: Yuhu Village. Cost: $40 000
Collaboration: Yeo Kangshua, Cheong Kenghua, Lim Guanxiong

Located at an altitude of over 2700 meters near the Jade Dragon Snow Mountain, the village of Yuhu is in the Naxi region on northwestern Yunnan Province. A primary school for the village had been built in 2001, but required enlargement. With the help of donations from Singapore, China, and the local government, Li Xiaodong undertook the study and construction of the extension using local materials, techniques, and resources. Intended for 160 students, the facility is divided into three small buildings arranged in a Z pattern around a maple tree. A staircase in reinforced concrete with timber steps is one marked departure from local architectural traditions, but allowed the creation of supplementary classroom areas. A timber-frame structure was designed with local seismic conditions in mind, while local limestone and cobblestones were used extensively. Because of the danger of earthquakes, masonry elements are all non-load bearing. Traditional ornamentation of roof designs are reduced to the simplest possible expression, while retaining something of the spirit of the space.

Das Dorf Yuhu liegt auf einer Höhe von über 2700 m in einem von der Minorität der Naxi bewohnten Gebiet im Nordwesten der Provinz Yunnan, unweit vom Jadedrachen-Schneeberg. Eine 2001 im Dorf gebaute Grundschule musste erweitert werden. Mithilfe von Spenden aus Singapur, China und der Kommunalverwaltung übernahm Li Xiaodong die Planung und Ausführung des Anbaus mit heimischen Materialien, Techniken und Hilfsmitteln. Die für 160 Schüler gedachte Einrichtung ist auf drei kleine Gebäude verteilt, die in Form eines Z um einen Ahornbaum angeordnet sind. Mit einer Treppe aus Stahlbeton mit Holzstufen weicht der Bau von heimischen Architekturtraditionen ab, aber die Treppe ermöglichte die Erschließung weiterer Klassenzimmer. Im Hinblick auf die hier herrschenden seismischen Bedingungen wurde der Bau als Holzrahmenkonstruktion errichtet. Im Übrigen wurde ausgiebiger Gebrauch von heimischem Kalkstein und Kopfsteinen gemacht. Wegen der Erdbebengefahr sind sämtliche gemauerte Elemente nicht tragend. Traditionelle Schmuckelemente oder Dachgestaltungen wurden zwar auf die schlichtest mögliche Form reduziert, bewahren aber dennoch etwas vom Geist der Ortes.

Situé à plus de 2700 m d'altitude de la Montagne de dragon de jade enneigée, le village de Yuhu fait partie de la région de la minorité Naxi, dans le nord-ouest de la province du Yunnan. L'école primaire, construite en 2001, devait être agrandie. Grâce à des donations venues de Singapour, de Chine et de l'administration locale, Li Xiaodong entreprit l'étude et la construction de cette extension en faisant appel aux matériaux, techniques et ressources trouvés sur place. Les installations conçues pour 160 élèves sont divisées en trois petits bâtiments disposés en « Z » autour d'un érable. L'escalier en béton armé à marches de bois, un des seuls écarts avec les traditions architecturales locales, a permis la création de classes supplémentaires. L'ossature en bois a été conçue en pensant aux conditions sismiques de la région et aucun élément en maçonnerie n'est porteur. Le calcaire et les galets locaux ont été abondamment employés. Le style traditionnel des toitures est réduit à plus simple expression, tout en conservant, d'une certaine manière, l'esprit du lieu.

The layout of the school is relatively straightforward (plans below). The juxtaposition of rough wood and stone gives the building a hand-made quality that fits in well with its environment.

Die bauliche Anlage der Schule ist schlicht gehalten (Grundrisse unten). Der Kontrast von unbehandeltem Holz und Felsstein gibt dem Bau eine „handwerkliche" Qualität, die sich selbstverständlich in das Umfeld fügt.

La dispositions des bâtiments de l'école est relativement simple (plans ci-dessous). La juxtaposition de bois brut et de pierre leur confère une qualité de « fait main » qui s'intègre bien à l'environnement.

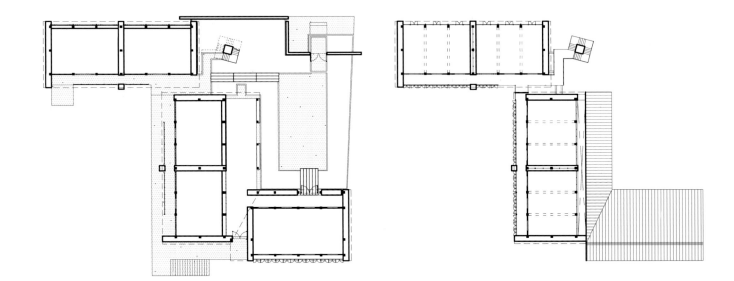

The kind of contrasting, often rough, surfaces seen elsewhere in contemporary Chinese architecture have a different fundamental justification here, namely, that of the extremely remote setting of the school.

Die kontrastierenden, häufig rauen Oberflächen, die man andernorts in der zeitgenössischen Architektur Chinas antrifft, erhalten hier durch die extrem abgelegene Lage der Schule eine grundlegend andere Berechtigung.

Les surfaces brutes et contrastées que l'on observe dans l'architecture contemporaine chinoise prennent ici un sens différent, lié à la situation géographique éloignée de cette école.

Roughly finished wood and stone come together with somewhat more unexpected glazed surfaces opening to the natural setting.

Grob bearbeitetes Holz und Stein treffen auf eher unerwartete verglaste Oberflächen, die sich zur Landschaft der Umgebung öffnen.

Les habillages de bois brut et de pierre encadrent des plans vitrés inattendus, ouverts sur le cadre naturel.

The transition from wood to stone
and then to water creates a tactile
and visual interest which is in keeping with the place and with local
traditions.

*Der Übergang von Holz zu Stein und
Wasser schafft taktile und visuelle
Reize, die harmonisch an die Umgebung und lokale Traditionen anknüp-
fen.*

*Le passage du bois à la pierre, puis à
l'eau, crée un intérêt tactile et visuel
correspondant à l'endroit et aux traditions locales.*

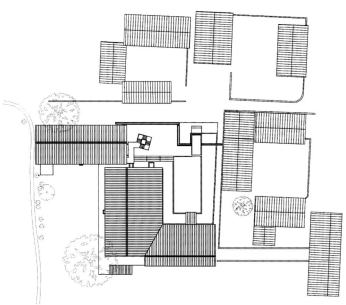

MIII ARCHITECTEN

MIII architecten
Generaal Berenschotlaan 211–213
2283 JM Rijswijk
The Netherlands

Tel: +31 70 394 43 49
Fax: +31 70 394 42 34
E-mail: info@m3architecten.com
Web: www.m3architecten.com

MIII ARCHITECTEN is an architectural design firm created in 1990 in Rijswijk, the Netherlands, and directed by Leendert Steijger, Edwin Smit, and Remko van Buren. Leendert Steijger, born in 1961 in Delft, attended the Faculty of Architecture of the Technical University in Delft (1981–90). He was Assistant Designer at the architectural office of Hoogstad Weeber en Van Tilburg and worked as an architect at KOW architects, before cofounding MIII in 1990. Edwin Smit was born in 1963 in Hoorn. He attended the Faculty of Architecture of the Technical University in Delft (1981–88) and worked in several architectural offices, including Broek & Bakema, before cofounding MIII. Remko van Buren was born in Sittard in 1966, attended the Faculty of Architectural Design at the Academy of Art and Design, St. Joost, Breda (1982–87), and gained experience in the office of Morphosis in Santa Monica, before working in the Netherlands (1987–99). He became a partner of MIII in 1999. Their design of the Quantum Homes gave them the status of pioneers in the area of sustainable building in the Netherlands. Their work includes the Environmental Education Center (Hoorn, 2001–03, published here); a housing project in Zoetermeer (2005); a waterfront restaurant (Capelle aan den IJssel, 2007); the Chess Office Building (Haarlem, 2008); and a district police station (Utrecht, 2008). Current projects are a facility center and hotel at Eindhoven Airport (2009), and housing projects in The Hague and Amsterdam (2009), all in the Netherlands.

MIII ARCHITECTEN ist ein 1990 in Rijswijk in den Niederlanden gegründetes Architekturbüro unter der Leitung von Leendert Steijger, Edwin Smit und Remko van Buren. Leendert Steijger, geboren 1961 in Delft, besuchte von 1981 bis 1990 die Fakultät für Architektur der Technischen Universität Delft. Anschließend war er Assistant-Designer im Architekturbüro Hoogstad Weeber en Van Tilburg. Bevor er 1990 MIII mitgründete, arbeitete er als Architekt bei KOW Architecture. Edwin Smit wurde 1963 in Hoorn geboren. Er studierte Architektur an der Technischen Universität Delft (1981–88) und war in verschiedenen Architekturbüros tätig, darunter auch Broek & Bakema, bevor er MIII mitgründete. Remko van Buren wurde 1966 in Sittard geboren, studierte Architektur an der Akademie für Kunst und Design St. Joost in Breda (1982–87) und arbeitete für Morphosis in Santa Monica, bevor er verschiedentlich in den Niederlanden tätig war (1987–99). 1999 wurde auch er Partner bei MIII. Der Entwurf der Quantum Homes machte MIII in den Niederlanden als Pioniere für nachhaltiges Bauen bekannt. Zu ihren Projekten zählen das Umweltbildungszentrum (Hoorn, 2001–03, hier vorgestellt), eine Wohnanlage in Zoetermeer (2005), ein Restaurant am Meer (Capelle aan den IJssel, 2007), das Bürogebäude Chess (Haarlem, 2008) sowie ein Polizeirevier (Utrecht, 2008). Aktuelle Projekte sind u. a. ein Funktionsgebäude und ein Hotel am Flughafen Eindhoven (2009) sowie Wohnbauprojekte in Den Haag und Amsterdam (2009), alle in den Niederlanden.

MIII ARCHITECTEN est une agence d'architecture créée en 1990 à Rijswijk, Pays-Bas, dirigée par Leendert Steijger, Edwin Smit et Remko van Buren. Leendert Steijger, né en 1961 à Delft a étudié à la faculté d'architecture de l'Université Polytechnique de Delft (1981–90). Il a été concepteur assistant dans l'agence Hoogstad Weeber en Van Tilburg et travaillé comme architecte chez KOW Architects avant de co-fonder MIII en 1990. Edwin Smit, né en 1963 à Hoorn, à étudié à la faculté d'architecture de l'Université Polytechnique de Delft (1981–88) et travaillé dans plusieurs agences, dont Broek & Bakema, avant de cofonder MIII. Remko van Buren, né à Sittard en 1966, a étudié à la faculté d'architecture de l'Académie d'art et de design de St. Joost à Breda (1982–87), et travaillé chez Morphosis à Santa Monica, puis dans plusieurs agences aux Pays-Bas (1987–99). Il est associé de MIII depuis 1999. Leur projet pour les Quantum Homes a fait d'eux des pionniers de la construction durable dans leur pays. Parmi leurs réalisations : le Centre d'éducation environnementale (Hoorn, 2001–03, publié ici) ; un projet d'immeuble de logements à Zoetermeer (2005) ; un restaurant en front de mer (Capelle a/d IJssel, 2007) ; l'immeuble de bureaux Chess (Haarlem, 2008) ; et un commissariat de police de quartier (Utrecht, 2008). Actuellement, ils travaillent sur les projets d'un hôtel et centre de services à l'aéroport d'Eindhoven (2009) et des immeubles de logements à La Haye et à Amsterdam (2009), le tout aux Pays-Bas.

ENVIRONMENTAL EDUCATION CENTER

Hoorn, The Netherlands, 2001–03

*Floor area: 511 m². Client: City of Hoorn
Cost: €500 000*

"For this project," according to the architects, "by order of the local government, the premise was to create a presence close to 'no intervention' in the landscape." Approximately 85% of the building is covered with a thick layer of soil, meaning that it disappears partially, and takes advantage of a particularly efficient form of natural insulation. A single large curved window emerges on one side, where there is a pond, and visitors are invited to observe the underwater habitat. On the opposite side of the structure, a single concrete door is incised into the hill that forms the visible volume of the structure. The architects write: "Ecological considerations affect the design, as well as the positioning of required functions, the technologies used, the building physics, and the choice of materials, in order to establish a coherent presence within the original scenery." In a sense, this is an extreme example of ecological and landscape considerations dictating the form of an architectural realization.

„Die Vorgaben der Kommunalverwaltung für dieses Projekt" hatten es den Architekten zufolge „zur Bedingung gemacht, einen Bau zu schaffen, der so gut wie ‚keinen Eingriff' in die Landschaft darstellte". Rund 85 % des Gebäudes sind mit einer dicken Erdschicht bedeckt, sodass der Bau teilweise verschwindet und zugleich von der besonders effizienten, natürlichen Dämmweise profitiert. Auf einer Seite, zum Teich hin, befindet sich ein großes, gewölbtes Fenster, durch das die Besucher das Leben unter Wasser beobachten können. Auf der gegenüberliegenden Seite des Baus wurde eine einzelne Betontür in den Hügel eingelassen, der das sichtbare Volumen des Gebäudes ausmacht. Die Architekten schreiben: „Einfluss auf den Entwurf hatten sowohl ökologische Überlegungen als auch die Positionierung der erforderlichen Funktionen, die zum Einsatz gebrachte Technik, die Bauphysik sowie die Materialwahl, um eine schlüssige Erscheinung in der ursprünglichen Landschaft gestalten zu können." In gewisser Weise ist dies ein Extrembeispiel dafür, wie ökologische und landschaftliche Überlegungen die formale Gestaltung eines architektonischen Entwurfs diktieren können.

« À la demande de la municipalité, expliquent les architectes, les nouvelles constructions se devaient d'avoir dans le paysage une présence proche de la "non-intervention". » Environ 85 % du bâtiment sont recouverts d'une épaisse couche de terre qui le fait disparaître en partie et assure une forme naturelle et efficace d'isolation. Une grande et unique fenêtre sur un côté donne sur un étang, et les visiteurs sont invités à observer le biotope aquatique. Sur l'autre façade, une unique porte de béton est découpée dans la colline que forme le volume de la structure. « Les considérations écologiques ont influé sur le projet, ainsi que le positionnement des fonctions prédéfinies, les technologies utilisées, les contraintes physiques du bâti et le choix des matériaux afin d'établir une présence cohérente avec le paysage d'origine », précise l'agence. En un sens, il s'agit d'un exemple extrême dans lequel les considérations écologiques et paysagères ont dicté la forme d'une réalisation architecturale.

The form of the building is integrated into the landscape with the rather traditional device of the green roof here functioning as a central part of the architectural design.

Formal wurde der Bau mit einem eher traditionellen Stilmittel in die Landschaft integriert: einem begrünten Dach, das hier integraler Bestandteil des architektonischen Entwurfs ist.

Le centre est comme enveloppé dans le paysage. Le recours assez traditionnel à la couverture végétalisée manifeste l'ambition écologique de ce projet architectural.

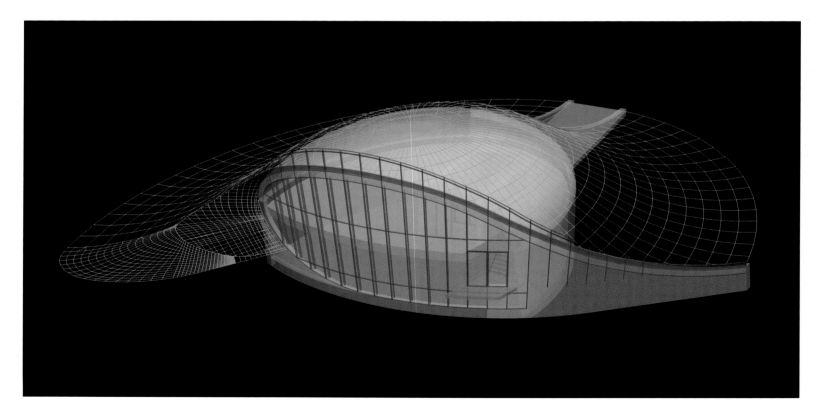

KEN SUNGJIN MIN

SKM Architects
SKM Building
60–15 Samseong-dong, Gangnam-gu
Seoul 135–896
South Korea

Tel: +82 2 543 2027
Fax: +82 2 548 2027
E-mail: skm@skma.com
Web: www.skma.com

KEN SUNGJIN MIN received his B.Arch degree from the University of Southern California, School of Architecture (1989), and his M.Arch in Urban Design (MAUD) from the Harvard GSD (1993). He created SKM Architects in 1996. The recent work of the firm includes the Hilton Namhae Golf and Spa (Nam-myeon, Namhae-gun, 2006); the Kumgang Ananti Golf & Spa Resort (Gangwon-do, North Korea, 2008, published here); Lake Hills Suncheon Country Club (Suncheon, JeollaNam-do, 2008); Asiana Airlines Weihai Point Golf & Resort (Weihai, China, 2009); Asiana Airlines Laolaob Bay Golf & Spa Resort (Saipan, Marianas, USA, 2009); Arumdaun Golf & Spa Resort (Chungcheongnam-do, 2009); Ananti Club Seoul (Gapyeoung-gun, Gyeonggi-do, 2009–10); Cheong Pyeong Village, 70 prestigious single-family houses (Gyeonggi-do, ongoing); and the Anmyeun Island Newtown Master Plan (Chungcheongnam-do, ongoing), all in South Korea unless stated otherwise.

KEN SUNGJIN MIN erwarb seinen B.Arch. an der Architekturfakultät der University of Southern California (1989) und seinen M.Arch. in Stadtplanung (MAUD) an der Harvard GSD (1993). 1996 gründete er sein Büro SKM Architects. Jüngere Projekte des Büros sind u.a. das Hilton Namhae Golf & Spa (Nam-myeon, Namhae-gun, 2006), das Kumgang Ananti Golf & Spa Resort (Gangwon-do, Nordkorea, 2008, hier vorgestellt), der Lake Hills Suncheon Country Club (Suncheon, JeollaNam-do, 2008), das Asiana Airlines Weihai Point Golf & Resort (Weihai, China, 2009), das Asiana Airlines Laolaob Bay Golf & Spa Resort (Saipan, Marianas, USA, 2009), der Arumdaun Golf & Spa Resort (Chungcheongnam-do, 2009), der Ananti Club Seoul (Gapyeoung-gun, Gyeonggi-do, 2009–10), das Cheong Pyeong Village, 70 Luxus-Einfamilienhäuser (Gyeonggi-do, in Planung) und der Masterplan für eine Neustadt auf der Insel Anmyeon (Chungcheongnam-do, in Planung), alle in Südkorea, sofern nicht anders angegeben.

KEN SUNGJIN MIN a obtenu son B.Arch. à l'École d'architecture de l'université de Caroline du Sud (1989) et son M.Arch. en urbanisme (MAUD) à la Harvard GSD (1993). Il a créé SKM Architects en 1996. Les réalisations récentes de l'agence comprennent le golf et spa Hilton Namhae (Nam-myeon, Namhae-gun, 2006) ; la station de golf thermale Kumgang Ananti (Gangwon-do, Corée-du-Nord, 2008, publié ici) ; le club de loisirs Lake Hills Suncheon (Suncheon, JeollaNam-do, 2008) ; la station & golf Asiana Airlines de Weihai Point (Weihai, Chine, 2009) ; la station de golf thermale Asiana Airlines de Laolaob Bay (Saipan, îles Mariannes, États-Unis, 2009) ; la station de golf thermale Arumdaun (Chungcheongnam-do, 2009) ; le club Ananti de Séoul (Gapyeoung-gun, Gyeonggi-do, 2009–10) ; le village Cheong Pyeong de 70 maisons individuelles de prestige (Gyeonggi-do, en cours) et le plan directeur d'une ville nouvelle sur l'île d'Anmyeun (Chungcheongnam-do, en cours), toutes en Corée-du-Sud sauf si spécifié.

KUMGANG ANANTI GOLF & SPA RESORT

Gangwon-do, North Korea, 2008

Address: Kumgang Mountain, Gangwon-do, North Korea,
+52 2 22 61 33 88, www.emersonpacific.co.kr
Area: 13 210 m². Client: Emerson Pacific Group. Cost: $24 million

This rather spectacular structure is surely the first in the Architecture Now! books to be located in North Korea, not generally known for its contemporary architecture.

Der beeindruckende Komplex ist sicherlich der erste Bau in der Buchreihe Architecture Now! in Nordkorea – einem Land, das sonst nicht für moderne Architektur bekannt ist.

Cette réalisation assez spectaculaire est certainement la première construction à paraître dans Architecture Now! qui vienne de Corée-du-Nord, un pays qui ne s'est pas fait remarquer jusque-là pour la qualité de son architecture contemporaine.

The architect makes use of an over-arching roof, as seen in the section below. The overall plan approaches an organic design, combining curves, straight lines, and skewed angles.

Der Architekt entschied sich für ein überhängendes Dach, wie der Schnitt unten zeigt. Der Gesamtplan folgt einer organischen Gestaltung, einer Kombination aus Kurven, geraden Linien und schrägen Winkeln.

L'architecte a dessiné une toiture enveloppante qui s'appuie sur des arcs (coupe ci-dessous). Le plan d'ensemble évoque une approche organique dans sa combinaison de courbes, de lignes droite et d'angles aigus.

Kumgang Mountain is admired in Korea as a beautiful natural location. The architect explains: "The key design issue in the **KUMGANG ANANTI GOLF & SPA RESORT** was the panoramic view created by the well-preserved natural environment. Instead of designing a resort for short-term use, it was designed to uphold the comparison to worldwide resorts when the North and South are unified." The master plan for the site put an emphasis on the preservation of the natural setting and the adaptation of the architecture to the natural topography. The hotels on the site all face Kumgang Mountain; and a skylight on the eastern side of the clubhouse, at the center of the site, and condominium building also face the summit. The use of concrete was minimized and a wooden post-and-beam structure employed. An exterior canopy echoes the interior lobby with its glulam arches.

Die Bergregion Kumgang gilt in Korea als besonders schönes Naturgebiet. Der Architekt erklärt: „Das entscheidende Thema beim **KUMGANG ANANTI GOLF & SPA RESORT** war die Panoramasicht auf diese geschützte, natürliche Umgebung. Wir haben es nicht als Erholungsgebiet für kurzfristige Nutzung geplant, sondern so, dass es einem weltweiten Vergleich standhält, wenn Nord- und Südkorea einmal vereinigt werden." Der Masterplan für das Gelände legte das Schwergewicht auf die Erhaltung der natürlichen Umgebung und die Anpassung der Architektur an die gegebene Topografie. Alle Hotels auf dem Gelände sind zum Berg orientiert, ein Oberlicht an der Ostseite des Klubhauses im Zentrum des Geländes und die Wohnanlage geben auch den Blick auf den Gipfel frei. Ein äußeres Vordach nimmt die Form der Eingangshalle mit Schichtholzbögen auf.

Les monts Kumgang sont considérés en Corée comme un magnifique cadre naturel. Selon l'architecte : « L'enjeu essentiel de la **STATION DE GOLF THERMALE KUMGANG ANANTI** était de conserver la vue panoramique de cet environnement naturel préservé. Au lieu de se contenter d'un *resort* pour séjours de brève durée, le projet a été conçu pour soutenir la comparaison avec les grandes installations touristiques internationales. » Le plan directeur du site met donc l'accent sur la préservation du cadre de la nature et l'adaptation de l'architecture à la topographie. Les hôtels font tous face aux monts Kumgang ainsi que l'immeuble d'appartements et la verrière sur la façade orientale du *club-house*. Le béton reste discret et la structure est à poutres et poteaux de bois. Un auvent à grands arcs de lamellé-collé fait écho à la structure du hall.

The elegant, asymmetrical arch of the dining area seen above allows for fully glazed walls on one side.

Die im Foto oben sichtbare elegante, asymmetrische Wölbung des Speisesaals ermöglichte die geschosshohe Verglasung auf einer Seite.

L'élégant arc asymétrique de la salle à manger (ci-dessus) a permis de créer un mur de façade entièrement vitré.

The laminated arches over the main space, seen to the right and on the left page, give a feeling of considerable space and openness.

Die rechts und auf der linken Seite sichtbaren laminierten Holzbögen über dem großen Raum lassen diesen sehr geräumig und offen erscheinen.

Les arcs en lamellé-collé du hall principal (à droite et page de gauche) créent un sentiment très fort d'ouverture et de volume.

Landscaped pond areas enrich the view from inside the building, while the wooden arches are continued on the exterior to form a canopy.

Landschaftlich gestaltete Bereiche mit Teichen machen den Blick nach draußen interessant. Die hölzernen Bogenbinder setzen sich außerhalb fort und bilden ein schützendes Vordach.

Des bassins paysagés agrémentent la vue à partir de l'intérieur du bâtiment. Les arcs se poursuivent à l'extérieur pour constituer un auvent.

MODUS

MODUS Architects Attia Scagnol
Via Fallmerayer 7
Bressanone 39042
Italy

Tel/Fax: +39 0472 201581
E-mail: info@modusarchitects.com
Web: www.modusarchitects.com

SANDY ATTIA was born in 1974 in Cairo, Egypt. She completed her Bachelor of Arts in Architecture in 1995 at the University of Virginia and her Master in Architecture at the Graduate School of Design at Harvard in 2000. **MATTEO SCAGNOL,** born in 1968 in Trieste, graduated from the University of Venice, IUAV in 1995. Shortly thereafter he worked two years in Naples before attending the Graduate School of Design at Harvard University where he completed a Master in Architecture in 1999 and was recognized as Best Designer of the graduating class. The two architects meet in the United States during their studies at the Graduate School of Design at Harvard University and began their work together in 2000. Their work includes Villa Terzer (Appiano, 2007–09); the Bressanone-Varna Ring road, (Bressanone, 2006–11); working farmhouse complex (Renon, 2010–12); artist's atelier and private residence (Castelrotto, 2010–12); Damiani Holz & Ko Headquarters (Bressanone, 2010–12, published here); elementary school addition and refurbishment (Ora, 2008–13); Brenner highway pedestrian passage (Brennero, 2011–13); and a mountain refuge (Dolomites, 2012–14), all in Italy.

SANDY ATTIA wurde 1974 in Kairo in Ägypten geboren. Sie erlangte ihren B.Arch. 1995 an der University of Virginia und ihren M.Arch. 2000 an der Harvard Graduate School of Design (GSD). **MATTEO SCAGNOL,** 1968 in Triest in Italien geboren, schloss sein Studium 1995 an der IUAV in Venedig ab. Er arbeitete zwei Jahre in Neapel und besuchte im Anschluss die Harvard GSD, wo er 1999 seinen M.Arch. machte und als „Best Designer" seiner Abschlussklasse ausgezeichnet wurde. Die zwei Architekten lernten sich beim Studium an der Harvard GSD kennen und praktizieren seit 2000 gemeinsam. Zu ihren Projekten zählen die Villa Terzer (Appiano, Provinz Bozen, 2007–09), die Umgehungsstraße Bressanone-Varna (Bressanone, Provinz Bozen, 2006–11), ein Hofkomplex (Renon, Provinz Bozen, 2010–12), ein Künstleratelier mit Wohnung (Castelrotto, Provinz Bozen, 2010–12), die Hauptniederlassung Damiani Holz & Ko (Bressanone, Provinz Bozen, 2010–12, hier vorgestellt), Sanierung und Erweiterung einer Grundschule (Ora, Provinz Bozen, 2008–13), ein Fußweg an der Brenner-Autobahn (Brennero, Provinz Bozen, 2011–13) sowie eine Berghütte (Dolomiten, Provinz Bozen, 2012–14), alle in Italien.

SANDY ATTIA est née en 1974 au Caire. Elle a obtenu son B.Arch. en 1995 à l'université de Virginie et son M.Arch. à la Harvard GSD en 2000. Né à Trieste en 1968, **MATTEO SCAGNOL** est diplômé de l'université IUAV de Venise (1995). Il a ensuite travaillé deux ans à Naples, avant de rejoindre la Harvard GSD où il a obtenu un M.Arch. en 1999 et a été couronné « meilleur designer » de sa promotion. Ils se sont rencontrés aux États-unis pendant leurs études à la Harvard GSD et ont commencé à travailler ensemble en 2000. Leurs réalisations comprennent la villa Terzer (Appiano, Bolzano, 2007–09) ; la rocade Bressanone-Varna (Bressanone, Bolzano, 2006–11) ; un complexe fermier (Renon, Bolzano, 2010–12) ; un atelier d'artiste et résidence privée (Castelrotto, Bolzano, 2010–12) ; le siège de Damiani-Holz & Ko (Bressanone, Bolzano, 2010–12, publié ici) ; l'extension et le réaménagement d'une école élémentaire (Ora, Bolzano, 2008–13) ; le passage piéton de la route nationale du Brenner (Brennero, Bolzano, 2011–13) et un refuge de montagne (Dolomites, Bolzano, 2012–14), toutes en Italie.

DAMIANI HOLZ & KO
HEADQUARTERS

Bressanone, Italy, 2010-12

*Area: 225 m². Client: Damiani Holz & Ko
Cost: €2,900,000*

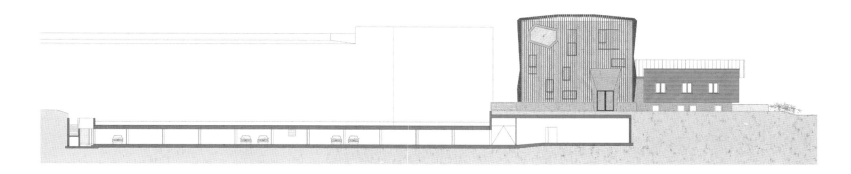

A section drawing shows the long underground parking area near the structure (top left). The sculpted wood form of the main building sits on its concrete base. Its form is neither fully regular nor fully irregular.

Ein Querschnitt zeigt die lange Tiefgarage neben dem Gebäude (oben links). Der skulpturale Holzaufbau ruht auf einem Betonsockel – seine Form ist weder vollkommen regelmäßig noch gänzlich unregelmäßig.

Le schéma en coupe fait apparaître le long parking souterrain qui jouxte la structure (en haut à gauche). La forme de bois sculptée qui constitue le bâtiment principal est posée sur une base de béton. Elle n'est ni parfaitement régulière, ni parfaitement irrégulière.

Unexpected window and door placement add to the ambiguity of the design, making function and internal structure impossible to guess.

Überraschende Platzierungen von Fenster- und Türöffnungen betonen die Mehrdeutigkeit des Entwurfs und machen es unmöglich, Funktion oder Innenaufteilung des Baus zu erraten.

La disposition surprenante de la fenêtre et de la porte ajoute à l'ambiguïté de l'ensemble et rend la fonction et la structure interne impossibles à deviner.

Winners of a 2008 invited competition, the architects undertook the refurbishment of and addition to the existing headquarters of a wood construction company. Since the company "designs and develops building systems in wood and pursues the use of environmentally conscientious wood building products and techniques," the project had to take these factors into account. The completed structure is something of a "showcase" for the methods and products of the firm. The structure has received a KlimaHaus Gold+ certification, the highest standard in energy efficiency and eco-compatible building materials set by the KlimaHaus council of Bolzano. The building is essentially a wooden monolith on a black concrete base. Wooden slats of varying density form a second skin, although the wood structure has load-bearing wall systems. The office addition is a five-story building with underground parking for 40 cars. Different floor designs in wood participate in the varied use of the company's products. All the furniture was custom designed and built with the exception of the chairs.

Nachdem sich die Architekten 2008 in einem geladenen Wettbewerb durchsetzen konnten, folgte die Sanierung und Erweiterung der Hauptniederlassung eines Holzbauunternehmens. Bei einer Firma, die „Holzbausysteme plant und entwickelt und sich auf umweltgerechte Holzbauprodukte und -techniken spezialisiert hat", galt es, entsprechende Faktoren bei der Planung zu berücksichtigen. Der realisierte Bau dient zugleich als Beispiel für die Techniken und Produkte des Unternehmens. Der Bau erhielt das Zertifikat KlimaHaus Gold+, die höchste Auszeichnung für Energieeffizienz und umweltgerechte Baustoffe, vergeben vom KlimaHaus-Gremium in Bozen. Der Bau ist ein Monolith aus Holz über einem schwarzen Betonsockel. Über die tragenden Wände der Holzkonstruktion zieht sich eine zweite Haut aus Holzleisten unterschiedlicher Stärke. Der Büroanbau, ein fünfstöckiger Komplex, verfügt über eine Tiefgarage mit 40 Stellplätzen. Die individuelle Gestaltung der einzelnen Etagen unterstreicht die vielfältige Nutzbarkeit der Holzprodukte der Firma. Alle Möbel mit Ausnahme der Stühle wurden eigens entworfen und gebaut.

Vainqueurs d'un concours organisé par l'entreprise en 2008, les architectes ont eu à réaliser le réaménagement et l'extension du siège d'une société de construction en bois. L'entreprise « crée et développe des systèmes de construction en bois et encourage l'utilisation de produits et techniques de construction en bois écologiquement responsables » et le projet devait tenir compte de ces facteurs. La structure réalisée est pour ainsi dire une « vitrine » des méthodes et produits de l'entreprise. Elle a reçu la certification « KlimaHaus Gold+ », la plus haute note qui récompense l'efficacité énergétique et l'utilisation de matériaux de construction éco-compatibles, décernée par le conseil « KlimaHaus » de Bolzano. Le bâtiment est essentiellement composé d'un bloc monolithique de bois sur une base de béton noir. Des lattes de bois aux densités variables forment une seconde peau – même si la structure en bois présente des systèmes de murs porteurs. L'extension qui abrite des bureaux est un immeuble de cinq étages doté d'un parking souterrain de 40 places. Différents motifs en bois au sol présentent les usages variés des produits du constructeur. Tout le mobilier a été conçu et construit sur mesure, à l'exception des chaises.

In the image above, the building is seen behind stacks of wood produced by the client. The relation between the product and the new structure is evident.

Oben ein Blick auf den Bau hinter Holzstapeln aus der Produktion des Auftraggebers. Die Beziehung zwischen Produkt und Neubau ist offensichtlich.

On voit ci-dessus le bâtiment derrière des piles de bois fourni par le client : la relation entre le produit et la nouvelle structure est évidente.

A closer view of the skin of the building gives it an even more organic appearance, like a living, wooden skin.

Bei näherer Betrachtung wirkt die Gebäudehülle noch organischer, wie eine lebendige, hölzerne Haut.

Une vue rapprochée de l'enveloppe du bâtiment lui donne une apparence encore plus organique, telle une peau de bois vivante.

Below, section drawings show the shed-like design of the building, with its underground area also visible.

Querschnitte (unten) zeigen, dass der Bau wie ein Schuppen entworfen ist. Auch die Ebenen im Untergeschoss sind zu erkennen.

Ci-dessous, les schémas en coupe font apparaître la forme de hangar du bâtiment, la partie souterraine étant elle aussi visible.

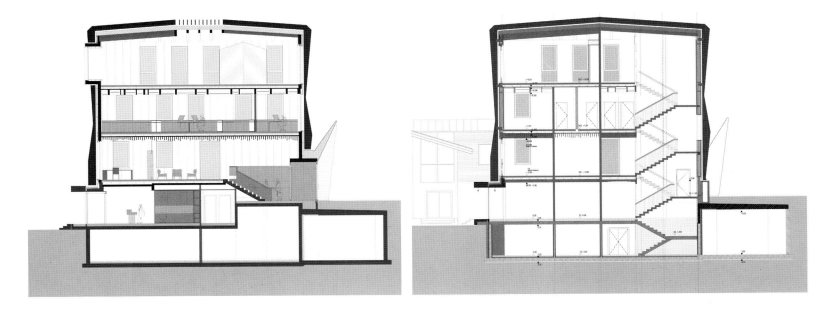

The architects have had the opportunity to give life to the wood design of the building on the interior as well, as seen in the alternation of rectilinear forms with irregular polygons in these ceiling views.

Auch im Innenbau hatten die Architekten Gelegenheit, die Holzkonstruktion lebendig zu gestalten – auf diesen Deckenansichten zu erkennen als Kombination von rechtwinkligen Formen und unregelmäßigen Polygonen.

Les architectes ont pu donner vie à leur création en bois à l'intérieur aussi, comme en témoigne l'alternance de formes rectilignes et de polygones irréguliers sur ces vues du plafond.

Left page, an overall plan shows the new building to the left of the drawing. On this page, the irregular polyhedron roof responds to the tilted window. Below, the large open space is set for a conference.

Ein Plan des Gesamtkomplexes (linke Seite) zeigt links den Neubau. Die unregelmäßige Deckenkassettierung aus Polyedern oben korrespondiert mit dem schiefwinkligen Fenster. Der große offene Raum unten steht für eine Tagung bereit.

À gauche, le plan d'ensemble montre le nouveau bâtiment du côté gauche. Sur cette page, le toit polyédrique irrégulier répond à l'inclinaison des fenêtres. Ci-dessous, le vaste espace ouvert va accueillir une conférence.

MORPHOSIS

Morphosis
3440 Wesley Street
Culver City, CA 90232
USA

Tel: +1 424 258 6200
Fax: +1 424 258 6299
E-mail: studio@morphosis.net
Web: www.morphosis.com

Morphosis principal **THOM MAYNE**, born in Connecticut in 1944, received his B.Arch in 1968 from the University of Southern California, Los Angeles, and his M.Arch degree from Harvard in 1978. He created Morphosis in 1979. He has taught at UCLA, Harvard, Yale, and SCI-Arc, of which he was a founding Board Member. Thom Mayne was the winner of the 2005 Pritzker Prize. Some of the main buildings by Morphosis are the Kate Mantilini Restaurant (Beverly Hills, California, 1986); Cedars-Sinai Comprehensive Cancer Care Center (Beverly Hills, California, 1987); Crawford Residence (Montecito, 1987–92); the Blades Residence (Santa Barbara, California, 1992–97); and International Elementary School (Long Beach, California, 1997–99). More recent work includes the NOAA Satellite Operation Facility in Suitland (Maryland, 2001–05); San Francisco Federal Building (San Francisco, California, 2003–07); 41 Cooper Square (New York, New York, 2006–09); and the Giant Interactive Group Corporate Headquarters (Shanghai, China, 2006–10, published here).They are working on the Museum of Nature and Science (Dallas, Texas) and the Alexandria Bay Port of Entry (Alexandria Bay, New York), all in the USA unless stated otherwise.

THOM MAYNE, Direktor von Morphosis, wurde 1944 in Connecticut geboren. Seine Studien schloss er 1968 mit einem B.Arch. an der University of Southern California, Los Angeles, sowie 1978 mit einem M.Arch. in Harvard ab. 1979 gründete er Morphosis. Mayne lehrte an der UCLA, in Harvard, in Yale und am Sci-Arc, zu dessen Gründungsmitgliedern er zählt. 2005 wurde Mayne mit dem Pritzker-Preis ausgezeichnet. Ausgewählte Bauten von Morphosis sind u.a. Kate Mantilini Restaurant (Beverly Hills, Kalifornien, 1986), Cedars-Sinai Krebsklinik (Beverly Hills, Kalifornien, 1987), Crawford Residence (Montecito, 1987–92), Blades Residence (Santa Barbara, Kalifornien, 1992–97) sowie die International Elementary School (Long Beach, Kalifornien, 1997–99). Jüngere Arbeiten sind u.a. das NOAA-Satellitenzentrum in Suitland (Maryland, 2001–05), das San Francisco Federal Building (2003–07), 41 Cooper Square (New York, 2006–09) und der Hauptsitz der Giant Interactive Group (Schanghai, China, 2006–10, hier vorgestellt). Das Büro arbeitet derzeit an einem Museum für Naturkunde (Dallas, Texas) sowie am Importhafen Alexandria Bay (Alexandria Bay, New York), alle in den USA, sofern nicht anders angegeben.

Directeur de l'agence Morphosis, **THOM MAYNE**, né dans le Connecticut en 1944, est titulaire d'un B.Arch. de l'université de Californie du Sud-Los Angeles (1968) d'un M.Arch. de Harvard (1978), et a fondé l'agence en 1979. Il a enseigné à l'UCLA, Harvard, Yale et SCI-Arc dont il est l'un des fondateurs. Il a reçu le prix Pritzker en 2005. Parmi ses principales réalisations : le restaurant Kate Mantilini (Beverly Hills, Californie, 1986) ; le Centre anticancéreux de Cedars-Sinai (Beverly Hills, Californie, 1987) ; la résidence Crawford (Montecito, Californie, 1987–92) ; la résidence Blades (Santa Barbara, Californie, 1992–97) et l'école élémentaire internationale de Long Beach (Californie, 1997–99). Plus récemment, il a construit le Centre opérationnel de communication par satellites NOAA (Suitland, Maryland, 2001–05) ; le San Francisco Federal Building (San Francisco, 2003–07) ; l'immeuble 41 Cooper Square (New York, 2006–09) et le siège social du Giant Interactive Group (Shanghai, Chine, 2006–10, publié ici). L'agence travaille sur un projet de Musée de la nature et de la science (Dallas, Texas) et le bâtiment de l'Alexandria Bay Port of Entry (Alexandria Bay, New York).

GIANT INTERACTIVE GROUP
CORPORATE HEADQUARTERS

Shanghai, China, 2006–10

*Area: 23 996 m². Client: Giant Interactive Group
Cost: not disclosed*

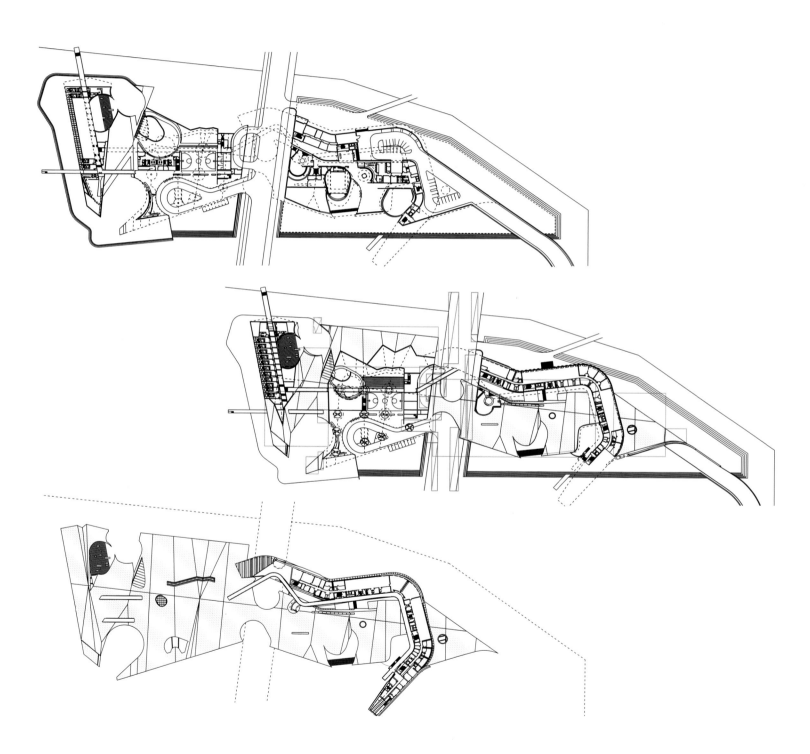

As the plans above and the photos on the right show, the large complex has an intricate form that appears to emerge from the landscaping, creating a natural, flowing feeling of continuity.

Wie Grundrisse (oben) und Aufnahmen (rechts) belegen, scheint die hochkomplexe Anlage geradezu aus der Landschaft herauszuwachsen. Es entsteht der Eindruck eines natürlichen, fließenden Kontinuums.

Comme le montrent les plans ci-dessus et les photos de la page de droite, cette vaste structure à la composition complexe semble émerger du sol dans un mouvement de flux continu.

Built on a 3.2-hectare site, this very large structure includes offices, an exhibition hall, conference rooms, auditorium, library, gymnasium, hotel, clubhouse, and pool. The site includes existing canals and a new man-made lake. According to the architects, the project seeks to join "architecture to landscape and environment to site. The forms of the architecture move in and out of a folded landscape plane." The East Campus building contains open, non-hierarchical office space, private offices, and executive suites, which cantilever over the lake. The landscape is used to house the auditorium, exhibition space, and a café in this area. The West Campus uses the same strategy to insert a pool, sports court, and relaxation and fitness spaces for employees beneath a green roof. The green roof, of course, also has energy-efficiency benefits. A hotel for company guests completes the installation to the west. Outdoor pedestrian walkways and plazas further connect users to the site. The office building has a narrow profile which maximizes the entry of natural light where it is beneficial to users.

Zu dem ungewöhnlich großen Komplex auf einem 3,2 ha großen Grundstück gehören Büroräume, eine Messehalle, Konferenzräume, ein Auditorium, eine Bibliothek, eine Sporthalle, ein Hotel, ein Klubhaus und ein Pool. Zum Gelände gehören außerdem einige ältere Kanäle sowie ein neuer künstlicher See. Den Architekten zufolge soll das Projekt „die Architektur an die Landschaft und das Umfeld an das Grundstück" anbinden. „Die Formen der Architektur schlängeln sich durch die gefaltete Landschaftsebene." Im Ostcampus sind offene, hierarchiefreie Büroflächen untergebracht, private Büros sowie Räume für das gehobene Management, die über den See hinausragen. In diesem Bereich der Landschaft sind auch das Auditorium, die Messehalle und ein Café angesiedelt. Der Westcampus folgt der gleichen Strategie mit einem Schwimmbad, Sporthallen und Entspannungs- sowie Fitnessräume für die Angestellten – alles unter einem begrünten Dach, das zur Energieeffizienz beiträgt. Abgerundet wird der Komplex im Westen durch ein Firmenhotel für Gäste. Fußwege und Plätze in den Außenanlagen schaffen zusätzliche Bindung zwischen Nutzern und Gelände. Das Bürogebäude hat ein schmales Profil, was den Einfall von Tageslicht dort maximiert, wo die Nutzer von ihm profitieren.

Édifié sur un terrain de 3,2 hectares, comprenant des canaux et un lac artificiel, ce vaste complexe regroupe des bureaux, une salle d'exposition, des salles de conférence, un auditorium, une bibliothèque, un gymnase, un hôtel, un club-house et une piscine. Le projet cherche à « lier l'architecture au paysage et l'environnement au site. Les formes architecturales se meuvent comme les plis du sol dans un paysage », expliquent les architectes. Le bâtiment du Campus Est contient des bureaux de plan ouvert non hiérarchisé, des bureaux fermés et des appartements pour la direction en surplomb au-dessus du lac. Dans la même zone se trouvent un auditorium privé, un espace d'exposition et un café. Le Campus Ouest applique une stratégie identique en intègrant une piscine, des terrains de sport et des espaces de relaxation et de remise en forme pour les employés, le tout réuni sous un toit végétalisé qui permet par ailleurs des économies d'énergie. À l'ouest, un hôtel pour les hôtes de l'entreprise complète ces installations. Des allées piétonnières et diverses places offrent des connexions supplémentaires avec le site. Le bâtiment des bureaux est étroit pour optimiser l'éclairage naturel des postes de travail.

The powerful cantilever of the building seen above contrasts with the insertion of other parts of the complex into the earth. The whole assumes the appearance of a kind of quasi-mechanical entity that is nonetheless earthbound.

Die beeindruckende Auskragung des Gebäudeflügels oben ist ein deutlicher Kontrast zu den teilweise in den Boden versenkten Teilen des Komplexes. Die Anlage wirkt fast maschinenhaft, aber dennoch erdverbunden.

Cet imposant porte-à-faux (ci-dessus) contraste avec l'enfoncement dans le sol d'autres bâtiments du complexe. L'ensemble présente un aspect quasi mécanique qui n'en reste pas moins étroitement lié à la terre.

An elevation and photos of the green roofs of the buildings emphasize the way in which it appears to emerge from the site, with its spaces formed at the interstitial point between the natural and the artificial.

Aufriss und Ansichten der begrünten Dächer machen deutlich, wie stark die Bauten aus dem Boden herauszuwachsen scheinen. Es entstehen Räume zwischen Natur und Technik.

Une élévation et des photos des toitures végétalisées font ressortir l'aspect « émergeant » de ce projet dont les volumes se déploient aux intersections du naturel et de l'artificiel.

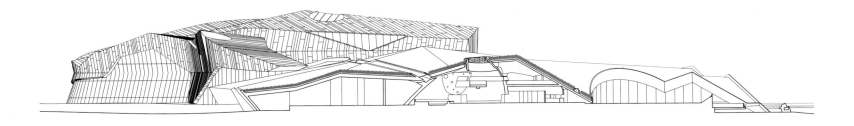

Spectacular curves and unexpected forms characterize both interior and exterior, as seen in these images. Thom Mayne and Morphosis continue to innovate and challenge architectural assumptions.

Innen- wie Außenbau überraschen mit dramatischen Kurven und Formen, wie diese Ansichten belegen. Thom Mayne und Morphosis verstehen es nach wie vor, architektonische Grundannahmen zu hinterfragen und innovativ zu erneuern.

Comme le montrent ces images, l'intérieur et l'extérieur se caractérisent par des courbes aussi spectaculaires qu'inattendues. Thom Mayne et Morphosis poursuivent leur veine innovante et leur remise en question des idées architecturales reçues.

A pool with a large curving window that opens out to the landscaped exterior from which the buildings emerge is visible here, together with elevations showing how the roof in some places dips down to the earth.

Ein Schwimmbad mit einem großen geschwungenen Fenster bietet einen Ausblick auf die Grünanlagen, aus denen die Bauten aufzusteigen scheinen. Aufrisse lassen erkennen, dass das Dach teilweise bis zum Boden hinuntergezogen ist.

Ci-dessus : piscine face à une grande baie de forme libre qui ouvre sur l'environnement paysager d'où émergent les bâtiments. Ci-dessous : élévations montrant la façon dont le toit plonge dans le sol à certains endroits.

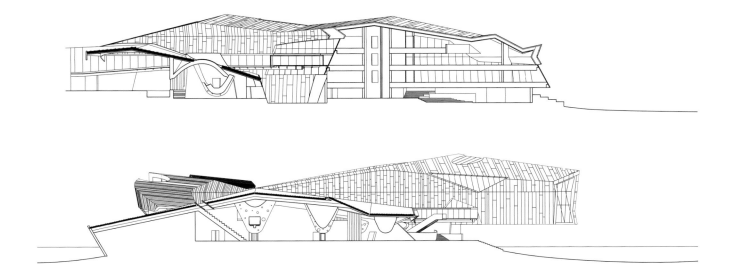

ALBERTO MOZÓ

Alberto Mozó Studio
Padre Letelier 0343
Providencia, Santiago de Chile
Chile

Tel: +56 2 494 1928
E-mail: alberto@mozo.cl

ALBERTO MOZÓ was born in 1963 in New York and emigrated with his family to Santiago de Chile, at the age of seven. After completing college in Santiago, he graduated in 1991 from the Pontificia Universidad Católica de Chile. His first architectural projects involved the creation of interior spaces and the design of furniture for bars. He was thus in the midst of the creation of meeting places for the young generation emerging after Chile's transition to democracy. Simultaneously he worked on the restoration of old houses in Santiago. In 2002 he received an award from the Province Council of Andalucia (Spain) for the rehabilitation of old houses situated in the Ibero-American historic districts. His recent work includes the Schkolnick Photo Studio (Sur Providencia, Santiago, 1999); Yankovic House (Aculeo, Santiago, 2002); Rivadeneira House (Tunquén, Valparaiso, 2004); and the BIP Computer Office and Shop (Providencia, Santiago, 2007, published here), all in Chile.

ALBERTO MOZÓ wurde 1963 in New York geboren und zog im Alter von sieben Jahren nach Santiago de Chile. Nachdem er dort das College absolviert hatte, schloss er 1991 sein Studium an der Pontificia Universidad Católica de Chile ab. Seine ersten architektonischen Projekte waren die Gestaltung von Innenräumen und der Entwurf von Möbeln für Bars. Auf diese Weise war er unmittelbar an der Gestaltung von Treffpunkten für die junge Generation nach Chiles Demokratisierung beteiligt. Gleichzeitig arbeitete er an der Sanierung von Altbauten in Santiago. 2002 wurde er von der Provinzverwaltung in Andalusien für die Renovierung von Altbauten in latein-amerikanischen Altstädten mit einem Preis ausgezeichnet. Zu seinen Projekten zählen das Fotoatelier Schkolnick (Sur Providencia, Santiago, 1999), die Casa Yankovic (Aculeo, Santiago, 2002), die Casa Rivadeneira (Tunquén, Valparaiso, 2004) sowie die Büro- und Ladenräume der Computerfirma BIP (Providencia, Santiago, 2007, hier vorgestellt), alle in Chile.

ALBERTO MOZÓ, né en 1963 à New York, s'est installé avec sa famille à Santiago du Chili quand il avait sept ans. Il est diplômé en architecture de la Pontifica Universidad Católica du Chili (1991). Ses premières commandes ont porté sur la création d'espaces intérieurs et de mobilier pour des bars. Il se trouvait ainsi au centre des lieux de rencontre de cette nouvelle génération apparue après le retour à la démocratie du Chili. Simultanément, il restaurait des maisons anciennes à Santiago. En 2002, il a reçu un prix du Conseil de la province d'Andalousie (Espagne) pour la réhabilitation de vieilles demeures dans les quartiers historiques de villes ibéro-américaines. Parmi ses réalisations récentes : le studio photo Schkolnick (Sur Providencia, Santiago, 1999) ; la maison Yankovic (Aculeo, Santiago, 2002) ; la maison Rivadeneira (Tunquén, Valparaiso, 2004) et les bureaux et boutique de BIP Computer (Providencia, Santiago, 2007, publiés ici), toutes au Chili.

BIP COMPUTER OFFICE AND SHOP

Providencia, Santiago de Chile, Chile, 2007

Floor area: 569 m². Client: Nicolas Moens de Hase. Cost: $450 000
Collaboration: Francisca Cifuentes, Mauricio Leal

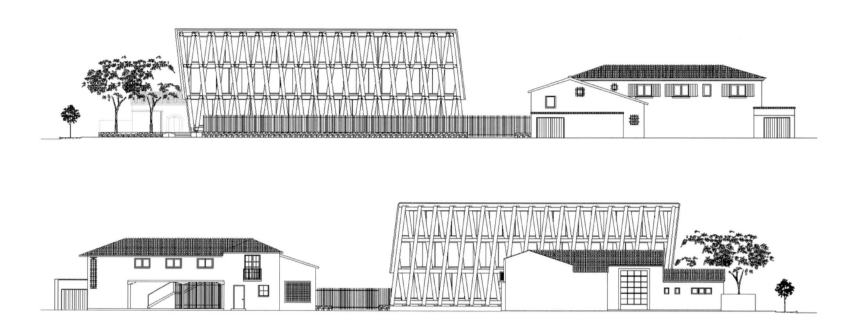

The BIP Computer Office was built between two restored old houses and is three stories high. The architect notes that local zoning regulations encourage a building of 12 stories in this particular location, yet he was determined to make his lower, essentially rectangular, and laminated wood structure easily dismountable. Wood 9 x 34.2 centimeters in size was chosen because it is a standard dimension used in Chile for reasons of efficiency. Mozó explains: "It is important to mention that the wood utilized is an incentive for reforestation, since it is a type of wood that comes from a renewable forest. Wood is the construction material that produces the lowest carbon emissions, a significant factor with respect to global warming." The architect further states that the BIP Building is the combined result of his "vision of the next building generation," which is environmentally friendly, easy to build, transitory, and economically viable.

Das Büro für die Computerfirma BIP wurden zwischen zwei sanierten zweistöckigen Altbauten errichtet und hat drei Stockwerke. Der Architekt weist darauf hin, dass die örtlichen Bebauungspläne sogar bis zu zwölf Etagen zugelassen hätten. Dennoch entschied man sich für eine bedeutend niedrigere, im Grunde rechteckige Konstruktion aus laminiertem Holz, die sich leicht demontieren lässt. Gearbeitet wurde mit 9 x 34,2 cm starken Holzbalken, ein Standardformat in Chile und deshalb besonders effizient. Mozó erklärt: „Es ist wichtig zu erwähnen, dass das gewählte Bauholz zugleich ein Anreiz zur Wiederaufforstung ist, da es aus einem nachhaltig bewirtschafteten Waldgebiet stammt. Holz ist das Baumaterial mit den geringsten CO_2-Emissionen, ein signifikanter Faktor im Hinblick auf die Erderwärmung." Darüber hinaus ist das BIP-Gebäude nach Aussage des Architekten Ergebnis seiner „Vision für Gebäude der nächsten Generation" – umweltfreundlich in der Konstruktion, temporär und wirtschaftlich.

L'immeuble de deux étages de BIP Computers a été construit entre deux maisons anciennes restaurées. Les architectes font remarquer que la réglementation de zonage locale encourageait la construction de 12 niveaux et qu'ils ont décidé de faire en sorte que cette structure rectangulaire en bois lamellé soit facilement démontable. Des poutres de bois de 9 x 34,2 cm de section ont été choisies car il s'agit d'une dimension standard utilisée par l'industrie du bois chilienne pour des raisons d'efficacité. Alberto Mozó explique qu'« il est important de mentionner que le bois utilisé encourage la reforestation puisque qu'il provient d'une forêt gérée écologiquement. Le bois est le matériau de construction au plus faible taux d'émissions de carbone, facteur important pour lutter contre le réchauffement global ». Cet immeuble, ajoute-t-il, est le résultat « de sa vision d'une nouvelle génération de constructions » qui sera respectueuse de l'environnement, facile à construire, transitoire et économiquement viable.

Contrary to many buildings, this office and shop is designed to be easily dismounted, a fact that contributes in a fundamental manner to its green credentials.

Anders als viele Bauten wurde dieses Bürohaus mit Ladengeschäft so entworfen, dass es leicht demontiert werden kann, ein Aspekt, der wesentlich zu seinem grünen Profil beiträgt.

Contrairement à de nombreuses réalisations, cet ensemble bureaux/ magasin a été conçu pour être facilement démontable, ce qui contribue de manière fondamentale à la qualité de son impact environnemental.

Stacked wood stairs and a volume that makes the building fit into its environment, where it might have been as many as 12 stories high, are part of its respectful design.

Bestandteil des umsichtigen Designs sind u. a. eine Treppe aus gestapelten Holzbohlen und der Baukörper selbst. Er wurde seinem Umfeld angepasst, obwohl er theoretisch bis zu 12 Geschosse hoch sein dürfte.

L'escalier fait de lourdes marches de bois empilées et le volume adapté à l'échelle du quartier (alors qu'il aurait pu compter jusqu'à 11 étages), font partie intégrante d'une approche respectueuse de l'environnement.

Wooden beams and columns are repetitive but animated, in the case of the columns, by their diagonal placement. The interior space is high and bright.

Träger und Stützen aus Holz sind regelmäßig angeordnet und wirken dennoch aufgelockert – im Fall der Stützen dank ihrer diagonalen Positionierung. Der Innenraum ist hoch und hell.

La disposition répétitive des poutres et des piliers de bois est animée, dans le cas des colonnes, par leur pose croisée. Le lumineux volume intérieur bénéficie d'une grande hauteur sous plafond.

NERI & HU

Neri & Hu Design and Research Office
88 Yuqing Road
Shanghai 200030
China

Tel: +86 21 6082 3777
Fax: +86 21 6082 3778
E-mail: info@nhdro.com
Web: www.nhdro.com

LYNDON NERI received his B.Arch degree from the University of California (Berkeley, 1987) and his M.Arch degree from Harvard (1992). He worked in the offices of Steven Harris (New York, 1992) and Michael Graves (Princeton, 1993–2003), before founding Design Republic (Shanghai, 2006) and Neri & Hu (Shanghai, 2004). **ROSSANA HU** also studied at the University of California (Berkeley, B.Arch, 1990) and then received a Master of Architecture and Urban Planning at Princeton (1995). After working with Skidmore, Owings & Merrill (New York, 1993) and Michael Graves (1996–99), she cofounded Design Republic and Neri & Hu with Lyndon Neri. The Waterhouse at South Bund (Shanghai, China, 2010, published here) is a recent project.

LYNDON NERI machte seinen B.Arch. an der University of California (Berkeley, 1987) und seinen M.Arch. in Harvard (1992). Er arbeitete in den Büros von Steven Harris (New York, 1992) und Michael Graves (Princeton, 1993–2003), bevor er Design Republic (Schanghai, 2006) und Neri & Hu (Schanghai, 2004) gründete. Auch **ROSSANA HU** studierte an der University of California (Berkeley, B.Arch. 1990) und erlangte ihren Master in Architektur und Stadtplanung in Princeton (1995). Nachdem sie für Skidmore, Owings & Merrill (New York, 1993) und Michael Graves (1996–99) gearbeitet hatte, gründete sie mit Lyndon Neri die Büros Design Republic und Neri & Hu. Das Waterhouse in South Bund (Schanghai, 2010, hier vorgestellt) ist ein aktuelles Projekt.

LYNDON NERI a obtenu son B.Arch. à l'université de Californie (Berkeley, 1987) et son M.Arch. à Harvard (1992). Il a travaillé dans les agences de Steven Harris (New York, 1992) et de Michael Graves (Princeton, 1993–2003) avant de fonder Design Republic (Shanghai, 2006) et Neri & Hu (Shanghai, 2004). **ROSSANA HU**, qui a également fait ses études à l'université de Californie (Berkeley, B.Arch. 1990), a passé son mastère en architecture et urbanisme à Princeton (1995). Après avoir travaillé pour Skidmore, Owings & Merrill (New York, 1993) et Michael Graves (1996–99), elle a fondé Design Republic et Neri & Hu avec Lyndon Neri. Ils ont récemment réalisé l'hôtel Waterhouse at South Bund (Shanghai, 2010, publié ici).

THE WATERHOUSE AT SOUTH BUND

Shanghai, China, 2010

Address: Maojiayuan Road No. 1–3, Zhongshan Road South, Huangpu District, Shanghai 200011,
China, +86 21 6080 2988, www.waterhouseshanghai.com
Area: 2800 m². Client: Cameron Holdings Hotel Management Limited. Cost: not disclosed
Collaboration: Debby Haepers, Cai Chun Yan, Markus Stoecklein, Jane Wang

This unusual four-story 19-room boutique hotel was created in the remains of a three-story Japanese Army headquarters building dating from the 1930s. It is part of the Cool Docks development area in the South Bund District. Additions built over the old concrete building were made using Cor-ten steel, a homage on the part of the architects to the industrial nature of the shipping activity on the neighboring Huangpu River. Inside, their design relies on "a blurring and inversion of the interior and exterior, as well as between the public and private realms." Peeks into private rooms from the public spaces or from rooms to the public areas are amongst the surprises created by Neri & Hu. Furnishings, also selected by the designers, include custom pieces, antiques, and items from Moooi, Magis, and Emeco, as well as Tom Dixon lights.

Das ungewöhnliche Boutique-Hotel mit vier Stockwerken und 19 Zimmern wurde in die baulichen Überreste eines dreistöckigen Hauptquartiers der japanischen Armee aus den 1930er-Jahren integriert. Das Hotel entstand im Zuge der Erschließung der sogenannten Cool Docks im Stadtteil South Bund. Anbauten an den Altbau aus Beton wurden aus Corten-Stahl realisiert: Eine Hommage der Architekten an den Schiffsverkehr auf dem nahe gelegenen Huangpu Jiang. Im Innern entfaltet das Design besonders durch „das Verschwimmen und die Umkehrung der Grenzen von innen und außen, sowie von öffentlichen und privaten Bereichen" seine Wirkung. Einige der Überraschungen, mit denen Neri & Hu aufwarten, sind Einblicke in private Räume aus den öffentlichen Bereichen bzw. aus den Zimmern in die öffentlichen Bereiche. Die ebenfalls von den Architekten ausgewählte Innenausstattung umfasst sowohl Maßanfertigungen als auch Antiquitäten und Objekte von Moooi, Magis und Emeco sowie Leuchten von Tom Dixon.

Ce curieux « hôtel-boutique » de 19 chambres sur quatre niveaux occupe les anciens locaux de l'état-major de l'armée japonaise dans les années 1930, inclus dans l'opération de rénovation urbaine des Cool Docks du quartier sud du Bund. Des extensions en acier Corten ont été ajoutées à l'ancien bâtiment en béton, en rappel des chantiers de construction navale du fleuve Huangpu tout proche. À l'intérieur, le projet repose sur « une confusion et une inversion de l'intérieur et de l'extérieur, des parties privatives et parties publiques ». On y découvre des surprises comme des perspectives sur l'intérieur des chambres à partir des circulations, ou le contraire. Le mobilier, choisi par les architectes, comprend des meubles spécialement réalisés pour le projet, des meubles anciens et des créations de Moooi, Magis, Emeco et Tom Dixon pour les luminaires.

Visitors to Shanghai know that next to its sleek modern towers a good number of older buildings, with a kind of patina of the past, do remain in some areas. The architects here have played on this presence of the relatively recent past.

Wer Schanghai kennt, weiß, dass neben den glatten modernen Hochhausbauten in manchen Gegenden auch eine Reihe alter Gebäude erhalten sind, an denen noch die Patina früherer Zeiten haftet. Die Architekten spielen mit diesen Überbleibseln der vergleichsweise jungen Vergangenheit.

Les visiteurs de Shanghai savent qu'au pied de ses innombrables tours subsiste dans certains quartiers un grand nombre de bâtiments anciens marqués par la patine du temps. Les architectes ont joué ici de la présence d'un passé relativement récent.

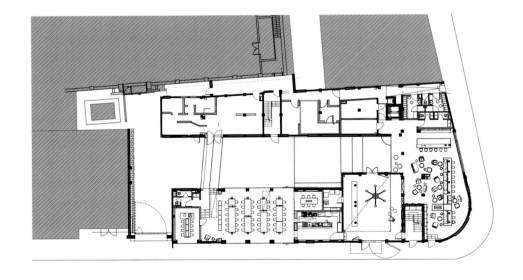

Rough, almost untreated surfaces are contrasted with a decided sense of trendy elegance in these images. To the right, the reception area (seen from the opposite side, above), and below, a section drawing of the hotel.

Raue, fast unbehandelte Oberflächen bilden auf diesen Aufnahmen ein Kontrastprogramm zur trendbewussten Eleganz des Baus. Rechts der Empfangsbereich (oben links aus einer anderen Perspektive), unten ein Querschnitt des Hotels.

Les surfaces non traitées, quasiment brutes, contrastent avec l'élégance tendance voulue de certains aménagements. À droite, la réception (vue ci-dessus de la perspective opposée) et ci-dessous, une coupe de l'hôtel.

Rough wood tables recall the atmosphere of the exterior of the hotel or its entrance lobby area, but the décor here tends toward more overt sophistication.

Tische aus grobem Holz knüpfen an die Atmosphäre des Außenbaus und den Eingangsbereich bzw. die Lobby an. Insgesamt ist die Ausstattung jedoch deutlich gehoben.

Les tables en bois brut rappellent l'atmosphère de l'extérieur de l'hôtel et de sa réception, même si le décor fait ici preuve d'une plus grande sophistication.

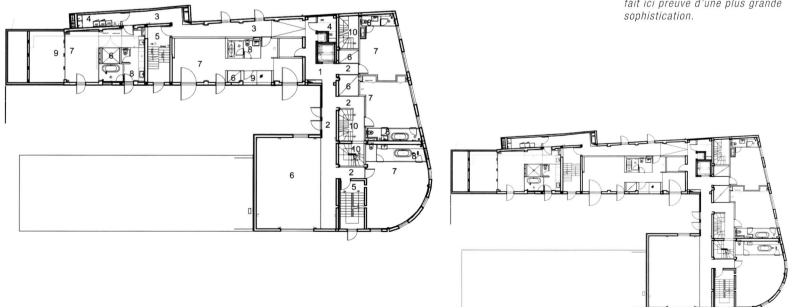

Guest rooms offer all of the comforts to which visitors to this type of hotel are accustomed. Surfaces alternate between opacity and transparency, or roughness and smoothness.

Die Zimmer bieten jeden Komfort, den Gäste von Hotels dieser Klasse erwarten. Die Oberflächen sind wechselweise opak oder transparent, rau oder glatt.

Les chambres offrent le confort auquel la clientèle de ce type d'hôtel est habituée. On observe l'alternance de plans opaques et transparents, lisses ou bruts.

VICTOR NEVES

*Victor Neves – Arquitectura e Urbanismo, Lda
Rua Das Trinas, N° 48–RC/ e 2°
1200–859 Lisbon
Portugal*

*Tel: +351 21 395 16 97
Fax: +351 21 395 59 61
E-mail: victneves@sapo.pt
Web: www.victorneves.com*

VICTOR NEVES was born in 1956 in Lisbon, Portugal. He obtained his doctorate at the ETSAB-UPC (Escuela Técnica Superior de Arquitectura de Barcelona Universidad – Politécnica de Cataluña, Spain). He is a Professor at the Faculty of Architecture of the Lusíada University (Lisbon). He created his own office Victor Neves – Arquitectura e Urbanismo, Lda in 1985. His work includes the Vale Flores Primary School (Feijó, Almada, 2000); a house in Cacela-a-Velha (2003); and the reorganization of the Esposende riverside (Esposende, 2006–07, published here). More recently, he has participated in competitions for a new psychiatric hospital (with Proconsultores and Cândido Gomes; Bejaia, Algeria, 2008); the redesign of the seafront of Pedra Alta (in collaboration with the architect Victor Mogadouro and landscape designer Francisca Pinto da Costa; northern Portugal, 2009); and a riverfront design for Caminha (also in collaboration with Francisca Pinto da Costa, Portugal, 2010).

VICTOR NEVES wurde 1956 in Lissabon, Portugal, geboren. Er promovierte an der ETSAB-UPC (Escuela Técnica Superior de Arquitectura de Barcelona/Universidad Politécnica de Cataluña, Spanien). Er ist Professor an der Architekturfakultät der Universität Lusíada in Lissabon. 1985 gründete er sein eigenes Büro Victor Neves – Arquitectura e Urbanismo, Lda. Zu seinen Arbeiten zählen die Grundschule Vale Flores (Feijó, Almada, 2000), ein privates Wohnhaus in Cacela-a-Velha (2003) und die Neugestaltung des Flussufers bei Esposende (Esposende, 2006–07, hier vorgestellt). Außerdem hat er an Wettbewerben teilgenommen, wie z. B. für den Neubau eines psychiatrischen Krankenhauses (mit dem Büro Proconsultores und Cândido Gomes, in Bejaia, Algerien, 2008), die Neugestaltung der Meeresküste von Pedra Alta (mit dem Architekten Victor Mogadouro und der Landschaftsplanerin Francisca Pinto da Costa, Nordportugal, 2009) sowie den Entwurf für das Flussufer in Caminha (ebenfalls mit Francisca Pinto da Costa, 2010). Alle Projekte befinden sich in Portugal, sofern nicht anders vermerkt.

VICTOR NEVES, né en 1956 à Lisbonne, est titulaire d'un doctorat en architecture de l'ETSAB-UPC (École supérieure technique d'architecture de l'université de Barcelone – Politécnica de Cataluña, Espagne). Il est professeur à la faculté d'architecture de l'université Lusíada (Lisbonne) et a créé l'agence Victor Neves, Arquitectura e Urbanismo, Lda, en 1985. Parmi ses réalisations : l'école primaire de Vale Flores (Feijó, Almada, 2000) ; une maison à Cacela-a-Velha (2003) ; la restructuration des berges à Esposende (2006–07, publié ici). Plus récemment, il a participé à des concours pour un nouvel hôpital psychiatrique (avec Proconsultores et Cândido Gomes, Bejaia, Algérie, 2008) ; la rénovation du front de mer de Pedra Alta (en collaboration avec l'architecte Victor Mogadouro et l'architecte paysagiste Francisca Pinto da Costa (nord du Portugal, 2009) et un projet de front de mer pour Caminha (également en collaboration avec Francisca Pinto da Costa, 2010), tous ces projets étant situés au Portugal, sauf mention contraire.

REORGANIZATION OF THE RIVERSIDE
OF ESPOSENDE

Esposende, Portugal, 2006–07

Address: Av. Eduardo Arantes, Esposende, Portugal. Area: 25 500 m²
Client: Câmara Municipal de Esposende and Instituto Marítimo-Portuário. Cost: €1.7 million
Collaboration: João Nunes (PROAP), Nuno Mota,
Joana Barreto, and Mafalda Meirinho (Landscape Architecture)

Esposende is a small village located in the north of Portugal. The project consisted essentially in the reorganization of the urban area, bordered by a riverside, in order to create a public leisure area, surrounded by several buildings related to nautical activities. The project originally included a number of five-meter glass cubes housing visitor information facilities, not erected for financial and regulatory reasons. The architect states: "The concept behind the whole proposal is to give priority to the natural landscape, denying the artificiality of formal excesses of the 'design' and also denying the profusion of materials often exhibited in recent urban interventions," and to increase awareness and knowledge of local flora and fauna.

Esposende ist ein kleines Dorf im Norden Portugals. Bei dem Projekt ging es vor allem um die Neugestaltung des Siedlungsbereiches, der an den Fluss grenzt. Hier sollte ein öffentliches Erholungsgebiet entstehen, das von Gebäuden gerahmt wird, die mit nautischen Aktivitäten verbunden sind. Ursprünglich war vorgesehen, hier auch mehrere 5 x 5 m große Glaskuben aufzustellen, in denen u. a. eine Touristeninformation untergebracht werden sollte. Dies wurde aus Kostengründen und aufgrund der geltenden Bauvorschriften nicht realisiert. Der Architekt kommentiert sein Projekt wie folgt: „Das Konzept des Gesamtentwurfs gründet sich auf den Anspruch, der Naturlandschaft Priorität einzuräumen und sich jeder Form der Künstlichkeit zu verweigern, die die formalen Exzesse des ‚Designs' mit sich bringen, ebenso die Materialschlacht zu vermeiden, wie sie leider so häufig bei neueren städtebaulichen Maßnahmen zu beobachten ist." Ziel ist es, die lokale Flora und Fauna ins Bewusstsein der Menschen zu rücken und Wissen darüber zu vermitteln.

Esposende est un petit village du nord du Portugal. Le projet consistait essentiellement à restructurer la zone urbaine en bordure de rivière pour créer une aire publique de loisirs entourée de quelques bâtiments affectés aux activités nautiques. Il comportait à l'origine un certain nombre de constructions en forme de cubes de verre de 5 m, abritant divers services d'information pour les visiteurs, qui n'ont pas été réalisées pour des raisons financières et réglementaires. «Le concept de l'ensemble de cette proposition est de donner la priorité au paysage naturel, en rejetant l'aspect artificiel des excès de "design" et la profusion de matériaux que l'on trouve souvent dans les interventions urbaines récentes», explique l'architecte. Le projet encourage les passants à prendre conscience de la flore et de la faune locales, et à mieux les connaître.

The architect has intentionally made his interventions minimal, not only for cost reasons, but also in a spirit of rejection of what he sees as the excessive nature of other similar projects in other locations.

Der Architekt hat seine Eingriffe mit Absicht auf ein Minimum beschränkt. Dies geschah nicht nur aus Kostengründen, sondern auch aus einer gewissen Ablehnung übertriebenen Designs, wie man es oft bei ähnlichen Projekten findet.

L'intervention de l'architecte est restée volontairement minimale, non seulement pour des raisons de coût, mais aussi pour marquer sa désapprobation des excès d'aménagements que provoque parfois ce type d'intervention.

With its light walkway set just off the river banks, the design makes the economy of means into a visible virtue, allowing walkers to discover their own town from an entirely different angle.

Mit diesem leichten Steg, der nah am Flussufer entlangführt, wird der sparsame Einsatz der Mittel zu einer sichtbaren Tugend, können doch die Fußgänger ihre Stadt von hier aus einem völlig neuen Blickwinkel betrachten.

Grâce à cette allée suspendue à quelques mètres de la rive, ce projet qui fait de l'économie de moyens une vertu permet aux promeneurs de découvrir leur ville sous un angle entièrement différent.

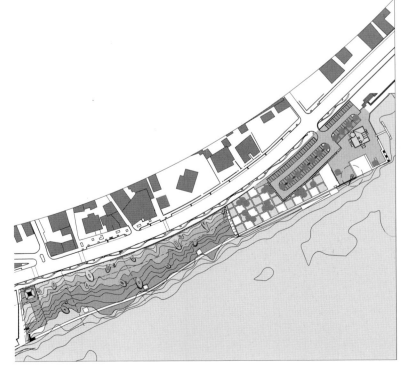

NIKKEN SEKKEI

Nikken Sekkei Ltd.
2-18-3 Iidabashi
Chiyoda-ku, Tokyo
102-8117 Japan

Tel: +81 3 6893 3055
Fax: +81 3 5226 3052
E-mail: global@nikken.co.jp
Web: www.nikken.co.jp

Nikken Sekkei started its existence at the turn of the 20th century as a group of 29 architects formed for the construction of a new library in Osaka. In 1964, they became the first architectural practice in Japan to use computers. The firm today has over 2,500 employees and projects in 40 countries. Their headquarters are in Tokyo, with foreign branch offices in Shanghai, Dalian, Dubai, Hanoi, Ho Chi Minh City, and Seoul. **TOMOHIKO YAMANASHI**, the designer of the Sony City Osaki Building (Tokyo, 2011, published here) is presently Executive Officer and principal-in-charge of Nikken Sekkei. He was born in 1960 in Kanagawa Prefecture, and graduated in 1984 from the Tokyo National University of Fine Arts and Music. In 1986, he completed a Master's degree in Engineering at the University of Tokyo and began his career at Nikken Sekkei. His notable buildings include the Sumitomo Mitsui Banking Corporation Headquarters (Tokyo, 2010); Hoki Museum (Chiba, 2010); Nomura Kougei Headquarters (Tokyo, 2007) and the Jimbo-Cho Theater Building (Tokyo, 2007). Tomohiko Yamanashi won the 2011 Grand Prix of The Japan Institute of Architects for the Hoki Museum.

Nikken Sekkei wurde Anfang des 20. Jahrhunderts ins Leben gerufen, als sich eine Gruppe von 29 Architekten zum Bau einer neuen Bibliothek in Osaka zusammenschloss. 1964 begann das Architekturbüro als erstes landesweit, mit Computern zu arbeiten. Heute hat das Büro 2500 Mitarbeiter und betreut Projekte in 40 Ländern. Neben der Zentrale in Tokio unterhält es Dependancen in Schanghai, Dalian, Dubai, Hanoi, Ho Chi Minh City und Seoul. **TOMOHIKO YAMANASHI,** verantwortlich für den Entwurf des Sony City Osaki Building (Tokio, 2011, hier vorgestellt), ist derzeit Geschäftsführender Direktor bei Nikken Sekkei. Er wurde 1960 in der Präfektur Kanagawa geboren und schloss sein Studium 1984 an der Nationaluniversität Tokio für Kunst und Musik ab. 1986 machte er einen Master in Bauingenieurwesen an der Universität Tokio und begann seine Laufbahn bei Nikken Sekkei. Zu seinen wichtigsten Bauten zählen die Zentrale von Nomura Kougei (Tokio, 2007), das Jimbo-Cho-Theater (Tokio, 2007), die Hauptniederlassung der Sumitomo Mitsui Banking Corporation (Tokio, 2010) sowie das Museum Hoki (Chiba, 2010). 2011 wurde Tomohiko Yamanashi für das Museum Hoki mit dem Grand Prix des Japan Institute of Architects ausgezeichnet.

Nikken Sekkei a commencé sa carrière au tournant du XXe siècle dans un groupe de 29 architectes constitué pour la construction d'une nouvelle bibliothèque à Osaka. En 1964, ils sont devenus la première agence japonaise à travailler avec des ordinateurs. Aujourd'hui, la société compte plus de 2500 employés et des projets dans 40 pays. Le siège est Tokyo, avec des bureaux étrangers à Shanghai, Dalian, Dubaï, Hanoi, Ho Chi Minh-Ville et Séoul. **TOMOHIKO YAMANASHI**, l'auteur de l'immeuble Sony City Osaki (Tokyo, 2011, publié ici), est actuellement directeur administratif et principal responsable de Nikken Sekkei. Il est né en 1960 dans la préfecture de Kanagawa et a obtenu son diplôme de l'université nationale des beaux-arts et de musique de Tokyo en 1984. Il a ensuite passé un master en ingénierie en 1986 à l'université de Tokyo et a débuté sa carrière à Nikken Sekkei. Ses constructions les plus notables comprennent le siège de la société bancaire Sumitomo Mitsui (Tokyo, 2010) ; le musée Hoki (Chiba, 2010) ; le siège de Nomura Kougei (Tokyo, 2007) et le théâtre Jimbo-Cho (Tokyo, 2007). En 2011, Tomohiko Yamanashi a remporté le grand prix de l'Institut japonais des architectes pour le musée Hoki.

SONY CITY OSAKI

Tokyo, Japan, 2009–11

Area: 124,041 m². Client: Sony Corporation
Cost: not disclosed

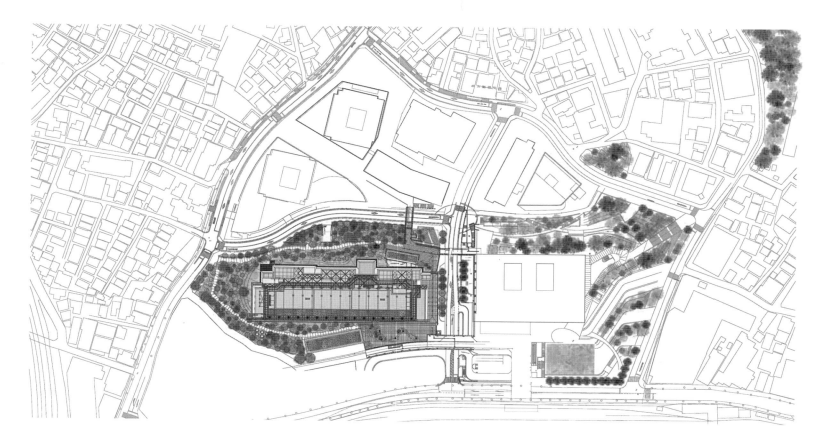

This office building for Sony's R&D department, takes the form of a thin vertical plate to ensure good views. The form also minimizes the "heat island effect" by positioning its narrow sides against prevailing winds, thus allowing the breeze to flow in from Tokyo Bay without hindrance. According to the architects, "The building was then conceived as a massive cooling device that performs in much the same way as a natural forest." The building's mechanisms are integrated into the façades, and the narrow floor plates have column-free plans. Elevators and stairways were placed on the western façade to block the afternoon sun. Protruding solar panels on the south elevation also work as shading devices, generating electricity while at the same time blocking out the heat. This is the first structure to use BIOSKIN, a new exterior system based on the principles behind *sudare*, or traditional Japanese screens usually made by thin bamboo. BIOSKIN reduces the heat island effect by cooling the exterior of the building with rainwater collected from the roof area and then feeding it through special porous ceramic pipes. As the water evaporates, it reduces the surface temperature of the ceramic pipes subsequently cooling the adjacent air.

Das Bürogebäude für Sonys Forschungsabteilung wurde als Scheibenhochhaus realisiert, um einen idealen Ausblick zu gewähren. Die Gebäudeform trägt außerdem zur Reduzierung des „Wärmeinseleffekts" bei, da die Schmalseite des Baus an der vorherrschenden Windrichtung orientiert ist und so die Luftströme von der Bucht von Tokio nicht blockiert. Die Architekten konzipierten „das Gebäude als überdimensioniertes Kühlmedium, nach demselben Wirkungsprinzip wie ein natürlicher Wald". Die Haustechnik ist in die Fassaden integriert, die schmalen Geschossplatten haben stützenfreie Grundrisse. Aufzüge und Treppen wurden an die Westseite verlegt, um vor der Nachmittagssonne zu schützen. An der Südfassade dienen auskragende Solarpaneele ebenso als Sonnenschutz wie der Stromerzeugung. Das Hochhaus ist das erste Gebäude, bei dem BIOSKIN zum Einsatz kommt, eine neuartige Gebäudehülle inspiriert von den Prinzipien klassischer japanischer Wandschirme, der *sudare*, die in der Regel aus dünnem Bambus gefertigt sind. BIOSKIN sorgt für eine Reduzierung des Wärmeinseleffekts, indem es die Außenfassaden des Baus mit Regenwasser kühlt, das auf dem Dach gesammelt und durch spezielle poröse Keramikrohre abgeleitet wird. Wenn es verdunstet, kühlt das Wasser die Keramikrohre und damit die Luft.

Le bâtiment de bureaux pour le service R&D de Sony a la forme d'une fine plaque verticale qui garantit de belles vues. Cette configuration permet par ailleurs de minimiser l'effet « îlot de chaleur » car ses petits côtés sont orientés face aux vents dominants, de sorte que la brise peut y pénétrer sans rencontrer le moindre obstacle depuis la baie de Tokyo. Les architectes expliquent que « le bâtiment a été conçu comme un énorme appareil de refroidissement qui fonctionne pour l'essentiel de la même manière qu'une forêt naturelle ». Les différents mécanismes sont intégrés aux façades et les étroites plaques de sol ne sont traversées d'aucun pilier. Les ascenseurs et les cages d'escaliers ont été placés sur la façade ouest afin de piéger le soleil de l'après-midi. Les panneaux solaires faisant saillie sur l'élévation sud assurent également l'ombrage et produisent de l'électricité, tout en empêchant la chaleur de pénétrer. Pour la première fois dans cette structure, on a utilisé le BIOSKIN, un nouveau système extérieur basé sur les principes des *sudare*, de fins écrans japonais traditionnellement en bambou. BIOSKIN réduit l'effet d'îlot de chaleur en refroidissant l'extérieur du bâtiment avec de l'eau de pluie récupérée du toit qui circule dans des tubes en céramique poreuse spécifiquement conçus à cet effet : lorsque l'eau s'évapore, la température de surface des tubes diminue, ce qui refroidit l'air environnant.

A site plan (left) shows the building on its left side. Above, the structure stands out like a massive singularity from the lower buildings behind it in this image.

Ein Lageplan (linke Seite) zeigt links das Gebäude. Der Bau erhebt sich auf der Aufnahme oben als massiver Solitär über der niedrigeren Bebauung im Hintergrund.

Plan du site (à gauche) avec le bâtiment du côté gauche. Ci-dessus, l'ensemble se détache ici des plus petits bâtiments de derrière telle une excentricité massive.

A detail of the façade (left) shows the ceramic pipe system called Bioskin that is intended to cool the building using the traditional Japanese principle of the sudare *screen.*

Eine Detailaufnahme der Fassade (links) zeigt das Keramikrohrsystem Bioskin, das den Bau nach den Prinzipien des klassischen japanischen Wandschirms sudare *kühlt.*

Détail de la façade (à gauche) avec le système de tubes en céramique Bioskin, conçu pour rafraîchir le bâtiment selon le principe traditionnel japonais des écrans sudare.

On this page, solar panel arrays on the roof and another façade view with a more solid appearance.

Die Aufnahmen auf dieser Seite zeigen Solarpaneele auf dem Dach und eine weitere, geschlossener wirkende Fassadenansicht.

Rangées de panneaux solaires sur le toit et autre vue de la façade à l'aspect plus fermé.

ROLF CARL NIMMRICHTER

Nimmrichter CDA Ltd.
Rietstr. 38
8702 Zollikon
Switzerland

Tel: +41 44 554 4154
Fax: +41 44 554 4150
E-mail: rcn@nimmrichter.com
Web: www.nimmrichter.com

Born in 1968, **ROLF CARL NIMMRICHTER** received his diploma from the ETH in Zurich in 1996. After that he was a research and teaching assistant at the ETH, working with professors Paul Meyer and Marc Angélil. He also worked for Interbrand Zintzmeyer and Lux (Zurich), Bétrix & Consolascio (Erlenbach), and with Machado & Silvetti Associates (Boston). Since 1999 he has worked as an independent architect and corporate designer in Zurich. Recent work includes the S House (Dietlikon, 2008, published here) and the competition entry for the Werkhof St. Gallen (2009), both in Switzerland.

Der 1968 geborene **ROLF CARL NIMMRICHTER** machte 1996 sein Diplom an der Eidgenössischen Technischen Hochschule (ETH) Zürich. Danach war er als Assistent der Professoren Paul Meyer und Marc Angélil an der ETH in Forschung und Lehre tätig. Er arbeitete auch bei Interbrand Zintzmeyer und Lux (Zürich), Bétrix & Consolascio (Erlenbach) und Machado & Silvetti Associates (Boston). Seit 1999 ist er selbstständiger Architekt und Designer in Zürich. Zu seinen aktuellen Arbeiten zählen das Haus S (Dietlikon, 2008, hier vorgestellt) sowie der Wettbewerbsentwurf für den Werkhof St. Gallen (2009), beide in der Schweiz.

Né en 1968, **ROLF CARL NIMMRICHTER** est diplômé de l'ETH de Zurich (1996). Il a été assistant de recherche et d'enseignement à l'ETH, travaillant avec les professeurs Paul Meyer et Marc Angélil. Il a également travaillé pour Interbrand Zintzmeyer et Lux (Zurich), Bétrix & Consolascio (Erlenbach) et Machado & Silvetti Associates (Boston). Depuis 1999, il est architecte et designer indépendant à Zurich. En Suisse, il a récemment réalisé la maison S (Dietlikon, 2008, publiée ici) et a participé au concours pour le Werkhof de Saint-Gall (2009).

S HOUSE
Dietlikon, Switzerland, 2008

*Address: Eichenbühlweg, 8004 Dietlikon, Switzerland
Area: 160 m². Client: not disclosed. Cost: not disclosed*

The house has slightly staggered or notched levels that make room for terraces. The horizontal wood siding gives a modern appearance.

Die Ebenen dieses Hauses sind leicht gestaffelt oder offen gelassen, um Platz für Terrassen zu gewinnen. Die horizontale Holzverkleidung gibt ihm ein modernes Aussehen.

La maison présente des niveaux légèrement décalés ou découpés qui permettent d'intégrer des balcons et des loggias. Le bardage horizontal en bois lui confère une apparence très moderne.

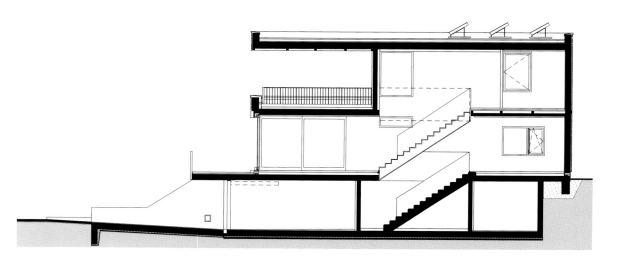

The plan of the house is slightly inclined on the side of the small swimming pool, seen above.

Der Grundriss des Hauses ist, wie oben erkennbar, auf der Seite des kleinen Swimmingpools leicht abgewinkelt.

Le plan de la maison marque un léger retrait devant une petite piscine (ci-dessus).

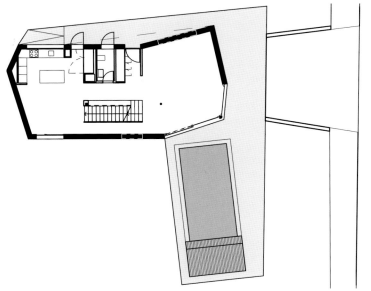

The architect states that the "box is the spatially defining element" for this detached house in Dietlikon on a site where there was already a house and pool. Rolf Nimmrichter was awarded this commission against the competition of a modular house manufacturer. The outside of the three-story house is faced in open-jointed cedar batten cladding. A garage is located in the basement, while the ground floor has a large living, cooking, and dining area. Three bedrooms and a recessed balcony are located on the upper floor. The architect also designed the interiors with their chestnut facing. The floor is finished in dark, rough concrete. The architect states: "The building is Minergie® certified, a registered quality label for low-energy buildings. The energy concept includes making use of the neighboring house's existing heating system and using solar panels to heat water for both houses."

Der Architekt erklärt, dass „die Kiste das raumbildende Element" dieses frei stehenden Hauses sei. Es wurde auf einem Grundstück in Dietlikon errichtet, wo sich bereits ein Haus und ein Swimmingpool befanden. Rolf Nimmrichter erhielt diesen Auftrag in Konkurrenz zu einer Fertigbaufirma. Außen ist das dreigeschossige Gebäude mit in Abständen verlegten Zedernlatten verkleidet. Im Untergeschoss befindet sich die Garage; im Erdgeschoss liegen ein großer Wohnraum, die Küche und der Essbereich, im Obergeschoss drei Schlafzimmer und eine Loggia. Nimmrichter entwarf auch die Innenausstattung mit einer Verkleidung aus Kastanienholz. Der Boden besteht aus rauem, dunklem Beton. Der Architekt erklärt: „Das Gebäude ist Minergie®-zertifiziert, eine eingetragene Qualitätsbezeichnung für Niedrigenergiehäuser. Zum Energiekonzept gehört die Nutzung der bestehenden Heizanlage des Nachbarhauses und von Solarzellen zur Warmwasserversorgung beider Häuser."

La « boîte est l'élément spatial qui définit » cette maison à Dietlikon, explique l'architecte. Le terrain était déjà occupé par une autre résidence et une piscine. Rolf Nimmrichter a remporté cette commande contre un fabricant de logements modulaires. L'extérieur de la maison de trois niveaux est habillé d'un bardage en lattes de cèdre à joint ouvert. Un garage occupe le sous-sol tandis que le rez-de-chaussée est réservé à un vaste séjour et une zone cuisine/repas. Les trois chambres et un balcon en loggia se répartissent l'étage. L'architecte a également conçu l'intérieur qu'il a habillé de noyer. Les sols sont en béton brut à finition de couleur sombre. « La maison est certifiée Minergie®, un label de qualité pour les constructions à faible consommation d'énergie. L'approche a consisté ici à se brancher sur le système de chauffage de la maison voisine existante et à utiliser des panneaux solaires pour la production d'eau chaude des deux résidences », précise l'architecte.

Contrasting surfaces and lighting enliven the interior appearance of the house.

Kontrastierende Oberflächen und Beleuchtung bereichern die Innenausstattung des Hauses.

Les surfaces contrastées et l'éclairage étudié animent l'atmosphère intérieure de la maison.

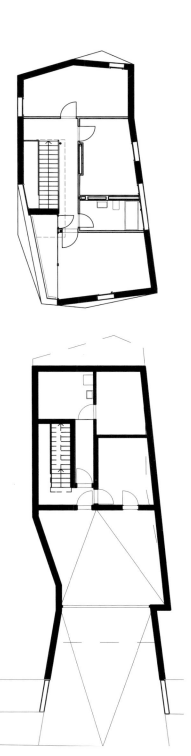

With its slightly irregular albeit rectilinear plan, the interior of the house provides for a number of spatial surprises, as seen in the stairway above, for example.

Mit seinem leicht unregelmäßigen, aber geradlinigen Grundriss bietet das Haus im Innern überraschende Raumwirkungen, wie z. B. im Treppenhaus (oben) erkennbar.

À travers son plan légèrement irrégulier bien que rectiligne, l'intérieur de la maison réserve un certain nombre de surprises spatiales, comme cet escalier par exemple.

OFFICE DA

Office dA
1920 Washington Street, #2
Boston, MA 02118
USA

Tel: +1 617 541 5540
Fax: +1 617 541 5535
E-mail: da@officeda.com

NADER TEHRANI was born in England in 1963 and is of Iranian descent. He received a B.A. in Fine Arts (1985) and a B.Arch (1986) from the Rhode Island School of Design, and an M.Arch in Urban Design from the Harvard GSD in 1991. He teaches at MIT as an Associate Professor of Architecture, and has taught at the Harvard GSD, Rhode Island School of Design, and Georgia Institute of Technology, where he served as the Thomas W. Ventulett III Distinguished Chair in Architectural Design. **MONICA PONCE DE LEON** was born in 1965 in Venezuela. She received a B.A. from the University of Miami in 1989, followed by an M.Arch in Urban Design from the Harvard GSD in 1991. Ponce de Leon is a Professor at the Harvard GSD and became the Dean of the A. Alfred Taubman College of Architecture and Urban Planning at the University of Michigan in the fall of 2008. They formed their partnership in 1991 in Boston. In 2006 Office dA designed the main library for the Rhode Island School of Design in Providence. In addition Office dA won the first-place award in the Villa Moda Competition for a mixed-use building in Kuwait, which includes housing, retail, multiplex, convention area, and sport facilities. Office dA recently completed the first LEED-certified, multi-housing building in Boston, the Macallen Building, with over 140 environmentally sensitive condominium units (2005–07). Helios House, the first LEED-rated gas station, was completed in Los Angeles in 2007 (published here).

NADER TEHRANI wurde 1963 in England geboren, seine Familie stammt aus dem Iran. Er erwarb einen B.A. in bildender Kunst (1985) sowie einen B.Arch. (1986) an der Rhode Island School of Design und schließlich 1991 einen M.Arch. in Stadtplanung an der Harvard Graduate School of Design (GSD). Er lehrt als außerordentlicher Professor für Architektur am MIT und unterrichtete auch an der Harvard GSD, der Rhode Island School of Design sowie dem Georgia Institute of Technology, wo er den Thomas-W.-Ventulett-III-Lehrstuhl für architektonisches Entwerfen innehatte. **MONICA PONCE DE LEON** wurde 1965 in Venezuela geboren. Sie erwarb 1989 einen B.A. an der Universität von Miami und 1991 einen M.Arch. in Stadtplanung an der Harvard GSD. Ponce de Leon ist Professorin an der Harvard GSD und wurde im Herbst 2008 Dekanin des A. Alfred Taubman College für Architektur und Stadtplanung an der Universität von Michigan. 1991 begannen die beiden in Boston ihre Partnerschaft. 2006 entwarf Office dA die Hauptbibliothek der Rhode Island School of Design in Providence, Rhode Island. Zudem gewann das Büro den ersten Preis im Villa-Moda-Wettbewerb für einen Baukomplex mit gemischter Nutzung in Kuwait, zu dem Wohnungen, Geschäfte, ein Kino, ein Messeareal und Sporteinrichtungen gehören. Vor Kurzem konnte Office dA den ersten LEED-zertifizierten Wohnkomplex in Boston fertigstellen, das Macallen Building mit über 140 umweltgerechten Eigentumswohnungen (2005–07). Das Helios House, die erste LEED-zertifizierte Tankstelle, wurde 2007 in Los Angeles realisiert (hier vorgestellt).

NADER TEHRANI est né en Grande-Bretagne, en 1963, de parents iraniens. Il est titulaire d'un B.A. en Beaux-Arts (1985), d'un B.Arch. (1986) de la Rhode Island School of Design et d'un M.Arch. d'urbanisme à la Harvard GSD (1991). Il enseigne au MIT comme professeur associé d'architecture et a professé à la Harvard GSD, la Rhode Island School of Design et au Georgia Institute of Technology, où il a occupé la Thomas W. Ventulett III Distinguished Chair de conception architecturale. **MONICA PONCE DE LEON**, née au Venezuela en 1965, a obtenu un B.A. à l'université de Miami (1989) et un M.Arch. d'urbanisme à la Harvard GSD (1991). Elle est professeur à la Harvard GSD et doyenne de l'A. Alfred Taubman College of Architecture and Urban Planning de l'université du Michigan depuis l'automne 2008. Ils se sont associés à Boston en 1991. En 2006, Office dA a conçu la bibliothèque principale de la Rhode Island School of Design à Providence. L'agence a remporté le concours de la Villa Moda pour un immeuble mixte à Koweït, qui comprend des logements, des commerces, une salle multiplexe, un centre de congrès et des équipements sportifs. Elle a récemment achevé le premier immeuble mixte certifié LEED à Boston, le Macallen Building, qui compte plus de 140 appartements en copropriété (2005–07). Helios House, première station-service certifiée LEED, a été achevée en 2007 (Los Angeles, publiée ici).

HELIOS HOUSE

Los Angeles, California, USA, 2006–07

Floor area: 975 m². Client: BP Corporation of North America
Cost: not disclosed. Architect of Record: Johnston Marklee
Collaboration: BIG at Ogilvy & Mather

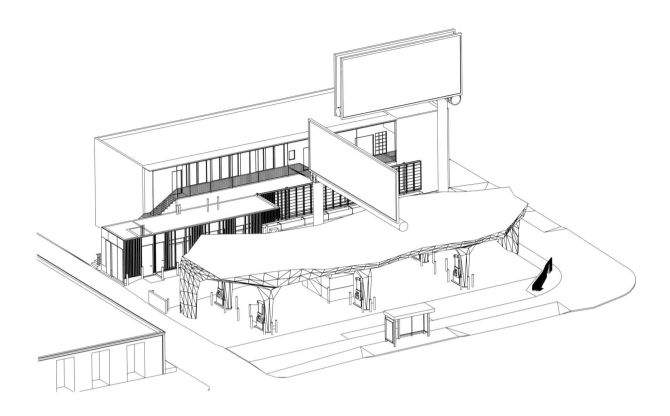

The idea of an ecological design for a gas station might seem contradictory, but the client and the architects have taken it up with energy and originality.

Das Konzept einer ökologisch gestalteten Tankstelle mag zunächst widersprüchlich erscheinen, doch Auftraggeber und Architekten stellten sich der Herausforderung engagiert und mit Originalität.

L'idée de conception écologique d'une station-service peut sembler contradictoire en soi, mais le client et les architectes l'ont traitée avec originalité et énergie.

P 522

Though its essential function is that of a gas station, **HELIOS HOUSE** was intended to be a "learning lab," to stimulate dialogue, promote education, and foster discussion on the topic of environmental stewardship. Built to maximize sustainability and energy efficiency, the structure is located at the intersection of Robertson and Olympic Boulevards in the location of a former conventional gas station. Existing billboards and bus stops were maintained "to attract attention to the station's experimental and educational mission." The architects make reference to the rich history of gas station architecture in America, while calling attention to "green" issues. A triangulated prefabricated steel-panel structure makes use of what the architects call "mass-customization" of the building elements. All potentially contaminated runoff water from the site is collected and placed in an underground cistern, filtered, and used to water plants. Ninety solar panels on the canopy roof "provide approximately 15 000 kWh of energy to the station—enough electricity to power two to three typical American homes for a year." Energy-efficient lights are used and the canopy was designed to reflect light, reducing electricity consumption by 16% as compared to conventional stations. Sensors further optimize the use of artificial light through a 24-hour cycle. Recycled materials were used wherever possible, and the project is LEED certified. Energy-related videos are visible for customers.

Trotz der Hauptfunktion als Tankstelle war **HELIOS HOUSE** als „Lernlabor" gedacht, um Gespräche anzuregen, Wissen zu vermitteln und Diskussionen zum Umgang mit der Umwelt anzustoßen. Die Konstruktion, bei deren Bau auf Maximierung von Nachhaltigkeit und Energieeffizienz geachtet wurde, liegt an der Kreuzung von Robertson und Olympic Boulevard, wo vorher eine konventionelle Tankstelle stand. Bereits vorhandene Werbetafeln und Bushaltestellen wurden übernommen, um „Aufmerksamkeit auf die experimentelle und informative Mission der Tankstelle zu lenken". Die Architekten nehmen Bezug auf die facettenreiche Geschichte der Tankstellenarchitektur in Amerika, jedoch mit der Besonderheit, Aufmerksamkeit auf „grüne" Aspekte zu lenken. Eine in Dreiecke segmentierte Plattenkonstruktion aus vorgefertigten Metallelementen überspannt die gesamte Anlage. Für die Produktion der einzelnen Bausegmente griffen die Architekten auf maßgeschneiderte, aber in Massenfertigung hergestellte Teile zurück. Das gesamte potenziell verunreinigte Ablaufwasser auf dem Grundstück wird in einer unterirdischen Zisterne gesammelt, gefiltert und zur Bewässerung der Bepflanzung genutzt. 90 Solarmodule auf dem Dach „erzeugen rund 15 000 kWh Strom für die Tankstelle – ausreichend Elektrizität, um zwei bis drei durchschnittliche amerikanische Eigenheime pro Jahr zu versorgen". Energiesparleuchten wurden eingesetzt, zudem wurde das Dach lichtreflektierend gestaltet, was den Stromverbrauch im Vergleich zu herkömmlichen Tankstellen um 16 % reduziert. Darüber hinaus optimieren Sensoren den Einsatz künstlicher Beleuchtung rund um die Uhr. Wo möglich, wurden für das LEED-zertifizierte Projekt recycelte Materialien verwendet. Videos zum Thema Energie werden für alle Kunden sichtbar gezeigt.

Bien que sa fonction essentielle soit d'être une station-service, **HELIOS HOUSE** avait aussi pour vocation d'être « un laboratoire d'apprentissage » pour stimuler, dialoguer, promouvoir la formation, et susciter le débat sur l'économie des sujets environnementaux. Construite avec la volonté d'optimiser sa durabilité et son efficacité énergétique, cette structure se trouve à l'angle des boulevards Robertson et Olympic à la place d'une ancienne station-service. Les arrêts de bus et les panneaux d'affichage existants ont été conservés « pour attirer l'attention sur la mission expérimentale et éducative de la station ». Les architectes se sont référés à la riche histoire des stations-service aux États-Unis, mais avec une importante nuance : attirer l'attention sur les enjeux écologiques. Une structure triangulée en panneaux d'acier préfabriqués recouvre toute la construction et les fonctions dans un effort de ce que les architectes appellent « une personnalisation massive » des éléments constructifs. Toute l'eau, potentiellement contaminée, collectée par cette structure est collectée et envoyée vers une citerne souterraine, avant d'être filtrée et de servir à arroser les plantes. Les 90 panneaux solaires placés sur le toit « fournissent environ 15 000 kWh d'électricité, suffisamment pour alimenter trois maisons américaines typiques pendant un an ». Des ampoules économiques ont été mises en place, et l'auvent a été dessiné de façon à refléter la lumière et réduire la consommation d'électricité de 16 % par rapport aux stations-service classiques. Des capteurs optimisent en permanence la consommation de l'éclairage artificiel. À chaque fois que c'était possible, des matériaux recyclés ont été utilisés et le projet a reçu une certification LEED. Des vidéos sur le thème de l'énergie informent les clients.

The articulated triangular panel canopy over the pumps morphs into the roof of the gas station itself.

Das dynamisch artikulierte Baldachindach aus dreieckigen Paneelen über den Zapfsäulen geht nahtlos in das Dach der Tankstelle über.

L'auvent des pompes, composé d'un assemblage articulé de triangles, se fond dans la couverture de la station-service.

In the image below, it is clear that the roof is also an arching protective wall, with its triangular forms becoming larger as it reaches the ground.

Im Bild unten ist deutlich zu sehen, wie sich das Dach zu einer geschwungenen Wand entwickelt, deren Dreieckselemente umso größer werden, je näher sie dem Boden kommen.

Dans l'image ci-dessous, le toit semble se transformer en mur de protection, les triangles s'agrandissant en se rapprochant du sol.

The folded shape of the station is seen in the drawings below, as well as in the images, which demonstrate the flexibility of the concept, bending to each planned use in the program.

Der Falteffekt der Tankstelle zeigt sich besonders gut an den Zeichnungen unten und den Aufnahmen, die die Flexibilität des Konzepts verdeutlichen, das sich jeder vorgesehenen Nutzung des Programms anpasst.

Les effets de pliage de la station-service sont détaillés dans les dessins ci-dessous. Les photos montrent la souplesse de ce concept qui s'adapte à chaque spécification du programme.

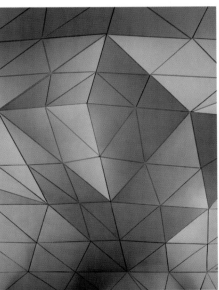

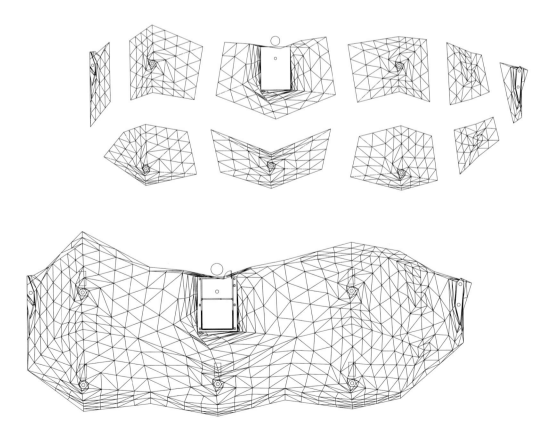

The architects explain, "The bathrooms incorporate farmed wood and uniquely designed tile mosaics, made from 100% recycled glass."

Die Architekten erläutern: „Für die Toiletten wurde mit Plantagenholz und individuell gestalteten Fliesenmosaiken aus 100 % recyceltem Glas gearbeitet."

Descriptif de l'architecte : « Les toilettes sont en bois naturel et mosaïque de céramique spécialement créée en verre 100 % recyclé. »

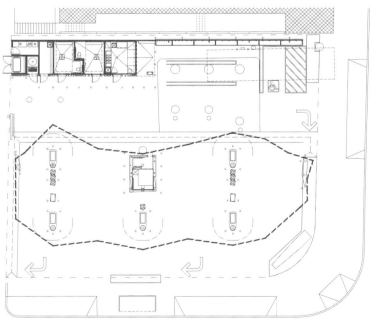

CARLOS OTT

Carlos Ott Architect
Zonamerica Business and Technology Park
Ruta 8 Km 17.5, Edificio Beta 4 of. 103, Montevideo 91600, Uruguay
Tel: +598 2 518 2235 / Fax: +598 2 518 2234
E-mail: info@carlosott.com / Web: www.carlosott.com

Edgar Baruzze
Cebollati 1698 apto. 203, Montevideo 11200, Uruguay
Tel: +598 2 410 8893 / E-mail: edbar@adinet.com.uy

CARLOS OTT was born in Montevideo, Uruguay, in 1946. He received his M.Arch degrees from the Washington University School of Architecture (Saint Louis, Missouri) and Hawaii University (Honolulu) in 1972. Carlos Ott became an international figure when he won the open, anonymous international competition for the Opera Bastille in Paris (1989). Ott created his current firm in 1992 with a head office in Montevideo, Uruguay, and branches in Shanghai, Abu Dhabi, Toronto, Paris, and Montréal. The firm employs about 60 architects. Completed projects include the National Bank of Dubai (Dubai, 1998); Dubai Hilton Hotel (Dubai, 2001); National Bank of Abu Dhabi (Abu Dhabi, 2003); Etisalat Headquarters (Abu Dhabi, 2003), all in the UAE; and the Hangzhou Grand Theater (Zhejiang, China, 2004). Other current work includes Calgary Federal Court House (Alberta, Canada, 2005–07); Seasons Tower (Punta del Este, Uruguay, 2005–08); Artech Residential Building (Aventura, Florida, USA, 2006–08); the AAM Tower (Dubai, UAE, 2008); Rambla Rep. Del Perú Residencial Building (Montevideo, Uruguay, 2005–09); Jade Ocean Residential Tower (North Miami Beach, Florida, USA, 2005–09); and Ushuaia International Airport Extension (Tierra del Fuego, Argentina, 2007–09). He was associated with Edgar Baruzze for the Playa Vik (Faro José Ignacio, Maldonado, Uruguay, 2007–10, published here).

CARLOS OTT wurde 1946 in Montevideo, Uruguay, geboren. Er schloss sein Architekturstudium an der Washington University (Saint Louis, Missouri) und der Hawaii University (Honolulu) 1972 jeweils mit einem M.Arch. ab. Carlos Ott wurde international bekannt, als er den offenen anonymen Wettbewerb für die Opéra Bastille in Paris (1989) gewann. Ott gründete sein aktuelles Büro 1992 mit Hauptsitz in Montevideo und Niederlassungen in Schanghai, Abu Dhabi, Toronto, Paris und Montreal. Das Büro beschäftigt 60 Architekten. Realisierte Projekte sind u.a. die Nationalbank von Dubai (1998), das Dubai Hilton (2001), die Nationalbank von Abu Dhabi (2003), die Zentrale von Etisalat (Abu Dhabi, 2003), alle in den VAE, sowie das Hangzhou-Grand-Theater (Zhejiang, China, 2004). Zu Otts weiteren Projekten zählen das Bundesgerichtsgebäude in Calgary (Alberta, Kanada, 2005–07), der Seasons Tower (Punta del Este, Uruguay, 2005–08), die Wohnanlage Artech (Aventura, Florida, 2006–08), der AAM Tower (Dubai, 2008), die Wohnanlage an der Rambla Rep. Del Perú (Montevideo, Uruguay, 2005–09), das Apartmenthochhaus Jade Ocean (North Miami Beach, Florida, 2005–09) sowie die Erweiterung des internationalen Flughafens von Ushuaia (Tierra del Fuego, Argentinien, 2007–09). Gemeinsam mit Edgar Baruzze entwarf er die Ferienanlage in Playa Vik (Faro José Ignacio, Maldonado, Uruguay, 2007–10, hier vorgestellt).

CARLOS OTT, né à Montevideo (Uruguay) en 1946 a obtenu ses diplômes M.Arch. à l'École d'architecture de l'université de Washington (Saint Louis, Missouri) et à l'université d'Hawaii (Honolulu, 1972). Il a acquis une notoriété internationale en remportant le concours ouvert et anonyme lancé pour la construction de l'Opéra Bastille à Paris (1989). Son agence actuelle, qui compte une soixantaine d'architectes, possède son siège à Montevideo et des bureaux à Shanghai, Abou Dhabi, Toronto, Paris et Montréal. Parmi ses projets réalisés figurent la Banque nationale de Dubaï (Dubaï, 1998); l'hôtel Hilton Dubaï (Dubaï, 2001); la Banque nationale d'Abou Dhabi (Abou Dhabi, 2003); le siège d'Etisalat (Abou Dhabi, 2003) et le Grand Théâtre d'Hangzhou (Zhejiang, Chine, 2004). Il a également réalisé le bâtiment de la Cour fédérale de Calgary (Alberta, Canada, 2005–07); la Seasons Tower (Punta del Este, Uruguay, 2005–08); l'immeuble résidentiel Artech (Aventura, Floride, 2006–08); la tour AAM (Dubaï, EAU, 2008); l'immeuble résidentiel Rambla Rep. Del Perú (Montevideo, Uruguay, 2005–09); la tour d'appartements Jade Ocean (North Miami Beach, Floride, 2005–09) et l'extension de l'aéroport international d'Ushuaia (Terre de Feu, Argentine, 2007–09). Il s'est associé avec Edgar Baruzze pour le projet de complexe de vacances de Playa Vik (Faro José Ignacio, Maldonado, Uruguay, 2007–10, publié ici).

PLAYA VIK

Faro José Ignacio, Maldonado, Uruguay, 2007–10

Address: Calle Los Cisnes y Los Horneros, Faro José Ignacio, Maldonado, Uruguay, +598 94 60 5212,
www.playavik.com. Area: 2022 m². Client: Bermick S.A. Cost: $14 million
Collaboration: Edgar Baruzze (Associated Architect)

This beach resort is on the south Atlantic coast of Uruguay. Its central feature is called the "Sculpture" by the owners and is a double-curved titanium and glass building with a 16.8-meter-wide sliding glass wall. An L-shaped pavilion made of six houses that can serve as individual residences is arrayed around the Sculpture. A collection of contemporary art, including works by such figures as Anselm Kiefer and James Turrell, is part of the complex. A 23-meter-long black granite pool and wooden deck cantilever over the beach, located ten meters below. Green roofs, water recycling, radiant heat, natural ventilation, and an "intelligent" system to control energy usage are part of the overall "environmentally friendly" strategy of the architect and owners.

Die Ferienanlage liegt am Strand der Südatlantikküste von Uruguay. Zentrales Merkmal ist das Hauptgebäude, von den Eigentümern „Skulptur" genannt, mit seiner zweifach geschwungenen Fassade aus Glas und Titan mit einer 16,8 m breiten Glasschiebetür. Ein L-förmiger Pavillon aus sechs Wohnbauten, die individuell genutzt werden können, gruppiert sich um die „Skulptur". Zum Komplex gehört auch eine Sammlung zeitgenössischer Kunst mit Werken von u. a. Anselm Kiefer und James Turrell. Ein 23 m langer Pool aus schwarzem Granit und ein Holzdeck kragen in 10 m Höhe über dem Strand aus. Als Teil der „umweltfreundlichen" Strategie von Architekt und Eigentümern entschied man sich für begrünte Dächer, Fußbodenheizung, natürliche Belüftung und ein „intelligentes" System zur Steuerung des Energieverbrauchs.

Ce complexe de vacances situé sur la côte uruguayenne de l'Atlantique Sud se signale par ce que ses propriétaires appellent « la sculpture », un bâtiment de verre à murs inclinés en titane, dont une façade est une paroi vitrée coulissante de 16,8 m de large. Il est entouré d'une composition en L de six résidences utilisables en maisons individuelles. Le petit complexe possède une collection d'œuvres d'art contemporain, dont des pièces d'Anselm Kiefer et James Turrell. Une piscine de 23 m de long en granit noir et entourée d'un platelage en bois se projette en porte-à-faux au-dessus de la plage, située à 10 m en contrebas. Des toitures végétalisées, un système de recyclage des eaux, des chauffages radiants, la ventilation naturelle et un système intelligent de contrôle de l'utilisation de l'énergie font partie de la stratégie « écologique » voulue par l'architecte et les propriétaires.

The spectacular oceanside setting of the hotel is emphasized by the long narrow pool that projects beyond the outside deck. As the elevation drawings above and these photos show, Playa Vik is built on a sloping site.

Durch den langen schmalen Pool, der über das Terrassendeck hinaus auskragt, kommt die dramatische Lage des Hauses am Meer besonders zur Geltung. Wie auf Aufrissen und Ansichten zu sehen, liegt die Playa Vik auf einem Hanggrundstück.

Le cadre spectaculaire de l'hôtel face à l'océan est sublimé par un long couloir de nage qui se poursuit au-delà de sa bordure. Les élévations et les photographies montrent que Playa Vik a été construite sur un terrain incliné.

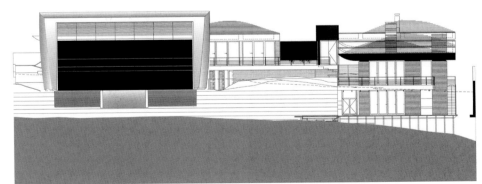

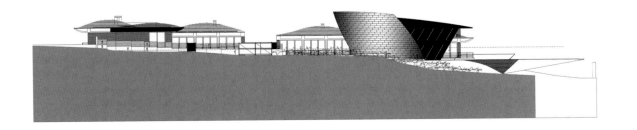

Bungalow-type structures offer clients private decks and uninterrupted views of the ocean. The architect mixes wooden exterior elements with a more mineral aspect in the actual buildings.

Die bungalowähnlichen Häuser bieten Besuchern private Terrassen und einen unverstellten Blick aufs Meer. Holzelemente am Außenbau kombiniert der Architekt mit eher mineralischen Elementen im Innenbereich.

Les bâtiments de type pavillon offrent à leurs hôtes des terrasses et des vues panoramiques sur l'océan. L'architecte a tempéré l'aspect minéral des constructions par des composants extérieurs en bois.

The pool leads to the main building of
the Playa Vik in an axial arrangement
that emphasizes the continuity from
the land to the ocean.

*Der Pool läuft auf das Hauptgebäude
von Playa Vik zu. Die axiale Komposition verknüpft Land und Meer zu
einem Kontinuum.*

*La piscine part du bâtiment principal
de Playa Vik, orientée sur un axe qui
souligne la continuité entre la terre et
l'océan.*

SERGIO PALLERONI

Sergio Palleroni
School of Architecture
PO Box 751
Portland, OR 97207
USA

Tel: +1 503 725 8403
E-mail: sergio@basicinitiative.org
Web: www.basicinitiative.org

SERGIO PALLERONI, born in Berkeley, California, in 1955, received his B.Arch degree at the University of Oregon and an M.S. in Architectural Studies (History, Theory, and Criticism) at MIT. He was Associate Professor of Architecture at the University of Washington, Seattle (1993–2004), Research Fellow and Associate Professor at the Center for Sustainable Development, University of Texas, Austin (2004–08) and is currently Professor and Fellow at the Center for Sustainable Processes and Practices, Portland State University. He was Director and cofounder of the Building Sustainable Communities (BaSiC) Initiative, University of Washington, University of Texas, Penn State University, University of Wisconsin; a member of the United Nations Think Tank on Climate Change (SBCI TTWG); and of the Luce Foundation Workshop on Sustainable Development (University of Texas). Through the BaSiC Initiative, Sergio Palleroni has worked with his students to build housing, clinics, and schools in poor communities in the rural United States, Mexico, Africa, and India; in addition to sustainability and eco-design projects like the Zhong-Xiao Boulevard Urban Ecological Corridor (Taipei, Taiwan, 2005–07, published here). From 2008 to 2009 he was Co-Principal Investigator with Jen-Hui Tsai for an Urban Development Grant, National Taipei University of Technology (NTUT, Taiwan).

SERGIO PALLERONI, geboren 1955 in Berkeley, Kalifornien, erwarb seinen Grad des B.Arch. an der Universität von Oregon und einen M.S. in Architektur (Geschichte, Theorie und Kritik) am Massachusetts Institute of Technology (MIT). Er war außerordentlicher Professor für Architektur an der Universität von Washington, Seattle (1993–2004), Forschungsmitarbeiter und außerordentlicher Professor am Center for Sustainable Development, Universität von Texas in Austin (2004–08), und ist derzeit Professor und Mitglied am Center for Sustainable Processes and Practices an der Portland State University. Er war Direktor und Mitbegründer der Initiative „Building Sustainable Communities" (BaSiC) der Universitäten Washington und Texas, der Penn State University sowie der Universität von Wisconsin. Palleroni war Mitglied des Thinktanks der Vereinten Nationen zum Klimawandel (SBCI TTWG) und des Arbeitskreises Nachhaltige Entwicklung der Luce Foundation (Universität von Texas). Im Rahmen der BaSiC-Initiative arbeitete Palleroni gemeinsam mit seinen Studenten an Wohnungs-, Klinik- und Schulbauprogrammen in finanziell benachteiligten Gemeinden in den ländlichen Gegenden der USA, Mexikos, Afrikas und Indiens sowie für nachhaltige und umweltfreundliche Projekte wie den hier vorgestellten Zhong-Xiao Boulevard Urban Ecological Corridor (Taipei, Taiwan, 2005–07). 2008 bis 2009 war er gemeinsam mit Jen-Hui Tsai Forschungsleiter für das Stipendium für Stadtentwicklung an der Technischen Nationaluniversität Taipei (NTUT, Taiwan).

SERGIO PALLERONI, né à Berkeley en 1955, a obtenu un B.Arch. à l'université de l'Oregon et un M.S. en études sur l'architecture au MIT. Professeur associé en architecture à l'université de Washington, Seattle (1993–2004), chercheur et professeur associé au Center for Sustainable Development de l'université du Texas, à Austin (2004–08), il est membre et professeur titulaire du Center for Sustainable Processes and Practices de l'université d'État de Portland. Il a fondé et dirigé la Building Sustainable Communities (BaSiC) dans diverses universités : université de Washington, du Texas, du Wisconsin, université Penn State ; membre du Comité de réflexion des Nations unies sur le changement climatique (SBCI TTWG) et de l'atelier de la Fondation Luce sur le développement durable (université du Texas). Dans le cadre de la BaSiC Initiative, Sergio Palleroni a travaillé avec ses étudiants sur la construction de logements, de cliniques et d'écoles pour des communautés pauvres rurales aux États-Unis, au Mexique, en Afrique et en Inde ainsi qu'à des projets soutenables et d'eco-design tel le corridor écologique Zhong-Xiao Boulevard Urban (Taipei, Taiwan, 2005–07, publié ici). De 2008 à 2009 il a été chercheur principal, avec Jen-Hui Tsai, pour le Fonds de développement urbain de l'Université nationale de technologie de Taipei (NTUT, Taïwan).

ZHONG-XIAO BOULEVARD URBAN ECOLOGICAL CORRIDOR

Taipei, Taiwan, 2005–07

Site area: 50 000 m² (urban landscape and rooftops); 140 m² (building)
Client: National Taipei University of Technology, Taipei City Government. Cost: not disclosed
Collaboration: Sergio Palleroni, Jen-Hui Tsai, James Adamson

This project includes a campus garden designed and built by a group of architecture, planning, and engineering students; a "green" pavilion designed by students, built with assistance from the local construction industry, and other initiatives. An entrance to the campus along Zhong-Xiao Boulevard formerly occupied by a long wall is the location for a garden and bioswale. A bioswale is a landscape element designed to remove silt and pollution from surface runoff water. It consists of a drainage course with gently sloped sides filled with vegetation or compost. Solar panels used as window shades on campus buildings power the pumps used for the project. Planting was carried out with the assistance of the local community. The so-called Lotus Pavilion is a large room that makes use of passive cooling and low-energy lighting. Rising almost ten meters above the ground, the structure captures passing breezes for cooling and also makes use of solar panels. The partially planted roof serves as insulation. An exterior bamboo rain screen tops the insulation, leaving a gap for air to flow through, thus further reducing solar gain. Students participating in this project went on to install various green devices, including solar panels and mesh screens for vines to grow on around the bioswale. This initiative is exemplary both in terms of student, community, and professional participation, and also in the mixture of different techniques employed, ranging from the expected passive strategies to landscape solutions.

Zum Projekt gehören ein Campusgarten, der von einer Gruppe von Architektur-, Stadtplanungs- und Ingenieurstudenten entworfen und gebaut wurde, sowie ein „grüner" Pavillon, der von Studenten geplant und mithilfe ortsansässiger Bauunternehmen und weiterer Initiativen gebaut wurde. Am Eingang des Campusgeländes am Zhong-Xiao-Boulevard stand früher eine lange Mauer. Heute befinden sich hier ein Garten und eine ökologisch angelegte Bodensenke, deren obere Schicht das Sickerwasser filtert. Eine ökologisch konzipierte Bodensenke ist ein Landschaftselement, das Schlick und Schadstoffe aus Stauwasser filtert. Sie besteht aus einem abgesenkten, mit Pflanzen oder Kompost versehenen Dränagelauf. Solarmodule auf den Campusbauten dienen als Fensterläden und liefern Strom für die Pumpanlagen des Projekts. Die Bepflanzung wurde mit der Hilfe von Anwohnern realisiert. Der sog. Lotuspavillon ist ein großer Raum, der passiv gekühlt wird und mit Energiesparlampen ausgestattet ist. Der fast 10 m über dem Boden aufgeständerte Bau fängt den kühlenden Luftzug ein und nutzt zudem Solarmodule. Das teilweise begrünte Dach wirkt dämmend. Ein außen zum Schutz vor Regen angebrachter Wandschirm aus Bambus verstärkt die Isolierung, durch eine Lücke kann Luft ziehen, was den solaren Wärmegewinn minimiert. Die am Projekt beteiligten Studenten installierten außerdem Rankhilfen im Bereich der Bodensenke, etwa Solarmodule und Drahtgitter, an denen Wein emporwachsen kann. Vorbildfunktion hat die Initiative sowohl im Hinblick auf die Einbindung von Studenten, Anwohnern und Fachleuten als auch durch die Kombination verschiedener Ansätze – von den zu erwartenden Passivstrategien bis hin zur Landschaftsgestaltung.

Ce projet comprend un jardin de campus conçu et réalisé par un groupe d'étudiants en architecture, urbanisme et ingénierie, et un pavillon « vert » dessiné par les étudiants et construit avec l'assistance d'entreprises et autres partenaires locaux. La zone d'entrée du campus donnant sur le Boulevard Zhong-Xiao anciennement masquée par un grand mur est l'emplacement choisi pour le jardin et une zone de biorétention. Une zone de biorétention est un élément de paysage qui réduit le limon et la pollution des eaux d'écoulement de surface. Il consiste en plans de drainage dont les côtés, légèrement inclinés, sont recouverts de plantes ou de compost. Des panneaux solaires qui font également fonction d'écrans de protection solaire sur les bâtiments du campus fournissent l'énergie aux pompes utilisées sur place. Les plantations ont été effectuées par les gens du quartier. Le pavillon du Lotus est une vaste pièce qui bénéficie d'un refroidissement passif de l'atmosphère et d'un éclairage à faible consommation. De près de 10 m de haut, il capte les vents utilisés pour la ventilation naturelle et utilise également des panneaux solaires. Le toit en partie planté apporte une isolation thermique. Il est entouré d'un écran en bambou dont les ouvertures laissent circuler l'air et participent à la protection solaire. Les étudiants ont mis en place divers dispositifs dont des panneaux solaires et des écrans en treillis métallique sur lesquels poussent des plantes grimpantes. Cette initiative est exemplaire tant en termes de participation des étudiants, de la communauté et des professionnels locaux que d'association de techniques variées, allant de stratégies passives à des solutions qui relèvent de l'aménagement du paysage.

This intervention has turned space that was otherwise unused and uncared for into useful, ecologically productive gardens.

Diese Intervention ist zugleich die Umnutzung eines Raums, der zuvor brach lag und nicht gepflegt wurde, als ökologisch produktiver Garten.

Cette intervention a permis de transformer des lieux inutilisés et mal entretenus en jardins écologiques productifs.

This pavilion is basically one large
room, with an open loft over the
southern portion. Set on steel stilts,
the lightweight metal-stud structure
rises to a height of 9.7 meters above
the ground to catch available breezes.

Dieser Pavillon ist im Prinzip ein
einziger großer Raum mit einem offenen Loftbereich über dem südlichen
Abschnitt. Die Leichtbau-Metall-
skelett-Konstruktion erhebt sich
9,7 m hoch über dem Boden, um
den verfügbaren Luftzug zu nutzen.

Ce pavillon est en fait une vaste
pièce avec atelier ouvert au sud.
Posée sur des pilotis d'acier, cette
structure métallique légère s'élève
jusqu'à une hauteur de 9,7 m au-
dessus du sol pour capter la brise.

Student initiatives include a green
roof on top of an existing building,
and channeled water runoff to irrigate
the plants.

Studenteninitiativen legten ein
begrüntes Dach auf einem bestehenden Gebäude und ein Kanalisierungs-
system für das Ablaufwasser zur
Bewässerung der Pflanzen an.

Parmi les initiatives des étudiants
figurent un jardin sur le toit d'un
bâtiment existant et l'utilisation
de l'eau de pluie pour irriguer les
plantes.

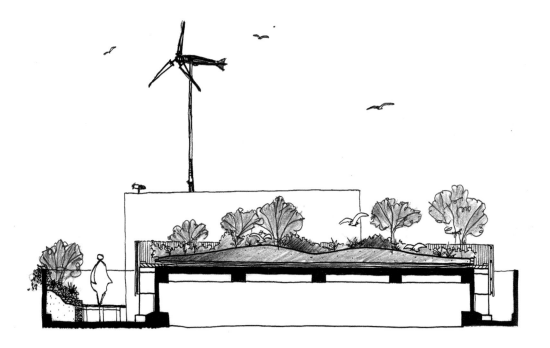

Palleroni's initiatives in an educational environment show that ecologically driven projects can be woven into an existing urban environment.

Palleronis Studenteninitiativen beweisen, dass sich ökologisch motivierte Projekte in ein bestehendes urbanes Umfeld integrieren lassen.

Les initiatives éducatives de Palleroni montrent que des projets de nature écologique peuvent s'intégrer à un environnement urbain existant.

PERKINS+WILL

Perkins+Will
1315 Peachtree Street NE
Atlanta, Georgia 30309
USA

Tel: + 1 404 873 2300
Web: www.perkinswill.com
E-mail: paula.vaughan@perkinswill.com

PHILIP HARRISON is the President and CEO of Perkins+Will. He joined the firm in 1993 after completing his architectural training at the Harvard GSD. He provided owner oversight and perspective for the project 1315 Peachtree Street (Atlanta, Georgia, USA, 2010, published here). **MANUEL CADRECHA** is the Design Director for the Atlanta office of Perkins+Will and was the Principal in Charge for the project. He received his architecture degrees from the Georgia Institute of Technology. **BRUCE MCAVOY** studied architecture at the Georgia Institute of Technology and at the École d'Architecture de Paris La Villette. He was the Design Principal for 1315 Peachtree Street. **PAULA VAUGHAN,** who studied architecture and sustainable design at Auburn University, is Co-Director of Perkins+Will's Sustainable Design Initiative (SDI) and was sustainability advisor for 1315 Peachtree Street. Recent Perkins+Will projects include the VanDusen Botanical Garden Visitor Center (Vancouver, Canada, 2010–11); Oklahoma Medical Research Foundation Research Tower (Oklahoma City, Oklahoma, USA, 2011); Rush University Medical Center (Chicago, Illinois, USA, 2011); University of British Columbia's Center for Interactive Research on Sustainability (Vancouver, Canada, 2011); University of British Columbia's Earth Systems Building (Vancouver, Canada, 2012); and the Edmonton City Center Redevelopment Master Plan (Edmonton, Canada, 2012).

PHILIP HARRISON ist Hauptgeschäftsführer bei Perkins+Will. Er schloss sich dem Büro 1993, nach seinem Architekturstudium an der Harvard Graduate School of Design, an. Er leitete das Projekt 1315 Peachtree Street (Atlanta, Georgia, 2010, hier vorgestellt) als Bauherr und gab ihm seine Ausrichtung. **MANUEL CADRECHA** ist leitender Architekt in der Perkins+Will-Niederlassung in Atlanta und zeichnete verantwortlich für die Projektleitung. Er schloss sein Architekturstudium am Georgia Institute of Technology ab. **BRUCE MCAVOY** studierte Architektur am Georgia Institute of Technology und der Ecole d'Architecture de Paris La Villette. Er verantwortete die Entwurfsleitung für 1315 Peachtree Street. **PAULA VAUGHAN,** die Architektur und nachhaltige Planung an der Auburn University studierte, ist Kodirektorin der Sustainable Design Initiative (SDI) bei Perkins+Will und war für die Nachhaltigkeit am Gebäude 1315 Peachtree Street zuständig. Jüngere Projekte von Perkins+Will sind u. a. die Haltestellen des Canada Line Skytrain (Vancouver, 2010), das Besucherzentrum im Botanischen Garten VanDusen (Vancouver, 2010–11), der Oklahoma Medical Research Foundation Research Tower (Oklahoma City, USA, 2011); das Rush University Medical Center (Chicago, USA, 2011); das interaktive Forschungszentrum für Nachhaltigkeit der University of British Columbia (Vancouver, 2011), das Earth Systems Building der University of British Columbia (Vancouver, 2012) sowie der Masterplan für die bauliche Neugestaltung von Edmonton (2012), alle in Kanada, soweit nicht anders vermerkt.

PHILIP HARRISON est président et directeur général de Perkins+Will. Il a rejoint la société en 1993 après avoir achevé sa formation en architecture à la Harvard GSD. Il a supervisé le projet du 1315 Peachtree Street (Atlanta, Georgie, 2010, publié ici). **MANUEL CADRECHA** est chef du design au bureau d'Atlanta de Perkins+Will et a été le principal responsable de l'immeuble 1315 Peachtree Street. Il est diplômé en architecture de l'Institut de technologie de Georgie. **BRUCE MCAVOY** a étudié l'architecture à l'Institut de technologie de Georgie et à l'École d'architecture de Paris La Villette. Il a dirigé le design du 1315 Peachtree Street. **PAULA VAUGHAN** a étudié l'architecture et le design durable à l'université d'Auburn, elle est codirectrice de l'initiative pour le design durable (SDI) de Perkins+Will et a été consultante pour la durabilité du 1315 Peachtree Street. Les projets récents de Perkins+Will comprennent le centre d'accueil des visiteurs du jardin botanique VanDusen (Vancouver, 2010–11) ; la tour de la recherche de la fondation pour la recherche médicale Oklahoma (Oklahoma City, Oklahoma, 2011) ; le centre médical universitaire Rush (Chicago, Illinois, 2011) ; le Centre de recherche interactive sur la durabilité de l'université de Colombie-Britannique (Vancouver, 2011) ; le bâtiment des sciences de la terre de l'université de Colombie-Britannique (Vancouver, 2012) et le plan directeur du réaménagement du centre d'Edmonton (2012), tous au Canada.

1315 PEACHTREE STREET

Atlanta, Georgia, United States, 2010

Area: 7,246 m². Cost: not disclosed. Client: 1315 Peachtree Street LLC
Collaboration: Bruce McEvoy, Design Principal; Manuel Cadrecha, Principal in Charge;
Phil Harrison, CEO

This renovated office building is the new Atlanta headquarters of Perkins+Will, located near the High Museum of Art. Office space is shared with the Peachtree Branch of the Atlanta-Fulton County Public Library and the Museum of Design Atlanta (MODA). The Perkins+Will Atlanta office occupies the main level lobby and the top four floors, with office space for up to 240 employees. Exterior design includes a more energy efficient window system and alterations to the western façade. An exterior terrace with a garden on the fifth floor serves as a lunch, meeting, and office social space. A trigeneration system includes turbines on the building's roof, which use natural gas to produce electricity. Radiant heating and cooling and shading devices are employed throughout. Rainwater is re-circulated as graywater and low-flow toilets and sinks decrease water consumption. LED fixtures and natural daylighting also decrease the building's energy needs. Building interior materials were aggressively screened to reduce toxic substances. The building achieved North America's highest LEED NC 2009 Platinum certification.

Im sanierten Bürogebäude unweit des High Museum of Art liegt das neue Hauptbüro von Perkins+Will in Atlanta. Das Gebäude wird auch von der Peachtree-Zweigstelle der Atlanta-Fulton-County-Bücherei und dem Museum of Design Atlanta (MODA) genutzt. Die Büros von Perkins+Will Atlanta liegen auf der Lobbyebene und in den vier obersten Stockwerken und bieten Platz für 240 Mitarbeiter. Der Bau erhielt ein energiesparendes Fenstersystem, und die westliche Fassade wurde umgebaut. Eine Terrasse in der fünften Etage dient als Kantine, für informelle Meetings und als Gemeinschaftsbereich. Zu einem Kraft-Wärme-Kälte-Kopplungssystem gehören Turbinen auf dem Dach, die aus Erdgas Strom erzeugen. Im ganzen Haus gibt es eine Fußbodenheizung sowie Kühl- und Sonnenschutzvorrichtungen. Regenwasser wird als Grauwasser genutzt; Sparsysteme in Toiletten und Waschbecken reduzieren den Wasserverbrauch. Auch LED-Leuchtmittel und natürliches Tageslicht tragen zur Energieersparnis bei. Das Baumaterial wurde sorgfältig ausgewählt, um Giftstoffe zu reduzieren. Das Gebäude wurde mit dem LEED-NC-2009-Platin-Zertifikat ausgezeichnet.

Cet immeuble de bureaux rénové est le nouveau siège d'Atlanta de Perkins+Will, près du High Museum of Art. Il est partagé avec la section de Peachtree de la bibliothèque publique du comté d'Atlanta-Fulton et le Musée du design d'Atlanta (MODA). Les bureaux de Perkins+Will occupent le centre du niveau principal et les quatre derniers étages offrant un espace de travail à 240 employés. Le design extérieur comprend un système de fenêtres à haute efficacité énergétique et des modifications de la façade ouest. Au cinquième étage, une terrasse avec jardin offre un lieu de restauration, de réunion et d'espace social. Sur le toit du bâtiment, un système de trigénération comprend des turbines qui produisent de l'électricité à partir de gaz naturel. Un chauffage à rayonnement et des dispositifs de refroidissement et d'ombrage sont utilisés. L'eau de pluie est remise en circulation sous forme d'eau ménagère, tandis que des toilettes et lavabos à faible débit diminuent la consommation d'eau. Des luminaires à LED et l'éclairage naturel font également baisser les besoins en énergie du bâtiment. Le bâtiment a obtenu la première certification LEED platine NC 2009 d'Amérique du Nord.

An exterior terrace on the fifth floor serves as lunch, meeting, and office social space. It also features a garden for employees.

Eine Terrasse in der fünften Etage dient zum Mittagessen, für informelle Meetings und als Gemeinschaftsbereich. Hier befindet sich auch ein Garten für die Angestellten.

Au cinquième étage, une terrasse sert de lieu de restauration, de réunion et d'espace social. Elle comporte également un jardin pour les employés.

The building has demountable interior partitions and open office workstations, making the available space fully flexible.

Die Raumteiler im Gebäude lassen sich versetzen. In Kombination mit offenen Büroflächen entsteht so ein äußerst flexibler Raum.

L'intérieur du bâtiment comporte des cloisons internes démontables et des postes de travail et bureaux ouverts qui confèrent à l'espace une flexibilité totale.

DOMINIQUE PERRAULT

Dominique Perrault Architecture
6 rue Bouvier
75011 Paris
France

Tel: +33 1 44 06 00 00 / Fax: +33 1 44 06 00 01
E-mail: dpa@d-p-a.fr
Web: www.perraultarchitecte.com

DOMINIQUE PERRAULT was born in 1953 in Clermont-Ferrand, France. He studied in Paris and received his diploma as an architect from the École des Beaux-Arts in 1978. He received a further degree in Urbanism at the École nationale des Ponts et Chaussées in 1979, as well as a Master's in History at the EHESS (École des hautes études en sciences sociales) in 1980. He created his own firm in 1981 in Paris. His most significant projects include the French National Library in Paris (1989–95); and the Velodrome and Olympic Swimming Pool (Berlin, Germany, 1992–99). Recent buildings include the Media Library in Vénissieux (France, 1997–2001); the design of several supermarkets for the MPreis chain in Austria (1999–2003); the master plan for Donau City in Vienna (Austria, 2002–03); and the refurbishment of Piazza Gramsci (Cinisello Balsamo, Milan, Italy, 1999–2004). More recent projects include the ME Barcelona Hotel Tower (Barcelona, Spain, 2002–07); an extension of the Court of Justice of the European Communities (Luxembourg, 2004–08); the Ewha Womans University in Seoul (South Korea, 2004–08, published here); Priory Park Pavilion (Reigate, UK, 2007–08); the NH–Fieramilano Hotel (Milan, Italy, 2006–09); the Arganzuela Footbridge in Madrid (Spain, 2005–10); and the Fukoku Tower (Osaka, Japan, 2008–10). Recent ongoing projects include the DC Towers in Vienna (Austria, 2004–12); the new Grand Albi Theater (France, 2009–13); the extension of the Dobrée Museum in Nantes (France, 2010–15); the development of the new FFS station district at Locarno (Switzerland, 2009–); and the city center redevelopement of Sofia (Bulgaria, 2009–).

DOMINIQUE PERRAULT wurde 1953 in Clermont-Ferrand geboren. Er studierte in Paris und machte sein Architekturdiplom 1978 an der Ecole des Beaux-Arts. 1979 folgte ein weiterer Abschluss in Städtebau an der Ecole nationale des Ponts et Chaussées sowie 1980 ein Master in Geschichte an der EHESS (Ecole des hautes études en sciences sociales). 1981 gründete er sein eigenes Büro in Paris. Seine bedeutendsten Projekte sind u. a. die Französische Nationalbibliothek in Paris (1989 bis 1995) und die Schwimm- und Sprunghalle Velodrom (Berlin, 1992–99). Weitere realisierte Bauten sind u. a. die Mediathek in Vénissieux (Frankreich, 1997–2001), die Gestaltung mehrerer Filialien der Supermarktkette MPreis in Österreich (1999–2003), der Masterplan für die Donau City in Wien (2002–03) sowie die Sanierung der Piazza Gramsci (Cinisello Balsamo, Mailand, 1999–2004). Zu den jüngeren Projekten zählen der ME Barcelona Hotel Tower in Barcelona (2002–07), die Erweiterung des Europäischen Gerichtshofs (Luxemburg, 2004–08), die Ewha Womans University in Seoul (Südkorea, 2004–08, hier vorgestellt), der Priory-Park-Pavillon (Reigate, Großbritannien, 2007–08), das NH-Fieramilano Hotel (Mailand, 2006–09), die Fußgängerbrücke Arganzuela in Madrid (2005–10) und der Fukoku Tower (Osaka, Japan, 2008 bis 2010). Laufende Projekte sind u. a. die DC Towers in Wien (Österreich, 2004–12), das neue Grand Theater in Albi (Frankreich, 2009–13), die Erweiterung des Dobrée Museums in Nantes (Frankreich, 2010–15), die Planung des neuen FFS Bahnhofsareals in Locarno (Schweiz, seit 2009) sowie die Umgestaltung der Innenstadt von Sofia (Bulgarien, seit 2009).

DOMINIQUE PERRAULT est né en 1953 à Clermont-Ferrand (France). Il est diplômé d'architecture de l'École des beaux-arts de Paris (1978), et d'urbanisme de l'École nationale des ponts et chaussées (Paris, 1979). Il est également titulaire d'une maîtrise d'histoire à l'École des hautes études en sciences sociales (Paris, 1980). Il crée son agence en 1981 à Paris. Parmi ses principales réalisations figurent la Bibliothèque de France (Paris, 1989–97) ; le vélodrome et la piscine olympique de Berlin (1992–99) ; la médiathèque de Vénissieux (France, 1997–2001) ; plusieurs supermarchés pour la chaîne M-Preis en Autriche (1999–2003) ; le plan directeur de Donau City à Vienne (Autriche, 2002–03) et la rénovation de la Piazza Gramsci (Cinisello Balsamo, Milan, 1999–04). Ses projets actuels comprennent le nouveau théâtre Mariinsky (Saint-Pétersbourg, 2003–) ; la tour de l'hôtel ME Barcelona Hotel (Barcelone, 2002–07) ; une extension de la Cour de justice des Communautés européennes (Luxembourg, 2004–08) ; l'université féminine EWHA à Séoul (Corée du Sud, 2004–08, publiée ici) ; le pavillon de Priory Park (Reigate, GB, 2007–08) ; l'hôtel NH–Fieramilano (Milan, 2006–09) ; la passerelle de l'Arganzuela à Madrid (2005–10) et la tour Fukoku (Osaka, 2008–10). Actuellement, il travaille sur les projets des tours DC à Vienne (Autriche, 2004–12) ; le nouveau Grand théâtre d'Albi (2009–13) ; l'extension du musée Dobrée à Nantes (France, 2010–15) ; le plan de développement du nouveau quartier de la gare FFS station à Locarno (Suisse, 2009–) et le plan de rénovation du centre de Sofia (Bulgarie, 2009–).

EWHA WOMANS UNIVERSITY

Seoul, South Korea, 2004–08

Address: 11–1 Daehyungdong, Seodaemun-gu, Seoul 120–750, South Korea, www.ewha.ac.kr
Area: 70 000 m². Client: Ewha Womans University. Cost: not disclosed
Collaboration: Baum Architects, Seoul

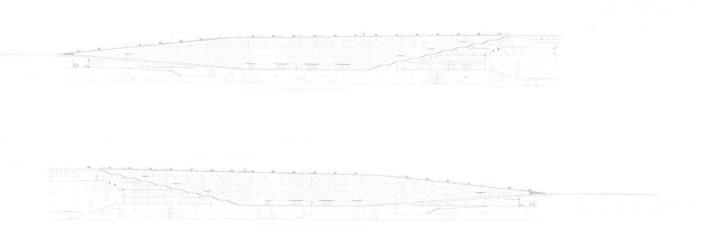

Drawings of the structure show its slightly angled form, following the lines of the topography of the site.	*Auf Zeichnungen des Gebäudes ist seine leicht schräge Form zu erkennen, die der Topografie folgt.*	*Les plans ci-dessus montrent la forme légèrement inclinée de l'université, qui suit la topographie.*

Founded in 1886, **EWHA** has 22 000 female students. Dominique Perrault won the international competition to design these new facilities in 2003, inaugurating the building on April 29, 2008. The program includes spaces for study, sports, including outdoor areas, offices, a cinema, and parking. A great emphasis was put on the energy efficiency of the structure, with its green roof, water-use efficiency, and renewable energy sources. In winter fully 80% and in summer 70% of the power demands are provided by natural resources, such as geothermal energy or natural ventilation. The project resembles a work of landscape architecture as much as it does more traditional structures—with its long avenue slicing through the middle of the site and revealing the academic spaces below the green roof. The architect calls the main spaces the Sports Strip and the Campus Valley—emphasizing the landscape elements of the design. As he wrote at the beginning of the project: "A new seam slices through the topography revealing the interior of the Ewha campus center. A void is formed, a hybrid place, in which a variety of activities can unfold. It is an avenue, gently descending, controlling the flow of traffic, leading to a monumental stair carrying visitors upwards, recalling the Champs Elysees or the Campidoglio in Rome."

Die 1886 gegründete Universität **EWHA** hat 22 000 weibliche Studierende. Dominique Perrault gewann den Wettbewerb für die neuen Einrichtungen 2003, eingeweiht wurde der Bau am 29. April 2008. Das Programm umfasst Räume für Lehre und Studium, Sport (einschließlich Außenanlagen), Büros, ein Kino sowie Parkplätze. Besondere Aufmerksamkeit wurde der Energieeffizienz des Komplexes gewidmet, was durch ein begrüntes Dach, effiziente Wassernutzung und den Einsatz erneuerbarer Energien unterstützt wurde. Im Winter werden gut 80 %, im Sommer 70 % des Energieverbrauchs durch natürliche Ressourcen gedeckt, etwa durch Erdwärme oder natürliche Belüftung. Das Projekt wirkt teilweise wie Landschaftsarchitektur und erinnert zugleich an traditionelle Bauten – eine lange Schneise zieht sich mitten durch das Gelände, unter den begrünten Dächern liegen die akademischen Einrichtungen. Der Architekt nennt die Hauptzonen des Komplexes „Sportstreifen" und „Campustal" und betont damit die landschaftlichen Aspekte des Entwurfs. Zu Beginn des Projekts formulierte er: „Eine neue Nahtstelle verläuft quer durch die Topografie und enthüllt das Innenleben des Ewha-Campuszentrums. Es entsteht ein Leerraum, ein hybrider Raum, in dem sich die verschiedensten Aktivitäten entfalten können. Eine sanft abfallend Chaussee regelt den Verkehrsfluss und mündet in einer monumentalen Treppe, die die Besucher nach oben führt und an die Champs-Elysées oder den Campidoglio in Rom erinnert."

Fondée en 1886, l'université d'**EWHA** compte 22 000 étudiantes. Dominique Perrault a remporté, en 2003, le concours international lancé pour ce nouveau bâtiment, dont l'inauguration a eu lieu le 29 avril 2008. Le programme comprend des installations pour l'étude, le sport, y compris de plein air, des bureaux, un cinéma et des parkings. La consommation énergétique a été particulièrement étudiée, ce qui se traduit entre autres par une toiture végétalisée, une gestion efficace de l'eau et l'appel à des sources d'énergie renouvelables. En hiver, 80 % de la consommation électrique, pour 70 % en été, sont fournis par des ressources naturelles, comme la géothermie ou la ventilation naturelle. Le projet fait penser à une œuvre d'architecture paysagère par sa longue avenue centrale en tranchée sur laquelle donnent les salles d'étude protégées par une toiture végétalisée. Dans cet esprit, l'architecte a appelé les deux éléments principaux « Boucle des sports » et « Vallée du campus ». Il explique : « L'université féminine s'organise autour d'une clôture géométrique modelée à partir d'une faille naturelle, et cette profonde incision dans le terrain, qui sert aussi d'axe de circulation piétonne, est complétée par une bande horizontale à usage sportif. Comme une peinture suprématiste, le projet se résout ainsi en deux gestes topographiques catégoriques […] qui font disparaître l'architecture dans un paysage violemment altéré par la géométrie … »

Images of the central walkway and
the site show how the architect has
inserted the buildings into the earth,
almost like a piece of functional
land art.

Ansichten der zentralen Wegschneise
und des Geländes verdeutlichen, wie
der Architekt die Bauten in den Boden
integriert hat – beinahe wie eine funk-
tional nutzbare Land-Art-Installation.

Les images de l'avenue centrale et
du site montrent comment l'architecte a intégré les bâtiments dans le
profil du terrain, un peu comme une
œuvre de land art fonctionnel.

Because of the way it is cut into the earth, the university complex allows daylight to penetrate interior areas. Below, a site plan, showing the long rectangular path of the main walkway.

Dank der Art, wie der Universitäts-komplex in den Boden eingelassen wurde, fällt Tageslicht in die Innen-räume. Unten ein Grundstücksplan, auf dem die längliche Wegschneise zu erkennen ist.

La profonde tranchée dans le sol permet à la lumière naturelle de pénétrer dans tous les volumes inté-rieurs. Ci-dessous, un plan montrant la longue tranchée centrale.

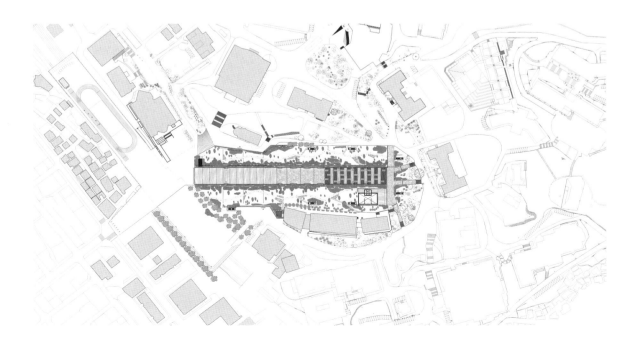

RENZO PIANO

Renzo Piano Building Workshop
Via P. Paolo Rubens 29, 16158 Genoa, Italy
Tel: +39 010 617 11 / Fax: +39 010 617 13 50
E-mail: italy@rpbw.com
Web: www.rpbw.com

RENZO PIANO was born in 1937 in Genoa, Italy. He studied at the University of Florence and at Milan's Polytechnic Institute (1964). He formed his own practice (Studio Piano) in 1965, associated with Richard Rogers (Piano & Rogers, 1971–78)—completing the Pompidou Center in Paris in 1977—and then worked with Peter Rice (Piano & Rice Associates, 1978–80), before creating the Renzo Piano Building Workshop in 1981 in Genoa and Paris. Piano received the RIBA Gold Medal in 1989. Built work after 2000 includes Maison Hermès (Tokyo, Japan, 1998–2001); Rome Auditorium (Italy, 1994–2002); conversion of the Lingotto Factory Complex (Turin, Italy, 1983–2003); the Padre Pio Pilgrimage Church (San Giovanni Rotondo, Foggia, Italy, 1991–2004); the Woodruff Arts Center Expansion (Atlanta, Georgia, USA, 1999–2005); the renovation and expansion of the Morgan Library (New York, New York, USA, 2000–06); and the New York Times Building (New York, New York, USA, 2005–07). Recently completed work includes the Broad Contemporary Art Museum (Phase 1 of the LACMA expansion, Los Angeles, California, USA, 2003–08); the California Academy of Sciences (San Francisco, California, USA, 2005–08, published here); the Modern Wing of the Art Institute of Chicago (Chicago, Illinois, USA, 2005–09); Saint Giles Court mixed-use development (London, UK, 2002–10); the Resnick Pavilion (Phase 2 of the LACMA expansion, Los Angeles, 2006–10); the Poor Clare Monastery at Ronchamp (France, 2006–11); and the London Bridge Tower (London, UK, 2000–12). Ongoing work includes the Stavros Niarchos Foundation Cultural Center (Athens, Greece, 2008–); Valletta City Gate (Valletta, Malta, 2008–); and the Botin Art Center (Santander, Spain, 2010–).

RENZO PIANO wurde 1937 in Genua in Italien geboren. Er studierte bis 1964 an der Universität Florenz und am Polytechnikum in Mailand. 1965 gründete er sein eigenes Büro (Studio Piano), von 1971 bis 1978 leitete er mit Richard Rogers das Büro Piano & Rogers, das 1977 das Centre Pompidou in Paris fertigstellte. Von 1978 bis 1980 arbeitete Piano mit Peter Rice (Piano & Rice Associates), bevor er 1981 in Genua und Paris den Renzo Piano Building Workshop gründete. Renzo Piano erhielt 1989 die Goldmedaille des RIBA. Zu seinen nach 2000 entstandenen Werken gehören das Maison Hermès in Tokio (1998–2001), das Auditorium in Rom (1994–2002), der Umbau des Fabrikgebäudes Lingotto in Turin (1983–2003), die Pilgerkirche Padre Pio in San Giovanni Rotondo, Foggia, Italien (1991–2004), der Erweiterungsbau des Woodruff Arts Center in Atlanta, Georgia, USA (1999–2005), die Renovierung und Erweiterung der Morgan Library (2000–06) und das New York Times Building (2005 bis 2007), beide in New York. In letzter Zeit fertiggestellt wurden das Broad Contemporary Art Museum (1. Bauabschnitt der Erweiterung des LACMA in Los Angeles, 2003 bis 2008), die California Academy of Sciences in San Francisco (2005–08, hier vorgestellt), der Modern Wing des Art Institute of Chicago (Illinois, 2005–09), die Neubebau-ung mit Mischnutzung im Stadtteil Saint Giles Court (London, 2002–10), der Resnick Pavillon (2. Bauabschnitt der Erweiterung des LACMA in Los Angeles, 2006–10), das Klarissenkloster in Ronchamp, Frankreich (2006–11), und das Hochhaus London Bridge Tower (2000–12). Momentan im Bau befinden sich das Kulturzentrum der Stavros Niarchos Foundation (Athen, Griechenland, seit 2008), das Valletta City Gate (Valletta, Malta, seit 2008) sowie das Kunstzentrum der Stiftung Botín in Santander (Spanien, seit 2010).

RENZO PIANO, né en 1937 à Gênes (Italie), a étudié à l'université de Florence et à l'Institut polytechnique de Milan (1964). Il crée son agence Studio Piano en 1965, puis s'associe à Richard Rogers (Piano & Rogers, 1971–78) et réalise le Centre Pompidou à Paris en 1977. Il collabore avec Peter Rice (Piano & Rice Associates, 1978–80) avant de fonder le Renzo Piano Building Workshop en 1981 à Gênes et à Paris. Il a reçu la médaille d'or du RIBA en 1989. Parmi ses réalisations après 2000 : la Maison Hermès (Tokyo, 1998–2001); l'auditorium Parco della Musica (Rome, 1994–2002); la reconversion du site industriel du Lingotto (Turin, 1983–2003); l'église de pèlerinage Padre Pio (San Giovanni Rotondo, Foggia, Italie, 1991–2004); l'extension du Centre d'art Woodruff (Atlanta, Géorgie, 1999–2005); la rénovation et l'agran-dissement de la Morgan Library (New York, 2000–06) et le New York Times Building (New York, 2005–07). Parmi ses œuvres récentes : le Broad Contem porary Art Museum (Phase 1 de l'extension du LACMA, Los Angeles, 2003–08); la California Academy of Sciences (San Francisco, 2005–08, publiée ici); l'aile moderne de l'Art Institute de Chicago (Illinois, 2005–09); Saint Giles Court, immeubles mixtes (Londres, 2002–10); le Resnick Pavilion (Phase 2 de l'extension du LACMA, Los Angeles, 2006–10); le monastère Sainte-Claire à Ronchamp (France, 2006–11) et la London Bridge Tower (Londres, 2000–12). Il travaille actuellement au projet du Centre culturel de la Fondation Stavros Niarchos (Athènes, 2008–); de la porte de la ville de La Valette (Malte, 2008–) et du Centre d'art Botín (Santander, Espagne, 2010–).

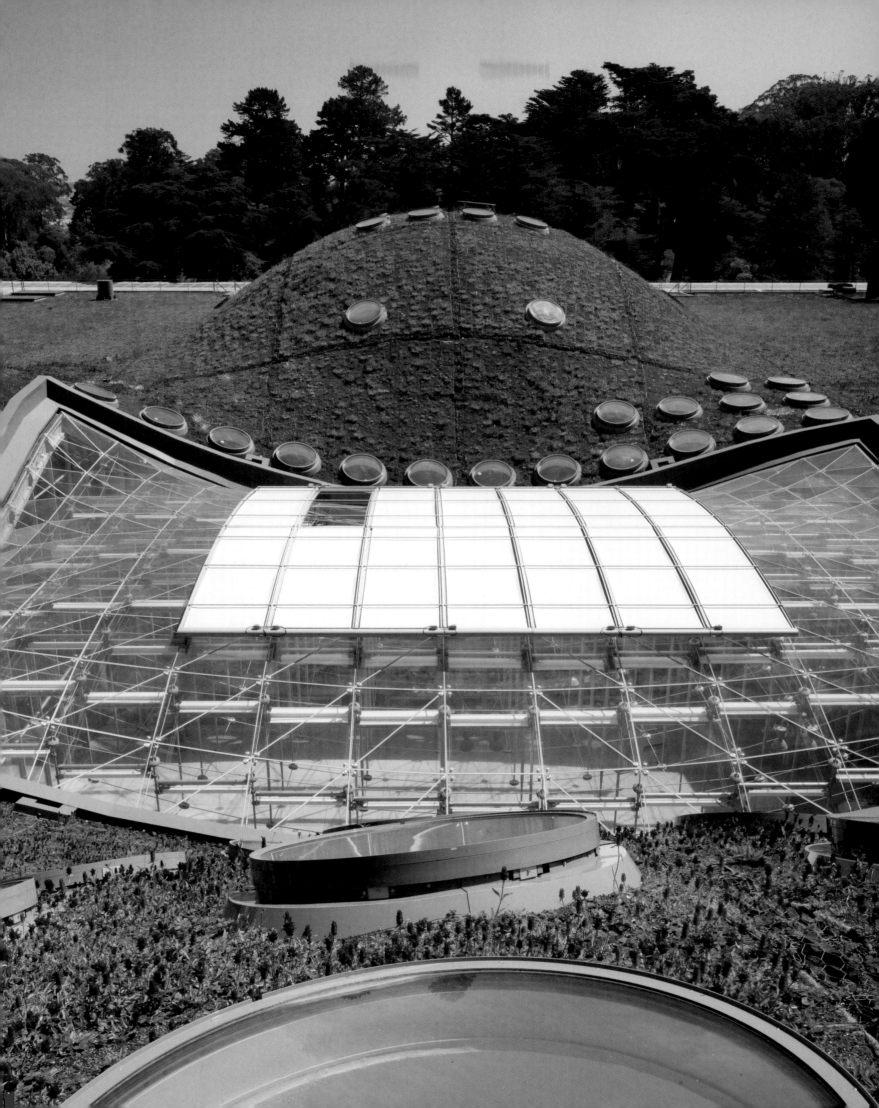

RENOVATION AND EXPANSION
OF THE CALIFORNIA ACADEMY OF SCIENCES

San Francisco, California, USA, 2005–08

*Address: 55 Music Concourse Drive, Golden Gate Park, San Francisco, CA 94118, USA, +1 415 379 8000,
www.calacademy.org. Area: 74 322 m² (site), 34 374 m² (floor area). Client: California Academy of Sciences
Cost: $370 million, including exhibition program and costs associated with the Academy's temporary housing
Collaboration: Gordon H. Chung and Partners, San Francisco*

The green roof of the California Academy of Sciences is one of the most outstanding features of the architecture, making up an artificial landscape of considerable proportions. Skylights admit overhead daylight into the building.

Das grüne Dach der California Academy of Sciences ist eines der auffälligsten Merkmale dieser Architektur. Es ist eine recht große künstliche Dachlandschaft. Über die Oberlichter gelangt Tageslicht in das Innere des Gebäudes.

La toiture végétalisée de la California Academy of Sciences est l'un des éléments les plus remarquables de ce projet. Elle constitue en soi un paysage artificiel de dimensions considérables. Des verrières assurent l'éclairage diurne de l'intérieur du bâtiment.

One of the 10 largest natural history museums in the world, the **CALIFORNIA ACADEMY OF SCIENCES** was founded in 1853. The institution declared: "The new CAS will be at the forefront of green building design, showcasing world-class architecture that fully integrates green building features to reflect its mission to protect the natural world." The completed structure has a LEED Platinum rating reflecting its strategies to conserve energy and to use environmentally friendly building materials. The undulating roof of the structure, with a surface of over one hectare, is covered with 1.8 million native California plants. Careful study of the plants themselves, but also of the seismic implications of a planted roof, was part of the preparation of this aspect of the design that is open to visitors. It is calculated that the design of the roof reduces temperatures inside the museum by about 6°C. A rainwater collection system is designed to store and reuse about 13 500 cubic meters of water each year, reused for irrigation and gray water. The roof's shape and, indeed, the entire design of the museum were conceived to form a continuum with the surrounding park environment. Intended for schoolchildren and the general public, the academy focuses on education and research on conserving natural environments and habitats.

Die 1853 gegründete **CALIFORNIA ACADEMY OF SCIENCES** gehört zu den zehn größten Naturhistorischen Museen der Welt. Die Museumsleitung erklärt: „Die neue CAS wird an vorderster Stelle der nach ‚grünen' Maßstäben entworfenen Gebäude stehen, mit einer Weltklassearchitektur, die alle Merkmale des nachhaltigen Bauens in sich vereint und dadurch der Aufgabe des CAS entspricht, die Natur zu schützen." Das gesamte Gebäude ist wegen der Energiesparmaßnahmen und den umweltfreundlichen Baumaterialien nach der US-Klassifizierung für ökologisches Bauen, LEED, mit der höchsten Kategorie „Platinum" zertifiziert. Das gewellte Dach mit einer Fläche von etwa 1 ha ist mit 1,8 Millionen in Kalifornien heimischen Pflanzen bedeckt und öffentlich zugänglich. Sorgfältige Pflanzenstudien, aber auch Untersuchungen bezüglich der Auswirkungen von Erdbeben auf das begrünte Dach wurden im Vorfeld durchgeführt. Laut den Berechnungen mindert die Dachgestaltung die Innenraumtemperaturen des Museums um etwa 6 °C. Dank eines Regenwassersammelsystems können etwa 13 500 m³ Grauwasser pro Jahr für Bewässerung wiederverwendet werden. Der Museumsentwurf einschließlich des Dachs bildet ein nahtloses Kontinuum mit der umliegenden Parklandschaft. Die Institution richtet sich sowohl an Schüler als auch das allgemeine Publikum und beschäftigt sich mit Bildung und Forschung über den Erhalt der natürlichen Umwelt und der Habitate.

L'un des dix plus grands musées d'histoire naturelle au monde, la **CALIFORNIA ACADEMY OF SCIENCES** date de 1853. Orientée vers le grand public et le public scolaire, elle se consacre à l'éducation et à la recherche sur la conservation des environnements et habitats naturels. Lors de la présentation du projet, l'institution a déclaré : «La nouvelle CAS sera à l'avant-garde de la construction écologique, la vitrine d'une architecture de niveau international, qui intègre pleinement les exigences de la construction durable dans sa mission de protéger le monde naturel.» Le bâtiment a obtenu la classification LEED Platine qui récompense les stratégies mises en œuvre pour conserver l'énergie et utiliser des matériaux de construction durables. Ouverte aux visiteurs, la toiture à ondulations de plus de un hectare a été plantée de plus de 1,8 million d'espèces californiennes. L'étude de ces végétaux, mais aussi des implications du poids élevé de la toiture en cas de tremblement de terre ont joué un rôle important. On a calculé que ce type de toit réduit la température à l'intérieur du musée de 6 °C environ. Un système de collecte des eaux de pluie permet de stocker et de réutiliser environ 13 500 m³ d'eau par an pour l'irrigation et les eaux sanitaires. La forme du toit et l'ensemble du musée forment un continuum avec le parc environnant.

The building is itself located in a park and, as can be seen in the image and the elevation drawing above, greenery in various forms is present above and within the structure.

Das Gebäude liegt in einem Park, wie man auf dem Bild und der Fassaden-abwicklung oben erkennen kann. Grün ist in verschiedenen Formen auf und im Gebäude vorhanden.

Le bâtiment est situé dans un parc, comme le montrent les images et le dessin de coupe ci-dessus. La ver-dure est présente sous toutes ses formes à l'intérieur comme alentour.

PUSHAK

PUSHAK AS
Sivilarkitekter MNAL
Arbeidersamfunnets Plass 1
0181 Oslo
Norway

Tel: +47 22 60 60 40
E-mail: post@pushak.no
Web: www.pushak.no

CAMILLA LANGELAND was born in Oslo, Norway, in 1975. She studied Art History at Oslo University (1995), attended the University of Lund (1999), and received her degree in Architecture from the Oslo School of Architecture (2001). She worked for Lund & Slaatto (1999–2000), and for div.A Architects (2002–04) before cofounding PUSHAK in 2004. **SISSIL MORSETH GROMHOLT** was born in 1974 in Oslo, studied at Bergen University (1999), and received an architecture degree from the Oslo School of Architecture (2001) before becoming a principal of PUSHAK in 2004. **MARTHE MELBYE** was born in 1973 in Oslo and received her degree from the Oslo School of Architecture in 2001 before becoming a partner of PUSHAK in 2004. **GYDA DRAGE KELIVA** was born in Oslo in 1972, received an architecture degree from the Oslo School of Architecture in 2000, and was also a founding partner of PUSHAK in 2004. The firm was created by all four partners in 2004 and has actually been called PUSHAK since 2006. The practice has completed Rest Stop Snefjord (Finnmark, 2005); Lillefjord (Måsøy, Finnmark, 2006, published here); Rest Stop Torskfjorddalen (Finnmark, 2007); Rest Stop Reinoksevatn (Finnmark, 2007); Imagine Rommen (Rommen, Groruddalen, Oslo, 2008–); Vestfold Crematorium (Sandefjord, Vestfold, 2010); Solstad Kindergarten (Stavern, Vestfold, 2010); and a Summer Cabin (Hvaler, 2011), all in Norway. It is currently working on Rest Stop Storberget (Finnmark, 2011).

CAMILLA LANGELAND wurde 1975 in Oslo geboren. Sie studierte Kunstgeschichte an der Universität Oslo (1995), besuchte die Universität Lund (1999) und beendete 2001 ihr Architekturstudium an der Oslo School of Architecture. Sie arbeitete im Büro Lund & Slaatto (1999–2000) und bei div.A Architekter (2002–04), bevor sie 2004 PUSHAK mitgründete. **SISSIL MORSETH GROMHOLT** wurde 1974 in Oslo geboren, studierte an der Universität Bergen (1999) und beendete 2001 ihr Studium an der Oslo School of Architecture. 2004 wurde sie Leiterin von PUSHAK. **MARTHE MELBYE** wurde 1973 in Oslo geboren und schloss 2001 ihr Studium an der Oslo School of Architecture ab. 2004 wurde sie Partnerin von PUSHAK. **GYDA DRAGE KELIVA** wurde 1972 in Oslo geboren, beendete 2000 ihr Studium an der Oslo School of Architecture und war 2004 ebenfalls Mitgründerin von PUSHAK. Die Firma wurde 2004 gegründet und heißt seit 2006 PUSHAK. Das Büro hat folgende Bauten ausgeführt: Raststätte Snefjord (Finnmark, 2005), Lillefjord (Måsøy, Finnmark, 2006, hier vorgestellt), Raststätte Torskfjorddalen (Finnmark, 2007), Raststätte Reinoksevatn (Finnmark, 2007), Imagine Rommen (Rommen, Groruddalen, Oslo, seit 2008), das Krematorium Vestfold (Sandefjord, Vestfold, 2010), der Kindergarten Solstad (Stavern, Vestfold, 2010) sowie ein Ferienhaus (Hvaler, 2011), alle in Norwegen. Im Bau befindet sich die Raststätte Storberget (Finnmark, 2011).

CAMILLA LANGELAND, née à Oslo en 1975, a étudié l'histoire de l'art à l'université d'Oslo (1995), puis à l'université de Lund (1999) et a reçu son diplôme d'architecte de l'École d'architecture d'Oslo (2001). Elle a travaillé pour Lund & Slaatto (1999–2000) et div.A Architekter (2002–04) avant de participer à la fondation de PUSHAK en 2004. **SISSIL MORSETH GROMHOLT**, née en 1974 à Oslo, a étudié à l'université de Bergen (1999), est diplômée de l'École d'architecture d'Oslo (2001) et a rejoint les partenaires de PUSHAK en 2004. **MARTHE MELBYE**, née en 1973 à Oslo, a suivi le même parcours, ainsi que **GYDA DRAGE KELIVA**, née à Oslo en 1972. L'agence fondée par ses quatre partenaires en 2004 a pris le nom de PUSHAK en 2006. L'agence a réalisé, toujours en Norvège : le restaurant d'autoroute Snefjord (Finnmark, 2005) ; Lillefjord (Måsøy, Finnmark, 2006, publié ici) ; le restaurant d'autoroute Torskfjorddalen (Finnmark, 2007) ; le restaurant d'autoroute Reinoksevatn (Finnmark, 2007) et Imagine Rommen (Rommen, Groruddalen, Oslo, 2008–) ; le crématorium de Vestfold (Sandefjord, Vestfold, 2010) ; le jardin d'enfants Solstad (Stavern, Vestfold, 2010) et un chalet d'été (Hvaler, 2011). Elle travaille actuellement au restaurant d'autoroute Storberget (Finnmark, 2011–).

LILLEFJORD

Måsøy, Finnmark, Norway, 2006

Address: Rv 889, Måsøy, Finnmark, Norway
Area: not applicable. Client: National Tourist Route Project
Cost: not disclosed

Part of a series of other projects, this installation in northern Norway involved benches, a shelter, and a toilet at the start of a trail to a mountain waterfall. PUSHAK proposed to create a steel-frame bridge with a wooden interior that leads visitors to an old trail. The architects state: "The steel frame was prefabricated, minimizing work on site in this rough climate. Materials were chosen to minimize maintenance."

Diese Anlage ist eines von mehreren Projekten im Norden Norwegens und umfasst Bänke, einen Schutzbau und Toiletten am Beginn eines Wanderwegs zu einem Wasserfall in den Bergen. PUSHAK schlug den Bau einer Brücke mit Stahlkonstruktion und einem Innenraum in Holz vor, die die Besucher zu einem alten Fußweg leitet. Die Architektinnen erklären: „Die Stahlkonstruktion wurde vorgefertigt, um die Arbeit vor Ort in diesem rauen Klima zu reduzieren. Es wurden Materialien gewählt, die nur minimaler Wartung bedürfen."

Élément d'une série de projets, cette installation mise en place dans le nord de la Norvège comprend des banquettes, un abri, des toilettes et le départ d'un parcours vers une cascade dans les montagnes. PUSHAK a proposé de créer une passerelle à ossature d'acier et tablier en bois qui oriente les visiteurs vers un ancien chemin. « La structure en acier est préfabriquée, ce qui a réduit la durée du chantier sous un climat difficile. Les matériaux ont été choisis pour minimiser la maintenance », ont expliqué les architectes.

The architects use pine planks and metal to create both a proximity to the natural setting and an intentional, manufactured distance, as seen in the frame.

Die Architektinnen wählten Kiefernholzbretter und Metall, um Nähe zur natürlichen Umgebung zu erreichen und – wie an der Einfassung erkennbar – zugleich bewusst eine Distanz herzustellen.

Les architectes ont volontairement choisi des habillages en pin pour créer une proximité avec le cadre naturel et une ossature en métal pour installer une distance.

The elongated wooden structure seems to flow into and over the bridge, narrowing as it reaches the opposite bank of the stream.

Die lang gestreckte Holzkonstruktion führt scheinbar in und über die Brücke und verengt sich auf der anderen Uferseite.

La superstructure en bois semble se projeter de la petite construction vers le pont qu'elle franchit en se rétrécissant lorsqu'elle atteint la rive opposée.

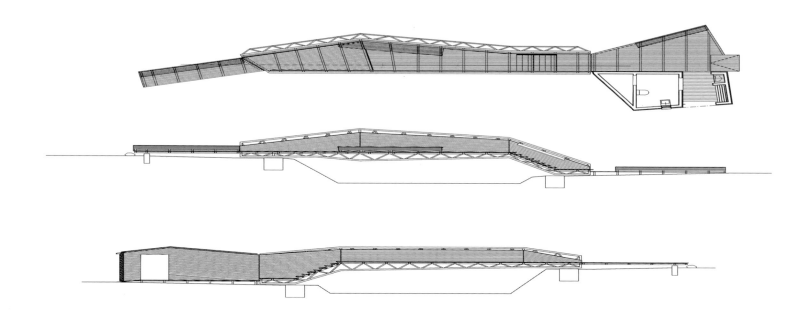

The horizontal planking and angled surfaces contribute to an impression of a flowing, almost mobile design that runs into the landscape itself.

Die horizontale Bretterverkleidung und die abgewinkelten Flächen tragen zur fließenden, beinahe mobilen Wirkung der Brücke bei.

Le bardage horizontal et les plans inclinés contribuent à donner une impression de fluidité, presque de mobilité.

HIROSHI SAMBUICHI

Hiroshi Sambuichi Architects
8–3–302 Nakajima naka-ku
730–0811 Hiroshima
Japan

Tel: +81 82 544 1417
Fax: +81 82 544 1418
E-mail: samb@d2.dion.ne.jp

HIROSHI SAMBUICHI was born in 1968. He graduated from the Department of Architecture in the Faculty of Science and Technology at Tokyo University of Science. After working for Shinichi Ogawa & Associates, he established Sambuichi Architects and began design work in Hiroshima. His work includes the Running Green Project (Yamaguchi, 2001); Air House (Yamaguchi, 2001); Miwa-gama (Yamaguchi, 2002); Sloping North House (Yamaguchi, 2003); Stone House (Shimane, 2005); and the Inujima Art Project Seirensho (Okayama, 2006–08, published here), all in Japan.

HIROSHI SAMBUICHI wurde 1968 geboren. Sein Architekturstudium schloss er an der Fakultät für Naturwissenschaften und Technik an der Tokyo University of Science ab. Nachdem er zunächst für Shinichi Ogawa & Associates gearbeitet hatte, gründete er sein Büro Sambuichi Architects und begann in Hiroshima zu praktizieren. Zu seinen Projekten zählen u. a.: Running Green Project (Yamaguchi, 2001), Air House (Yamaguchi, 2001), Miwa-gama (Yamaguchi, 2002), Sloping North House (Yama-guchi, 2003), Stone House (Shimane, 2005) sowie das Inujima Art Project Seirensho (Inujima, Okayama, 2006–08, hier vorgestellt), alle in Japan.

Né en 1968, **HIROSHI SAMBUICHI** est diplômé du département d'architecture de la faculté des sciences et technologies de l'Université des sciences de Tokyo. Après avoir travaillé pour Shinichi Ogawa & Associates, il a fondé l'agence Sambuichi Architects et commencé à travailler à Hiroshima. Ses réalisations comprennent le Running Green Project (Yamaguchi, 2001) ; l'Air House (Yamaguchi, 2001) ; Miwa-Gama (Yamaguchi, 2002) ; la Sloping North House (Yamaguchi, 2003) ; la Stone House (Shimane, 2005) et le projet artistique Seirensho d'Inujima (Okayama, 2006–08, publié ici), le tout au Japon.

INUJIMA ART PROJECT SEIRENSHO

Inujima, Okayama, Japan, 2006–08

Area: 790 m². Client: Soichiro Fukutake
Cost: not disclosed

This one-story wood-and-steel structure is located on a 5212-square-meter site on the small Inland Sea island of Inujima. The client, Soichiro Fukutake, is the head of the Benesse Corporation, which is also at the origin of Tadao Ando's projects on the nearby island of Naoshima. Like Naoshima, the island was marked by an industrial presence, in this case a copper refinery that operated between 1909 and 1919, leaving only ruins behind. The architect says: "I thought that all the existing materials are regenerable resources, such as the old architecture of the ruins, the geography, open spaces, the infrastructure of the factories, wastes, and so on. There are six different levels of height on the site, and I considered these as landscapes for making use of the necessary potential energy. I decided to use levels one to four in this project, and planned architectural figures to utilize and activate chimneys and accumulate energy for years and years." He used waste slag in the floor and walls. Timber is used above ground, as it was in the original plant, and the slag used in the floors contains iron oxide from the plant. The museum contains four main spaces, a cooling corridor that uses the heat of the earth, a sun gallery that collects the energy of the sun, an energy hall and chimney, and a landscape "controlling the circulation of vegetation and water." Rather than "large hidden machinery," the architect has used the energy of the earth and sun to "power" this museum.

Der einstöckige Bau aus Holz und Stahl liegt auf einem 5212 m^2 großen Grundstück auf der kleinen Insel Inujima in der Seto-Inlandsee. Soichiro Fukutake, Bauherr des Projekts und Direktor der Firma Benesse, war schon Auftraggeber der Tadao-Ando-Bauten auf der nahe gelegenen Insel Naoshima. Wie Naoshima so ist auch Inujima von seiner industriellen Vorgeschichte geprägt, in diesem Fall von einer Kupferraffinerie, die zwischen 1909 und 1919 in Betrieb war und von der noch Ruinen erhalten sind. Der Architekt erklärt: „Meine Überlegung war, alle vorhandenen Materialien als erneuerbare Ressourcen zu verstehen – die Architektur der Ruinen, die Geografie, die offenen Räume, die Infrastruktur der Fabriken, den Schutt und so weiter. Das Gelände hat sechs Höhenniveaus, die ich als Landschaften und potenzielle Energieerzeuger interpretiert habe. Ich beschloss, die Niveaus eins bis vier in das Projekt zu integrieren, und entwarf eine Architekturkonstellation, in der sich die Schornsteine aktivieren und nutzen lassen, um so Energie auf Jahre hinaus speichern zu können." Für Böden und Wände griff der Architekt auf alte Schlacken zurück. Über Grund wurde, wie in der alten Fabrik, mit Holz gearbeitet. Die Schlacken der Bodenbeläge enthalten Eisenoxid aus dem alten Werk. Zum Museum gehören vier Bereiche, ein Kühlkorridor, der mit Erdwärme arbeitet, eine Sonnengalerie, die Solarenergie erzeugt, eine Energiehalle mit Schornstein und eine Landschaft, die „den Kreislauf von Vegetation und Wasser steuert". Statt „aufwendiger Technik hinter den Kulissen" nutzt der Architekt Erde und Sonne, um dieses Museum mit Energie zu versorgen.

Cette construction en bois et acier d'un seul niveau est implantée sur un terrain de 5212 m^2 sur la petite île d'Inujima, dans la Mer intérieure du Japon. Le client, Soichiro Fukutake – qui dirige la Benesse Corporation – est par ailleurs à l'initiative des projets de Tadao Ando sur l'île voisine de Naoshima. Comme à Naoshima, les lieux étaient marqués par la présence d'une raffinerie de cuivre qui avait opéré de 1909 à 1919 et laissé une friche de ruines industrielles. Selon l'architecte : « J'ai pensé que tous ces matériaux abandonnés étaient des ressources réutilisables, de même que l'architecture ancienne de ces ruines, la géographie, les espaces ouverts, l'infrastructure des usines, les déchets, etc. Il existe six niveaux de hauteur sur le site que j'ai considérés comme un paysage dont il fallait extraire le potentiel énergétique nécessaire. J'ai décidé d'investir les niveaux un à quatre, et j'ai conçu des formes architecturales pour utiliser et activer les cheminées et l'énergie accumulée depuis des années et des années. » Hiroshi Sambuichi s'est servi de scories pour les sols (mâchefer chargé d'oxyde de fer) et les murs. Le bois est utilisé pour les structures au-dessus du sol, comme dans l'usine originelle. Le musée contient quatre volumes principaux, un corridor de refroidissement qui utilise la chaleur de la terre, une galerie solaire qui collecte l'énergie du soleil, un hall de l'énergie et la cheminée, et un paysage aménagé « contrôlant la circulation de la végétation et de l'eau ». Plutôt qu'une « grosse machinerie dissimulée », l'architecte s'est servi de l'énergie de la terre et du soleil pour « ancrer » cette réalisation.

The museum occupies the site of a former copper refinery on a small, remote island, giving the ruins a certain poetic presence.

Das Museum liegt auf einer kleinen entlegenen Insel, auf dem Gelände einer ehemaligen Kupferraffinerie. Die Ruinen wirken geradezu poetisch.

Le musée occupe le site d'une ancienne raffinerie de cuivre située sur une petite île isolée. Les ruines dégagent une certaine poésie.

The tall smokestack of the former refinery marks the location of the museum. The architect has deftly combined new elements with the existing architecture.

Der große Schornstein der ehemaligen Raffinerie markiert den Standort des Museums. Gekonnt kombiniert der Architekt neue Elemente mit bestehender Architektur.

La haute cheminée de l'ancienne raffinerie signale le site du musée. L'architecte a habilement associé des éléments architecturaux anciens à des composants nouveaux.

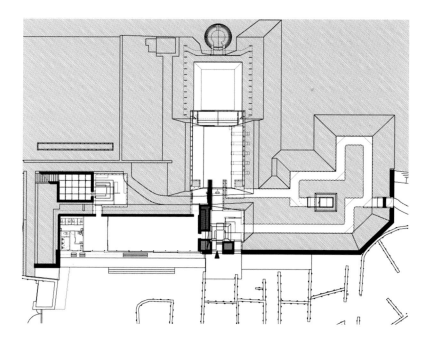

Hiroshi Sambuichi has used natural light and energy to the exclusion of artificial sources that would have been hard to come by on this abandoned site. He mixes existing spaces and elements with new ones in a way that makes it difficult to distinguish one from the other.

Hiroshi Sambuichi nutzt natürliches Licht und Energie und verzichtet auf künstliche Energiequellen, die an diesem entlegenen Standort auch schwerlich verfügbar sind. Er kombiniert bestehende Räumlichkeiten und Elemente so geschickt mit neuen, dass kaum Unterschiede erkennbar sind.

Hiroshi Sambuichi s'est servi de la lumière et de l'énergie naturelles à l'exclusion de toute source artificielle, difficile à mettre en œuvre sur un site aussi isolé. Il a mixé les volumes existants à de nouveaux éléments d'une telle façon qu'il est difficile de les distinguer.

Located near the Island of Naoshima, where Tadao Ando has built numerous art-related projects for the same client, the museum is intended to bring this abandoned industrial site back to life.

Das Museum – unweit der Insel Naoshima, auf der Tadao Ando verschiedene Kunstprojekte für denselben Auftraggeber realisierte – will das verlassene Industriegelände wieder zum Leben erwecken.

Situé non loin de l'île de Naoshima sur laquelle Tadao Ando a réalisé de nombreux projets d'ordre artistique pour le même client, ce musée devrait redonner vie à ce site industriel abandonné.

SARC ARCHITECTS

SARC Architects
Tammasaarenlaituri 3
00180 Helsinki
Finland

Tel. +358 9 6226 180
Fax: +358 9 6226 1840
E-mail: sarc@sarc.fi
Web: www.sarc.f

ANTTI-MATTI SIIKALA was born in 1964 in Turku, Finland, and obtained an M.S. degree in Architecture from the Helsinki University of Technology in 1993. He is a partner of SARC and a Professor of Building Technology, Department of Architecture, Helsinki University of Technology / Aalto University (2002–). **SARLOTTA NARJUS** was born in 1966 in Turku. She obtained her M.S. degree in Architecture from the Helsinki University of Technology in 1996. She worked with Heikkinen-Komonen Architects (1989–98) before becoming a partner of SARC in 1998. Their work includes Expo 2000 Finnish Pavilion (Hannover, Germany, 2000); University of Oulu, Faculty of Medicine, Main Building (Oulu, 2003); Metla, the Finnish Forest Research Institute (Joensuu; 2004, published here); Oulu City Hall (Oulu, 2008); and the Tapiola Headquarters (Espoo, 2010), all in Finland unless stated otherwise.

ANTTI-MATTI SIIKALA wurde 1964 in Turku in Finnland geboren und machte 1993 seinen Master in Architektur an der Technischen Universität Helsinki. Er ist Partner von SARC und Professor für Bautechnik an der Architekturabteilung der Technischen Universität Helsinki/Aalto-Universität (seit 2002). **SARLOTTA NARJUS** wurde 1966 in Turku geboren und machte ihren Master 1996 an derselben Universität. Sie arbeitete bei Heikkinen-Komonen Architects (1989–98) und wurde 1998 Partnerin bei SARC. Zu den Werken dieses Büros zählen der finnische Pavillon auf der Expo 2000 (Hannover, 2000), das Hauptgebäude der medizinischen Fakultät an der Universität Oulu (2003), Metla, das finnische Institut für Waldforschung (Joensuu; 2004, hier vorgestellt), das Rathaus von Oulu (2008) und die Hauptverwaltung von Tapiola (Espoo, 2010), alle in Finnland, sofern nicht anders angegeben.

ANTTI-MATTI SIIKALA, né en 1964 à Turku en Finlande est titulaire d'un M.Sc. en architecture de l'Université de technologie d'Helsinki (1993). Il est partenaire de l'agence SARC et professeur de technologie de la construction du département d'architecture de l'Université de technologie d'Helsinki/université Aalto (2002–). **SARLOTTA NARJUS**, née en 1966 à Turku, est également titulaire d'un M.Sc. en architecture de l'Université de technologie d'Helsinki (1996). Elle a travaillé chez Heikkinen-Komonen Architects (1989–98) avant de devenir partenaire de SARC en 1998. Parmi leurs réalisations, presque toutes en Finlande : le Pavillon finlandais pour Expo 2000 (Hannovre, Allemagne, 2000) ; le bâtiment principal de la faculté de médecine de l'University d'Oulu (Oulu, 2003) ; Metla, Institut finlandais de recherche forestière (Joensuu, 2004, publié ici) ; l'hôtel de ville d'Oulu (Oulu, 2008) et le siège de Tapiola (Espoo, 2010).

METLA, FINNISH FOREST RESEARCH INSTITUTE

Joensuu, Finland, 2004

Address: Joensuu Research Unit, Yliopistokatu 6, Box 68, FI-80101 Joensuu, Tel. +358 10 2111, www.metla.fi
Area: 7400 m². Client: Finnish Forest Research Institute. Cost: not disclosed

This building, an expansion of the existing institute, intended for a staff of 150–170 employees, is located on the Joensuu University campus, near the city center. The institute does applied forestry research and research on wooden materials. The architects explain: "The primary goal of the project was to use Finnish wood in innovative ways. Hence, wood is the main material used throughout the building, from the post-beam-slab system in the structural frame to the exterior cladding." The work areas are arrayed around a central courtyard and lobby. The walls of the entrance to the courtyard are made up of 100-year-old timber. Tall pines grow through the terrace in the courtyard. A conference space "resembles an overturned boat and fish-chest-inspired tilted wooden columns."

Dieses Gebäude, eine Erweiterung des bestehenden Instituts, bietet 150 bis 170 Arbeitsplätze und steht auf dem Campus der Universität Joensuu in der Nähe des Stadtzentrums. Das Institut führt angewandte Forschungen über Waldwirtschaft und über Materialien aus Holz durch. Die Architekten erklären: „Oberstes Ziel dieses Projekts war die Nutzung finnischen Holzes auf innovative Weise. Daher wurde Holz als Hauptbaumaterial für das gesamte Gebäude verwendet, von der Ständerkonstruktion des Tragwerks bis zur Außenverkleidung." Die Arbeitsbereiche sind um einen zentralen Innenhof und eine Lobby angeordnet. Die Wände des Eingangsbereichs zu diesem Innenhof bestehen aus 100 Jahre altem Holz. In diesem Hof wachsen hohe Kiefern durch die Terrasse. Die Form des Konferenzraums „ähnelt einem umgedrehten Boot und einer Fischkiste und wurde von den gebogenen Holzstützen bestimmt".

Ce bâtiment, qui est une extension de l'Institut installé sur le campus de l'université de Joensuu, près du centre-ville, a été conçu pour un personnel de 150 à 170 chercheurs et employés. L'Institut mène des recherches sur la forêt et les matériaux en bois. Selon les architectes : « L'objectif premier du projet est d'utiliser le bois finlandais selon des techniques novatrices. C'est pourquoi le bois est le principal matériau utilisé dans l'intégralité du bâtiment, du système d'ossature à poutres et poteaux sur dalle au parement extérieur. » Les zones de travail se répartissent autour d'une cour centrale et d'un hall d'accueil. Les murs de l'entrée qui donne sur la cour sont en bois de cent ans d'âge. De grands pins poussent dans la cour. On note un espace de conférences « ressemblant à une coque de bateau renversée et des colonnes en bois en forme de navettes inclinées ».

The Metla building demonstrates that wood can, indeed, be used to create an elegant, modern structure on a large scale.

Der Metla-Bau beweist, dass Holz in der Tat auch für elegante, moderne Bauten in großem Maßstab verwendet werden kann.

Le bâtiment du Metla montre que le bois peut servir à créer des constructions modernes et élégantes de grandes dimensions.

The basic plan of the building
(see below) is square with a notched,
interior courtyard. Splayed columns
made of wood connect the wood
ceiling to the tiled floor.

*Die Grundform des Gebäudes
(unten) ist quadratisch mit einem
eingeschnittenen Innenhof. Schräg
gestellte Stützen aus Holz verbinden
die Holzdecke mit dem Fliesenboden.*

*Le plan du bâtiment décrit un carré
(ci-dessous) dans lequel a été découpée une cour intérieure. Des colonnes
inclinées en bois font le lien entre le
plafond de bois et le sol carrelé.*

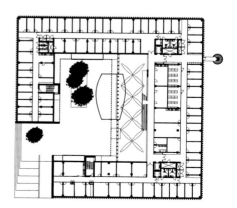
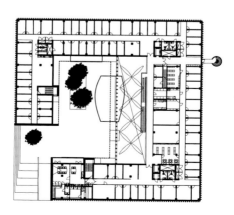
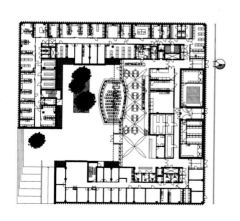

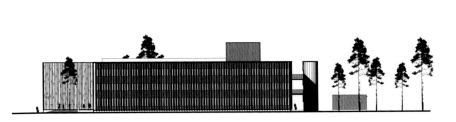

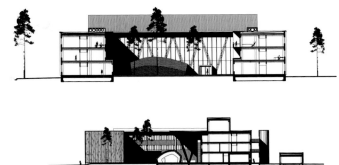

Glazed façades alternate with the more closed surfaces seen in the elevations above. Below, the space seen on the left page from a different angle.

Verglaste Flächen wechseln mit geschlossenen, wie die Ansichten oben zeigen. Unten: der auf der linken Seite dargestellte Innenraum aus einem anderen Blickwinkel.

Des façades vitrées alternent avec des plans plus fermés comme le montrent les élévations ci-dessus. Ci-dessus, l'espace de la page de gauche vu sous un angle différent.

SAUNDERS & WILHELMSEN

Todd Saunders
Saunders Architecture
Vestre Torggate 22
5015 Bergen, Norway

Tel: +47 55 36 85 06
E-mail: post@saunders.no
Web: www.saunders.no

Tommie Wilhelmsen
Wilhelmsen Arkitektur
Kvitsøygata 15
4006 Stavanger, Norway

E-mail: post@tommie-wilhelmsen.no
Web: www.tommie-wilhelmsen.no

TODD SAUNDERS was born in 1969 in Gander, Newfoundland, Canada. He obtained a Bachelor of Environmental Planning from the Nova Scotia College of Art and Design (1988–92) and his M.Arch from McGill University (Montreal, Canada, 1993–95). Since 1997, he has worked in Austria, Canada, Germany, Russia, Latvia, and Norway. His work includes the Summer House (Hardanger Fjord, Norway, 2003, published here); Aurland Look-Out (Aurland, Norway, 2006, with Tommie Wilhelmsen); as well as the Fogo Island Studios, four of which have been completed out of a program of six (Fogo Island, Newfoundland, Canada, 2010–11). **TOMMIE WILHELMSEN**, born in 1973, is Norwegian and was educated as an architect at the Bergen Architecture School. He has worked in Norway and Germany (with Behnisch & Behnisch in 1998). Recent work includes a number of private houses in Stavanger, Sandnes, and other nearby towns in Norway. The two were associated in Saunders & Wilhelmsen in 2002, and more recently created separate firms respectively located in Bergen and in Stavanger.

TODD SAUNDERS wurde 1969 in Gander im kanadischen Neufundland geboren. Er machte einen Bachelor of Environmental Planning am Nova Scotia College of Art and Design (1988–92) und einen M.Arch. an der McGill University (Montreal, 1993–95). Ab 1997 war er in Österreich, Kanada, Deutschland, Russland, Lettland und Norwegen tätig. Zu seinen Entwürfen zählt das Sommerhaus (Hardanger-Fjord, Norwegen, 2003, hier vorgestellt), ein Aussichtspunkt in Aurland (Norwegen, 2006, mit Tommie Wilhelmsen) sowie die Fogo Island Studios, von denen vier der insgesamt sechs geplanten Bauten bisher realisiert wurden (Fogo Island, Neufundland, 2010–11). **TOMMIE WILHELMSEN**, 1973 in Norwegen geboren, studierte an der Hochschule für Architektur in Bergen. Er war in Norwegen sowie in Deutschland tätig (Behnisch & Behnisch, 1998). Zu seinen jüngeren Arbeiten zählen einige Privathäuser in Stavanger, Sandnes und anderen nahe gelegenen Städten in Norwegen. Die beiden gründeten 2002 das Büro Saunders & Wilhelmsen. Vor Kurzem haben die Architekten eigene Büros in Bergen und Stavanger etabliert.

TODD SAUNDERS, né à Gander (Terre-Neuve, Canada) en 1969, est titulaire d'un Bachelor en programmation environnementale du Nova Scotia College of Art and Design (1988–1992) et d'un M.Arch. de la McGill University (Montréal, 1993–1995). Depuis 1997, il a travaillé au Canada, en Autriche, Allemagne, Russie, Lettonie et Norvège. Ses réalisations incluent une maison d'été (Hardanger Fjord, Norvège, 2003, publiée ici) ; le poste d'observation d'Aurland (Aurland, Norvège, 2006, avec Tommie Wilhelmsen), ainsi que les Fogo Island Studios, dont quatre sur six ont été achevés (île Fogo, Terre-Neuve, Canada, 2010–11). **TOMMIE WILHELMSEN**, né en 1973, est Norvégien et a étudié l'architecture à l'École d'architecture de Bergen. Il a travaillé en Norvège et en Allemagne (chez Behnisch & Behnisch, 1998). Ses projets récents incluent des maisons privées à Stavanger, Sandnes, ainsi que dans d'autres villes aux alentours de Norvège. Les deux architectes étaient associés dans l'agence Saunders & Wilhelmsen en 2002. Récemment, ils ont créé deux entités différentes, désormais situées à Bergen et Stavanger.

SUMMER HOUSE

Hardanger Fjord, Norway, 2003

Client: private. Floor area: 20 m² + 30 m²
Costs: €30 000 (site included)

On a site they bought to create experimental architecture in order to convince potential clients of their abilities, Saunders and Wilhelmsen imagined a two-part structure. The first is a 20-square-meter "anything goes room" or bedroom, atelier, writer's studio etc. The second, 30-square-meter section includes the kitchen and living area, plus a bedroom, shower, and toilet. It is possible to walk up onto the roof via an integrated stairway. The deck is made of local spruce and the building is unexpectedly insulated with recycled newspapers. The folding structure is made of birch plywood that has been treated with cold-pressed linseed oil. The site is on the west coast of Norway, about 70 km from Bergen on one of the largest and most beautiful fjords of the country. As the architects describe this adventure, "We made a structure that would be a part of the natural surroundings, yet in a sensitive contrast to the dramatic landscape. A long thin floating outdoor floor connects the two parts of the structure. This outdoor floor made the space twice as large in the summer, and connected the two buildings… The front of this arrangement faces the fjords, but the inner space towards the mountain creates an evening space that can be complemented by a small fire."

Auf einem Grundstück, das sie kauften, um dort mit neuen, experimentellen Architekturformen potenzielle Auftraggeber von ihrem Können zu überzeugen, realisierten Saunders und Wilhelmsen einen zweiteiligen Entwurf. Der erste Bauteil besteht aus einem 20 m² großen Raum, der als „Alles-ist-möglich-Raum" oder Schlafzimmer, Künstleratelier, Arbeitsraum eines Schriftstellers u. Ä. genutzt werden kann. Der zweite, 30 m² große Teil enthält die Küche und den Wohnraum, dazu ein Schlafzimmer, eine Dusche und Toilette. In seinem Innern führt eine Treppe auf das Dach. Die Terrasse ist aus lokalem Fichtenholz gefertigt, während das Gebäude originellerweise mit recyceltem Zeitungspapier isoliert wurde. Die gefaltete Konstruktion besteht aus Birkensperrholz, das mit kalt gepresstem Leinsamenöl behandelt wurde. Das Grundstück liegt an der Westküste Norwegens, etwa 70 km von Bergen entfernt, an einem der größten und schönsten Fjorde des Landes. Die Architekten beschreiben ihr Abenteuer so: „Wir entwarfen ein Gebäude, das Teil der natürlichen Umgebung ist und dennoch einen sensiblen Kontrast zur dramatischen Landschaft bildet. Die Vorderseite der beiden Baukörper, die durch eine lang gestreckte Bodenfläche miteinander verbunden sind, wendet sich dem Fjord zu. Der zum Berg ausgerichtete Innenraum bietet dagegen einen Bereich für den Abend, der durch ein kleines Kaminfeuer vervollständigt werden kann."

Sur un terrain spécialement acquis pour expérimenter leurs idées architecturales et convaincre leurs clients potentiels de leur capacité, Saunders et Wilhelmsen ont imaginé une construction en deux parties. La première est une « pièce à tout faire », ou chambre, atelier, bureau d'écrivain, etc., de 20 m². La seconde, de 30 m², comprend une cuisine, un séjour, une chambre, une douche et des toilettes. On peut monter sur le toit via un escalier intégré. La terrasse est en lattes d'épicéa local et l'isolation du bâtiment est assurée par des journaux recyclés. La structure pliable est en contreplaqué de bouleau traité à l'huile de lin pressée à froid. Le site se trouve sur la côte ouest de la Norvège, à 70 km environ de Bergen, au bord de l'un des plus vastes et plus magnifiques fjords du pays. Les architectes décrivent ainsi leur aventure : « Nous avons réalisé une construction qui est un élément de l'environnement naturel tout en contrastant avec le paysage spectaculaire. Une mince plate-forme extérieure flottante réunit les deux parties. Elle double l'espace disponible en été… Son avancée donne sur le fjord, mais sa partie intérieure, orientée vers les montagnes, offre le soir un séjour extérieur réchauffé par une petite cheminée. »

The idyllic setting where the architects have installed this summer house naturally contributes to its effect, but their simple, elegant design has obvious merits.

Die idyllische Lage, in der dieses Sommerhaus aufgestellt ist, trägt natürlich zu dessen Wirkung bei, doch ihr schlichtes und elegantes Design hat seine eigenen Qualitäten.

Le cadre idyllique de cette maison d'été contribue à son effet, même si l'élégance et la simplicité de son dessin présentent des mérites évidents.

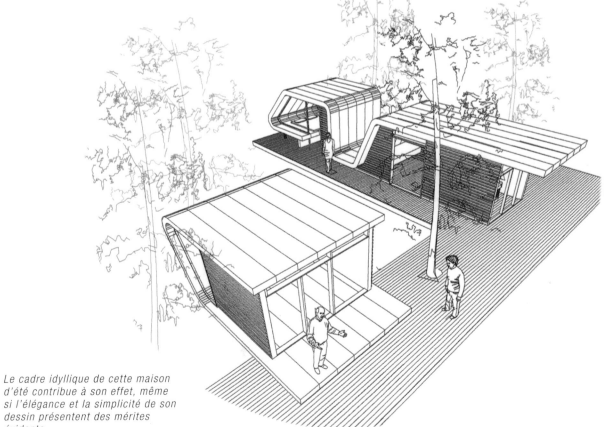

The wooden platform extends the usable surface of the house and allows its inhabitants to enjoy the surroundings, just as the ample glazing of the house opens the view out and allows light in.

Die Holzplattform vergrößert die Nutz-fläche des Hauses und erlaubt seinen Bewohnern, die Umgebung zu genie-ßen. Hierzu tragen auch die großzügi-gen Verglasungen bei, die den Blick nach draußen freigeben und Licht hereinlassen.

La plate-forme en bois agrandit la surface utile de la maison et permet à ses habitants de profiter de l'envi-ronnement, de même que les vastes baies vitrées qui laissent entrer la lumière naturelle.

Original in its simplicity and in the way it is perched on the water, this small house is a model for modest vacation residences.

Originell in seiner Schlichtheit und Platzierung am Uferrand, könnte das kleine Haus als Vorbild für einfache Ferienhäuser dienen.

Originale dans sa simplicité et dans son positionnement au-dessus de l'eau, cette petite maison est un modèle de résidence modeste pour les vacances.

SEARCH

SeARCH
Hamerstraat 3
1021 JT Amsterdam
The Netherlands

Tel: +31 20 7 88 99 00
E-mail: info@search.nl
Web: www.search.nl

SeARCH is an architecture office, established in Amsterdam in 2002 by **BJARNE MASTENBROEK** and Ad Bogerman. Bjarne Mastenbroek was born in 1964, attended the TU Delft Faculty of Architecture (1982–89) and then worked in the Van Gameren Mastenbroek project team that was part of Architectengroep in Amsterdam from 1993. SeARCH currently employs 20 people. SeARCH has worked on Triade, the conversion and extension of a cultural education center (Den Helder, 1997–2001); Bredero College, extension to a trade school (Amsterdam Noord, 1998–2001); and buildings in Lelystad and Alemere. They also completed the Posbank Tea Pavilion (National Park Veluwe Zoom, Rheden, 1998–2002; published here); the Dutch Embassy in Addis Ababa (Ethiopia, 1998–2005); the TwentseWelle museum in Enschede (2003–08); a watchtower in Putten (2004–09); and the Villa Vals (Vals, Switzerland, 2005–09, with Christian Müller), which is the work of SeARCH (Bjarne Mastenbroek), all in the Netherlands unless stated otherwise. Recent projects include the LJG Synagogue (Amsterdam, 2005–10); Isberget apartment complex (Aarhus, Denmark, 2008–12); Natura Docet museum extension (Denekamp, 2011–under construction); and an extension of the Geerte Groote College (Amsterdam, 2010–under construction).

Das Architekturbüro SeARCH wurde 2002 von **BJARNE MASTENBROEK** und Ad Bogerman in Amsterdam gegründet. Bjarne Mastenbroek wurde 1964 geboren, studierte an der Fakultät für Architektur der TU Delft (1982–89) und arbeitete anschließend im Projektteam Van Gameren Mastenbroek, das ab 1993 Teil der Architectengroep in Amsterdam war. Derzeit beschäftigt SeARCH 20 Mitarbeiter. SeARCH arbeitete an Triade, dem Umbau und der Erweiterung eines Kulturbildungszentrums (Den Helder, 1997–2001), der Erweiterung einer Handelsschule am Bredero College (Amsterdam Noord, 1998–2001) sowie Bauten in Lelystad und Alemere. Sie realisierten auch den Posbank Teepavillon (Nationalpark Veluwe Zoom, Rheden, 1998–2002, hier vorgestellt), die niederländische Botschaft in Addis Abeba (Äthiopien, 1998–2005), das Museum TwentseWelle in Enschede (2003–08), einen Wachturm in Putten (2004–09) und die Villa Vals (Vals, Schweiz, 2005–09, mit Christian Müller). Zu den jüngeren Projekten zählen die Synagoge der Liberalen Jüdischen Gemeinde in Amsterdam (2005–10), der Appartementkomplex Isberget (Aarhus, Dänemark, 2008–12); die Erweiterung des Museums Natura Docet (Denekamp, seit 2011) und eine Erweiterung des Geerte Groote College (Amsterdam, seit 2010), alle in den Niederlanden, sofern nicht anders angegeben.

SeARCH est une agence créée à Amsterdam en 2002 par **BJARNE MASTENBROEK** et Ad Bogerman. Bjarne Mastenbroek, né en 1964, a étudié à la faculté d'architecture de la TU de Delft (1982–89), puis dans l'équipe de projet de Van Gameren Mastenbroek faisant partie de l'Architectengroep d'Amsterdam à partir de 1993. SeARCH emploie actuellement vingt personnes. SeARCH a réalisé Triade, conversion et extension d'un centre éducatif culturel (Den Helder, 1997–2001) ; le Bredero College, extension d'une école de commerce (Amsterdam Noord, 1998–2001) et des immeubles à Lelystad et Alemere. Ils ont également réalisé le pavillon de thé de la Posbank (parc national Veluwe Zoom, Rheden, 1998–2002, publié ici) ; l'ambassade néerlandaise à Addis Abeba (Éthiopie, 1998–2005); le musée TwentseWelle à Enschede (2003–08) ; une tour de guet à Putten (2004–09) et la villa Vals (Vals, Suisse, 2005–09, avec Christian Müller), œuvre de SeARCH (Bjarne Mastenbroek), le tout aux Pays-Bas, sauf mention contraire. Parmi leurs projets récents : la synagogue LJG (Amsterdam, 2005–10) ; un complexe résidentiel (Aarhus, Danemark, 2008–12) ; l'extension du musée Natura Docet (Denekamp, 2011–en construction) et l'extension du Geerte Groote College (Amsterdam, 2010–en construction).

POSBANK TEA PAVILION

Rheden, 1998–2002

Area: 760 m². Client: Vereinigung Natuurmonumenten, 's-Gravezand
Cost: €1.4 milion

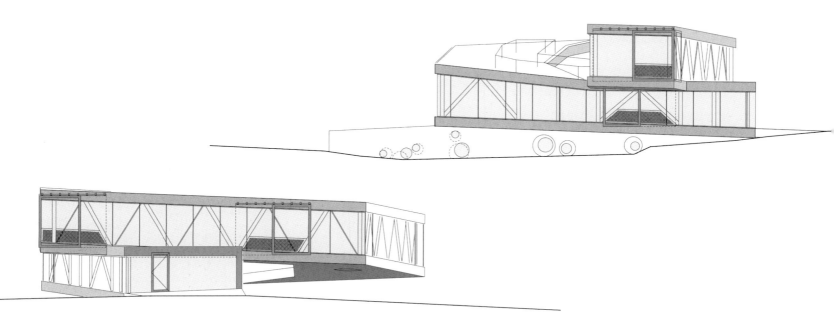

Section drawings make it clear how the segmented structure is inserted into or above the sloped site.

Querschnitte veranschaulichen die Einbindung des modulhaften Baus in den Hang.

Les vues en coupe montrent parfaitement la manière dont la structure segmentée est insérée au site en pente.

Bjarne Mastenbroek completed this project working with his former firm De Architectengroep Rijnboutt Ruijssenaars Hendriks Van Gameren Mastenbroek bv. Working for the Dutch Nature Conservancy (Natuurmonumenten), the architect was given the mission to build "a natural restaurant in a natural environment," but he immediately counters that this is precisely what he did not do. Looking at the site, he says, "Two hundred years ago this was farmland; before that it was a forest, and it's a forest again today. Its 'natural' environment is not only manufactured, but also, to a certain extent, kitsch, except for the elevations. The experience of nature is already artificial. The design is about the schizophrenic idea that a nature organization would build something. It is a building that aims a sly wink at naturalness." The supporting wood struts are real oak tree trunks with the bark removed, but the "boulders" that dot the building are fakes created by an American rock mold maker and they conceal structural elements. Floors are covered with two-centimeter-thick slices of acacia trees set in epoxy. The building has no right angles and the entire structure was drawn with 3D-coordinate AutoCad. The Posbank Pavilion was one of the four finalists of the AM NAI Prize 2004 for Young Architects.

Bjarne Mastenbroek erarbeitete dieses Projekt noch mit seinem früheren Büro De Architectengroep Rijnbout Ruijssenaars Hendriks Van Gameren Mastenbroek bv. Den Auftrag zum Bau eines „natürlichen Restaurants in einer natürlichen Umgebung" erteilte ihm der niederländische Naturschutzbund (Natuurmonumenten). Mastenbroek betont, genau das habe er nicht getan habe. Er blickt über das Gelände und erklärt: „Vor 200 Jahren war dies Ackerland, davor war es Wald und heute ist es wieder ein Wald. Die ‚natürliche' Umgebung ist demnach nicht nur vom Menschen gemacht, sondern bis auf die ursprüngliche Topografie auch in gewisser Weise klischeehaft. Schon das Erlebnis dieser Natur ist also künstlich. Der Entwurf thematisiert die fast widersprüchliche Ausgangssituation, dass ein Naturverband etwas bauen möchte. Der Pavillon ist ein verschmitzter Kommentar zum Thema Natürlichkeit." Die tragenden Holzstreben bestehen aus echten Eichenstämmen, von denen die Rinde entfernt wurde; die im Gebäude verteilten „Felsblöcke" sind dagegen Nachbildungen, die von einem amerikanischen Hersteller für Felsgussformen angefertigt wurden und die Bauteile verbergen. Der Fußbodenbelag besteht aus 2 cm dicken, in Epoxidharz gegossenen Akazienholzscheiben. Im ganzen Pavillon gibt es keinen rechten Winkel; das Gebäude wurde vollständig mit dem 3-D-Programm AutoCAD entworfen. Der Posbank Pavillon gehörte zu den vier Finalisten des AM-NAI-Preises 2004 für junge Architekten.

Bjarne Mastenbroek a achevé son projet alors qu'il travaillait encore pour son ancienne agence Architectengroep Rijnboutt Ruijssenaars Hendriks Van Gameren Mastenbroek bv. La mission confiée par le Conservatoire des monuments naturels néerlandais (Natuurmonumenten) était de construire « un restaurant naturel dans un environnement naturel ». Il précise immédiatement que c'est précisément ce qu'il n'a pas fait. « Il y a deux cents ans, ce terrain était agricole. Avant c'était une forêt et c'est de nouveau une forêt. Cet environnement « naturel » est en fait une production humaine mais aussi, dans une certaine mesure, kitsch, à l'exception des élévations. L'expérience de la nature y est déjà artificielle. La conception traite de cette idée schizophrénique qu'une organisation pour la défense de la nature construirait quelque chose. C'est une construction qui adresse un clin d'œil à la notion de nature. » Les poutres de soutien sont de vrais troncs d'arbres dégagés de leur écorce, mais les « rochers » qui parsèment le bâtiment sont des faux créés par un spécialiste américain de fausse rocaille pour dissimuler des éléments structurels. Les sols sont recouverts de ronds d'acacia de 2 cm d'épaisseur pris dans un lit d'époxy. Le bâtiment entièrement dessiné à l'aide d'un logiciel AutoCad 3D ne présente aucun angle droit. Il a figuré parmi les quatre finalistes du Prix des jeunes architectes AM Netherlands Architecture Institute 2004.

In this pavilion, what appears to be natural is "fake" and vice versa. In any case, the architect has succeeded in giving an impression of being close to nature and has created a space that is very much in contact with its wooded setting.

In diesem Pavillon ist künstlich, was natürlich scheint, und umgekehrt. Zweifellos vermittelt der Architekt gekonnt Nähe zur Natur und gestaltet einen Raum, der deutliche Bezüge zu seiner waldigen Umgebung hat.

Dans ce pavillon, tout ce qui semble naturel est « truqué » et vice-versa. L'architecte est cependant parfaitement parvenu à donner une impression de proximité avec la nature et a créé un espace en contact étroit avec les bois qui l'entourent.

An interior view (left) contrasts with the willful integration into the natural setting, seen in the images on this page. Green remains the color of choice in both cases however.

Das Interieur links kontrastiert auffällig mit der gewollten Integration des Baus in seine landschaftliche Umgebung (diese Seite). In beiden Fällen jedoch ist Grün die Farbe der Wahl.

Cette vue intérieure (à gauche) contraste avec l'intégration délibérée au cadre naturel qui apparaît sur les autres photos de cette page. Le vert reste néanmoins la couleur de choix dans les deux cas.

SELGASCANO

selgascano
Guecho 27–SC
28023 Madrid
Spain

Tel: +34 91 30 76 481
E-mail: selgas1@gmail.com
Web: www.selgascano.net

JOSÉ SELGAS was born in Madrid, Spain, in 1965. He received his architecture degree at the ETSA Madrid in 1992 and then worked with Francesco Venezia in Naples, Italy (1994–95). **LUCIA CANO** was also born in Madrid in 1965, and received her degree from the ETSA Madrid in 1992. She worked with Julio Cano Lasso from 1997 to 2003. Selgascano have won a number of first prizes in competitions, including Ideas Competition for Social Housing (Madrid, 1993); the competition for the Badajoz Center (1999–2006), for the Cartagena Conference and Auditorium (2001–08), and for a similar facility in Plasencia (2005–09). They also participated in the "On-Site: New Architecture in Spain" exhibition at the Museum of Modern Art, New York (2006). The architects have completed a congress center and auditorium in Badajoz (1999–2006); Silicon House (La Florida, Madrid, 2002–06); Studio in the Woods (Madrid, 2006–09, published here); an auditorium and congress center in Cartagena (2004–11); Mérida Factory Youth Movement (Mérida, 2009–11, also published here); a congress center and auditorium in Plasencia (2005–12); House in a Fault (Madrid, 2009–12); and Garden Villas in Vallecas (Madrid, 2008–12), all in Spain.

JOSÉ SELGAS wurde 1965 in Madrid geboren. Er schloss sein Architekturstudium 1992 an der ETSA Madrid ab und arbeitete bei Francesco Venezia in Neapel (1994–95). Auch **LUCIA CANO,** ebenfalls 1965 in Madrid geboren, schloss ihr Studium 1992 an der ETSA Madrid ab. Von 1997 bis 2003 war sie für Julio Cano Lasso tätig. Selgascano gewannen verschiedene Wettbewerbe, darunter den Ideenwettbewerb für ein Projekt im sozialen Wohnungsbau (Madrid, 1993), den Wettbewerb für das Kongresszentrum in Badajoz (1999–2006), für das Kongresszentrum in Cartagena (2001–08) und einen ähnlichen Komplex in Plasencia (2005–09). Sie waren außerdem vertreten in der Ausstellung „On-Site: New Architecture in Spain" im Museum of Modern Art in New York (2006). Das Büro realisierte das Kongresszentrum mit Auditorium in Badajoz (1999–2006), das Haus Silicon (La Florida, Madrid, 2002–06), ein Kongresszentrum mit Auditorium in Cartagena (2004–11), das Studio im Wald (Madrid, 2006–09, hier vorgestellt), das Mérida Factory Youth Movement (Mérida, 2009–11, ebenfalls hier vorgestellt), ein Kongresszentrum mit Auditorium in Plasencia (2005 bis 2012), das Haus in der Kluft (Madrid, 2009–12) sowie Gartenvillen in Vallecas (Madrid, 2008–12), alle in Spanien.

JOSÉ SELGAS est né à Madrid en 1965. Il a obtenu son diplôme en architecture à l'ETSA de Madrid en 1992 et a ensuite travaillé avec Francesco Venezia à Naples (1994–95). **LUCIA CANO** est également née à Madrid en 1965 et a obtenu son diplôme en architecture à l'ETSA de Madrid en 1992. Elle a travaillé avec Julio Cano Lasso de 1997 à 2003. Selgascano a remporté de nombreux premiers prix à des concours, parmi lesquels : le concours Ideas du logement social (Madrid, 1993) ; le concours pour le centre de Badajoz (1999–2006) ; pour l'auditorium et centre de conférences de Carthagène (2001–08) et pour un établissement semblable à Plasencia (2005–09). Ils ont également participé à l'exposition « On-Site: New Architecture in Spain » du Musée d'art moderne de New York (2006). Ils ont réalisé un centre des congrès et auditorium (Badajoz, 1999–2006) ; la maison Silicon (La Florida, Madrid, 2002–06) ; le Studio dans les bois (Madrid, 2006–09, publié ici) ; un auditorium et centre de congrès (Carthagène, 2004–11) ; le centre de loisirs Factory Youth Movement de Mérida (2009–11, également publié ici) ; le centre des congrès et auditorium (Plasencia, 2005–12) ; la Maison dans une faille (Madrid, 2009–12) et des villas avec jardins à Vallecas (Madrid, 2008–12), tous en Espagne.

STUDIO IN THE WOODS

Madrid, Spain, 2006–09

Area: 70 m². Cost: not disclosed
Client: selgascano. Web: www.selgascano.net

Partially dug into its rectilinear footprint, the structure is fully glazed on one side, giving those working there the impression that they are fully integrated with the natural setting.

Der teilweise im Baugrund versenkte rechteckige Bau ist auf einer Seite vollständig verglast und vermittelt den Mitarbeitern den Eindruck, ganz in den landschaftlichen Kontext eingebunden zu sein

Enfouie en partie dans son empreinte rectiligne, la structure est entièrement vitrée sur un côté, donnant l'impression à ceux qui y travaillent de se trouver au cœur même du décor naturel.

As the architects say, their goal in designing this studio was to "work under the trees." This implied having a transparent roof without too much direct sunlight. The northern section of the structure is covered with a bent sheet of 20-millimeter colorless Plexiglas, while the southern side has a double sheet of fiberglass and polyester with translucent insulation. A cantilevered metal structure was placed inside the "sandwich" covering. Despite the relatively simple concept, the input of several manufacturers was required, but difficult to obtain because of the small quantities of their products concerned. Partially buried, the structure sits on poured concrete made with wooden formwork, and wooden floors. The architects write of their office: "And to finish off, we have given it a slightly less... slightly more... wet touch: when raindrops hit the plastic... sometimes more, sometimes less, sometimes a lot... sometimes there is a sound..."

Ausgangspunkt des Entwurfs, so die Architekten, sei der Wunsch gewesen, „unter Bäumen zu arbeiten". Gefordert waren also ein transparentes Dach und kontrollierter Lichteinfall. Die Nordseite der Konstruktion wurde aus gewölbtem, 20 mm starkem klarem Plexiglas realisiert, die Südseite hat eine Doppelhaut aus Fiberglas und Polyester mit lichtdurchlässiger Isolierung. Integriert in die „Sandwich"-Hülle ist eine Auslegerkonstruktion aus Metall. Trotz des relativ einfachen Konzepts war die Mitarbeit mehrerer Hersteller gefordert, jedoch nicht leicht zu bekommen, da jeweils nur geringe Auftragsmengen gefragt waren. Die teilweise im Boden versenkte Konstruktion ruht auf einem in eine Holzschalung gegossenen Betonsockel und einem Holzboden. Die Architekten schreiben über ihr Büro: „Schließlich spielt Wasser mal mehr ... mal weniger ... eine Rolle: Wenn Regen auf die Kunststoffflächen fällt ... mal mehr, mal weniger, mal heftig ... dann ist das zu hören ..."

Les architectes expliquent que leur objectif en créant ce studio était de « travailler sous les arbres ». Cela supposait un toit transparent et un ensoleillement direct pas trop important. La partie nord de l'ensemble est couverte d'une feuille courbe de Plexiglas transparent épaisse de 20 mm, tandis que la partie sud présente une double feuille de fibre de verre et de polyester à isolation translucide. Un structure métallique en porte-à-faux a été placée à l'intérieur de la couverture « sandwich ». Malgré un concept relativement simple, l'intervention de plusieurs constructeurs a été nécessaire, mais difficile à obtenir en raison des petites quantités des différents produits requis. La structure en partie souterraine est posée sur du béton coulé réalisé avec un coffrage en bois et des sols également en bois. Les architectes disent de leur bureau : « Et pour terminer, nous avons apporté une touche un peu moins... un peu plus... humide : lorsque des gouttes de pluie frappent le plastique... parfois plus, parfois moins, parfois beaucoup... on entend parfois un bruit... »

With its very fine columns and thin roof, the building appears to sit very lightly on the land despite being inserted into it.

Mit seinen filigranen Stützen und dem dünnen Dach scheint der Bau nur leicht auf dem Boden aufzuliegen, obwohl er in ihn versenkt ist.

Avec ses colonnes très fines et son toit mince, le bâtiment semble posé très légèrement sur le sol, alors qu'il y est enfoncé.

The rectilinear plan is exceedingly
simple, while the curved Plexiglas
roof becomes the front "wall" of the
studio as well.

Der rechteckige Grundriss ist von
äußerster Schlichtheit. Das gewölbte
Plexiglasdach wird zur „Vorderwand".

Le plan rectiligne est extrêmement
simple, le toit en Plexiglas courbe se
prolonge en « mur » avant du studio.

An end wall of the studio flips out to allow fresh air in. Left, in a closed position, the building is an enigmatic object in the garden.

Eine Stirnseite des Studios lässt sich öffnen, um frische Luft hereinzulassen. In geschlossenem Zustand (links) zeigt sich der Bau als rätselhafte Präsenz im Garten.

L'un des murs de l'extrémité du studio s'ouvre pour faire entrer l'air frais. À gauche, en position fermée, le bâtiment forme un mystérieux objet à poser dans un jardin.

Shiny surfaces and bright green col-
oring or red chairs make the interior
of the studio come alive, whether by
day or at night. Below, a section
drawing with figures drawn to scale.

Tags und nachts lassen glänzende
Oberflächen und die intensiven
grünen Farbakzente und roten Stühle
das Innere lebendig werden. Unten
ein Querschnitt mit maßstabsge-
treuen Figuren

De jour ou de nuit, les surfaces
brillantes et le vert vif ou les chaises
rouges animent l'intérieur du studio.
Ci-dessous, schéma en coupe avec
personnages à l'échelle.

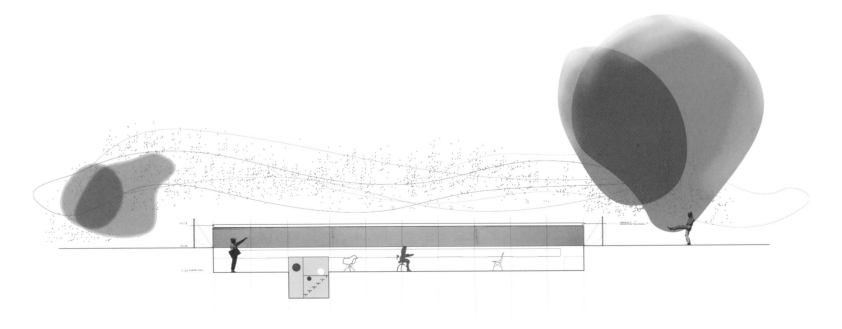

MÉRIDA FACTORY YOUTH MOVEMENT

Mérida, Spain, 2009–11

Area: 1550 m². Client: Government of Extremadura
Cost: €1.2 million

The steel space frame for this structure was assembled on site in a period of two months. The polycarbonate roof is orange on its upper side and white on the underside. Roman ruins were found in the course of the preparation of the site, and thus the structure is set at 1.5 meters above street level. Steel columns, placed at the perimeter, support the roof. The program called for a skate park, a climbing wall, an exterior theater, three 75-square-meter multipurpose rooms, and 25 square meters of storage areas, together with an office, meeting room, a storage area for climbing materials, and toilets. The climbing wall was made with 18-millimeter laminated and waterproofed plywood. When asked what their inspiration was, the architects respond: "We don't believe in inspiration. We don't even believe in architectural issues if they aren't recognizable by future users. Our only inspiration was to let whoever wants to be there, and to do what they want under a large canopy open to the whole city." They speak also of a project in layers—the Roman history of Mérida, the concrete play surface, the steel canopy structure, and the polycarbonate roof.

Das Stahlfachwerk für den Bau wurde in nur zwei Monaten vor Ort montiert. Die Oberseite des Polycarbonatdachs ist orange, die Unterseite weiß. Da bei den Vorbereitungen römischer Ruinen gefunden wurden, wurde der Komplex 1,5 m über Straßenniveau realisiert. Stahlstützen am Rand der Konstruktion tragen das Dach. Das Programm sah einen Skatepark, eine Kletterwand, eine Freiluftbühne, drei 75 m² große Mehrzweckräume und 25 m² Abstellfläche vor, ein Büro, einen Gruppenraum, einen Abstellraum für Kletterausrüstungen und die Toiletten. Die Kletterwand wurde aus 18 mm starkem, imprägniertem Sperrholz gefertigt. Auf die Frage nach ihrer Inspiration antworten die Architekten: „Wir glauben nicht an Inspiration. Wir glauben nicht einmal an architektonische Themen, wenn sie den künftigen Nutzer nichts sagen. Unsere Inspiration war, jedem Raum zu geben, die Möglichkeit, unter dem großen, der ganzen Stadt offenen Dach zu tun, wozu sie Lust haben." Sie sprechen von einem Projekt in Schichten – der römischen Geschichte von Mérida, den Spielflächen aus Beton, der Dachkonstruktion aus Stahl und schließlich dem Polycarbonatdach.

Le cadre en acier de la structure a été assemblé sur place au cours d'une période de deux mois. Le toit de polycarbonate est orange par-dessus et blanc par-dessous. Des ruines romaines ont été découvertes pendant la préparation du terrain, c'est pourquoi l'ensemble est surélevé à 1,5 m au-dessus du niveau de la rue. Des colonnes en acier sur le périmètre du bâtiment soutiennent le toit. Le projet prévoyait un parc de skate, un mur d'escalade, un théâtre de plein air, trois salles polyvalentes de 75 m² et 25 m² d'espace de stockage, ainsi qu'un bureau, une salle de réunion, un espace de rangement pour le matériel d'escalade et des toilettes. Le mur d'escalade a été réalisé en contreplaqué laminé et imperméabilisé de 18 mm. Lorsqu'ils sont interrogés sur l'origine de leur inspiration, les architectes répondent : « Nous ne croyons pas à l'inspiration. Nous ne croyons même pas à l'intérêt architectural s'il n'est pas reconnaissable et accessible aux futurs utilisateurs. Notre seule inspiration a été de donner accès à tous ceux qui le veulent pour faire ce qu'ils veulent sous une immense voûte ouverte à la ville entière. » Ils parlent aussi d'un projet en strates – l'histoire romaine de Mérida, la surface de jeu en béton, la voûte en acier de la structure et le toit en polycarbonate.

Bright colors and patterns and an amoeboid roof bring together the functions of the joyfully artificial structure.

Markante Farben und Muster sowie ein amöbenförmiges Dach halten die verschiedenen Funktionen des heiter-künstlichen Baus zusammen.

Les couleurs et motifs vifs et colorés associés à la forme amiboïde du toit réunissent les fonctions de cette structure joyeusement artificielle.

Open and yet offering varied, sheltered spaces, the building is obviously attractive to the young both for play and to just meet and talk.

Die offene Konstruktion, die abwechslungsreiche, geschützte Räume definiert, ist offensichtlich bei Kindern und Jugendlichen beliebt, die hier gemeinsam spielen oder sich einfach treffen und reden können.

Ouvert mais n'en proposant pas moins des espaces abrités variés, le bâtiment est manifestement attirant pour les jeunes, qu'il s'agisse de venir y jouer ou simplement de se retrouver et de discuter.

KEN SMITH

*WORKSHOP: Ken Smith Landscape Architect
450 West 31st Street, Fifth Floor
New York, NY 10001, USA*

*Tel: +1 212 791 3595 / Fax: +1 212 732 1793
E-mail: info@kensmithworkshop.com
Web: www.kensmithworkshop.com*

KEN SMITH was born in 1953, and graduated from Iowa State University with a B.S. in Landscape Architecture (Ames, Iowa, 1975). He attended the Harvard GSD (Master of Landscape Architecture program, 1986). He worked as a Landscape Architect for the State Conservation Commission in Iowa (1979–84), as a consultant for the Department of Environmental Management (Massachusetts, 1984–86), in the office of Peter Walker and Martha Schwartz (New York, San Francisco, 1986–89) and with Martha Schwartz Ken Smith David Meyer Inc. (San Francisco, 1990–92), before creating his present firm, Ken Smith Landscape Architect, in New York. His current and recent landscape work includes Lever House Landscape Restoration (New York, New York, 2000); the MoMA Decorative Rooftop (Museum of Modern Art, New York, New York, 2004–05); 7 World Trade Center, Triangle Park (New York, New York, 2002–06); 40 Central Park South, Courtyard Garden (New York, New York, 2005–06); H-12 Office Complex (Hyderabad, India, 2007); Santa Fe Railyard Park and Plaza (Santa Fe, New Mexico, 2006–08, published here); 17 State Street Plaza (New York, New York, 2008); and the East River Waterfront (New York, New York, 2006–). Other current work includes Brooklyn Academy of Music Cultural District Public Space and Streetscape (Brooklyn, New York, 2006–); the Croton Water Treatment Plant (Bronx, New York, 2006–); and Orange County Great Park (Irvine, California, 2007–), all in the USA unless stated otherwise.

KEN SMITH wurde 1953 geboren und schloss 1975 sein Studium an der Iowa State University mit einem Bachelor in Landschaftsarchitektur ab (Ames, Iowa). 1986 machte er seinen Master in Landschaftsarchitektur an der Harvard GSD. Er arbeitete von 1979 bis 1984 als Landschaftsarchitekt bei der State Conservation Commission in Iowa, von 1984 bis 1986 als Berater beim Department of Environmental Management (Massachusetts), von 1986 bis 1989 im Büro von Peter Walker und Martha Schwartz (New York und San Francisco) und von 1990 bis 1992 im Büro Martha Schwartz Ken Smith David Meyer Inc. (San Francisco). Danach gründete er sein eigenes Büro Ken Smith Landscape Architect in New York. Zu seinen jüngeren landschaftsarchitektonischen Projekten gehören die Restaurierung der Gartenanlagen des Lever House (New York, 2000), der Dachgarten des MoMA (Museum of Modern Art, New York, 2004–05), 7 World Trade Center, Triangle Park (New York, 2002–06), 40 Central Park South, Innenhofgestaltung (New York, 2005–06), der Bürokomplex H-12 (Hyderabad, Indien, 2007), die Park- und Platzanlage auf den ehemaligen Gleisanlagen in Santa Fe (New Mexico, 2006–08, hier vorgestellt), die 17 State Street Plaza (New York, 2008) und die Ufergestaltung des East River (New York, seit 2006). Als weitere laufende Projekte sind zu nennen der öffentliche Freiraum und die Straßengestaltung im Kulturviertel der Musikakademie von Brooklyn (Brooklyn, New York, seit 2006), die Wasseraufbereitungsanlage Croton Water Treatment Plant (Bronx, New York, seit 2006) und der Great Park von Orange County (Irvine, Kalifornien, seit 2007), alle in den USA, sofern nicht anders angegeben.

Né en 1953, **KEN SMITH** est titulaire d'un B.S. de paysagisme de l'université d'Iowa (Ames, Iowa, 1975). Il a également étudié à la Harvard GSD (Master of Landscape Architecture Program, 1986). Il a été architecte paysagiste pour la Commission de préservation de l'État d'Iowa (1979–84) et consultant pour le Département de gestion environnementale (Massachusetts, 1984–86). Il a travaillé pour l'agence de Peter Walker et Martha Schwartz (New York, San Francisco, 1986–89) et pour Martha Schwartz Ken Smith David Meyer Inc. (San Francisco, 1990–92), avant de créer sa propre agence, Ken Smith Landscape Architect, à New York. Parmi ses interventions récentes (toutes aux États-Unis, sauf mention contraire) : la restauration de l'aménagement paysager de Lever House (New York, 2000) ; la toiture paysagée du MoMA (Museum of Modern Art, New York, 2004–05) ; le parc triangulaire du 7 World Trade Center (New York, 2002–06) ; le jardin de la cour du 40 Central Park South (New York, 2005–06) ; le complexe de bureaux H-12 (Hyderabad, Inde, 2007) ; le Railyard Park et Plaza de Santa Fe (Nouveau-Mexique, 2006–08, publié ici) ; la 17 State Street Plaza (New York, 2008) ; l'aménagement des berges de l'East River (New York, 2006–) ; les espaces publics et l'aménagement des rues du Brooklyn Academy of Music Cultural District (Brooklyn, New York, 2006–) ; les installations de traitement des eaux de Croton (Bronx, New York, 2006–) et le Orange County Great Park (Irvine, Californie, 2007–).

SANTA FE RAILYARD PARK AND PLAZA

Santa Fe, New Mexico, USA, 2006–08

Address: corner of Guadalupe Street and Paseo De Peralta Santa Fe, NM 87501, USA, www.railyardpark.org
Area: 4.85 hectares. Client: The Trust for Public Land. Cost: $13 million
Collaboration: Frederic Schwartz, Mary Miss (Artist)

An "iconic water tank" (below) serves as a point of collection for water harvested from rain that is used to irrigate the park area. The overall plan of the park and plaza is seen on the right page.

In einem „typischen Wassertank" (unten) wird das Regenwasser für die Bewässerung des Parks gesammelt. Der Gesamtlageplan von Park und Plaza ist auf der rechten Seite zu sehen.

Un « réservoir d'eau typique » (ci-dessous) récupère les eaux de pluies qui servent à l'irrigation du parc. Un plan d'ensemble du parc et de la place est visible sur la page de droite.

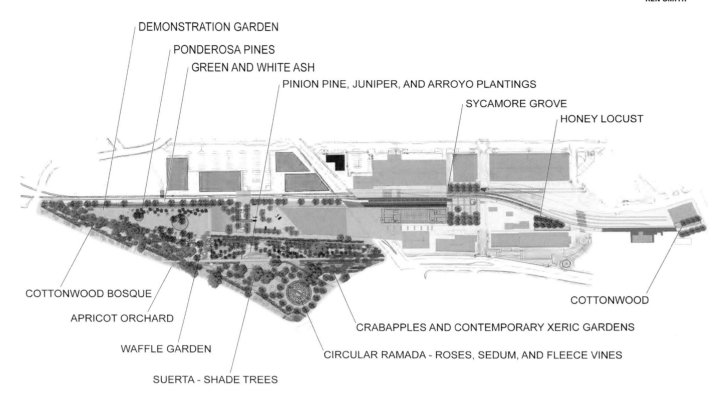

DEMONSTRATION GARDEN
PONDEROSA PINES
GREEN AND WHITE ASH
PINION PINE, JUNIPER, AND ARROYO PLANTINGS
SYCAMORE GROVE
HONEY LOCUST

COTTONWOOD BOSQUE
APRICOT ORCHARD
WAFFLE GARDEN
SUERTA - SHADE TREES
CIRCULAR RAMADA - ROSES, SEDUM, AND FLEECE VINES
CRABAPPLES AND CONTEMPORARY XERIC GARDENS
COTTONWOOD

The history of Santa Fe as a railway point of passage goes back to the late 19th century. Ken Smith was called on, in collaboration with the artist Mary Miss and the architect Frederic Schwartz, to redevelop railyards located near downtown Santa Fe. The resulting park includes a plaza, a tree-shaded promenade, and "sophisticated water conservation features." According to Ken Smith, the "design draws on traditional northern New Mexican traditions but the expression is contemporary. Along the paths, we designed benches of simple large wood rectangles, local bricks, and other local material… As the centerpiece of a newly revitalized mixed-use district, the park makes strong connections with the neighborhood and cultural institutions including SITE Santa Fe, the Santa Fe Farmers' Market, El Museo Cultural de Santa Fe, Warehouse 21, and other local institutions." A 400-year-old irrigation ditch runs through the site, a fact that Ken Smith seized on to emphasize the continuity of the stewardship of the landscape by local residents. Smith states: "Throughout the park, water is captured from neighboring roof areas, stored, and used as a visible element in the park design. An iconic water tank in the new plaza is the central water storage component for harvested water. Beneath it, a drip fountain recalls the watershed of the Santa Fe River and this harvested water supports xeric plantings, native grasses, and garden environments."

Die Geschichte von Santa Fe als bedeutendem Eisenbahndrehkreuz geht bis in das späte 19. Jahrhundert zurück. Ken Smith wurde gemeinsam mit der Künstlerin Mary Miss und dem Architekten Frederic Schwartz eingeladen, das Bahngelände nahe der Innenstadt von Santa Fe neu zu gestalten. Zum neuen Park gehören eine Plaza, eine Schatten spendende Allee und „raffinierte Maßnahmen zum Gewässerschutz". Smith erläutert, dass der Entwurf „auf die Traditionen von New Mexico Bezug nimmt, aber in seiner Umsetzung zeitgenössisch ist. Für die Wege haben wir einfache, große, rechteckige Bänke aus Holz, lokalem Klinker und anderen ortstypischem Material entworfen … Der Park bildet das Zentrum eines sanierten Stadtviertels mit Mischnutzung und stellt enge Verbindungen mit der Nachbarschaft und Kulturinstitutionen wie der SITE Santa Fe, dem Bauernmarkt von Santa Fe, dem Museo Cultural de Santa Fe, dem Warehouse 21 und anderen örtlichen Einrichtungen her." Durch das Gelände verläuft ein 400 Jahre alter Bewässerungsgraben, für Ken Smith ein Symbol dafür, dass die Menschen hier schon immer die umgebende Landschaft gestaltet haben. Er sagt: „Im gesamten Park wird das Wasser von den Gebäudedächern gesammelt und als sichtbares Gestaltungselement eingesetzt. Ein typischer Wassertank auf dem neuen Platz dient als Reservoir für den Park. Darunter greift ein Brunnen das Motiv des Santa Fe River und seines Einzugsgebiets auf. Das hier gespeicherte Wasser versorgt die Wüstenpflanzen, die heimischen Gräser und die Gartenanlagen."

L'histoire de Santa Fe en tant que nœud ferroviaire remonte à la fin du XIXᵉ siècle. Ken Smith a été sollicité, avec l'artiste Mary Miss et l'architecte Frederic Schwartz, pour reconvertir des friches ferroviaires à proximité du centre-ville. Le nouveau parc comprend une place, une promenade ombragée par des arbres et « des systèmes de stockage de l'eau sophistiqués ». Ken Smith explique que « le projet s'appuie sur les traditions du nord du Nouveau-Mexique, mais dans une expression contemporaine. Le long des allées, nous avons dessiné des banquettes qui sont de simples grands rectangles en bois, brique rouge et autres matériaux locaux… Élément central d'un quartier d'usage mixte récemment revitalisé, le parc établi de solides connexions avec son voisinage et des institutions culturelles comme SITE Santa Fe, le Santa Fe Farmers Market, El Museo Cultural de Santa Fe ou Warehouse 21 ». Smith s'est emparé d'un fossé d'irrigation vieux de quatre siècles qui traversait le site pour souligner la continuité de l'appropriation du paysage par les habitants. « Dans l'ensemble du parc, l'eau est récupérée à partir des toitures avoisinantes, stockée et réutilisée sous forme visible. Un réservoir de forme typique, sur la nouvelle place, constitue l'élément central du stockage des eaux de récupération. En dessous, une fontaine rappelle la Santa Fe River et l'eau récupérée sert à arroser des plantes xérophiles, des graminées de variétés locales et des environnements traités en jardins. »

Mixing stone, gravel, plants, and wood, the designers create a stimulating and unexpected environment, a park full of surprises.

Mit dieser Mischung von Naturstein, Schotter, Pflanzen und Holz schaffen die Planer ein stimulierendes und unerwartetes Ambiente, einen Park voller Überraschungen.

En mélangeant la pierre, le gravier, les plantes et le bois, les paysagistes ont créé un environnement à la fois stimulant, inattendu et plein de surprises.

WERNER SOBEK

Werner Sobek Stuttgart GmbH & Co. KG
Albstr. 14
70597 Stuttgart
Germany
Tel: +49 711 767 50 38 / Fax: +49 711 767 50 44
E-mail: stuttgart@wernersobek.com
Web: www.wernersobek.com

WERNER SOBEK was born in 1953 in Aalen, Germany. He studied architecture and civil engineering at the University of Stuttgart (1974–80) and did postgraduate research in "Wide-Span Lightweight Structures" at the University of Stuttgart (1980–86). He received his Ph.D. in Civil Engineering at the same university in 1987. He worked as a structural engineer in the office of Schlaich, Bergermann and Partner (Stuttgart, 1987–91), before creating his own office in 1991. Since 1995 he has been a Professor at the University of Stuttgart, where he succeeded Frei Otto as Director of the Institute for Lightweight Structures and Conceptual Design (ILEK). He is the Mies van der Rohe Professor at the Illinois Institute of Technology. His projects include the Ecole Nationale d'Art Décoratif (Limoges, France, 1991–94); the Dome Service Hall, Deutsche Bank (Hanover, Germany, 1992–95); Art and Media Science Center (Karlsruhe, Germany, 1992–97); Façade Interbank (with Hans Hollein, Lima, Peru, 1996–99); a private residence at Römerstr. 128 (Stuttgart, Germany, 1998–2000); New Bangkok International Airport (with Murphy/Jahn, Thailand, 1995–2004); H16 (Tieringen, Germany, 2005–06, published here); and fair pavilions for Audi and BMW. In 2007, WSGreenTechnologies was cofounded by Klaus Sedlbauer and Werner Sobek in Stuttgart. WSGreenTechnologies "offers integrated planning of buildings taking into consideration all phases of construction, use, and deconstruction." Sobek has been a member of the supervisory board of the German Sustainable Building Council (DGNB) since 2007, and served as its President from 2008 to 2010. Included among recent work are D10 (Biberbach an der Riss, Germany, 2009–10); and F87 (Berlin, Germany, 2011).

WERNER SOBEK, geboren 1953 in Aalen in Deutschland, studierte Architektur und Bauingenieurwesen an der Universität Stuttgart (1974–80) und arbeitete nach seinem Abschluss an einer Arbeit zum Thema „Flächentragwerke und Leichtbaukonstruktionen" an der Universität Stuttgart (1980–86). 1987 promovierte er an derselben Hochschule. Er arbeitete zunächst als Statiker bei Schlaich, Bergermann und Partner (Stuttgart, 1987–91) und gründete 1991 sein eigenes Büro. Seit 1995 ist er Professor an der Universität Stuttgart, wo er die Nachfolge von Frei Otto antrat und das heutige Institut für Leichtbau, Entwerfen und Konstruieren (ILEK) leitet. Er ist Mies-van-der-Rohe-Professor am Illinois Institute of Technology. Zu seinen Projekten zählen die Ecole Nationale d'Art Décoratif (Limoges, Frankreich, 1991–94), die Kuppel in der Schalterhalle der Deutschen Bank in Hannover (1992–95), das ZKM in Karlsruhe (1992–97), die Fassade der Interbank (mit Hans Hollein, Lima, Peru, 1996–99), das Privatwohnhaus R128 (Stuttgart, 1998–2000), der neue Internationale Flughafen Bangkok (mit Murphy/Jahn, Thailand, 1995–2004), das H16 (Tieringen, Deutschland, 2005–06, hier vorgestellt) sowie Messepavillons für Audi und BMW. 2007 gründeten Klaus Sedlbauer und Werner Sobek gemeinschaftlich WSGreenTechnologies. Das Büro „bietet einen integrierten Planungsprozess für alle Arten von Gebäuden. Dieser Planungsprozess berücksichtigt alle Phasen eines Lebenszyklus des Gebäudes." Seit 2007 ist Sobek Mitglied des Präsidiums der Deutschen Gesellschaft für Nachhaltiges Bauen (DGNB), deren Präsident er von 2008 bis 2010 war. Zu seinen jüngeren Entwürfen zählen auch die Projekte D10 (Biberbach an der Riss, Deutschland, 2009–10) und F87 (Berlin, 2011).

WERNER SOBEK est né en 1953 à Aalen, en Allemagne. Il a fait des études d'architecture et de génie civil à l'université de Stuttgart (1974–80), puis des recherches de troisième cycle sur « les structures légères de grande envergure » (1980–86). Il a obtenu son Ph.D en génie civil à la même université en 1987. Il a travaillé comme ingénieur constructeur dans l'agence de Schlaich, Bergermann und Partner (Stuttgart, 1987–91) avant de créer sa propre société en 1991. Depuis 1995, il est professeur à l'université de Stuttgart où il a succédé à Frei Otto au poste de directeur de l'Institut des structures légères et de design conceptuel (ILEK). Il est également titulaire de la chaire Mies van der Rohe à l'Illinois Institute of Technology. Ses projets comprennent l'École nationale d'art décoratif (Limoges, 1991–94) ; le hall de services du Dome, Deutsche Bank (Hanovre, Allemagne, 1992–95) ; le Centre scientifique des arts et médias (Karlsruhe, Allemagne, 1992–97) ; la façade de l'Interbank (avec Hans Hollein, Lima, Pérou, 1996–99) ; une résidence privée Römerstr. 128 (Stuttgart, 1998–2000) ; le nouvel aéroport international de Bangkok (avec Murphy/Jahn, 1995–2004) ; H16 (Tieringen, Allemagne, 2005–06, publié ici) et des pavillons d'exposition pour Audi et BMW. WSGreenTechnologies a été fondé en 2007 par Klaus Sedlbauer et Werner Sobek à Stuttgart. La société « propose la planification intégrée de bâtiments en tenant compte de toutes les phases de construction, exploitation et déconstruction ». Sobek est membre du bureau de surveillance du Conseil allemand pour le bâtiment durable (DGNB) depuis 2007 et en a été le président de 2008 à 2010. Parmi ses réalisations récentes comptent D10 (Biberbach an der Ris, Allemagne, 2009–10) et F87 (Berlin, 2011).

H16

Tieringen, Germany, 2005–06

*Floor area: 454 m². Client: Helmut and Georgia Link
Cost: not disclosed*

Seen from a distance the house adapts a decidedly discreet profile, integrating glass and stone elements in an unexpected way.

Aus der Ferne gesehen beweist das Haus ein ausgesprochen diskretes Profil und kombiniert Elemente aus Glas und Stein auf überraschende Weise.

Vue à distance, la maison présente un profil volontairement discret, intégrant divers éléments en verre ou en pierre de façon inattendue.

This house is described as a logical progression and improvement on the widely published R128 house. Located south of Stuttgart, the structure seeks "maximum transparency and a minimum of structure, full recyclability … and zero emissions." Careful attention was also paid to the integration of the house into its site. An all-glass cube, shielded from the street by a hedge, contains an open living space, while a second black cube, located below, houses private spaces. A third, light-colored cube, connected to the black cube by a steel terrace, contains the garage and utilities room. The supporting steel structure of the entire house can be dismantled "within a couple of days." The black volume is built with prefabricated architectural concrete sections. Geothermal heating with a heat pump, as well as photovoltaic panels, reduces energy consumption. The sophisticated climate control system also contributes to a minimum use of electricity. The architects write, not without a certain amount of pride: "H16 is a tribute to outstanding icons of modern architecture, such as the ones designed by Mies van der Rohe. The building combines sustainability (by zero emissions and full recyclability), state-of-the-art design, and first-class building technologies, thus making it an achievement from an architectural, technical, and aesthetic point of view."

Dieses Wohnhaus wurde als logische Fortführung und Verfeinerung des weithin publizierten R128 bezeichnet. Der im Süden von Stuttgart gelegene Bau strebt nach „maximaler Transparenz und einem Minimum an Struktur, vollständiger Recyclingfähigkeit … und Emissionsfreiheit". Besondere Aufmerksamkeit galt der Einbindung des Hauses in sein Umfeld. In einem voll verglasten Kubus, der zur Straße hin durch eine Hecke abgeschirmt ist, befindet sich ein offener Wohnbereich; in einem zweiten schwarzen, darunterliegenden Kubus liegen private Räume. In einem dritten, hellgrauen Kubus, der über eine Stahlterrasse mit dem schwarzen Kubus verbunden ist, sind Garage und Haustechnik untergebracht. Das tragende Stahlgerüst des gesamten Hauses lässt sich „innerhalb weniger Tage" demontieren. Das schwarze Volumen wurde aus Betonfertigbauteilen erbaut. Eine Erdwärmeheizung mit Wärmepumpe sowie Solarmodule reduzieren den Energieverbrauch. Auch das ausgefeilte Klimasteuerungssystem trägt zur Minimierung des Stromverbrauchs bei. Die Architekten schreiben nicht ohne Stolz: „H16 ist eine Hommage an herausragende Ikonen der Architektur, wie etwa die Bauten Mies van der Rohes. Der Bau vereint Nachhaltigkeit (durch Emissionsfreiheit und vollständige Recycelbarkeit) mit anspruchsvollem Design und erstklassigen Bauverfahren, was ihn zu einer Leistung in architektonischer, technischer und ästhetischer Hinsicht macht."

Cette maison est présentée comme la progression logique et le perfectionnement du projet de la maison R128 largement publié. Située au sud de Stuttgart, elle recherche « un maximum de transparence et un minimum de structure, une recyclabilité totale… et zéro émissions ». Une grande attention a été portée à son intégration dans le site. Un cube entièrement vitré, protégé de la rue par une haie, contient un séjour ouvert, tandis qu'un second cube, noir cette fois, situé en dessous, abrite les chambres. Un troisième cube, de couleur claire, connecté au précédent par une terrasse en acier contient un garage et des pièces de service. La structure en acier qui soutient l'ensemble de la maison peut être démontée « en deux jours ». Le volume noir est en béton architectural préfabriqué. Un chauffage géothermique à pompe à chaleur ainsi que des panneaux photovoltaïques réduisent la consommation d'électricité. Le système sophistiqué de contrôle de la climatisation contribue également à ces économies. Les architectes précisent, non sans une certaine fierté : « H16 est un hommage aux icônes les plus célèbres de l'architecture moderne, comme celles conçues par Mies van der Rohe. Cette construction combine la durabilité (zéro émissions et recyclabilité totale), une conception d'avant-garde et des technologies de construction de haut niveau, qui en font un accomplissement sur les plans architecturaux, techniques et esthétiques. »

Seen from below, the glass box forming the upper level almost seems to
float on its base.

Von unten betrachtet scheint die
Glasbox der oberen Etage fast über
ihrem Sockel zu schweben.

Vu en contre-plongée, le cube vitré
du niveau supérieur semble flotter
au-dessus de sa base.

The upper volume of the house is an extremely light box made of glass, extending out to a wooden deck.

Le volume supérieur est une boîte vitrée extrêmement légère, qui se prolonge par une terrasse en bois.

Der obere Baukörper des Hauses ist eine extrem leichte Box aus Glas, an die sich eine Holzterrasse anschließt.

As might be expected, the interior of the house is very bright and open, an impression emphasized here by the choice of modern furniture.

Wie zu erwarten, ist das Interieur des Hauses hell und offen, ein Eindruck, der hier durch die Wahl moderner Möbel noch unterstrichen wird.

Comme on peut l'imaginer, l'intérieur de la maison est très ouvert et lumineux, impression renforcée par le choix d'un mobilier moderne.

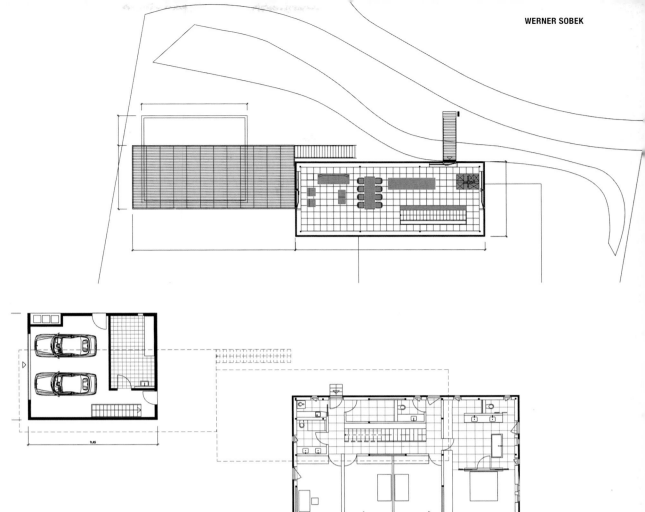

If anything, the house proves that a very modern house with large window surfaces need not be considered ecologically wasteful—in particular with an engineer such as Werner Sobek as its author.

Das Haus stellt fraglos unter Beweis, dass sich ein explizit moderner Bau mit großen Fensterflächen keineswegs mangelndes ökologisches Energiebewusstsein vorwerfen lassen muss – insbesondere, wenn ein Ingenieur wie Werner Sobek als Autor verantwortlich zeichnet.

La maison prouve, entre autres, qu'une résidence très moderne à grandes baies vitrées peut éviter les gaspillages énergétiques, en particulier lorsqu'un ingénieur comme Werner Sobek en est l'auteur.

GERMÁN DEL SOL

Germán del Sol, Arquitecto
Camino Las Flores 11441
Las Condes, Santiago
Chile

Tel: +562 214 12 14
Fax: +562 214 11 47
E-mail: contacto@germandelsol.cl
Web: www.germandelsol.cl

GERMÁN DEL SOL was born in Santiago de Chile in 1949. He graduated in 1973 from the Escuela Técnica Superior de Arquitectura de Barcelona, Spain. He created his own firm in Barcelona (1973–79) before returning to Santiago, where he worked on his own (1980–83), before spending two years in the office of R. Elmore in Palo Alto, California (1984–86). He then returned to his own practice in Santiago, where he has been based since 1986. Between 1988 and 1998, he created and directed Explora, a company dedicated to creating new travel destinations in remote places in South America. Between 1995 and 1998, he created and directed Viña Gracia, a new Chilean vineyard. Germán del Sol then created and directed a new hot springs complex, next to the Villarrica Vulcano, in Pucón (Chile, 2001–05). His built work includes the Hotel Explora en Atacama (San Pedro de Atacama, 1998); horse stables (San Pedro de Atacama, 1999); saunas and pools (Atacama, 2000); Puritama Hot Springs Complex (Atacama, 2000); Geometricas Hot Springs Complex (Villarrica, 2004); Hotel Remota (Puerto Natales, Patagonia, 2005–06, published here); and Remota Spot (Patagonia, 2007), all in Chile. In 2008 he completed an apartment building in Vallecas (Madrid). He won the National Association of Chilean Architects Award in 2006.

GERMÁN DEL SOL wurde 1949 in Santiago de Chile geboren. Sein Studium schloss er 1973 an der Escuela Técnica Superior de Arquitectura de Barcelona in Spanien ab. Nachdem er zunächst in Barcelona ein eigenes Büro betrieb (1973–79), kehrte er nach Santiago zurück, wo er selbstständig arbeitete (1980–83), bevor er zwei Jahre lang für R. Elmore in Palo Alto, Kalifornien, tätig war (1984–86). Schließlich kehrte er zu seinem eigenen Büro in Santiago zurück, von wo aus er seit 1986 arbeitet. Von 1988 bis 1998 leitete er die von ihm gegründete Agentur Explora, die sich auf die Erschließung neuer Reiseziele an abgelegenen Orten Südamerikas spezialisiert hatte. Von 1995 bis 1998 führte er das von ihm gegründete chilenische Weingut Viña Gracia. Schließlich baute und leitete Germán del Sol auch eine Hotelanlage an den Thermalquellen am Vulkan Villarrica in Pucón (Chile, 2001–05). Zu seinen realisierten Projekten zählen das Hotel Explora en Atacama (San Pedro de Atacama, 1998), Pferdeställe (San Pedro de Atacama, 1999), Saunen und Pools (Atacama, 2000), die Thermalquellen Puritama (Atacama, 2000), der Thermalquellenkomplex Geometricas (Villarrica, 2004), das Hotel Remota (Puerto Natales, Patagonien, 2005–06, hier vorgestellt) sowie Remota Spot (Patagonien, 2007), alle in Chile. 2008 wurde ein Apartmentgebäude in Vallecas (Madrid) fertiggestellt. 2006 wurde er mit dem Preis des Nationalen Architektenverbands in Chile ausgezeichnet.

GERMÁN DEL SOL, né à Santiago du Chili en 1949, est diplômé de la Escuela Técnica Superior de Arquitectura de Barcelona, Espagne (1973). Il fonde son agence à Barcelone (1973–79), avant de revenir à Santiago où il travaille à son compte (1980–83). Il collabore deux années avec l'agence de R. Elmore à Palo Alto, en Californie (1984–86), puis retourne à Santiago. De 1988 à 1998, il crée et dirige Explora, société qui propose de nouvelles destinations de voyages dans des lieux isolés d'Amérique du Sud. Entre 1995 et 1998, il fonde et dirige « Viña Gracia », un nouveau domaine viticole. Il a ensuite créé et dirigé un nouveau complexe touristique autour de sources d'eau chaude près du volcan de Villarrica, à Pucón (Chili, 2001–05). Parmi ses réalisations, toutes au Chili : l'hôtel Explora à Atacama (San Pedro de Atacama, 1998) ; des écuries (San Pedro de Atacama, 1999) ; des saunas et piscines (Atacama, 2000) ; le complexe thermal de Puritama (Atacama, 2000) ; le complexe thermal Geometricas (Villarrica, 2004) ; l'hôtel Remota (Puerto Natales, Patagonie, 2005–06, publié ici) et Remota Spot (Patagonie, 2007). En 2008, il a achevé un immeuble d'appartements à Vallecas (Madrid). Il a remporté le prix de l'Association nationale des architectes chiliens en 2006.

HOTEL REMOTA
Puerto Natales, Patagonia, Chile, 2005–06

Floor area: 5215 m². Client: Immobiliaria mares del sur. Cost: $9.5 million
Team: José Luis Ibañez, Francisca Schüler, Carlos Venegas

Inspired by the sheep farming buildings of Patagonia, the Hotel Remota has a central courtyard occupied only by several boulders at its center. The architect states: "Latin America has an ancient tradition of architecture that stands in the midst of nature, where shepherds or merchants used to pass or stay the night, or where people gather once in a while to celebrate their ancient rites." Germán del Sol describes Remota as resembling a "big black barn" from a distance with an unexpectedly refined interior. Pillars, slabs, and interior walls are made of concrete. Waterproof industrial plywood panels coated with a synthetic asphalt membrane and a 25-centimeter-thick layer of expanded polyurethane cover the building and act as insulation. Double-glazed thermal window panes "form a continuous sequence of vertical openings in the exterior walls." The natural grasses found on the site are allowed to grow wild around the building, and on its landscaped roof. The three buildings that form the hotel are connected by wooden corridors. Within, the architect has placed spartan geometric dark wood furniture made by carpenters on site from dead wood culled in the Patagonian lowlands near the sea. Low-energy light bulbs, low-water consumption bathroom fittings, and an orientation intended to make use of passive solar energy are part of the overall sustainability strategy employed.

Das Hotel Remota, inspiriert von den Schaffarmen Patagoniens, hat einen zentralen Innenhof, in dem nur einige Findlinge liegen. Der Architekt erklärt: „Lateinamerika hat eine uralte architektonische Tradition von Bauten, die inmitten der Landschaft liegen, dort, wo einst Schäfer oder Händler vorüberzogen und die Nacht verbrachten oder sich Menschen versammelten, um uralte Riten zu feiern." Germán del Sol zufolge wirkt Remota aus der Ferne wie eine „große schwarze Scheune" mit unerwartet raffiniertem Interieur. Stützen, Platten und Innenwände sind aus Beton. Verkleidet und gedämmt wurde der Bau mit wasserfesten industriellen Sperrholzpaneelen, die mit einer synthetischen Asphaltmembran und einer 25 cm starken Schicht aus Polyurethan-Hartschaum ummantelt sind. Doppelwärmeschutzfenster „bilden eine uniforme Sequenz vertikaler Öffnungen in den Außenwänden". Die auf dem Gelände beheimateten natürlichen Gräser wachsen wild um das Gebäude ebenso wie auf dem begrünten Dach. Die drei Hotelgebäude sind durch Holzkorridore miteinander verbunden. Die Innenräume stattete der Architekt mit „spartanischen" geometrischen dunklen Holzmöbeln aus, die von Schreinern vor Ort aus totem Holz aus der patagonischen Tiefebene an der Küste gefertigt wurden. Energiesparlampen, Wasser sparende Installationen in den Bädern und die Ausrichtung des Baus für die passive Nutzung von Solarenergie sind Bestandteile der hier angewandten Nachhaltigkeitsstrategie.

Inspiré des formes des bergers de Patagonie, l'hôtel Remota se caractérise par une cour centrale uniquement occupée en son centre par quelques rochers. L'architecte explique ainsi son projet : « L'Amérique latine possède une tradition ancienne d'architecture en pleine nature, où bergers et colporteurs séjournaient ou passaient la nuit, où des gens se réunissaient de temps en temps pour célébrer des rites anciens. » Il considère Remota comme « une grosse grange noire » vue de loin, mais possédant un intérieur au raffinement inattendu. Les piliers, les dalles des sols et les murs intérieurs sont en béton. Le bâtiment est habillé et isolé par des panneaux industriels en contreplaqué à membrane d'asphalte synthétique et couche de polyuréthane expansé de 25 cm d'épaisseur. Des fenêtres à double vitrage de verre thermique « forment une séquence continue d'ouvertures verticales dans les murs extérieurs ». Les herbes naturelles trouvées sur le site grandissent librement autour du bâtiment et sur son toit végétalisé. Les trois constructions qui constituent l'hôtel sont réunies par des corridors en bois. À l'intérieur, l'architecte a disposé un mobilier en bois de formes géométriques « spartiate », réalisé sur place par les menuisiers à l'aide de bois mort récupéré dans les marais patagonien au bord de la mer. Des ampoules à basse consommation, des équipements de salles de bains qui économisent l'eau, et une orientation qui favorise l'utilisation passive de l'énergie solaire font partie de la stratégie de durabilité utilisée.

Lying low in the ground, with its three buildings connected by wooden corridors, the hotel has a somewhat austere appearance.

Das Hotel besteht aus drei durch Holzgänge verbundenen Bauten. Es scheint sich dicht an den Boden zu kauern und wirkt geradezu streng.

Se détachant à peine du sol, les trois bâtiments de l'hôtel reliés par des corridors en bois sont d'aspect assez austère.

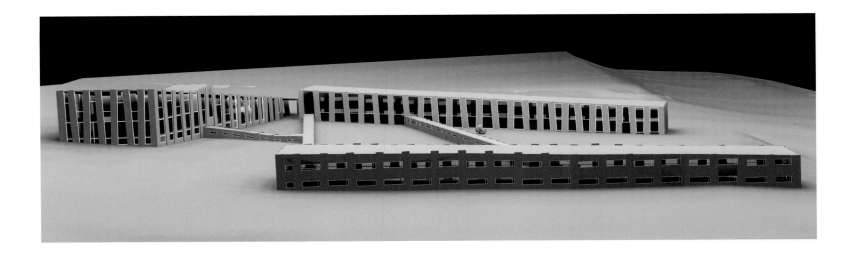

Even the landscaping of the hotel participates in its overall impression of frugality generated by the architects in this sparse natural setting.

Selbst die Landschaftsgestaltung des Hotels trägt zum beinahe spartanischen Gesamteindruck bei, den die Architekten in dieser spröden Umgebung geschaffen haben.

Même l'aménagement paysager participe à l'impression générale d'économie de moyens voulue par les architectes pour ce cadre naturel sévère.

Although simple, the interiors give a greater impression of warmth than the outside of the hotel.

Trotz seiner Schlichtheit vermittelt das Interieur mehr Wärme als die Außenansicht des Hotels.

Bien que sobres, les intérieurs sont plus chaleureux que l'aspect extérieur de l'hôtel.

STUDIO MUMBAI

Studio Mumbai Architects
561/63 N. M. Joshi Marg
Byculla West
Mumbai
Maharashtra 400 001
India

Tel: +91 22 6577 7560
Fax: +91 22 2302 1973
E-mail: contact@studiomumbai.com
Web: www.studiomumbai.com

BIJOY JAIN was born in Mumbai, India, in 1965 and received his M.Arch degree from Washington University in Saint Louis in 1990. He worked in Los Angeles and London between 1989 and 1995, and returned to India in 1995 to found his practice. As the architects define their firm: "The essence of the work lies in the relationship between land and architecture. The endeavor is to show the genuine possibility of creating buildings that emerge through a process of collective dialogue, a face-to-face sharing of knowledge through imagination, intimacy, and modesty." Recent projects of the firm include the Reading Room (Nagaon, Maharashtra, 2003); Tara House (Kashid, Maharashtra, 2005); Palmyra House (Nandgaon, Maharashtra, 2006–07, published here); Leti 360 Resort (Leti, Uttaranchal, 2007); House on Pali Hill (Bandra, Mumbai, 2008); Utsav House (Satirje, Maharashtra, 2008); Belavali House (Belavali, Maharashtra, 2008); Copper House II (Chondi, Maharashtra, 2010); "In-Between Architecture," Victoria & Albert Museum (London, UK, 2010); and the exhibition "Work-Place," Venice Biennale (Venice, Italy, 2010), all in India unless stated otherwise.

BIJOY JAIN wurde 1965 in Mumbai, Indien, geboren und schloss sein Studium an der Washington University in Saint Louis 1990 mit einem M.Arch. ab. Von 1989 bis 1995 arbeitete er in Los Angeles und London und kehrte 1995 nach Indien zurück, wo er sein Büro gründete. Die Architekten beschreiben ihr Profil wie folgt: „Das wesentliche Element unserer Arbeit ist das Verhältnis von Landschaft und Architektur. Unser Ziel ist es zu zeigen, dass es tatsächlich möglich ist, Bauten zu schaffen, die aus einem Prozess des kollektiven Dialogs entstehen, durch persönliches Teilen von Wissen, mithilfe von Fantasie, Vertrautheit und Bescheidenheit." Jüngere Projekte des Büros sind u. a. der Reading Room (Nagaon, Maharashtra, 2003), das Tara House (Kashid, Maharashtra, 2005), das Palmyra House (Nandgaon, Maharashtra, 2006–07, hier vorgestellt), die Hotelanlage Leti 360 (Leti, Uttaranchal, 2007), ein Haus auf Pali Hill (Bandra, Mumbai, 2008), das Utsav House (Satirje, Maharashtra, 2008), das Belavali House (Belavali, Maharashtra, 2008), das Copper House II (Chondi, Maharashtra, 2010), In-Between Architecture, Victoria & Albert Museum (London, GB, 2010), sowie die Ausstellung Work-Place, Biennale Venedig (Venedig, Italien, 2010), alle in Indien, sofern nicht anders angegeben.

BIJOY JAIN, né à Mumbai en 1965, a obtenu son M.Arch. à l'université Washington à Saint Louis (1990). Il a travaillé à Los Angeles et Londres de 1989 à 1995, puis est revenu en Inde en 1995 pour y fonder son agence dont il définit ainsi les objectifs : « L'essence de notre travail réside dans la relation entre la terre et l'architecture. Notre préoccupation constante est de montrer qu'il est véritablement possible de créer des constructions issues d'un processus de dialogue collectif, d'un échange personnel de connaissances, où l'imagination, l'intimité et la modestie ont leur place. » Parmi les projets récents de l'agence, essentiellement en Inde, figurent : une salle de lecture (Nagaon, Maharashtra, 2003) ; la maison Tara (Kashid, Maharashtra, 2005) ; la maison Palmyra (Nandgaon, Maharashtra, 2006–07, publiée ici) ; l'hôtel de tourisme Leti 360 (Leti, Uttaranchal, 2007) ; la maison sur la colline de Pali (Bandra, Mumbai, 2008) ; la maison Utsav (Satirje, Maharashtra, 2008) ; la maison Belavali (Belavali, Maharashtra, 2008) ; la maison Copper II (Chondi, Maharashtra, 2010) ; l'exposition « In-Between Architecture », Victoria & Albert Museum (Londres, 2010), et l'exposition « Work-Place » à la Biennale de Venise 2010.

PALMYRA HOUSE

Nandgaon, Maharashtra, India, 2006–07

Area: 300 m². Client: not disclosed. Cost: not disclosed
Collaboration: Jeevaram Suthar, Punaram Suthar, Pandurang Malekar

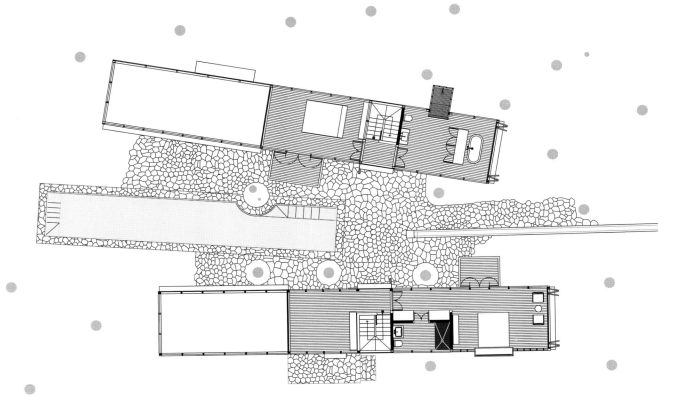

Above, a site plan shows that the two structures are slightly skewed apart. The rectangular basin separates them and forms a third rectangle in the plan.

Ein Lageplan rechts zeigt die leicht schiefwinklige Anordnung der beiden Bauten. Das rechteckige Wasserbecken, das sie trennt, erscheint als drittes Rechteck auf dem Grundriss.

À droite, plan du terrain montrant que les deux constructions ne sont pas parallèles. Le bassin rectangulaire qui les sépare forme le troisième rectangle du plan.

In this house, air and light are filtered through two louvered wood boxes set on stone plinths within a coconut plantation situated outside Mumbai. The louvers are made from the trunks of local palmyra palms, whence the name of the residence. These louvers naturally supply passive cooling, as do the neighboring trees. Water from three on-site wells is stored in a water tower that arrives through force of gravity in the house. The architects write: "Sky, sea, and landscape overlap as one moves between and through the spaces of the home. A network of stone aqueducts, inhabited by moss, lichen, and ferns, irrigate the plantation, drawing water from artesian wells as has been the practice for generations." The plan of the house is made up of a series of strict, long rectangles. This is a two-story timber house built as a weekend retreat south of Mumbai.

Bei diesem Haus werden Luft und Licht durch eine Gebäudehülle aus Lamellen gefiltert, die die zwei hölzernen Boxen auf ihrem Steinfundament umfangen. Das Haus liegt inmitten einer Kokosnussplantage außerhalb von Mumbai. Die Sonnenschutzblenden wurden aus dem Holz der heimischen Palmyrapalme gefertigt, von der sich auch der Name des Hauses ableitet. Die Blenden sorgen für natürliche passive Kühlung, zu der auch der Baumbestand beiträgt. Wasser für das Haus wird auf dem Gelände in drei Brunnen gesammelt, gefiltert und in einem Wasserturm gespeichert, der das Haus durch natürlichen, gefällebedingten Wasserdruck versorgt. Die Architekten schreiben: „Himmel, Meer und Landschaft gehen ineinander über, sobald man sich zwischen den Bauten und durch die Räume des Hauses bewegt. Die Plantage wird durch ein Netzwerk steinerner Aquädukte voller Moos, Flechten und Farne bewässert, die durch artesische Brunnen gespeist werden, eine seit Generationen bestehende Praxis." Der Grundriss des Hauses besteht aus einer Reihe strenger, lang gestreckter Rechtecke. Die zweistöckige Holzkonstruktion wird als Wochenendhaus südlich von Mumbai genutzt.

Dans cette maison située au milieu d'une palmeraie de cocotiers au sud de Mumbai, l'air et la lumière sont filtrés par les persiennes des deux structures en bois reposant sur leurs socles en pierre. Les persiennes sont en palmier de Palmyre local, d'où le nom de la résidence. Elles assurent un rafraîchissement naturel passif qui complète celui fourni par les arbres environnants. L'eau tirée de trois puits est conservée dans un château d'eau qui alimente la maison par simple gravité. « Le ciel, la mer et le paysage semblent se superposer lorsqu'on se déplace à l'intérieur des volumes de la maison. Un réseau de petits aqueducs de pierre, où poussent des mousses, des lichens et des fougères, irrigue la plantation. Il est alimenté par des puits artésiens selon des pratiques qui remontent à des générations », précisent les architectes. Le plan de cette maison de week-end se compose de deux parallélépipèdes allongés, de deux niveaux chacun, construits en bois.

This very light wooden box structure is seen with its sliding walls opened to the warm environment. Sitting lightly on the earth, it might almost appear to be a temporary structure.

Ein Blick auf die zwei besonders leichten Baukörper aus Holz mit Schiebewänden, die sich im heißen Klima nach außen öffnen lassen. Die Bauweise wirkt sehr leicht, fast als handele es sich um temporäre Bauten.

Photo des deux parties de la maison composée de deux structures très légères en bois, à parois coulissantes ouvertes sur l'environnement tropical. Elles sont si délicatement posées sur le sol qu'elles pourraient faire penser à des constructions temporaires.

With the folding louvered walls in the open position, the interior of the house and its generous volumes are fully open to the natural setting. In elevation (below) the structure remains just as simple and rectilinear.

Sind die Lamellentüren aufgeklappt, öffnet sich das großzügige Interieur des Hauses vollständig zur Landschaft. Im Aufriss (unten) wirkt der Bau ebenso schlicht und geradlinig.

Parois à persiennes ouvertes, l'intérieur de la maison aux généreux volumes s'inscrit pleinement dans son cadre naturel. L'élévation ci-dessous illustre la forme simple et rectiligne de chaque pavillon.

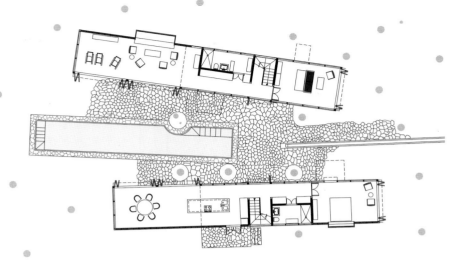

Floor plans reveal the basic simplicity of the interior design, echoing the architecture itself, as can be seen in the image below.

Etagengrundrisse zeugen von der grundlegenden Schlichtheit des Interieurs, die sich auch in der Architektur des Hauses widerspiegelt, wie die Ansicht unten belegt.

Les plans au sol expriment la simplicité élémentaire de l'aménagement intérieur qui vient en écho à l'architecture extérieure, comme le montre l'image ci-dessous.

TAYLOR CULLITY LETHLEAN

Taylor Cullity Lethlean
385 Drummond Street
Carlton, VIC 3053
Australia

Tel: +61 3 9380 4344
Fax: +61 3 9348 1232
E-mail: agata.k@tcl.net.au
Web: tcl.net.au

Taylor Cullity Lethlean is directed by three principals, Kevin Taylor, Kate Cullity, and Perry Lethlean. **KEVIN TAYLOR** was born in 1953 in Clarence Park, Australia. He graduated from RMIT in Landscape Architecture and from the University of South Australia in Architecture. **KATE CULLITY** was born in 1956 in Perth and received degrees in Botany and Education from the University of Western Australia. **PERRY LETHLEAN** graduated from RMIT in Landscape Architecture (Bachelor of Applied Science) in 1985. He received a Master of Urban Design from the same university in 1992, and his Ph.D. in 2010. They founded Taylor Cullity Lethlean in 1991. Their work includes the Geelong Waterfront Development, not far from Melbourne (Geelong, 1999–2001); Birrarung Marr (Melbourne, 2002); the Kangaroo Island National Park, located on Kangaroo Island 112 kilometers southwest of Adelaide (1999–2003); noise barriers for the Craigieburn Bypass Freeway (Melbourne, 2003); Tidbinbilla Nature Reserve, located between the Tidbinbilla and Gibraltar Ranges to the south of Canberra (2005); and Manly Corso (Sydney, 2005). The firm is currently working on the Canberra International Arboretum (with TGZ Architects, 2005–); Lonsdale Street (Dandenong, Victoria, 2007–); the Auckland Waterfront (New Zealand, 2009–); and the Royal Botanic Gardens published here (Cranbourne, Melbourne, 1995; Stage 1 complete; Stage 2 ongoing).

Das Büro Taylor Cullity Lethlean wird von drei Partnern geführt: Kevin Taylor, Kate Cullity und Perry Lethlean. **KEVIN TAYLOR** wurde 1953 in Clarence Park, Australien, geboren. Er machte seinen Universitätsabschluss an der RMIT in Landschaftsarchitektur sowie einen Abschluss als Architekt an der University of South Australia. **KATE CULLITY** wurde 1956 in Perth geboren und schloss ihr Studium in Botanik und Pädagogik an der University of Western Australia ab. **PERRY LETHLEAN** schloss 1985 sein Studium der Landschaftsarchitektur an der RMIT (Bachelor of Applied Science) ab. Dort machte er 1992 den Master in Stadtplanung und promovierte 2010. Das Büro Taylor Cullity Lethlean wurde 1991 gegründet. Zu ihren Arbeiten gehören die Neugestaltung und Bebauung der Meeresuferzone von Geelong, das nicht weit von Melbourne entfernt ist (1999–2001), Birrarung Marr (Melbourne, 2002), der Kangaroo Island National Park auf der Insel Kangaroo Island, 112 km südwestlich von Adelaide (1999–2003), Lärmschutzwände an der Ringstraße um Craigieburn (Melbourne, 2003), das Tidbinbilla-Naturreservat, das zwischen dem Tidbinbilla und den Gibraltar Ranges südlich von Canberra (2005) liegt, und die Gestaltung der Einkaufsstraße Manly Corso in Sydney (2005). Derzeit realisiert das Büro das Internationale Arboretum von Canberra (mit dem Architekturbüro TGZ Architects, seit 2005), die Gestaltung der Lonsdale Street (Dandenong, Victoria, seit 2007), die Ufergestaltung von Auckland (Neuseeland, seit 2009) und den hier vorgestellten Botanischen Garten (Cranbourne, Melbourne, Bauabschnitt 1 wurde 1995 fertiggestellt, Bauabschnitt 2 ist noch in Arbeit).

L'agence Taylor Cullity Lethlean est dirigée par trois associés : Kevin Taylor, Kate Cullity et Perry Lethlean. **KEVIN TAYLOR**, né en 1953 à Clarence Park (Australie), est titulaire d'un diplôme d'architecture du paysage du RMIT (Melbourne) et d'un diplôme d'architecture de l'université d'Australie du Sud. **KATE CULLITY**, née en 1956 à Perth, est diplômée en botanique et en éducation de l'université d'Australie occidentale. **PERRY LETHLEAN** est diplômé en architecture du paysage du RMIT (Bachelor of Applied Science, 1985) et titulaire d'un M.A. (1992) et d'un Ph.D. (2010) d'urbanisme de la même université. Ils ont fondé Taylor Cullity Lethlean en 1991. Parmi leurs réalisations en Australie, sauf mention contraire : l'aménagement du front de mer de Geelong, près de Melbourne (Geelong, 1999–2001); le parc de Birrarung Marr (Melbourne, 2002); le parc national de Kangaroo Island, 112 km au sud-ouest d'Adélaïde (1999–2003); des barrières antibruit pour la rocade de Craigieburn (Melbourne, 2003); la réserve naturelle de Tidbinbilla, entre les chaînes de montagnes de Tidbinbilla et de Gibraltar, au sud de Canberra (2005) et le Manly Corso (Sydney, 2005). L'agence travaille actuellement sur le projet du Canberra International Arboretum (avec TGZ Architects, 2005–); la Lonsdale Street (Dandenong, Victoria, 2007–); le front de mer d'Auckland (Nouvelle-Zélande, 2009–) et les Royal Botanic Gardens (Cranbourne, Melbourne, 1995; phase 1 achevée, phase 2 en cours, publiés ici).

ROYAL BOTANIC GARDENS

Cranbourne, Melbourne, Australia, 1995 (Stage 1 complete; Stage 2 ongoing)

Address: 1000 Ballarto Road, Cranbourne, VIC 3977, Australia, +61 3 5990 2200,
www.rbg.vic.gov.au. Area: 1.25 hectares. Client: Royal Botanic Gardens. Cost: $18 million
Collaboration: Paul Thompson, Mark Stoner, Edwina Kearney, Greg Clark (Artists)

This project, called the Australian Garden, is located 30 kilometers south of Melbourne at the **ROYAL BOTANIC GARDENS** in Cranbourne. The designers point out that usually botanic gardens are based on European predecessors. "The Australian Garden by contrast," they say, "uses the Australian landscape as its inspiration to create a sequence of powerful sculptural and artistic landscape experiences that recognize its diversity, breadth of scale, and wonderful contrasts. The project seeks to stimulate and educate visitors of the potential use and diversity of Australian flora." They have sought to express the tension between Australian reverence for nature and the continual drive to modify it. Thus the western side of the garden is more free flowing and inspired directly by nature, while the eastern side contains "highly designed exhibition gardens" by various landscape architects. Logically, the center of the project is the Sand Garden, evoking the "dry red center of the Australian continent." Water features with variable rates of flow are used as the "mediating element" between these contrasting views of Australian nature. Biodiversity, sustainability, and other ecological concerns are integrated into the park design. Artworks by Greg Clark and Mark Stoner are included in the park as are structures by Kerstin Thompson and Greg Burgess. Based on the success of the first phase of this project, the client asked Taylor Cullity Lethlean and Paul Thompson to work on a second phase expansion.

Dieses Projekt, der Australische Garten, liegt 30 km südlich von Melbourne auf dem Gelände der **ROYAL BOTANIC GARDENS** in Cranbourne. Die Planer weisen darauf hin, dass sich Botanische Gärten normalerweise an europäischen Vorbildern orientieren. „Der Australische Garten dagegen nutzt die Landschaft Australiens als Inspiration, um eine Folge von kraftvollen skulpturalen und künstlerischen Landschaftserfahrungen mit ihrer gesamten Vielfalt, ihren unterschiedlichen Maßstäben und den wunderbaren Kontrasten zu schaffen. Das Projekt versucht, die Besucher anzuregen und ihnen die Potenziale und Vielfalt der australischen Flora zu zeigen." Die Planer wollen die Spannung aufzeigen zwischen der Verehrung der Natur und dem ständigen Drang, eben diese zu verändern. So ist der westliche Gartenbereich eher in freien, unmittelbar von der Natur beeinflussten Formen angelegt, wohingegen im östlichen Bereich „durchgestylte Ausstellungsgärten" von mehreren Landschaftsarchitekten präsentiert werden. Den Mittelpunkt dieses Projekts bildet logischerweise der „Sand Garden", der an die „trockene rote Mitte des australischen Kontinents" erinnert. Als „vermittelnde Elemente" zwischen diesen gegensätzlichen Betrachtungsweisen der australischen Natur dienen unterschiedliche Wasserelemente. Biodiversität, Nachhaltigkeit und andere ökologische Aspekte sind Bestandteile des Parkentwurfs. Im Park befinden sich Werke von Greg Clark und Mark Stoner sowie Bauten von Kerstin Thompson und Greg Burgess. Da der erste Bauabschnitt des Projektes ein großer Erfolg war, beauftragte der Bauherr das Büro Taylor Cullity Lethlean und Paul Thompson mit der Ausarbeitung einer zweiten Erweiterungsphase.

Ce projet, l'Australian Garden, a été réalisé dans les **ROYAL BOTANIC GARDENS** de Cranbourne, à 30 km au sud de Melbourne. Ses créateurs notent que les jardins botaniques s'appuient en général sur le modèle établi par leurs prédécesseurs européens. « Par contraste, expliquent-ils, l'Australian Garden s'inspire du paysage australien pour créer une séquence d'explorations éloquentes du paysage, sculpturales et artistiques, qui prennent en compte sa diversité, l'ampleur de son échelle et ses merveilleux contrastes. Le projet veut stimuler le visiteur et lui montrer les usages potentiels et la diversité de la flore australienne. » L'agence a cherché à exprimer la tension entre le respect des Australiens pour la nature et leur tendance permanente à la modifier. Le côté ouest du jardin est traité en flux plus libres et directement inspirés de la nature, tandis que le côté est regroupe « des jardins d'exposition très dessinés » par divers architectes paysagistes. Dans une logique géographique, le centre du projet est le Sand Garden qui évoque « la région centrale sèche et rouge du continent australien ». Divers bassins et éléments aquatiques servent d'« éléments de médiation » entre ces visions contrastées de la nature australienne. La biodiversité, la durabilité et d'autres préoccupations écologiques ont été intégrées dans le projet, de même que des œuvres d'art de Greg Clark et Mark Stoner et des constructions de Kerstin Thompson et de Greg Burgess. Face au succès de la première phase de ce projet, les Royal Botanic Gardens ont chargé Taylor Cullity Lethlean et Paul Thompson de travailler sur une seconde phase.

An overall plan of the project and an aerial view (seen from a different angle) show the attention of the designers to creating a variety of different environments, some more "painterly" as seen here, and others more "natural."

Der Gesamtplan des Projekts und die Luftaufnahme, die aus einem anderen Blickwinkel gemacht wurde, zeigen, mit welcher Sorgfalt die Planer vorgegangen sind, um eine Vielfalt unterschiedlicher Naturumfelder darzustellen. Manche sind eher „malerisch" wie hier, andere eher „naturnah" umgesetzt.

Un plan d'ensemble du projet et une vue aérienne mettent en évidence l'attention portée par les paysagistes à la création d'environnements différents et variés, certains plus « picturaux » comme ici, et d'autres plus « naturels ».

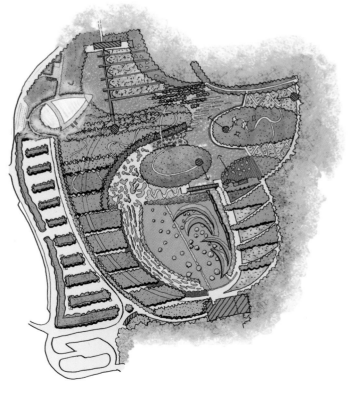

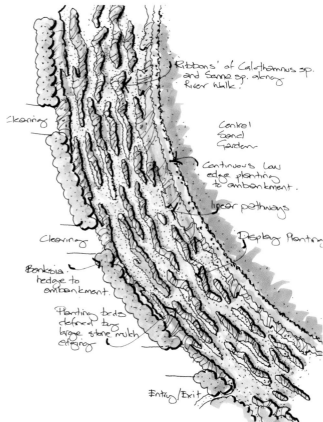

Ribbons' of Calothamnus sp.
and Senna sp. along
River Walk.

Clearing

Central
Sand
Garden

Continuous Low
edge planting
to embankment.

linear pathways

Display Planting

Clearing

Banksia
hedge to
embankment.

Planting beds
defined by
large stone mulch
edging.

Entry/Exit

The brief for the project requires that it should "explore and illustrate the role of native flora in shaping the nature of Australia; display native flora in creative ways; and celebrate the role of Australian plants in Australian life and culture."

In der Auftragsbeschreibung für dieses Projekt wurde verlangt, es solle „die Rolle der heimischen Flora untersuchen und darstellen, wie sie der Natur in Australien ihre Gestalt gibt; die heimische Flora in kreativer Art und Weise vorstellen und die Rolle der australischen Pflanzen im Leben und in der Kultur Australiens herausarbeiten".

Le cahier des charges du projet spécifiait qu'il devait « explorer et illustrer le rôle de la flore locale dans la nature australienne ; présenter cette flore de manières créatives et célébrer le rôle des plantes australiennes dans la vie et la culture du pays ».

The designers state: "Utilizing
100 000 species of flora, some never
before seen in cultivation, the garden
illustrates the enormous potential of
our flora in creating distinctive, bold,
and memorable garden experiences."

Die Planer stellen fest: „Mit 100 000
Pflanzenarten, von denen einige nie
zuvor kultiviert wurden, ist dieser
Garten mit seinen unverwechselba-
ren, kühnen und unvergesslichen
Erlebnissen Beweis für das enorme
Potenzial unserer Pflanzenwelt."

« Mettant en scène 100 000 espèces
de plantes, dont certaines encore
jamais cultivées, le jardin illustre
l'énorme potentiel de notre flore de
créer des opportunités de découverte
originales, audacieuses et inou-
bliables », précisent les paysagistes.

MATTEO THUN

Matteo Thun & Partners
Via Appiani 9
20121 Milan
Italy

Tel: + 39 02 655 6911
Fax: + 39 02 657 0646
E-mail: info@matteothun.com
Web: www.matteothun.com

MATTEO THUN was born in 1952 in Bolzano, Italy. He studied at the Salzburg Academy with the painter Oskar Kokoschka and received his doctorate in Architecture in Florence in 1975. He began working with Ettore Sottsass in Milan in 1978 and was a cofounding member of the Memphis group with Sottsass in 1981. He was the Chair for Product Design and Ceramics at the Vienna Academy for Applied Arts (1982–96), and created his own office, Matteo Thun & Partners, in Milan in 1984. He served as Creative Director for Swatch from 1990 to 1993. According to his description, in his studio, Matteo Thun attempts "to offer a complete service to his international clients, developing projects covering different fields, such as architecture, design, and communication." Matteo Thun & Partners comprises a team of 40 professionals, graphic designers, product designers, and architects, who work on an interdisciplinary basis. The work of the studio ranges from resorts and hotels, like the Vigilius Mountain Resort (Lana, Merano, Italy, 2001–03, published here), to low-energy prefabrication systems, watches for Bulgari or Swatch, furniture for Kartell, or lighting systems for AEG and Zumtobel.

MATTEO THUN wurde 1952 in Bozen geboren. Er studierte an der Sommerakademie Salzburg bei Oskar Kokoschka und promovierte 1975 in Florenz in Architektur. 1978 begann er in Mailand seine Zusammenarbeit mit Ettore Sottsass, mit dem er 1981 zum Mitbegründer der Gruppe Memphis wurde. Er war Professor für Design an der Hochschule für Angewandte Kunst in Wien (1982–96) und gründete 1984 sein eigenes Büro Matteo Thun & Partners in Mailand. Von 1990 bis 1993 war er Kreativdirektor bei Swatch. Mit seinem Studio will Matteo Thun „einen Rundumservice für internationale Auftraggeber bieten und entwickelt Projekte in verschiedenen Disziplinen wie Architektur, Design und Kommunikation". Matteo Thun & Partners hat 40 Mitarbeiter, darunter Grafikdesigner, Produktdesigner und Architekten, die interdisziplinär zusammenarbeiten. Die Projekte des Studios reichen von Hotels – wie das hier veröffentlichte Vigilius Mountain Resort (Lana, Merano, Italien, 2001–03) – bis hin zu Niedrigenergie-Fertigbausystemen, von Armbanduhren für Bulgari oder Swatch über Möbel für Kartell bis hin zu Lichtsystemen für AEG und Zumtobel.

MATTEO THUN est né en 1952 à Bolzano, Italie. Après avoir étudié à l'Académie de Salzbourg auprès du peintre Oskar Kokoschka, il reçoit son diplôme d'architecte à Florence en 1975. Il commence à travailler avec Ettore Sottsass à Milan en 1978, puis à participer avec lui à la fondation du groupe Memphis en 1981. Il dirige le département de design produit et de céramique à l'Académie des arts appliqués de Vienne (1982–96) et crée sa propre agence, Matteo Thun & Partners, à Milan, en 1984. Il a été directeur de la création de Swatch de 1990 à 1993. Matteo Thun & Partners propose « d'offrir à des clients internationaux un service complet de développement de projets, couvrant différents domaines comme l'architecture, le design et la communication ». L'agence emploie 40 collaborateurs, graphistes, designers et architectes travaillant sur une base interdisciplinaire. Les interventions du studio vont d'hôtels – tel le complexe hôtelier Vigilius Mountain Resort (Lana, Merano, Italie, 2001–03, publié ici) – à des systèmes de construction préfabriquée à faible consommation d'énergie, en passant par des montres pour Bulgari ou Swatch, des meubles pour Kartell ou des systèmes d'éclairage pour AEG et Zumtobel.

VIGILIUS MOUNTAIN RESORT

Lana (Merano), Italy, 2001–03

Area: 11 500 m². Cost: not disclosed
Client: not disclosed

Located at an altitude of 1500 meters, this resort was designed as an extension to the existing Vigiljoch Hotel. Accessible only by funicular or on foot, the complex includes 35 bedrooms and 6 suites, together with a wellness center, swimming pool, conference room, library, and restaurants. Matteo Thun explains that the design of the new structures is based on local wood construction used in an innovative manner. Stone, wood, clay, and glass are significant building materials. Integrated into its surroundings to the greatest possible extent, the resort has a green roof covered with vegetation. Other energy-saving gestures include a façade with adjustable louvers. Large, planted terraces and an insistence on opening the architecture out onto the surrounding natural setting emphasize the close rapport between the buildings and the site. As the architect says: "The willingness to integrate completely with nature is evident in the 'Paradise Garden,'" a hill planted with larch trees in the inner part of the complex. The **VIGILIUS MOUNTAIN RESORT** is a good example of the present and future potential for ecotourism, based on responsible architecture in spectacular natural settings.

Das Ferienhotel, gelegen auf 1500 Metern Höhe, ist ein Erweiterungsbau des Hotel Vigiljoch. Erreichbar nur per Seilbahn oder zu Fuß, umfasst der Komplex 35 Zimmer und 6 Suiten, ein Wellnesscenter, ein Schwimmbad, einen Konferenzsaal, eine Bibliothek und Restaurants. Matteo Thun weist darauf hin, dass das Design der Neubauten lokale Holzbautraditionen aufgreift und innovativ umsetzt. Stein, Holz, Lehm und Glas sind die bestimmenden Baumaterialien. Das Resort wurde so weit wie möglich in sein Umfeld integriert und hat ein begrüntes Dach. Zu den weiteren energiesparenden Maßnahmen zählt auch die Fassade mit justierbaren Sonnenschutzblenden. Großzügige begrünte Terrassen und die konsequente Öffnung der Architektur zur Landschaft unterstreichen die enge Beziehung von Gebäuden und Standort. Der Architekt merkt an: „Die Bereitschaft, sich ganz in die Natur zu integrieren wird auch am ‚Paradiesgarten' deutlich," einem mit Lärchen bepflanzten Hügel im Herzen des Komplexes. Das **VIGILIUS MOUNTAIN RESORT** ist ein gutes Beispiel für das gegenwärtige und zukünftige Potenzial des ökologischen Tourismus, der auf verantwortliche Architektur und spektakuläre Landschaften baut.

Situé à 1500 m d'altitude, ce complexe est une extension de l'hôtel Vigiljoch. Accessible uniquement à pied ou par funiculaire, il compte 35 chambres, 6 suites, un centre de remise en forme, une piscine, une salle de conférences, une bibliothèque et des restaurants. Matteo Thun explique que la conception des bâtiments a fait appel à des principes de construction en bois locaux, mais utilisés de façon innovante. La pierre, le bois et le verre sont ainsi les principaux matériaux mis en jeu. Intégré au maximum dans son environnement, le complexe hôtelier possède un toit recouvert de végétation. Parmi les autres dispositifs d'économies d'énergie figure une façade à persiennes réglables. De vastes terrasses plantées et l'accent mis sur l'ouverture de l'architecture sur son cadre naturel soulignent les liens étroits entre les bâtiments et le site. Pour Thun : « La volonté de s'intégrer complètement à la nature est évidente dans le "jardin du Paradis", » une colline plantée de mélèzes à l'intérieur du complexe. Le **VIGILIUS MOUNTAIN RESORT** est un bon exemple du potentiel actuel et futur d'un écotourisme fondé sur une architecture responsable au cœur de sites naturels spectaculaires.

Lying relatively low in its car-free, isolated site, the resort makes a strong case for "ecotourism," or the discovery of the natural environment, as opposed to ecologically unsound exploitation of a site.

Das relativ niedrige Ferienhotel liegt an einem autofreien, entlegenen Ort und ist ein eindrückliches Plädoyer für „ökologischen Tourismus" und die Entdeckung der natürlichen Umgebung, statt einer ökologisch unverantwortlichen Ausbeutung des Standorts.

Relativement discret dans ce site sans voitures, cet hôtel est un argument pour l'écotourisme ou la découverte de l'environnement naturel et s'oppose à l'exploitation anti-écologique de certaines régions.

MICHAEL VAN VALKENBURGH

Michael Van Valkenburgh Associates, Inc.,
Landscape Architects, PC
16 Court Street, 11th Floor
Brooklyn, NY 11241, USA

Tel: +1 718 243 2044 / Fax: +1 718 243 1293
E-mail: mvva_ny@mvvainc.com
Web: www.mvvainc.com

MICHAEL VAN VALKENBURGH received a B.S. degree from the Cornell University College of Agriculture (Ithaca, New York, 1973) and a Master of Fine Arts in Landscape Architecture from the University of Illinois (Champaign/Urbana, 1977). He oversees both the New York and Cambridge (Massachusetts) offices of the firm he founded in 1982—Michael Van Valkenburgh Associates, Inc. (MVVA)—and is involved in some way in every project. Other firm Principals are **MATTHEW URBANSKI,** who is a lead designer for many of the firm's public projects, and **LAURA SOLANO,** who is a specialist in landscape technology. Matthew Urbanski joined MVVA in 1989 after receiving a Master of Landscape Architecture degree from Harvard the same year. Laura Solano has worked at MVVA since 1991. She received a Bachelor of Landscape Architecture from Ohio State University in 1983. Their work includes Tahari Courtyards (Millburn, New Jersey, 2002–03); Alumnae Valley Landscape Restoration, Wellesley College (Wellesley, Massachusetts, 2001–05); the Connecticut Water Treatment Facility (with Steven Holl; New Haven, Connecticut, 2001–05, published here); Teardrop Park (New York, New York, 1999–2006); the ASLA Green Roof (Washington, D.C., 2005–06); and Harvard Yard Restoration (Cambridge, Massachusetts, 1993–2009). Ongoing work of the firm includes Brooklyn Bridge Park (Brooklyn, New York, 2003–); Princeton University (master plan and various projects, Princeton, New Jersey, 2006–); North Grant Park (Chicago, Illinois, 2009–); and CityArchRiver 2015 (Saint Louis, Missouri, 2010–), all in the USA.

MICHAEL VAN VALKENBURGH machte 1973 seinen Bachelor am College of Agriculture der Cornell University (Ithaca, New York) und 1977 seinen Master in Landschaftsarchitektur an der University of Illinois (Champaign/Urbana). Er leitet beide von ihm 1982 gegründeten Büros in New York und in Cambridge (Massachusetts) – Michael Van Valkenburgh Associates, Inc. (MVVA) – und ist in jedes Projekt eingebunden. Zu seinen Büropartnern gehören **MATTHEW URBANSKI,** Chefdesigner für viele öffentliche Projekte des Büros, und **LAURA SOLANO,** Spezialistin für Landschaftstechnologie. Matthew Urbanski kam nach Abschluss seines Masterstudiums in Landschaftsarchitektur in Harvard 1989 zu MVVA. Laura Solano arbeitet dort seit 1991. Sie machte 1983 ihren Bachelor in Landschaftsarchitektur an der Ohio State University. Zu den von MVVA ausgeführten Projekten gehören die Tahari Courtyards (Millburn, New Jersey, 2002–03), die Sanierung des Alumnae Valley am Wellesley College (Wellesley, Massachusetts, 2001–05), die hier vorgestellte Wasseraufbereitungsanlage Connecticut Water Treatment Facility (mit Steven Holl, New Haven, Connecticut, 2001–05), der Teardrop Park (New York, 1999–2006), das Gründach der American Society of Landscape Architects (ASLA) in Washington, D. C. (2005–06), und die Restaurierung des Parks Harvard Yard (Cambridge, Massachusetts, 1993–2009). Zu den derzeit laufenden Projekten des Büros zählen der Brooklyn Bridge Park (Brooklyn, New York, seit 2003), der Masterplan und mehrere Projekte für die Princeton University (Princeton, New Jersey, seit 2006), der North Grant Park (Chicago, seit 2009) und die Parkanlage CityArchRiver 2015 (Saint Louis, seit 2010), alle in den USA.

MICHAEL VAN VALKENBURGH est titulaire d'un B.S. du Cornell University College of Agriculture (Ithaca, New York, 1973) et d'un M.F.A. d'architecture du paysage de l'université de l'Illinois (Champaign/Urbana, 1977). Il dirige les bureaux de New York et de Cambridge (Massachusetts) de son agence – Michael Van Valkenburgh Associates, Inc. (MVVA) – et s'implique dans chaque projet. Les autres dirigeants sont **MATTHEW URBANSKI**, concepteur de projets pour le secteur public, et **LAURA SOLANO**, spécialiste des technologies du paysage. Matthew Urbanski a rejoint MVVA en 1989 après avoir obtenu son Master of Landscape Architecture à Harvard. Laura Solano, à MVVA depuis 1991, est titulaire d'un B.A. en architecture du paysage de l'université de l'Ohio (1983). Parmi leurs réalisations aux États-Unis : les Tahari Courtyards (Millburn, New Jersey, 2002–03) ; la restauration paysagère de l'Alumnae Valley au Wellesley College (Wellesley, Massachusetts, 2001–05) ; la Connecticut Water Treatment Facility (avec Steven Holl, New Haven, Connecticut, 2001–05, publiée ici) ; le Teardrop Park (New York, 1999–2006) ; le toit vert de l'ASLA (Washington, 2005–06) et la restauration du Harvard Yard (Cambridge, Massachusetts, 1993–2009). L'agence travaille actuellement sur le Brooklyn Bridge Park (Brooklyn, New York, 2003–) ; l'université de Princeton (plan directeur et divers projets, Princeton, New Jersey, 2006–) ; le North Grant Park (Chicago, Illinois, 2009–) et le CityArchRiver 2015 (Saint Louis, Missouri, 2010–).

CONNECTICUT WATER TREATMENT FACILITY

New Haven, Connecticut, USA, 2001–05

*Area: 5.67 hectares. Client: South Central Connecticut Regional Water Authority
Cost: $2.88 million. Collaboration: A. Paul Seck (Senior Associate),
Robert Rock (Associate)*

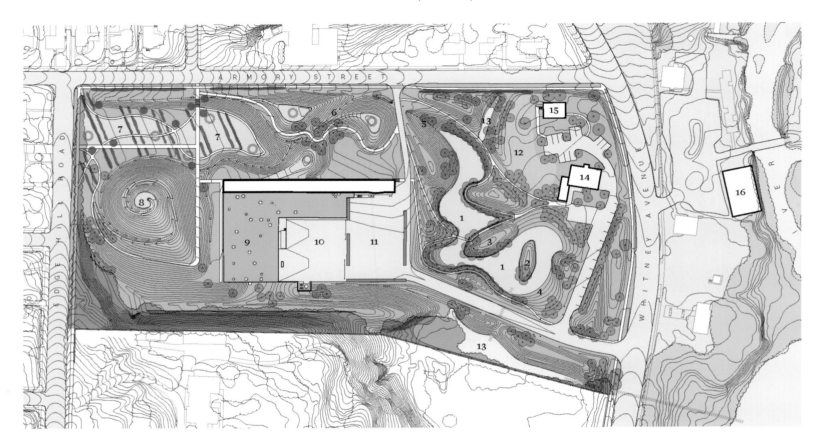

This project is located on the outskirts of New Haven. The facility concerned is a reserve water source for the South Central Connecticut Regional Water authority, drawing water from Lake Whitney. The architect of the facility was Steven Holl. MVVA was given a limited budget of approximately $5 per square foot for the landscaping. The landscape architects state: "The use of the most elemental of landscape architectural tools—soil, water, and plants—offsets the sleek form of the facility building. The design creates topographical variety and interest through sustainable reuse of excavated soil. Swales replace a traditional engineered drainage system. The planting program, inspired by restoration ecology, is at once primal and sophisticated in its extent and complexity." Stormwater and runoff from the facility roof are run through the landscape and filtered. MVVA used native species that require no fertilizers or pesticides to thrive. They also sought to create "seasonal variation in color and texture" with the plant selection.

Dieses Projekt befindet sich außerhalb von New Haven. Die Anlage dient als Wasserreservoir für die regionale Wasserbehörde South Central Connecticut, die das Wasser aus dem Whitney-See bezieht. Architekt des Gebäudes war Steven Holl. MVVA wurde nur ein beschränktes Budget von etwa 5 US-Dollar pro Quadratmeter zugestanden. Die Landschaftsarchitekten bemerken dazu: „Die Verwendung der grundlegenden Gestaltungselemente der Landschaftsarchitekten – Erde, Wasser und Pflanzen – dient als Ausgleich für die schlanke Form des Gebäudes. Der Entwurf schafft eine topografische Vielfalt und ist wegen der nachhaltigen Wiederverwendung des Aushubmaterials interessant. Bodensenken ersetzen das herkömmliche technische Drainagesystem. Das Bepflanzungsprogramm beruft sich auf die Ökologie der Sanierung und ist in seinem Umfang und seiner Komplexität sowohl einfach als auch sorgfältig durchdacht." Das Regen- und Abflusswasser vom Gebäudedach wird in die Naturlandschaft geleitet und gefiltert. MVVA verwendete heimische Pflanzen, die weder Dünger noch Pestizide benötigen, um zu gedeihen. Die Pflanzen wurden so ausgesucht, dass sich je nach Jahreszeit einen Wechsel von Farben und Texturen ergibt.

Le projet est situé dans la banlieue de New Haven. Il portait sur une réserve d'eau naturelle, pompée dans le lac Whitney par le Département régional des eaux du centre-sud du Connecticut. Les bâtiments des installations techniques ont été réalisés par Steven Holl. MVVA disposait d'un budget limité d'environ 5 $ par mètre carré pour l'aménagement paysager. « Le recours aux outils les plus basiques de l'architecture paysagère – la terre, l'eau et les plantes – vient contrebalancer la forme lisse du bâtiment. Le projet apporte une diversité topographique et suscite un intérêt visuel grâce à la réutilisation de la terre extraite lors du creusement du sol. Des baissières remplacent les systèmes traditionnels de drainage. Le programme des plantations, inspiré de principes écologiques de restauration, est à la fois élémentaire et sophistiqué dans sa complexité et son étendue », explique l'architecte. MVVA a utilisé des espèces végétales locales qui ne demandent ni engrais ni pesticides et ont permis de mettre en scène des « variations saisonnières de couleurs et de textures ». Les eaux de pluie et celles récupérées par l'intermédiaire du toit du bâtiment sont canalisées et filtrées à travers le paysage.

KOEN VAN VELSEN

Koen van Velsen
Spoorstraat 69a
1200 BJ Hilversum
The Netherlands

Tel: +31 35 6 22 20 00
Fax: +31 35 62 88 89 91
E-mail: mail@koenvanvelsen.com
Web: www.koenvanvelsen.com

Born in Hilversum, the Netherlands, in 1952, **KOEN VAN VELSEN** graduated from the Academy of Architecture in Amsterdam in 1983. He started his own firm in Hilversum in 1977. His major works include the Discotheque Slinger (Hilversum, 1978–79); the van Velsen shop and house (Hilversum, 1980–81); a public library in Zeewolde (1985–89); the Rijksakademie van Beeldende Kunsten (Amsterdam, 1985–92); a multiplex cinema on Schouwburgplein in Rotterdam (1992–96); the Town Hall of Terneuzen (extension of the 1972 building by Van den Broek & Bakema, 1994–97); the Film Academy in Amsterdam (1995–99); and the Media Authority Building (Hilversum, 1998–2002, published here). More recently, he has completed the Groot Klimmendaal Rehabilitation Center, a finalist in the 2011 Mies van der Rohe Awards (Arnhem, 2010); and the Het Loo Palace Visitor Center (Apeldoorn, 2011), all in the Netherlands.

KOEN VAN VELSEN, geboren 1952 in Hilversum in den Niederlanden, schloss sein Studium 1983 an der Academie van Bouwkunst in Amsterdam ab. Sein Büro in Hilversum gründete er 1977. Zu seinen wichtigsten Projekten zählen die Diskothek Slinger (Hilversum, 1978–79), das Geschäfts- und Wohnhaus van Velsen (Hilversum, 1980–81), die Stadtbibliothek Zeewolde (1985–89), die Reichsakademie der bildenden Künste (Amsterdam, 1985–92), ein Multiplexkino am Schouwburgplein in Rotterdam (1992–96), das Rathaus Terneuzen (Erweiterung des Bestandsbaus von 1972 von Van den Broek & Bakema; 1994–97), die Filmakademie Amsterdam (1995–99) sowie die Niederländische Medienaufsicht in Hilversum (1998–2002, hier vorgestellt). In jüngster Zeit realisierte er das Rehabilitationszentrum Groot Klimmendaal (Arnhem, 2010), Finalist für den Mies-van-der-Rohe-Preis 2011, sowie das Besucherzentrum am Schloss Het Loo (Apeldoorn, 2011), alle in den Niederlanden.

Né à Hilversum aux Pays-Bas en 1952, **KOEN VAN VELSEN** est diplômé de l'Académie d'architecture d'Amsterdam (1983). Il a ouvert son agence à Hilversum en 1977. Ses principales réalisations comprennent la discothèque Slinger (Hilversum, 1978–79) ; la boutique et maison van Velsen (Hilversum, 1980–81) ; une bibliothèque publique à Zeewolde (1985–89) ; l'Académie royale des beaux-arts (Amsterdam, 1985–92) ; un cinéma multiplex place Schouwburgplein à Rotterdam (1992–96) ; l'hôtel de ville de Terneuzen (extension du bâtiment construit en 1972 par Van den Broek & Bakema, 1994–97) ; l'Académie du cinéma d'Amsterdam (1995–99) et l'immeuble de l'autorité des médias (Hilversum, 1998–2002, publié ici). Plus récemment, il a réalisé le centre de rééducation Groot Klimmendaal qui a été finaliste pour l'attribution du prix Mies van der Rohe 2011 (Arnhem, 2010) et le centre d'accueil du public du palais Het Loo (Apeldoorn, 2011), tous aux Pays-Bas.

MEDIA AUTHORITY BUILDING

Hilversum, The Netherlands, 1998–2002

Area: 2048 m² (floor). Client: Commissariaat voor de Media, Hilversum
Cost: €3.42 milion

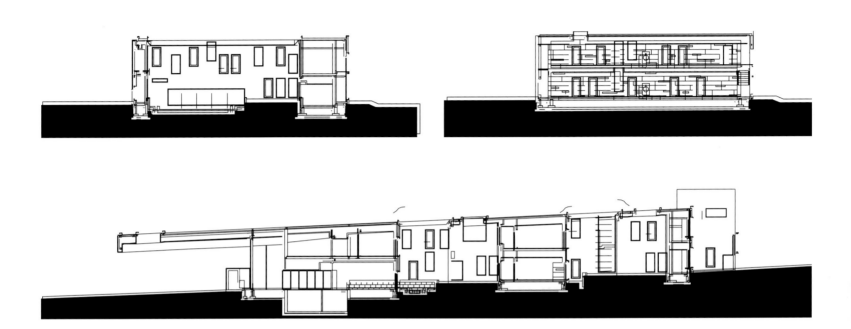

Located near Schiphol airport between Amsterdam and The Hague, Hilversum is a wealthy suburban neighborhood, where W. M. Dudok (1884–1974) built the town hall in the 1930s, and where Richard Meier erected his first building in the Netherlands, the KNP BT Headquarters (1987–92). Koen van Velsen is from Hilversum where his **MEDIA AUTHORITY BUILDING** is located next to the Media Park. The structure was built with as much respect for the wooded site and for nature as possible. Patios have been cut into the building volume to avoid cutting down several existing trees. This is also true of the roof overhang whose form was altered to make way for trees. Within the building, corridors are aligned along the two longer façades. Openings and large areas of glass in the façade offer glimpses of the surrounding landscape. Work areas, by contrast, face out onto internal patios that have been designed with care by the architect. Unlike the glass and metal exterior façades, the patio areas present "a differentiated composition of staggered windows, masonry walls and various splashes of color." Koen van Velsen acted in this instance as the architect, interior designer, and landscape architect. His avowed intention is to create a feeling of calm and well-being, a goal that he apparently attained. With a floor area of 2048 m², the structure cost a total of €3.42 million.

Die Stadt Hilversum liegt in der Nähe des Flughafens Schiphol, zwischen Amsterdam und Den Haag. Willem Marinus Dudok (1884–1974) baute hier in den 1930er-Jahren das Rathaus und Richard Meyer von 1987 bis 1992 sein erstes Gebäude in den Niederlanden, die KNP BT Hauptniederlassung (1987–92). Koen van Velsen stammt aus Hilversum, sein **GEBÄUDE DER NIEDERLÄNDISCHEN MEDIENAUFSICHT** liegt neben dem Media Park. Die Gestaltung respektiert so weit wie möglich den Baumbestand und die natürliche Vegetation des Grundstücks. Innenhöfe wurden eingefügt, um das Abholzen von Bäumen zu vermeiden. Auch die Form des Dachüberstands wurde verändert, um Bäumen Platz zu machen. Im Inneren liegen Flure unmittelbar hinter den zwei längeren Fassaden. Öffnungen und große Glasflächen bieten Ausblicke in die Landschaft. Im Gegensatz dazu sind die Arbeitsräume den Innenhöfen zugewandt, die der Architekt sorgfältig gestaltete. Anders als die Außenfassaden aus Glas und Metall präsentieren sich die Innenhöfe als eine »gegliederte Komposition aus versetzt angeordneten Fenstern, gemauerten Wänden und unterschiedlichen Farbtupfern«. Koen van Velsen war hier als Architekt, Innenarchitekt und Landschaftsplaner tätig. Seine erklärte Absicht, ein Gefühl von Ruhe und Wohlbefinden zu erzeugen, hat er ganz offensichtlich verwirklicht. Die Gesamtkosten für das Gebäude mit 2048 m² Bruttogeschossfläche betrugen 3,42 Millionen Euro.

Près de l'aéroport de Schiphol entre Amsterdam et La Haye, Hilversum est une banlieue aisée dont W. M. Dudok (1884–1974) avait édifié l'hôtel de ville dans les années 1930 et où Richard Meier a réalisé son premier projet aux Pays-Bas, le siège de KNP BT (1987–92). Koen van Velsen est originaire de cette ville où est situé **L'IMMEUBLE DE L'AUTORITÉ DES MÉDIAS** près du Media Park. Le bâtiment a été construit dans le plus grand respect du terrain boisé et de la nature. Des patios ont été découpés dans le volume pour éviter d'avoir à abattre certains arbres. À l'intérieur, les corridors sont alignés dans l'axe des deux façades longues. Des ouvertures et de vastes surfaces vitrées permettent d'apercevoir le paysage environnant. Par contraste, les zones de travail donnent sur des patios intérieurs dessinés avec le plus grand soin. Contrairement aux façades extérieures en verre et métal, celles des patios présentent « une composition différenciée de fenêtres, de murs de maçonnerie et de diverses masses de couleurs étagées ». Koen van Vels a agi ici en tant qu'architecte, architecte d'intérieur et paysagiste. Son intention revendiquée est de créer un sentiment de calme et de bien-être, objectif qu'il semble avoir atteint. D'une surface totale de 2048 m², ce bâtiment a coûté 3,42 millions d'euros.

The building, as seen in the image above, appears to hover around the existing trees that have been protected by large cutouts. Right, generous glazed areas and a modest scale make the building approachable and convivial.

Wie oben im Bild zu sehen, umfängt der Bau scheinbar schwebend den Baumbestand, der dank großer Aussparungen erhalten werden konnte. Großzügige Glasfronten und die eher geringe Höhe lassen den Bau zugänglich und freundlich wirken.

Le bâtiment, vu ci-dessus, semble flotter autour des arbres qui ont été protégés par d'amples découpures. À droite, les surfaces généreusement vitrées et l'échelle modeste du bâtiment le rendent très accessible et convivial.

An orchestration of windows, doors, and volumes, which might bring to mind De Stijl, in some views, like the one above, actually participates in a very contemporary play on opacity and transparency, as seen in the entrance and façades to the right.

Die Komposition aus Fenstern, Türen und Baumassen, die aus manchen Blickwinkeln (wie oben) an De Stijl erinnert, gehört zu einem sehr zeit-genössischen Spiel mit Opazität und Transparenz, wie man am Eingang und den Fassaden rechts sieht.

Le jeu des fenêtres, portes et volumes, qui pourrait rappeler le mouvement DeStijl sur certaines vues comme celle-ci-dessus, fait partie d'un travail très contemporain sur l'opacité et la transparence, comme on le voit à l'entrée et aux façades à droite.

With its full-height glazing opening out onto green areas, the structure is filled with natural light and in general embodies a kind of lightness that is not that common in the Netherlands.

Dank geschosshoher Verglasung und Blick ins Grüne ist der Bau lichtdurch- flutet und von einer Helligkeit, die für die Niederlande eher untypisch ist.

Avec son vitrage sur toute sa hauteur qui ouvre sur des espaces verts, l'ensemble est baigné de lumière naturelle et incarne plus généralement une clarté peu courante aux Pays-Bas.

WHY ARCHITECTURE

wHY Architecture
9520 Jefferson Boulevard
Studio C
Culver City, CA 90232
USA

Tel: +1 310 839 5106
Fax: +1 310 839 5107
E-mail: work@why-architecture.com
Web: www.why-architecture.com

WHY ARCHITECTURE was founded in 2003 by Yo-ichiro Hakomori and Kulapat Yantrasast. Hakomori received his M.Arch degree from UCLA, and his doctorate from the University of Tokyo. Yantrasast, born in 1968 in Thailand, received his B.Arch degree in Thailand and his M.Arch degree and Ph.D. from the University of Tokyo. The two met at the University of Tokyo and they collaborated on several design competitions and research projects. After completing his studies, Hakomori worked for the late Frank Israel and for Arthur Erickson. Yantrasast became a key member of Tadao Ando's team in Osaka, working on the Modern Art Museum of Fort Worth, the Armani Teatro in Milan, the Foundation François Pinault for Contemporary Art in Paris, the Calder Museum project in Philadelphia, and the Clark Art Institute in Williamstown, Massachusetts. Their work includes the Grand Rapids Art Museum published here (Grand Rapids, Michigan, 2004–07); the Art Bridge (Los Angeles, California, 2008–09); the Malibu Residence (Malibu, California, 2007–10); and the redesign of a number of galleries for the Art Institute of Chicago (2008–); all in the USA.

WHY ARCHITECTURE wurde 2003 von Yo-ichiro Hakomori und Kulapat Yantrasast gegründet. Hakomori schloss sein Studium an der UCLA mit einem M.Arch. ab und promovierte an der Universität Tokio. Yantrasast, 1968 in Thailand geboren, erwarb seinen B.Arch. in Thailand und seinen M.Arch. an der Universität Tokio, wo er ebenfalls promovierte. Die beiden lernten sich an der Universität Tokio kennen, beteiligten sich zusammen an verschiedenen Entwurfswettbewerben und arbeiteten gemeinsam an Forschungsprojekten. Nach Abschluss seines Studiums arbeitete Hakomori für den inzwischen verstorbenen Frank Israel und für Arthur Erickson. Yantrasast wurde zu einer der Schlüsselfiguren in Tadao Andos Team in Osaka und war u.a. am Modern Art Museum in Fort Worth, Texas, dem Armani Teatro in Mailand, der Fondation François Pinault pour l'Art Contemporain in Paris, dem Calder-Museumsprojekt in Philadelphia sowie dem Clark Art Institute in Williamstown, Massachusetts, beteiligt. Zu den Projekten des Büros zählen das hier vorgestellte Grand Rapids Art Museum (Grand Rapids, Michigan, 2004–07), die Art Bridge (Los Angeles, 2008–09), die Umgestaltung verschiedener Ausstellungsräume am Art Institute of Chicago (seit 2008) sowie die Malibu Residence (Malibu, Kalifornien, 2007–10).

L'agence **WHY ARCHITECTURE** a été fondée en 2003 par Yo-ichiro Hakomori et Kulapat Yantrasast. Hakomori est titulaire d'un M.Arch. de l'UCLA et docteur de l'université de Tokyo. Yantrasast, né en 1968 en Thaïlande, a obtenu son B.Arch. dans ce pays et son mastère et son doctorat à l'université de Tokyo. Ils se sont rencontrés à l'université et ont collaboré à l'occasion de plusieurs concours et projets de recherche. Après avoir achevé ses études, Hakomori à travaillé pour Frank Israël et pour Arthur Erickson. Yantrasast est devenu l'un des principaux collaborateurs de l'équipe de Tadao Ando à Osaka. Il a travaillé sur les projets du musée d'Art moderne de Fort Worth, le théâtre Armani à Milan, la Fondation François Pinault pour l'art contemporain à Paris ; le projet du musée Calder à Philadelphia ; et celui du Clark Art Institute à Williamstown, Massachusetts. Parmi leurs réalisations : le Grand Rapids Art Museum (Grand Rapids, Michigan, 2004–07, publié ici) ; l'Art Bridge (Los Angeles, Californie, 2008–09) ; la rénovation d'un certain nombre de galeries pour l'Art Institute of Chicago (2008-) et la résidence Malibu (Malibu, Californie, 2007–10).

GRAND RAPIDS ART MUSEUM

Grand Rapids, Michigan, USA, 2004–07

Floor area: 11 613 m². Client: Grand Rapids Art Museum. Cost: $75 million
Collaboration: Design Plus

The **GRAND RAPIDS ART MUSEUM**'s new building, located one block from the city center, was the first art museum in the world to receive a LEED certification. This is not surprising given the necessary temperature, lighting, or humidity controls required in art museums. In fact, obtaining LEED certification was one condition of the 2001 donation by local philanthropist Peter Wege, a known defender of environmental causes. The facility includes approximately 5000 square meters of exhibition space. A large, sheltering canopy hovers over the facility and has its lobby, restaurant, education center, and pavilions "formed like fingers extending into the green of the park." The museum also faces a sculptural work by Maya Lin called *Ecliptic*, an oval square. The main museum space is a three-level gallery tower with natural overhead lighting for the top floor. The use of natural light in the structure is planned to reduce energy consumption where possible. Ten percent of the construction materials for the project were recycled, and rainwater is recycled for toilets, plant watering, and a reflecting pool. A vapor-mist air-conditioning system emits no hydrochlorofluorocarbons. With its strong, simple lines, the Grand Rapids Art Museum makes it clear that Kulapat Yantrasast learned from a master, in particular when he worked on the Modern Art Museum of Fort Worth.

Der einen Block vom Stadtzentrum entfernte Neubau des **GRAND RAPIDS ART MUSEUM** war weltweit das erste Kunstmuseum, das eine LEED-Auszeichnung erhielt. Angesichts der in Kunstmuseen erforderlichen Steuerung von Temperatur-, Licht- und Luftfeuchtigkeitsverhältnissen erstaunt dies kaum. Tatsächlich war die Spende des ortsansässigen Philanthropen Peter Wege, der für sein Engagement in Umweltschutzfragen bekannt ist, daran gebunden, dass der Bau eine LEED-Zertifizierung erhielt. Die Einrichtung umfasst rund 5000 m² Ausstellungsfläche. Ein großes, schützendes Baldachindach schwebt über dem Bau. Lobby, Restaurant, museumspädagogische Einrichtungen und Pavillons wurden „wie Finger gestaltet, die in das Grün des Parks hineinragen". Dem Museum gegenüber befindet sich eine Skulptur von Maya Lin mit dem Titel *Ecliptic*, ein ovaler Platz. Der zentrale Bereich des Museums ist ein dreistöckiger Turm mit Ausstellungsräumen, die vom obersten Stockwerk aus durch ein Oberlicht natürlich belichtet werden. Der Einsatz von natürlichem Licht soll den Energieverbrauch wo immer möglich reduzieren. 10 % der Baumaterialien sind recycelt, Regenwasser wird aufbereitet und für Toiletten, die Bewässerung der Pflanzen und ein Wasserbecken genutzt. Die Verdunstungsklimaanlage produziert kein FCKW. Mit seinen klaren, schlichten Linien macht das Grand Rapids Art Museum deutlich, dass Kulapat Yantrasast bei einem Meister in die Lehre gegangen ist, insbesondere während seiner Mitarbeit am Modern Art Museum in Fort Worth.

Le nouveau bâtiment du **GRAND RAPIDS ART MUSEUM**, situé à un bloc du centre-ville, est le premier musée au monde à avoir reçu la certification LEED. Ce n'est pas surprenant, compte tenu de la problématique complexe de température, d'éclairage ou de contrôle de l'humidité posée par un musée d'art. En fait, l'obtention de cette certification était la condition pour recevoir une donation du philanthrope local, Peter Wege, défenseur connu de la cause environnementale. Les installations comptent 5000 m² environ d'espaces d'expositions. Un vaste auvent est suspendu au-dessus du musée dont le hall d'accueil, le restaurant, le centre éducatif et les pavillons « forment comme des doigts qui s'étendent vers l'espace vert du parc ». Le musée fait face à une œuvre sculpturale de Maya Lin intitulée Ecliptic, qui est une place de forme ovale. Le volume principal est une tour de galeries de trois niveaux à éclairage zénithal. La lumière naturelle permet de diminuer la consommation d'électricité. Dix pour cent des matériaux de construction sont d'origine recyclée, et l'eau de pluie est récupérée pour les toilettes, l'arrosage des plantes et un bassin. Un système de conditionnement de l'air à émission de brouillard artificiel n'émet aucun hydrofluorocarbone. Par ses lignes simples et puissantes, ce musée témoigne de l'influence du maître auprès duquel Kulapat Yantrasast a appris, en particulier lorsqu'il travaillait sur le projet du musée d'Art moderne de Fort Worth.

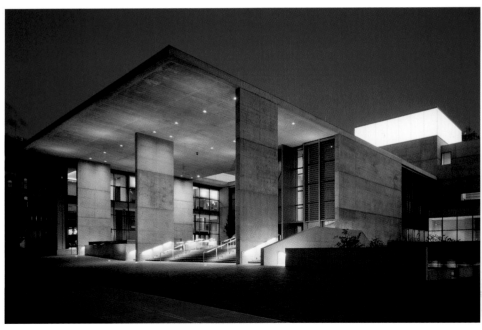

The entrance to the Grand Rapids Art Museum is clearly signaled by its great overhanging canopy roof.

Der Eingang zum Grand Rapids Art Museum wird von einem monumentalen, ausgreifenden Vordach markiert.

L'entrée du musée est fortement signalée par son grand toit en porte-à-faux.

The architects have engaged in a careful assemblage of essentially Euclidean volumes, keeping in mind the ecological concerns of the client at all times.

Die Architekten schufen eine ausgewogene Komposition aus einfachen euklidischen Körpern und behielten dabei stets die ökologischen Vorgaben des Mäzens im Blick.

Les architectes ont réalisé un assemblage soigné de volumes essentiellement euclidiens en tenant compte en permanence des préoccupations écologiques de leur client.

A grand entry sequence with its
ramped stairway may recall some
gestures of Tadao Ando. Left, a large
window opens the museum to the
nearby city center.

Der beeindruckende Eingangsbereich
mit seiner rampenförmigen Treppe
mag an gewisse Gesten Tadao Andos
erinnern. Ein großes Fenster (links)
öffnet das Museum zum nahe gelegenen Stadtzentrum.

L'impressionnante séquence d'entrée
et le grand escalier pourraient rappeler certains gestes de Tadao Ando.
À gauche, une grande baie ouvre sur
le centre-ville tout proche.

WMR

WMR Arquitectos
San Patricio 4150
Matanzas s/n Navidad
Santiago 7630287
Chile

Tel: +56 9744 2439
E-mail: info@wmraq.cl
Web: www.wmrarq.cl

FELIPE WEDELES TONDREAU was born in 1977. He obtained his degree in Architecture at the Finis Terrae University in Santiago (1994–2001). He was a founding partner of the firm DAW (Santiago, 2001–03), and then cofounded WMR in 2005. **JORGE MANIEU BRICEÑO** was born in 1976. He also studied at the Finis Terrae University, obtaining his degree in Architecture in 1999. He worked with Manuel Casanueva and Felipe Assadi prior to cofounding WMR. **MACARENA RABAT ERRAZURIZ** was born in 1982, and also completed her architecture studies at Finis Terrae, before working at ZS arquitectos in Santiago and cofounding WMR in 2005. The acronym WMR is derived from the partners' names: Wedeles Manieu Rabat. Their recent work includes Hotel Surazo (Matanzas, 2008–10); the Mandakovic and Till Houses (Navidad, Los Arcos, 2010, published here); the Ingrid House (La Boca, 2010–11); Espinoza House (Matanzas, 2011); Cipres Surf Shop (Pichilemu, 2011–12); and Carlos Cortes House (Matanzas, 2011–12). They are currently working on the Awakova Hotel (Farellones, 2012–); and the La Sirena Hotel (Curanipe, 2012–), all in Chile.

FELIPE WEDELES TONDREAU wurde 1977 geboren. Sein Architekturdiplom erlangte er an der Finis Terrae University in Santiago (1994–2001). Er war zunächst Gründungspartner bei DAW (Santiago, 2001–03) und 2005 Mitbegründer von WMR. **JORGE MANIEU BRICEÑO,** Jahrgang 1976, studierte ebenfalls an der Finis Terrae University, wo er sein Architekturstudium 1999 abschloss. Vor der Gründung von WMR arbeitete er mit Manuel Casanueva und Felipe Assadi. Auch **MACARENA RABAT ERRAZURIZ,** geboren 1982, schloss ihr Architekturstudium an der Finis-Terrae-Universität ab, arbeitete bei ZS arquitectos in Santiago, bevor sie 2005 WMR mitbegründete. WMR steht für die Namen der Partner: Wedeles, Manieu, Rabat. Jüngere Projekte sind das Hotel Surazo (Matanzas, 2008–10), die Häuser Mandakovic und Till (Navidad, Los Arcos, 2010, hier vorgestellt), das Haus Ingrid (La Boca, 2010–11), das Haus Espinoza (Matanzas, 2011), der Cipres Surf-Shop (Pichilemu, 2011–12) sowie das Haus Carlos Cortes (Matanzas, 2011–12). Derzeit arbeitet das Büro am Hotel Awakova (Farellones, seit 2012) sowie dem Hotel La Sirena (Curanipe, seit 2012), alle in Chile.

FELIPE WEDELES TONDREAU est né en 1977. Il a obtenu son diplôme en architecture à l'université Finis Terrae de Santiago (1994–2001). Il est l'un des partenaires fondateurs de l'agence DAW (Santiago, 2001–03) et a ensuite cofondé WMR en 2005. **JORGE MANIEU BRICEÑO** est né en 1976. Il a également fait ses études à l'université Finis Terrae et a obtenu son diplôme en architecture en 1999. Avant de cofonder WMR, il a travaillé avec Manuel Casanueva et Felipe Assadi. **MACARENA RABAT ERRAZURIZ** est née en 1982 et a, elle aussi, fait des études d'architecture à Finis Terrae avant de travailler à ZS arquitectos à Santiago et de cofonder WMR en 2005. L'acronyme WMR est tiré des noms des partenaires : Wedeles Manieu Rabat. Leurs réalisations récentes comprennent l'hôtel Surazo (Matanzas, 2008–10) ; les maisons Mandakovic et Till (Navidad, Los Arcos, 2010, publiées ici) ; la maison Ingrid (La Boca, 2010–11) ; la maison Espinoza (Matanzas, 2011) ; la boutique de surf Cipres (Pichilemu, 2011–12) et la maison Carlos Cortes (Matanzas, 2011–12). Ils travaillent actuellement à l'hôtel Awakova (Farellones, 2012–) et à l'hôtel La Sirena (Curanipe, 2012–), tous au Chili.

TILL HOUSE
Navidad, Los Arcos, Chile, 2010

Client: Till Kreytenberg
Cost: $120,000. Area: 85 m² + 100 m² of terraces

The **TILL HOUSE** and the Mandakovic House, both published here, are for different clients but are situated very close to each other on a 200-meter-high cliff along the ocean. The smaller Till House was designed for a German-Chilean couple. Designed with 3.2 x 3.2-meter wooden modules, the structure leaves its beams and columns visible. The skeleton is colored black while the walls are dark brown, giving way to an all-white interior, with wooden floors. Local timber and labor were used for construction. The two bedrooms, living, dining, and kitchen areas share the same space, but can be divided by doors for privacy. Terraces, including one on the roof, take full advantage of the sun and views. A wood-fired jacuzzi is placed to the south on an exterior terrace.

Die hier vorgestellten Häuser Till und Mandakovic wurden für verschiedene Bauherren realisiert, liegen jedoch in unmittelbarer Nähe an einer 200 Meter hohen Steilküste über dem Meer. Das kleinere **HAUS TILL** wurde für ein deutsch-chilenisches Paar entworfen. Träger und Stützen des Baus aus 3,2 x 3,2 m großen Holzmodulen sind freigelegt. Das Skelett ist schwarz, die Wandflächen sind dunkelbraun gebeizt; das Interieur mit Holzböden ist ganz in Weiß gehalten. Für den Bau wurde mit lokalem Holz und Firmen gearbeitet. Die beiden Schlafzimmer, Wohn-, Ess- und Küchenbereich liegen in einem Raum, lassen sich jedoch durch Türen abtrennen. Die Terrassen, einschließlich einer Dachterrasse, profitieren optimal von Sonnenlicht und Aussicht. Ein holzbeheizter Jacuzzi liegt südlich auf einer der Außenterrassen.

La **MAISON TILL** et la maison Mandakovic, toutes deux publiées ici, ont été réalisées pour deux clients différents mais sont très proches l'une de l'autre, sur une falaise de 200 m de haut au bord de l'océan. La maison Till, plus petite, a été créée pour un couple germano-chilien. Conçue en modules de bois de 3,2 x 3,2 m, les poutres et colonnes de la structure sont apparentes. La charpente est teinte en noir, tandis que les murs sont brun foncé, ouvrant sur un intérieur entièrement blanc au sol en bois. La construction a eu recours au bois et à la main d'œuvre locaux. Les deux chambres à coucher, le salon, la salle à manger et la cuisine partagent un espace commun mais peuvent être fermés par des portes pour plus d'intimité. Les terrasses, dont une sur le toit, tirent un profit maximal du soleil et de la vue. Un jacuzzi chauffé au bois est placé au sud sur une terrasse.

Seen from a distance on its spectacular cliff-top setting, the house seems like a fragile outpost on the edge of the abyss.

Aus der Ferne gesehen wirkt das Haus mit seiner spektakulären Lage am Steilhang wie ein fragiler Außenposten am Rande eines Abgrunds.

Vue de loin à son emplacement spectaculaire en haut de la falaise, la maison semble un avant-poste fragile au bord de l'abîme.

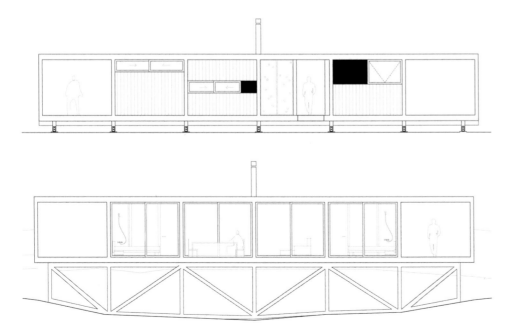

Above, the wood-fired jacuzzi with its remarkable view of the ocean. Below, drawings demonstrate the simplicity of the design, located on a slightly curved then sloping lot.

Oben der holzbeheizte Jacuzzi mit beeindruckendem Blick auf das Meer. Zeichnungen (unten) belegen die Schlichtheit des Entwurfs auf seinem sanft geschwungenen, dann steil abfallenden Grundstück.

Ci-dessus, le jacuzzi chauffé au bois et sa vue extraordinaire sur l'océan. Ci-dessous, les schémas témoignent de la simplicité du design, sur le terrain d'abord légèrement courbe, puis en pente.

A sweeping wood terrace overlooks the ocean and a canopy shields the fully glazed interior.

Eine große Terrasse bietet einen Blick auf das Meer; ein Vordach schützt den geschosshoch verglasten Innenraum.

Une vaste terrasse de bois surplombe l'océan et un auvent abrite l'intérieur entièrement vitré.

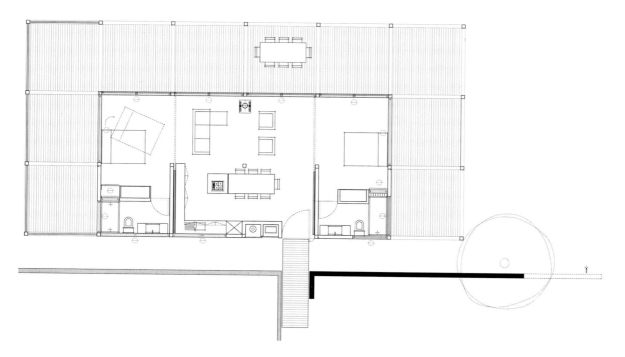

Left, a floor plan. Right, terrace and bedroom spaces share a completely open design with views on three sides.

Links ein Grundriss. Terrasse und Schlafzimmer (rechts) sind gänzlich offen gehalten und bieten Ausblicke an drei Seiten.

À gauche, un plan. À droite, la terrasse et les chambres à coucher partagent une conception entièrement ouverte avec vue sur trois côtés.

MANDAKOVIC HOUSE

Navidad, Los Arcos, Chile, 2010

Client: Carlos Cortes Simon
Cost: $160,000. Area: 150 m²

The **MANDAKOVIC HOUSE** was built for a couple with two children. The two-story house was designed with timber, stone, and glass, and its plan is rectangular. A stairway divides the living room from the dining and kitchen area on the ground level. The bedrooms are above. The ground floor is a plinth made from local stone, with a line of glass above it, offering 180° views of the scenery. The shell of the house, made of wood, envelops the main volume and also serves to cover the forward terraces on the ocean side. It is difficult to imagine a more spectacular view of the Pacific, a fact that is the very basis for the architecture, which has been realized with an admirable economy of means.

Das **HAUS MANDAKOVIC** wurde für ein Paar mit zwei Kindern geplant. Der zweistöckige Entwurf mit rechteckigem Grundriss wurde aus Holz, Stein und Glas realisiert. Im Erdgeschoss gliedert eine Treppe Wohnbereich, Essbereich und Küche. Die Schlafzimmer sind im Obergeschoss untergebracht. Über einem Sockel aus lokalem Naturstein schließt sich ein Fensterband an, das 180°-Blicke in die Landschaft erlaubt. Die Gebäudehülle aus Holz umfängt nicht nur den Baukörper an sich, sondern überdacht auch die vordere Terrasse zum Meer. Ein spektakulärerer Blick auf den Pazifik lässt sich kaum vorstellen – eine Tatsache, die den eigentlichen Anlass zum Bau des Hauses gab, eine Architektur, die mit bewundernswert sparsamen Mitteln realisiert wurde.

La **MAISON MANDAKOVIC** a été construite pour un couple avec deux enfants. À deux étages, elle est construite en bois, pierre et verre selon un plan rectangulaire. Un escalier sépare le salon de l'espace salle à manger et cuisine au rez-de-chaussée. Les chambres à coucher sont à l'étage. Le rez-de-chaussée se compose d'un socle en pierre locale surmonté d'un bandeau de verre qui offre une vue à 180° du paysage. L'enveloppe de la maison, en bois, enrobe le volume principal et sert aussi à couvrir les terrasses à l'avant, côté océan. On peut difficilement imaginer une vue plus fantastique du Pacifique, elle constitue la base même de l'architecture qui a été réalisée avec des économies de moyens admirables.

A wood-clad box, the house is cantilevered in the direction of the cliff top and the ocean beyond. The wood shell continues outward to become a canopy for the terraces of the house. Right, section drawings.

Das Haus, ein kastenförmiger, holzverschalter Bau, kragt in Richtung Steilhang und Meer aus. Die Verkleidung aus Holz ist zum Terrassendach verlängert. Rechts Querschnittszeichnungen.

Cube revêtu de bois, la maison est en porte-à-faux vers le sommet de la falaise et l'océan en contrebas. La coque de bois se prolonge vers l'extérieur et forme un auvent pour les terrasses. À droite, schémas en coupe.

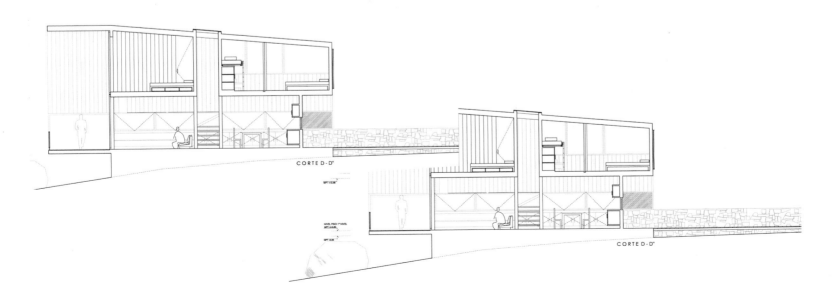

CORTE D-D'

CORTE D-D'

Wood is present everywhere in the house. Wooden floors, ceilings, and walls alternate here with full-height glazing and a steel staircase.

Holz ist überall im Haus zu finden. Holzböden, -decken und -wände wechseln sich hier mit raumhoher Verglasung und einer Stahltreppe ab.

Le bois est omniprésent dans toute la maison. Les sols, plafonds et murs en bois alternent avec le vitrage sur toute la hauteur de la pièce et un escalier en acier.

The relatively simple lines of the house (drawings below) translate into generous, open space with grand views of the ocean located just below the cliffside site.

Die schlichten Linien des Hauses (Zeichnungen unten) definieren groß-zügige, offene Räume mit großartigen Ausblicken auf den Ozean unterhalb des Hanggrundstücks.

Les lignes plutôt simples de la mai-son (schémas ci-dessous) donnent naissance à un espace ouvert et généreux avec une vue grandiose sur l'océan en bas de la falaise.

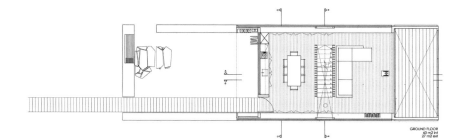

GROUND FLOOR
60 m2 int
27 m2 ext

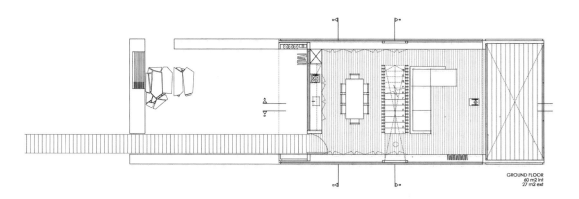

GROUND FLOOR
60 m2 int
27 m2 ext

P 672

Putney Mountain House

KYU SUNG WOO

Kyu Sung Woo Architects
488 Green Street
Cambridge, MA 02139
USA

Tel: +1 617 547 0128
E-mail: kswa@kswa.com
Web: www.kswa.com

KYU SUNG WOO was born in Seoul, Korea, and received B.Sc. and M.Sc. degrees in Architectural Engineering at Seoul National University. He moved to the United States to continue his architectural studies, receiving Master's degrees in Architecture from Columbia University (New York, 1968) and in Urban Design from Harvard (Cambridge, Massachusetts,1970). He worked in the office of José Luis Sert at Sert, Jackson & Associates (Cambridge, Massachusetts, 1970–74), and as an urban designer for a new town development in South Carolina. He was senior Urban Designer for the Mayor's office Midtown Planning and Development (New York, 1975), and then founded his own practice in Cambridge, Massachusetts, in 1978 initially as Woo Associates, and since 1990, as Kyu Sung Woo Architects. Recent significant projects include the Heller School for Social Policy and Management at Brandeis University (Waltham, Massachusetts, 2006); Putney Mountain House (Putney, Vermont, 2005–07, published here); Nerman Museum for Contemporary Art (Overland Park, Kansas, 2007); Harvard Graduate Student Housing (Cambridge, Massachusetts, 2008); Northeastern University Student Housing (Boston, Massachusetts, 2009), all in the USA; and the Asian Culture Complex (Gwangju, South Korea, 2012).

KYU SUNG WOO kam im koreanischen Seoul zur Welt und erlangte einen B.Sc. und einen M.Sc. in Bauingenieurwesen an der Nationaluniversität Seoul. Zur Fortsetzung seines Architekturstudiums zog er in die USA, wo er mit einem Master in Architektur an der Columbia University (New York, 1968) sowie in Stadtplanung in Harvard (Cambridge, Massachusetts, 1970) seine Studien abschloss. Er arbeitete für José Luis Sert bei Sert, Jackson & Associates (Cambridge, Massachusetts, 1970 bis 1974) sowie als Stadtplaner an einem Neubaugebiet in South Carolina. Er war leitender Stadtplaner im Büro des Bürgermeisters für die Planung und Entwicklung von Midtown (New York, 1975) und gründete 1978 sein eigenes Büro in Cambridge, Massachusetts, zunächst als Woo Associates. Seit 1990 firmiert das Büro unter dem Namen Kyu Sung Woo Architects. Bedeutende jüngere Projekte sind die Heller School for Social Policy and Management an der Brandeis University (Waltham, Massachusetts, 2006), das Putney Mountain House (Putney, Vermont, 2005–07, hier vorgestellt), das Nerman Museum for Contemporary Art (Overland Park, Kansas, 2007), ein Wohnheim für Universitätsstudenten in Harvard (Cambridge, Massachusetts, 2008), ein Studentenwohnheim an der Northeastern University (Boston, Massachusetts, 2009), alle in den USA, sowie der Asian Culture Complex (Gwangju, Südkorea, 2012).

KYU SUNG WOO, né à Séoul (Corée), a obtenu son B.Sc. et son M.Sc. en ingénierie architecturale de l'Université nationale de Séoul. Parti poursuivre ses études aux États-Unis, il a obtenu un M.Arch. de l'université Columbia (New York, 1968) et un second en urbanisme de Harvard (Cambridge, Massachusetts,1970). Il a travaillé dans l'agence de José Luis Sert – Sert, Jackson & Associates (Cambridge, Massachusetts, 1970–74) – et comme urbaniste sur un projet de ville nouvelle en Caroline du Sud. Il a été urbaniste senior au Bureau du maire pour l'urbanisme et le développement de Midtown à New York (1975), puis a fondé sa propre agence à Cambridge (Massachusetts) en 1978, initialement sous le nom de Woo Associates et, depuis 1990, de Kyu Sung Woo Architects. Parmi ses projets récents les plus importants : Heller School for Social Policy and Management à l'université Brandeis (Waltham, Massachusetts, 2006) ; la maison de Putney Mountain (Putney, Vermont, 2005–07, publiée ici) ; le Nerman Museum for Contemporary Art (Overland Park, Kansas, 2007) ; des logements pour étudiants à Harvard (Cambridge, Massachusetts, 2008) et à Northeastern University (Boston, Massachusetts, 2009) ; et le complexe de la culture asiatique (Gwangju, Corée-du-Sud, 2012).

PUTNEY MOUNTAIN HOUSE

Putney, Vermont, USA, 2005–07

Area: 372 m². Client: Kyu Sung Woo. Cost: not disclosed
Collaboration: Brett Bentson (Project Architect), Waclaw Zalewski (Structural Concept),
Reed Hilderbrand Associates Inc. (Landscape)

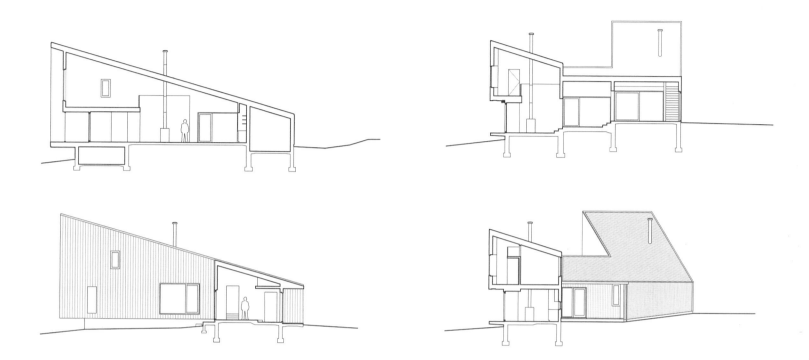

This is the architect's own vacation residence. It has a concrete foundation and was built with standard dimensional lumber and a single long-span wood truss. Western red cedar, corrugated, galvanized steel, Vermont granite, maple, and mahogany are the main building materials. Views of the Green Mountains are framed by the composition through large aluminum-frame windows. According to the architect, the house seeks to reinterpret "the simple volumes of Vermont rural architecture." Organized in three elements around a rock outcropping, the house is intended to provide shelter in the harsh winters, while allowing a maximum amount of contact with the exterior. One volume contains a workshop and storage area, while the two main connected elements respectively contain private family living space for three generations, and a public studio and meditation space. High-performance insulation and photovoltaic panels reduce energy consumption. Wood stoves and radiant heat floors are also part of the energy scheme of the residence.

Dieses Haus ist das Ferienhaus des Architekten. Gebaut wurde es auf einem Betonfundament mit Bauholz in Standardmaßen und einem einzigen Weitspannträger aus Holz. Hauptmaterialien sind Holz vom Riesenlebensbaum, feuerverzinktes Wellblech, Granit aus Vermont, Ahorn und Mahagoni. Große Aluminiumfenster wurden so positioniert, dass sie Ausblicke auf den Green Mountain rahmen. Dem Architekten zufolge ist das Haus der Versuch, „die schlichten Baukörper der ländlichen Architektur Vermonts" neu zu interpretieren. Das in drei Elementen um einen Felsvorsprung gruppierte Haus soll während der harten Winter Zuflucht bieten und dennoch maximalen Kontakt nach außen gewähren. In einem der Baukörper sind eine Werkstatt und Abstellräume untergebracht, während sich in den beiden anderen, miteinander verbundenen Volumina private Wohnräume für die drei Generationen der Familie sowie ein öffentlich zugängliches Atelier und ein Meditationsraum befinden. Eine leistungsstarke Dämmung und Solarpaneele senken den Energieverbrauch. Auch Holzöfen und eine Fußbodenheizung sind in das Energiekonzept des Hauses integriert.

Cette maison est la résidence de vacances de l'architecte. Elle repose sur des fondations en béton et la construction fait appel à des éléments de bois de dimensions standard, et à une ferme préfabriquée de longue portée. Ses principaux matériaux sont le cèdre rouge, la tôle ondulée d'acier, le granit du Vermont, l'érable et l'acajou. Les vues sur les Green Mountains sont cadrées par de grandes fenêtres à châssis en aluminium. Selon l'architecte : la maison cherche à réinterpréter « les volumes simples de l'architecture rurale du Vermont ». Organisée en trois éléments autour d'un affleurement rocheux, la maison devait résister aux hivers rudes de cette région, tout en permettant le maximum de contacts avec l'extérieur. Un volume contient un atelier et un espace de rangement, tandis que les deux éléments principaux, reliés entre eux, abritent les diverses pièces nécessaires à trois générations, un atelier et un espace de méditation. Une isolation haute performance et des panneaux photovoltaïques permettent de réduire la consommation d'énergie. La stratégie énergétique déployée comprend également des poêles à bois et des sols chauffants.

With its steep single sloped roofs and generous glazing (right, top and bottom), the house exudes a combination of structural simplicity and sophistication that allows residents to take in the setting in comfort.

Mit seinen steilen Pultdächern und der großflächigen Verglasung (rechts unten) wirkt das Haus konstruktiv ebenso schlicht wie anspruchsvoll. So können die Bewohner die Umgebung des Hauses ganz bequem genießen.

À travers ses toits fortement inclinés et ses généreux vitrages (en bas à droite), la maison exprime à la fois une simplicité structurelle et une sophistication qui permettent à ses occupants de profiter confortablement de son cadre.

Left, plans of the house show its angled design, made up of attached, rectangular boxes. Above, a living room interior, with large glazed surfaces, wood floors, and an overall, elegant simplicity.

Links: Die Grundrisse des Hauses zeigen die winklige Anordnung der kastenförmigen Elemente. Oben: Der Wohnbereich mit großflächigen Verglasungen und Holzboden in seiner schlichten Eleganz.

À gauche, les plans de la maison illustrent sa composition d'ensemble, faite de boîtes rectangulaires reliées entre elles. Ci-dessus, un séjour aux grandes ouvertures vitrées et à plancher de bois d'une élégante simplicité.

Angled surfaces and numerous openings animate the interior spaces, which have been decorated in a sober, attractive way that corresponds well to the architecture.

Winklige Flächen und zahlreiche Öffnungen beleben die Innenräume, welche in nüchterner, ansprechender Weise eingerichtet wurden, die gut mit der Architektur harmoniert.

Les plafonds inclinés et de nombreuses ouvertures animent des volumes intérieurs décorés de manière sobre et séduisante, dans l'esprit de l'architecture.

WORK ARCHITECTURE COMPANY

WORK Architecture Company
156 Ludlow Street, 3rd Floor
New York, NY 10002
USA

Tel: +1 212 228 1333
Fax: +1 212 228 1674
E-mail: office@work.ac
Web: www.work.ac

Born in Beirut, Lebanon, **AMALE ANDRAOS** received her B. Arch at McGill University (1996) and her Master's degree from Harvard University (1999). She worked with Rem Koolhaas / OMA (Rotterdam, 1999–2003), before founding WORK AC in New York in 2003. **DAN WOOD**, born in Rhode Island, received his Bachelor's degree (in Film Theory) from the University of Pennsylvania (1989) and his M.Arch from Columbia University (1992). He lived in Paris and the Netherlands, before moving to New York in 2002. He worked with Rem Koolhaas / OMA (Rotterdam, 1994–2000) and was President and Founder of AMO, Inc. in New York (2000–03) and a partner with Rem Koolhaas / OMA in New York (2000–03), before cofounding WORK AC with Amale Andraos. Their work includes the Diane von Furstenberg Studio Headquarters (New York, 2007); Public Farm 1 (Long Island City, New York, 2008, published here); Wild West Side (New York, New York, 2008); designs for the Shenzhen Metro Tower (Shenzhen, China, 2010); Wuhan University Library (Wuhan, China, 2010); Kew Gardens Hills Library (Queens, New York, 2011); Children's Museum of the Arts (New York, 2011); and Edible Schoolyard, PS 216 (Brooklyn, New York, 2011), all in the USA unless stated otherwise.

AMALE ANDRAOS wurde in Beirut geboren und machte 1996 ihren Bachelor in Architektur an der McGill University und 1999 ihren Master an der Harvard University. Bevor sie 2003 ihr eigenes Büro WORK AC in New York gründete, arbeitete sie von 1999 bis 2003 im Büro Rem Koolhaas/OMA in Rotterdam. **DAN WOOD,** der in Rhode Island geboren wurde, machte 1989 seinen Bacholor in Filmtheorie an der University of Pennsylvania und 1992 seinen Master in Architektur an der Columbia University. Bevor er nach New York ging, lebte er in Paris und in den Niederlanden. Von 1994 bis 2000 war er Mitarbeiter im Büro von Rem Koolhaas in Rotterdam und von 2000 bis 2003 sowohl Geschäftsführer und Gründer der AMO, Inc., in New York als auch Büropartner von Rem Koolhaas/OMA in dessen New Yorker Büro, bis er mit Amale Andraos WORK AC gründete. Zu ihren Arbeiten gehören die Diane von Furstenberg Studio Headquarters in New York (2007), die Public Farm 1 in Long Island City, New York (2008, hier vorgestellt), die Wild West Side in New York (2008), Entwürfe für das Hochhaus Shenzhen Metro Tower in Shenzhen (China, 2010), die Universitätsbibliothek der Universität in Wuhan (China, 2010), die Kew Gardens Hills Library in Queens (New York, 2011), das Kinderkunstmuseum in New York (2011) und der Essbare Schulhof, PS 216 (Brooklyn, New York, 2011). Alle Projekte befinden sich in den USA, sofern nicht anders angegeben.

Née à Beyrouth, **AMALE ANDRAOS** est titulaire d'un B.Arch. de l'université McGill (1996) et d'un M.Arch. de l'université Harvard (1999). Elle a travaillé pour Rem Koolhaas/OMA (Rotterdam, Pays-Bas, 1999–2003), avant de fonder l'agence WORK AC à New York en 2003. **DAN WOOD**, né dans le Rhode Island, est titulaire d'un B.A. en théorie du cinéma de l'université de Pennsylvanie (1989) et d'un M.Arch. de l'université Columbia (1992). Il a vécu à Paris et aux Pays-Bas avant de s'installer à New York en 2002. Il a travaillé pour Rem Koolhaas/OMA (Rotterdam, Pays-Bas, 1994–2000) et a été président-fondateur d'AMO, Inc. à New York (2000–03) et partenaire de Rem Koolhaas/OMA à New York (2000–03), avant de fonder WORK AC avec Amale Andraos. Parmi leurs réalisations : le siège de Diane von Furstenberg Studio (New York, 2007) ; Public Farm 1 (Long Island City, New York, 2008, publiée ici) ; Wild West Side (New York, 2008) ; des installations pour la tour Metro de Shenzhen (Shenzhen, Chine, 2010) ; la bibliothèque de l'université de Wuhan (Wuhan, Chine, 2010) : la bibliothèque de Kew Gardens Hills (Queens, New York, 2011) ; le Children's Museum of the Arts (New York, 2011) et le projet Edible Schoolyard de la PS 216 (Brooklyn, New York, 2011).

PUBLIC FARM 1

Long Island City, New York, USA, 2008

*Address: 22–25 Jackson Avenue at the intersection of 46th Avenue,
Long Island City, New York, NY 11101, USA, www.ps1.org. Area: 1011 m²
Client: Museum of Modern Art (MoMA). Cost: $180 000*

This project was the winning entry for the 2008 MoMA/PS1 Young Architect Program. Built in the P.S.1 Contemporary Art Center's courtyards, the temporary installation introduced a quarter acre fully functioning urban farm in the form of a folded plane made of structural cardboard tubes. The project was built entirely with recyclable materials, powered by solar energy, and irrigated by a rooftop rainwater collection system. The farm actually produced over 50 varieties of organic fruit, vegetables, and herbs that were used by the museum's café, served at special events, and harvested directly by visitors. Each of these crops was planted in six tubes of varying diameter arrayed around a central tube that was part of the structural support. The columns were also used to house videos about farms, solar powered fans, and a mobile phone charger. The architects state: "As a live urban farm, PF1 was a testament to the possibilities of rural engagement in urban environments and proposed that cities be reinvented to become a more complete and integrated system capable of producing their own food, producing their own power, and reusing their own water while creating new shared spaces for social interaction and public pleasure."

Dieser Entwurf gewann 2008 den Wettbewerb MoMA/PS1 Young Architect Program. Er wurde als temporäre Installation in den Innenhöfen des P.S.1 Contemporary Art Center angelegt. Auf gut 1000 m² wurde ein voll funktionierender urbaner Bauernhof in Form einer abgeknickten Ebene angelegt, die aus Pappröhren bestand. Das gesamte Projekt wurde aus recycelbaren Materialien errichtet, mit Solarenergie gespeist und mithilfe eines Regenwassersammelsystems bewässert. Die Farm zog mehr als 50 Sorten Obst, Gemüse und Kräuter, die im Museumscafé serviert und von den Besuchern geerntet wurden. Alle Pflanzen wurden jeweils in sechs unterschiedlich großen Röhren angebaut, die um eine zentrale Röhre angeordnet waren, die Teil der Konstruktion war. In den Pappröhren wurden auch Videos über Bauernhöfe abgespielt, sie enthielten Solarventilatoren und eine Ladestation für Handys. Die Architekten meinen: „PF1 beweist, dass Landwirtschaft in einem urbanen Umfeld möglich ist, und regt dazu an, dass sich Städte zu neuen Systemen entwickeln, die in der Lage sind, sich mit Essen und Energie selbst zu versorgen und das vor Ort anfallende Wasser wiederzuverwenden. Zugleich entstehen neue gemeinschaftlich genutzte Freiräume, die zum sozialen Dialog einladen und als öffentliche Erholungsräume dienen."

Ce projet a remporté le concours du programme des jeunes architectes du MoMA/PS1 en 2008. Réalisée dans les cours du PS1 Contemporary Art Center, cette installation temporaire a recréé une exploitation agricole pleinement opérationnelle d'environ 1000 m² sur un plan incliné plié en tubes de carton structurel. Le projet, réalisé en matériaux recyclables, était alimenté par l'énergie solaire et irrigué par les eaux récupérées des toitures. La ferme a produit plus de 50 variétés de fruits, de légumes et d'herbes, servis dans le café du musée lors de manifestations ou directement récoltés par les visiteurs. Chaque variété était plantée dans six tubes de divers diamètres, disposés autour d'un tube central solidaire du système structurel. Les colonnes étaient également utilisées pour proposer des vidéos sur les fermes, des ventilateurs solaires et un chargeur de téléphones mobiles. «En tant que ferme urbaine vivante, PF1 illustrait la possibilité d'une présence de la ruralité dans des environnements urbains et proposait que les villes se réinventent pour devenir des systèmes plus complets et plus intégrés, capables de produire leur propre nourriture, leur énergie et réutiliser leurs eaux, tout en créant de nouveaux espaces de partage visant à l'interaction sociale et au plaisir des visiteurs», ont expliqué les architectes.

The array of cardboard tubes that forms the Public Farm 1 project are essentially placed on an angled plane that leads up from and down to the ground level.

Die Pappröhren des Projekts Public Farm 1 sind größtenteils auf einer doppelt geneigten Ebene angeordnet.

Les tubes de carton qui constituent la Public Farm 1 sont pour l'essentiel disposés sur un plan doublement incliné, descendant vers le sol et en remontant.

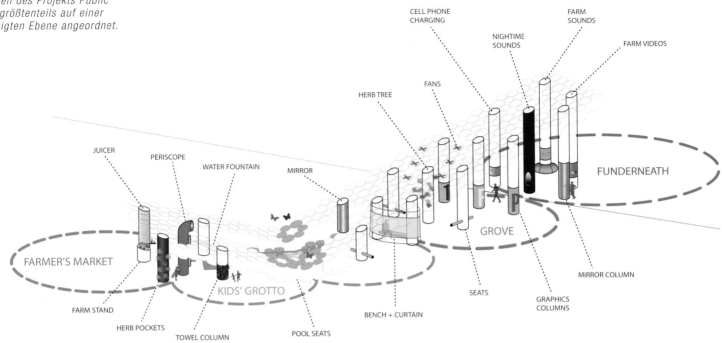

The installation made use of a rooftop rainwater collection system and featured 50 different vegetables, fruits, and herbs.

Für die Installation wurde ein Regenwassersammelsystem genutzt, in dem das Dachflächenwasser aufgefangen wurde, und es gab 50 verschiedene Gemüse- und Obstsorten sowie Küchenkräuter.

L'installation fonctionnait à l'aide d'un système de récupération des eaux de pluie et permettait de cultiver une cinquantaine de variétés de légumes, de fruits et d'herbes.

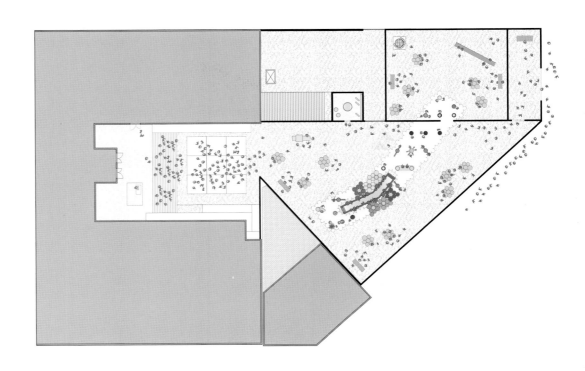

A diagram on the right shows the careful selection of plants as outlined by the designers. This project might be considered to be a cross between architecture, landscape design, and ecological consciousness-raising.

Das Diagramm rechts zeigt die sorg-fältige Pflanzenauswahl, auf die die Planer hinweisen. Dieses Projekt kann man als eine Mischung aus Architektur, Landschaftsgestaltung und Vermittlung ökologischen Bewusstseins bezeichnen.

Le plan de droite montre la sélection de plantes voulue par les aména-geurs. Ce projet est au croisement de l'architecture, de l'aménagement paysager et de la prise de conscience des enjeux écologiques.

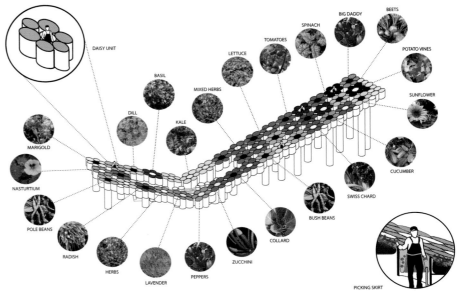

DAISY UNIT

BASIL
MIXED HERBS
LETTUCE
TOMATOES
SPINACH
BIG DADDY
BEETS
POTATO VINES
SUNFLOWER
DILL
KALE
MARIGOLD
CUCUMBER
NASTURTIUM
SWISS CHARD
BUSH BEANS
POLE BEANS
COLLARD
RADISH
ZUCCHINI
HERBS
PEPPERS
LAVENDER
PICKING SKIRT

ZHU XIAOFENG
SCENIC ARCHITECTURE

Scenic Architecture Office
No. 6 Lane 365 Xinhua Road
Building 9 – 3A
200052 Shanghai
China

Tel : +86 21 6294 8898
Fax : +86 21 6289 8381
E-mail: office@scenicarchitecture.com
Web: www.scenicarchitecture.com

Born in Shanghai, China, in 1972, **ZHU XIAOFENG** received his B.Arch degree from the Shenzen University School of Architecture (1994) and his M.Arch from the Harvard GSD (1997). He worked at Kohn Pedersen Fox (New York, 1999–2004), and created his firm, Scenic Architecture, in Shanghai in 2004. His work since leaving KPF includes the Qingpu New Downtown Xiayang Lake Lot 6, a hotel, recreation, office, and retail complex (Shanghai, 2004); Renjie Riverfront Club Villa clubhouse (Shanghai, 2004); the Qingpu Bus Station Plaza, office and retail (Shanghai, 2004); Jingze Church (Shanghai, 2004–05); the Green Pine Garden clubhouse, restaurant, and landscape (Shanghai, 2004–05, published here); Sunrise Plaza office building (Shanghai, 2005); Vanke Chunshen Community Center (Shanghai, 2005); Lai Zhi Fu Boutique Hotel and Restaurant, renovation and extension (Shanghai, 2006); and Presidential Hotel, restaurants and cultural facilities (Nanjing, 2006). More recent work includes the Dashawan Beach Facilities (Liandao Island, 2008), and the Zhujiajiao Museum of Fine Arts (Shanghai, 2011), all in China.

ZHU XIAOFENG, 1972 in Schanghai, China, geboren, absolvierte seinen B. Arch. an der Architekturfakultät der Universität Shenzen (1994) und einen M. Arch. an der Harvard GSD (1997). Nachdem er zunächst bei Kohn Pedersen Fox (New York, 1999–2004) tätig war, gründete er 2004 sein Büro Scenic Architecture in Schanghai. Seither realisierte Projekte sind u. a. der Hotel-, Freizeit-, Büro- und Geschäftskomplex Qingpu New Downtown Xiayang Lake Lot 6 (Schanghai, 2004), ein Klubhaus für die Renjie Riverfront Club Villa (Schanghai, 2004), ein Vorplatz mit Büro- und Geschäftsflächen am Busbahnhof Qingpu (Schanghai, 2004), die Jingze-Kirche (Schanghai, 2004–05), Klubhaus, Restaurant und Landschaftsgestaltung für den Green Pine Garden Club (Schanghai, 2004–05, hier vorgestellt), das Bürogebäude Sunrise Plaza (Schanghai, 2005), das Bürgerzentrum Vanke Chunshen (Schanghai, 2005), Sanierung und Erweiterung des Boutique-Hotels Lai Zhi Fu mit Restaurant (Schanghai, 2006) sowie Restaurants und Kultureinrichtungen für das Presidential Hotel (Nanjing, 2006). Jüngere Projekte sind die Strandanlagen in Dashawan (Insel Liandao, 2008) sowie das Kunstmuseum Zhujiajiao (Schanghai, 2011), alle in China.

Né à Shanghai en 1972, **ZHU XIAOFENG** a obtenu son B.Arch. à l'école d'architecture de l'université de Shenzen (1994) et son M.Arch. à la Harvard GSD (1997). Il a travaillé chez Kohn Pedersen Fox (New York, 1999–2004) et a ouvert son agence, Scenic Architecture, à Shanghai en 2004. Ses projets depuis qu'il a quitté KPF comprennent le lot 6 du nouveau centre ville de Qingpu sur le lac Xiayang – complexe hôtelier, de loisirs, de bureaux et de commerces (Shanghai, 2004) ; la club-house du Renjie Riverfront Club (Shanghai, 2004) ; l'aire, bureau et commerce de la gare routière de Qingpu (Shanghai, 2004) ; l'église de Jingze (Shanghai, 2004–05) ; la club-house, le restaurant et le parc du Green Pine Garden (Shanghai, 2004–05, publié ici) ; l'immeuble de bureaux Sunrise Plaza (Shanghai, 2005) ; le centre communautaire Vanke Chunshen (Shanghai, 2005) ; la rénovation et l'extension de l'hôtel-boutique et restaurant Lai Zhi Fu (Shanghai, 2006) et les restaurants et équipements culturels du Presidential Hotel (Nankin, 2006). Parmi ses réalisations plus récentes : les équipements de plage de Dashawan (île de Liandao, 2008) et le musée des beaux-arts de Zhujiajiao (Shanghai, 2011), toutes en Chine.

THE GREEN PINE GARDEN

Qingpu, Shanghai, 2004–05

*Area: 1603 m² (floor). Client: Yiluhua Industry Development Co. Ltd
Cost: $380 000. Collaboration: Guo Dan*

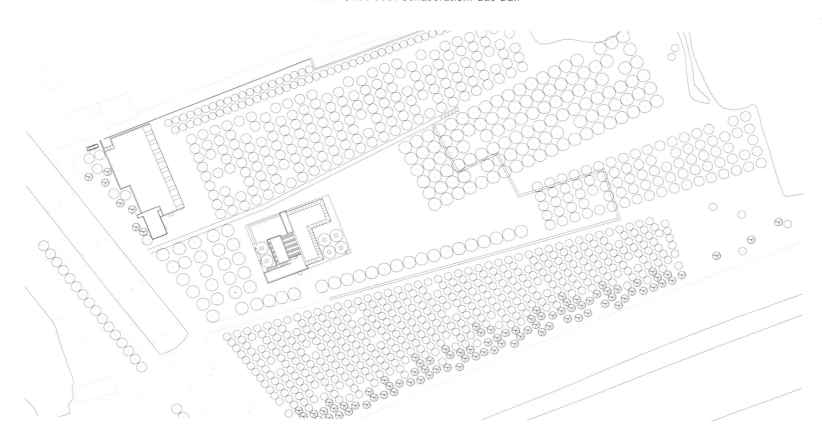

Located near the highway from Shanghai to Zhujiajiao, this project involved the renovation of two factory buildings and their conversion into a restaurant and bar. Zhu states that "the reorganization of volume and space of the two buildings follows the logic of the originals." Set in an extensively planted 30 000-square-meter green area, the restaurant building is characterized on its eastern side by a folding screen made of a local pine battens. The screen provides "privacy for the VIP dining rooms and creates an exterior space for the air conditioning unit." Similar wooden screens are applied in a more removed way on the eastern side of the bar building, while solid brick marks the west façade to limit traffic noise inside. Alternating thick and thin gray bricks typical of construction in southeastern China are applied here in a modern way. Zhu Xiaofeng demonstrates here that the local materials and existing buildings can be converted to a new use without recurring to Western models, and without any hint of pastiche.

Das unweit der Autobahn von Schanghai nach Zhujiajiao gelegene Projekt umfasste die Sanierung und den Umbau von zwei Fabrikgebäuden in ein Restaurant mit Bar. Zhu erklärt: „Die Neuorganisierung der Volumen und Räume der zwei Gebäude folgen der Logik des Bestands." Das Restaurantgebäude, eingebettet in weitläufige, 30 000 m² große Grünflächen, fällt durch seine gefaltete Ostfassade aus Holzlatten auf. Der Wandschirm schafft „Privatsphäre für die VIP-Bereiche und bietet zugleich Platz für die Technik der Klimaanlage". An der Ostfassade des Bargebäudes findet sich eine Abwandlung dieser Holzwandschirme. Die gemauerte Westfassade reduziert den Straßenlärm im Bau. Das Mauerwerk aus alternierenden schmalen und breiten grauen Ziegeln ist eine typisch südchinesische Bauform, die hier modern interpretiert wurde. Zhu Xiaofeng stellt unter Beweis, dass Bestandsbauten mit lokalen Materialien saniert und umgenutzt werden können, ohne auf westliche Vorbilder zurückzugreifen oder sie zu persiflieren.

Ce projet portait sur la rénovation de deux bâtiments d'usine en bordure de l'autoroute de Shanghai à Zhujiajiao et leur conversion en bar et restaurant. Zhu explique que « la réorganisation du volume et de l'espace des deux bâtiments suit la logique des constructions d'origine ». Dans un espace vert de 30 000 m² abondamment planté, le restaurant se caractérise sur la façade par un écran repliable en lattes de pin local. Il offre « l'intimité aux salles à manger des VIP et délimite un espace extérieur pour l'installation de la climatisation ». Des écrans de bois similaires sont utilisés de façon moins affirmée sur la façade est du bâtiment du bar, tandis que la façade ouest est traitée en brique pleine pour limiter la pollution sonore due à la circulation automobile. L'alternance de briques grises fines et épaisses est un procédé de construction typique du Sud-Est de la Chine, mais appliqué ici de façon moderne. Zhu Xiaofeng prouve ce faisant que les matériaux locaux et les bâtiments existants peuvent être convertis à un nouvel usage sans faire appel aux modèles occidentaux ni à la moindre trace de pastiche.

Folding pine screens that certainly evoke the traditions of Chinese architecture are visible in the image to the right.

Faltwände aus Kiefernholz, die an traditionelle chinesische Architektur erinnern, sind auf dem Bild rechts zu sehen.

Les écrans en pin pliants qui évoquent les traditions de l'architecture chinoise sont visibles à droite.

P 690

Set in a large site, the buildings are attached, but almost appear to be separate entities when they are photographed.

Die auf einem großen Gelände stehenden Bauten sind miteinander verbunden, wirken aus bestimmten Blickwinkeln jedoch wie separate Einheiten.

Implantés sur un vaste terrain, les bâtiments sont reliés entre eux, mais semblent presque séparés selon certains angles de vue.

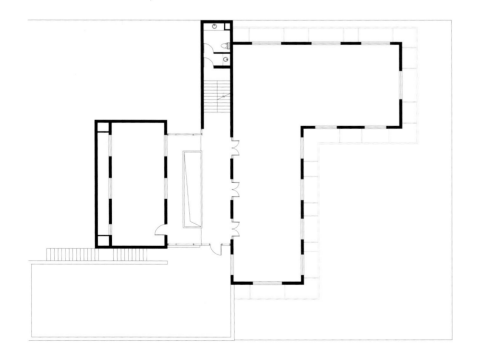

The architect has created an unusual composition in which cladding and the accumulation of essentially geometric forms speak more of modernity than anything else.

Der Architekt schuf eine unkonventionelle Anlage, bei der die Verkleidung und Häufung geometrischer Grundformen am ehesten an die Moderne denken lässt.

L'architecte a su créer une composition originale dans laquelle l'habillage et l'accumulation de formes essentiellement géométriques évoquent davantage la modernité que la tradition.

INDEX OF BUILDINGS, NAMES, AND PLACES

0-9
1315 Peachtree Street 544
24H Architecture 12
70F 18

A
Active Nature, Saclay, France 38
Adhiwira, Effan 18
AFF 32
Agence Babylone 38
Aldinger Architekten 44
Ambasz, Emilio 48
Anti-Smog, Paris, France 126
Anttolanhovi Art and Design Villas, Mikkeli, Finland 378
Auer+Weber+Assoziierte 54
Australia
  Cape Schanck, Victoria, Cape Schanck House 338
  Cranbourne, Melbourne, Royal Botanic Gardens 634
  Mudgee, NSW, Permanent Camping 158
Auttila, Pieta-Linda 62

B
Balmori Associates 68
Ban, Shigeru 7, 9, 11, 74
Bangladesh
  Dinajpur, Rudrapur, Handmade School 286
Barclay, Charles 84
Barlindhaug Consult AS 90
Bergne, Sebastian 98
BIG 104
BIP Computer Office and Shop, Santiago de Chile, Chile 486
Blanc, Patrick 7, 9, 11, 110
Bohlin Cywinski Jackson 114
Bubbletecture H, Sayo-cho, Hyogo, Japan 216
Buildings in Botanical Garden Shanghai, Shanghai, China 54

C
Cafeteria and Day Care Center, Waldorf School, Stuttgart, Germany 44
CaixaForum Vertical Garden, Madrid, Spain 110

Vincent Callebaut Architects 126
Camouflage House, Green Lake, Wisconsin, USA 384
Canada
  Osoyoos, British Columbia, Nk'Mip Desert Cultural Center 304
Cape Schanck House, Cape Schanck, Victoria, Australia 338
Carney Logan Burke Architects 138
Carter + Burton Architecture 144
Casagrande, Marco 150
Casey Brown 158
Chen House, Sanjhih, Taipei, Taiwan 150
Chesa Futura, St. Moritz, Switzerland 244
Chile
  Lake Rupanco, Fuente Nueva Chapel 202
  Los Arcos, Navidad, Mandakovic House 668
  Los Arcos, Navidad, Till House 660
  Puerto Natales, Patagonia, Hotel Remota 620
  Quintero, Valparaíso, La Baronia House 188
  Santiago de Chile, BIP Computer Office and Shop 486
China
  Lijiang, Yunnan, Yuhu Elementary School 454
  Quingpu, Shanghai, The Green Pine Garden 686
  Shanghai, Buildings in Botanical Garden Shanghai 54
  Shanghai, Giant Interactive Group Corporate Headquarters 478
  Shanghai, The Waterhouse at South Bund 492
  Shenzhen, Vanke Center / Horizontal Skyscraper 292
Coconut Grove, Florida Garden, Coconut Grove, Florida, USA 396
Connecticut Water Treatment Facility, New Haven, Connecticut, USA 644
Cullinan, Edward 164

D
Damiani Holz & Ko Headquarters, Bressanone, Italy 470
dECOi Architects 170
Denmark
  Copenhagen, The Mountain 104
Diller Scofidio + Renfro 178
Djurovic, Vladimir 7, 9, 11, 182
Downland Gridshell, Singleton, UK 164
dRN Architects 188
Dumay + Fones + Vergara 202

E

Ecoboulevard of Vallecas, Madrid, Spain   208

Ecolodge, Siwa, Egypt   228

Ecosistema Urbano   208

Eden Project, Bodelva, UK   266

Egypt

  Siwa, Ecolodge   228

Endo, Shuhei   216

Environmental Education Center, Hoorn, The Netherlands   460

ETH-Studio Monte Rosa / Bearth & Deplazes   222

Ewha Womans University, Seoul, South Korea   548

F

FELIX-DELUBAC   228

Finland

  Helsinki, Wisa Wooden Design Hotel   62

  Joensuu, Metla, Finnish Forest Research Institute   572

  Kärsämäki, Kärsämäki Church   440

  Mikkeli, Anttolanhovi Art and Design Villas   378

Float   236

Foster, Norman   244

France

  Mulhouse, Social Housing, Cité Manifeste   434

  Paris, Anti-Smog   126

  Saclay, Active Nature   38

Fuente Nueva Chapel, Lake Rupanco, Chile   202

G

Gehry, Frank O.   254

Germany

  Herne, Mont-Cenis Center   390

  Rostock, Hedge Building   404

  Stuttgart, Cafeteria and Day Care Center, Waldorf School   44

  Oberwiesenthal, Tellerhäuser, "Hutznhaisl," Protective Hut

    on Fichtelberg Mountain   32

  Tieringen, H16   612

Giant Interactive Group Corporate Headquarters, Shanghai, China   478

Glass Wood House, New Canaan, Connecticut, USA   424

Glavovic Studio   260

Grand Rapids Art Museum, Grand Rapids, Michigan, USA   654

Grand Teton Discovery and Visitor Center, Moose Junction, Grand Teton

  National Park, Wyoming, USA   114

Green School, Badung, Bali, Indonesia   24

Greenhouses, Japanese Pavilion, Venice, Italy   330

Grimshaw, Nicholas   266

Gustafson Guthrie Nichol   272

H

H16, Tieringen, Germany   612

Handmade School, Rudrapur, Dinajpur, Bangladesh   286

Hedge Building, Rostock, Germany   404

Helios House, Los Angeles, California, USA   518

Heringer, Anna and Eike Roswag   286

Holl, Steven   292

Homestead House   362

Hotel Remota, Puerto Natales, Patagonia, Chile   620

Hotson Bakker Boniface Haden   304

"Hutznhaisl," Protective Hut on Fichtelberg Mountain, Tellerhäuser,

  Oberwiesenthal, Germany   32

HWKN (Hollwich Kushner)   320

Hypar Pavilion Lawn, New York, New York, USA   178

I

India

  Maharashtra, Nandgaon, Palmyra House   626

Indonesia

  Bali, Badung, Green School   24

Inujima Art Project Seirensho, Inujima, Okayama, Japan   568

IROJE KHM Architects   320

Ishigami, Junya   330

Italy

  Bressanone, Damiani Holz & Ko Headquarters   470

  Lana, Merano, Vigilius Mountain Resort   640

  Venice, Greenhouses, Japanese Pavilion   330

  Venice-Mestre, Ospedale dell'Angelo   48

J

Jackson Clements Burrows   338

Jacobs, Chris   344

James Corner Field Operations / Diller Scofidio + Renfro   354

Jantzen, Michael   362

Japan

  Hyogo, Sayo-cho, Bubbletecture H   216

  Kochi, Yusuhara, Yusuhara Marché   430

  Okayama, Inujima, Inujima Art Project Seirensho   568

  Tokyo, Nomadic Museum   7, 9, 11, 80

  Tokyo, Sony City Osaki   506

Jensen & Skodvin Architects   366

Johansson, Emma and Timo Leiviskä   378

Johnsen Schmaling Architects   384

Jourda, Françoise-Hélène   390

Jungles, Raymond   396

Juvet Landscape Hotel, Gudbrandsjuvet, Norway   374

K

Kärsämäki Church, Kärsämäki, Finland   440

Kempe Thill   404

Kielder Observatory, Kielder, Northumberland, UK   84

KieranTimberlake   410

Klotz, Mathias   416

Kuma, Kengo   424

Kumgang Ananti Golf & Spa Resort, Gangwondo, North Korea   464

L

La Baronia House, Quintero, Valparaíso, Chile   188

La Roca House, Punta del Este, Uruguay   416

Lacaton & Vassal   434

Lassila Hirvilammi Architects   440

Laurance S. Rockefeller Preserve, Moose, Grand Teton National Park,

  Wyoming, USA   138

Lebanon
Beirut, Samir Kassir Square — 7, 9, 11, 182
LEGO Greenhouse, London, UK — 98
Lehoux, Nic and Jacqueline Darjes — 446
Li Xiaodong — 454
Lillefjord, Måsøy, Finnmark, Norway — 562
Lim Geo Dang, Go Yang, South Korea — 320
Lurie Garden, Chicago, Illinois, USA — 272

M
MIII architecten — 460
Mandakovic House, Navidad, Los Arcos, Chile — 668
Masdar Institute, Abu Dhabi, UAE — 250
Media Authority Building, Hilversum, The Netherlands — 648
Mérida Factory Youth Movement, Mérida, Spain — 602
Metla, Finnish Forest Research Institute, Joensuu, Finland — 576
Min, Ken Sungjin — 464
MODUS — 470
Mont-Cenis Center, Herne, Germany — 390
Morphosis — 478
Mozó, Alberto — 486

N
Neri & Hu — 492
The Netherlands
Almere, Petting Farm — 18
Hilversum, Media Authority Building — 648
Hoorn, Environmental Education Center — 460
Rheden, Posbank Tea Pavilion — 588
Neves, Victor — 500
New Monte Rosa Hut SAC, Zermatt, Switzerland — 222
Nikken Sekkei — 506
Nimmrichter, Rolf Karl — 512
Nk'Mip Desert Cultural Center, Osoyoos, British Columbia, Canada — 304
Nomadic Museum, New York, New York, USA; Santa Monica, California, USA; Tokyo, Japan — 7, 9, 11, 80
North Korea
Gangwondo, Kumgang Ananti Golf & Spa Resort — 464
Norway
Finnmark, Måsøy, Lillefjord — 562
Gudbrandsjuvet, Juvet Landscape Hotel — 374
Hardanger Fjord, Summer House — 582
Svalbard, Longyearbyen, Svalbard Global Seed Vault — 90
Tautra Island, Tautra Maria Convent — 366

O
Office dA — 518
One Main, Cambridge, Massachusetts, USA — 170
Ospedale dell'Angelo, Venice-Mestre, Italy — 48
Ott, Carlos — 528

P
Palleroni, Sergio — 536
Palmyra House, Nandgaon, Maharashtra, India — 626
Panyaden School, Chiang Mai, Thailand — 12

Papertainer Museum, Seoul, South Korea — 74
Perkins+Will — 544
Permanent Camping, Mudgee, NSW, Australia — 158
Perrault, Dominique — 548
Petting Farm, Almere, The Netherlands — 18
Piano, Renzo — 556
PUSHAK — 562
Playa Vik, Faro José Ignacio, Maldonado, Uruguay — 528
Portugal
Esposende, Reorganization of the Riverside of Esposende — 500
Posbank Tea Pavilion, Rheden, The Netherlands — 588
Public Farm 1, Long Island City, New York, USA — 678
Putney Mountain House, Putney, Vermont, USA — 672

R
Renovation and Expansion of the California Academy of Sciences, San Francisco, California, USA — 556
Reorganization of the Riverside of Esposende, Esposende, Portugal — 500
Royal Botanic Gardens, Cranbourne, Melbourne, Australia — 634

S
S House, Dietlikon, Switzerland — 512
Sambuichi, Hiroshi — 568
Samir Kassir Square, Beirut, Lebanon — 7, 9, 11, 182
Santa Fe Railyard Park and Plaza, Santa Fe, New Mexico, USA — 606
SARC Architects — 576
Saunders & Wilhelmsen — 582
SeARCH — 588
selgascano — 594
Serpentine Gallery Pavilion, London, UK — 254
Shenandoah Retreat, Warren County, Virginia, USA — 144
Sidwell Friends School, Washington, D.C., USA — 410
Smith, Ken — 606
Sobek, Werner — 612
Social Housing, Cité Manifeste, Mulhouse, France — 434
Sol, Germán del — 620
Sony City Osaki, Tokyo, Japan — 506
South Korea
Go Yang, Lim Geo Dang — 320
Seoul, Ewha Womans University — 548
Seoul, Papertainer Museum — 74
Spain
Bilbao, The Garden That Climbs the Stairs — 68
Madrid, CaixaForum Vertical Garden — 110
Madrid, Ecoboulevard of Vallecas — 208
Madrid, Studio in the Woods — 594
Mérida, Mérida Factory Youth Movement — 602
Studio in the Woods, Madrid, Spain — 594
Studio Mumbai — 626
Summer House, Hardanger Fjord, Norway — 582
Svalbard Global Seed Vault, Longyearbyen, Svalbard, Norway — 90
Switzerland
Dietlikon, S House — 512
St. Moritz, Chesa Futura — 244
Zermatt, New Monte Rosa Hut SAC — 222

T

Taiwan

Taipei, Sanjhih, Chen House ... 150

Taipei, Zhong Xiao Boulevard Urban Ecological Corridor ... 536

Tautra Maria Convent, Tautra Island, Norway ... 366

Taylor Cullity Lethlean ... 634

Thailand

Chiang Mai, Panyaden School ... 12

The Garden That Climbs the Stairs, Bilbao, Spain ... 68

The Green Pine Garden, Quingpu, Shanghai, China ... 686

The High Line, New York, New York, USA ... 354

The Lilypad, Point Roberts, Washington, USA ... 446

The Mountain, Copenhagen, Denmark ... 104

The Waterhouse at South Bund, Shanghai, China ... 492

Thun, Matteo ... 640

Till House, Navidad, Los Arcos, Chile ... 660

U

UAE

Abu Dhabi, Masdar Institute ... 250

UK

Bodelva, Eden Project ... 266

London, LEGO Greenhouse ... 98

London, Serpentine Gallery Pavilion ... 254

Northumberland, Kielder, Kielder Observatory ... 84

Singleton, Downland Gridshell ... 164

Uruguay

Maldonado, Faro José Ignacio, Playa Vik ... 528

Punta del Este, La Roca House ... 416

USA

California, Los Angeles, Helios House ... 518

California, San Francisco, Renovation and Expansion of
    the California Academy of Sciences ... 556

California, Santa Monica, Nomadic Museum ... 80

Connecticut, New Canaan, Glass Wood House ... 424

Connecticut, New Haven, Connecticut Water Treatment Facility ... 644

Florida, Coconut Grove, Florida Garden, Coconut Grove ... 396

Florida, Hollywood, Young Circle ArtsPark ... 260

Georgia, Atlanta, 1315 Peachtree Street ... 544

Illinois, Chicago, Lurie Garden ... 272

Massachusetts, Cambridge, One Main ... 170

Michigan, Grand Rapids, Grand Rapids Art Museum ... 654

New Mexico, Santa Fe, Santa Fe Railyard Park and Plaza ... 606

New York, Harlem, Vertical Farm ... 344

New York, Long Island City, Public Farm 1 ... 678

New York, New York, Hypar Pavilion Lawn ... 178

New York, New York, Nomadic Museum ... 80

New York, New York, The High Line ... 354

New York, Queens, Long Island City, MoMA PS1, Wendy ... 320

Oregon, Willamette Valley, Watershed ... 236

Vermont, Putney, Putney Mountain House ... 672

Virginia, Warren County, Shenandoah Retreat ... 144

Washington, D.C., Sidwell Friends School ... 410

Washington, Point Roberts, The Lilypad ... 446

Wisconsin, Green Lake, Camouflage House ... 384

Wyoming, Grand Teton National Park, Moose Junction,
    Grand Teton Discovery and Visitor Center ... 114

Wyoming, Grand Teton National Park, Moose,
    Laurance S. Rockefeller Preserve ... 138

V

Valkenburgh, Michael van ... 644

Vanke Center / Horizontal Skyscraper, Shenzhen, China ... 292

Velsen, Koen van ... 648

Vertical Farm, Harlem, New York, USA ... 344

Vigilius Mountain Resort, Lana, Merano, Italy ... 640

W

Watershed, Willamette Valley, Oregon, USA ... 236

Wendy, MoMA PS1, Long Island City, Queens, New York, USA ... 320

wHY Architecture ... 654

Wisa Wooden Design Hotel, Helsinki, Finland ... 62

WMR ... 660

Woo, Kyu Sung ... 672

WORK Architecture Company ... 678

Y

Young Circle ArtsPark, Hollywood, Florida, USA ... 260

Yuhu Elementary School, Lijiang, Yunnan, China ... 454

Yusuhara Marché, Yusuhara, Kochi, Japan ... 430

Z

Zhong Xiao Boulevard Urban Ecological Corridor, Taipei, Taiwan ... 536

Zhu Xiaofeng Scenic Architecture ... 686

CREDITS

PHOTO CREDITS — **354** © James Corner Field Operations / **355–361** © Iwan Baan / **362** © Michael Jantzen / **366, 374–377** © Jensen & Skodvin / **378** © Arkkitehtitoimisto Emma Johansson/Timo Leiviskä / **379–383** © Jussi Tiainen / **384, 386** © Johnsen Schmaling Architects / **385, 387–388** © John Macaulay / **389** © Kevin Miyazaki / **390** © Jean–Pierre Porcher / **391–395** © Paul Raftery/Arcaid / **396** © Raymond Jungles, Inc. / **397–403** © Annie Schlechter / **404** © Kempe Thill / **405–409** © Ulrich Schwarz / **410** © KieranTimberlake / **411–415** © Michael Moran / **416** © Mathias Klotz / **417–423** © Roland Halbe / **424** © Kengo Kuma & Associates / **425–433** © Kengo Kuma & Associates for Glass Wood House / **434** © Lacaton & Vassal / **435–439** © Philippe Ruault / **440** © Lassila Hirvilammi / **441–445** © Jussi Tiainen / **446–453** © Nic Lehoux / **454** © Li Xiaodong / **455–459** © Melvin Tan / **460** © MIII Architecten / **461–463** © Olaf Klyn Photography / **464** © SKM Architects / **465–469** © Kim Yong Kwan / **470** © Marco Pietracupa / **471–477** © Günther Wett / **478** © Morphosis / **479–485** © Roland Halbe / **486** © Alberto Mozó / **487–491** © Cristóbal Palma / **492–493, 497, 499 top and bottom right** © Neri & Hu Design and Research Office / **494–496, 498, 499 bottom left** © Pegenaute / **500–505** © Victor Neves / **506** © Nikken Sekkei Ltd. / **507–511** © Yutaka Suzuki / **512** © Nimmrichter CDA Ltd. / **513–517** © Bruno Helbling Fotografie / **518** © Office dA / **519–527** © Eric Staudenmaier / **528** © Carlos Ott Architect / **529–535** © Cristóbal Palma / **536** © Sergio Palleroni / **537–543** Hong-Wei Chen © Palleroni/Tsai / **544** © Perkins+Will / **545–547** © Eduard Hueber/archphoto / **548** © Dominique Perrault Architecture / **549–555** © André Morin / **556** © Renzo Piano Building Workshop / **557–561** © Nic Lehoux / **562–567** © PUSHAK / **568** © Sambuichi Architects / **569–575** © Iwan Baan / **576** © SARC Architects / **577–581** © Jussi Tiainen / **582** © Saunders & Wilhelmsen / **583–587** © Bent Renè Synnevåg / **588** © SeARCH / **589–593** © Christian Richters / **594** © selgascano / **595–597** © Iwan Baan / **598–601, 603–605** © Roland Halbe / **602** © selgascano / **606** © Ken Smith Landscape Architect / **607–611** © Peter Mauss/Esto / **612** © Wilfried Dechau / **613–619** © Zooey Braun Photography / **620** © Germán del Sol / **621–625** © Cristóbal Palma / **626** © Studio Mumbai Architects / **627–633** © Rajesh Vora/Aga Khan Trust for Culture / **634, 636, 638–639** © Taylor Cullity Lethlean / **635, 637** © Peter Hyatt/fabpics / **640** © Matteo Thun / **641–643** © Gerhard Hagen/arturimages / **644** © Michael Van Valkenburgh Associates, Inc. / **645–647** © Elizabeth Felicella / **648** © Koen van Velsen / **649–653** © Duccio Malagamba / **654, 658 bottom, 659 top** © wHY Architecture / **655–657, 658 top** © Steve Hall@Gedrich Blessing / **659 bottom** © Scott McDonald@Hedrich Blessing / **660** © WMR arquitectos / **661–671** © Sergio Pirrone / **672** © Lucy Cobos Photography / **673–677** © Timothy Hursley / **678** © Andy French / **679–685** © WORK Architecture Company / **686** © Scenic Architecture Inc. / **687–690, 691** © Shen Zonghai

CREDITS FOR PLANS / DRAWINGS / CAP DOCUMENTS — **363–365** © Michael Jantzen / **374** © Jensen & Skodvin / **380, 382–383** © Arkkitehtitoimisto Emma Johansson/Timo Leiviskä / **386, 388** © Johnsen Schmaling / **398, 400** © Raymond Jungles, Inc. / **408–409** © Kempe Thill / **412** © KieranTimberlake / **427–428, 430, 432–433** © Kengo Kuma & Associates / **437 bottom, 438 bottom** © Lacaton & Vassal / **443, 445** © Lassila Hirvilammi / **457, 459** © Li Xiaodong / **462** © MIII Architecten / **467** © SKM Architects / **472, 475–477** © MODUS architects / **480, 483, 485** © Morphosis / **488, 490** © Alberto Mozó / **495–498** © Neri & Hu Design and Research Office / **505** © Victor Neves / **508** © Nikken Sekkei Ltd. / **514–515, 517** © Nimmrichter CDA Ltd. / **521, 525–526** © Office dA / **531** © Carlos Ott Architect / **538, 540, 542** © BASIC Initiative / **547** © Perkins+Will / **550, 555** © Dominique Perrault Architecture / **561** © Renzo Piano Building Workshop / **565** © PUSHAK / **572, 574** © Hiroshi Sambuichi / **580–581** © SARC Architects / **585** © Saunders & Wilhelmsen / **590** © SeARCH / **599, 601, 603–604** © selgascano / **609** © Ken Smith Landscape Architect / **616, 619** © Werner Sobek / **623** © Germán del Sol / **628, 632–633** © Studio Mumbai Architects / **637–638** © Taylor Cullity Lethlean / **646** © Michael Van Valkenburgh Associates, Inc. / **650** © Koen van Velsen / **663, 666, 669, 671** © WMR arquitectos / **674, 676** © Kyu Sung Woo Architects / **681, 683, 685** © WORK Architecture Company / **688, 691** © Scenic Architecture Inc.

Kyu Sung Woo, Putney 672
dECOi Architects, Cambridge 170

Bohlin Cywinski Jackson, Finger Lakes Region 120

wHY Architecture, Grand Rapids 654

Gustafson Guthrie Nichol, Chicago 272

Johnsen Schmaling Architects, Green Lake 384

Bohlin Cywinski Jackson, Grand Teton National Park 114
Carney Logan Burke Architects, Grand Teton National Park 138

Hotson Bakker Boniface Haden, Osoyoos 304

Nic Lehoux and Jacqueline Darjes, Point Roberts 446

Float, Willamette Valley 236

Renzo Piano, San Francisco 556

Shigeru Ban, Santa Monica 80
Glavovic Studio, Hollywood 260
Office dA, Los Angeles 518

Ken Smith, Santa Fe 606

Carter + Burton Architecture, Warren County 144
Gustafson Guthrie Nichol, Washington, D.C. 278
KieranTimberlake, Washington, D.C. 410

Perkins+Will, Atlanta 544

Raymond Jungles, Coconut Grove 396

70F, Almere 18
MIII architecten, Hoorn 460
Koen van Velsen, Hilversum 648

Charles Barclay, Kielder 84

Sebastian Bergne, London 98
Frank O. Gehry, London 254

Edward Cullinan, Singleton 164

Nicholas Grimshaw, St. Austell 266

Balmori Associates, Bilbao 68

Patrick Blanc, Madrid 110
Ecosistema Urbano, Madrid 208
selgascano, Madrid 594

Victor Neves, Esposende 500

selgascano, Mérida 602

80 **Shigeru Ban**, New York
178 **Diller Scofidio + Renfro**, New York
320 **HWKN (Hollwich Kushner)**, Long Island City
344 **Chris Jacobs**, Harlem
354 **James Corner Field Operations /**
     Diller Scofidio + Renfro, New York
424 **Kengo Kuma**, New Canaan
644 **Michael Van Valkenburgh**, New Haven
678 **WORK Architecture Company**,
     Long Island City

dRN Architects, Quintero, Valparaíso 188
Alberto Mozó, Santiago de Chile 486
WMR, Los Arcos 660

416 **Mathias Klotz**, Punta del Este
528 **Carlos Ott**, José Ignacio, Maldonado

Dumay + Fones + Vergara, Lake Rupanco 202

dRN Architects, Chiloé Island 188

Germán del Sol, Puerto Natales 620